W9-DGS-425

MUSIC REFERENCE AND RESEARCH MATERIALS

MUSIC REFERENCE AND RESEARCH MATERIALS

An Annotated Bibliography

Fourth Edition, Revised

Vincent H. Duckles
Michael A. Keller

SCHIRMER BOOKS
An Imprint of Macmillan Publishing Company
New York

Maxwell Macmillan Canada
Toronto

Maxwell Macmillan International
New York   Oxford   Singapore   Sydney

Copyright©1988, 1994 by Schirmer Books
                    An Imprint of Macmillan Publishing Company
Copyright©1967, 1974 by Vincent Duckles
Copyright©1964 by The Free Press
                    A Division of Macmillan Publishing Co., Inc.

All rights reserved. No part of this publication may be reproduced or
transmitted in any form or by any means, electronic or mechanical,
including photocopying, recording, or by any information storage
and retrieval system, without permission in writing from the
Publisher.

Schirmer Books   Maxwell Macmillan Canada, Inc.
An Imprint of Macmillan Publishing Company   1200 Eglinton Avenue East
866 Third Avenue   Suite 200
New York, N.Y. 10022   Don Mills, Ontario M3C 3N1

Macmillan Publishing Company is part of the Maxwell Communication Group
of Companies.

Library of Congress Catalog Card Number: 92-12386

Printed in the United States of America

printing number
1 2 3 4 5 6 7 8 9 10

Library of Congress Cataloging-in-Publication Data
Duckles, Vincent H. (Vincent Harris), 1913–1985
    Music reference and research materials: an annotated bibliography
/Vincent H. Duckles, Michael A. Keller. - 4th. ed., rev.
        p.   cm.
    Includes indexes.
    ISBN 0-02-870822-9
    1. Music-Bibliography. 2. Music-History and Criticism—
—Bibliography. 3. Bibliography—Bibliography—Music.   I. Keller,
Michael A. II. Title.
ML113.D83 1992
016.78—dc20   92-12386
                                                                    CIP
                                                                    MN

The paper used in this publication meets the minimum requirements of American
National Standard for Information Sciences—Permanence of Paper for Printed
Library Materials. ANSI Z39.48-1984.∞™

Contents

LIBRARY
ALMA COLLEGE
ALMA, MICHIGAN

Contents

MISCELLANEOUS AND BIBLIOGRAPHICAL TOOLS 570

INDEXES 585

Introduction to the Fourth Edition, Revised

The fourth edition of *Music Reference and Research Materials* was produced using a computerized data base system to facilitate its timely publication and to expedite the eventual publication of future editions. In retrospect, our efforts—both in the choice of a particularly unsuited computer program and in the often unwieldy manuscript preparation that the software required—were less prudent than they should have been. The fourth edition was plagued by a number of typographical errors, formatting problems, out-of-sequence citation numbers, and false cross-references. We are acutely aware of the difficulties these errors caused for users, who have come to rely on *Music Reference and Research Materials* for complete and accurate information, and we have made every effort to correct each error in this revised edition. In fact, over the last two years our attempts to integrate corrections in the original data base have proven fruitless, and we have prepared this revised edition through the admittedly old-fashioned and yet still effective method of copyediting from hard copy and proofreading galleys and page proofs.

An overview of the revisions made may be useful to some readers. First, the number of simple typographic and formatting errors has been reduced to the lowest level possible. Second, virtually all duplicate citations, which had been thought to be a convenience, have been removed, and in their places cross-references have been inserted. Third, a large number of citations and annotations have been updated, expanded, and corrected. There are still a few citations without annotations, but in such cases the title is sufficiently self-explanatory and descriptive. Fourth, advantage was taken of the revision to add a few new entries, some embarrassing omissions of works published before 1986 but not included in the fourth edition and a very few published after 1986. The ones with a post-1986 publishing date chosen for inclusion in this revised fourth edition were selected because of their crucial significance to the field. Among them are *The New Grove Dictionary of Jazz* edited by Barry Kernfeld, J. F. Weber's *A Gregorian Chant Discography*, and Richard Spottswood's *Ethnic Music on Records*. In response to criticism of the thematic catalog section, citations for some of the "classics," old and new, have been added, but the focus of the section remains on thematic catalogs published since Barry S. Brook's *Thematic Catalogues in Music*.

Astute readers will also note that titles like Brook's *Thematic Catalogues in Music* have been moved to the head of the section of specific works for which they have relevance as an essential "reference work of reference works." This practice was begun in the fourth edition, but is now more fully enacted in the revised fourth edition. Also, the last chapter has been reduced in size and reorganized; entries are placed in five sections, only one of which is truly miscellaneous. Finally, a separate *Index of Selected Music Bibliographic Series* has been created, which lists titles in numerical order within each series, without annotations, but with references to their appearance in the bibliography proper.

In general, tenets of *The Chicago Manual of Style*, thirteenth edition, have been employed to resolve questions of presentation in this bibliography. All but first words transcribed in titles in citations and see references are in lowercase, except for nouns in German-language titles, which are capitalized. Titles of books mentioned in annotations are presented in italics and nouns are capitalized. Abbreviations have been eliminated, except for two: throughout, *MGG* refers to *Die Musik in Geschichte und Gegenwart* (no. 43) and the *New Grove* refers to *The New Grove Dictionary of Music and Musicians* (no. 46).

As painful as has been the realization of the degree of revision and correction required to make the fourth edition the kind of reference work it has been in the past and ought to be in the present, the process of revision itself has been salutary, made so by the criticism and suggestions contributed by a number of persons about to be mentioned. First among the readers and contributors is Ida Reed, Music Librarian at the University of North Carolina at Chapel Hill. Her devotion to this revision always produced suggestions and queries that have made this revision more accurate and more consistent. To have had such a colleague as Ida Reed has been marvelous. Professor Richard D. Green of Northwestern University, David C. Hunter, Music Librarian at the University of Texas at Austin, and Daniel Zager, Music Librarian of the Oberlin Conservatory Music Library of Oberlin College, each read the entire fourth edition and made numerous detailed suggestions for the revision. Their careful attention to every aspect of the book has stimulated and challenged the compiler and the publisher to make the revised fourth edition—as well as succeeding editions—much better books. The publisher and the compiler are grateful for these suggestions and for the careful thought behind them.

A number of other professionals contributed to the revision: Professor Bertil van Boer of Wichita State University; Richard Griscom, Music Librarian at University of Louisville; Linda M. Fidler, formerly Music Librarian at Bowling Green State University; John Roberts, my successor at the University of California at Berkeley; Judy Tsou, Assistant Music Librarian at the University of California at Berkeley; Mimi Tashiro, Reference Librarian of the Music Library at Stanford University; Barbara Sawka, Head of the Archives of Recorded Sound and Acting Music Librarian at Stanford University; Kären Nagy, Director of Academic Information Services at Stanford University; Gordon Thiel, Music Librarian at the University of California at Los Angeles; Professor Angelo Pompilio, Departamento di Musica e Spettacolo of the Università degli Studi di Bologna; Clemens Gruber at the Internationales Opern Archiv in Vienna; Gudrun Kilburn, Chief Cataloger of the Music Library at the State University of New York at Buffalo; Jerry Call, Archivist of the Musicological Archives for Renaissance Studies at the University of Illinois at Urbana; James Farrington, Music Librarian at Wesleyan University; Professor Jeffrey Titon of Brown University; Marjorie Hassen, Music Librarian at the University of Pennsylvania; and Gillian B. Anderson, Reference Librarian in the Music Division of the Library of Congress. To all of these fine colleagues and friends go my thanks.

The contributions of Yale colleagues once again have been illustrative of one of the many reasons people find working in and for the Yale Library such a productive and pleasant experience. Ken Crilly, Public Services Librarian in the Jackson Music Library, made crucial discoveries and extended his services extraordinarily to me time and again. Richard Warren, Curator of the Historical Sound Recording Collection, Cesar Rodriguez, Curator of the Latin American Collection, Hideo Kaneko, Curator of the East Asian Collection, and Tanya Lorkovic, Curator of the Slavic and Eastern European Collections, each made their special knowledge and skills available generously. David-Marc Finley, Director of the Yale Russian Chorus and my administrative assistant, lent himself willingly to the dual tasks of making me efficient in the revision process itself and shielding me from most of the demands of my position at Yale in the final stage of the revision. Joyce Ogburn, Steven Eichner, and Carol Lawrence read the manuscript and made valuable suggestions. No one has shared the agony of this revision more than Maribeth Anderson Payne, the Editor-in-chief of Schirmer Books. While suffering, she has alternately consoled and goaded me, talked with many people in the field, and through it all, reiterated the faith Schirmer Books has in the importance and utility of *Music Reference and Research Materials*. A more patient and understanding editor one could not have.

Despite all of this assistance, errors and omissions may remain, for which the compiler of course accepts responsibility.

With this visible result of the process of criticism and contributions made by colleagues, it is perhaps unnecessary to reiterate the call for more suggestions, more comments, and more criticism, in order that the next edition will continue to meet the needs of scholars and librarians in the pursuit of their work with the resources of musical research.

Michael A. Keller
Yale University Library
New Haven, Connecticut
1993

Introduction to
the Fourth Edition

During the long interval between the third and fourth editions of this book, Vincent H. Duckles gathered and evaluated new titles, and wrote annotations for inclusion in the fourth edition. In 1984 he recognized that his declining health would not permit him to complete this edition without assistance and he called upon me, his successor as Music Librarian at the University of California at Berkeley, to become his coauthor. Duckles died in mid-July of 1985, but had continued to work on *Music Reference and Research Materials* until he was hospitalized a few months before his death. In the short time we worked together, we agreed on some modest innovations, although this edition was completed on the basis of the previous editions, albeit with the substantial mechanical assistance of computers.

Music Reference and Research Materials continues to be a select, not comprehensive, and annotated bibliography of published reference works and research tools concerned with musical topics. It is intended that this work serve the scholar as a bibliographic handbook, a repertory of sources for information covering the broadest expanse of the art of music. Music librarians and general reference librarians should find this classified bibliography helpful in pursuing their dual responsibilities of building and interpreting library collections. However, it is the students of music for whom this book principally was compiled. Long tested in introductory courses in musicology at Berkeley, this edition has benefited also from experiences in similar courses I taught at Cornell and Stanford.

The bibliography itself is an accumulation and synthesis of information, but in the selection of works to be included, it is a critical work. The theoretical basis for the work is evident in part by its organization of the repertory of titles into genres and subjects. The annotations are as much analytical as they are descriptive. The subject index is an interpretation of the contents, item by item.

If the decade of the 1970s was the era of reprinters, the decade of the 1980s has been the era of the makers of reference works. As computers and especially microcomputers become commonplace tools used by more and more of our colleagues, we should expect to see more reference works and research tools compiled and available solely on high technology equipment. None of the several "music processing" systems in some ways analogous to word processing systems were included because they have not been tested sufficiently in support of musical research. Data base managers abound and these have already begun to assist musicologists in their work, but as these programs are not specifically musical in themselves, they have not been cited. Thousands of traditionally published works with potential for inclusion in this book were examined. Many works cited in earlier editions have been weeded from this one. Because of the great number of new books and articles potentially relevant, those printed after 1986 were not included; works published after this year will be included in the fifth edition. The section *Music for Instruction and Performance* has been reorganized to bring works for like or similar instruments together under their own headings. There is a new section on *Women in Music*, although many of the works cited there are duplicated elsewhere in the bibliography. In the chapters *Bibliographies of Music* and *Discographies*, jazz and popular music have been separated. There is a new popular music section in the chapter *Bibliographies of Music Literature*. Many more names and titles are indexed than in previous editions and there is a new scheme for subject indexing. The divided indexes have been retained in the belief that most readers were best served by them.

As in the previous editions, people too numerous to name individually have provided assistance. A few persons have been so diligent and have contributed so much that we must acknowledge them in this introduction. The fourth edition would not have appeared without the persistence and forbearance of Madeline Duckles and Carol A. Lawrence. Ruth Siebenmorgen, Eva Einstein, and the indefatigable Harriet Nicewonger were of great assistance to Vincent H. Duckles. As the responsibility for completion fell entirely on me, my knowledgeable and energetic assistant at Berkeley, Keith Stetson, became a key figure in the work. Jeffrey Dean and Cynthia Underhill were instrumental in the Berkeley phase of my efforts. Once in New Haven, the Jackson Music Library of Yale University became my principal resource; its staff under Harold Samuel was supportive and helpful. Conrad Jacoby, a Yale student, provided some much-needed assistance at a crucial stage. Again and again the bibliographic resources of the Research Libraries Information Network (or RLIN) came to the rescue. Research for this edition has been based primarily on the collections of the Berkeley and the Yale music libraries, but it became apparent that even these great research collections did not have everything of interest. Interlibrary loan and recourse to colleagues helped bring in the needed works. Among the most assiduous of the "foreign correspondents" was Kären Nagy, Music Librarian at Stanford University, but thanks to electronic mail and BITNET, colleagues from North America and Europe assisted me in gathering information for the book as well. Hideo Kaneko, Curator of Yale's East Asia Collection, and Anthony Marr, his colleague, provided substantial assistance with titles in Japanese and Chinese. Diane Perushek, Curator of the Gest Oriental Library and East Asia Collections at Princeton, provided assistance with some Chinese and Japanese titles as well. I am indebted to these and many other kind and generous people who have contributed to the completion of this edition.

Every book, particularly every bibliography, involves compromises of some sort. As in the past, readers with suggestions and criticisms of *Music Reference and Research Materials* are urged to send their comments to me. Assistance of this sort has made each edition a better book, and it is anticipated that the fifth edition will benefit in a comparable way.

Michael A. Keller
Yale University Library
New Haven, Connecticut
Spring 1988

Introduction to
the Third Edition

Since the second edition of this work appeared in 1967, there have been substantial gains in the area of music reference and research materials, both in quantity and in quality. Quantity is indicated by the fact that this third edition incorporates more than 600 new entries; quality is represented in a number of distinguished new works that have come into existence during the past five years—for example, Barry Brook's *Thematic Catalogues in Music*; Rita Benton's *Directory of Music Research Libraries*, volumes 2 and 3; and several important additions to the series issued under the auspices of the International Inventory of Musical Sources. The reprint publishers have been increasingly active during the past few years, and their work has restored a great many valuable music reference books to the shelves. A special effort has been made to call these titles to the attention of our readers.

No significant changes have been made in the organization of the work. A new section covering *Music History in Pictures* has been added. New catalogs treating *Individual Composers* and *Music of Individual Composers* have been introduced. These sections are far from comprehensive; however, they are intended to call attention to useful types of reference tools that might otherwise be overlooked by the student. In spite of the increased size and scope of this volume, selectivity has remained the rule. Those who look for complete or comprehensive coverage in any category will be disappointed. In some cases the selection has been involuntary, based as it is upon the resources of a particular music research library here at Berkeley. But more often than not the selection has been deliberate, intended to highlight the kinds of questions raised by graduate students in music and to suggest approaches to the solution of their research problems. Over the years I have accumulated an increasing debt to those generous users who have both called my attention to errors and omissions in the text and suggested improvements. They are too numerous to mention individually, but their collective impact on this new edition of *Music Reference and Research Materials* has been considerable.

Vincent Duckles
Berkeley, California
1974

Introduction to the Second Edition

The plea for corrections and additions that concluded the Introduction to the first edition of this work has not gone unheeded. Responses have come from a wide group of music students, teachers, and librarians. The chagrin at having one's oversights pointed out has been more than balanced by the pleasure at finding that this bibliography has been extensively and searchingly used. I am particularly grateful for suggestions made by my own students at the University of California, and to my colleague Daniel Heartz. John Davies, Music Librarian of the British Broadcasting Corporation, London, made many helpful comments, as did Jan La Rue, New York University, Frederick Crane, Louisiana State University, and George Skapski of San Fernando Valley State College. For assistance in the preparation of the manuscript of this edition, I am indebted to Lee Rosen.

Apart from the corrections of old entries and the addition of new, no major changes have been introduced in this edition. A few minor revisions in organization should be noted, however. These include (1) an added section on *Jazz and Popular Music* under *Bibliographies of Music*; (2) the printed and manuscript sources of early music have been combined under one alphabet rather than two; and (3) *Catalogs of Private Collections* have been extracted from the general list of music library catalogs and entered in a section of their own. A substantial number of new book reviews have been added, and much attention has been given to making the *Index* more usable from a subject point of view.

The bibliography of music is an actively growing field. This is reflected not only in the fact that more than 200 new entries have been added to this edition, but also in the high quality of the work that is being done. The International Inventory of Musical Sources has been progressing slowly but surely toward its goal. The publication of the catalogs of major Italian music libraries has been moving ahead under the direction of Claudio Sartori in the series Bibliotheca Musicae. In this country we have the exemplary bibliography of *Instrumental music printed before 1600* by Howard Brown and the long-awaited *Index of Festschriften* by Walter Gerboth. Our control over the materials of popular song has been greatly enhanced by the appearance of Richard Wolfe's bibliography of *Secular music in America, 1801–25* and by the work of James Fuld and Nat Shapiro. Two new series devoted exclusively to music bibliography are off to a promising start: the Detroit Studies in Music Bibliography and the Music Library Association Index Series.

Vincent Duckles
1966

Introduction to
the First Edition

A bibliography can be regarded as the relatively inert by-product of scholarly activity, or it can be treated as an active ingredient in the learning process. The latter perspective has been adopted in this guide to *Music Reference and Research Materials*. While no one but a professional bibliographer may be expected to come for his leisure reading to a list of books, most of us can respond with interest to an organized survey of the literature of a particular field. A bibliography, in fact, offers one of the best means of gaining an over-all impression of a subject area. It throws the essential patterns of a discipline into relief, casting light on what has been accomplished and drawing attention to the shadows where work still needs to be done. This guide has been designed to illuminate the bibliographical resources for musical scholarship. It is, above all, intended to serve a teaching purpose. Implicit in its organization is the concept that bibliography is an approach to knowledge, a way in which the student can progress toward mastery in his chosen field of specialization within the larger dimensions of the field of music. The guide was developed, through a series of editions beginning in 1949, as a text for a graduate seminar entitled "An Introduction to Musical Scholarship" given in the Music Department of the University of California at Berkeley. If its pattern has been determined to some extent by the way in which music bibliography is taught in a specific institution, its structure is still flexible enough to permit other teachers to use it in their own way.

The work is actually intended to fulfill the requirements of two groups: graduate students who need to become acquainted with the resources of musical research, and music reference librarians whose job it is to help others find the information they want. While the needs of the two have much in common, there are points at which their interests diverge. Much more is listed here than will be required for reference services in any but a large music research library, and there is material included which the scholar would rarely need to consult unless he moved outside of the traditional framework of historical musicology.

The present volume is much larger than any of its predecessors, yet it remains a selective list. One limitation in coverage, strictly enforced, is the selection of titles that pertain directly or exclusively to music. This criterion eliminates a great deal of valuable reference material, particularly important in areas that lie on the borderline between musicology and other disciplines: liturgics, the theater arts, literature, the dance, etc. No musicologist can afford to neglect such general reference tools as the *Encyclopedia of Religion and Ethics*, or Cabrol's *Dictionnaire d'archéologie chrétienne et de liturgie*, or, in another area, the *Census of Medieval and Renaissance Manuscripts in the U.S. and Canada*, by Seymour de Ricci, or Paul O. Kristeller's valuable survey of the catalogs of *Latin Manuscript*

Books before 1600. The fact that these tools are indispensable only serves to demonstrate that musicology is far from being a self-sufficient and self-contained discipline. But an attempt to list all of the peripheral resources would inflate the present work and destroy its focus. There are excellent bibliographies of general reference works currently available. Perhaps the best service to be offered to the young musicologist here is to direct him to Constance M. Winchell's *Guide to Reference Books* (7th ed., 1951, and later supplements) or to Theodore Besterman's *World Bibliography of Bibliographies* (3rd ed., 1955–56). If all else fails, he should be urged to rely on that universal repository of fact and resource, the reference librarian, who sits behind a desk in every large library, prepared to guide the inquiring student through the complex paths of information retrieval. But there is a distinct advantage to be gained in approaching the general reference tools from the musician's point of view. Recently Keith E. Mixter has furnished such an approach in his manual on *General Bibliography for Music Research* (1962), published as Number 4 in the Detroit Studies in Music Bibliography. It is a pleasure to be able to point to that work as a useful complement to this one.

A few further statements should be added to make clear what ground this guide is, and is not, intended to cover. It does not represent the well-rounded library of musical literature; it contains no entries for biography, no local histories, no monographs or studies devoted to most of the subject areas into which the field of music can be subdivided. It is certainly not a basic list of titles which every music library should acquire; but it does provide a list from which the essential materials for a music reference collection can be selected. It can best be described as a bibliography of music bibliographies, its emphasis being on those works which themselves serve as points of departure for further investigations: lists, inventories, alphabetized compilations of facts about music. The one section which falls most conspicuously outside of this pattern of bibliographic emphasis is the section on *Histories and Chronologies.* This is the only category in which books are listed for what they contain intrinsically rather than for their function as guides to further information.

In its preliminary forms this book has been put to use in a number of courses in music bibliography throughout the country, and as a result has benefited from the suggestions of several generous-minded critics. I am particularly indebted to Professor Albert T. Luper of the State University of Iowa, and to Professor Otto Albrecht of the University of Pennsylvania for their help in this respect. The form of the annotations owes much to Richard Angell of the Library of Congress, who placed his notes at my disposal. My colleagues in the Music Library of the University of California at Berkeley, Harriet Nicewonger and Minnie Elmer, have made their influence felt on nearly every page in matters that have to do with the selection of titles, the framing of the annotations, and the reading of proof.

One feature which has been introduced for the first time in the current edition is the citation of book reviews. These are offered as practical aids to the evaluation of the items. No effort has been made to achieve complete coverage: reviews are cited only for the more recent items, and are confined largely to those published in the English-language journals.

The entries are numbered throughout this book, and for the most part, each title is entered once. There are some instances of duplicate entries, however, when the content of the item calls for its listing in more than one category. Eitner's *Quellen-Lexikon* is a case in point. This title is entered once as a dictionary of biography, and again as a bibliography of early music.

Abbreviations are used sparingly. What they save in space in a work of this kind is rarely commensurate to the inconvenience caused to the user. They are confined to the standard symbols for the dictionaries and journals most frequently cited in reviews: *Grove* for *Grove's Dictionary of Music and Musicians*, 5th edition; *MGG* for *Die Musik in Geschichte und Gegenwart; Acta M* for *Acta Musicologica; JAMS* for *Journal of the American Musicological Society; MQ* for the *Musical Quarterly*; and *Notes* for *Music Library Association Notes*, 2nd series.

A bibliographer's work is never done. Even as this edition goes to press, I am troubled by the submerged voices of would-be entries which may have been overlooked, and entries which may have been misplaced or misrepresented. Other music bibliographers proceed, unconcerned, with their work, the results of which will eventually call for supplements, or even substantial revisions in our present pattern of organization. But if one were too attentive to such considerations a work of this kind would never reach the point of publication. Now that it has made its appearance, I hope that it will attract collaboration, in the form of corrections, additions, or suggestions for improvement, from all who have occasion to use it.

Vincent Duckles
1964

MUSIC
REFERENCE
AND
RESEARCH
MATERIALS

Dictionaries and Encyclopedias

The most comprehensive bibliography of music dictionaries and encyclopedias is James B. Coover's *Music Lexicography*, 3rd edition, 1971 (no. 689), which offers some 1,800 titles. Other convenient listings appear in the article "Lexika der Musik," by Hans Heinrich Eggebrecht, in *MGG*, vol. 8, and in the "Sachteil" of the Riemann *Musik-Lexikon*, 12th edition, 1967. Coover's article in the *New Grove*, "Dictionaries and Encyclopedias of Music" (no. 688), includes a selective listing arranged by country or region, a listing by language, and another by subject.

Two works published since the 3rd edition of *Music Reference and Research Materials* are of prime importance. The first is the *New Grove*, edited by Stanley Sadie (no. 46). It was based almost entirely on new research and is the fruit of mainly Anglo-American musical scholarship, though many of the contributors were from other countries. The second is *The New Harvard Dictionary of Music*, edited by Don M. Randel (no. 385). Both of these substantial new research tools succeeded in breaking away from the practice of depending heavily upon earlier dictionaries and encyclopedias for their texts.

The present list includes the most important music dictionaries and encyclopedias in current use, in modern languages, cited as far as possible under their latest editions. It also includes a selection of titles of those early works that are available in modern reprints or that are of continuing value for reference purposes.

GENERAL

1. Abert, Hermann J. Illustriertes Musik-Lexikon. Stuttgart: J. Engelhorns Nachf., 1927. 542 p.

A popular general dictionary based on Riemann (no. 53) and *Das neue Musiklexikon* (no. 102). 503 pictures on 72 plates and numerous short musical examples. Contributing editors: Hermann Abert, Friedrich Blume, Rudolf Gerber, Hans Hoffman, and Theodor Schwartzkopff.

2. Algemene muziekencyclopedie. Onder leiding van A. Corbet en Wouter Paap. J. Robijns: Redactiesecretaris. Antwerpen: Zuid-Nederlandse Uitg., 1957–63. 6 v.

7th volume issued in 1972: Aanvullend deel.

Comprehensive coverage of all aspects of music, including ethnomusicology, popular music, jazz. Brief biographies include performers, musicologists, composers, dancers. Major articles signed by contributors from England, Israel, United States, U.S.S.R., etc. Subject bibliographies, discographies, and brief lists of works for composers and musicologists. Valuable for its wide biographical range. Illustrated.

3. **Allorto, Riccardo and Alberto Ferrari.** Dizionario di musica. Milano: Casa Editrice Ceschina, 1959. 576 p.

A popular dictionary of terms and biography. Brief biographical entries mentioning representative works of minor composers and giving full tabulations of works of major composers. Well printed and illustrated, 8 plates in color. No bibliographical references.

4. **Ammer, Christine.** Harper's dictionary of music. 2nd ed. New York: Harper & Row, 1986. 493 p.

1st edition, 1972. 414 p.

A dictionary for the general music lover.

5. **Arma, Paul and Yvonne Tiénot.** Nouveau dictionnaire de musique. Paris: Éditions Ouvrières, 1947. 285 p.

A "pocket" dictionary comprising some 2,000 biographical entries and 6,000 terms. 365 illustrated and short musical examples. Brief articles and summary listings of composers' works. Table of abbreviations.

6. **Arnold, Denis, ed.** The new Oxford companion to music. Oxford: Oxford University Press, 1983. 2 v.

First published in 1938 and reissued in 10 more editions as the *Oxford Companion to Music*.

Still intended for the general reader, the *New Oxford Companion* is the work of a team of scholars and writers on music, among them the originator of the *Companion*, Percy Scholes, several of whose articles have been incorporated. The *New Companion* is intended to be complete in itself, but bibliographies are appended to few articles and the *New Grove* is cited as the source for "more facts." The inclusion of jazz, some popular music, and non-Western music signals the broader worldview of the authors and their readers. Nevertheless, the articles on "colour and music" by Scholes, any of the geographical articles ("Russia," "Scandinavia"), and the articles on several formal terms ("sonata," "symphony") signal somewhat dated styles and intentions.

Review of the 8th ed. by Charles Warren Fox in *Notes*, 8 (1950), p. 177–78; of the 9th ed. by Vincent Duckles in *Notes*, 13 (1955), p. 70–72. For a further evaluation of this work, see the article "Music Lexicography," by Vincent Duckles, in *College Music Symposium*, 11 (1971), p. 121 ff.

7. **Blom, Eric.** New everyman dictionary of music. 6th edition. Originally compiled by Eric Blom; edited by David Cummings. New York: Weidenfeld and Nicolson, 1989. 876 p.

Also published in London by Dent, 1988. 5th edition of 1971 revised by Jack Westrup, John Caldwell, Edward Olleson, and R. T. Beck.

First pub. in 1946; U.S. ed., 1948; rev. ed., 1965; further rev. ed., 1968.
A popular quick-reference book of terms and biography. Small in size but exceedingly rich in information. Excludes living performers. Summary listings of composers' works.
Review of the 1954 ed. by Vincent Duckles in *Notes*, 13 (1955), p. 70–72.

8. Bonaccorsi, Alfredo. Nuovo dizionario musicale Curci. Milano: Curci, [1954]. 557 p.
Emphasis on terms and forms, but with essential biographies. Brief bibliographies for most articles, including references to modern republications for composers.
Review in *Rassegna Musicale*, 24 (1954), p. 389–91.

9. Bonniers musiklexikon. [Edited by] Folke H. Törnblom. Stockholm: Bonniers Förlag, 1983. 528 p.
First published in 1975 based on entries in the *Bonniers Lexikon* of 1961–64. 446 p.
The endpapers carry a chronological chart of music history with parallel columns devoted to art, literature, philosophy, and political history.
Danish edition cited in no. 27.

10. Borba, Tómas and Fernando Lopes Graça. Dicionário de música ilustrado. Lisboa: Edições Cosmos, 1956. 2 v.

11. Bottenheim, S. A. M. Prisma encyclopedie der muziek. Bewerkt en ingeleid door Wouter Paap. [2. druk.] Utrecht: Het Spectrum, 1957. 2 v.

12. Coeuroy, André. Dictionnaire critique de la musique ancienne et moderne. Paris: Payot, 1956. 413 p.
Primarily biographical, its chief value is in the section "Écoles modernes" (p. 92–191), which provides chronological lists by country, giving brief stylistic characteristics and one or two works for each composer. Important modern composers are entered in the main alphabet. Appropriate cross-references.

Collins music encyclopedia. See Westrup, Jack A. and F. Ll. Harrison.
The new college encyclopedia of music..., no. 68.

13. Cooper, Martin. The concise encyclopedia of music and musicians. 4th ed. London: Hutchinson, 1978. 480 p.
First edition published in London by Hutchinson and in New York by Hawthorne Books, 1958. 516 p.

> It is [the] "average music lover" for whom the present work is designed. The expert and connoisseur are already well catered for with twelve-volume dictionaries and detailed studies of particular musical fields, but my task has been to present in a concise, easily digestible form the history and technical rudiments of an art which plays an increasing part in our life. [*Foreword*]

Biographical entries are brief. Longer discussions of major terms and forms. No bibliographies. Well illustrated with 16 color plates and more than 100 in monochrome. 17 contributors in addition to the editor.

14. Dahlhaus, Carl and Hans Heinrich Eggebrecht. Brockhaus Riemann Musik-lexikon. Wiesbaden: F. A. Brockhaus; Mainz: Schott, 1978–79. 2 v.

A general music dictionary based on the format laid out in the *Musik-Lexikon* of Hugo Riemann, 1882.

Reviews by Wolfgang Burde in *Neue Zeitschrift für Musik*, 140 (1979), p. 74–75, and by Hubert Unverricht in *Musik und Bildung*, 11 (1979), p. 127–128.

DBG-Musiklexikon. See Herzfeld, Friedrich. Ullstein Musiklexikon, no. 30.

15. Della Corte, Andrea and G. M. Gatti. Dizionario di musica. 6. ed. Torino: G.B. Paravia, [1959]. 724 p.

First published in 1925.

Includes personal names, subjects, instruments, and cities, covering all countries and periods, but with emphasis on Italian names and topics. Brief biographies list major works, with fair coverage of republication of old music, especially for Italian composers.

16. Diccionario enciclopédico de la música. [Dirección general A. Albert Tor-rellas]. Barcelona: Central Catalana de Publicaciones, [1947]–52. 4 v.

Supersedes *Diccionario de la Música Ilustrado*, 1927–29. 2 v.

Contributors include composers and musicologists from Spain, Portugal, and Latin America.

Vol. 1: "Terminología, tecnología, morfología, instrumentos." Technical terms in all languages, including Greek and Oriental (transliterated). No bibliography or documentation.

Vols. 2–3: "Biografías, bibliografía, monografías, historia, argumentos de operas." Biographies of composers, performers, musicologists, with emphasis on Spanish and South American musicians. Lists of works for major composers; classified listing for minor figures. Historical articles under names of countries. Extended articles for Spanish provinces, covering folk music, history, composers, institutions, etc. No bibliographical references.

Vol. 4: "Apéndice, por A. Albert Torrellas...."

17. Dizionario enciclopedico universale della musica e dei musicisti. Diretto da Alberto Basso. Torino: UTET, 1983–. 4 v. dictionary of terms and 8 v. biographical dictionary; 1 v. appendix.

Successor to *La musica* (no. 41).

Prima parte: *La Lessico*, vols. 1–4 (1983–84).

Seconda parte: *Le Biografie*, vols. 1–8. (1985–86).

The dictionary of terms consists of extensive signed articles with many illustrations, charts, and tables. Cross-references.

The biographical section features signed articles on composers, musicians, and other musical figures. Articles on composers have works lists. International in scope. Selective bibliographies.

This is the leading Italian encyclopedia of music.

Review by Hans Lenneberg in *Notes*, 40 (1986), p. 538–40.

18. Dizionario Ricordi della musica e dei musicisti. [Direttore: Claudio Sartori; redattori: Fausto Broussard *et al.*] [Milano]: Ricordi, 1959. 1,155 p.

Wide biographical coverage, including living performers, important composers of light music, musicologists. Concise articles, excellent bibliographies and lists of compositions.

See also the *Nuovo Dizionario Ricordi* (no. 48).

Review by Jack A. Westrup in *Music and Letters*, 41 (1960), p. 80–81; by James B. Coover in *Notes*, 17 (1960), p. 564–66.

19. Enciclopédia da música Brasileira: erudita, folclórica, popular. General editor: Marcos Antônio Marcondes. São Paulo: Art Editora, 1977. 2 v.

Includes entries on Brazilian musical persons, terms, genres, and instruments. Extensive lists of works in biographical entries. Many useful appendices: discography by composer and medium; chronological list of Brazilian operas; Brazilian music periodicals; Brazilian theaters; first-line index of music. General bibliography.

Accompanied by 2 LP recordings.

20. Enciclopedia Salvat de la música. Barcelona; Madrid; Buenos Aires; Mexico; Caracas; Bogotá; Rio de Janeiro: Salvá, 1967. 4 v.

This is a Spanish adaptation of the *Encyclopédie de la Musique* published by Fasquelle (no. 21).

Review by Daniel Devoto in *Revue de Musicologie*, 57 (1971), p. 87–88.

21. Encyclopédie de la musique. [Publié sous la direction de François Michel en collaboration avec François Lesure et Vladimir Fédorov, et un comité de rédaction composé de Nadia Boulanger *et al.*]. Paris: Fasquelle, [1958–61]. 3 v.

Preceding the dictionary proper is a series of essays (vol. 1, p. 1–238) devoted to general information about music in society: festivals, concerts, radio, the music press, education in France, copyright laws, institutions, and associations. A "Livre d'Or," p. 35–76, gives portraits and facsimile pages from the manuscripts of leading contemporary composers. Chronological table of music history, p. 203–38.

Much emphasis on ideas and principles rather than on individuals and works. Biographical articles are short. Bibliographical references, many to *MGG* (no. 43). Lists of works for major composers; fuller treatment of subjects. Many signed articles. Excellent illustrative material, musical and pictorial. Especially valuable for its coverage of modern music.

For Spanish adaptation see no. 20.

Review by James B. Coover in *Notes*, 16 (1959), p. 381–83.

22. Encyclopédie de la musique et dictionnnaire du conservatoire. Fondateur: Albert Lavignac; Directeur: Lionel de La Laurencie. Paris: C. Delagrave, 1913–31. 2 parts in 11 v.

Originally published in fascicles.

Part I: "Histoire de la musique." Part II: "Technique, esthétique, pédagogie."

The work was designed, in the tradition of the French encyclopedists, as a universal repository of musical knowledge. It is international in scope, although most of the contributors are French. Many of the studies are full-scale monographs and still rank among the most important surveys of their fields. History is treated by country. Among the chief contributors are Maurice Emmanuel, Amédée Gastoué, Oscar Chilesotti, Romain Rolland, Henry Expert, and Rafael Mitjana.

Part II deals with music theory, instruction, and aesthetics in all aspects, including acoustics, notation, instrument making, choreography, and institutions. Major articles by Charles Koechlin, Paul Rougnon, and Vincent d'Indy. Illustrated; numerous musical examples.

The *Encyclopédie* lacks an index, and for this reason the detailed tables of contents at the end of each part are most useful as a guide to its contents. A partial index was compiled by Robert Bruce and published in *Notes*, ser. 1 (May 1936), p. 1–40.

23. Encyclopédie methodique, ou par ordre de matières; par une société de gens de lettres, de savans et d'artistes ... *La Musique*, publiée par MM. [Nicholas Étienne] Framery et [Pierre Louis] Ginguené. Paris: Chez Panckoucke, 1791–1818. 2 v.

Vol. 1: A–G, 760 p. Vol. 2: H–Z, 558 p.

Publisher varies. Tome II, Paris, Chez Mme. veuve Agasse. In this volume the name of Jerome Joseph de Momigny is added to that of the two other compilers. Vol. 1 contains a musical appendix of 74 p.; vol. 2, of 114 p.

The *Encyclopédie Methodique* is a large general reference work of which the two volumes cited are concerned with music. These volumes are of considerable historical importance since they incorporate articles from Rousseau's *Dictionnaire de Musique* (no. 387) and from the Diderot-d'Alembert *Encyclopédie* along with more recent commentary. Articles are signed.

24. Encyclopedie van de muziek. Hoofdredactie: Louis M. G. Arntzenius *et al.* Met bijzondere medwerking van J. Kunst *et al.* Amsterdam: Elsevier, 1956–57. 2 v.

Vol. 1: A–H. Vol. 2: I–Z.

25. Encyklopedia muzyczna PWM. [kolegium red. i komitet red. Zofia Lissa (przewodn.), *et al.*]. Kraków: Polskie Wydawn. Muzyczne, 1979–80. 6 v.

The modern Polish encyclopedia of music, providing bio-bibliographical information and entries on terms and topics.

26. Entsiklopedicheskii muzykal'nyi slovar'. Otvetstvennyi redaktor: G. V. Vsevolodovich sostaviteli B. S. Shteinpress i I. M. Iampol'skii. Moskva: Gos. Nauk. Izd. "Bol'shaia sovetskaia entsiklopediia," 1959. 326 p.

A 2nd edition appeared in 1966. 631 p.

One of the standard Soviet encyclopedias of music, containing partially revised articles from the general *Bol'shaia Sovetskaia Entsiklopediia.*

27. Gads musikleksikon. Redigeret af Søren Sørensen, John Christiansen, Finn Slumstrup. København: G.E.C. Gad, 1976. 502 p.

Based on the *Bonniers Musiklexikon* of 1975 (no. 9).

Grove's dictionary of music and musicians. See The new Grove dictionary of music and musicians, no. 46.

28. Gurvin, Olav and Ø. Anker. Musikleksikon. Ny revidert utg. Oslo: Dreyer, [1959]. 902 cols.

First published in 1949.

Biography, including jazz musicians, performers, and composers. Title entries for dramatic works, familiar art songs, and folk songs. Terms, short articles, partial lists of works, occasional bibliographical references. Popular.

29. Hamburger, Povl. Aschehougs musikleksikon. København: Aschehoug, 1957–58. 2 v.

Supersedes the *Illustreret Musikleksikon*, edited by Hortense Panum and William Behrend, published in 1940.

Intended for popular use, international in scope, but with emphasis on Scandinavia.

30. Herzfeld, Friedrich. Ullstein Musiklexikon. Mit 4500 Stichwörtern, 600 Notenbeispielen, 1000 Abbildungen, und 32 Tafelseiten. Berlin; Frankfurt; Wien: Verlag Ullstein, 1965. 631 p.

Also published under the title *DBG-Musiklexikon* by the Deutsche Buch-Gemeinschaft, Berlin.

A one-volume music dictionary for ready reference. Profusely illustrated with small-scale portraits and musical examples. References to recordings.

31. Honegger, Marc. Dictionnaire de la musique. I: Les hommes et leurs œuvres. II: Science de la musique: techniques, formes, instruments. Paris: Bordas, 1970–76. 4 v.

Part I reprinted in 1974 and a new edition, also 2 v., issued in 1986.

The most substantial modern French music encyclopedia. Excellent coverage particularly of French topics, albeit with brief entries. A handsome, well-illustrated work, produced with the collaboration of some 186 authorities; international in scope.

32. Hyōjun ongaku jiten. [Standard music dictionary. Sansaku Meguro, ed.] Tokyo: Ongaku no Tomo Sha, 1966–73. 2 v.

For a Japanese multi-volume encyclopedia of music, see no. 61.

33. Jacobs, Arthur. The new Penguin dictionary of music. Rev. ed. Harmondsworth: Penguin, 1978. 458 p.

First published as *A New Dictionary of Music* in 1958, followed by a hardcover edition with a new introduction and corrections published in London and Chicago, 1961, and a 2nd edition in 1967, 425 p.

A pocket dictionary for the inquiring music lover, with brief identifications of people (mostly composers and performers), terms, operatic and other specific titles, and all sorts of musical topics. [*Notes*, 16 (1958), p. 68]

Review of the 1961 edition by Harold E. Samuel in *Notes*, 20 (1963), p. 657–58.

34. Keller, Gerard and Philip Kruseman. Geïllustreerd muzieklexicon, onder redactie van G. Keller en Philip Kruseman, met medewerking van Sem Dresden, Wouter Hutschenruijter, Willem Landré.... 's-Gravenhage: J. P. Kruseman, 1932. 966 p.

Supplement of 319 p. published in 1949; then reissued in two volumes (vol. 1, p. 1–664; vol. 2, p. 665–966).

Brief articles, bibliographical references, and lists of major works for composers. Similar to Abert (no. 1) in form and content, but useful in connection with contemporary Dutch names.

35. Kennedy, Michael. The Oxford dictionary of music. Oxford and New York: Oxford University Press, 1985. 810 p.

An enlargement and revision of the 3rd ed. of the *Concise Oxford Dictionary of Music* (1980, 724 p.), based on the original by Percy A. Scholes, first published in 1952. A second edition was issued in 1964 and reissued as a paperback in 1968.

Primarily a reduction of the *New Oxford Companion* (no. 6). Includes hundreds of short biographical entries for vocal and instrumental performers and conductors, as well as some hundreds of entries concerning individual compositions. About 11,000 entries, 4,000 biographical. This edition adds many new articles to supplement articles remaining from previous editions.

36. Larousse de la musique. Edited by Antoine Goléa and Michel Vignal. Paris: Larousse, 1982. 2 v.

A one-volume abridged version appeared in 1985. The 1st edition (1957, 2 v.) was edited by Norbert Dufourcq with the assistance of Félix Raugel and Armand Machabey. An Italian version of the 1st edition was issued as *Dizionario Musicale Larousse*, edited by Delfino Nava (Milan: Edizioni Paoline, 1961. 3 v.)

An encyclopedic dictionary with more than 8,000 entries, principally on Western music from its origins to the present time. Brief but authoritative articles: biographies (composers, performers, musicologists, editors, makers of instruments, critics, and writers); works (operas, ballets, manuscripts); subjects (terms, places, schools, forms and genres). There are some articles on non-Western music. Some French emphasis. Color illustrations.

There is a bibliography at the end of the second volume arranged by entry. Name and title index.

Reviews of the 1st edition by Paul Henry Lang in *Musical Quarterly*, 45 (1959), p. 120–23, and by James B. Coover in *Notes*, 16 (1959), p. 381–83.

37. Malá encyklopédia hudby. Spracoval kolektiv autorov. Vedúci autorského kolektívu Marian Jurík. Vedecký redaktor Dr. Ladislav Mokrý, CSc. Bratislava: Obzor, 1969. 642 p.

A Slovak dictionary of music and bio-bibliography. P. 629–42: bibliography. Illustrated. No bibliographical references with the articles.

38. Mendel, Hermann. Musikalisches Conversations-Lexikon. Eine Encyklopädie der gesammten musikalischen Wissenschaften. Für Gebildete aller Stände, unter Mitwirkung der Literarischen Commission des Berliner Tonkünstlervereins.... Berlin: L. Heimann; New York: J. Schuberth, 1870–79. 11 v.

Reprint of the 2nd ed., 12 v., by Georg Olms, Hildesheim.

2nd ed. with supplementary volume, "Ergänzungsband," Berlin: R. Oppenheim, 1880–83. 3rd ed., "Neue wohlfeile Stereotyp-Ausgabe," Leipzig: List & Francke [1890–91].

Founded by Mendel, continued (vols. 7–11) by August Reissmann. One of the major 19th-century general music encyclopedias. Superseded in most respects, but still useful for obscure names and earlier concepts and criticism. Partial lists of works; few bibliographical references.

39. Moore, John W. Complete encyclopaedia of music, elementary, technical, historical, biographical, vocal, and instrumental. Boston: J. P. Jewett, 1854 [copyright notice, 1852]. 1,004 p.

Appendix containing events and information occurring since the main work was issued. Boston: Oliver Ditson, 1875, 45 p.

Reprinted by Ditson in 1880.

The first comprehensive American musical dictionary, containing more than 5,000 terms, 4,000 biographical citations, 200 articles, many of which are drawn from Gerber, Choron and Fayolle, Burney, Hawkins, Hogarth, Calcott, Gardiner, Busby, Hamilton, Schilling, and Fétis. Substantial additional material from *Dwight's Musical Journal* and the *New York Musical Times*. Especially rich in notices of 18th- and 19th-century musicians, although somewhat weak in early Americana.

40. Moser, Hans J. Musik Lexikon. Vierte, stark erweiterte Aufl. Hamburg: H. Sikorski, 1955. 2 v. Nachtrag, 1958. 71 p.

First published in 1932–35; 2nd ed., 1943; 3rd ed., 1951. Ergänzungsband A–Z, 1963. 287 p.

Brief, authoritative articles, with special emphasis on bibliographies and lists of early music in new editions. Addressed to German readers, but increasingly international in scope with the late editions. The 4th edition, first to appear in two volumes, is extensively revised, with many new articles and bibliographical additions.

41. La musica. Sotto la direzione di Guido M. Gatti, a cura di Alberto Basso. Torino: Unione Tipografico-editrice Torinese, 1966–68. 6 v.

Predecessor to no. 17.

Parte prima: *Enciclopedia Storica*, v. 1–4 (1966).

Parte seconda: *Dizionario*, v. 5–6 (1968).

A large-scale, handsomely illustrated reference tool. There are only 196 entries in the *parte prima*, of which 81 are biographies. All of the articles are extended, averaging 16 to 18 pages each. Useful tabulations of composers' works. The contributors are chiefly Italian but include a number of international authorities.

The dictionary, *parte seconda*, serves as an index to the *Enciclopedia*, articulating with it and offering brief entries for terms and the biographies of minor musicians.

Review of the *Enciclopedia Storica* by Vincent Duckles in *Notes*, 24 (1947), p. 263–64; reviews of the *Dizionario* by Hans Lenneberg in *Notes*, 27 (1970), p. 51–52, and by Georg Karstadt in *Die Musikforschung*, 24 (1971), p. 458–61.

42. Musiikin tietokirja. Toimituskunta: Tiovo Haapanen *et al.* Helsingissä: Kustannososkeyhtiö Otava, [1948]. 573 p.

Terms, subjects, operas, biographies (including performers, publishers, musicologists, many contemporary composers). Emphasis on Scandinavian musicians. Partial lists of works.

43. Die Musik in Geschichte und Gegenwart. Allgemeine Enzyklopädie der Musik.... Edited by Friedrich Blume. Kassel u. Basel: Bärenreiter Verlag, 1949–1986. 17 v.

The work consists of 14 volumes with the principal articles and continues in two *Ergänzungs Bänden*, 1973–79. A *Register Band*, edited by Elisabeth Heckmann and Harald Heckmann, was published 1986.

MGG is a comprehensive music reference work of the highest scholarly merit. In German, but international in scope and coverage. Articles contributed by specialists throughout the world. Gives complete listings of some composers' works and detailed monographs, embodying the latest research. Many illustrations.

The *Ergänzungs Bände* both supplement and correct information in the first 14 volumes. The first supplement volume provides individual entries for composers and musicians who were originally treated in very large family articles. The *Register Band* is an extensive and very valuable index, making many otherwise obscured matters accessible.

Reviewed by Willi Apel in *Journal of the American Musicological Society*, 3 (1950), p. 142–45; 5 (1952), p. 56–57, and p. 138–39; by Charles Warren Fox in *Notes*, 7 (1950), p. 466–67, 10 (1953), p. 451–52, 12 (1954), p. 92–93; by Paul Henry Lang in *Musical Quarterly*, 36 (1950), p. 141–43, 38 (1952), p. 477–79. Reviewed in *Die Musikforschung* by Rudolph Steglich, 6 (1953), p. 260–64; by Hans Ehinger, 8 (1955), p. 92–96; by Kurt von Fischer, 9 (1956), p. 331–36, and 10 (1957), p. 423–28; by Hellmut Federhofer in 12 (1959), p. 338–41.

Publication of the 5th edition of *Grove* in 1954 provided the occasion for some critical comparisons between *Grove* and *MGG*. See Richard S. Hill in *Notes*, 12 (1954), p. 85–92, and A. Hyatt King, "*Grove V* and *MGG*," in the *Monthly Musical Record*, 85 (1955), p. 115–19, p. 152–57, and p. 183–85. For a fascinating discussion of the genesis, organization, and production of a great music reference work, see "*Die Musik in Geschichte und Gegenwart*: a postlude," by Friedrich Blume in *Notes*, 24 (1967), p. 217–44. Blume also wrote a "Preface" to the Supplement to *MGG* published in *Notes*, 26 (1970), p. 5–8. Paul Henry Lang in "*Die Musik in Geschichte und Gegenwart*: Epilogue," in *Notes*, 36 (1979), p. 271–81, presents a panegyric to Blume and others who had worked on *MGG* as well as a comment on the state of musicology.

See also Jack Westrup, "Kritische Anmerkungen zu *Die Musik in Geschichte und Gegenwart*, volumes 9–14," trans. by Ludwig Finscher in *Die Musikforschung*, 22 (1969), p. 217–25.

Two of Blume's major survey articles have been translated by M. D. Herter Norton and published separately by W. W. Norton: 1. *Renaissance and Baroque Music, a Comprehensive Survey* (1967), 180 p.; and 2. *Classic and Romantic Music, a Comprehensive Survey* (1970), 213 p. The former is reviewed by Vernon Gotwals in *Notes*, 24 (1968), p. 488–89.

For an index to facsimiles of polyphonic music in *MGG*, see no. 1742.

44. Muzička enciklopedija. [Glavni redaktor: Josip Andreis]. Zagreb: Izdanje i naklada leksikografskog zavoda, 1958–63. 2 v.

Vol. 1: A–J, 760 p. Vol. 2: K–Z, 286 p. Rev. ed., 1971–77. 3 v.

Contributors: Yugoslavian musicologists. Major articles signed.

Condensed biographical, extended subject entries. Well-organized bibliographies and lists of works. Living performers excluded. International coverage, with emphasis on Slavic composers. Excellent in content and appearance.

Review by Josef Brozek in *Notes*, 21 (1963–64), p. 128–29.

45. Muzykal'naia entsiklopediia. Gl. red. Iurii Vsevolodovich Keldysh. Moscow: Sov. Entsiklopediia—Sov. Kommozitor, 1973–82. 6 v.

The official musical encyclopedia of the U.S.S.R. Extensive, signed articles. Many with bibliographies and works lists. International in scope, but clearly more coverage of figures in socialist countries. Many of the biographical articles cover musical figures cited in no other reference work. The reader is rewarded for the difficult task of decoding the Cyrillic characters by the acquisition of information and opinion otherwise unavailable.

46. The new Grove dictionary of music and musicians. Edited by Stanley Sadie. London: Macmillan, 1980. 20 v.

First published in 1879–89; 2nd ed., 1904–10, ed. by J. A. Fuller-Maitland; 3rd ed., 1927–28, ed. by H. C. Colles; 4th ed., 1940, ed. by H. C. Colles. A supplementary volume to the 3rd edition appeared in 1940, covering the period from 1928 to 1940, with new information pertaining to earlier entries. An American supplement, edited by W. S. Pratt, containing material on the U.S., Canada, and South and Central America, was published in 1920 and again in 1928. A 5th edition, edited by Eric Blom, was published in 1954 by Macmillan. A supplementary volume to the 5th edition, ed. by Eric Blom; assoc. ed., Denis Stevens; 1961. 493 p.

The 5th edition was issued in an unabridged paperback reprint by St. Martin's Press, New York, 1970.

The *New Grove* is the standard comprehensive music encyclopedia in English. It contains entries on music history, theory, and practice, instruments, and terms. The longer biographical entries include lists of works and extensive bibliographies; the shorter ones summarize works lists and bibliographies. Entries are signed. This edition clearly favors the interests of music scholars rather than those of informed amateurs and performers. It succeeds *MGG* as the major reference work supporting and informing musical scholarship. The *New Grove* is marred by the lack of a general index; there is an index to ethnomusicological terms, but a vast body of information is made less accessible by this editorial decision. See Ann P. Basart's index to manuscripts cited in the "Sources" articles (mentioned in no. 1711). For other indexes see no. 1126.

The publication of the *New Grove* in 1980 brought a flood of commentary, most of it highly favorable. The work was projected on an international scale, with contributions from scholars throughout the world. Stanley Sadie, the general editor, has provided an account of the complexities in such a vast publication in 20 volumes and 20,000 entries in the article "The New Grove" in *Notes*, 32 (1975), p. 259–68. The text of the *New Grove* was set using a computer and parts of it have reappeared since 1980, revised in a varied series of volumes. The whole work has been reprinted with a few alterations.

The editor of the *Musical Quarterly* devoted an entire issue (v. 68, 1982, p. 153–286) to assessments of coverage of certain broad topics in the new edition: Bruno Nettl—ethnomusicology; Allen Forte—theory; Robert Cogan—music, science and technology; Lance W. Brunner—Medieval music; Frank Tirro—Renaissance music; Denis Stevens—Baroque music; Bathia Churgin—music of the Classic era; Aubry S. Garlington—opera; Jon W. Finson—19th-century music; Richard Crawford—music of pre-20th-century America; Robert P. Morgan—20th-century music; Billy Taylor—jazz; Paul Wittke—American music theater.

Similar treatment was afforded in *Notes*, 38 (1981) by Susan T. Sommer, William Morris, Virgil Thomson, Michael Tilson Thomas, and the reference staff of the Music Division of the New York Public Library. Joshua Rifkin reviewed the *New Grove* in *Journal of the American Musicological Society*, 35 (Spring 1982), p. 182–99, as did Desmond Shawe-Taylor in the *New Yorker* (23 Nov. 1981), p. 218–25. A controversial and perhaps the longest review is that of Charles Rosen in the *New York Review of Books* issue of 28 May 1981; Rosen concentrates mostly on the treatment of Western art music, focusing principally on biography and theory in the *New Grove*. Donald W. Krummel's review in *Choice* of February 1981, p. 762–66, is well worth reading. There is a review in the *New Statesman* of 27 February 1981 by Andrew Clements. Andrew Jones, Robin Orr, and Michael Greenhalgh reviewed portions of the *New Grove* in the March 1981 issue of the *Musical Times* and reviews by Christopher Hogwood and Derrick Puffett appeared in the April 1981 issue.

Articles from the *New Grove* are cited as nos. 635, 688, 824, 905, 1712, 1722, 1737, 1771, 1852, and 2683.

47. Norlind, Tobias. Allmänt musiklexikon. 2 omarbetade uppl. Stockholm: Wahlström & Widstrand, 1927–28. 2 v.

First published in parts, 1912–16.

Many biographies, with full lists of compositions, including information on dates and publishers.

48. Nuovo dizionario Ricordi della musica e dei musicisti, a cura di Riccardo Allorto; redattori Lily Allorto Bozzano, Franco Armani, Irlando Danieli. Milano: G. Ricordi, 1976. 730 p.

Utilizes parts of the *Dizionario Ricordi* (no. 18). The entries are short and the bibliographies brief. Well printed, with handsome color plates; notation practices illustrated.

49. Pena, Joaquín. Diccionario de la música Labor; iniciado por Joaquín Pena, continuado por Higinio Anglés, con la colaboración de Miguel Querol y otros distinguidos musicólogos españoles y extranjeros. Barcelona: Labor, 1954. 2 v.

Begun in 1940 as an adaptation of Riemann (no. 53), but developed as a new dictionary of music for Spanish-speaking countries. Contributors are Spanish and Spanish-American. Foreign biographies drawn from Riemann, Grove, Baker, Schmidl, etc. Covers bio-bibliography, technique, and history. Designed for professional musicians and for general use.

50. Pratt, Waldo S. The new encyclopedia of music and musicians. New and rev. ed. New York: Macmillan, 1929. 969 p.

First published in 1924.

Originally planned as an abridgment of the second edition of *Grove* but developed as an independent work. Arranged in three main alphabets: terms, biographies, and institutions and organizations. Appendixes for bibliography, musicians before 1700, and operas and oratorios produced since 1900. Covers primarily the 18th–20th centuries, with emphasis on the living musicians and the American scene. Excellent definitions of musical terms.

51. Reiss, Jósef Władysław. Mala encyklopedia muzyki. [Redaktor naczelny tefan Sledzinski Wyd. 1]. Warszawa: Państwowe Wydawn. Naukowe, 1970. 1,269 p.

First issued in 1924; later editions issued in 1960 and 1968.

Popular dictionary, international coverage, with definitions of terms, fairly extensive articles on topics, and brief biographies of composers, performers, critics, etc. Short bibliographies for major subjects. Illustrated. An interesting feature is the biographical index, which assembles all references to individuals.

52. Ricordi enciclopedia della musica. Direttore: Claudio Sartori. Vice-direttore: Riccardo Allorto. Milano: Ricordi, 1963–64. 4 v.

A major modern Italian encyclopedia of music. Well printed and illustrated, including color plates. Contributions by some 232 international specialists. Long articles signed. Good bibliographical coverage.

53. Riemann, Hugo. Musik-Lexikon. 12. völlig neubearbeitete Auflage in drei Bänden. Hrsg. von Willibald Gurlitt. Mainz: B. Schott's Söhne, 1959–67. 3 v.

Vol. 1: *Personenteil*, A–K, 1959. 986 p. Vol 2: *Personenteil*, L–Z, 1961. 976 p. Vol. 3: *Sachteil*, 1967. 1,087 p. (Vol. 3 ed. by Hans Heinrich Eggebrecht.) Two supplementary volumes, *Ergänzungsbände* to the *Personenteil*, have been published. The first, A–K, appeared in 1972, edited by Carl Dahlhaus. The second, L–Z, appeared in 1975.

The 12th edition is the latest in the series based on Riemann's work, first published in 1882. The present edition is the first in which terms and biography are treated in separate alphabets. Alfred Einstein was editor of the 9th, 10th, and 11th editions and added much to the scope and authority of the work.

Riemann's *Musik-Lexikon* is a universal dictionary of music covering all times and places and incorporating the achievements of German musical scholarship. Superior to Moser (no. 40) in typography and organization, and to Baker (no. 71) in bibliographical coverage. Lists of works are included within the bodies of the articles; modern editions of early works and bibliographical references are given in separate paragraphs.

The *Ergänzungsbände* incorporate new information, corrections, and additions to the articles and bibliographies in the main volumes. There are new articles as well. The L–Z volume includes a supplementary necrology covering persons in the dictionary who died before 1975.

Riemann's work has been widely translated, and most of the translations have incorporated new materials of national interest. The principal translations are as follows:

Dictionnaire de Musique. Traduit d'après la 4me édition par Georges Humbert. Paris: Perrin, 1895–1902. 2me éd., Paris: Perrin, 1913. 3me éd., entièrement refondue et augm. sous la direction de A. Schaeffner, avec la collaboration de M. Pincherle, Y. Rokseth, A. Tessier. Paris: Payot, 1931.

Dictionary of Music. New edition, with many additions by the author. Trans. by J. S. Shedlock. London: Augener, 1893. Also published in 1897 as *Encyclopedic Dictionary of Music.* Later editions in 1902 and 1908. Reprint of the 1908 edition by Da Capo Press, New York, 1970.

Muzykal'nyi Slovar'.... Moskva: P. Iurgenson, 1901–1904. A Russian translation from the 5th German edition.

Nordisk Musik-lexikon, udarbeidet af H. V. Schytte, København: 1888–92, 2 v., with a *Supplement* (c. 1906).

Reviews of the 12th ed. *Personenteil* by Vincent Duckles in *Notes*, 16 (1959), p. 240–42, and 18 (1961), p. 572–74; by Paul Henry Lang in the *Musical Quarterly*, 45 (1959), p. 563–66; by Hans H. Eggebrecht in *Die Musikforschung*, 12 (1959), p. 221–23; and by Charles van den Borren in *Revue Belge de Musicologie*, 14 (1960), p. 137–38.

Reviews of the 12th ed. *Sachteil* by Jack Alan Westrup in *Music and Letters*, 49 (1968), p. 256–57; by François Lesure in *Revue de Musicologie*, 54 (1968), p. 115–16; by Hans Oesch in *Melos*, 36 (1969), p. 15; and by Vincent Duckles in *Notes*, 27 (1970), p. 256–58. See also the review-article by Walter Wiora, "Hugo Riemann und der 'neue Riemann,'" in *Die Musikforschung*, 22 (1969), p. 348–55.

The *Ergänzungsbände* were briefly reviewed by Stephen M. Fry in *Notes*, 32 (1976), p. 782.

54. Roche, Jerome and Elizabeth Roche. A dictionary of early music: from the troubadors to Monteverdi. New York: Oxford University Press, 1981. 208 p.

> The aim ... is to deal ... with the instruments, musical forms, technical terms, and composers [of the period until the death of Monteverdi]. [*Introduction*]

Some entries include brief bibliographical citations.

Review by François Lesure in *Fontes Artis Musicae*, 29 (1982), p. 149.

55. Rororo Musikhandbuch. Hrsg. u. bearb. von Heinrich Lindlar in Zusammenarb. mit d. Fachred. Musik d. Bibliograph. Inst. Reinbek bei Hamburg: Rowohlt, 1973. 2 v.

Originally issued as *Meyers Handbuch über die Musik*, 1961.

Contents: Bd. 1. Musiklehre und Musikleben; Bd. 2. Lexikon der Komponisten, Lexikon der Interpreter, Gesamtregister.

As in the *Meyers Handbuch*, a miscellaneous array of facts about music and musical life, especially from a European perspective. Lists of libraries, societies, research institutes, performers, etc. Wide scope, shallow coverage.

56. Rubertis, Victor de. Pequeño diccionario musical, tecnológico y biográfico. 6 ed., corregida y aumentada. Buenos Aires: Ricordi Americana, 1962. 349 p.

57. Sandved, Kjell Bloch. Musikkens verden. Musik fra A–Z. Udg. ved Kjell B. Sandved. [Øvers. fra norsk] Gennemset og revideret af Vagn Kappel. Redaktionssekrataer: K. Claussen. [Ny udg.] Høvedred.: Sverre Hagerup Bull. København: Musikkens Verden, 1964. 2,272 cols.

Published in German as *Die Welt der Musik* (Stuttgart: Deutsche Volksbücher, 195–. 2,264 cols.), in English as *The World of Music* (New York: Abradale Press; London: Waverly, 1963. 4 v. 2,239 p.), and in Swedish as *Musikens värald* (Göteborg: Kulturhistoriska förlaget, 1973. 2,236 cols.).

A Danish general dictionary of music.

58. Schilling, Gustav. Encyclopädie der gesammten musikalischen Wissenschaften, oder, Universal-Lexikon der Tonkunst. Stuttgart: F. H. Köhler, 1835–37. 6 v.

Supplement-Band, hrsg. von Gustav Schilling, 1842.

Reprinted by Georg Olms, Hildesheim, including the supplement, in 1974.
One of the leading 19th-century repositories of musical knowledge. A comprehensive work with emphasis on the subject aspects, but including numerous biographies displaced or reduced in later reference works.

59. Schilling, Gustav. Universal-Lexikon der Tonkunst. Neue Hand-Ausgabe in einem Bande. Mit Zugrundlegung des grösseren Werkes neu bearbeitet, ergänzt und theilweise vermehrt von Dr. F. S. Gassner.... Stuttgart: F. Köhler, 1849. 918 p.
A one-volume condensation of the preceding six-volume work. Remarkably full of information. In many instances the entries are more comprehensive and up-to-date than in the original edition.

60. Seeger, Horst. Musiklexikon in zwei Bänden. Leipzig: Deutscher Verlag für Musik, 1966. 2 v.
Vol. 1, A–K. Vol. 2, L–Z.
Represents the Marxist (East German) approach to music lexicography. Articles by 44 East European contributors. Summary listings of composers' works; no bibliographies for articles on major topics. Illustrated.

61. Shimonaka, Yasazuro, ed. Ongaku jiten. Tokyo: Heibonsha, 1954–57. 12 v.
The major Japanese encyclopedia of music.
Vol. 12 is an index in Japanese and English.

62. Sohlmans musiklexikon. Editor-in-chief Hans Åstrand. Stockholm: Sohlmans Förlag, 1975–78. 5 v.
First edition was published 1948–52.
An extensive dictionary in Swedish providing brief entries on a very wide variety of musical topics, including biographical entries. Pop music, ethnic dance forms, musical technologies, and geographical topics are covered. The larger articles are signed and include bibliographies. There are many unusual illustrations, photographs, and charts. Excellent and extensive coverage of the contemporary musical scene. The last volume provides a classified index to topical articles. The major modern Swedish music encyclopedia. Contributions by leading Scandinavian musicologists.
Reviewed by Sven Hansell in *Fontes Artis Musicae*, 24 (1977), p. 194–96. Briefly reviewed by Stephen M. Fry in *Notes*, 33 (1976), p. 307.

63 Thompson, Oscar, ed. The international cyclopedia of music and musicians. 11th ed. by Bruce Bohle. New York: Dodd, Mead, 1985. 2,609 p.
First published in 1939. 8th ed. (1958) edited by Nicolas Slonimsky. 9th ed. (1964) edited by Robert Sabin. 10th ed. (1975) edited by Bruce Bohle.
The 11th edition includes an appendix of additional new articles and new information added to articles appearing in the 10th edition; it is thus a reprint of the 10th edition with a section of addenda and corrigenda.
A good one-volume general dictionary of music in English. Strong list of contributors, with extended signed articles for major persons and subjects. Large numbers of title entries. Particularly valuable for detailed lists, given in tabulated form, of works by major composers. Through the 8th

edition the work carried an appendix of opera plots and an extensive bibliography of music literature. The 11th edition includes an appendix of additional new articles and new information to articles appearing in the 10th edition.

Review of the 5th edition by Charles Warren Fox in *Notes*, 7 (1950), p. 291–92; of the 9th edition by Irene Millen in *Notes*, 22 (1965), p. 733–35.

64. Tonkonsten, Internationellt musiklexikon. Stockholm: Nordiska Uppslagsböcker, [1955–57]. 2 v.

Popular, illustrated dictionary giving pronunciations of foreign names, lists of works and bibliographies for major composers, bibliographical references on important topics. Covers popular music. Signed articles by Scandinavian contributors.

65. Tschierpe, Rudolf. Kleines Musiklexikon, mit systematischen Übersichten und zahlreichen Notenbeispielen. [6. ergänzte Auflage]. Hamburg: Hoffman und Campe, 1959. 414 p.

First published in 1946; 2. Aufl., 1948; 3 Aufl., 1949; 4. Aufl., 1951; 5. Aufl., 1955.

Excellent small general dictionary. Brief but inclusive. Representative works listed for major composers. Bibliographical references. Tables illustrating dance forms, theory, and history. Appendix lists major writers on music with their fields of specialization; another lists titles of operas, operettas, oratorios, choral and orchestral works.

66. Viotta, Henri Anastase. Lexicon der toonkunst. Met medewerking van de heeren Peter Benoit, Frans Coenen, F. Gernsheim, L. van Gheluwe, F. A. Heinze, Richard Hol, Dan. de Lange, W. F. G. Nicolai, etc. Amsterdam: P. N. van Kampen, 1883–85. 3 v.

First printed in 1881–85.

The standard 19th-century Dutch encyclopedia of music. The emphasis is on biography.

67. Walther, Johann G. Musikalisches Lexicon, oder musikalische Bibliothek. Leipzig: Wolffgang Deer, 1732. 659 p., 22 fold. plates.

Facsimile reprint edited by Richard Schaal (1953 and 1986) and published by Bärenreiter in the series *Documenta Musicologica* (Erste Reihe, 3).

Walther's *Lexicon* established the pattern for modern dictionaries that combine terms and biography, as in Riemann and Moser. It also constitutes a primary source of information about late Baroque musical knowledge and practice.

68. Westrup, Jack A. and Frank Ll. Harrison. The new college encyclopedia of music. Revised by Conrad Wilson. New York: W. W. Norton, 1976. 608 p.

Published first in England, in 1959, as the *Collins Music Encyclopedia* and then in the U.S. as the *New College Encyclopedia of Music* in 1960. 739 p. The present edition was also published in Britain as the *Collins Encyclopedia of Music*. The 1976 American edition was reprinted in 1981.

A dictionary less scholarly than informative. Focus on common composers, terms, and titles, but with brief attention to earlier and more modern topics. Most important composers are provided with summaries of works. There are occasional bibliographical references in the articles. Some illustrations with musical quotations.

Review of the 1960 edition by James B. Coover in *Notes*, 17 (1960), p. 564–66.

69. Willemze, Theo. Spectrum muzieklexicon. Utrecht: Het Spectrum, 1975. 4 v.

Composers, authors and titles of pieces of music, as well as definitions of terms, are found in this compendium of very brief entries. Plentiful cross-references from the major European languages to Dutch. Extensive coverage of a broad span of Low Countries' musical culture.

70. Zenei Lexikon. [írtak] Bence Szabolcsí [és] Aladár Tóth. Átdolgozott új loadás, förszerkesztö: Dénes Bartha, szerkesztö: Margit Tóth. Budapest: Zenemükiadó Vallalat, 1965. 3 v.

This is a revision and expansion of a work that was first issued in 1930–31.

A general music encyclopedia of high quality. Major articles signed by outstanding musicologists, Hungarian and foreign. Long articles on national music, forms, music for various instruments. Biographical articles discuss major works and list others by category. Short bibliographies.

Revue by J. Gerely in *Revue de Musicologie*, 53 (1967), p. 185–87.

BIOGRAPHY, INTERNATIONAL

Listed here are dictionaries and encyclopedias, international in coverage, in which the emphasis is exclusively or mainly on persons engaged in activities related to music: composers, performers, scholars, critics, impresarios, etc. The line that separates biographical dictionaries from volumes of collected biography is a rather arbitrary one. The distinction is essentially between works that contain numerous brief entries, alphabetically arranged, and works that consist of collections of essays on a fairly limited group of musicians. Works in the latter category have been excluded, and for this reason the user should not expect to find entries for such titles as Joachim Kaiser's *Grosse Pianisten in unserer Zeit* (Mainz, 1989), Harold D. Rosenthal's *Great Singers of Today* (London, 1966), *Das Atlantisbuch der Dirigenten* (Zürich, 1985), or Denis Arnold's *Italian Baroque Masters* (New York and London, 1984).

71. Baker, Theodore. Baker's biographical dictionary of musicians. 7th ed. revised by Nicolas Slonimsky. New York: Schirmer Books, 1984. 2,577 p.

First published in 1900; subsequent editions in 1905, 1919, 1940, 1958, and 1978. The 1958 edition was reprinted in 1965, with a 143-page *Supplement.* There was also a 1971 *Supplement* of 262 p.

Baker's is by far the most authoritative and extensive biographical dictionary in English, a standard work from its beginning. It focuses mainly on musicians and musical figures in the world of "art music." Through the 3rd edition early figures were treated briefly, with references to *Grove* and Eitner. For the 4th edition, these biographies were rewritten as independent articles (by Gustave Reese, Gilbert Chase, and Robert

Geiger). The 5th edition was greatly enlarged and checked carefully for accuracy. The 6th edition was extensively revised from the 5th edition and the 7th from the 6th. Lists of works.

Reviews of 5th edition by Brooks Shepard, Jr., in *Notes*, 16 (1959), p. 239–40; by Philip L. Miller in *Musical Quarterly*, 45 (1959), p. 255–58. Review of the 1971 *Supplement* by Gloria Rose in *Notes*, 29 (1972), p. 253–54. Review of the 7th edition by François Lesure in *Fontes Artis Musicae*, 33 (1986), p. 218.

72. Bertini, Giuseppe. Dizionario storico-critico degli scrittori di musica, e de'piu celebri artisti di tutte le nazioni si' antiche che moderne. Palermo: Dalla Tipografia reale di Guerrà, 1814–15. 4 v. in 2.

Tomo primo: Discorso preliminare, p. i-lvi, AA–BU. 167 p.

Tomo secondo: C–KU. 234 p.

Tomo terzo: LA–RU. 245 p.

Tomo quarto: SA–Z. 145 p.

An early Italian dictionary of musical biography. Bertini leans heavily on Choron and Fayolle (no. 76) for his information but adds much new material. His "Discorso preliminare" is a perceptive discussion of the role of bibliography in enhancing musical knowledge.

73. Bingley, William. Musical biography; memoirs of the lives and writings of the most eminent musical composers and writers who have flourished in the different countries of Europe during the last three centuries. London: H. Colburn, 1814. 2 v.

2nd ed., 1834. Reprint of the 2nd ed. by Da Capo Press, New York, 1971.

Brief, anecdotal accounts grouped chronologically and by national schools.

74. Brown, James Duff. Biographical dictionary of musicians, with a bibliography of English writings on music. Paisley and London: A. Gardner, 1886. 637 p.

Reprint by Georg Olms, Hildesheim, 1970.

International in coverage but with pronounced British slant.

75. Carlson, Effie B. A bio-bibliographical dictionary of twelve-tone and serial composers. Metuchen, New Jersey: Scarecrow Press, 1970. 233 p.

Entries for 80 twelve-tone and serial composers, from Gilbert Amy to Bernd Alois Zimmermann.

76. Choron, Alexandre É. and F. J. M. Fayolle. Dictionnaire historique des musiciens, artistes et amateurs, morts ou vivans, qui se sont illustrés en une partie quelconque de la musique et des arts qui y sont relatifs.... Paris: Valade, 1810–11. 2 v.

Another printing, 1817. Reprint by Olms, Hildesheim, 1970.

The first French biographical dictionary of importance. International in scope. Partial lists of works for major composers. A valuable guide to early 19th-century musical opinion. The dictionary proper (by Fayolle) is preceded by an 81-page "Sommaire de l'histoire de la musique" by Choron.

Translated and expanded in the English *A Dictionary of Musicians*, 1824. See no. 78.

Cohen, Aaron I. International encyclopedia of women composers. See no. 2980.

77. A dictionary of modern music and musicians. Edited by Arthur Eaglefield-Hull. London: J. M. Dent; New York, E. P. Dutton, 1924. 543 p.

Reprint of the 1924 ed. by Da Capo Press, New York, 1971; by the Scholarly Press, 1972; and by AMS Press, New York, 1973.

Primarily biographical, although there are entries for terms related to modern music. For the period c. 1880–1920, the best international coverage of any dictionary of its time. Written with the aid of numerous foreign collaborators. Also includes publishers, musicologists, organizations, new instruments, etc. Corrections and additions included in Slonimsky's *Music since 1900* (no. 621). Corrected and enlarged German edition (no. 102).

78. A dictionary of musicians, from the earliest ages to the present time, comprising the most important biographical contents of the works of Gerber, Choron and Fayolle, Count Orloff, Dr. Burney, Sir John Hawkins, etc., together with more than 100 original memoirs of the most eminent living musicians and a summary of the history of music. London: Sainsbury, 1824. 2 v.

Reprinted in 1827.

Reprint of the original edition by Da Capo Press, New York, 1966. The reprint incorporates an essay on the work by H. G. Farmer, originally printed in *Music and Letters*, 12 (1931), p. 384–92.

The Sainsbury *Dictionary* has been shown recently to have been copied and paraphrased from Bingley (no. 73) and from other contemporaneous English publications. The first major biographical dictionary of musicians in English. Its tone is popular and anecdotal, but the work furnishes an excellent picture of contemporary taste and opinion. The compiler is not identified, but the work has been attributed to its publisher, John Sainsbury. See the article by Lawrence I. Ritchey, "The untimely death of Samuel Wesley; or the perils of plagiarism," in *Music and Letters*, 60 (1984), p. 45–59.

Review of the reprint edition by Vincent H. Duckles in *Notes*, 23 (1967), p. 737–39.

79. Eitner, Robert. Biographisch-bibliographisches Quellen-Lexikon der Musiker und Musikgelehrten der christlichen Zeitrechnung bis zur Mitte des 19. Jahrhunderts.... Leipzig: Breitkopf & Härtel, 1898–1904. 10 v.

Eitner's *Quellen-Lexikon* is mainly a bibliography of primary sources, but it does contain much useful biographical information, often helpful with respect to obscure names. For fuller information on this important reference work, see no. 1739.

80. The Etude music magazine. Portraits of the world's best known musicians, an alphabetical collection of notable musical personalities of the world covering the entire history of music. Compiled and edited by Guy McCoy. Philadelphia: Theodore Presser, [1946]. 251 p.

Portraits and brief identifications of 4,748 composers, performers, and other musicians, largely reprinted from *Etude*, 1932–40. Geographical index of American names.

One of the few dictionaries of its kind. Of limited value, however, since the portraits are reproduced at little more than postage-stamp size.

19

81. Ewen, David. Composers of yesterday: A biographical and critical guide to the most important composers of the past. New York: H. W. Wilson, 1937. 488 p.

Reprint by the Scholarly Press, St. Clair Shores, Michigan, 1977.

Biographies, lists of major works, bibliographies, lists of recordings, and portraits of about 200 composers from Dunstable to the end of the 19th century. Selected on the basis of current acceptance or importance in music history.

82. Ewen, David. Composers since 1900: a bibliographical and critical guide. New York: H. W. Wilson, 1969. 639 p.

First Supplement...., 1981. 328 p.

Supersedes *Composers of Today* (1934 and 1936); *American Composers of Today;* and *European Composers Today* (1954). Partially superseded by no. 203.

Portraits, listing of major works, and short bibliographies of writings about the composers under consideration.

Reviewed in the *Booklist*, 66 (July 1970), p. 1290–91.

83. Ewen, David. Musicians since 1900: Performers in concert and opera. New York: H. W. Wilson, 1978. 974 p.

Supersedes Ewen's *Living Musicians* (1940) and its supplement (1957) with a work wider in scope.

Ewen, David. Popular American composers... See no. 239.

84. Fétis, François J. Biographie universelle des musiciens et bibliographie générale de la musique. 2me éd. Paris: Firmin Didot Frères, 1866–70. 8 v.

First published in 1835–44. *Supplément et Complément*, pub. sous la direction de M. Arthur Pougin. Paris, 1878–80. 2 v.

Reprint of the 2nd edition, with the supplements by Arthur Pougin, by Édition Culture et Civilisation, Brussels (1973), with a critical introduction by L. Weemaels, P. Huyskens, and G. Thines. 10 v.

Fétis's work once set the standard for modern biographical research in music. A significant achievement for its time, it contains biographical and bibliographical information (much of which modern scholarship has shown to be less than accurate), lists of major works, and—occasionally—annotated lists of books about composers. Although outdated and marred by the author's personal critical bias, it has been a starting point for research.

85. Gerber, Ernst Ludwig. Historisch-biographisches Lexikon der Tonkünstler, welches Nachrichten von dem Leben und Werken musikalischer Schriftsteller, berühmter Componisten, Sänger, usw. ... enthält. Leipzig: J. G. I. Breitkopf, 1790–92. 2 v.

See annotation for no. 86.

86. Gerber, Ernst Ludwig. Neues historisch-biographisches Lexikon der Tonkünstler.... Leipzig: A. Kühnel, 1812–13. 4 v.

The Gerber *lexica* are early biographical dictionaries of great historical importance. The compiler expanded the biographical content of Walther's *Lexikon* (no. 67) and produced the first major self-contained dictionary of musical biography. The four-volume edition of 1812–14 supplements but does not supersede the earlier two-volume edition (no. 85). Both compilations must be used for complete coverage.

The two Gerber *lexica* have been reprinted by Akademische Druck- u. Verlagsanstalt, Graz, under the editorship of Othmar Wessely. Wessely has also edited a supplementary volume containing additions and corrections made by Gerber's contemporaries and published in the *Leipzig Allgemeine Musikalische Zeitung* and other journals. Also included are the author's manuscript revisions. A full transcription of the title of the reprint edition is given as follows:

Historisch-Biographisches Lexikon der Tonkünstler (1812–14) und Neues historisch-biographisches Lexikon der Tonkünstler (1812–14). Mit den in den Jahren 1792 bis 1834 veröffentlichten Ergänzungen sowie der Erstveröffentlichung handschriftlicher Berichtigungen und Nachträge. Hrsg. von Othmar Wessely. Graz: Akademische Druck- u. Verlagsanstalt, 1966–69. 4 v.

87. Gilder, Eric. The dictionary of composers and their music; a listener's companion. New, revised edition. New York: Holt, Rinehart and Winston, 1986. 592 p.

First published in 1978; 2nd ed. 1985.

Brief biographical entries on 426 composers most likely to be encountered on programs of classical music. Works lists arranged in chronological order for each composer and a survey of compositions listed in chronological order. Time lines for the lives of composers in the book. Includes a time line showing when each cited composer was born and died, and with whom each was contemporaneous.

Reviewed by Ann P. Basart in *Fontes Artis Musicae*, 35 (1988), p. 208–9.

88. Le Grandi Voci. Dizionario critico-biografico dei cantanti, con discografia operistica. Roma: Istituto per la Collaborazione Culturale, 1964. 1,044 cols.

Published under the direction of Rodolfo Celletti; consultants for the discographies, Raffaele Vegeto and John B. Richards; editor, Luisa Pavolini.

An illustrated dictionary of opera singers, historical and contemporary, with the discographies of the major artists.

89. Greene, David Mason. Greene's biographical encyclopedia of composers. Garden City, New York: Doubleday, 1985. 1,348 p.

A popular dictionary limited to composers of art music. Entries arranged chronologically by birth date. Alphabetical list of composers.

Review by Richard Koprowski in *Notes*, 42 (1985), p. 787.

90. Griffiths, Paul. The Thames and Hudson encyclopaedia of 20th-century music. New York: Thames and Hudson, 1986. 207 p.

91. Hughes, Rupert. The biographical dictionary of musicians. Originally compiled by Rupert Hughes, completely revised and newly edited by Deems Taylor and Russell Kerr. Over 8,500 entries, together with a pronouncing dictionary of given names and titles and a key to the pronunciation of 16 languages. New York: Blue Ribbon Books, 1940. 481 p.

Reprinted by the Scholarly Press, St. Clair Shores, Michigan, 1972.

A popular reference work. Brief entries with representative works for composers mentioned. Useful for the abundant citations of obscure performers.

92. International who's who in music and musical gazetteer. A contemporary biographical dictionary and a record of the world's musical activity. Edited by César Saerchinger. New York: Current Literature Pub. Co., 1918. 861 p.

The geographical index and directory of schools and organizations are now only of historical interest, but the biographical section is still useful for minor figures of the first two decades of the century. Composers, performers, critics, musicologists, teachers—their education, field of activity, principal works, and addresses.

93. International who's who in music and musicians' directory. 10th ed., 1985. Cambridge, England: International Who's Who in Music of the International Bibliographical Centre; Melrose Press, 1984. 1,178 p.

Began publication in 1935. Title 1962–72, *Who's Who in Music and Musicians' International Directory.* Resumed under the present title with 7th ed., 1975; 8th ed., 1977; 9th ed., 1980.

Résumés of almost 8,000 musicians, musicologists, music critics, managers, publishers, librarians, and others in the field. Each entry initially supplied by the subject. Includes addresses of subjects. Emphasis on western European and Western hemisphere figures. International lists of organizations with addresses by various categories: orchestras, competitions, libraries, conservatories, etc.

Review of the 1962 ed. by Fred Blum in *Notes*, 19 (1962), p. 442–43.

94. Kurzgefasstes Tonkünstler-Lexikon [von Paul] Frank [und Wilhelm] Altmann; fortgeführt von Burchard Bulling, Florian Noetzel [und] Helmut Rösner. 15. Aufl. Zweiter Teil: Ergänzungen und Erweiterungen seit 1937. Wilhelmshaven: Heinrichshofen's Verlag, 1974–78. 2 v.

Erster Teil, a reprint of Merseburger's *Kurzgefasstes Tonkünstler-Lexikon*, 14. Aufl. (no. 97), published in 1974.

This edition corrects and augments the 14th, adding more than 16,000 new entries.

Review by Rudolf Klein in *Österreichische Musik Zeitschrift*, 30 (1975), p. 422, and by Nyal Williams in *Notes*, 29 (1973), p. 478.

95. Kutsch, K. J. and Leo Riemens. A concise biographical dictionary of singers, from the beginning of recorded sound to the present. Translated from German, expanded and annotated by Harry Earl Jones. Philadelphia, Pennsylvania: Chilton Book Co., 1969. 487 p.

First printed in German under the title *Unvergängliche Stimmen*, Bern and Munich: Francke Verlag, 1962, 1975, 1979, 1982.

Brief biographies of great singers who have flourished since the invention of sound recording. Entries include information on the singers' principal roles, the character of the voice, and the labels under which recordings were made. No detailed discographies.

Review by Philip L. Miller in *Library Journal* (15 Oct. 1969), p. 3638.

96. Mattheson, Johann. Grundlage einer Ehren-Pforte, woran die tüchtigsten Capellmeister, Componisten, Musikgelehrten, Tonkünstler, etc. erscheinen sollen. Zum fernern Ausbau angegeben von Mattheson, Hamburg, 1740. Vollständiger, originalgetreuer Neudruck mit gelegentlichen bibliographischen Hinweisen und Matthesons Nachträgen, hrsg. von Max Schneider. Berlin: Leo Liepmannssohn, 1910. 428 p. with *Anhang* of 51 p.

Reprints issued in 1969 by Bärenreiter, Kassel, and by Die Akademische Druck- und Verlagsanstalt, Graz.

Mattheson's work is, strictly speaking, a volume of collected biography rather than a biographical dictionary. But the volume stands first, chronologically, among all self-contained works of musical biography, establishing the precedent for Gerber's *Lexikon* (nos. 85 and 86) and subsequent dictionaries of musical biography. Most of the essays were contributed by the subjects themselves.

97. Merseburger, Carl W. Kurzgefasstes Tonkünstler-Lexikon für Musiker und Freunde der Musik. Begründet von Paul Frank [pseud.] Neu bearbeitet und ergänzt von Wilhelm Altmann. 14. stark erweiterte Auflage. Regensburg: G. Bosse, 1936. 730 p.

First published in 1860 as P. Frank's *Kleines Tonkünstler-Lexikon.* Title varies slightly in subsequent editions. Subsequently published as part 1 of the Frank-Altmann *Kurzgefasstes Tonkünstler-Lexikon* in 1974 (no. 94).

One of the most popular of the pre-war German dictionaries of musical biography. Extremely wide coverage, but with minimum data. Over 18,000 entries, including composers, librettists, performers, and musicologists. Many minor figures. No lists of works or bibliographical references. Useful for quick reference.

Review of the 15th edition by Nyal Williams in *Notes*, 29 (1973), p. 448.

98. Mirkin, Mikhail Iur'evich. Kratkii biograficheskii slovar' zarubezhnykh kompozitorov. [Brief biographical dictionary of foreign composers.] Moskva: Sovetskii Kompozitor, 1969. 265 p.

A biographical dictionary covering some 2,500 musicians, excluding Russian and Soviet composers.

99. Moore, John W. A dictionary of musical information, containing also a vocabulary of musical terms, and a list of modern musical works published in the United States from 1640 to 1875. New York: AMS Press, 1977. 211 p.

Reprint of the 1st edition published by Oliver Ditson, Boston, 1876. Previously reprinted by B. Franklin, New York, 1971.

The "musical information" is chiefly biographical. The "vocabulary of musical terms" is a pronouncing dictionary. The "list of modern musical works" is alphabetical by title.

100. Les musiciens célèbres. [Publié sous la direction de Jean Lacroix....] [Genève]: L. Mazenod, 1946. 385 p.

Also published in German under the title *Die berühmten Musiker.* Genève, 1946. Reprinted by Magenod, Paris, 1950. 357 p.

An "art" publication, chiefly valuable for its fine full-page portraits of musicians. Has 66 individual biographies and several group articles, chronologically arranged. P. 293–349: brief identifications of other composers.

101. Musikens Hven-Hvad-Hvar. Politikens musikleksikon. Udarbejdet af Nelly Backhausen og Axel Kjerulf. København: Politikens Forlag, 1950. 3 v.

Vol. 1: "Musikhistorie." Chronology from antiquity to 1900, with composer index. Vols. 2–3: Biographies (composers, performers, musicologists) indicating field of activity and principal works. Vol. 3: p. 141–414. Title list of 15,000 entries, including operas, repertory works, popular and musical comedy songs, folk songs. For each, identification, composer, and date if known.

A new edition of vols. 2–3, the biographies section, appeared in 1961, edited by Ludwig Ernst Bramsen Jr.

102. Das neue Musiklexikon, nach dem *Dictionary of Modern Music and Musicians*, hrsg. von A. Eaglefield-Hull, übersetzt und bearb. von Alfred Einstein. Berlin: M. Hesse, 1926. 729 p.

A German translation of no. 77, with many additions and corrections by Einstein. Most of the information in this revision is incorporated in the 11th edition of the *Riemann Musik-Lexikon* (no. 53).

103. Parker, John R. A musical biography; with new introduction by Frederick Freedman. Detroit, Michigan: Information Coordinators, 1975. 250 p.

Reprint of the 1825 edition published by Stone & Fovell, Boston.

Includes bibliographical references in the introduction.

104. Pedigo, Alan. International encyclopedia of violin-keyboard sonatas and composer biographies. Booneville, Arkansas: Arriaga, 1979. 135 p.

Most useful for the national lists of composers and the brief biographies of composers.

105. Prieberg, Fred K. Lexikon der neuen Musik. Freiburg & München: K. Alber, 1958. 495 p.

Primarily biographical, but with a few articles on aspects of and trends in contemporary music (film music, radio operas, polytonality, 12-tone music, *musique concrète*, etc.). Factual rather than critical, covering education, activities, and principal works of the 20th-century composers.

106. Ricart Matas, José. Diccionario biográfico de la música. [3rd. ed.] Barcelona: Editorial Iberia, 1980. 1,143 p.

A Spanish dictionary of international musical biography. Brief biographical entries. Lists of works for major composers together with bibliographical references.

107. Rostand, Claude. Dictionnaire de la musique contemporaine. Paris: Larousse, 1970. 256 p.

A pocket dictionary of contemporary music, primarily biographical. Major works are mentioned, but no attempt is made to provide full lists of works.

108. Sakka, Keisei. Meikyoko jiten. [Dictionary of famous music and musicians.] Tokyo: Ongaku no Tomosha, 1969. 702 p.

A general bio-bibliography in Japanese.

109. Schäffer, Boguslaw. Leksykon kompozytorów XX wieku. Kraków: Polskie Wydawnictwo Muzyczne, 1963–65. 2 v.
Vol. 1: A–L. Vol. 2: M–Z.
A Polish-language dictionary of 20th-century composers. International in coverage but particularly strong in Slavic musicians. Portraits, bibliographies.

110. Schmidl, Carlo. Dizionario universale dei musicisti. Milano: Sonzogno, [1928?–29]. 2 v.
Supplemento, 1938. 806 p.
First pub. 1888–89 in 1 v.
A major bio-bibliography in Italian and good general biographical source for obscure Italian musicians. Emphasis on native composers, librettists, and performers, with full articles on well-known persons and brief accounts of minor ones. Dates of first productions of dramatic works. Lists of works, including modern republications. Particularly valuable for articles on Italian literary figures and their relation to music. All forenames are Italianized.

111. Schnoor, Hans. Oper, Operette, Konzert. Ein praktisches Nachschlagebuch für Theater- und Konzertbesucher, für Rundfunkhörer, Fernsehteilnehmer und Schallplattenfreunde. Gütersloh: C. Bertelsmann, 1963. 575 p.
First printed in 1955. Reprinted in 1969 by Rowohlt-Taschenbücher-Verlag and in 1970 by Bertelsmann.
Issued also in an edition with additions by Stephan Pflicht entitled *Mosaik-Opernführer, Konzertführer mit Operetten und Musicals.* München: Mosaik-Verlag, 1979, 504 p.
A handbook for the musical amateur and concertgoer. Organized biographically, but with emphasis on the composers' works in the current repertory. Some 347 musical examples and numerous illustrations. With an appended glossary and indexes of persons and subjects.

112. Seeger, Horst. Musiklexikon: Personen A–Z. Leipzig: Deutscher Verlag für Musik, 1981. 860 p.
Originally issued in 1966 in 2 v.
Very brief biographical sketches followed by categorized lists of major works. International scope, but better coverage for persons from the Eastern bloc.

113. Simpson, Harold. Singers to remember. Lingfield, England: Oakwood Press, 1973. 223 p.

I have not attempted an exhaustive survey of these singers' careers or their recordings. Rather it has been my aim to provide data which will encourage searchers in the vocal record field to probe further into the legacy of discs left by the artists mentioned. [Author's *Introduction*]

Biographies of some 100 singers, with selected discographies.

114. Southern, Eileen. Biographical dictionary of Afro-American and African musicians. Westport, Connecticut: Greenwood Press, 1982. 478 p. (Greenwood encyclopedia of black music)
Biographies include citations of sources. Lists of periods and places of birth, musical occupations. Index.
Reviews by Doris Evans McGinty in *Black Perspective in Music*, 11 (1987), p. 79–82, and by Dominique-René De Lerma in *Ethnomusicology*, 27 (1983), p. 543–44.

115. Suppan, Wolfgang. Lexikon des Blasmusikwesens. Im Auftrag des Bundes Deutscher Blasmusikverbände, hrsg. in Zusammenarbeit mit Fritz Thelen und weiteren Fachkollegen. 2., ergänzte und erweiterte Auflage. Freiburg im Breisgau: F. Schulz, 1976. 342 p.
First published in 1973. Also known as *Blasmusikwesen.*
Extensive introductory chapters on history, supporting organizations, arrangements, repertoire, conducting, and bibliography of wind bands. Biographies of composers, conductors, and performers, each accompanied by a brief bibliography. Most extensive coverage of German-speaking areas of Europe.
Review by Georg Karstädt in *Die Musikforschung*, 32 (1979), p. 193–94.

Unvergängliche Stimmen. See Kutsch, K. J. (no. 95).

116. Vinton, John. Dictionary of contemporary music. New York: E. P. Dutton; London: Thames and Hudson, 1974. 834 p.
London edition titled *Dictionary of Twentieth-Century Music.*
A dictionary consisting of articles focusing on concert music of the Western tradition. Entries on composers were based on questionnaires completed by the composers. Entries on topics were written by distinguished scholars. "Perhaps a ... way to use this book is to regard it as a slice of history reported in large part by some of its makers" (author's preface). Articles include lists of principal compositions and bibliographies.

Who's who in music. . . . See nos. 92, 93, and 222.

117. Willemze, Theo. Componistenlexicon. Utrecht: Spectrum, 1981. 2 v. 785 p.
A Dutch biographical dictionary with international coverage. Includes bibliographical references.

118. Young, Percy M. Biographical dictionary of composers, with classified list of music for performance and study. New York: Crowell, 1954. 381 p.
Published in England under the title *A Critical Dictionary of Composers and Their Music.* London: Dobson, 1954; British edition reprinted by Hyperion Press of Westport, Connecticut, 1979.
Selective list of 500 composers. Brief critical surveys of each, titles of representative works, and references to further sources of information, usually in English. Intended for the general student rather than the specialist.

BIOGRAPHY, NATIONAL

Any dictionary of musical biography may be expected to be strong in names within its own language group. There are numerous specialized dictionaries of biography devoted specifically to the musicians of particular countries. Only the most important of such dictionaries are listed here, with the emphasis on recent publications. Entries are arranged by country or by region (e.g., Latin America).

ARGENTINA

119. Arizaga, Rodolfo. Enciclopedia de la música Argentina. Buenos Aires: Fondo Nacional de las Artes, 1971. 371 p.

Chiefly a biographical dictionary of Argentine musicians but including some terms for dance forms, musical institutions, and the like. Partial lists of composers' works. Chronological tables covering the history of Argentine music from 1901 to 1970.

120. Senillosa, Mabel. Compositores argentinos. 2. ed., a umentada. Buenos Aires: Casa Lottermosser, 1956. 451 p.

1st ed. issued as *Homenaje al Artista Argentino, Músicos*, 1948.

Some entries supplied by the composers themselves.

AUSTRALIA

121. MacKenzie, Barbara and Findlay MacKenzie. Singers of Australia from Melba to Sutherland. Melbourne: Lansdowne Press, 1967. 309 p.

Also published in London by Newnes, 1968.

Biographies, with a liberal selection of portraits. Bibliography and index; data on results of vocal competitions in Australia.

122. McCredie, Andrew D. Catalogue of 46 Australian composers and selected works.... Canberra: Commonwealth Assistance to Australian Composers, 1969. 20 p. (Music by Australian Composers, survey no. 1)

AUSTRIA

123. Knaus, Herwig. Die Musiker im Archivbestand des Kaiserlichen Obersthofmeisteramts (1637–1705). Wien: Hermann Böhlaus Nachf., 1967. 2 v. (Österreichische Akademie der Wissenschaften ... Veröff. der Kommission für Musikforschung, Heft 7 u. 8)

An archival study of early Austrian musicians, made up of transcriptions of documents pertaining to musical activity in Austrian courts, chapels, and municipalities. Each volume has an index of names.

For a similar study based on French archives, see no. 2270.

124. Suppan, Wolfgang. Steirisches Musiklexikon. Im Auftrage des Steirischen Tonkünstlerbundes unter Benützung der "Sammlung Wamlek" bearb.... Graz: Akademische Druck- und Verlagsanstalt, 1962–66. 676 p. 56 plates.

Issued serially between 1962 and 1966.

A biographical dictionary of musicians associated with Graz and other parts of Styria. Comprehensive for pre-1800 names, selective for post-1800. Good bibliographical coverage for composers' works and for writings on the musicians.

Review by Fritz Racek in *Die Musikforschung*, 22 (1969), p. 388–89.

BELGIUM

125. Centre Belge de Documentation Musicale. Music in Belgium: contemporary Belgian composers. Brussels: Published in cooperation with the CeBeDeM, by A. Manteau, 1964. 158 p.

A publication designed to stimulate interest in contemporary Belgian music. Biographical sketches of 48 modern Belgian composers, with lists of their major works. Portraits. Index of names and brief lists of recordings.

126. Hemel, Victor van. Voorname belgische toonkunstenaars uit de 18de, 19de, en 20ste eeuw. Beknopt overzicht van hun leven en œuvre. Derde bijgewerkte druk. Antwerpen: Cupidouitgave, 1958. 84 p.

Brief biographies of 101 Belgian musicians, covering the period from Loeillet to the present.

127. Vannes, René with André Souris. Dictionnaire des musiciens (compositeurs). Bruxelles: Maison Larcier, 1947. 443 p.

Belgian composers from the 15th century to 1830, with comprehensive lists of works, published or in manuscript, and references to other sources of information.

Comments by Richard S. Hill in *Notes*, 6 (1949), p. 607–608.

BULGARIA

128. Entsiklopediia na Bŭlgarskata muzikalna kultura. Edited by Venelin Krŭstev. Sofia: Bulgarska Akademiia na Naukite, 1967. 465 p.

A Bulgarian bio-bibliographical dictionary of musicians. Illustrated. Contains much information on Bulgarian instruments and musical institutions.

CANADA

129. Canadian Broadcasting Corporation. Catalogue of Canadian composers. Rev. and enl. ed. Edited by Helmut Kallmann. Ottawa: Canadian Broadcasting Corporation [1952?]. 254 p.

Reprint by the Scholarly Press, St. Clair Shores, Michigan, 1972.

356 brief biographical sketches, giving activities, education, addresses. Listings of works as complete as possible, giving titles, dates of publications, medium, duration, publishers. Unpublished works included. Lists of Canadian publishers and composers' organizations.

Contemporary Canadian Composers. See no. 1058.

130. Encyclopedia of music in Canada. Edited by Helmut Kallmann, Gilles Potvin, and Kenneth Winters. Toronto: University of Toronto Press, 1981. 1,076 p.
French version published in 1982 as *Encyclopédie de Musique au Canada.*

About music in Canada and Canada's musical relations with the rest of the world ... relates the activities and contributions of Canadian individuals and organizations ... and discusses general topics in their Canadian aspects. [*Introduction*]

Truly encyclopedic in scope. Lengthy articles, many illustrated. Includes tables, lists, and bibliographies. Superb indexes.
Review by George A. Proctor in *Fontes Artis Musicae*, 29 (1983), p. 92, and by François Lesure in *Fontes Artis Musicae*, 30 (1983), p. 224–25.

CROATIA

131. Kovačević, Krešimir. Hrvatski kompozitori i njihova djela. Zagreb: Naprijed, 1960. 553 p.
Biographies of 50 Croatian composers, for the most part contemporary, with descriptive accounts of their principal works. Summaries in English. Classified index of works analyzed; general index.

CUBA

132. Orovio, Helio. Diccionario de la música cubana; biográfico y técnico. Ciudad de la Habana: Editorial Letras Cubanas, 1981. 442 p.
Primarily a biographical dictionary, but with entries for terms, institutions and organizations, and instruments.

133. Ramírez, Serafín. La Habana artistica. Apuntes historicos. Habana: Imp. del E. M. de la Capitania general, 1891. 687 p.
Early attempt to record activity in 19th-century Cuba, includes notes on 19th-century Cuban dances. Includes a 200-p. dictionary of composers and another 100 p. discussing the literature of music. An index of "composiciones musicales" is on p. 671–87.

CZECH REPUBLIC AND SLOVAKIA

134. Československý Hudební Slovník, osob a institucí. Praha: Státní hudební vydavatelství, 1963–65. 2 v.
Editors: Gracian Černušák, Bohumír Štedroň, and Zdenko Nováček.
A Czech and Slovak bio-bibliographical dictionary. Also includes entries under names of places and institutions.
Review by Camillo Schoenbaum in *Die Musikforschung*, 18 (1965), p. 347–49.

135. Dlabač, Jan Bohumir. Allgemeines historisches Künstlerlexikon für Bohmen und zum Theil auch für Mähren und Schlesien. Auf Kosten der hochlöblichen Herrenstände Böhmens hrsg. Prag: Gedruckt bei G. Haase, 1815. 3 v.
Reprint by Frits A. M. Knuf, Hilversum, Holland.
An early dictionary of Czech (Bohemian and Moravian) musicians.

136. Gardavský, Čenĕk, ed. Contemporary Czechoslovak composers. Prague: 1965. 562 p.
Biographies and bibliographical information on more than 300 Czech composers. English text. Also published in French.

DENMARK

137. Kappel, Vagn. Contemporary Danish composers against the background of Danish musical life and history. 3rd rev. ed. Copehagen: Det Danske Selskab, 1967. 88 p.
A public relations document, first issued in 1948 and published in a 2nd edition in 1950. 116 p.
Biographical sketches of 14 Danish composers. Representative works cited, but no full lists. Discography of Danish music, p. 97–113.

FRANCE

138. Benoit, Marcelle. Musiques de cour, chapelle, chambre, écurie. Recueil de documents 1661–1733. Paris: Éditions A. et J. Picard, 1971. 553 p. (La vie musicale en France sous les rois Bourbons, 20)
A rich documentary study of musicians active in the French court from 1661 to 1733 based on material in the national archives and the Bibliothèque Nationale.

139. Brossard, Yolande de. Musiciens de Paris, 1535–1792; actes d'État civil d'après le Fichier Laborde de la Bibliothèque Nationale. Préf. de Norbert Dufourcq. Paris: A. et J. Picard, 1965. 302 p. (La vie musicale en France sous les rois Bourbons, 11)
A directory of early Parisian musicians based on a card file compiled by Leon de Laborde (d. 1869). Comprises some 6,624 cards listing musicians of all kinds active in Paris during the period covered. Index of musicians arranged chronologically under their specialties.

140. Dictionnaire des musiciens français. Paris: Seghers, 1961. 379 p.
A pocket, illustrated dictionary of French musicians. Coverage is selective, particularly for contemporary figures. Brief summaries of the major works of composers; no full listings or bibliographical references.

141. Favati, Guido. Le biografie trovadoriche, testi provenzali dei secc. XIII e XIV, edizione critica ... Bologna: Libreria Antiquaria Palmaverdi, 1961. 523 p. (Biblioteca degli studi mediolatine e volgari, 3)
Not a French biographical dictionary in the ordinary sense, but a critical edition of the original 13th- and 14th-century biographical descriptions of the troubadour composers.

For specialists in Romance philology and medieval music; to be used in connection with Gennrich (no. 1749) and Pillet (no. 1775).

Jurgens, Madeleine. Documents du Minutier Central.... See no. 2271.

142. Müller, René. Anthologie des compositeurs de musique d'Alsace. Strasbourg: Féderation de sociétés catholiques de chant et de musique d'Alsace, 1970. 190 p.

143. Tablettes de renommée des musiciens, auteurs, compositeurs, virtuoses, amateurs et maîtres de musique vocale et instrumentale, les plus connus en chaque genre. Genève: Minkoff Reprints, 1971. 125 p.
Reprint of the edition of Cailleau, Paris, 1785.
A bio-bibliographical work focusing primarily on musicians of Paris.

GERMANY

144. Fellerer, Karl G., ed. Rheinische Musiker. Köln: Arno Volk-Verlag, 1960–74. (Beiträge zur rheinischen Musikgeschichte, 43, 53, 58, 64, 69, 80, 97)
A series of volumes giving biographical and bibliographical information on musicians of the Rhineland. Issued serially. Each volume is alphabetically complete in itself, but the indexing is cumulative. Numerous contributors. Beginning with Folge 6 (1969), the editor is Dietrich Kamper. The work follows the pattern of Mattheson's *Grundlage einer Ehren-Pforte* (1740) (no. 96) in that many of the biographies of living musicians are self-compiled.

145. Fey, Hermann. Schleswig-Holsteinische Musiker, von den ältesten Zeiten bis zur Gegenwart; ein Heimatbuch. Hamburg: C. Holler, 1922. 126 p.
Dictionary arrangement. Full bibliographies of compositions, with authority references. "Quellennachweis," p. 125–126.

146. Kossmaly, Karl and C. H. Herzel. Schlesisches Tonkünstler-Lexikon, enthaltend die Biographieen aller schlesischen Tonkünstler, Componisten, Cantoren, Organisten, Tongelehrten, Textdichter, Orgelbauer, Instrumentenmacher ... hrsg. von Kossmaly und Carlo (pseud.). Breslau: E. Trewendt, 1846–47. 332 p.
Reprinted by G. Olms, Hildesheim, 1982.
Issued in four parts, each in a separate alphabet. Long articles giving classified lists of compositions, roles for performers, concert programs.

147. Kürschners Deutscher Musiker-Kalender 1954. Zweite Ausgabe des Deutschen Musiker-Lexikons. Herausgeber: Hedwig Müller von Asow und E. H. Müller von Asow. Berlin: Walter de Gruyter, 1954. 1,702 cols.
First published in 1929 under the title *Deutsches Musiker-Lexikon.* Edited by Erich H. Müller.
Biographies of living German, Austrian, and Swiss musicians in all categories and German-born musicians in foreign countries. Entries give essential biographical information and detailed lists of works. Excessive use

of abbreviations. Indexes of names by date of birth (1854–1939) and date of death (1929–54).

148. Ledebur, Carl F. H. W. P. J., Freiherr von. Tonkünstler-Lexikon Berlins von den ältesten Zeiten bis auf die Gegenwart. Berlin: L. Rauh, 1861. 704 p.
Reprint by Hans Schneider, Tutzing, 1965.
An important early dictionary of Berlin musicians. Entries for composers, publishers, performers, and amateurs who were born or active in Berlin, with detailed bibliographies of compositions.

149. Lipowsky, Felix J. Baierisches Musik-Lexikon. München: Giel, 1811. 338 (438) p.
Reprint of the original edition by G. Olms, Hildesheim, 1982.
An early dictionary of some historical importance. Covers Bavarian composers and performers, listing major compositions. Occasional title-page transcriptions.

150. Musik und Musiker am Mittelrhein: ein biographisches, orts- und landesgeschichtliches Nachschlagewerk in Verbindung mit den Musikwissenschaftlichen Instituten der Universitäten Frankfurt a.M.... [et al.] unter Mitarbeit zahlreicher Musik- und Lokalgeschichtsforscher und mit Unterstützung durch Franz Bösken herausgegeben von Hubert Unverricht; Bd. 2 Unter Mitwirkung von Kurt Oehl. Mainz: Schott, 1974–81. 2 v. (Beiträge zur mittelrheinischen Musikgeschichte, 20–21)
A biographical work concentrating upon musical figures from the area around Frankfurt. Bibliographies.

151. Verband Deutscher Komponisten und Musikwissenschaftler. Komponisten und Musikwissenschaftler der Deutschen Demokratischen Republik. Kurzbiographien und Werkverzeichnisse. Berlin: Verlag Neue Musik, 1959. 199 p.
2nd edition expanded, Berlin, 1967. 239 p.
Brief biographical sketches of East German composers and musicologists, with listings of their major works. Preceded by a group of essays on musical life and institutions in East Germany. Portraits.

GREAT BRITAIN

152. Baptie, David. Musical Scotland, past and present. Being a dictionary of Scottish musicians from about 1400 till the present time, to which is added a bibliography of musical publications connected with Scotland from 1611. Paisley: J. and R. Parlane, 1894. 53 p.
Reprint by Georg Olms, Hildesheim, 1972.

153. Brown, James D. and Stephen S. Stratton. British musical biography: a dictionary of musical artists, authors, and composers born in Britain and its colonies. Birmingham: Stratton, 1897. 462 p.
Reprint by Da Capo Press, New York, 1971.
The emphasis is on composers living at the time of publication. Great masters treated briefly to afford room for the obscure. Includes a large

number of British names that cannot be found elsewhere, with excellent bibliographies.

154. Highfill, Philip H. A biographical dictionary of actors, actresses, musicians, dancers, managers & other stage personnel in London, 1660–1800. By Philip H. Highfill, Kalman A. Burnim and Edward A. Langhans. Carbondale: Southern Illinois University Press, 1973–. 14 v. to date.

When completed this work will comprise perhaps 20 volumes, each containing about 1,000 biographical entries detailing all the facts that exhaustive research has produced about the performers and other theatrical personnel listed.

Humphries, Charles and William C. Smith. Music publishing in the British Isles.... See no. 2634.

155. Huntley, John. British film music. Forward by Muir Mathieson. London: Skelton Robinson, 1947. 247 p.

Reprinted by Arno Press, New York, 1972.

P. 189–229: biographical index of British film composers. Lists many names not to be found in other reference sources together with a listing of film scores.

Kidson, Frank. British music publishers.... See no. 2641.

156. Palmer, Russell. British music. London: Skelton Robinson, 1948. 283 p.

Biographical index of contemporary British musicians and musical organizations. Portraits.

157. Pulver, Jeffrey. A biographical dictionary of old English music. London: Kegan Paul; New York, Dutton, 1927. 537 p.

Reprints by the Da Capo Press, New York, 1973, with a new introduction by Gilbert Blount, and by Bert Franklin, New York, 1969.

English musicians active from about 1200 to the death of Purcell (1695). Cites manuscript sources, contemporary publications, and occasionally modern editions. Somewhat discursive in style, with lists of works scattered through the bodies of the articles, but useful as a starting point for the study of early English musicians. See also the author's companion volume covering old English musical terms (no. 383).

HOLLAND

See THE NETHERLANDS

HUNGARY

158. Contemporary Hungarian Composers. Responsible editor: Gyula Czigány. 4th ed., revised and enlarged. Budapest: Editío Musica, 1979. 219 p.

First published in 1970.
A bio-bibliographical work including a discography of works by Hungarian composers.

159. Molnár, Imre. A magyar muzsika könyve. Budapest: Merkantil-Nyomda, 1936. 632 p.
Institutions, organizations, and biographical entries for composers, performers, and other musicians.

INDIA

160. Sambamoorthy, P. A dictionary of South Indian music and musicians. 2nd ed. Madras: Indian Music Publishing House, 1984. 3 v.
Originally issued in 3 v. covering only A–F, 1952–71.
Portraits of composers and performers.

161. Who's who of Indian musicians. New Delhi: Sangeet Natak Akademi, 1984. 160 p.
First published in 1968. 100 p.
Brief biographical data on living Indian musicians, giving date of birth, area of specialization, addresses.

IRELAND

162. A catalogue of contemporary Irish composers. Edited by Edgar M. Deale. 2nd ed. Dublin: Music Association of Ireland, 1974. 108 p.
Data on the works of contemporary Irish composers, including brief biographical information, addresses, full descriptions of works: titles, media, timing, instrumentation, availability. List of publishers and list of abbreviations.

ISRAEL (AND JEWISH MUSICIANS IN GENERAL)

163. Gradenwitz, Peter. Music and musicians in Israel: a comprehensive guide to modern Israeli music. 3rd ed. Tel Aviv: Israeli Music Publications, 1978. 227 p.
Originally published in Jerusalem, 1952. Subsequently appeared in Tel Aviv, 1959. 226 p.
Biographies, varying in length, of about 60 composers, grouped by school. Appendix, p. 133–63, contains an alphabetical listing of composers and their works, but without reference to the biography section. Also given is a list of publishers and a group of publishers' catalogs.

164. Saleski, Gdal. Famous musicians of Jewish origin. New York: Bloch, 1949. 716 p.
First published in 1927 under the title *Famous Musicians of a Wandering Race.* 463 p.
Informal biographies, classified according to type of musical activity: composers, conductors, violinists, etc. About 400 entries. No bibliogra-

phies, but major works are mentioned in the articles. Portraits. P. 679–716: Israeli musicians.

165. Shalita, Israel and Hanan Steinitz. Encyclopedia of music. Vol. 1: a biographical dictionary of Jewish and world musicians; vol. 2: a dictionary of terms, theory, instruments, forms and history of Jewish and world music. Tel Aviv: Joshua Chachik, 1965. 2 v.
In Hebrew with indexes of Hebrew equivalents for English names and terms. International in scope.

166. Stengel, Theophil and Herbert Gerigk. Lexikon der Juden in der Musik, mit einem Titelverzeichnis jüdischer Werke. Berlin: B. Hahnefeld, 1943. 404 cols. (Veröffentlichungen des Instituts der NSDAP zur Erforschung der Judenfrage ..., 2)
First published in 1940. 380 p.
Among the more shameful products of German National Socialism were dictionaries of Jewish musicians compiled to further the purposes of anti-Semitism. This one and the Girschner *Repertorium* (no. 540) are cited as examples of this vicious genre.

167. Who is who in ACUM. Authors, composers, and music publishers. Biographical notes and principal works. Compiled and edited by Ravina Ravina and Shlomo Skolsky. Tel Aviv: ACUM Ltd., Société d'auteurs, compositeurs et éditeurs de musique en Israel, 1965. 95 p.
Addenda and Corrigenda published in 1966. 10 p.
Brief biographies, with lists of works and of authors, composers, and publishers affiliated with ACUM, a performing-rights organization in Israel.

ITALY

168. Alcari, C. Parma nella musica. Parma: M. Fresching, 1931. 259 p.
A biographical dictionary of musicians born in Parma. Emphasis is placed on 19th-century figures. Extended bibliographies for the most important musicians (e.g., Verdi, Pizzetti).

169. Angelis, Alberto de. L'Italia musicale d'oggi. Dizionario dei musicisti: compositori, direttori d'orchestra, concertisti, insegnanti, liutari, cantanti, scrittori musicali, librettisti, editori musicali, ecc. 3rd ed., corredate di una appendice. Roma: Ansonia, 1928. 523, 211 p.
First published in 1918; 2nd edition, 1922.
Living Italian musicians, with comprehensive lists of works.

170. Berutto, Guglielmo. Il Piemonte e la musica 1800–1984. Torino: Guglielmo Berutto, 1984. 421 p.
A bio-bibliographical dictionary arranged in sections: *musicisti, cantanti, editori, impresari, registri, scenografi, danzi-bande musicali, società corali, teatri scomparsi ed esistenti.* A final section gives brief historical sketches.

171. Damerini, Adelmo and Franco Schlitzer. Musicisti toscani; scritti di G. Barblan *et al.*, settembre 1955. Siena: Ticci, 1955. 81 p.
A publication of the Accademia Musicale Chigiana.
Musicians of Tuscany.

172. Masutto, Giovanni. I maestri di musica italiana del secolo XIX. Notizie biografiche.... Terza edizione, corretta ed aumentata. Venezia: G. Cechini, 1882. 226 p.
First printed in 1880 by Fontana, Venice.

LATIN AMERICA

173. Mariz, Vasco. Dicionário bio-bibliográfico musical (brasileiro e internacional). Pref. de Renato Almeida. Rio de Janeiro: Livraria Kosmos, 1948. 246 p.
Brief biographies of the best-known figures in music since the Renaissance, including performers. Useful chiefly for Brazilian musicians.

174. Mayer-Serra, Otto. Música y músicos de Latinoamérica. México: Editorial Atlante, 1947. 2 v.
Primarily biographical, although some terms, dance forms, and instruments are included. Listings of composers' works vary from brief resumes to full tabulations for major composers. Portraits.

175. Pan American Union Music Section. Composers of the Americas, biographical data and catalogs of their works. Washington, D.C.: Pan American Union, 1955–79. Nos. 1–19.
Each issue contains from 4 to 16 composers, alphabetically arranged, with brief biographies in English and Spanish. Portraits. Dates from scores, sometimes autographs. Works are given chronologically within principal media, with dates of composition, timing, publishers, and recordings, if any. Lists unpublished works.

THE NETHERLANDS

176. Gregoir, Édouard G. J. Biographie des artistes-musiciens néerlandais des XVIIIe et XIXe siècles, et des artistes étrangers résidant ou ayant résidé en Néerlands à la même époque. Anvers: L. de la Montagne, 1864. 238 p.
Based on and supplementing his *Essai Historique sur la Musique*, Brussels, 1861.
Brief biographies of Dutch musicians. Careers summarized, major works mentioned for composers, but no full listings.

177. Letzer, J. H. Muzikaal Nederland, 1850–1910. Bio-bibliographisch woordenboek ... 2.uitgaff met aanvulligen en verbeteringen. Utrecht: J. L. Beijers, 1913. 201 p., with 10 p. of additions.
Composers, musicologists, performers, etc., active in The Netherlands 1850–1910. Biographies, lists of works, occasional dates of first performances.

178. Straeten, Edmond S. J. vander. La musique aux pays-bas avant le XIXe siècle. Documents inédits et annotés. Compositeurs, virtuoses, théoriciens, luthiers, opéras, motets, airs nationaux, académies, maîtrises, livres, portraits, etc. Bruxelles: C. Muquardt, 1867–88. 8 v.

Vols. 2–7 published by G. A. Van Trigt; vol. 8 by Schott. Reprint by Dover, New York, 1968, 4 v.

Not strictly a biographical dictionary but an invaluable collection of documents, transcripts of records, biographical and bibliographical notes related to the activities of Flemish musicians (Dutch and Belgian). Vol. 6 is devoted to Flemish musicians in Italy; vols. 7–8, to Flemish musicians in Spain. Rich in information of the greatest interest to students of early European music.

179. Het toonkunstenaarsboek van Nederland 1956. Edited by Jos. Smits van Waesberghe. Amsterdam: Nederlandse Toonkunstenaarsraad, 1956. 240 p.

A sourcebook of information on Dutch organizations, institutions, and persons connected with music. Members of the Dutch society of composers are listed alphabetically, with addresses and a key to their activities and affiliations. They are also listed by place.

PARAGUAY

180. Boettner, Juan Max. Música y músicos del Paraguay. Asunciön: Editorial de Autores Paraguayos Asociados, 1957. 294 p.

Includes biographical dictionary of Paraguayan musicians. Bibliography.

POLAND

181. Chominski, Josef. Slownik muzyków polskich. Warsaw: Polskie Wydawnictwo Muzyczne, 1962. 2 v.

At head of title: Instytut Sztuki Polskiej Akademii Nauk. Vol. 1: A–L. Vol. 2: M–Z.

A biographical dictionary of Polish musicians of all periods, including organists, lutenists, and other obscure figures. Strong in 19th-century figures. Works lists and brief bibliographies provided. Addenda to vol. 1 provided at the end of vol. 2. List of commonly used reference and research sources.

182. Chybiński, Adolf. Slownik muzyków dawnej Polski do roku 1800. Kraków: Polskie Wydawnictwo Muzyczne, 1949. 163 p.

Biographical dictionary of musicians (composers and performers) active in Poland in 1800. Brief articles mentioning principal works. List of references for each entry. Preface discusses sources of information such as Fétis, Eitner, and many Polish publications and archives.

183. Sowinski, Wójciech. Les musiciens polonais et slaves, anciens et modernes; dictionnaire biographique ... Précédé d'un résumé de l'histoire de la musique en Pologne.... Paris: A. Le Clerc, 1857. 599 p.

Another edition, in Polish, published in 1874. Reprint by the Da Capo Press, New York, 1971.

"Résumé de l'histoire de la musique en Pologne," p. 1–44. "Anciens in-struments de musique chez les polonais et les slaves," p. 45–58. Long bio-graphical articles, with full bibliographies for major composers.

PORTUGAL

184. Amorim, Eugénio. Dicionário biográfico de musicos do norte de Por-tugal. Porto: Edições Maranus, 1935. 110 p.
Chiefly 19th-century and living musicians. Some extended articles, with compositions listed in the body of the text.

185. Mazza, José. Dicionário biográfico de musicos portugueses, com pre-fácio e notas do José Augusto Alegria.... Lisboa: [1945?]. 103 p.
"Extraido de revista, *Ocidente*, 1944–45."
A dictionary compiled around 1790 and preserved in manuscript in the Biblioteca Publica de Évora. Entries arranged by Christian names; many names of members of religious orders. The dictionary occupies p. 13–40; additional biographical information supplied by the editor from other sources, p. 41–103.

186. Vasconcellos, Joaquim A. da Fonseca E. Os musicos portuguezes. Biogra-phia-bibliographia. Porto: Imprenza Portugueza, 1870. 2 v.
Long biographical articles, lists and discussions of compositions. Useful for early names, library locations of manuscripts, etc. Discussions of op-eras include dates and places of first performances.

187. Viera, Ernesto. Diccionario biographico de musicos portuguezes; his-toria e bibliographia da musica em Portugal. Lisboa: Moreira e Pinheiro, 1900–1904. 2 v.
More inclusive than Vasconcellos (no. 186). Comprehensive lists of works for major composers. Vol. 2 includes much supplementary material and a chronological index.

ROMANIA

188. Cosma, Viorel. Muzicieni români. Compozitori si muzicologi. Lexicon. [Romanian musicians, composers, and musicologists; a dictionary.] Bucu-resti: Uniunii Compozitorilor, 1970. 475 p.
Expansion of a work first issued in 1965.
Biographical data and information on the works of the most prominent Romanian composers and musicologists. Includes musicians of earlier times, but stresses the contemporary scene. Portraits and discographies.

RUSSIA

189. Bélza, Igor' Fedorovich. Handbook of Soviet musicians. Edited by Alan Bush. London: Pilot Press, 1944. 101 p.
First printing, 1943. Reprints by the Greenwood Press, Westport, Con-necticut, 1971, and by the Scholarly Press, St. Clair Shores, Michigan, 1972.

40 short biographies. Portraits. Separate bibliographical section giving a list of each composer's works. English titles, dates given when known.

190. Sovetskie kompozitory, kratkii biograficheskii spravochnik. Sostaviteli: G. Bernandt e A. Dolzhanskii. Moskva: Sovetskii Kompozitor, 1957. 695 p.

Biographical sketches of 1,072 composers, with a full listing of their compositions arranged by medium, with dates of first performance for large works. Literary works by the musicians are also listed.

Review by Fred K. Prieberg in *Musical America*, 78 (July 1958), p. 28–29.

191. Vordarsky-Shiraeff, Alexandria. Russian composers and musicians, a biographical dictionary. New York: H. W. Wilson, 1940. 158 p.

Reprint by the Greenwood Press, New York, 1969.

Brief biographies of outstanding figures: composers, performers, teachers, critics. Classified lists of major works, bibliographical references. Cross-references to variant spellings of Russian names.

SCANDINAVIA

192. Sundelin, Torsten. Norrländskt musikliv. Uppsala: Almqvist & Wiksell, 1946. 358 p.

SOUTH AFRICA

193. Huskisson, Yvonne. The Bantu composers of southern Africa. South African Broadcasting Corporation, 1969. 335 p.

Text in English and Afrikaans.

Portraits of musicians, index of composers, and a study of the traditional instruments of the Bantu.

194. South African music encyclopedia. General editor: Jacques P. Malan. Cape Town: Oxford University Press, 1979–86. 4 v.

"A publication of the Human Sciences Research Council, Pretoria."

Entries limited to the period 1652–1960. Coverage of the music of European and indigenous South Africans. Biographical entries include comprehensive lists of works. Bibliographies follow many articles.

SPAIN

195. Alcahili y de Mosquera, José Maria Ruiz de Lihori y Pardines, Baron de. La música en Valencia. Diccionario biográfico y crítico... Valencia: Domenech, 1903. 445 p.

Biographies of widely varying length, with summary lists of works for major composers. Under "Anonimos," p. 39–170, the compiler introduces long literary digressions concerning liturgical drama, dance music, military music, etc. with musical examples.

SWITZERLAND

196.   Refardt, Edgar. Historisch-biographisches Musikerlexikon der Schweiz. Leipzig/Zürich: Hug u. Co., 1928. 355 p.

Comprehensive biographical coverage for names connected with Swiss music from the Middle Ages to the end of the 16th century. Musicians and instrument makers of the 17th and 18th centuries; composers only for the 19th and 20th centuries. Lists of works.

197.   Schweizer Musiker-Lexikon. Dictionnaire des musiciens suisses.... Im Auftrag des Schweizerischen Tonkünstlervereins bearbeitetvon ... Rédigé à la demande de l'Association des Musiciens Suisses par Willi Schuh *et al.* Zürich: Atlantis Verlag, 1964. 421 p.

A 15-page supplement was issued in 1965.

The expansion of a biographical dictionary of Swiss musicians that appeared originally as vol. 2 of the *Schweizer Musikbuch* (Zürich, 1939). Treats Swiss musicians of all periods as well as foreign musicians resident in Switzerland or associated with the music of that country. Articles in French and German. Excellent bibliographical coverage.

198.   Swiss Composers' League. 40 contemporary Swiss composers. Amriswil: Bodensee Verlag, 1956. 222 p.

Brief biographies and critical comment. A few representative works are described and a larger selection listed, with imprints and instrumentation given. Recordings. Portraits. Text in English.

TURKEY

199.   Öztuna, T. Yilmaz. Türk musikisi ansiklopedisi. Istanbul: M. E. B. Devlet Kitaplari, 1969–74. 2 v.

Based on his *Türk Musikisi Lugati.*

Turkish dictionary of terms and biography. Terms are general musical concepts, but the biographies are restricted to Turkish figures. Bibliographical references.

UNITED STATES OF AMERICA

200.   American Society of Composers, Authors and Publishers. ASCAP Biographical dictionary. 4th ed. Compiled for the American Society of Composers, Authors and Publishers by Jacques Cattell Press. New York: R. R. Bowker, 1980. 589 p.

1st edition published 1948. 2nd edition, 1952. 3rd edition, 1966.

Brief biographies of over 8,000 members of ASCAP, including lyricists and composers of popular and serious music. Major works listed. Separate list of publisher members.

Review by Alan Hoffman in *Notes*, 39 (1982), p. 103–104.

201.   Anderson, E. Ruth. Contemporary American composers: a biographical dictionary. 2nd ed. Boston: G. K. Hall, 1982. 578 p.

First published in 1976 with 513 p.

Approximately 4,500 composers listed.

Criteria for inclusion: birth date no earlier than 1870; American citizenship or extended residence in the U.S.; at least one original composition published, commercially recorded, or performed in an urban area.

Lists representative works; composers' addresses cited.

202. Claghorn, Charles Eugene. Biographical dictionary of American music. West Nyack: Parker Publishing, 1973. 491 p.

5,200 entries covering persons engaged in a wide range of musical styles and genres. Entries also for ensembles, listing principal members.

Reviewed in ALA *Booklist*, February 1, 1975.

203. Edwards, George Thornton. Music and musicians of Maine. Being a history of progress of music in the territory which has come to be known as the State of Maine, from 1604 to 1928. New York: AMS Press, 1970.

Reprint of the 1928 edition.

Many illustrations and a biographical dictionary.

204. Ewen, David. American composers, a biographical dictionary. New York: G. P. Putnam's Sons, 1982. 793 p.

Partially supersedes *Composers since 1900*, no. 82.

Biographical information and stylistic characterizations for 300 American composers from William Billings to the present. Index of titles of music discussed.

Ewen, David. Popular American composers.... See no. 239.

205. Granniss, Lewis C. Connecticut composers. New Haven: Connecticut State Federation of Music Clubs, 1935. 125 p.

Brief biographies with lists of major works. Lists early tune book writers. Chronological list of composers.

206. Historical Records Survey. District of Columbia. Bio-bibliographical index of musicians in the United States of America from colonial times. Sponsored by the Board of Commissioners of the District of Columbia. 2nd ed. Washington, D.C.: Music Section, Pan American Union, 1956. 439 p.

First printed in 1941. Unaltered reprint, 1970, by the AMS Press, New York, and the Scholarly Press, St. Clair Shores, Michigan, 1972.

An index to biographical information contained in 66 works (dictionaries, histories, etc.) on American music published between 1846 and 1941, with page references to the volumes indexed.

207. Jablonski, Edward. The encyclopedia of American music. New York: Doubleday, 1981. 629 p.

The work is organized in roughly chronological order under the following headings:

1. In the beginning;
2. A time of revolutions;
3. From the second awakening to the second New England School;
4. The Romantics and Classicists;
5. The Twenties;
6. The time of trouble: Depression and war.

41

Appendix: American music on records.
Review by Susan T. Sommer in *Notes*, 38 (1982), p. 607–608.

208.   Jacobi, Hugh William. Contemporary American composers based at American colleges and universities. Consultant: Margaret DeVoss. Paradise, California: Paradise Arts Publishers, 1975. 240 p.

Biographies interpolating citations of major works. Quotations from composers following each alphabetical section. Supplement 2, p. 238–40.

Brief review by Stephen M. Fry in *Notes*, 32 (1975), p. 302.

209.   Mangler, Joyce Ellen. Rhode Island music and musicians, 1733–1850. Detroit, Michigan: Information Service, 1965. 90 p. (Detroit studies in music bibliography, 7)

Primarily a directory of early Rhode Island musicians; indexed by profession and by chronology.

Supplement I: organ builders and installations in Rhode Island churches. Supplement II: membership in the Psallonian Society 1816–32. Bibliography of primary and secondary sources.

Review by Donald W. Krummel in *Notes*, 23 (1966), p. 265.

210.   Music and dance in California and the West. Edited by Richard D. Saunders. Hollywood, California: Bureau of Musical Research, 1948. 311 p.

Earlier editions with slightly varying titles in 1933 and 1940.

This and the following six titles (nos. 208–213) are a series of regional reference works covering different sections of the United States. Long articles on the development of musical and dance activities. Biographical sketches of composers, performers, conductors, educators, etc. Portraits. Pronounced emphasis on the commercial aspects of music.

211.   Music and dance in New York State. Sigmund Spaeth, editor-in-chief. William J. Perlman, director and managing editor. New York: Bureau of Musical Research, 1951. 435 p.

212.   Music and dance in Pennsylvania, New Jersey and Delaware. Sigmund Spaeth, editor-in-chief. William J. Perlman, director and managing editor. New York: Bureau of Musical Research, 1954. 339 p.

213.   Music and dance in Texas, Oklahoma and the Southwest. Edited by E. Clyde Whitlock and Richard D. Saunders. Hollywood, California: Bureau of Musical Research, 1950. 256 p.

214.   Music and dance in the central states. Richard D. Saunders, editor; William J. Perlman, compiler. Hollywood, California: Bureau of Musical Research, 1952. 173 p.

215.   Music and dance in the New England states. Sigmund Spaeth, editor-in-chief. William J. Perlman, director and associate editor. New York: Bureau of Musical Research, 1951. 347 p.

216. Music and dance in the southeastern states. Sigmund Spaeth, editor-in-chief. William J. Perlman, director and managing editor. New York: Bureau of Musical Research, 1952. 331 p.

217. The new Grove dictionary of American music. Edited by H. Wiley Hitchcock and Stanley Sadie. London: Macmillan, 1986. 4 v.

A work consisting of reworked articles from the *New Grove* (no. 46) and newly commissioned ones "to reflect the essence of American music" (*Preface*). Covers American music and musicians broadly considered, with concise articles summarizing works of lesser-known persons, and broad, illustrated pieces with works lists and lengthy bibliographies for well-known persons. Many of the articles bring bits of information together for the first time. Detailed coverage of popular styles and genres, including sketches of important popular groups. Numerous descriptions of uniquely American musical instruments. Historical sketches of musical publishers. Copiously illustrated, provided with an excellent introduction and a list of contributors. Signed articles. The principal reference work on American music, but not without significant flaws and omissions.

An extensive review by Mary Wallace Davidson *et al.* appears in *Notes*, 44 (1987), p. 43–47. Review essays by Allen P. Britton in *American Music*, 5 (1987), p. 194–203, and by Richard A. Crawford, in *College Music Symposium*, 27 (1987), p. 172–86. Review by Gary Giddins in *Village Voice*, 35 (13 January 1987), p. 75–76.

218. North Carolina Federation of Music Clubs. North Carolina musicians, a selective handbook. Chapel Hill: University of North Carolina Library, 1956. 82 p. (Univ. of North Carolina Library Extension pub., vol. 21, no. 4.)

219. Reis, Claire R. Composers in America; biographical sketches of contemporary composers with a record of their works. Rev. and enl. ed. New York: Macmillan, 1947. 399 p.

First published in 1930 under the title *American Composers....*

A survey of music written by American serious composers, 1915 to 1947. Biographies of 332 composers, with a classified listing of their works, manuscripts included (date, publishers, duration). Supplementary list of 424 names without further biographical data.

Review by Lee Fairley in *Notes*, 4 (1947), p. 458–59.

220. Schiavo, Giovanni Ermenegildo. Italian-American history. New York: Arno Press, 1975. 2 v. (The Italian American experience)

Vol. 2 also has a special title: The Italian contribution to the Catholic church in America. Reprint of the edition published by Vigo Press, New York, 1947–49.

One of a series of volumes devoted to Italian-American cultural relations. The first volume of this set includes a section on Italian music and musicians in America and a "Dictionary of musical biography."

221. Thomson, Virgil. American music since 1910. With an introduction by Nicolas Nabokov. New York: Holt, Rinehart and Winston, 1970. 204 p. (Twentieth-century composers, 1)

Primarily a collection of critical essays, but contains a biographical dictionary of 106 American composers, p. 118–85. Brief biographies with stimulating commentary. Principal works cited.

222. Who's who in American music: classical. 2nd ed. Edited by Jacques Cattell Press. New York; London: Bowker, 1985. 783 p.

Brief biographical entries compiled from information provided by the subjects themselves. Entries include résumés of professional careers and mailing addresses. 9,038 entries in alphabetical order. Geographical and professional classification indexes.

Review by George Hill in *Notes*, 41 (1985), p. 518–19.

See also nos. 95 and 96.

223. Works Projects Administration. Northern California. Celebrities in El Dorado, 1850–1906. Cornel Lengyel, editor. San Francisco: Works Project Administration of California and sponsored by the City and County of San Francisco, 1940. 270 leaves (typescript). (The history of music in San Francisco, 4)

A biographic record of 111 prominent musicians who have visited San Francisco and performed there from the earliest days of the gold rush era to the time of the great fire, with additional lists of visiting celebrities (1909–1940), chamber music ensembles, bands, orchestras, and other music making bodies. [Editor's *Note*]

YUGOSLAVIA

Kompositori i Muzicki Pisci Jugoslavije. See no. 1306.

DICTIONARIES AND ENCYCLOPEDIAS OF JAZZ, POPULAR, AND FOLK MUSIC

Resources for reference and research in the areas of jazz, popular, and folk music have increased since the last edition of this work. Numerous dictionaries, encyclopedias, and other related works are now widely available, though frequently these contain few references to the sources of data for the information provided. The rise of popular music as a commercial enterprise has in turn stimulated an enormous number of books intended for the uncritical reader; few such works are cited here. Related information will be found in the sections *Jazz* under "Bibliographies of Music Literature," *Jazz* and *Popular Music* under "Bibliographies of Music," and *Collectors' Guides to Jazz Recordings, Collectors' Guides to Popular Recordings,* and *Ethnic and Folk Music on Records* under "Discographies."

224. Anderson, Robert and Gail North. Gospel music encyclopedia. New York: Sterling, 1979. 320 p.

Illustrated popular biographical work with variable quantities of data presented. Useful lists of winners of awards and broadcast gospel programs.

Discography.

225. Baggelaar, Kristen and Donald Milton. The folk music encyclopedia. London: Omnibus Press, 1977. 419 p.
Also published in the U.S. as *Folk Music: More than a Song* by Crowell in 1976.
Entries on persons and groups, incorporating biographical, political, social, musical, and discographical information. Does not cite sources. Illustrated.

226. Bane, Michael. Who's who in rock. Researcher: Kenny Kertok. New York: Everest House, 1982. 259 p.

227. Berry, Lemuel, Jr. Biographical dictionary of black musicians and music educators. Vol. 1. Guthrie, Oklahoma: Educational Book Publishers, 1978.
Entries on individuals and ensembles. Many appendixes. Indexes to names and specialties.

228. Bogaert, Karel. Blues lexikon. Blues, cajun, boogie woogie, gospel. Antwerp: Standaard, 1972. 480 p.
Biographical information, with discographies for hundreds of blues performers. Bibliography and index. Introduction by John Godrich provides a survey of significant blues literature.

229. Brown, Len and Gary Friedrich. Encyclopedia of rock and roll. New York: Tower Publications, 1970. 217 p.
A bio-bibliographic work.

230. Charters, Samuel B. Jazz: New Orleans. Rev. ed. New York: Oak Publications, 1963. 173 p.
First published in 1958 by Walter C. Allen.
Brief descriptions of musicians and groups, under chronological periods. Appendix consisting of discography; index to names of musicians and bands, halls, cabarets, and tune titles. Illustrated.

231. Chilton, John. Who's who of jazz: Storyville to Swing Street. 4th ed. London: Macmillan, 1985. 373 p.
First published in London by the Bloomsbury Book Shop, 1970, 447 p., and subsequently in Philadelphia by the Chilton Book Co., 1972, 419 p. There is a paper edition produced in 1989 by Papermac in London.
Brief biographies of more than 1,000 jazz musicians tracing their affiliations with various groups. Portraits. A partial listing of bandleaders mentioned in the text (p. 416–18).

232. Clifford, Mike. The Harmony illustrated encyclopedia of rock. 5th ed. New York: Harmony Books, 1986. 272 p.
Published in Great Britain as *The Illustrated Rock Handbook*. Revised from previous editions of 1981–84. Revised edition of *The Illustrated New Musical Express Encyclopedia of Rock*, 1978.

233. Craig, Warren. The great songwriters of Hollywood. San Diego, California: A. S. Barnes, 1980. 287 p.

Simultaneously published in London by Tantivy Press.
A biographical work covering composers and librettists. Includes lists of songs and song indexes.

234. Craig, Warren. Sweet and lowdown: America's popular song writers. Metuchen, New Jersey: Scarecrow, 1978. 645 p.
Biographical sketches of Tin Pan Alley figures followed by chronological lists of productions and songs. Claims to rectify factual errors in other works on the same subject. Indexes to song titles and productions.
Review by Julian Hodgson in *Brio*, 16 (1979), p. 23–24. Review by John Shepherd in *Notes*, 36 (1979), p. 372–73.

235. Davidson, Harry C. Diccionario folclórico de Colombia; musicos, instrumentos y danzas. Bogotá: Banco de la Républica, Departmento de Talleres Gráficos, 1970. 3 v.
Entries on genres, forms, instruments, and terms of the folk music and dance of Colombia, from adagio to *zumba*. Sources are cited in context. Some of the articles are quite extensive (e.g., El arpa) and one, on the dance form *bambuco*, occupies 400 p. Index to names, forms, and instruments.

236. Dellar, Fred, Roy Thompson and Douglas B. Green. The illustrated encyclopedia of country music. Foreword by Roy Acuff. New York: Harmony Books, 1977. 256 p.
A publication intended for the enthusiast, but with sufficient information and cross-references to be a useful source. Covers personalities, groups, and occasional places. Profusely illustrated. Discographic information provided.

237. Enciclopedia del rock, [di] Massimo Bassoli [*et al.*]. Milano: Teti, 1981. 222 p.
A biographical work covering both individuals and groups. Better coverage of European figures.

238. Enciclopedia rock anni '60, a cura di Riccardo Bertoncelli. Milano: Arcana, 1985. 512 p.
An Italian dictionary on rock music of the 1960s, includes biographical entries with discographic citations. Brief general bibliography.

239. Ewen, David. Popular American composers, from revolutionary times to the present. New York: H. W. Wilson, 1962. 217 p.
First Supplement, 1972. 121 p.
A bibliographical reference guide to 130 of the most important American composers of popular music, from William Billings to André Previn. Portraits. Chronological list of the composers, with an index to some 3,500 songs. The *First Supplement* updates the information in 1962 volume and adds 31 new biographies. See also no. 201.

240. Feather, Leonard G. The encyclopedia of jazz. Completely revised, enlarged and brought up to date. New York: Horizon Press, 1960. 527 p.

First published in 1955. Supplement, 1956. Reprinted by Quartet Books, London and New York, 1978, and by Da Capo, New York, 1985.

Introductory essays on the history, sociology, and structure of jazz (p. 13–90); biographies of jazz musicians, outlining their careers and summarizing their recording activities (p. 96–473). Addresses given.

241. Feather, Leonard G. The encyclopedia of jazz in the sixties. Foreword by John Lewis. New York: Horizon Press, 1966. 312 p.

Reprinted by Da Capo, New York, 1986.

Similar in content and organization to the preceding. Numerous portraits. Biographies stress affiliations with recording companies. Short essays on the state of jazz, the results of jazz polls, etc.

242. Feather, Leonard G. and Ira Gitler. The encyclopedia of jazz in the seventies. Introduction by Quincy Jones. New York: Horizon Press, 1976. 393 p.

Reprinted by Da Capo Press, New York, 1987. Also published by Quartet Books, London, 1978.

As in the preceding, a compilation of biographies surrounded with short, topical essays. Covers events from mid-1966 to mid-1976.

"A guide to available jazz films," by Leonard Maltin, p. [382]–386.

Reviews in *Jazz Podium*, 26 (1977), p. 39, and in *Down Beat*, 44 (15 December 1977), p. 52, 60.

243. Gammond, Peter and Peter Clayton. Dictionary of popular music. New York: Philosophical Library, 1961. 274 p.

A dictionary of names, terms, and titles of major popular songs. Listing of works and recordings for the principal composers of popular music. Pronounced British slant.

244. Gentry, Linnell. A history and encyclopedia of country, western, and gospel music. 2nd edition, completely revised. Nashville, Tennessee: Claimon Corp., 1969. 598 p.

First published in 1961 by the McQuiddy Press, Nashville.

A major reference work in its field. Part II is an anthology of magazine articles on country, western, and gospel music since 1904. Part III: country musical shows since 1924. Part IV: biographies of country, western, and gospel singers, musicians, and comedians.

245. Harris, Sheldon. Blues who's who: a biographical dictionary of blues singers. New York: Da Capo Press, 1981. 775 p.

A reprint of the 1979 publication by Arlington House, New Rochelle, N.Y.

Covering 571 blues singers active from 1900 to 1977. Bibliography of sources. Film, radio, television, theater, song, and names and place indexes. Numerous photographs.

Review by Raymond F. Kennedy in *Notes*, 37 (1980), p. 327–28.

246. Helander, Brock. The rock who's who: a biographical dictionary and critical discography, including rhythm-and-blues, soul, rockabilly, folk, country, easy listening, punk, and new wave. New York: Schirmer Books; London: Collier Macmillan, 1982. 686 p.

Includes articles about nonmusical figures. Bibliography and index.

47

247. Herzhaft, Gérard. Encyclopédie du blues: étude bio-discographique d'une musique populaire négro-americaine. Lyon: Fédèrop, 1979. 346 p.

Entries on individuals, genres, trends, and styles. Occasional discographic citations. General bibliography, but no bibliographies for individuals. Name index.

248. Jasper, Tony and Derek Oliver. The international encyclopedia of hard rock & heavy metal. Revised ed. London: Sidgwick & Jackson, 1986. 388 p.

Previously published by Facts on File, New York, 1983. 400 p.

Entries for almost 1,500 groups and individual musicians. International in scope. Entries include basic biographical facts, some attempts at critical analysis, and a discography.

249. Kienzle, Richard. Great guitarists; the most influential players in jazz, country, blues and rock. New York: Facts on File, 1985. 246 p.

Extensive biographies on about 50 performers in popular genres. Includes discographies and index.

250. Kinkle, Roger D. The complete encyclopedia of popular music and jazz, 1900–1950. New Rochelle, New York: Arlington House, 1974. 4 v.

Contents: vol. 1. Music year by year, 1900–1950; vol. 2. Biographies, A–K; vol. 3. Biographies, L–Z; vol. 4. Indexes and appendixes.

Covers musicians whose careers began before 1950 and therefore may include works actually written up to the early 1970s. Vol. 1 contains lists of significant works organized by year of appearance (Broadway musicals, popular songs, movie musicals, representative recordings). Biographies in vol. 2 and vol. 3 provide works and recordings lists, but no bibliographic citations. Vol. 4 contains lists of winners of polls and prizes, indexes of names, titles, and popular songs. This is an essential reference work for the genre and the period it covers.

Review by Felicity Howlett in *Notes*, 32 (1975), p. 44–46.

251. Lacombe, Alain and Claude Rode. La musique du film. Paris: Éditions Francis Van de Velde, 1979. 516 p.

Preceded by five chapters on the nature of film music, there are biographical entries on composers, each with lists of films for which music was provided. Lists of 20th-century composers whose music has been adapted to film. Indexes of names and titles.

252. Lawless, Ray McKinley. Folksingers and folksongs in America; a handbook of biography, bibliography, and discography. Illustrated from paintings by Thomas Hart Benton and others and from designs in Steuben glass. New revised edition with special supplement. New York: Duell, Sloan and Pearce, 1965. 750 p.

First published in 1960.

A general book of knowledge for folk song enthusiasts, with information pertaining to singers, song collecting, sources, and recordings. The largest part of the work is devoted to biographical information on American folksingers.

Review of the first edition by Rae Korson in *Notes*, 18 (1960), p. 62.

253. The new Grove dictionary of jazz. Edited by Barry Kernfeld. New York: Grove's Dictionaries of Music; London: Macmillan Press, 1988. 2 v.

The first truly scholarly dictionary on jazz including "a comprehensive treatment of terminology and theory, articles on musical instruments, record labels, festivals, venues, films, institutions, individuals who are not performers, and also an extensive bibliography" as well as articles on individual performers, ensembles, and styles of jazz. A model of scholarly breadth and rigorous methodology, the work carries over entries from *The New Grove Dictionary of Music and Musicians* and *The New Grove Dictionary of American Music*. However:

> It is the largest dictionary of the music ever published; it contains the broadest coverage of the subject to appear in one work and seeks to give detailed attention to all periods and styles of jazz from many countries, in an effort to counteract the factionalism noticeable in some jazz literature.... While the purpose of an encyclopedic work is to reflect the current understanding of its subject, it is important to note that a large amount of information is published for the first time here, and that many of the major articles represent new thinking on the ways jazz may be approached.... The dictionary includes extensive bibliographies supplemented by references to holdings of oral history collections.... Close and wide-ranging attention is paid to the music itself; numerous musical terms are precisely defined, musical structures, procedures, and styles are described in detail, and there are informed analytical surveys (with music examples) of such theoretical topics as forms, harmony, and improvisation. [from the introductory remarks]

Focuses on jazz and not on related popular and commercial music, from the genesis of the music—principally from black Americans at the turn of the 20th century—to the mid-1980s. Includes extensive articles on topics like "arrangement" and "recording." These synthetic and often segmented articles present many examples, facts, and even directories of information. There are bibliographies for virtually every article; articles on performers and ensembles include selected lists of recordings. There is a substantial general bibliography. Articles are signed by contributors and there is a list of contributors identifying their articles. Well-illustrated and handsomely produced with wide margins.

254. Nite, Norm N. Rock on: the illustrated encyclopedia of rock n' roll, updated edition. New York: Harper & Row, 1982–85. 3 v.

v. 1: *The solid gold years*, updated edition. Originally published as *The solid gold years* by T. Y. Crowell in New York, 1974.

v. 2: *The years of change, 1964–1978*, updated edition with Ralph M. Newman; published by Harper & Row, New York, 1984. 749 p. Originally published as *The modern years, 1964–present* by T. Y. Crowell in New York, 1978. 590 p.

v. 3: *The video revolution, 1978–present*, with Charles Crespo; published by Harper & Row, New York, 1985. 444 p.

Brief biographical entries on individuals and groups active in rock and roll and related genres. Includes lists of principal recordings. Indexes of song titles.

255. Panassie, Hughes and Madeleine Gautier. Dictionnaire du jazz. Préface de Louis Armstrong. Nouvelle édition, revue et augmenté. Paris: Albin Michel, 1980. 378 p.

First published by Robert Laffont, Paris, 1954. Subsequently published by Albin Michel in Paris, 1971, 360 p. This edition is a reprint of the 1971 edition with a supplement of 9 pages of new entries and a postface. English translation under the title *Guide to Jazz*, translated by Desmond Flower (New York: Houghton Mifflin, 1956).

The *Dictionnaire* is a standard source book on jazz; it is chiefly biographical but with some terms included. Portraits.

256. Paulin, Don. Das Folk-Music-Lexikon. Frankfurt: Fischer-Taschenbuch-Verlag, 1980. 128 p.

A bio-bibliographical work covering individuals and ensembles. Better coverage of European figures. Entries include discographical information. Index and bibliography.

Rachlin, Harvey. The encyclopedia of the music business. See no. 3014.

257. Rice, Edward le Roy. Monarchs of minstrelsy, from "Daddy" Rice to date. New York: Kenny Publishing Co., 1911. 366 p.

Colorful biographical sketches of the leading performers in American minstrel shows of the late 19th century. Illustrated. The information is arranged in rough chronological order.

258. The Rolling Stone encyclopedia of rock & roll. Edited by Jon Pareles, consulting editor, and Patricia Romanowski. New York: Rolling Stone Press/Summit Books, 1983. 615 p.

Entries on significant and insignificant persons, groups, terms, record companies, etc., contributing to the rock industry. Entries on performers include chronological lists of recordings giving brief titles and manufacturers' name, but not catalog numbers. Entries for groups list back-up personnel; back-up personnel frequently have individual entries. Definitions of terms include those for dance styles.

259. Rose, Al and Edmond Souchen. New Orleans jazz family album. rev. ed. Baton Rouge: Louisiana State University Press, 1978. 322 p.

First published in 1967, 304 p., and then in two more editions.

Copiously illustrated with many early photographs. Special sections devoted to the musicians, the ensembles, and the places where they performed.

Roxon, Lillian. Rock encyclopedia. See no. 1525.

260. Schmidt-Joos, Siegfried and Barry Graves. Rock-Lexikon; mit Diskographien von Bernie Sigg. Reinbeck bei Hamburg: Rowohlt, 1975. 445 p.

Biographical dictionary of rock performers, as individuals and groups. Brief entries with cross-references and selected discographies. Appendix of entries on terms and recording companies. Extensive bibliography. Index to names cited in articles.

261. Sevran, Pascal. Dictionnaire de la chanson française. Paris: M. Lafron, 1986. 379 p.

Successor to an edition by France Vernillat and Jacques Charpentreau and published by Larousse, Paris, 1968. 256 p.

A biographical dictionary of French popular song. Coverage extends from the 13th century to the present day, but with emphasis on singers of the 19th and 20th centuries. The dictionary is preceded by a "petite histoire de la chanson française." Includes both terms and biographies. No bibliographical references. Illustrated.

262. Shaw, Arnold. Dictionary of American pop/rock: rock, pop, rhythm and blues, folk, country, blues, gospel, jazz films, musical theater, recordings and music business. New York: Schirmer Books, 1982. 440 p.

Brief entries on the terminology of the field and on important individuals. Entries on persons discuss style characteristics and contributions. Cross-references. Entries on important clubs and locations. Index to names and terms.

263. Shestack, Melvin. The country music encyclopedia. New York: T. Y. Crowell Co., 1974. 410 p.

Contains 200 entries and 250 black-and-white photographs. Describes the institutions of country music and relates its history.

264. Stambler, Irwin. Encyclopedia of pop, rock & soul. New York: St. Martin's Press, 1977. 609 p.

First printed in 1974. Successor to the *Encyclopedia of Popular Music,* 1965. 359 p.

Preceded by three essays on the genres, most of the dictionary consists of biographical entries, with a few terms and trends defined or discussed. There are articles on films and musicals included. Lists of winners of various prizes. Bibliography.

265. Stambler, Irwin and Grulun Landon. Encyclopedia of folk, country, and western music. New York: St. Martin's Press, 1984. 902 p.

First published in 1969, 396 p.

Consists chiefly of biographical entries on performers and groups. Appendixes include special articles on "Changing attitudes toward folk music" by Sam Hinton, "The rise and fall of country music" by Bill Anderson, and "Country and pop music: development and relationship" by Ed Kahn. Also, award listings and a selective discography and bibliography.

266. Ténot, Frank. Dictionnaire du jazz. Paris: Larousse, 1967. 256 p. (Les dictionnaires de l'homme du XXe siècle)

One of the popular, subject-oriented Larousse dictionaries. Good, brief discussions, chiefly biographical but with some jazz terms. Illustrated.

267. Walker, Leo. The big band almanac. Rev. ed. New York: Da Capo, 1989. 466 p.

Corrected reprint of the first edition by Ward Ritchie Press in Pasadena, California, 1978.

A biographical dictionary principally of band leaders flourishing from the early 1920s to the mid-1950s in America. Each entry includes information on band affiliation, sidemen, principal vocalists, theme songs, and recording company contracts.

268. Who's new wave in music: an illustrated encyclopedia, 1976–1982 (the first wave). Compiled and edited by David Bianco. Ann Arbor, Michigan: Pierian Press, 1985. 430 p.
Bibliography: p. 333–38. Includes discographies and indexes.

269. York, William. Who's who in rock music. Rev. edition. New York: Scribner, 1982. 413 p.
First published by Atomic in Seattle, Washington, 1978. 260 p.
Collates information gleaned from rock album covers and therefore covers "sidemen" broadly, if with dubious authority.

MUSICAL INSTRUMENTS: MAKERS AND PERFORMERS

There is a substantial group of reference books concerned with the construction, performance, and iconography of musical instruments. A great deal of work has been done with respect to the violin, and there is an increasing number of reference tools devoted to keyboard and to wind instruments. For specific descriptions, prices, and illustrations of individual instruments, particularly those of the string family, the student should not neglect the catalogs of various dealers: Hamma, Herrmann, Hill, Lyon and Healy, Wurlitzer, etc. These are not included in our listing. For the iconography of musical instruments, see Buchner (no. 282), Besseler (no. 587), Kinsky (no. 595), and Komma (no. 596). See also "Bibliographies of Music Literature" (no. 671 ff.) and "Catalogs of Musical Instrument Collections" (no. 2495 ff.).

270. Ames, David W. and Anthony V. King. Glossary of Hausa music and its social contexts. Evanston, Illinois: Northwestern University Press, 1971. 184 p. plus 10 p. of photographs.
A technical glossary of musical instruments and sound production providing indicators of the sociocultural context of musical performance of the sub-Saharan Hausa culture. Indexes of Hausa terms and English equivalents.

271. Avgerinos, Gerassimos. Lexikon der Pauke. Frankfurt am M.: Verlag das Musikinstrument, 1964. 105 p. (Das Musikinstrument, 12)
A dictionary of terms, chiefly German, connected with drums and drum playing.

272. Bächi, Julius. Berühmte Cellisten: Porträts der Meistercellisten von Boccherini bis Casals und von Paul Grümmer bis Rostropovitch. 3. Aufl. Zürich: Atlantis, 1981. 168 p.

273. Bachmann, Alberto A. An encyclopedia of the violin. Translated by Frederick H. Martens, edited by Albert E. Wier. New York: D. Appleton, 1925. 470 p.
Reprinted, with a new preface by Stuart Canin, by Da Capo Press, New York, 1966.

A sourcebook on the violin, its history, construction, literature, and performers. Organized by chapters, many of which contain lexicons and bibliographies: for example, Chap. II, "Violin makers in Europe"; Chap. III, "Violin makers in America"; Chap. XXI, "Glossary of musical terms"; Chap. XXII, "Biographical dictionary of violinists"; Chap. XXIII, "Literature relating to the violin"; Chap. XXV, "A list of music for the violin." Portraits and illustrations.

274. Bachmann, Alberto A. Les grands violinists du passé.... Paris: Fischbacher, 1913. 468 p.

Biographies of 40 violinist-composers, varying in length but with lists of works and a number of full or partial thematic catalogs (e.g., Corelli, Kreutzer, Leclair, Rode, Sarasate, Tartini, Viotti, Vivaldi, etc.).

275. Baines, Anthony. European and American musical instruments. London: Batsford, 1966. 824 p.

A "pictorial museum" of musical instruments selected from American and European collections. Instruments are grouped by families: stringed, woodwind, brass, and percussion. Much precise technical information along with historical background. All instruments are identified as to present location.

Review by Albert Protz in *Die Musikforschung*, 21 (1968), p. 388–89.

276. Bechler, Leo and Bernhardt Rahm. Die Oboe und die ihr verwandten Instrumente, nebst biographischen Skizzen der bedeutendsten ihrer Meister. Anhang: Musikliteratur für Oboe und englisch Horn, zusammengestellt von Dr. Phillip Losch. Leipzig: C. Merseburger, 1914. 98 p., 32 p. (Anhang).

Reprint of the 1914 edition by Sändig, Wiesbaden, 1972, and by Knuf, Buren, 1978.

A history of the oboe and related instruments, with brief biographical sketches of famous players. Supplementary list of works for oboe and English horn, solo and with other instruments.

277. Boalch, Donald H. Makers of the harpsichord and clavichord, 1440 to 1840. Oxford: Clarendon Press, 1974. 225 p.

First published by G. Ronald, London, [1956], 169 p.

Lists more than 820 makers of early keyboard instruments and describes over 1,000 of their instruments, giving dates, registers, compasses, histories, and present ownership. Photographs of instruments.

Review by Frank Hubbard in *Notes*, 14 (1957), p. 572–73. Review in the *Times Literary Supplement*, 21 Dec. 1956.

278. Bone, Philip James. The guitar and mandolin: biographies of celebrated players and composers. [2nd ed., enl.] London and New York: Schott, 1954. 388 p.

First published in 1914. Reprint by Schott, London, 1972.

Performers and composers, including "standard" composers who have written for guitar or mandolin. Major works are mentioned, but there are no complete listings. Portraits.

Review by Richard Capell in *Music and Letters*, 35 (1954), p. 254.

279. Bowers, Q. David. Encyclopedia of automatic musical instruments. Cylinder music boxes, disc music boxes, piano players and player pianos, coin-operating pianos, orchestrions, photoplayers, organettes, fairground organs, calliopes, and other self-playing instruments mainly of the 1750–1940 era. Including a dictionary of automatic musical instrument terms. Vestal, New York: Vestal Press, 1972. 1,008 p.

Profusely illustrated. Much documentary information. A book for collectors of automatic musical instruments.

280. Bragard, Roger and Ferdinand J. de Hen. Musical instruments in art and history. Preface by G. Thibault. Translated by Bill Hopkins. New York: Viking Press, n.d. 281 p. 119 plates.

Originally published in French. German translation by Dieter Krickeberg. Stuttgart: Belser Verlag, 1968.

An attractive "picture book" of early instruments, with popular commentary.

Review of the German edition by J. H. van der Meer in *Die Musikforschung*, 24 (1971), p. 481–83; of the English edition by Edmund A. Bowles in *Notes*, 25 (1969), p. 735–36, and by Mary Remnant in *Music and Letters*, 50 (1969), p. 301–303.

281. Brinser, Martin. Dictionary of twentieth century Italian violin makers. Irvington, New Jersey: American Graphic, 1978. 111 p.

282. Buchner, Alexander. Musical instruments through the ages. Translated by Iris Urwin. London: Spring Books, [1956]. 37 p. 323 plates.

First published, with the text in Czech, by Artia, Prague. German edition: *Musikinstrumente im Wandel der Zeiten*. Published in a new translation by Borek Vancurel as *Musical Instruments, an Illustrated History* by Crown Books, New York, 1973, 274 p.

Not a dictionary or encyclopedia, but important as a collection of beautifully reproduced plates, some 323 in number, of musical instruments and representations of musical performance in painting, engraving, and sculpture.

283. Buchner, Alexander. Musikinstrumente der Völker. [Ins Deutsche übers. von O. Guth. Grafische Gestaltung von M. Houska. Notenbeispiele gezeichnet von J. Milota.] [Hanau/Main]: Dausien, [1968]. 295 p.

Simultaneous publication of *Hudební Nástroje Národú* (Prague: Artia). Published in an English translation, *Folk Music Instruments*, in 1972 by Crown in New York.

A pictorial work with focus on European folk music instruments.

284. Carfagna, Carlo and Mario Gangi. Dizionario chitarristico italiano. (Chitarristi, liutisti, tiorbisti, compositori, liutai ed editori.) Ancona: Bèrben, 1968. 97 p.

In two alphabets, the first devoted to guitarists, lutenists, theorbo players and composers, the second to instrument makers and editors.

285. Clarke, A. Mason. A biographical dictionary of fiddlers, including performers on the violoncello and double bass, past and present, containing sketches of their artistic careers. Together with notes of their compositions. London: W. Reeves, 1895. 390 p.

Reprint of the original edition by the Scholarly Press, St. Clair Shores, Michigan, 1972.

Anecdotal accounts.

286. Crane, Frederick. Extant medieval musical instruments: a provisional catalogue by types. Iowa City: University of Iowa Press, 1972. 105 p.

Brief descriptions of the surviving medieval musical instruments in art and archaeological museums throughout the world. The instruments are classified according to the Hornbostel-Sachs system (idiophones, chordophones, and aerophones). Rather crude pen sketches of 30 of the instruments.

P. 91–105: bibliography.

287. The Diagram Group. Musical instruments of the world; an illustrated encyclopedia. Compiled by the Diagram Group. London: Paddington Press, 1976. 320 p.

Simultaneously published in New York by Facts on File. Subsequently published in New York by Bantam, 1978, 320 p. Portions published as the *Scribner Guide to Orchestral Instruments* (New York: C. Scribner's Sons, 1983), 121 p.

Drawings of instruments, some with diagrams showing details of construction or methods of sound production and music making. Drawings are accompanied by brief prose explications. Index and bibliography.

288. Fairfield, John H. Known violin makers. Coral Gables, Florida: Virtuoso Press, 1983. 218 p.

First published by Bradford Press, New York, 1942, 192 p. Reprinted with supplements in 1973 and 1980.

Separate listings of European makers from the 16th century and American makers. For each, a brief biography, description of works, and the current price range of the instruments.

289. Gorgerat, Gérald. Encyclopédie de la musique pour instruments à vent. Lausanne: Éditions Rencontre, [1955]. 3 v.

A pretentious work that attempts to cover all information pertaining to the making and performance of wind instruments and much more that has no particular relevance. Useful fingering charts for all winds. Several special lists, as follows:

Vol. 3, p. 243–83: Principal works for wind instruments, solo and ensemble. Vol. 3, p. 285–340: Dictionary of composers cited in the text. Brief identifications; no page references. Vol. 3, p. 341–524: Table of French terms with their equivalents in Italian, German, English, and Spanish.

290. Hamma, Fridolin. German violin makers; a critical dictionary.... Translated by Walter Stewart. London: W. Reeves, [1961]. 49 p. 80 plates.

Translated from the 1948 German edition, *Meister deutscher Geigenbaukunst.* Stuttgart: Schuler-Verlag, 1948.

Alphabetical listing of 550 names of important German makers, with plates illustrating their work.

Review by Cynthia L. Adams in *Notes*, 19 (1962), p. 261–62.

291. Hamma, Walter. Geigenbauer der deutschen Schule des 17. bis 19. Jahrhunderts. Violin makers of the German school from the 17th to the 19th century. Luthiers de l'école allemande du 17e au 19e siècle. Tutzing: H. Schneider, 1986. 2 v.

Parallel texts in English, French, and German.

292. Hamma, Walter. Meister italienischer Geigenbaukunst. (Zum 100 jähr. Bestehen der Firma Hamma & Co., Stuttgart, im Jahre 1964. Engl. Übers: Walter J. Stewart. Franz. Übers.: Aristide Wirsta.) München: Schuler, 1976. 727 p.

Revision and expansion of a work first published in 1931. Subsequently published in Stuttgart by Schuler, 1965. 728 p.

Describes more than 300 instruments made by Italian masters. Descriptions arranged alphabetically by maker, with biographical information and photographic plates of details.

293. Handbuch der europäischen Volksmusikinstrumente, hrsg. vom Institut für Deutsche Volkskunde Berlin in Zusammenarbeit mit dem Musikhistorischen Museum Stockholm durch Ernst Emsheimer und Erich Stockmann. Leipzig: Deutscher Verlag für Musik, 1967–. 4 v.

Contents: Series I —

Bd. 1. *Die Volksmusikinstrumente Ungarns* von Bálint Sárosi. 1968. 148 p.

Bd. 2. *Die Volksmusikinstrumente der Tschechoslowakei* von Ludvík Kunz. 1974. 2 v.

Bd. 4. *Die Volksmusikinstrumente der Schweiz* von Brigitte Bachmann Geiser. 1981. 134 p.

Bd. 5. *Die Volksmusikinstrumente in Slowenien* von Zmaga Kumer (Ljubljana: Slovenska akademija znanosti in umetnosti, Znanstvenorazis-kovalni center SAZU, Institut za slovensko narodopisje, 1986. 107 p.)

See also no. 335.

294. Hartnack, Joachim W. Grosse Geiger unserer Zeit. München: Rütten & Loening, 1967. 335 p.

Includes discography.

295. Haupt, Helga. "Wiener Instrumentenbauer von 1791 bis 1815." In *Studien zur Musikwissenschaft, Beihefte der Denkmäler der Tonkunst in Österreich*. Bd. 24. Graz: Hermann Böhlau, 1960. P. 120–84.

Alphabetical listing of Viennese instrument makers in all categories. Addresses, dates of activity. A well-documented study.

296. Henley, William. Universal dictionary of violin and bow makers. 2nd ed. [Managing editor: Cyril Woodcock.] Brighton: Amati Pub. Co., 1973. 1,268 p.

1st edition published in 1959–69. 7 v.

Includes a dictionary of contemporary violin and bow makers and a price guide and appendix.

Biographies in the dictionary are of varying length. Long accounts of important figures with descriptions of famous instruments. Maintains a rather subjective and literary tone.

The "Price guide" gives listings for English and for American dealers.

297. Herzog, Hans Kurt. Piano-Nummern deutscher, europäischer und überseeischer Instrumente: Klaviere, Flügel, Cembali, Harmonien. Piano serial numbers of German, European and foreign uprights, grands, harpsichords, harmoniums... 6., wesentlich erw. und erg. Aufl. Frankfurt/M.: E. Bochinsky, 1984. 100 p. (Schriftenreihe Das Musikinstrument, 2)

First edition published under title *Taschenbuch der Piano-Nummern deutscher, europäischer und überseeischer Instrumente.* Cover title: *Europe Piano Atlas.*

Text in English, French, German, Italian, and Swedish.

298. Hirt, Franz Josef. Meisterwerke des Klavierbaus. Stringed Keyboard Instruments. Geschichte der Saitenklaviere von 1440 bis 1880. Olten: Urs Graf Verlag, 1981. 235 p.

First German edition published in 1955, 521 p. Original German edition translated by M. Boehme-Brown and published as *Stringed Keyboard Instruments, 1440–1880* in Boston, 1968. 465 p.

Parallel text in English and German.

Beautifully illustrated book with information about the history, design, construction, makers, etc., of keyboard instruments. Full-page photographic plates, useful sections of biography and bibliography.

299. Irwin, Stevens. Dictionary of pipe organ stops. 2nd ed. New York, Schirmer Books, 1983. 422 p.

First edition 1962. 264 p. Revised edition appeared in 1965. 276 p.

Detailed descriptions of more than 600 stops together with definitions of many other terms connected with the organ and an examination of the acoustical properties of many types of pipes and the various divisions of the organ. Illustrated. Includes a short bibliography.

300. Jacquot, Albert. Dictionnaire pratique et raisonné des instruments de musique anciens et modernes. 2nd ed. Paris: Fischbacher, 1886. 280 p.

Many names of Eastern instruments included. Some illustrations. Brief definitions. No bibliography.

301. Jahnel, Franz. Die Gitarre und ihr Bau. 3. Aufl. Technologie von Gitarre, Laute, Mandoline, Sistern, Tanbur und Saite. Frankfurt am Main: Verlag das Musikinstrument, 1977. 240 p.

English edition, *Manual of Guitar Technology; The History and Technology of Plucked String Instruments*, translated by J. C. Harvey, published by Verlag das Musikinstrument, 1981. 229 p.

A compendium of information on the construction of the guitar and other fretted instruments. Bibliography, numerous tables and lists, detailed plans, and technical data. A handsomely designed and printed volume, invaluable for the musical instrument maker or interested performer.

302. Jalovec, Karel. Enzyklopädie des Geigenbaues. Leiden: E. J. Brill, 1965. 2 v.

Simultaneous publication also by Dausien, Hanau am Main, and Artia, Prague.

Vol. 1: 940 p.; 51 colored illustrations on 24 plates. Vol. 2: 405 illustrations on 595 plates; 3,000 reproductions of violin makers' labels.

English translation, *Encyclopedia of Violin Makers*, by J. B. Kozak, published by Hamlyn, London, 1968.

303. Jalovec, Karel. German and Austrian violin makers. Translated from the Czech by George Theiner. Edited by Patrick Hanks. London: Hamlyn, 1967. 439 p.

304. Jalovec, Karel. Italian violin makers. Rev. ed. London: P. Hamlyn, 1964. 445 p.

First published in Prague, 1952; published in London, 1958, with text in Czech and English.

Accounts of Italian violin makers, with descriptions and dimensions of important instruments. Many illustrations, some in color. Index by place; scale plans, facsimiles of labels.

305. Jalovec, Karel. The violin makers of Bohemia; including craftsmen of Moravia and Slovakia. London: Anglo-Italian Publication, [1959]. 129 p. 392 plates.

Originally published in Czech under the title *Cesti Houslari*, Prague, 1959. German edition, 1959.

Covers the work of some 1,200 Czech violin makers. Photographs of instruments and a section of makers' labels in facsimile.

306. Langwill, Lyndesay Graham. Church and chamber barrel-organs: their origin, makers, music and location; a chapter in English church music, by Lyndesay G. Langwill and the late Noel Boston. 2nd ed. rev. and enl. Edinburgh: L. G. Langwill, 1970. 125 p.

First ed. by N. Boston and L. G. Langwill published in 1967. 120 p.

307. Langwill, Lyndesay Graham. An index of musical wind-instrument makers. 6th ed., rev., enl., and illus. Edinburgh: L. G. Langwill, 1980. 331 p.

First published in 1960; 2nd edition, 1962; 3rd edition, 1972; 4th edition, 1974; 5th edition, 1977.

Alphabetical index of musical wind-instrument makers with accompanying bibliographical references and locations of examples of early instruments in museums and private collections. Bibliography with occasional annotations. List of collections. A short selection of makers' marks. Index of makers by place.

Review of first edition by Josef Marx in *Notes*, 18 (1961), p. 234–36; of the second edition by Georg Karstadt in *Die Musikforschung*, 18 (1965), p. 90–91; of the third edition by Anthony Baines in *Galpin Society Journal*, 25 (July 1975), p. 134–35.

308. Lunelli, Renato. "Dizionario degli organari Veneti o attivi nel Veneto." In *Studi e Documenti di Storia Organaria Veneta*, p. 145–236. Firenze: L. S. Olschki, 1973. 279 p. (Studi di musica veneta, 3)

Following the dictionary is a bibliography of sources.

309. Lütgendorff, Willibald Leo. Die Geigen- und Lautenmacher vom Mittelalter bis zur Gegenwart, nach den besten Quellen bearbeitet.... 4. mit der

3. übereinstimmende Aufl. Frankfurt am Main: Frankfurter Verlags-Anstalt, 1922. 2 v.
First published in 1904, in 1 volume. Reprinted by Kraus, Nendeln, 1968, and by H. Schneider, Tutzing, 1975.
Vol. 1: History of the making of stringed instruments by country. Index of manufacturers by city, with dates of birth and death. Bibliography, p. 403–420. Many illustrations.
Vol. 2: Biographical dictionary of makers of stringed instruments. P. 583–668: facsimiles of trademarks and labels.

310. Lüttmann, Reinhard. Das Orgelregister und sein instrumentales Vorbild in Frankreich und Spanien vor 1800. Kassel: Bärenreiter, 1979. 365 p. (Münster. Universität, Orgelwissenschaftliche Forschungsstelle, Veröffentlichungen, 10)

311. Lyle, Wilson. A dictionary of pianists. New York: Schirmer Books, 1984. 343 p.
Simultaneously published in London by Hale.
International in scope. Covers 4,000 concertizing pianists with brief biographical sketches mentioning instructors and pupils, prizes won, stylistic characteristics. Cites compositions, if any, and lists principal recordings. Performers on historical instruments not covered well. Appendix of winners of international piano competitions and medalists of conservatories and schools. Addresses of competition organizers. No sources cited.

312. Marcuse, Sibyl. Musical instruments; a comprehensive dictionary. Corrected edition. New York: Norton, 1975. 608 p.
First published in New York by Doubleday, 1964. 608 p. Reprinted by Country Life, London, 1966.
Intended to serve English readers as Sachs' *Real-Lexikon* (no. 333) does German. World coverage, although the author acknowledges incompleteness with respect to non-European and folk instruments.
P. 603–608: listing of 206 sources of information about instruments.

313. Michel, Norman Elwood. Historical pianos, harpsichords and clavichords. Pico Rivera, California: [1963]. 209 p.
Reprinted in 1970. 236 p.
A volume of photographs of pianos. P. 1–46: pianos, birthplaces, family homes, and historical societies related to 35 presidents of the U.S. P. 47–86: pianos and homes of statesmen, actors, etc. P. 87–135: photos from libraries, historical societies, museums, and other institutions. P. 136–209: photos of musical instruments from all over the world. A curious exercise in bibliographical name-dropping.

314. Michel, Norman Elwood. Michel's organ atlas; organs, melodeons, harmoniums, church organs, lap organs, barrel organs. Pico Rivera, California: N. E. Michel, [1969]. 128 p.
"Book contains 141 photographs, 128 pages, 869 names of organs, etc." Known also as the *Organ Atlas*.

315. Michel, Norman Elwood. Michel's piano atlas. Contains names of pianos, dates of manufacture, and serial numbers. Pico Rivera, California: [1961]. 272 p.

Subsequently published as *Pierce Piano Atlas* (no. 322).

6,580 names of pianos. For some of these, there is no information other than name; for others, complete lists of serial numbers.

316. Möller, Max. The violin-makers of the low countries (Belgium and Holland). Amsterdam: M. Möller, 1955. 165 p.

A historical survey of violin making in Belgium and Holland.

P. 23–129: photographic plates, chiefly of instruments in detail. P. 131–53: "Alphabetical Register," brief critical comments on the makers and their work. Glossary of terms in English, French, German, and Flemish.

317. Morris, W. Meredith. British violin makers, a biographical dictionary of British makers of stringed instruments and bows and a critical description of their work. 2nd ed., rev. and enl. London: R. Scott, 1920. 318 p.

First published in 1904.

P. 87–259: alphabetical dictionary of violin and bow makers. Some labels in facsimile. P. 261–94: "A list of present-day makers, and a few old makers recently discovered."

318. The new Grove dictionary of musical instruments. Edited by Stanley Sadie. London: Macmillan, 1984. 3 v.

Articles on Western and non-Western, historical and modern instruments, their makers and performance practices, many derived, but largely rewritten from articles in the *New Grove*. Extensive coverage of folk and ethnic instruments by scholars expert in the regions in which the instruments are located. Extensive cross-references linking articles and terms to one another make up for the lack of an index by culture or region. Copiously illustrated. Bibliographies. The dictionary of musical instruments is based on modern scholarship and is unique in its genre.

Review by Mary Rasmussen in *Notes*, 42 (1986), p. 529–32.

319. Niemann, Walter. Klavier-lexikon: Elementarlehre für Klavierspieler, Anleitung zur Aussprache des Italienischen, Tabelle der Abkürzungen in Wort- und Notenschrift, Literaturverzeichnis, ausführliches Fremdwörter-, Sach- und Personal-Lexikon. 4. völlig umgearb. und reich verm. Aufl. Leipzig: C. F. Kahnt, 1918. 365 p.

First published in 1912 as *Taschen-Lexikon für Klavierspieler.*

320. Norlind, Tobias. Systematik der saiteninstrumente. Stockholm: [Emil Kihlströms Tryckeri], 1936–39. 2 v.

At head of title: Musikhistorisches Museum, Stockholm.

Vol. 1: *Geschichte der Zither* (1936). Vol. 2: *Geschichte des Klaviers* (1939).

Detailed classification and description of stringed instruments based on the archive in the Musikhistorisches Museum in Stockholm, where records of some 40,000 instruments are maintained. Illustrated. Bibliographical references and locations given for specific instruments in European and American collections. The work was projected in four parts, only two of which were completed.

321. Páris, Alain. Dictionnaire des interprètes et de l'interprètation musicale au XXe siècle. Paris: Robert Laffont, 1982. 875 p.
A collection of essays on the situation and evolution of musical interpretation in the 20th century precedes a biographical section on individual artists and another section covering ensembles. Indexes arranged by performance medium.

322. Pierce piano atlas. 8th ed. Long Beach, Calif.: B. Pierce, 1982. 416 p.
Title varies: 1947–61, *Michel's Piano Atlas*; also known as *Piano Atlas*. Compiled and published, 1947–61, by Norman Elwood Michel (no. 315).
Contains "piano names, serial numbers, dates of manufacture."

323. Pincherle, Marc. Les violonistes, compositeurs et virtuoses. Paris: H. Laurens, [1922]. 126 p.
Not a dictionary, but provides biographical information on a number of violinists and composers for the instrument.

324. Poidras, Henri. Critical and documentary dictionary of violin makers old and modern, translated by Arnold Sewell.... Rouen: Imprimerie de la Vicomté, 1928–30. 2 v.
Originally published in French, 1924, with a 2nd edition in 1930. There is also a one-volume English edition, 1928. Reprint edition by the Scholarly Press, St. Clair Shores, Michigan, 1978.
Brief biographical notices with critical comments, arranged alphabetically under national schools: Italian, French, German, etc. Photographic plates of instruments; facsimiles of labels.

325. Powroźniak, Józef. Leksykon gitary. Kraków: Polskie Wydawn. Muzyczne, 1979. 212 p.
Simultaneously published in Berlin by Neue Musik as *Gitarren-Lexikon*, in a translation by Bernd Haag. 165 p.
A dictionary of terms and biography devoted entirely to the guitar and its practitioners.
Review of the German translation by Thomas F. Heck in *Notes*, 37 (1981), p. 588–89.

326. Prat, Marsol Domingo. Diccionario biográfico, bibliográfico, histórico, crítico de guitarras (instrumentos afines), guitaristas (profesores, compositores, concertistas, lahudistas, amateurs), guitarreros (luthiers), danzas y cantos, terminología. Buenos Aires: Casa Romero y Fernandez, [1934]. 468 p.
Reprinted as *A Biographical, Bibliographical, Historical, Critical Dictionary of Guitars (related instruments), guitarists (teachers, composers, performers, lutenists, amateurs), guitar-makers (luthiers), dances and songs, terminology*, with an introduction by Matanya Ophée, by Éditions Orphée, Columbus, Ohio, 1986. Known also as the *Dictionary of Guitarists*.
The main alphabet contains biographies and lists of compositions. P. 423–52: dance forms. P. 453–64: terminology.

327. Profeta, Rosario. Storia e letteratura degli strumenti musicali. Firenze: Marzocco, 1942. 659 p.

A history of instrumental music, its composers and performers, consisting chiefly of a recital of names of musicians grouped under their instruments and respective national schools. Minimal biographical and bibliographical information given.

328. **"Provisional index of present-day makers of historical musical instruments (non-keyboard)."** In the *Galpin Society Journal*, 13 (July 1960), p. 70–97.

A useful guide to sources of modern replicas of historical instruments. Makers of historical keyboard instruments are listed in an appendix, p. 86–87.

329. **Riley, Maurice W.** The history of the viola. Ann Arbor, Michigan: Braun-Brumfield, 1980. 396 p.

Reprint of original edition published in Ypsilanti, Michigan, by M. W. Riley in 1980.

"Brief biographies of violists": p. 312–76. Bibliography: p. 379–84.

Review by Marion Korda in *Notes*, 37 (1981), p. 855–56.

330. **Roda, Joseph.** Bows for musical instruments of the violin family. Chicago, Illinois: W. Lewis & Son, 1959. 335 p.

Brief history and description of the bow, including statistics as to dimensions and weight.

P. 119–325: biographical list of bow makers, with 47 excellent plates of their work.

331. **Roth, Henry.** Great violinists in performance; critical evaluations of over 100 twentieth-century virtuosi. Los Angeles: Panjandrum Books, 1986. 266 p.

Essays on Kreisler, Francescatti, Milstein, Oistrakh, Stern, and Kogan precede surveys of Russian, American, and Chinese violinists. Entries in the surveys are short, providing basic biographical information and critical comments on performance style and recordings featuring each artist. No bibliographical references are cited in the entries, but there is a general bibliography and index.

332. **Sachs, Curt.** Handbuch der Musikinstrumentenkunde. (Reprografischer Nachdruck der 2. Aufl., Leipzig, 1930.) Hildesheim: Olms; Wiesbaden: Breitkopf u. Härtel, 1967. 419 p. (Kleine Handbücher der Musikgeschichte nach Gattungen, 12)

First published in 1920.

Not precisely a dictionary but a systematic and historical description of musical instruments classified according to their methods of sound production: idiophones, membranophones, chordaphones, aerophones, etc. Much of the same ground is covered in Sachs' *The History of Musical Instruments* (New York, Norton, 1940), in which the approach is chronological and by cultural areas.

Also listed in no. 551.

333. **Sachs, Curt.** Real-Lexikon der Musikinstrumente, zugleich ein Polyglossar für das gesamte Instrumentengebiet. [Rev. and enl. ed.] New York: Dover Publications, 1964. 451 p.

First published in Berlin, 1913; unaltered reprint of the original edition issued by G. Olms, Hildesheim, 1962.

A technical and historical dictionary of instruments of all periods and countries. Names of instruments and parts of instruments in some 120 languages and dialects—European, African, and Asian. Locations of examples in instrument collections. Illustrations; some bibliographies. This is Sachs's great work in this field and one of the best sources of information on instruments.

For an English-language dictionary inspired by the *Real-Lexikon*, see Marcuse's *Musical Instruments* (no. 312).

Review by Guy Oldham in *Musical Times*, 107 (Dec. 1966), p. 1064–65.

Review by J. A. Westrup in *Music and Letters*, 43 (July 1966), p. 277–78.

334. Samoyault-Verlet, Colombe. Les facteurs de clavecins Parisiens, notices biographiques et documents, 1550–1793. Paris: Société Française de Musicologie, 1966. 191 p. (Publications de la Société Française de Musicologie, Ser. 2, 11)

Biographies of some 140 Parisian makers of keyboard instruments, based largely on archival documents.

Review by Maurice A. Byrne in the *Galpin Society Journal*, 25 (July 1972), p. 136–37.

335. Sárosi, Bálint. Die Volksmusikinstrumente Ungarns. Leipzig: Deutscher Verlag für Musik, 1968. 147 p. (Handbuch der europäischen Volksmusikinstrumente I, 1)

Sárosi's work is the first of a series projected to cover folk instruments in Czechoslovakia, Bulgaria, the Soviet Union, Greece, Portugal, Turkey, and Norway.

The Hungarian folk instruments are grouped according to type, with detailed commentary, illustrations, and transcription of music. Bibliography, and glossary of Hungarian instrument names.

Review by Fritz Bose in *Literature, Music, Fine Arts*, 1 (1968), p. 230–31.

Also listed in no. 293.

336. Schimmel, Klaus. Piano-Nomenclatur. Ein Bildwörterbuch der Teile von Klavier und Flügel: Deutsch, Englisch, Französisch, Italienisch und Norwegisch. 2. Aufl. (Mitarbeit und Übersetzungen: Pianofortefabrik Wilhelm Schimmel [u.a.]) Frankfurt a. M.: Verlag Bochinsky/Das Musikinstrument, 1983. 127 p. (Fachbuchreihe Das Musikinstrument, 14)

Terms in German, English, French, Italian, Norwegian, and Spanish.

337. Schwarz, Boris. Great masters of the violin; from Corelli and Vivaldi to Stern, Zukerman, and Perlman. New York: Simon and Schuster, 1983. 671 p.

Like Pincherle's *Les Violonistes, Compositeurs et Virtuoses*, not a dictionary, but a valuable source of biographical information about violin virtuosi. Bibliography.

Review by Sonya Monosoff in *Notes*, 41 (1984), p. 63–64.

338. Shead, Herbert A. The anatomy of the piano. Old Woking, England: Unwin Brothers Ltd., 1978. 177 p.
An illustrated dictionary of the piano.

339. Stainer, Cecilia. A dictionary of violin makers, compiled from the best authorities. Rev. ed. London: Novello, 1909. 102 p.
First edition, 1896. 102 p. Reprinted by Milford House, Boston, 1973, and Longwood Press, Boston, 1977.
A useful biographical dictionary of violin makers with critical evaluations of their work. Still in print. Contains a bibliography of literature on violin making.

340. Stiller, Andrew. Handbook of instrumentation. Illustrations by James Stamos. Berkeley: University of California Press, 1985. 553 p.
A thorough, well-illustrated compendium of information about a wide range of instruments. Bibliography.

341. Straeten, Edmund S. J. vander. The history of the violin, its ancestors and collateral instruments from the earliest times to the present day; with 48 plates and numerous illustrations in the text. London: Cassell, [1933]. 2 v.
Reprinted by Da Capo, New York, 1968.
Vol. 1, p. 55–416, and the whole of vol. 2 consist primarily of biographies of violinists grouped by period, and under period by country. Biographical index, vol. 2, p. 443–73. Information on many obscure violinist-composers not elsewhere readily accessible, with lists of works by category.

342. Straeten, Edmund S. J. vander. History of the violoncello, the viola da gamba, their precursors and collateral instruments: with biographies of all the most eminent players of every country. 1st AMS ed. New York: AMS Press, 1976. 2 v.
Reprint of the 1915 edition published by W. Reeves, London. Another reprint edition published by W. Reeves, London, 1971. 700 p.

343. Thornsby, Frederick W. Dictionary of organs and organists. London: G. A. Mate, 1921. 476 p.
First published by H. Logan, Bournemouth, 1912 (?). 364 p.
Chiefly concerned with 19th-century British organs and organists. "Brief specifications of the principal organs in the British Isles." "The organist's *Who's Who*: Brief biographical notes of the leading British organists." A bibliography on the organ by J. H. Burn.

344. Tintori, Giampiero. Gli strumenti musicali. Ricerca iconografia di Alberto Basso. Turin: Unione tipografico-editrice torinese, [1971]. 2 v. 138 plates.
The main organization is geographical, with subdivisions covering the various types of instruments. Numerous musical examples, a comprehensive bibliography and glossary; general index.

345. Valdrighi, Luigi Francesco. Nomocheliurgografia antica e moderna, ossia Elenco di fabbricatori di strumenti armonici con note esplicative e documenti estratti dall'Archivio di Stato in Modena. Bologna: Forni, 1967. 327 p. (Bibliotheca musica Bononiensia, I, 3)

Reprint of the Modena 1884 edition, with supplements originally published 1888–94.

P. 2–106: an alphabetical listing of 3,516 instrument makers, giving name, nationality, dates of birth and death, name of special instrument, and the school, style, or system. Many of these names are given fuller biographical treatment in the section following p. 107 to end.

346. Vannes, René. Dictionnaire universel des luthiers. Bruxelles: Les Amis de la Musique, 1979. 2 v. in 1.

Reprint of 2nd edition (1951–59) and 3rd edition (1971–75).

First published in 1932, Paris, Fischbacher, under the title *Essai d'un Dictionnaire Universel....*

Most comprehensive of all dictionaries of violin makers. Each volume has its own alphabet of biographical entries. Bibliographical references. Both volumes combined give 3,400 facsimiles of makers' labels. Index of makers by place of birth or center of activity.

Review by Doris Commander in *Violins and Violinists*, 12 (Nov. 1951), p. 326; review of *Tome Second* by Albert van der Linden in *Revue Belge de Musicologie*, 14 (1960), p. 144, and by William Lichtenwanger in *Notes*, 17 (1960), p. 577.

347. Vercheval, Henri. Dictionnaire du violinist.... Paris: Fischbacher, 1923. 192 p.

Also published as *Dizionario del Violinista* ... by Casa Musicale Editrice ditta Cesare Sarti, Bologna, 1924. 249 p.

Part I, p. 9–141, includes terms of interest to violinists, history of stringed instruments, etc. Part II, p. 143–92, is a biographical dictionary of violinists, composers, teachers, violin and bow makers, giving dates and nationalities.

348. Winternitz, Emanuel. Musical instruments of the Western world. Photographs by Lilly Stunzi. New York and Toronto: McGraw-Hill Book Co.; London: Thames & Hudson, 1967. 259 p. 60 plates.

This work was published in German under the title *Die schönsten Musikinstrumente des Abendlandes.*

A magnificent picture book of music.

Review by Howard Mayer Brown in *Notes*, 25 (1968), p. 223–25.

349. Worthmuller, Willi. "Die Nürnberger Trompeten- und Posaunenmacher des 17. und 18. Jahrhunderts." In *Mitteilungen des Vereins für Geschichte der Stadt Nürnberg*. Bd. 46 (1955). P. 372–480.

Also published separately.

A musicological study, the major portion of which is a dictionary of 40 Nuremberg brass instrument makers of the Baroque period with a listing of their surviving instruments. Tracing of monograms and other makers' devices. 5 plates.

350. Wright, Rowland. Dictionnaire des instruments de musique; étude de lexicologie. London: Battley Bros., 1941. 192 p.

An etymological dictionary of names for musical instruments mentioned in French writings from ancient times to the end of the 19th century. Extremely well documented; precise bibliographical references. One of the few dictionaries of terms to employ a thoroughly etymological approach.

351. Zingel, Hans Joachim. Lexicon der Harfe: ein biographisches, bibliographisches, geographisches und historisches Nachschlagewerk von A–Z. Regensburg: Laaber, 1977. 207 p.
An errata slip was issued.
Very brief articles. Fails to cite works for the instrument even when appropriate to do so. Bibliography of sources.

352. Zuth, Josef. Handbuch der Laute und Gitarre. Wien: Verlag der Zeitschrift für die Gitarre, 1926. 297 p.
Reprinted by Olms, Hildesheim, 1972.
Terms; biographies of performers, instrument makers, and composers giving titles of compositions, publishers, and dates. International coverage for all periods, including many early names. A scholarly work with supported statements and bibliographical references.

TERMS

Dictionaries of terms have a longer history than any other form of music lexicology. Their prototype is Johannes Tinctoris' *Terminorum Musicae Diffinitorium* (no. 398), a work compiled in the late 15th century. Almost equally significant is Sebastien de Brossard's *Dictionnaire de Musique*, 1701 (no. 358), one of the first in the long line of "modern" dictionaries of music.

A few specialized dictionaries of terms will be found under other headings in this volume. See nos. 299 and 310 (pipe organ stops); no. 350 (names of musical instruments); no. 410 (liturgical music terms).

353. Albina, Diāna. Mùzikas terminu vardnica. Redigejis J. Licitis. Riga: Latvijas valsts izdevnieciba, 1962. 303 p.
A Latvian dictionary of musical terms.

354. Baker, Theodore. Dictionary of musical terms containing upwards of 9,000 English, French, German, Italian, Latin and Greek words and phrases used in the art and science of music ... with a supplement containing an English-Italian vocabulary for composers. New York: G. Schirmer, [1923]. 257 p.
First published in 1895. Reprinted by Saphrograph, New York, 1975.
Reprint of the 1923 edition, New York, AMS Press, 1970 and 1975.
Useful small manual, with brief definitions of English and foreign words, especially those used in performance. More extended articles on topics such as pitch, notation, instruments. More than 9,000 terms treated.

355. Balter, G. Fachwörterbuch Musik, deutsch-russisch und russisch-deutsch. Moscow and Leipzig: VEB Deutscher Verlag für Musik, 1976. 484 p.
Additional title page in Russian. Basically a bilingual glossary.

356. Bobillier, Marie. Diccionario de la música, histórico y técnico. Tradducíon de la última edición francesa, revisada y notablemente ampliada con multitud de artículos nuevos ... por Jose B. Humbert, J. Ricart Matas, and Aurelio Capmany. Barcelona: Iberia, J. Gil, [1964]. 548 p.
Translation of the 2nd edition of the following, revised and with special emphasis on Spanish terms and Latin and South American terminology and folklore. Profusely illustrated.

357. Bobillier, Marie. Dictionnaire pratique et historique de la musique, par Michel Brenet (pseud.). Paris: A. Colin, 1926. 487 p.
2nd edition, 1930.
The standard French dictionary of terms, including terms from Greek and Medieval music theory, historical sketches of musical forms. Fairly long articles, excellent small illustrations. No bibliographies.

358. Brossard, Sébastien de. Dictionnaire de musique, contenant une explication des termes grecs, latins, italiens & français les plus usitez dans la musique.... Paris: Christophe Ballard, 1703. 112 p.
A preliminary edition appeared in 1701, in octavo format.
The first folio edition (1703) has been reprinted in facsimile by Antiqua, Amsterdam, 1964, and translated and edited by Albion Gruber in an edition published by the Institute of Mediaeval Music, Henryville, Pa., 1982. 252 p. (Musical theorists in translation, 12). An octavo edition, Paris, 1705, has been reprinted, with an introduction by Harald Heckmann, by Frits A. M. Knuf, Hilversum, 1965.
Brossard's *Dictionnaire* is the prototype for all modern dictionaries of musical terms. It is also a pioneer work in music bibliography, since it contains a listing of more than 900 authors who have written about music from antiquity to Brossard's time.
For an early English music dictionary based on Brossard, see Grassineau no. 372.
Review of the 1964 (Amsterdam) reprint by Vincent Duckles in *Notes*, 24 (1968), p. 700–701.

359. Carter, Henry H. A dictionary of Middle English musical terms. Bloomington: Indiana University Press, [1961]. 655 p. (Indiana University humanities series, 45)
Reprint by Kraus, New York, 1968.
Terms are not only defined but quoted in their original contexts with citation of their sources. P. 569–604: bibliography of works quoted; p. 605–649: works consulted but not quoted.
Review by Leonard Ellinwood in *Notes*, 19 (1962), p. 262–63.

360. Chetrikov, Svetoslav. Muzikalen terminologischen rechnik. 2. izd. Sofiia: Muzika, 1979. 448 p.
A Bulgarian dictionary of musical terms.

361. Dembski, Stephen. Lexique musical international. International vocabulary of music. Lessico musicale internazionale. Par Stephen Dembski, Gerard Gubisch, Jorge Labrouve, Patrick Marcland. Paris: Éditions Transatlantiques, 1979. 151 p.

A polyglot dictionary of terms in English, French, Italian, and Spanish.

362. Dolzhanskii, Aleksandr Naumovich. Kratkii muzykal'nyi slovar'. Izd. 5. Leningrad: Muzyka, 1965. 517 p.

First published in Leningrad, 1952.

363. Eggebrecht, Hans Heinrich. Handwörterbuch der musikalischen Terminologie. Im Auftrag der Kommission für Musikwissenschaften und der Literatur zu Mainz.... Wiesbaden: F. Steiner, 1972–.

A work providing the most thorough and scientific treatment of musical terms. An exhaustive historical and etymological analysis of term families, showing their changes in meaning and citing quotations from the literature. The dictionary is compiled in loose-leaf format, with dividers and indexes.

By 1986, 13 Auslieferungen in 3 v. including over 100 articles had been issued.

For a preliminary notice and discussion, see *Archiv für Musikwissenschaft*, 25 (1968), p. 241–77, and 27 (1970), p. 214–22.

364. Eimert, Herbert and Hans Ulrich Humpert. Das Lexikon der electronischen Musik. Regensburg: Gustav Bosse Verlag, 1973. 428 p.

Brief terminological articles citing musical works where appropriate. Bibliography. Index to persons mentioned.

365. Elsevier's dictionary of cinema, sound and music, in six languages: English/American, French, Spanish, Italian, Dutch, and German. Compiled and arranged on an English alphabetical base by W. E. Clason. Amsterdam and New York: Elsevier Publishing Co., 1956. 948 p.

One of a series of polyglot technical dictionaries relating to special fields of science and industry. 3,213 terms, with brief definitions and the equivalent phrases in French, Spanish, Italian, Dutch, and German. Indexes in each of the five other languages.

366. Fink, Robert and Robert Ricci. The language of twentieth century music: a dictionary of terms. New York: Schirmer Books, 1975. 125 p.

Covering all 20th-century music genres and styles. Includes technical terms, instruments, analysis, and performance practice. Appendix of terms arranged topically.

367. Garvey, Barbara Jackson and Joel Berman. The A.S.T.A. dictionary of bowing terms for string instruments. 2nd ed. Urbana, Illinois: American String Teachers Association, 1976. 53 p.

368. Gerigk, Herbert. Fachwörterbuch der Musik. Bayreuth: Gondrom, 1983. 213 p.

First published in Münchberg i. Bayern by Hahnefeld in 1954, 206 p.

A small, useful dictionary of German definitions of the most common musical terms in French, Italian, and Latin, with some in English.
Review by Richard Schaal in *Die Musikforschung*, 8 (1955), p. 245.

369. Gold, Robert S. A jazz lexicon. New York: Knopf, 1964. 363 p.
A dictionary of terms from the world of jazz. Both musical and sociological interest. Date of usage is specified where possible. Informative introduction and bibliography.

370. Gold, Robert S. Jazz talk. Indianapolis, Indiana: Bobbs-Merrill Co., 1975. 322 p.
Reprinted in 1982 by Da Capo.

A dictionary of the colorful language that has emerged from America's own music. [Author's *Preface*]

A dictionary of slang terms providing definitions, sometimes word origins, and quotations from the literature of jazz. Extensive bibliography.
Brief review by Stephen M. Fry in *Notes*, 32 (1975), p. 302.

371. Grant, Parks. Handbook of music terms. Metuchen, New Jersey: Scarecrow Press, 1967. 476 p.

The availability of several excellent music dictionaries and encyclopedias intended for the scholar, the music professor, and the musicologist points up the need for a book less advanced (though not too brief) intended for persons who make only a modest claim to musical knowledge. [Author's *Preface*]

Review by James W. Pruett in *Notes*, 24 (1968), p. 720–21.

372. Grassineau, James. A musical dictionary; being a collection of terms and characters, ancient as well as modern; including the historical, theoretical, and practical parts of music.... London: Printed for J. Wilcox, 1740. 347 p.
Reprint by Broude Brothers, New York, 1967. (Monuments of music and music literature in facsimile, ser. 2, vol. 40)
Grassineau can be described as the first important dictionary of music in English. It is largely an adaptation of Brossard (no. 358), but with some important additions. A later edition, 1769, has an appendix containing additional terms from Rousseau's *Dictionnaire* (no. 387).

373. Grigg, Carolyn Doub. Music translation dictionary. An English, Czech, Danish, Dutch, French, German, Hungarian, Italian, Polish, Portuguese, Russian, Spanish, Swedish vocabulary of musical terms. Westport, Connecticut: Greenwood Press, 1978. 330 p.
A polyglot glossary of 1,300 musical terms with an index of all terms in one alphabet for words in Roman characters and in another for those in Cyrillic. Bibliography.
Review by Nanna Schiødt in *Notes*, 27 (1980), p. 122.

374. Hoyle, John. A complete dictionary of music. Réimpr en facs. de l'éd. de Londres, 1791. Genève: Minkoff Reprint, 1976. 162 p.
1st edition published in 1770 under title *Dictionarium Musica*. Reprint of the 1791 edition printed for H. D. Symonds, London.

375. Janovka, Tomas Baltazar. Clavis ad thesaurum magnae artis musicae, seu eluciadarium omnium ferè rerum & verborum, in musica figurali tam vocali, quam instrumentali obvenietum. Consistens potissimum in definitionibus & divisionibus; quibusdam recentioribus de scala, tono, cantu, & genere musicae &c. sententijs, variísque exqvisitis observationibus ... alphabetico ordine compositum à Thoma Balthasare Janovka. Vetero-Pragae: In Magno collegio Carolino typis Georgij Labaun, 1701. 324 p.

Reprinted by Frits Knuf, Hilversum, 1973, as vol. 3 of the series *Facsimile Reprints of Early Music Dictionaries.*

This volume shares with Brossard (no. 358) the distinction of being one of the first modern dictionaries of musical terms. The two compilers worked simultaneously but independently of each other.

376. Katayen, Leila and Val Telberg. Russian-English dictionary of musical terms. New York: Telberg Book Corp., 1965. 125 leaves (typescript).

Russian-English equivalents in musical terminology. No definitions, short bibliography.

377. Koch, Heinrich Christoph. Musikalisches Lexikon: welches die theoretische und praktische Tonkunst, encyclopädisch bearbeitet, alle alten und neuen Kunstwörter erklärt, und die alten und neuen Instrumente beschrieben, enthält.... Frankfurt a. M.: A. Hermann dem Jüngern, 1802. 2 v.

One of the first of a long line of German dictionaries of terms. Particularly important for definitions and concepts pertaining to late Baroque and classic music and instruments.

A revised edition, by Arrey von Dommer, printed in Heidelberg, 1865, has very little resemblance to the original.

Reprint publication by Georg Olms, Hildesheim, 1964 and 1975.

378. Leuchtmann, Horst. Wörterbuch Musik. Dictionary of terms in music: Englisch-Deutsch/Deutsch-Englisch. 3. [erw.] Aufl. München, etc.: K.G. Saur; Hamden, Connecticut: Linnet Books, 1981. 560 p.

First published as *Langenscheidts Fachwörterbuch, Musik* by Langenscheidt, Berlin, 1964. 359 p. 2nd edition published by Verlag Documentation in Munich, 1977. 433 p.

An English-German, German-English dictionary of terms. No definitions, merely verbal equivalents. Some unusual features: a list of 950 popular titles of musical works and a section devoted to the vocabulary of change ringing.

379. Levarie, Siegmund and Ernst Levy. Musical morphology: a discourse and a dictionary. Kent, Ohio: Kent State University Press, 1983. 344 p.

An earlier edition of this work [*A Dictionary of Musical Morphology*] was published by the Institute of Mediaeval Music, Binningen, Switzerland [and Henryville, Pennsylvania, 1980], despite the objections of the authors, who took the position that it was unauthorized, incorrect, and not truly representative of their work. The present edition is fully authorized. [*verso of title page*]

A dictionary covering few terms with lengthy entries. Appended illustrations. Index to composers and works cited in the entries.

380. Lichtenthal, Pietro. Dizionario e bibliografia della musica. Milano: A. Fontana, 1836. 4 v.

First published in 1826 in 2 v. Reprint of 1836 edition by Forni, Bologna (Biblioteca musica Bononiensis, I, 6), 1970.

The first two volumes of this work are a dictionary of terms, the last two a bibliography of music literature based on Johann Nikolaus Forkel's *Allgemeine Litteratur der Musik* (see no. 697). A French edition of the dictionary of terms, "traduit et augmenté par Dominique Mondo," appeared in Paris in 1839.

381. Limenta, Fernando. Dizionario lessicografico musicale italiano-tedesco-italiano. Milano: Hoepli, 1940. 391 p.

Designed to provide precise Italian equivalents for German technical terms not adequately treated in most dictionaries.

382. Padelford, Frederick M. Old English musical terms. Bonn: P. Hanstein, 1899. 112 pages. (Bonner Beiträge zur Anglistik, 4)

Reprinted by Milford House, Boston, 1973, and by Longwood Press, Portland, Maine, 1976.

383. Pulver, Jeffrey. A dictionary of old English music and musical instruments. London: Kegan Paul; New York: E. P. Dutton, 1923. 247 p.

Terms used by Tudor and early Stuart musicians. Fairly long articles, with references to early literary and musical sources for the terms. 10 plates of early English instruments. See also no. 157.

384. Randel, Don Michael. Harvard concise dictionary of music. Cambridge, Massachusetts: Belknap Press, 1978. 577 p.

Successor to the *Harvard Brief Dictionary of Music* by Willi Apel and Ralph T. Daniel (Cambridge: Harvard University Press, 1960), 341 p.

Published in Spanish as *Diccionario Harvard de Música* by Editorial Diana, Mexico City, 1984. 559 p.

Intended as a companion for students enrolled in a college-level music appreciation course. Short articles on topics and persons.

385. Randel, Don Michael, ed. The new Harvard dictionary of music. Cambridge, Mass.: Belknap Press of Harvard University Press, 1986. 942 p.

Completely revised edition of the *Harvard Dictionary of Music* by Willi Apel, 2nd ed. (Cambridge: Belknap, 1969. 935 p.)

First printed in 1944. The fifth printing, 1947, contains a section of addenda and corrigenda to the original entries. The second edition, 1969, was completely reset.

The standard reference work in English for nonbiographical information, designed to provide accurate and pertinent information on all musical topics. The emphasis is on the historical approach and on Western art music, but there is coverage of non-Western and popular musics. Good, basic bibliographies; excellent brief historical articles. Signed articles, numerous musical examples and illustrations.

There is a thoughtful article on the place of music lexicography in musicology by Don Randel entitled "Defining music" in *Notes*, 43 (1987), p. 751–66.

Review of the second edition by Charles Rosen in the *New York Review of Books*, 14 (Feb. 1970), p. 11–15; in the *Booklist*, 66 (May 1970), p. 1055-6l; by Vincent Duckles in *Notes*, 27 (1970), p. 256–58.

Entries cited as nos. 1698, 1793, and 2972.

386. Reid, Cornelius L. A dictionary of vocal terminology: an analysis. New York: Joseph Patelson Music House, 1983. 457 p.

Definition of principal terms "in common use by the vocal profession from the early 17th century to the present." Includes scientific terms and cross-references. Bibliography.

Review by Dee Baily in *Notes*, 41 (1985), p. 517–18.

387. Rousseau, Jean J. Dictionnaire de musique. Paris: Duchesne, 1768. 548 [i.e., 556] p. 13 folded plates.

Reprint by G. Olms, Hildesheim, and by Johnson Reprint Corp., New York, 1969.

Several editions published in Paris and Amsterdam during the 18th century. An English edition, translated by William Waring, published under the title *A Complete Dictionary of Music*, 2nd edition, London, 1779. Reprint of the 1779 Waring edition by AMS Press, New York, 1975. 470 p. Reprint of the Aubree edition of Paris, 1832, by Art & Culture, Paris, 1977. 2 v.

Based on articles written by Rousseau for the Diderot and d'Alembert *Encyclopédie*, but not included in that work. Reflects the stimulating and highly personal views of an 18th-century man of letters. Wide influence and considerable historical importance.

388. Sacher, Jack, ed. Music A to Z. Based on the work of Rudolf Stephan. [Translators: Miecslaw Kolinski and others.] New York: Grosset & Dunlap, 1963. 432 p.

A translation, with additions and corrections, of Rudolf Stephan's music dictionary in the Fischer *Lexikon* series (no. 406).

Review by Theodore Karp in *Journal of the American Musicological Society*, 17 (1964), p. 394–95; by Harold Samuel in *Notes*, 20 (1963), p. 658–59.

389. Schaal, Richard. Abkürzungen in der Musik-Terminologie. Eine Übersicht. Wilhelmshaven: Heinrichshofen's Verlag, 1969. 165 p. (Taschenbücher zur Musikwissenschaft, 1)

A dictionary of the abbreviations most frequently used to refer to musical practice, bibliography, institutions. Intended primarily for German music students, but of general utility.

390. Schaal, Richard. Fremdwörterlexikon Musik. Englisch-Französisch-Italienisch. Wilhelmshaven: Heinrichshofen's Verlag, 1970. 2 v. (Taschenbücher zur Musikwissenschaft, 2, 3)

Vol. 1: A–Ist. Vol. 2: Jac–Zur.

A polyglot dictionary of English, French, and Italian terms with their German equivalents. Contains more than 15,000 foreign terms.

391. Siliakus, H. J. 500 German musical terms and their English translations together with 500 useful phrases. Adelaide: University of Adelaide, 1968. 113 p.

This booklet is not a dictionary, but a special word list for musicologists who need a reading knowledge of German. It will only be useful for those who have mastered the elements of the German language, since we assume a knowledge of basic grammar and familiarity with about 1,000 basic words. [Author's *Preface*]

392. Sinzig, Pedro. Dicionário músical. Rio de Janeiro: Kosmos, 1947. 613 p.

A Portuguese-language dictionary of terms. Based largely on Apel and Riemann. Bibliographical references.

393. Smith, W. J. A dictionary of musical terms in four languages. London: Hutchinson, [1961]. 195 p.

English terms with equivalents in French, Italian, and German. Pronunciations given in phonetic symbols. No definitions.

394. Stainer, Sir John and W. A. Barrett. Dictionary of musical terms. Hildesheim: Olms, 1970. 456 p.

Reprint of the 2nd ed., Novello, 1898. Reprint of 1889 ed. by the Scholarly Press, St. Clair Shores, Michigan, 1974.

Terms in Italian, French, Latin, German, Hebrew, Greek, Russian, Spanish, and Arabic, with brief English definitions.

395. Stephan, Rudolf. Musik. [Frankfurt am Main]: Fischer Verlag, [1957]. 382 p.

This work has been translated and expanded in Sacher's *Music A to Z* (no. 388).

General articles cover major topics, with more detailed information approached through an index. Topical bibliographies, p. 355–64. 10 plates. A scholarly summation of musical knowledge for the general reader.

396. Terminorum musicae index septem linguis redactus: Polyglottes Wörterbuch der musikalischen Terminologie: Polyglot dictionary of musical terms.... [Prepared by a joint committee of the International Musicological Society and the International Association of Music Libraries; Editor: Horst Leuchtmann]. Budapest: Akadémiai Kiadó; Kassel: Bärenreiter, 1978. 798 p.

A polyglot dictionary of musical terms in English, German, French, Italian, Spanish, Russian, and Hungarian. Also known as the *Terminorum Musicae Index*. German is the basic language, but all terms in all seven languages are indexed. Introductory material in each of the seven languages. Cyrillic index. Diagrams.

Review by Dale Higbee in *American Recorder*, 19 (1979), p. 173.

397. Thiel, Eberhard. Sachwörterbuch der Musik. 4. verb. Aufl. Stuttgart: Alfred Kroner Verlag, 1984. 739 p.

1st ed., 1962; 2nd ed., 1973; 3rd ed., 1977.

Review by Harold Samuel in *Notes*, 20 (1963), p. 658.

398. Tinctoris, Johannes (Jean). Dictionary of musical terms. An English translation of *Terminorum Musicae Diffinitorium* together with the Latin text. Translated and annotated by Carl Parrish [with a bibliographical essay by James B. Coover]. New York: Free Press, [1963]. 108 p.

A 15th-century dictionary of musical terms, and one of the first books on music to be printed. 291 terms defined. Important for an understanding of Renaissance music theory and practice. The Latin text was reprinted in Coussemaker's *Scriptorum* (1867), in Forkel's *Allgemeine Literatur der*

Musik (1792), and with a German translation in Chrysander's *Jahrbuch der Musikwissenschaft*, I (1863).

It appeared in a French translation with introduction and commentary by Armand Machabey (Paris, 1951) and in an Italian translation by Lionello Cammarota (Rome, 1965). The Free Press edition of 1963 was reprinted by Da Capo in 1978 with an introduction by James W. McKinnon. A facsimile edition was published in 1983 by Bärenreiter, Kassel, with an introduction by Heinrich Bellermann and and afterword by Peter Gülke (Documenta musicologica, I, 37).

399. Tovey, Donald F. Musical articles from the *Encyclopaedia Britannica*. London and New York: Oxford University Press, 1944. 256 p.

Paperback edition: New York, Meridian Books, 1956, as *The Forms of Music*. Reprint of *The Forms* ... by Oxford University Press, London, 1967. Reprint of the *Musical Articles* ... by the Scholarly Press, St. Clair Shores, Michigan, 1977.

28 articles on the larger aspects of music. Shorter ones (madrigal, sonata, etc.) are briefly historical; others (harmony, sonata forms, etc.) are comprehensive and analytical. Reprinted from Tovey's contributions to the 11th edition of the *Britannica*.

400. Vannes, René. ... Essai de terminologie musicale. Dictionnaire universel comprenant plus de 15,000 termes de musique en italien-espagnol-portugais-français-anglais-allemand-latin et grec.... Thann: "Alsatia," 1925. 230 p.

Reprint by Da Capo Press, New York, 1970.

Most extensive manual of its kind, containing 15,000 entries in eight languages. Includes forms, terms, instruments in current use. Brief definitions given under the original or characteristic language, with equivalents in other languages. No explanatory or historical material.

401. Wallon, Simone. L'allemand musicologique. Paris: Beauchesne, 1980. 161 p. (Guides musicologiques, 2)

A phrase book devoted solely to musicological terms, translating German to French.

402. Wotton, Tom S. A dictionary of foreign musical terms and handbook of orchestral instruments. Leipzig: Breitkopf & Härtel, 1907. 226 p.

Reprint by the Scholarly Press, St. Clair Shores, Michigan, 1972.

Less comprehensive than Vannes (no. 400). Designed as an aid to score reading, including orchestral terms, instruments, tempo indications, etc. Primarily in French, German, and Italian.

CHURCH MUSIC

This section begins with a list of several general dictionaries relating to church music. Robin Leaver's article on the reference sources on hymnals (no. 426) precedes a list of handbooks on the hymnology of various Protestant groups, with citations under the denominations represented. Such handbooks are essentially bibliographies of sacred music, but most of them contain enough biographical and factual information to justify listing them among the encyclopedias and dictionaries of church music.

403. Carroll, J. Robert. Compendium of liturgical music terms. Toledo, Ohio: Gregorian Institute of America, 1964. 86 p.

An attempt to provide a single source for information most frequently requested by students and working church musicians. [*Preface*]

Claghorn, Charles Eugene. Women composers and hymnists. See no. 2979.

404. Davidson, James Robert. A dictionary of Protestant church music. Metuchen, New Jersey: Scarecrow Press, 1975. 349 p.

Brief entries on terms and subjects, most with bibliographies.
Brief review by Stephen M. Fry in *Notes*, 32 (1975), p. 301.

405. Encyclopédie des musiques sacrées. Publiée sous la direction de Jacques Porte. Paris: Éditions Lagergerie, 1968–70. 4 v. [Vol. 4 consists of 16 7-in. phonodiscs.]

Vol. I: "L'expression du sacré en Orient, Afrique, Amérique du Sud."
Vol. II: "Traditions chrétiennes—des premiers siècles aux cultes révolutionnaires."
Vol. III: "Traditions chrétiennes (suite et fin)—essence, nature et moyens de la musique chrétienne."
A handsomely designed publication. Numerous full-page color plates. The editor is assisted by a large group of authorities, chiefly French. The contributions are all extended articles; no definitions of terms.

406. Fischer, Albert F. W. Kirchenlieder-Lexikon; hymnologisch-literarische Nachweisungen über c. 4500 der wichtigsten und verbreitesten Kirchenlieder aller Zeiten in alphabetischer Folge nebst einer Übersicht der Liederdichter. Hildesheim: Georg Olms, 1967. 2 v. in 1.

Originally published in Gotha, 1878–79.
Contents: I. A–J — II. K–Z ; Alphabetisches Verzeichnis der Dichter.

407. Foote, Henry W. Three centuries of American hymnody. [Hamden, Connecticut]: Shoe String Press, 1961. 418, [23] p.

Reprint of original publication by Harvard University Press in 1940.
Not a dictionary, but a history that can serve as a kind of handbook.

408. Hatfield, Edwin Francis. The poets of the church; a series of biographical sketches of hymn writers with notes on their hymns. Detroit, Michigan: Gale Research, 1978. 719 p.

A reprint of the 1884 edition.

409. Hayden, Andrew J. and Robert F. Newton. British hymn writers and composers; a check-list giving their dates & places of birth & death. Croydon, England: Hymn Society of Great Britain and Ireland, 1977. [94] p.

410. Hughes, Anselm. Liturgical terms for music students; a dictionary. Boston: McLaughlin & Reilly, [1940]. 40 p.

Reprint (1972) by the Scholarly Press, St. Clair Shores, Michigan.
Concise definitions of terms likely to occur in the literature of ancient ecclesiastical music of the West. Tables give structure of mass and office. Includes terms from the church calendar, terms referring to notation, and texts with explanations of their places in the liturgy.

411. Julian, John. A dictionary of hymnology, setting forth the origin and history of Christian hymns of all ages and nations. Rev. ed. with new suppl. London: J. Murray, 1907. 1,768 p.
Unaltered reprint in two volumes, New York, Dover, 1957, and by Kregel Publications, Grand Rapids, Michigan, in 1985.
First published in 1892.
Entries under authors, titles, and subjects of hymn texts. Brief but adequate biographical notices. Long articles on American, English, Latin, etc. hymnody. For individual hymns gives original publication and location in other hymnals. Contains a vast amount of information on musical and literary aspects of Christian hymnody.

412. Key words in church music; definition essays on concepts, practices, and movements of thought in church music. Edited by Carl Schalk. St. Louis, Missouri: Concordia Pub. House, 1978. 365 p.
Focusing principally on Lutheran practices, but of general relevance. A dictionary of ideas that relate to the history and use of music in the Christian church. Includes bibliographical references.

413. Kornmüller, P. Utto. Lexikon der kirchlichen Tonkunst.... 2. verb. und verm. Aufl. Regensburg: A. Coppenrath, 1891–95. 2 v. in 1.
First published in 1870. Reprint by Olms, Hildesheim, 1975.
Vol. 1: Dictionary of subjects, terms, and instruments connected with Catholic church music, with a subject index of topics discussed in extended articles.
Vol. 2: Biographical dictionary of church musicians. Published works cited for early names, categories of compositions for recent ones.

414. Kümmerle, Salomon. Encyclopädie der evangelischen Kirchenmusik. Gütersloh: E. Bertelsmann, 1888–95. 4 v.
Originally published in Lieferungen, 1883–95.
Reprinted by Olms, Hildesheim, 1974.
Terms and biographies related to Protestant church music. Entries for chorale titles, with full musical quotations of the melodies. The author was responsible for basic research on the melodies of the Lutheran chorale.
Review by Friedrich Spitta in *Vierteljahrschrift für Musikwissenschaft*, 1 (1885), p. 235–38.

415. McCutchan, Robert G. Hymn tune names, their sources and significance. Nashville, Tennessee: Abingdon Press, [1957]. 206 p.
Reprinted by the Scholarly Press, St. Clair Shores, Michigan, 1976.
Alphabetical listing of tunes, giving their metrical structures and thematic incipits in letter notation. Commentary related to authors, composers, and sources. Numerous cross-references. Melodic index. First-line index of texts, with author, translator, and tune name.

416. Miller, Josiah. Singers and songs of the church; being biographical sketches of the hymn-writers in all the principal collections, with notes on their psalms and hymns. 2nd ed. Louisville, Kentucky: Lost Cause Press, 1981. 617 p.

A microfiche edition of the original published in London by Longmans, Green in 1869.

417. Mizgalski, Gerard. Podreczna encyklopedia muzyki kościelnej. Poznan; Warszawa; Lublin: Ksiegarnia Sw. Wojciecha, 1959. 566 p.

A Polish dictionary of sacred music. Biographical articles all stress contributions to church music. Illustrated.

418. Nulman, Macy. Concise encyclopedia of Jewish music. New York: McGraw-Hill Book Co., 1975. 276 p.

A highly selective work including both terms and biography. Information is presented in chronological order, with emphasis on current practices. Includes a 4-page "Highlights in the history of Jewish music."

Brief review by Stephen M. Fry in *Notes*, 32 (1976), p. 556.

419. Ortigue, Joseph Louis d'. Dictionnaire liturgique, historique et théorique de plain-chant et de musique d'église, au moyen âge et dans les temps modernes. Paris: J. P. Migne, 1853. 1,563 p.

Reprinted by Da Capo, New York, 1971.

A pioneer reference work on liturgical music, of considerable historical importance. Documented with frequent references to the works of the leading 18th- and 19th-century specialists in church music.

420. Perry, David W. Hymns and tunes indexed by first lines, tune names, and metres compiled from current English hymnbooks. Croydon, England: Hymn Society of Great Britain and Ireland: Royal School of Church Music, 1980. 310 p.

See also nos. 1827 and 1838 for other indexes to hymnbooks.

421. Richter, Gottfried Lebrecht. Allgemeines biographisches Lexikon alter und neuer geistlicher Liederdichter. Leipzig: Zentralantiquariat der Deutschen Demokratischen Republik, 1970. 487 p.

A reprint of the Leipzig, 1804 edition.

422. Stubbins, George W. A dictionary of church music. London: Epworth Press, [1949]. 128 p.

A practical reference book for the use of church organists and choir directors. Short explanations of technical terms and concise information on topics related to church music.

423. Studwell, William E. Christmas carols; a reference guide. Indexes by David A. Hamilton. New York: Garland, 1985. 278 p.

The book has four sections: 1. general background material on the carol; 2. a bibliography; 3. a historical dictionary which lists 789 carols, provides historical and other information about them, and in most cases locates them in one or more publications; 4. title, persons and group, and place indexes to the historical dictionary. [*Foreword*]

Entries for the carols are arranged alphabetically, but in the original language. The title index brings together all versions and languages; there are no cross-references. There is also a carol chronology.

424. Thomson, Ronald W. Who's who of hymn writers. London: Epworth Press, 1967. 104 p.

Brief biographies of the principal Protestant hymn text writers with a representative selection of their hymns.

425. Weissenbäck, Andreas. Sacra musica; Lexikon der katholischen Kirchenmusik. Klosterneuburg: Augustinus Druckerei, [1937]. 419 p.

Biography, terms, and subjects in one alphabet. Articles on religious organizations and music publishing houses. More comprehensive in coverage than Kornmüller (no. 413), but the articles are briefer.

HANDBOOKS ON HYMNOLOGY

426. Leaver, Robin A. "Hymnals, hymnal collections and collection development." In *Notes*, 47 (1990), p. 331–54.

A discussion of some of the principal bibliographical resources relating to hymnals, together with a listing of hymnal-based reference materials. [introductory paragraphs]

In addition to citing numerous general reference sources of use in identifying hymnals and related works, provides a "basic" bibliography of hymnals, hymnal companions, and handbooks arranged in three broad sections: North America, arranged by denomination; the English-speaking world outside of North America, arranged by denomination; non-English-language traditions, arranged by language. The last section is very selective.

Anglican/Episcopal

427. Church of England. Historical companion to Hymns ancient and modern. Edited by Maurice Frost. London: Printed for the Proprietors by William Clowes & Sons, [1962]. 716 p.

The latest revision of a work compiled in 1909 by W. H. Frere under the title *Historical Edition of Hymns Ancient and Modern;* revised in 1950. P.1–124: Introduction, with contributions by Egon Wellesz, Ruth Messenger, C. E. Pocknee, and Lowther Clarke covering the history of hymnody and of the Anglican hymnal. P. 125–478: Texts and commentary for 636 hymns, including the language of the original if translated. Index of first lines, brief biographies of hymn writers, chronological list of authors and translators, alphabetical index of tunes, index of plainsong. Notes on the composers, with chronology, list of publications and tunes, metrical index.

428. Moorsom, Robert Maude. A historical companion to hymns ancient and modern: containing the Greek and Latin; the German, Italian, French, Dan-

ish, and Welsh hymns; the first lines of the English hymns; the names of all authors and translators; notes and dates. 2nd ed. London: C. J. Clay, 1903. 380 p.
Includes bibliographic references.

429. Protestant Episcopal Church in the U.S.A. The *Hymnal 1940* companion. [3rd ed. rev.] New York: Church Pension Fund, 1956. 741 p.
First published in 1949.
Contains historical essays on texts and tunes; biographies of authors, composers, translators, and arrangers. List of organ works based on hymn tunes, with publishers. Index of scriptural texts; general index; melodic index; index of tunes; first-line index.

Congregational

430. Companion to congregational praise. Edited by Kenneth L. Parry, with notes on the music by Erik Routley. London: Independent Press, [1953]. 580 p.
P. 1–336: Notes on the words and music for 884 hymns and chants. P. 337–550: biographical notes on hymn writers and composers. Chronological listing of 396 musical sources. Index of tune names and first-line index of hymns.

Evangelical and Reformed

431. Haeussler, Armin. The story of our hymns: the handbook to the hymnal of the Evangelical and Reformed Church. St. Louis, Missouri: Eden Publishing House, 1952. 1,088 p.
Commentary on 561 hymns and other liturgical pieces. Biographies of hymn writers and notes on sources. Bibliography. Index of scriptural texts, topical index, metrical index, indexes of tune names, composers, arrangers, and sources. First-line index.

432. Hustad, Don. Dictionary-handbook to hymns for the living church: with the history of Hope Publishing Company ... by George H. Shorney, Jr. Carol Stream, Illinois: Hope Pub. Co., 1978. 364 p.

Lutheran

433. Handbuch zum evangelischen Kirchengesangbuch. Hrsg. von Christhard Mahrenholz und Oskar Söhngen, unter Mitarbeit von Otto Schliske. Göttingen: Vanderhoeck & Ruprecht, 1956–1970. Band I–III (5 v.).
Supplementary volume: *Die Lieder unserer Kirche*, by Johannes Kulp. Göttingen, 1958.
A compendium of information related to the German Lutheran hymnal, in five volumes.
Summary of contents:
Bd. 1. 1.T. *Wort- und Sachkonkordanz* (Word and subject concordance). 2. durchgesehene Aufl. (1956).

Bd. 1. 2.T. *Die biblischen Quellen der Lieder* (The biblical sources of hymns), von Rudolf Köhler (1957).
Bd. 2. 1.T. *Lebensbilder der Liederdichter und Melodisten* (Biographical sketches of the poets and the composers).
Bd. 2. 2.T. *Geschichte des Kirchenliedes* (History of the hymns).
Bd. 3. 1.T. *Liederkunde, Lied 1 bis 175* (Studies of the individual hymns and their melodies) (1975).

434. Polack, William G. The handbook of the Lutheran hymnal. 3rd and rev. ed. St. Louis, Missouri: Concordia, [1958]. 681 p.
Reprinted in Milwaukee by the Northwestern Publishing House, 1975.
Texts of and commentary on 660 Lutheran hymns. Biographical and historical notes on the authors and composers. Index of biblical references, table of hymns for feasts and festivals, first-line index (including stanzas of hymns), index of tunes, metrical index, topical index, index of authors and translators.

435. Stulken, Marilyn Kay. Hymnal companion to the Lutheran book of worship. Philadelphia, Pennsylvania: Fortress Press, 1981. 647 p.
Begins with seven brief essays on the general history of the hymns in the Lutheran hymnal, with some emphasis on German and Nordic origins. The major portion of the book is composed of entries on hymns arranged by first line of text. Each entry discusses sources, translators, tunes, and substantial biographical information about the person responsible for the text. There is usually a paragraph about the hymn tune. Extensive appendixes: bibliography; calendar of the church year citing hymns appropriate for use in each season and for each feast; chronological list of tunes; chronological list of first lines by original language. Indexes to: authors, composers, and sources; tunes; first lines of canticles; first lines of hymns in original languages and translations.

Mennonite

436. Hostetler, Lester. Handbook to the Mennonite hymnary. Newton, Kansas: General Conference of the Mennonite Church of North America, Board of Publications, 1949. 425 p.
Commentary on 623 Mennonite hymns and other liturgical pieces. Bibliography. Indexes.

Methodist

437. Gealy, Fred Daniel. Companion to the hymnal; a handbook to the 1964 Methodist hymnal. Nashville, Tennessee: Abingdon Press, [1970]. 766 p.

438. McCutchan, Robert G. Our hymnody, a manual of the Methodist hymnal. 2nd ed. New York: Abingdon Press, [1942]. 619 p.
First published in 1937.
Commentary on 664 hymns and other liturgical pieces. Hymn calendar, bibliography, and nine special indexes.

439. Rogal, Samuel J. Guide to the hymns and tunes of American Methodism. Westport, Connecticut: Greenwood Press, c1986. 318 p. (Music reference collection, 7)

Mormon

440. Cornwall, J. Spencer. Stories of our Mormon Hymns. 4th enlarged printing. Salt Lake City, Utah: Deseret Book Co., 1975. 304 p.

A popular companion to the Mormon hymnal, giving information on composers and writers of texts for approximately 311 hymns used in the Mormon church.

Presbyterian

441. Covert, William Chalmers. Handbook to the Hymnal. Calvin Weiss Laufer, associate editor. Philadelphia, Pennsylvania: Presbyterian Board of Christian Education, 1935. 566 p.

Unitarian

442. Foote, Henry W. American Unitarian hymn writers and hymns. Compiled for the Hymn Society of America for publication in the Society's proposed Dictionary of American Hymnology. Cambridge, Massachusetts: [Author], 1959. 270 leaves (typescript).

Contains a historical sketch of American Unitarian hymnody, a catalog of American Unitarian hymn books, an alphabetical list of hymn writers, biographical sketches, and a first-line index of published hymns.

United Church of Christ

443. Ronander, Albert C. and Ethel K. Porter. Guide to the Pilgrim hymnal. Philadelphia, Pennsylvania: United Church Press, [1966]. 456 p.

OPERA AND THEATER MUSIC

Dictionaries of opera and theater music are of two principal kinds: (1) compilations of facts related to the history or the production of musical dramatic works, in which case they can be cited as dictionaries or handbooks of opera; or (2) listings of operatic works, often in chronological order, associated with a particular place: city, country, or opera house. Works of the latter kind can properly be described as "Bibliographies of Music," and will be found cited under that heading in the subdivision "Local Opera Repertoires."

Listeners' guides to opera and collections of opera plots have been excluded.

One encyclopedia of theater arts demands mention at this point, although its coverage extends far beyond the realm of music. This is the *Enciclopedia dello Spettacolo*, Roma, Casa Editrice le Maschere, 1954–62. 9 v. (with an *Aggionamento, 1955–1965*, issued 1955–65, and an *Indice-repertorio*, issued 1968). This great illustrated reference work was published under the auspices of the Cini Foundation and covers all aspects of the theater, with contributions by outstanding authorities in the field.

Other reference works related to opera will be found cited under the entries Kutsch (no. 95), *Le Grandi Voci* (no. 88), and Highfill (no. 154).

444. Altmann, Wilhelm. Katalog der seit 1861 in den Handel gekommenen theatralischen Musik (Opern, Operetten, Possen, Musik zu Schauspielen, usw.) Ein musikbibliographischer Versuch.... Wolfenbüttel: Verlag für musikalische Kultur and Wissenschaft, 1935. 384 p. (incomplete).

This work was published in *Lieferungen*, of which four appeared, carrying the entries through "Siegmund, Josef."

Operas, ballets, and incidental music since 1861, arranged under composer with references from librettist, etc. Gives brief titles of works, type, librettist, date of first performance if known, type of score, language of text, and publisher. There is no key to the abbreviations of publishers' names, but most of these can be readily identified.

445. Bernandt, Grigorii B. Slovar' oper. Vpervye postavlennykh ili izdannykh v dorevoliutsionnoi rossii i v SSSR, 1736–1959. Moskva: Sovetskii Kompozitor, 1962. 554 p.

A dictionary of operas first performed or first published in Russia during the period 1736–1959. Entries are alphabetical by title. Information includes genre of the work, composer, first performance, librettist, literary source, and many details that relate to production. Indexed by composer, librettist, and author of the original literary source.

446. Bloom, Ken. American song: the complete musical theater companion. New York: Facts on File, 1985. 2 v.

Provides information on over 5,000 productions, on- and off-Broadway. Indexes individual songs in each production.

Reviews by Ed Glazier in *Notes*, 43 (1986), p. 303–305, and by Doris Evans McGinty in *Black Perspective in Music*, 13 (1985), p. 124–26.

447. Bordman, Gerald. American musical theatre: a chronicle. Expanded edition. New York: Oxford University Press, 1986. 782 p.

First published in 1978. 749 p.

Includes a chronologically ordered discussion of all sorts of musical theater presented in American theaters from 1735 to 1986. Information about each production includes opening date and theater, plot synopsis, characters and names of performers, and critical comments based on contemporaneous reviews. Title index. Index to sources upon which shows were based. Index to songs mentioned in the book, but not to all songs in each show. Index to persons.

448. Brockpähler, Renate. Handbuch zur Geschichte der Barockoper in Deutschland. Emsdetten: Verlag Lechte, 1964. 394 p.

A handbook of historical information related to German Baroque opera. Organized by place (47 municipalities), each entry includes a bibliography of relevant literature, sections devoted to the history of music or opera in particular in the place, and a listing of the works performed. Indexed by place, musicians, poets, and dancing masters.

449. Burton, Jack. The blue book of Broadway musicals; with additions by Larry Freeman. Watkins Glen, New York: Century House, [1975?]. 335 p.

Lists title, date, composer, author, principals, and musical numbers for more than 1,500 operettas, musical comedies, and revues from the 1890s to 1951. Arranged by decades, with a general introduction to each period.

The second book in a trilogy on popular music, the first of which was *The Blue Book of Tin Pan Alley* (no. 1510) and the third *The Blue Book of Hollywood Musicals* (no. 450).

450. Burton, Jack. The blue book of Hollywood musicals; songs from the sound tracks and the stars who sang them since the birth of the talkies a quarter-century ago. Watkins Glen, New York: Century House, [1953]. 296 p.

Complementing *The Blue Book of Tin Pan Alley* (1951) and *The Blue Book of Broadway Musicals* (1952), this present anthology completes a trilogy on popular music. [*Introduction*]

See also *The Blue Book of Tin Pan Alley* (1962), entered under "Bibliographies of Music: Popular" (no. 1510) and *The Index of American Popular Music* (no. 1511).

451. Busby, Roy. British music hall; an illustrated who's who from 1850 to the present day. London; Salem, New Hampshire: Paul Elek, 1976. 191 p.

A biographical dictionary of British popular entertainers.

452. Caselli, Aldo. Catalogo delle opere liriche pubblicate in Italia. Firenze: Leo S. Olschki, 1969. 891 p. (Historiae musicae cultores, Biblioteca, 27)

An ambitious attempt to cover all operas produced in Italy from 1600 to the present. Organized to permit approaches through the composer, city and theater, title, librettist. The effort to achieve comprehensiveness leads to some sacrifice in accuracy.

Review by Thomas Walker in *Notes*, 26 (1970), p. 758–59.

453. Clément, Félix and Pierre Larousse. Dictionnaire des opéras (Dictionnaire lyrique) contenant l'analyse et la nomenclature de tous les opéras, opéras-comiques, opérettes et drames lyriques représentés en France et à l'étranger depuis l'origine de ces genres d'ouvrages jusqu'à nos jours.... Rev. et mis à jour par Arthur Pougin. Paris: Librairie Larousse, [1905]. 1,203 p.

First published in 1869 under the title *Dictionnaire Lyrique*. Reprint of the 1905 edition by Da Capo Press, New York, 1969. 2 v.

Title entries (frequently under the French form, with references to other forms) for operas and comic operas presented in France and elsewhere from the beginnings to the date of publication. For each entry: language of text, number of acts, authors of words and music, place and date of first performance, brief sketch of plot, occasional criticism. Index of composers. A comprehensive work.

454. Dassori, Carlo. Opere e operisti (dizionario lirico 1541–1902). Elenco nominativo universale dei maestri compositori di opere teatrali, col prospetto cronologico dei loro principali lavori e catalogo alfabetico generale delle opere serie, semiserie, buffe, comiche e simili rappresentate … dall'origine dell'opera in musica fino ai d'i nostri, coll'indicazione di data e di luogo della prima rappresentazione, avuto speciale riguardo al repertorio italiano. Bologna: A. Forni, [1979]. 977 p. (Bibliotheca musica Bononiensis; III, 64)

Reprint of the original edition of Tipografia editrice R. Istituto Sordomuti, Genova, 1903.

Includes 15,406 operas by 3,628 composers. Author and title lists only, no descriptive or critical matter.

Part I: Alphabetical list of composers, with dates of birth and death, chronological list under composer of operas, with dates and places of first performances.

Part II: Title list of all operas that have been performed in Italy.

Directory of American and foreign contemporary operas and American opera premieres, 1967–1975. See no. 2926.

455. Directory of American contemporary operas. New York: Central Opera Service, 1967. 79 p.

A listing of operas by American composers premiered since 1930; arranged alphabetically by composer with information as to place of first performance, librettist, cast and number of acts, availability (from composer, publisher, etc.).

A special issue of the *Central Opera Service Bulletin*, v. 10, no. 2 (Dec. 1967); Maria F. Rich, editor.

456. Drone, Jeanette Marie. Index to opera, operetta, and musical comedy synopses in collections and periodicals. Metuchen, New Jersey: Scarecrow Press, 1978. 171 p.

…An index to 74 collections and four periodical titles … including 1,605 titles by 627 composers. [*Preface*]

Includes a bibliography of additional sources of synopses not indexed. Review by Frits Noske in *Fontes Artis Musicae*, 26 (1979), p. 92–93.

457. Eaton, Quaintance. Opera, a pictorial guide. New York: Abaris Books, 1980. 528 p.

458. Eaton, Quaintance. Opera production: a handbook. Minneapolis: University of Minnesota Press, [1961–74]. 2 v.

Reprint of vol. 1 by Da Capo, New York, 1974, with title *Opera Production I: A Handbook*. 266 p.

Vol. 1 contains useful information on 224 "long" and 148 "short" operas, including timings, difficulty of leading roles, instrumentation, source and cost of scores and parts, index to photographs of productions, lists of performing groups.

Vol. 2 treats more than 350 lesser-known operas and includes "Production problems of Handel's operas," by Randolph Mickelson.

Review by Boris Goldovsky in *Notes*, 32 (1975), p. 53–54.

459. The encyclopedia of opera. Edited by Leslie Orrey; advisory editor, Gilbert Chase. London: Pitman; New York: Charles Scribner's Sons, 1976. 376 p.

Signed articles of very short duration on people, characters, titles, terms, places, and subjects. Brief summary plots and descriptions of characters. Preceded by a short history of the bibliography of opera.

Review by Irwin Kraus in *Notes*, 34 (1977), p. 340–42. Review by Egon Voss in *Neue Zeitschrift für Musik*, 40 (1979), p. 421–22.

460. Ewen, David. New complete book of the American musical theatre. New York: Holt, Rinehart, and Winston, 1970. 800 p.

A sourcebook of information about American musical comedies and revues.

461. Ewen, David. The new encyclopedia of the opera. New York: Hill and Wang, 1971. 759 p.

First published in 1955; reissued with a supplement in 1963.

Composers, text incipits, terms, plots, singers, librettists, theaters, all in one alphabet.

Review by Piero Weiss in *Notes*, 28 (1972), p. 677–80.

462. Forbes, Elizabeth. Opera from A to Z. London: Kaye & Ward; South Brunswick, New Jersey: A. S. Barnes, 1977. 153 p.

A dictionary of opera including bibliographical references.

463. Gänzl, Kurt. The British musical theatre: volume 1, 1865–1914, and volume 2, 1915–1984. London: Macmillan Press Music Division; New York: Oxford University Press, 1986. 2 v.

A survey of British light musical theater, confining itself to works with texts and scores written particularly for the shows in question, excluding opera. Organized chronologically, each year's entries are preceded by a brief essay on the character of the times. Entries provide performance information and history, including references to TV/video productions. Characters and players are cited. Appendixes listing printed and recorded works. Index of names, titles, theaters, and titles of journals or newspapers cited. A substantial guide to this genre.

464. Green, Stanley. Broadway musicals, show by show. Milwaukee, Wisconsin: Hal Leonard Books, 1985. 316 p.

Organized chronologically, 300 entries provide brief histories, information on each production, and photographs. Indexes to titles, composers, lyricists, librettists, directors, choreographers, principal members of casts, and theaters.

465. Green, Stanley. Encyclopaedia of the musical film. New York: Oxford University Press, 1981. 344 p.

A companion to and using the same format as his *Encyclopedia of the Musical Theatre* (no. 466), this work contains "succinct" information regarding the musical screen's most prominent individuals, productions, and songs. The emphasis is on the Hollywood output (including feature-length cartoons), but British musical films and selected original television musicals are also covered. Western musicals (those of the singing cowboys, e.g., Gene Autry and Roy Rogers), short subjects, documentary musicals, foreign-language musicals, and silent films with accompanying scores are all excluded.

Entries for people contain year-by-year listings of every production with which they were associated. Production entries included major performers and their roles, songs, and singers, as well as songs intended for the film, but cut. Song entries include those primarily written for or first introduced in films. Some entries include bibliographic references. There is a list of Academy Award nominations and prize winners, a classified bibliography of biographies (classical composers, popular composers), a list of title changes for British and American versions of the same productions, a general bibliography, and a discography arranged by title.

466. Green, Stanley. Encyclopedia of the musical theatre: an updated reference guide to over 2,000 performers, writers, directors, productions, and songs of the musical stage, both in New York and London. New York: Da Capo Press, 1984. 492 p.

Reprint of the edition published by Dodd, Mead, New York, supplemented with photographs and addenda, 1976.

Bibliography and discography, p. 472–88. Supplementary listing of awards and prizes and long runs.

467. Green, Stanley. Rodgers and Hammerstein fact book: a record of their works together and with other collaborators. New York: Lynn Farnol Group, 1980. 762 p.

Previously published as *The Richard Rodgers Fact Book* by the same publisher in 1965. 582 p.

Three major divisions present information on Rodgers, on Hammerstein, and on Rodgers and Hammerstein as a partnership. The Rodgers section begins with information on his early, amateur career, then proceeds in chronological order with entries on each professional production. Each entry provides names of persons responsible (author, producer, director, etc.), places and dates of out-of-town tryouts, plot synopses, cast, lists of musical numbers by act, and excerpts of reviews, etc. The sections on Hammerstein and on the pair are similar in construction and content. There are some miscellaneous facts reported in three appendixes. Indexes to songs and productions, lists of songs by subject citing source musical production. Bibliography: p. 709–720. Discography: p. 721–34.

468. Green, Stanley. The world of musical comedy: the story of the American musical stage as told through the careers of its foremost composers and lyricists. Foreword by Deems Taylor. New York: Grosset & Dunlap, 1980. 480 p.

First published in 1960. Reprinted in 1962 (397 p.) and 1969 (541 p.).

Not properly a dictionary, this work nonetheless contains valuable information about the creators of this American genre. Musical productions and discography: p. 318–82.

469. Gruber, Clemens M. Opern-Uraufführungen: ein internationales Verzeichnis von der Renaissance bis zur Gegenwart; hrsg. von der Gesellschaft für Musiktheater. [Wien: Österreichische Verlagsanstalt, 1978–]. 2 v. to date.

Vol. 2. *Komponisten aus Deutschland, Österreich und der Schweiz, 1800–1899.* 1987. 397 p.

Vol. 3. *Komponisten aus Deutschland (der BRD und der DDR), Österreich und der Schweiz, 1900–1907.* 1978. 319 p.

Entries by composer giving dates and places of world premieres, number of acts, and names of librettists. Title and location indexes. *Anhang* and supplement. Vol. 1 covering pre-1800 premieres is expected.

Review by Gustav Pichler in the *Österreichische Musikzeitschrift,* 34 (1979), p. 388.

470. Herders Musiklexikon; Oper, Operette, Musical. 4. Aufl. Freiburg; Basel; Wien: Herder, 1976. 370 p.

Three sections with a brief history of each genre, followed by descriptions of the works including plot summaries, arranged by composer. Heavily weighted to German-language productions. There is a brief bio-bibliographical dictionary and a dictionary of terms. Indexes to arias and to names and titles.

471. Johnson, H. Earle. Operas on American subjects. New York: Coleman-Ross Co., 1964. 125 p.

An alphabetical listing, by composer, of operas from the 17th century to the present based on American subject matter or involving American characters. The entries supply much interesting information related to plot, performance, and estimates by contemporary critics. Topical, title, and general indexes.

Also see Julius Mattfeld's *A Handbook of American Operatic Premieres,1731–1962,* no. 1546.

472. Kürschners Biographisches Theater-Handbuch. Schauspiel, Oper, Film, Rundfunk: Deutschland, Österreich, Schweiz. Hrsg. von Herbert A. Frenzel and Hans Joachim Moser. Berlin: W. de Gruyter, 1956. 840 p.

Names, addresses, and activities of singers, music directors, actors, critics, dancers, choreographers, composers, librarians of theater collections, etc. Entries are for persons living as of 1956.

Also known as *Biographisches Theater-Handbuch.*

473. Lessing, Gotthold E. Handbuch des Opern-Repertoires. [Neubearbeitung.] London and New York: Boosey & Hawkes, 1952. 393 p.

An organized compilation of facts related to the performance of 392 operas in the current repertoire, including casts of characters, locales of action, instrumentation, duration of acts, dates of first performance, and publishers of music.

A work reference intended for the use of theatrical managers, conductors, dramatists and in libraries. [Author's *Preface*]

474. Loewenberg, Alfred. Annals of opera, 1597–1940. Compiled from the original sources, with an introduction by Edward J. Dent. 3rd ed., rev. and corrected. Totowa, New Jersey: Rowman and Littlefield; London: J. Calder, 1978. 1756 cols.

First published in 1943 by W. Heffer, Cambridge, 879 p., and subsequently published in a 2nd revised and corrected edition by Societas Bibliographica, Geneva, 1955, in 2 v. The 1955 edition was reprinted by Rowman and Littlefield, New York, 1970, and by the Scholarly Press, St. Clair Shores, Michigan, 1972.

Part 1: chronological listing of operas by dates of first performance, including (with a few exceptions) only works known to have been produced. The list is limited to older operas that are extant and modern ones that have created interest outside their countries of origin. Each entry includes composer's name, original title of the work, English translation for all languages except German, French, and Italian. Librettist identified; place and date of first performance given.

Part 2: indexes by title, composer, librettist, and a general index for other names, places, and subjects.

A work of distinguished scholarship; essential for the historical study of opera.

Review of 2nd ed. by Edward N. Waters, in *Notes*, 13 (1956), p. 285–86.

475. Manferrari, Umberto. Dizionario universale delle opere melodrama-tiche. Firenze: Sansoni, 1954–55. 3 v. (Contributi alla biblioteca bibliografica italica, 4, 8, 10)

One of the most comprehensive of all listings of opera before the work of Franz Stieger (no. 491). Entries under composer, giving title, librettist, place and date of first performances in other opera houses.

There is a typescript index of librettists cited in entries for operas composed before 1801 that was prepared in Venice in 1966.

476. Martin, George W. The companion to twentieth century opera. New York: Dodd, Mead & Co., 1984. 653 p.

Previously published as *The Opera Companion to Twentieth-Century Opera*, 1979.

Synopses of 78 opera plots, with statistics on repertoires of 23 major opera houses around the world.

477. Moore, Frank L. Crowell's handbook of world opera. New York: Thomas Y. Crowell, 1961. 683 p.

Reprinted by Greenwood Press, Westport, Connecticut, 1974.

Pub. in England under title *The Handbook of World Opera*, London, Arthur Baker, [1962], with introduction by Darius Milhaud.

Rich accumulation of facts under headings such as the operas, the people in opera, the characters in opera, first lines and titles of famous musical numbers, chronology of opera, glossary, themes of most famous musical numbers, recordings of complete operas. Numerous special indexes.

478. Northouse, Cameron. Twentieth century opera in England and the United States. Boston: G. K. Hall, 1976. 400 p.

A chronological list of first performances, 1900–1974, with another list organized by composer of operas lacking information to include them in the chronological list. Appendixes: a list of operas based on literary works and published operas. Index to composers, librettists, opera titles, literary titles, and literary authors.

479. L'opera: repertorio della lirica dal 1597. Capo redattore Riccardo Mezzanotte. Milano: A. Mondadori, 1977. 512 p.

Issued in an American version as *The Simon and Schuster Book of the*

Opera; a Complete Reference Guide—1597 to the Present by Simon and Schuster, New York, 1978. 512 p. Issued in a German version as *Oper; eine illustrierte Darstellung der Oper von 1597 bis zur Gegenwart* (Übersetzung aus dem Italienischen von Brigitte de Grandis Grossmann und Sigrid Oswald) by Laaber-Verlag, Laaber, and by Drei Lilien Verlag, Wiesbaden, both 1981 and both 508 p. Issued in a Spanish version as *La Ópera; Enciclopedia del Arte Lírico* [traducción del texto original en italiano por Juan Novella Domingo] by Aguilar, Madrid, 1981. 514 p.

Also issued in Britain as the *Phaidon Book of the Opera, a Survey of 780 Operas from 1597* (Oxford: Phaidon, 1979). 511 p.

Chronologically ordered descriptions and synopses, including first cast if known. Copiously illustrated. Indexes of titles and composers, librettists, and sources.

480. Opera manual: a handbook of practical operatic information. Edited by Mrs. Charles A. Matz and Marguerite Wickersham. New York: Central Opera Service, 1956. 36 p.

Contains lists of operas and chamber operas, citing voices and instruments needed, sets, duration, and source of music. Information on costume and scenery rentals. Bibliography of stagecraft materials; lists of awards for singers; opera activity in the U.S., 1955–56; addresses of publishers, opera groups; unpublished translations, sources of chamber operas, etc.

481. Osborne, Charles. The dictionary of the opera. New York: Simon & Schuster, 1983. 382 p.

A convenient source for the opera enthusiast, provides brief entries on over 300 composers, 800 singers, designers, conductors, directors, etc. as well as brief synopses of over 570 operas, including place and date of first performances. No bibliographic references are provided. There is a separate section devoted to short histories of leading opera houses. Illustrated.

482. Pipers Enzyklopädie des Musiktheaters: Oper, Operette, Musical, Ballet. Herausgegeben von Carl Dahlhaus und dem Forschungsinstitut für Musiktheater der Universität Bayreuth unter Leitung von Sieghart Döhring. München; Zürich: Piper, 1986–. 8 v. intended, 4 v. issued to date.

Vols. 1–5 will contain lengthy articles on composers and their works. Each entry provides information on individual works: authors of texts, first performances, characters, performing forces, performance characteristics. The origins of the story are described and discussed. A plot outline, commentary on the work, and a performance history are provided. There is bibliographical information on sources and editions as well as the literature about each work. Illustrated. An index and supplement volume is planned as are two volumes defining terms and discussing concepts. Vol. 1 treats composers through Donizetti in 726 p.

483. Regler-Bellinger, Brigitte, Wolfgang Schenck and Hans Winking. Knaurs grosser Opernführer. Redaktion, Brigitte Mudrak-Trost. München: Droemer Knaur, 1983. 672 p.

Earlier edition *Knaurs Opernführer* by Gerhart von Westermann and Karl Schumann and published by Droemer/Knaur, München and Zürich, 1969. 511 p. *Opera Guide*, edited and with an introduction by Harold D. Rosenthal and translated by Anne Ross, was adapted from the 1969

Knaurs Opernführer and published by E. P. Dutton, New York, 1965. 584 p.

Known as *Opernführer.*

Includes bibliographical references, a discography (p. 633–50), and indexes.

484. Rieck, Waldemar. Opera plots, an index to the stories of operas, operettas, etc., from the sixteenth to the twentieth century. New York: New York Public Library, 1927. 102 p.

Reprinted March 1927 from the *Bulletin of the New York Public Library* of January, February, March, April 1926.

> Over 200 books and editions published in English, French, German, and Danish during the past 80 years have been indexed; 998 composers are represented by more than 2,775 works in operatic form. [*Introduction*]

485. Riemann, Hugo. Opern-Handbuch. Repertorium der dramatisch-musikalischen Litteratur (Opern, Operetten, Ballette, Melodramen, Pantomimen, Oratorien, dramatische Kantaten, usw.). Leipzig: C. A. Koch, 1881–86. 862 p.

Originally published in fascicles, including a concluding supplement by C. A. Koch, 1881–86. Published by Koch in one volume, including the first supplement, in 1887. Intended as an opera supplement to Riemann's *Lexikon.*

Reprint of the reissue of the 1887 edition with the addition of the second supplement of 1892 by Olms, Hildesheim, 1979. 862 p.

Title articles give genre, number of acts, composer, librettist, first performance. Composer articles give dates, chronological list of operas. Librettist entries give dates and chief activity.

486. Rosenthal, Harold D. and John Warrack. Concise Oxford dictionary of opera. 2nd ed., reprinted with corrections. Oxford and New York: Oxford University Press, 1986. 561 p.

First published in 1964, subsequently issued in a corrected 1st edition in 1972. 2nd edition issued in 1971.

A richly informative pocket dictionary of opera. Special emphasis laid on the growth of opera in Eastern Europe, on literary backgrounds and relationships, and on singers.

Enlarged version of the earlier edition, considerably enhanced by a cross-referencing system, by more coverage of the development of opera in all countries, and by better coverage of localities. Singers are especially well represented. Includes a brief bibliography for further study.

Review by David Z. Kushner in *Notes*, 22 (1965–66), p. 906. Review by Clifford Bartlett in *Brio*, 16 (1979), p. 18.

487. Ross, Anne. The opera directory. London: John Calder; New York: Sterling Pub. Co., [1961]. 566 p.

A source book of current opera facts and figures. Introductions and headings in six languages (English, French, German, Italian, Spanish, Russian). Material organized under 13 headings, the most important of which are opera singers, conductors, producers and designers, technical staff, theaters and producing organizations, festivals, living composers, works by living composers, librettists, colleges and schools of music, casting index, glossary.

The identical volume is issued with various titles under the imprints of publishers in Paris, Geneva, Berlin, etc.

488. Schumann, Otto. Opernführer: von Monteverdi bis Penderecki unter Mitarbeit von Viktor Kreiner. Reinbeck bei Hamburg: Rowohlt, 1982. 963 p.
Revised and expanded edition of *Meyers Opernbuch*, published first in 1935.

489. Seeger, Horst. Opern Lexikon. Mitarbeit für die Gebiete Opernfiguren und -zitate, Eberhard Schmidt. 3., erw. Aufl. Wilhelmshaven: F. Noetzel Verlag "Heinrichshofen Bücher," 1978. 702 p.
"Lizenzausgabe für die Bundesrepublik Deutschland, Berlin (West), Österreich und die Schweiz."
Review by Egon Voss in *Neue Zeitschrift für Musik*, 40 (1979), p. 422.

490. Smith, William C. The Italian opera and contemporary ballet in London, 1789–1820; a record of performances and players with reports from the journals of the time. London: Society for Theatre Research, 1955. 191 p. (Society for Theatre Research. Annual publication, 1953–54)
Cites 618 works produced in the London theaters during the period under consideration, with commentary by the author and quotations from contemporary sources. Indexes of operas, burlettas, cantatas; of ballets and divertissements; of singers, ballet personnel, composers, and instrumentalists.

491. Stieger, Franz. Opernlexikon. Opera catalogue. Lexique des opéras. Dizionario operistico. Mit e. Einf. von Franz Grasberger. Tutzing: Schneider, 1975–83. 4 pts. in 11 v.
Contents: Titelkatalog, 3 v.; Komponisten, 3 v.; Librettisten, 3 v.; Nachträge, 2 v.
Each of the main volumes presents permutations of the same information: opera title, composer, librettist(s), premiere date & place, genre or opus number. All information is taken from the sources.
The *Nachträge* provide various chronological lists: opera composed before 1700; composers who were also librettists; an index to composers with additional full entries included; German opera and Singspiel, by period; Italian opera in Italy and elsewhere, by period; etc.

492. Suskin, Steven. Show tunes, 1905–1985: the songs, shows, and careers of Broadway's major composers. New York: Dodd, Mead, 1986. 728 p.
A study of 30 composers with a section on notable Broadway scores by other composers, a chronological list of productions, a collaborator reference listing, and a bibliography. Indexes to song titles, show titles, and persons.

493. Towers, John. Dictionary-catalogue of operas and operettas which have been performed on the public stage. Morgantown, West Virginia: Acme Pub. Co., [1910]. 1,045 p.
Reprint by Da Capo Press, New York, 1967. 2 v.
Title lists of 28,015 operas, giving for each composer his nationality and

birth and death dates. Alternative or translated titles included. Composer index. No information on librettists; no historical or descriptive material. Review by Donald Krummel in *Notes*, 24 (1968), p. 502–503.

494 Vallance, Tom. The American musical. London: A. Zwemmer; New York: A. S. Barnes, 1970. 192 p. (Screen series)
A biographical dictionary with brief entries and more lengthy lists of credits for persons appearing in staged or filmed musicals, including composers, authors, actors and actresses, and directors. No sources cited. Index to shows listed in the entries. Illustrated.

495. Várnai, Péter. Operalexikon. Budapest: Zeneműkiadó, 1975. 533 p.
A Hungarian dictionary of opera, especially strong on Eastern European opera.

496. Wallace, Mary Elaine and Robert Wallace. Opera scenes for class and stage. Carbondale: Southern Illinois University Press, 1979. 260 p.
Ready reference to over 700 excerpts from 100 operas by voice categories. A guide to opera ensembles for opera workshop use. Information includes identification of excerpts, duration, summary of the dramatic situation. Bibliography, index of operas, index of composers, index of arias and ensembles, index to editions of piano-vocal scores.

497. White, Eric Walter. A register of first performances of English operas and semi-operas: from the 16th century to 1980. London: Society for Theatre Research, 1983. 130 p.

498. Who's who in opera; an international biographical directory of singers, conductors, directors, designers, and administrators, also including profiles of 101 opera companies. Maria F. Rich, editor. New York: Arno Press, 1976. 684 p.
Provides information on 2,300 artists in 144 opera companies. Profiles of opera companies include recent repertories and budgets. There is also a directory of international agents.

MISCELLANEOUS

499. Barlow, Harold and Sam Morgenstern. A dictionary of musical themes. Rev. ed. New York: Crown Publishers, 1975. 642 p.
First published in 1948. Reissued in 1957 and 1966. This edition also published by E. Benn, London.
Contains 10,000 themes from instrumental works of the concert repertory, arranged alphabetically by composer. Indexed by scale degrees in letter notation, with all themes transposed to C major or minor. Title index.

500. Barlow, Harold and Sam Morgenstern. A dictionary of opera and song themes: including cantatas, oratorios, lieder, and art songs. Originally published as *A Dictionary of Vocal Themes*. Rev. ed. New York: Crown Publishers, 1976. 547 p.

First published in 1950 and reissued in 1960. This edition also published by E. Benn, London.

Contains themes from operas, cantatas, oratorios, art songs, and miscellaneous vocal works, arranged alphabetically by composer. Indexed by scale degrees as in the preceding work. Title and first-line index.

Review by Harold Spivacke in *Notes*, 8 (1951), p. 334–35.

501. Berger, Kenneth W. Band encyclopedia. Evansville, Indiana: Distributed by Band Associates, 1960. 604 p.

A compendium of information useful to band directors. Includes revisions of the author's earlier publications: *Band Bibliography; Band Discography;* and *Bandmen,* a biographical dictionary of band musicians.

Review by Keith Polk in *Notes*, 18 (1961), p. 424–26; by J. M. Lundahl in *Journal of Research in Music Education*, 10 (1962), p. 81–82.

502. Burrows, Raymond M. and Bessie C. Redmond. Concerto themes. New York: Simon and Schuster, 1951. 296 p.

A thematic catalog more inclusive than Barlow and Morgenstern (no. 499) for concertos. Alphabetical arrangement by composer. Indexed by concerto titles, keys, and solo instruments.

503. Burrows, Raymond M. and Bessie C. Redmond. Symphony themes. New York: Simon and Schuster, 1942. 295 p.

A thematic catalog of standard repertory symphonies. Table of contents includes references to scores, to analyses, and to printed program notes for each symphony cited in the catalog. Thematic incipits are opening measures and principal subjects of each movement. Arranged alphabetically by composer. Indexes by key and by titles of symphonies.

504. Cobbett, Walter W. Cyclopedic survey of chamber music. 2nd ed. London: Oxford Univ. Press, 1963. 3 v.

First published in 2 volumes, 1929–30.

Cobbet's Cyclopedia is a biographical and subject dictionary of chamber music, giving full lists of works in this category under composer. Solo works and piano compositions excluded. The main emphasis is critical and analytical. Excellent critical and bibliographical material, with signed articles by outstanding authorities.

The second edition is a reissue of the original two volumes with minor corrections, plus a third volume which brings the information up to date.

Volume 3 of the 1963 edition is made up of extended articles surveying chamber music since 1929 in Europe, Great Britain, the Soviet Union, and America. Editor and principal contributor is Colin Mason. The chapter on "Chamber music in America" is by Nicolas Slonimsky; the one on "Soviet chamber music" is by I. I. Martinov. Classified bibliography on chamber music; index of composers.

Review of the second edition by Homer Ulrich in *Notes*, 21 (1963–64), p. 124–26.

505. Comuzio, Ermanno. Film music lexicon. Pavia: Amministrazione Provinciale di Pavia, 1980. 304 p.

International in scope, providing biographical information on 580 musicians, listing the motion pictures for which they composed. "Filmografia" with entries from 1906 to 1980 on films with original music judged of particular value, films of a musical character (with subjects on symphonies, operas, ballets, or biographies of great musicians), musicals, and films featuring jazz, pop, and rock music. Index of names. Bibliography.

506. Heinzel, Erwin. Lexikon der Kulturgeschichte in Literatur, Bildender Kunst und Musik. Wien: Verlag Brüder Hollinek, 1962. 493 p.
A supplement to the succeeding work.

507. Heinzel, Erwin. Lexikon historischer Ereignisse und Personen in Kunst, Literatur und Musik. Wien: Verlag Brüder Hollinek, 1956. 782 p.
A dictionary treating the artistic, literary, and musical works based on the lives of historical persons or events. Entries arranged alphabetically with persons and events interfiled. The information includes a summary of the historical details followed by a classified listing of the works in which the person or event is represented.
Supplemented by no. 506. See also no. 509.

508. Hodgson, Julian. Music titles in translation; a checklist of musical compositions. London: Clive Bingley; Hamden, Connecticut: Linnet Books, 1976. 370 p.
A list of titles in one alphabetical sequence giving "the original or English language translation followed by the translation or original" of titles of musical compositions. The last name of the composer is included for each title. Excerpts are denoted by connection to the larger work.

509. Leipoldt, Friedrich. Lexikon der musischen Künste: Begriffe, Namen, Themen aus Musik, Malerei und Dichtung. Unter Mitarbeit von Clemens M. Gruber. Herrsching: M. Pawlak, [1986?]. 382 p.
A fascinating attempt to provide access to musical works by theme or reference to extramusical ideas. See also the work of E. Heinzel (no. 506 and 507).

510. Parsons, Denys. The directory of tunes and musical themes. Introduction by Bernard Levin. Cambridge, England: S. Brown, 1975. 288 p.
Identifies about 15,000 vocal and instrumental themes by representing the pitch direction of the first 16 notes in each theme. Includes a directory of popular tunes and a section on national anthems in musical notation coded to demonstrate the identification scheme.
Brief review by Stephen M. Fry in *Notes*, 32 (1976), p. 556–57.

511. Read, Gardner. Music notation: a manual of modern practice. 2nd ed. New York: Taplinger Pub. Co., 1979. 482 p.
First published in 1964.
A practitioner's guide to contemporary conventions of musical notation. Includes some discussion of advanced, radical solutions. See also no. 514.

512. Read, Gardner. Thesaurus of orchestral devices. New York: Pitman, 1953. 631 p.

Reprint by Greenwood Press, New York, 1969.

Intended to be a lexicon of instrumentation which will serve the student and/or professional orchestrator in the same manner and to the same degree that Bartlett's *Familiar Quotations* or Roget's *Thesaurus* aid both the student of literature and the established writer. [*Preface*]

Nomenclature in English, Italian, French, and German, with ranges of instruments, lists of devices, with reference to the page and measure number of the score. List of music publishers and their U.S. agents. Index of nomenclature and terminology. Also known familiarly as *Orchestral Devices*.

513. Reallexikon der Akustik. Herausgegeben von Michael M. Rieländer. Frankfurt am Main: Bochinsky, 1982. 461 p.

A technical dictionary with numerous diagrams and photographs. Bibliographic citations drawn almost entirely from German-language sources. There is a list of principal sources.

514. Risatti, Howard A. New music vocabulary. A guide to notational signs for contemporary music. Urbana, etc.: University of Illinois Press, 1975. 219 p.

This book has been organized into six chapters: Chapter I surveys general material pertinent to many instruments; succeeding chapters deal with one of the instrumental groups, and the sixth and final chapter deals with the voice. [Author's *Introduction*]

All the signs are graphically displayed, with explanation as to their meanings. There is a list of composers cited, a bibliography, and a general index. See also no. 511.

515. Schillinger, Joseph. Encyclopedia of rhythms: instrumental forms of harmony; a massive collection of rhythm patterns (evolved according to the Schillinger theory of interferences arrayed in instrumental form). New York: Da Capo, 1976. 250 p.

Reprint of edition of C. Colin, New York, 1966.

This is a practical handbook of rhythm patterns ... it presents ... the entire range of rhythm resources, making accessible to all who are interested in music the most normal, the most complex, and the most simple rhythm forms. [from the introductory remarks]

Arranged in two sections: rhythmic resultants; and analyzing rhythmic resultants with fractioning.

516. Slonimsky, Nicolas. Thesaurus of scales and melodic patterns. New York: Coleman-Ross, 1947. 243 p.

Reprinted by Duckworth, London, 1975.

Described by the author as "a reference book for composers in search of new materials." Contains nearly 1,000 scales, both traditional and contrived.

517. Whitfield, Jane Shaw. Songwriters' rhyming dictionary. Edited by Frances Stillman. North Hollywood, California: Melvin Powers, Wilshire Book Company, 1975. 283 p.

95

First published as *The improved rhyming dictionary*, 1951.

"Entries are grouped phonetically in orders of increasing syllabic complexity" [review by D. Martin Jenni in *Fontes Artis Musicae*, 23 (1976), p. 149–50]. Includes many non-English words. Includes a "Brief guide to English versification."

Histories and
Chronologies

We have been particularly selective in this area. The titles include only the standard general histories of music in the major European languages together with some of the more recent outline histories. Excluded are all histories devoted to the music of a particular national group and most early histories (pre-1850) unless—as in the case of Burney, Hawkins, Forkel, or Martini—they are of extraordinary interest and are currently available. Also excluded are histories of special periods and forms except as they occur as part of a comprehensive series. Music histories come and go, and few of those designed for the general reader, or for the music student, may be expected to outlive their time. This will account for the fact that some once-familiar occupants of library shelves, such as Dommer, Naumann, Rowbotham, and Rockstro, are missing from this list.

It is true of the early histories as it was of the early dictionaries that a number of titles have been restored to availability through modern reprint publication. We have indicated in the annotations which histories are available in reprint editions.

Warren Allen's *Philosophies of Music History* (no. 518) is not a history of music, but it is listed first in this chapter because it provides a "bibliography of literature concerning the general history of music in chronological order." This list covers works from 1600 to 1939. It is supplemented by S. T. Worsthorne's article "Histories" in the *Grove Dictionary of Music and Musicians*, 5th edition, vol. 4, p. 296–306, which provides chronological and systematic lists of histories of music.

HISTORIES

518 Allen, Warren D. "Bibliography of literature concerning the general history of music in chronological order." In his *Philosophies of Music History*. New York: American Book Co., 1939. P. 343–65.
Reprinted New York, Dover, 1962.
317 titles arranged chronologically from 1600 to 1939. Not all can be described as histories in the modern sense, but they have bearing on the development of music historiography.

519. Abbiati, Franco. Storia della musica. 2nd ed. Milano: Garzanti, 1944–54. 5 v.
A general history of music for Italian readers. Numerous pictorial and musical illustrations. Each major section is followed by an anthology of

excerpts from the writings of modern authorities on the period under consideration. There is a bibliography at the end of each volume.

Contents: Vol. I: *Roma, Medio Evo, Rinascimento.* Vol. II: *Seicento.* Vol. III: *Settecento.* Vol. IV: *Ottocento.* Vol. V: *Novecento.*

A revision was published in 1967–69 with a somewhat different organization of the material, compacting the Seicento and Settecento volumes into one.

520. Abraham, Gerald. The concise Oxford history of music. London, New York, Melbourne: Oxford University Press, 1979. 968 p.

A work that extends far beyond a condensation of *The New Oxford History of Music* (no. 564). It is one of the most informative of all one-volume histories, with extensive bibliographical references and an index.

Rev. by Paul Henry Lang in *Notes*, 37 (1980), p. 42–43, and by Kurt von Fischer in *Music and Letters*, 62 (1981), p. 68–70.

521. Adler, Guido. Handbuch der Musikgeschichte ... 2, vollständig durchgesehene und stark ergänzte Aufl. Berlin-Wilmersdorf: H. Keller, 1930. 2 v.

Unaltered reprint of the 2nd ed., Schneider, Tutzing, 1961, and Deutscher Taschenbuch-Verlag, München, 1975.

First printed in 1924 in one volume. Adler's *Handbuch* is the standard compendium of music history representing the fruits of German scholarship in its early period of expansion and influence. Major articles contributed by such authorities as Alfred Einstein, Wilhelm Fischer, Robert Haas, Friedrich Ludwig, Curt Sachs, Arnold Schering, Peter Wagner, and Egon Wellesz.

Contents: Bd. 1. Die Musik der Natur- und orientalischen Kulturvölker. Antike. Erste Stilperiode. Zweite Stilperiode. Bd. 2. Dritte Stilperiode.

522. Ambros, August Wilhelm. Geschichte der Musik... 3. gänzlich umbearb. Aufl. Leipzig: Leuckart, 1887–1911. 5 v.

Republication by Olms, Hildesheim, 1968.

One of the last major one-man histories of music. The author did not live to carry the fourth volume past the beginning of the 17th century. Based on original research, the work is particularly important for its coverage of the sources of Medieval and Renaissance music.

Bd. I: *Ancient Music.* 1862. 2nd ed., 1880. 3rd ed., 1887 (B. v. Sokolowsky, ed.).

Bd. II: *Music of the Middle Ages.* 1864. 2nd ed., 1880 (Otto Kade). 3rd ed., 1891 (Heinrich Riemann).

Bd III: *The Renaissance to Palestrina.* 1868. 2nd ed., 1893 (Otto Kade).

Bd. IV: (not completed by Ambros) *Italian Music, 1550–1650.* 1878 (Gustav Nottebohm and Carl F. Becker). 2nd ed., 1881. 3rd ed., 1909 (Hugo Leichtentritt).

Bd. V: *Musical Examples for Bd. III.* 1882 (Otto Kade). 2nd ed., 1887. 3rd ed., 1911.

The work by Wilhelm Langhans (no. 555) was intended to complete the Ambros history from the 17th through the 19th century.

523. Bernard, Robert. Histoire de la musique. [Paris]: F. Nathan, 1969–71. 5 v.

First published 1961–63. 3 v.

A history of music distinguished for its fine printing and rich illustrative material, including numerous plates in full color. The work lacks a bibliography or other documentation. Vol. 1 treats the history of European music to the end of the 18th century; vols. 2 and 3 are concerned with the 19th- and 20th-century developments in Europe and the Americas, with brief discussions of Oriental music.

A *Complément à l'Histoire de la Musique,* containing indexes and glossary, appeared in 1971.

524. Bourdelot, Pierre and Pierre Bonnet. Histoire de la musique et des ses effets. Paris: J. Cochart, 1715. 487 p.

Editions were also printed in Amsterdam, 1725, and The Hague, 1743. The Paris edition (1715) has been reprinted by Slatkine, Genève, 1969; the Amsterdam edition (1725) has been reprinted by the Akademische Druck- und Verlagsanstalt, Graz, 1966.

This is one of the first general histories of music. It was begun by Pierre Bourdelot, continued by his nephew, Pierre Bonnet, and finally completed and published by the brother of the latter, Jacques Bonnet.

525. Bücken, Ernst, ed. Handbuch der Musikwissenschaft. Wildpark-Potsdam: Akademische Verlagsgesellschaft Athenaion, [1927–31]. 13 v. in 10.

First issued serially in parts.

A series of monographs on various periods and aspects of music history by the leading German musicologists of the period. Well printed and profusely illustrated, including plates in color.

Reprinted by Musurgia, New York, 1949. 13 v. in 9.

[Vol. 1] Heinrich Besseler. *Die Musik des Mittelalters und der Renaissance* [1931]. 337 p.

[Vol. 2] Friedrich Blume. *Die evangelische Kirchenmusik* [1931]. 171 p. Re-edited under the title *Geschichte der evangelischen Kirchenmusik...* herausgegeben unter Mitarbeit von Ludwig Finscher, Georg Feder, Adam Adrio und Walter Blankenburg. Kassel: Bärenreiter, 1965.

Also published in an English translation as *Protestant Church Music: A History* with a foreword by Paul Henry Lang. (New York: W. W. Norton, 1974, and London: Victor Gollancz Ltd., 1975. 831 p.)

Review article by Werner Braun in *Die Musikforschung,* 21 (1968), p. 50–57.

Review of Blume's *Geschichte der evangelischen Kirchenmusik* by U. S. Leupold in *Notes,* 23 (1966), p. 45–46.

[Vol. 3] Ernst Bücken. *Geist und Form im musikalischen Kunstwerk* [1929]. 195 p.

[Vol. 4] Ernst Bücken. *Die Musik des 19. Jahrhunderts bis zur Moderne* [1929]. 319 p. Reprinted by Laaber Verlag, Laaber, 1979.

[Vol. 5] Ernst Bücken. *Die Musik des Rokokos und der Klassik* [1927]. 247 p.

[Vol. 6] Robert Haas. *Aufführungspraxis der Musik* [1931]. 298 p.

[Vol. 7] Robert Haas. *Die Musik des Barocks* [1929]. 290 p.

[Vol. 8, Pt. 1] Wilhelm Heinitz. *Instrumentenkunde* [1929]. 159 p.

[Vol. 8, Pt. 2] Robert Lachmann. *Die Musik der aussereuropäischen Natur- und Kulturvölker* [1929]. 33 p.

[Vol. 8, Pt. 3] Curt Sachs. *Die Musik der Antike* [1928]. 32 p.

[Vol. 8, Pt. 4] Peter Panóff. *Die Altslavische Volks- und Kirchenmusik* [1930]. 31 p.

[Vol. 9] Hans Mersmann. *Die moderne Musik seit der Romantik* [1928]. 225 p.

[Vol. 10] Otto Ursprung. *Die katholische Kirchenmusik* [1931]. 312 p.

526. Burney, Charles. A general history of music: from the earliest times to the present period. London: Printed for the author, 1776–89. 4 v.

Reprinted with critical and historical notes by Frank Mercer. London: Foulis; New York: Harcourt, 1935. 4 v. in 2. Reprint of the Mercer edition by Dover, New York, 1965. Reprinted by the Folio Society, London, 1969, and Eulenberg, London, 1974.

Burney shares with Sir John Hawkins (no. 546) credit for the emergence of music historiography in the latter part of the 18th century. In addition to its merits as a source of musical information, Burney's work is marked by high literary quality. It set a precedent for generations of music historians to follow.

527. Cannon, Beekman C., Alvin H. Johnson and William G. Waite. The art of music: a short history of musical styles and ideas. New York: Crowell, [1960]. 484 p.

Reprinted by Crowell in 1966.

Designed as an introduction to the history of music, presupposing little background. The "basic principles of music" are covered in an appendix. No bibliography. Brief musical examples in the text.

Review by Warner Imig in *Journal of Research in Music Education*, 9 (1961), p. 172.

528. Chailley, Jacques. 40,000 years of music. Translated from the French by Rollo Myers, with a preface by Virgil Thomson. London: Macdonald; New York: Farrar, Strauss & Giroux, 1964. 229 p.

Reprinted by Da Capo, New York, 1975.

Originally published by Libraries Plon, Paris, under the title *40,000 Ans de Musique*, 1961.

A provocative if somewhat disorganized approach to music history; treats the subject within the framework of sociology and the history of ideas.

529. Chi, Lien-k'ang. Ch'un ch'iu chan kuo yin yüeh shih liao. Hong Kong (?): 1980 or 1981. 104 p.

This is a selection of source readings from various Chinese classics of the Spring and Autumn period (722–481 B.C.) and the Warring States period (403–221 B.C.) concerning music. There is a bibliography of sources.

530. Combarieu, Jules. Histoire de la musique des origines au début du XXe siècle. Paris: A. Colin, 1946–60. 5 v.

Reprinted by Minkoff, Geneva, 1972.

Vols. 1–3 originally published 1913–19.

I: *Des origines à la fin du XVIe siècle.* II: *Du XVIIe siècle à la mort de Beethoven.* III: *De la mort de Beethoven au début du XXe siècle.* IV: *L'aube du XXe siècle* (by René Dumesnil, 1958). V: *La première moité du XXe siècle* (by René Dumesnil, 1960).

531. Confalonieri, Giulio. Storia della musica. Nuova edizione riveduta e aggiornata a cura di Alfredo Mandelli. Firenze: Sansoni; Milano: Accademia, 1968. 872 p.

First issued in 1958 by Nuova accademia editrice, Milano. 2 v.

A popular general history, lavishly printed on glossy paper, with 34 plates in full color and hundreds of black-and-white illustrations. No musical examples. Essential bibliography listed by chapter at the end of the second volume, where there is also a general index and an index of illustrations.

532. Contemplating music: source readings in the aesthetics of music. Selected and edited by Carl Dahlhaus and Ruth Katz. New York: Pendragon Press, 1986– . 4 v. (projected) (Aesthetics in music, no. 5–)
Projected in 4 v.
Contents: Vol. 1, *Substance* (1986); Vol. 2, *Import;* Vol. 3, *Essence;* Vol. 4, *Community of discourse.* Will include indexes.

533. Crocker, Richard L. A history of musical style. New York: McGraw-Hill, 1966. 573 p.
Reprinted by Dover, New York, 1986.
One of the few histories of music to focus attention consistently on musical style.
Crocker's book is discussed critically by Leo Treitler in "The present as history," an article in *Perspectives of New Music* (Spring–Summer 1969), p. 1–58.
Review by Martin Chusid in *Notes,* 23 (1967), p. 732–33; by Gwynn McPeek in *Journal of Research in Music Education,* 15 (1967), p. 333–36. Review by Henry Leland Clarke in *Journal of the American Musicological Society,* 21 (1968), p. 103–105.

534. Della Corte, Andrea. Antologia della storia della musica, dalla Grecia antica all'ottocento. 4. ed., rinnovata in uno volume. Torino: G. B. Paravia [1945]. 491 p.
First published in 1926 in 2 volumes.
An anthology of writings on music history, chiefly by modern European scholars, but with a few early documents (excerpts from Zarlino, Galilei, Caccini, Peri, etc.).

535. Della Corte, Andrea and Guido Pannain. Storia della musica. 4. riv. ed ampliata ed. Torino: Unione Tipografico-Editrice Torinese, 1964. 3 v.
First published in 1935; 2nd ed., 1942; reprinted, 1944.
The standard general history of music for Italian readers.
I: Dal medioevo al seicento. II: Il settecento. III: L'ottocento e il novecento.

536. Einstein, Alfred. A short history of music. 3rd American edition. New York: Knopf, 1947. 438 p.
Also issued as a paperback. Originally published in German, 1918.
One of the most perceptive and authoritative concise histories of music. Published in numerous editions and translations. Most editions incorporate a useful anthology of 39 musical examples, originally issued in 1917 as "Beispielsammlung zur älteren Musikgeschichte." The handsome illustrated edition edited by A. Hyatt King (London: Cassell, 1953) unfortunately does not contain the musical supplement.

537. Ferguson, Donald N. A history of musical thought. 3rd ed. New York: Appleton-Century-Crofts, [1959]. 675 p.

Reprinted by Greenwood Press, Westport, Connecticut, 1975. First published in 1935; 2nd ed., 1948.

An influential one-volume work designed for music history courses at college level. One of the first to propagate the results of German scholarship in America.

538. Finney, Theodore M. A history of music. Rev. ed. New York: Harcourt, 1947. 720 p.

Reprinted by Greenwood Press, Westport, Connecticut, 1976. First published in 1935. A well-organized student's history.

539. Forkel, Johann Nikolaus. Allgemeine Geschichte der Musik. Leipzig: im Schwikertschen Verlag, 1788–1801. 2 v.

Reprint by Olms, Hildesheim, 1962, and by the Akademische Druck- und Verlagsanstalt, Graz, 1967. Ed. by Othmar Wessely in the series *Die grossen Darstellungen der Musikgeschichte....*

The first full-scale history of music in German, by the scholar who has been called "the father of modern musicology." The work is incomplete, covering only as far as the early 16th century.

540. Girschner, Otto. Repetitorium der Musikgeschichte. Elfte Auflage. Köln: P. J. Tonger, 1941. 438 p.

A question-answer survey of music history produced during the Nazi era in Germany. Contains numerous anti-Semitic elements including, on p. 350–411, "Juden in der Musik," a biographical supplement first introduced in the 9th edition, 1936. See also the Stengel *Lexikon* (no. 166) as another example of a shameful practice.

541. Gleason, Harold. Music literature outlines. 2nd ed. Series 1–5. Bloomington: Frangipani Press, 1981. 5 v.

First published in Rochester by Levis Music Stores, 1949–55.

Ser. 1: *Music in the Middle Ages and Renaissance.* 2nd ed., 1951.
Ser. 2: *Music in the Baroque.*
Ser. 3: *Early American Music from 1620 to 1920.*
Ser. 4: *Contemporary American Music.*
Ser. 5: *Chamber Music from Haydn to Bartok.*

Historical outlines, or syllabi, with copious bibliographical references including discography. The organization of Series 1 and 2 follows closely that of the corresponding works by Reese and Bukofzer in the *Norton History of Music Series* (no. 566).

542. Grout, Donald Jay and Claude V. Palisca. A history of Western music. 4th ed. New York: Norton, 1988. 910 p.

First published in 1960, revised edition published in 1973. This work was issued under joint authorship first in 1980. All editions were also published in shortened form for use as a text, in 1964, 1973, and 1981. An anthology of scores, *The Norton Anthology of Western Music*, intended to accompany this book and edited by Claude Palisca, was issued first in 1980 and in a second edition in 1988.

Intended for undergraduate college music students or for the general reader. "An elementary knowledge of musical terms and of harmony ... has been assumed." Based on a stylistic approach. Contains numerous musical and pictorial illustrations. Annotated bibliography for further reading, a chronology of musical and historical events, and a glossary of terms.

Reviews of the 1960 edition by Albert T. Luper in *Notes*, 18 (1960), p. 47–48, by Warren Allen in *Journal of Research in Music Education*, 8 (1960), p. 124–26, and by Alec Harman in *Musical Times*, 103 (Dec. 1962), p. 845–47.

543. Gruber, Roman Il'ich. Istoriia muzykal'noi kyl'tury. Moskva: Gosudarstvennoe muzykal'noi izdatel stvo, 1941–59. 2 v.

A translation into Rumanian by Tatiana Nichitin was issued in Bucarest, 1963.

A general history of music from antiquity to the beginning of the 17th century, for Russian readers. Vol. 1, pt. 1, deals with Egypt, Mesopotamia, India, China, etc. as well as Greece and Rome. The final chapter of vol. 2 is concerned with the musical culture of the Western Slavs to the 17th century.

544. Handschin, Jacques. Musikgeschichte im Überblick. 2. ergänzte Auflage. Hrsg. von Franz Brenn. Luzern: Räber, 1964. 442 p.

First published in 1948. Reprint edition by Heinrichshofen, Wilhelmshaven, 1981. 450 p.

A stimulating short history weighted in the direction of medieval and Renaissance music. Chronological tables and a classified bibliography.

Review of the 2nd ed. by Joseph Müller-Blattau, in *Die Musikforschung*, 18 (1965), p. 441.

545. Harman, Alec and Wilfrid Mellers. Man and his music, the story of musical experiences in the West. New York and Oxford: Oxford University Press, 1962. 1,172 p.

First published in 1957–59 in four volumes covering medieval music through 20th-century music. Reprinted in London by Barrie & Rockcliffe, 1969, and by Barrie and Jenkins, 1977 and 1980.

A history designed for the intelligent layman, stressing the social and cultural backgrounds. Comparative chronology and a list of recommended books and music.

Review of vol. 2 by J. Merrill Knapp in *Notes*, 17 (1960), p. 569–70; of vols. 3 and 4 by William S. Newman in *Notes*, 15 (1957), p. 99–101; of the composite volume by Jack A. Westrup in *Music and Letters*, 43 (1962), p. 265–66.

546. Hawkins, Sir John. A general history of the science and practice of music. London: Payne and Son, 1776. 5 v.

New edition "with the author's posthumous notes," published by Novello, London, 1853, 3 v. (vol. 3 is an atlas of portraits); reprinted by Novello in 1875. Unabridged republication of the 1853 edition, with a new introduction by Charles Cudworth, New York: Dover, 1963. 2 v. Reprint by the Akademische Druck- und Verlagsanstalt, Graz, 1969. 2 v.

Hawkins' history appeared in the same year that the first volume of Charles Burney's history (no. 526) was published. The two works inevitably invite comparison, largely to Hawkins' disadvantage. His history, however, has much to recommend it. It contains extensive translations of excerpts from early theoretical works and includes many examples of early music.

Review by Bernard E. Wilson of the Dover reprint in *Notes*, 22 (1966), p. 1026–27.

547. Hermand, Jost, and James Steakley. Writings by German composers. New York: Continuum, 1984. 303 p.

Translated texts by 45 composers whose native language was German, from Johann Walther to Hans Werner Henze. Arranged in chronological order by composer and then chronologically within each composer's section. The acknowledgment section concluding the book provides a list of modern sources from which these texts were reprinted. Translators are credited.

548. Honolka, Kurt, ed. Knaurs Weltgeschichte der Musik. München and Zürich: Th. Knaur Nachf., 1968. 640 p.

Reprinted by the Rheingauer Verlagsgesellschaft, Wiesbaden, 1976, and by Doremer-Knaur, München and Zürich, 1979.

A general history with 500 illustrations and musical examples. 30 color plates.

Contributors: Hans Engel, Paul Nettl, Kurt Reinhard, Lukas Richter, and Bruno Stäblein.

549. Kiesewetter, Raphael Georg. Geschichte der europäisch-abendländischen oder unserer heutigen Musik. Darstellung ihres Wachsthumes und ihrer stufenweisen Entwicklung von dem ersten Jahrhundert des Christenthums bis auf unsere Zeit. Leipzig: Breitkopf und Härtel, 1834. 116 p.

A 2nd, enlarged edition appeared in 1846; this has been reprinted by Sändig, Wiesbaden, 1972. The work appeared in an English translation by Robert Müller (London: Newby, 1848). This, in turn, has been reprinted by Da Capo, New York, 1973, with a new introduction by Frank Ll. Harrison.

Kiesewetter's work is the first popular outline history of music in the modern sense. The author organizes his information in 17 different epochs, each characterized by the activity of one or more dominant musical individuals.

550. Knepler, Georg. Geschichte als Weg zum Musikverständnis: zur Theorie, Methode und Geschichte der Musikgeschichtsschreibung. 2., überarbeitete Aufl. Leipzig: Reclam, 1982. 664 p.

First published in 1977.

Knepler's *Geschichte* presents a thoroughly Marxist view of musical scholarship. Extensive bibliography.

551. Kretzschmar, Hermann. Kleine Handbücher der Musikgeschichte nach Gattungen. Leipzig: Breitkopf und Härtel, 1905–1922. 14 v. in 15.

All the volumes in this set have been reprinted by Olms, Hildesheim, 1967–72.

The Kretzschmar *Handbücher* are a series of historical monographs dealing with the development of specific musical forms or disciplines. Although superseded in many respects, these volumes remain basic studies in the areas with which they are concerned.

[Vol. 1] Arnold Schering. *Geschichte des Instrumentalkonzerts*.... 1905. 226 p. 2nd Aufl., 1927. Reprinted by Olms, Hildesheim, 1965 and 1972.

[Vol. 2] Hugo Leichtentritt. *Geschichte der Motette*. 1908. 453 p. Reprinted by Olms, Hildesheim, 1967, and Breitkopf und Härtel, Wiesbaden, 1967.

[Vol. 3] Arnold Schering. *Geschichte des Oratoriums*. 1911. 647 p. *Notenanhang*. 39 p. Reprinted by Olms, Hildesheim, 1966.

[Vol. 4.] Hermann Kretzschmar. *Geschichte des neuen deutschen Liedes*. Teil 1. Von Albert bis Zelter (all published). 1911. 354 p. Reprinted by Olms, Hildesheim and Breitkopf und Härtel, Wiesbaden, 1977.

[Vol. 5] Eugen Schmitz. *Geschichte der Kantate und des geistlichen Konzerts*. Teil 1. Geschichte der weltlichen Solokantate (all published). 1914. 327 p. 2nd. Aufl., 1955. Reprinted by Olms, Hildesheim, 1966.

[Vol. 6] Hermann Kretzschmar. *Geschichte der Oper*. 1919. 286 p. Reprinted by Sändig, Wiesbaden, 1970.

[Vol. 7] Hermann Kretzschmar. *Einführung in die Musikgeschichte*. 1920. 82 p. Also cited as no. 650.

[Vol. 8] Johannes Wolf. *Handbuch der Notationskunde*. Teil 1. Tonschriften des Altertums und des Mittelalters.... Teil 2. Tonschriften der Neuzeit, Tabulaturen, Partitur, Generalbass und Reformversuche. 1913–19. 2 v. Reprinted by Olms, Hildesheim, 1963. Also cited as no. 1811.

[Vol. 9] Hugo Botstiber. *Geschichte der Ouvertüre und der freien Orchesterformen*. 1913. 274 p. Reprinted by Sändig, Wiesbaden, 1969.

[Vol. 10] Georg Schünemann. *Geschichte des Dirigierens*. 1913. 359 p. Reprinted by Olms, Hildesheim, 1965.

[Vol. 11] Peter Wagner. *Geschichte der Messe*. Teil 1. Bis 1600 (all published). 1913. 548 p. Reprinted by Olms, Hildesheim, 1963.

[Vol. 12] Curt Sachs. *Handbuch der Musikinstrumentenkunde*. 1920. 412 p. Reprinted by Olms, Hildesheim, 1967. Also cited as no. 332.

[Vol. 13] Adolf Aber. *Handbuch der Musikliteratur*.... 1922. 696 cols. Reprinted by Olms, Hildesheim, and Breitkopf und Härtel, 1967. Also cited as no. 671.

[Vol. 14] Karl Nef. *Geschichte der Sinfonie und Suite*. 1921. 344 p. Reprinted by Sändig, Wiesbaden, 1970 and 1981.

552. De La Fage, J. Adrien. Histoire générale de la musique et de la danse. Tome premier. Paris: Antiquité Comptoir des Imprimeurs, 1844. 614 p.

30 p. of musical examples published separately with 28 plates of illustrations.

Noteworthy for its wide range of interest in music of other cultures, a forerunner of ethnomusicology.

553. Laborde, Jean Benjamin de. Essai sur la musique ancienne et moderne. Paris: Impr. de P. D. Pierres, et se vend chez E. Onfroy, 1780. 4 v.

Reprint by the Akademische Druck- und Verlagsanstalt, Graz, and by the AMS Press, New York, 1978.

Laborde's work is the major French contribution to music historiography of the 18th century, but it suffers by comparison to Burney and Hawkins because it is not a chronological history. The *Essai* is a vast assemblage of information on musical ethnology, iconography, organology, history, biography, and other humanistic concerns. Much attention is directed toward French lyric poetry and the chanson.

554. Lang, Paul Henry. Music in Western civilization. New York: Norton, 1941. 1,107 p.

This work has been widely translated (into German, Spanish, Portuguese, Czech, Japanese, etc.).

Music in the context of the social, political, and cultural currents of Western civilization. One of the most influential of all music histories produced in America, it coincided with, and contributed to, the general acceptance of music history in American higher education. Bibliography of literature in all languages in one alphabet, p. 1045–65.

555. Langhans, Wilhelm. Die Geschichte der Musik des 17. 18. und 19. Jahrhunderts in chronologischem Anschlusse an die Musikgeschichte von A. W. Ambros. Leipzig: F. E. C. Leuckart, 1884. 2 v.

Written as a continuation of Ambros' unfinished history (no. 522).

Manuel, Roland. See Roland-Manuel, no. 576.

556. Martini, Giovanni Battista. Storia della musica. Bologna: Lelio dalla Volpe, 1757–81. 3 v.

Reprint by the Akademische Druck- und Verlagsanstalt, Graz, 1967. Edited and supplied with an index by Othmar Wessely.

In spite of its archaic methodology, and the fact that Martini did not live to carry his history beyond the music of the ancients, it was an influential work and a sourcebook for later historians.

Review of the reprint edition by Jack A. Westrup in *Music and Letters*, 49 (1968), p. 55–57; and by Werner Kümmel in *Die Musikforschung*, 22 (1969), p. 238–39.

557. Music and aesthetics in the eighteenth and early nineteenth centuries. Edited by Peter Le Huray and James Day. Cambridge, England: Cambridge University Press, 1981. 597 p. (Cambridge readings in the literature of music)

Published in an abridged edition in 1988. 399 p.

> This first collection of materials is designed to illustrate some of the main aesthetic issues that were so hotly and continuously debated during the eighteenth and early nineteenth centuries. The second—which is to follow—will contain as it were evidence of the ways in which aesthetic attitudes were given practical expression—evidence in many forms, ranging from the musical novella to evaluations of individual composers and analyses of specific compositions. [*Preface*]

Almost 100 source readings in chronological order by about 80 writers. Each reading begins with an introduction setting the context and with suggestions for further reading. Sources are cited. There is a bibliography and an index of names, titles, and places as well as a general index.

558. Music in early Christian literature. Edited by James McKinnon. Cambridge and New York: Cambridge University Press, 1987. 180 p. (Cambridge readings in the literature of music)

Translations of writings from the Patristic period about music. This work is a Strunk *Source Readings* (no. 581) for the early medieval period. Bibliography. Index.

559. Music in the Western world, a history in documents. Selected and annotated by Piero Weiss and Richard Taruskin. New York: Schirmer Books; London: Collier Macmillan, 1984. 556 p.

A collection of source readings arranged chronologically intended for undergraduate students of Western music history. Sources noted and each is provided with an introduction establishing context. Glossary. Index of names, works, and subjects.

560. Muzykal'naia zhizn' Moskvy v pervye gody posle Oktiabria. Oktiabr 1917–1920. Khronika. Dokumenty. Materialy. [Musical life of Moscow in the first years after October.] [Compiled by] Svetlana Romanova Stepanova. Moskva: Sov. Kompozitor, 1972. 336 p.

A collection of source materials. Includes bibliographical references.

561. Muzykal'naia éstetika Rossii odinadtsatogo-vosemnadtsatogo vekov. [Dokumenty i materialy]. Sost. tekstov, perevody i obshchaia vstupit. stat'ia. [Compiled by] Aleksandr Ivanovich Rogova. Moskva: Muzyka, 1973. 245 p. (Pamiatniki muzykalno-ésteticheskoi mysli)

A collection of source documents on Russian musical aesthetics in the 11th–18th centuries. Includes bibliographical references.

562. Nef, Karl. An outline of the history of music. Translated by Carl Pfatteicher. New York: Columbia University Press, 1935. 400 p.

Originally published as *Einführung in die Musikgeschichte* in 1920. Many reprintings. An augmented French edition by Yvonne Rokseth appeared in 1931.

An excellent outline history for use in college or university courses. Brief yet comprehensive, readable yet scholarly. Rich in bibliographical information and musical examples in the text.

563. Neues Handbuch der Musikwissenschaft. Hrsg. von Carl Dahlhaus. Wiesbaden: Akademische Verlagsgesellschaft Athenaion; Laaber: Laaber-Verlag Müller-Buscher, 1980–. 10 v.

Contents:

Vol. 4: *Die Musik des 17. Jahrhunderts.* Hrsg. von Werner Braun.

Vol 5. : *Die Musik des 18. Jahrhunderts.* [Hrsg. von] Carl Dahlhaus, unter Mitarbeit von Ludwig Finscher, *et al.*

Vol. 6: *Die Musik des 19. Jahrhunderts.* [Hrsg. von] Carl Dahlhaus.

Vol. 7: *Die Musik des 20. Jahrhunderts.* [Hrsg. von] Hermann Danuser.

Vol. 8–9: *Aussereuropäische Musik* (Teil 1–2). [Hrsg. von] Hans Oesch, unter Mitarbeit von Peter Ackermann [und] Max Haas, *et al.*

Vol. 10: *Systematische Musikwissenschaft.* [Hrsg. von] Carl Dahlhaus [und] Helga de la Motte-Haber.

Each volume serves as a kind of guide to the study of the period or realm of musicology that is the topic of the volume, with each chapter prepared by an expert or team of experts in the specialty. In addition to discussions of methodology, problems, and directions, there are bibliographies, maps, discographies, tables of pertinent information, and indexes.

Volume 10 also cited as no. 665.

564. The new Oxford history of music. London and New York: Oxford University Press, 1954–. 10 v. to date.

Each volume is a composite work made up of contributions by scholars of international repute and edited by a specialist in the period. The set is planned in 10 volumes plus a volume of chronological tables and a general index.

There is an accompanying set of recordings issued under the title *The History of Music in Sound* with illustrated booklets designed for teaching purposes. All recordings and pamphlets have appeared.

Vol. 1: *Ancient and Oriental Music.* Ed. by Egon Wellesz. 1957. 530 p.

Review by Curt Sachs in *Notes*, 16 (1957), p. 97–99; by Roy Jesson in *Musical Quarterly*, 44 (1958), p. 245–53; by Charles Seeger in *Ethnomusicology*, 3 (1959), p. 96–97.

Vol. 2: *Early Middle Ages to 1300.* 2nd ed., by Richard Crocker and David Hiley. 1990. 795 p. Originally issued as *Early Medieval Music up to 1300.* Ed. by Anselm Hughes. 1955. 434 p.

Review by Charles Warren Fox in *Musical Quarterly*, 41 (1955), p. 534–47; by Jeremy Noble in *Music and Letters*, 36 (1955), p. 65–70.

Vol. 3: *Ars Nova and the Renaissance (1300–1540).* Ed. by Anselm Hughes and Gerald Abraham. 1960. Reprinted with corrections, 1986. 563 p.

Review by Richard H. Hoppin in *Musical Quarterly*, 47 (1961), p. 116–25; by Thurston Dart in *Music and Letters*, 42 (1961), p. 57–60.

Vol. 4: *The Age of Humanism, 1540–1630.* Ed. by Gerald Abraham. 1968. 978 p.

Review by Howard M. Brown in *Notes*, 26 (1969), p. 133–36; by Paul Doe in *Music and Letters*, 51 (1970), p. 66–69; by Claude V. Palisca in *Journal of the American Musicological Society*, 23 (1970), p. 133–36.

Vol. 5: *Opera and Church Music (1630–1750).* Ed. by Anthony Lewis and Nigel Fortune. 1975. Reprinted with corrections and revised bibliography, 1986. 869 p.

Vol. 6: *Concert Music (1630–1750).* Ed. by Gerald Abraham, 1986. 786 p.

Vol. 7: *The Age of Enlightenment (1745–1790).* Ed. by Egon Wellesz and Frederick Sternfeld. 1973. 724 p.

Review by Daniel Heartz in *Musical Times*, 115 (April 1974), p. 295–301.

Vol. 8: *The Age of Beethoven (1790–1830).* Ed. by Gerald Abraham. 1982, Reprinted with corrections, 1985. 747 p.

Vol. 9: *Romanticism* (1830–1890). Ed. by Gerald Abraham. 1990. 935 p.

Vol. 10: *The Modern Age (1890–1960).* Ed. by Martin Cooper. 1974. 764 p.

Vol. 11: Chronological tables and general index not yet published.

565. Nijenhuis, Emmie te. Musicological literature. Wiesbaden: Harrassowitz, 1977. 51 p. (A History of Indian literature, 6: Scientific and technical literature, Fasc. 1)

An essay on musicological works in India with a bibliography.

566. The Norton history of music series. New York: Norton, 1940–.

A publisher's series consisting of independent works on different periods in the history of music. The volumes by Reese, Austin, and Bukofzer are particularly rich in bibliographical content.

Curt Sachs. *The Rise of Music in the Ancient World, East and West.* 1943. 324 p.

Gustave Reese. *Music in the Middle Ages.* 1940. 502 p. Also cited in no. 987.

Also published in an Italian edition under the title *La Musica nel Medioevo* (Florence: Sansoni, 1964. 642 p.). Much new illustrative material has been added to this edition.

Gustave Reese. *Music in the Renaissance.* 1954. 1,022 p. Revised edition, 1959. Also cited in no. 988.

Review by Denis Stevens in *Music and Letters*, 36 (1955), p. 70–73; by Edgar H. Sparks in *Notes*, 17 (1960), p. 569.

Manfred Bukofzer. *Music in the Baroque Era, from Monteverdi to Bach.* 1947. 489 p.

Alfred Einstein. *Music in the Romantic Era.* 1947. 371 p.

William W. Austin. *Music in the 20th Century from Debussy through Stravinsky.* 1966. 708 p.

Also printed by Dent, London, 1967.

Review by Peter Evans in *Music and Letters*, 49 (1968), p. 43–47; by Henry Leland Clarke in *Journal of Research in Music Education*, 15 (1967), p. 174–76.

567. Norton introduction to music history series. New York: Norton, 1978– . 2 v. (to date).

Destined to supplant the *Norton History of Music Series* (no. 566).

Philip G. Downs: *Classical music; the era of Haydn, Mozart, and Beethoven*, 1992. 697 p. The *Anthology of Classical music* (Norton, 1992. 554 p.) is the score supplement.

Richard Hoppin: *Medieval Music*, 1978. 566 p. The *Anthology of Medieval Music* (Norton, 1978. 177 p.) is the score supplement.

Leon Plantinga: *Romantic Music; a History of Musical Style in Nineteenth-Century Europe*, 1984. 523 p. The *Anthology of Romantic Music* (Norton, 1984. 637 p.) is the score supplement.

Robert P. Morgan: *Twentieth-century music; a history of musical style in modern Europe and America*, 1990. 554 p. The *Anthology of twentieth-century music* (Norton, 1992. 452 p.) is the score supplement.

568. The Oxford history of music. 2nd ed. London: Oxford University Press, 1929–38. 7 v. (plus an introductory volume).

First printed in 1901–1905 in six volumes. Volumes 4–6 of the 2nd edition are reprints of the original volumes.

Introductory volume edited by Percy C. Buck. 1929. 239 p.

A symposium by nine scholars covering Greek and Hebrew music, notation, musical instruments, theory to 1400, plainsong, folk song, social aspects of music in the Middle Ages. Chapter bibliographies, p. 233–39.

Vols. 1–2: H. E. Wooldridge. *The Polyphonic Period.* 2nd rev. ed. by Percy C. Buck. 1928–32.

Vol. 3: C. Hubert Parry. *The Music of the 17th Century.* 1938. 486 p.

Vol. 4: A. J. Fuller-Maitland. *The Age of Bach and Handel.* 2nd ed. 1931. 362 p.

Vol. 5: W. H. Hadow. *The Viennese Period.* 1931. 350 p.

Vol. 6: Edward Dannreuther. *The Romantic Period.* 1931. 374 p.

Vol. 7: H. C. Colles. *Symphony and Drama, 1850–1900.* 1934. 504 p.

Still valuable, but succeeded by the *New Oxford History of Music* (no. 564).

569. The Pelican history of music. Edited by Alec Robertson and Denis Stevens. Harmondsworth, Middlesex: Penguin Books, 1960–69. 3 v.

Reissued by Barnes and Noble, New York, under the title *A History of Music*.

Vol. 1: *Ancient Forms to Polyphony.* Vol 2: *Renaissance and Baroque.* Vol. 3: *Classical and Romantic.*

A popular history of music with contributions from leading authorities, including the editors: Alec Robertson, "Plainchant"; Denis Stevens, "Ars antiqua"; Gilbert Reaney, "Ars nova"; Peter Crossley-Holland, "Non-Western music"; Hugh Ottaway, "The 19th century"; etc.

Review of vol. 3 by William S. Newman in *Notes*, 26 (1970), p. 504–506.

570. The Prentice-Hall history of music series. Englewood Cliffs, New Jersey: Prentice-Hall, 1965– .

A publisher's series for which H. Wiley Hitchcock serves as general editor. Short, one-volume surveys by leading American scholars covering the major historical periods as well as folk and non-Western music. The numbering of the volumes below is arbitrary.

[Vol. 1] Bruno Nettl. *Folk and Traditional Music of the Western Continents* with chapters on Latin America by Gérard Béhague. 2nd ed. 1973. 258 p.

Review by Alfred W. Humphreys in *Journal of Research in Music Education*, 13 (1965), p. 259–60; by Fritz Bose in *Die Musikforschung*, 21 (1968), p. 107–108; by Wolfgang Suppan in *Jahrbuch für Volksliedforschung*, 12 (1967), p. 217–18.

[Vol. 2] William P. Malm. *Music Cultures of the Pacific, the Near East, and Asia.* 2nd ed. 1977. 236 p.

[Vol. 3] Jeremy Yudkin. *Music in Medieval Europe.* 1989. 612 p. with two 90-minute cassettes of musical examples.

Yudkin's work succeeds that of Albert Seay, *Music in the Medieval World* (2nd ed. 1975. 182 p.).

[Vol. 4] Claude V. Palisca. *Baroque Music.* 3rd ed. 1991. 356 p.

Review by David Burrows in *Notes*, 25 (1969), p. 717–18.

[Vol. 5] Reinhard G. Pauly. *Music in the Classic Period.* 3rd ed. 1988. 265 p.

Review by Eugene Helm in *Notes*, 25 (1968), p. 40–41.

[Vol. 6] Rey M. Longyear. *Nineteenth-century Romanticism in Music.* 3rd ed. 1988. 367 p.

[Vol. 7] Eric Salzman. *Twentieth-century Music: An Introduction.* 3rd ed. 1988. 380 p.

[Vol. 8] H. Wiley Hitchcock. *Music in the United States: A Historical Introduction.* 3rd ed. 1988. 365 p.

Review by Ross Lee Finney in *Notes*, 26 (1969), p. 271–72.

[Vol. 9] Howard M. Brown. *Music in the Renaissance.* 1976. 384 p.

[Vol. 10] Bonnie C. Wade. *Music in India: The Classical Traditions.* 1978. 252 p.

[Vol. 11] Gérard Béhague. *Music in Latin America, an Introduction.* 1979. 369 p. Also cited as no. 1084.

571. Printz, Wolfgang Caspar. Historische Beschreibung der edelen Sing- und Kling kunst.... Dresden: J. C. Mieth, 1690. 240 p.

Reprint by the Akademische Druck- und Verlagsanstalt, Graz, 1964. Edited and indexed by Othmar Wessely.

This work has been described as the first history of music. Printz's observations are based largely on Biblical authority and legend, but his work exercised considerable influence on 18th century lexicographers and historians.

572. Prunières, Henry. A new history of music; the Middle Ages to Mozart. Trans. and ed. by Edward Lockspeiser. New York: Macmillan, 1943. 413 p. Originally published as *Nouvelle Histoire de la Musique.* Paris: 1934–36. 2 v. Reprint by Vienna House, New York, 1972.
Valuable for its emphasis on the earlier periods.

573. Readings in the history of music in performance. Selected, translated and edited by Carol MacClintock. Bloomington: Indiana University Press, 1979. 432 p.
Selected sources on the history of performance practice. Lacks index. Review by James Pruett in *Notes*, 36 (1980), p. 892–93.

574. Renner, Hans. Geschichte der Musik. Stuttgart: Deutsche Verlags-Anstalt, 1965. 704 p.
Also published as *Musikgeschichte der Büchergilde.*
A well-illustrated student's history. Traditional chronological arrangement with useful appendixes devoted to notation, voice ranges, the composition of orchestras, musical instruments, and glossary. Index of names and subjects.

575. Riemann, Hugo. Handbuch der Musikgeschichte. 2nd ed. [Edited by Alfred Einstein.] Leipzig: Breitkopf und Härtel, 1920–23. 2 v. in 4.
First published in 1904–1913. Reprint by Johnson Reprint Corporation, New York, 1972.
A product of one of the most vigorous and stimulating minds in German musicology, always provocative, frequently misleading. Extensive chapter bibliographies and sections devoted to brief biographies of musicians; the emphasis, however, is on musical styles and forms. Numerous transcriptions of early music, all of which must be viewed in the light of Riemann's unorthodox editorial methods.

576. Roland-Manuel, ed. Histoire de la musique. Nouv. ed. Paris: Gallimard, 1981. 2 v. (Encyclopédie de la Pléiade, 9 and 16)
First published 1960–63 and reprinted in 1977.
Vol. 1: *"Des origines à Jean-Sebastien Bach."* 2,238 p. Vol. 2: *"Du XVIIIe. siècle à nos jours."* 1,878 p.
An important work. The language is French but the approach is international, consisting of contributions by specialists from many different countries. Vol. 1 begins with a chapter on "Éléments et genèses," followed by surveys of the music of non-Western cultures, of ancient and oriental music, and of the music of the Moslem world. Thereafter the organization is chronological within individual countries. At the end of vol. 2 there are chapters devoted to contemporary music and to the history of musicology and of criticism. Each volume has a chronological table and index, plus an analytical table of contents.

577.   Rowen, Ruth Halle. Music through sources and documents. Englewood Cliffs, New Jersey: Prentice-Hall, 1979. 386 p.

Following in the tradition of Strunk's *Source Readings* (no. 581), chronologically ordered translations of excerpts of 103 source documents, each provided with historical and bibliographical background. Index of names and subjects.

Review by James W. Pruett in *Notes*, 36 (1980), p. 892–93.

578.   Sachs, Curt. Our musical heritage, a short history of music. 2nd ed. Englewood Cliffs, New Jersey: Prentice-Hall, 1955. 351 p.

First published in 1948. Reprinted by Greenwood Press, Westport, Connecticut, 1978.

Designed as a textbook for introductory courses in music history. References to essential bibliography.

579.   Salazar, Adolfo. La música en la sociedad europea. [México]: El Colegio di México, 1942–46. 9 parts in 4 v.

Reprinted by Alianza, Madrid, 1982.

A general history for Spanish readers, from antiquity to the end of the 19th century.

580.   Smijers, Albert, ed. Algemeene muziekgeschiedenis; geïlustreerd overzicht der Europeesche muziek van de oudheid tot heden. 4. bijgewerkte druk. Utrecht: W. de Haan, 1947. 518 p.

1st edition, 1938; 2nd edition, 1940.

A composite history in eight books, each written by a different Dutch or Flemish scholar. Short bibliographies after each book. Plates and numerous musical illustrations.

581.   Strunk, W. Oliver. Source readings in music history from classical antiquity through the romantic era. New York: Norton, 1950. 919 p.

Reissued in a paperback edition, 1965. 5 v.

87 items extracted from the writings of theorists, composers, teachers, critics, and practical musicians, arranged chronologically under topics. Each item is introduced with a few concise and illuminating comments by the editor. The translations are excellent, the editorial work exemplary. An indispensable volume in any library of music history.

Review by Manfred Bukofzer in *Notes*, 8 (1951), p. 517–18; by Erich Hertzmann in *Musical Quarterly*, 37 (1951), p. 430–32; by Leo Schrade in *Journal of the American Musicological Society*, 4 (1951), p. 249–51.

582.   Subirá, José. Historia de la música. 3. ed. reformada, amplicada, y puesta al dia. Barcelona: Editorial Salvat, 1958. 4 v.

First published in 1947; 2nd edition, 1951.

Handsomely printed and illustrated, musically and pictorially. Some emphasis on ethnomusicology. The approach is generally chronological, but with chapters on the development of notation, 17th-century theory, and performance practice.

583.   Time, place and music. An anthology of ethnomusicological observation c. 1550 to c. 1800, by Frank Ll. Harrison. Amsterdam: Frits Knuf, 1973. 221 p. (Source materials and studies in ethnomusicology, 1)

A compendium of written observations by travelers on non-Western musical cultures.

584. Ulrich, Homer and Paul Pisk. A history of music and musical style. New York: Harcourt, 1963. 696 p.

> The authors' purpose in writing this history of music has been to offer a clear, straightforward presentation of historical developments in musical style. [*Preface*]

Review by Susan Thiemann in *Notes*, 20 (1963), p. 638–42.

585. Wiora, Walter. The four ages of music. Translated by M. D. Herter Norton. New York: Norton, 1965. 233 p.

Originally issued by W. Kohlhammer Verlag, Stuttgart, 1961, under the title *Die vier Weltalter der Musik* (Urban-Bücher, 56). Also published in France as *Les Quatres Ages de la Musique, de la Préhistoire à l'Éra de la Technique*.

An original approach to music history and its periodization, treating the subject in the context of universal history and anthropology.

Review by Johannes Riedel in *Journal of Research in Music Education*, 13 (1965), p. 260–61; by Rose Brandel in *Notes*, 24 (1968), p. 695–97.

586. Wörner, Karl H. Geschichte der Musik. Ein Studien- und Nachschlagebuch. 7. durchgesehen und erg. von Ekkehard Kreft. Göttingen: Vandenhoeck u. Ruprecht, 1980. 692 p.

First published in 1954; 2nd ed., 1956; 3rd ed., 1961; 4th ed., 1965; 5th ed., 1972; 6th ed., 1975.

A well-organized outline history of music with excellent bibliographical information. Utilizes a variety of approaches: stylistic, national, biographical. Paragraphs are numbered for easy reference.

A 5th edition, in English translation, has been issued by the Free Press, New York, 1973.

MUSICAL ICONOGRAPHY

The change in the title of this section from the third edition's "Music History in Pictures" is meant to convey the change in emphasis in historical musicology. Increasingly musical iconography has become a branch of scholarship with its own principles, methodologies, and literature. At the same time, writers of histories of music have become more conscious of the value of including numerous well-chosen images in their texts. The tradition, begun in 1929 by George Kinsky in his *Geschichte der Musik in Bildern* (no. 595), is very much alive and flourishing. Meanwhile other scholars and publishers have compiled anthologies of images incorporating some reference to music as important adjuncts to the study of music by period, place, and genre; the extensive series *Musikgeschichte in Bildern* is an example of this activity.

There is an international body devoted to all aspects of musical iconography, the Répertoire Internationale d'Iconographie Musicale, with headquarters at the Graduate Center of the City University of New York. RIdIM produces a *Newsletter* that publishes important articles on the subject, relates the activities of the organization, and reports on scholarship in musical iconography that is under way or published elsewhere.

587. Besseler, Heinrich and Max Schneider, ed. Musikgeschichte in Bildern. Leipzig: Deutscher Verlag für Musik, 1961– . v. 1– .
A multivolume work projected to cover all periods in the history of music as well as some of the systematic branches. Publication of the volumes and their respective subsections (Lieferungen) has not necessarily followed in chronological order. Each issue contains numerous plates, with commentary, a bibliography, chronological tables, and indexes. The following issues have been released to date:

Band I: Musikethnologie

Lief. 1: Paul Collaer. *Ozeanien.* 1965. 234 p.
Review by Dieter Christensen in *Die Musikforschung*, 20 (1967), p. 339–41; by Bruno Nettl in *Notes*, 23 (1966), p. 276; by Wolfgang Suppan in *Jahrbuch für Volksliedforschung*, 16 (1971), p. 262–64.

Lief. 2: Paul Collaer. *Amerika: Eskimo und indianische Bevölkerung.* 1967. 211 p.
Review by Fritz Bose in *Die Musikforschung*, 22 (1969), p. 522–23; by Bruno Nettl in *Notes*, 24 (1968), p. 717–18.

Lief. 3: Paul Collaer, unter Mitarbeit von Emmy Bernatzik, [*et al.*]. *Südostasien.* 1979. 181 p.

Lief. 4: Alain Daniélou, trans. by Fritz Bose. *Südasien: die indische Musik und ihre Traditionen.* 1978. 146 p.

Lief. 8: Paul Collaer [und] Jürgen Elsner; unter der Mitarbeit von Brahim Bahloul, [*et al.*]. *Nordafrika.* 1983. 205 p.

Lief. 9: Jos Gansemans [und] Barbara Schmidt-Wrenger. *Zentralafrika.* 1986.

Lief. 10: Gerhard Kubik unter Mitarbeit von Jim de Vere Allen, [*et al.*]. *Ostafrika.* 1982. [252] p.

Band II: Musik des Altertums

Lief. 1: Hans Hickmann. *Ägypten.* 1961. 187 p.
Review by Caldwell Titcomb in *Journal of the American Musicological Society*, 17 (1964), p. 386–91; by Fritz Bose in *Die Musikforschung*, 17 (1964), p. 184–85.

Lief. 2: Subhi Anwar Rashid. *Mesopotamien.* 1984. 182 p.

Lief. 4: Max Wegner. *Griechenland.* 1964. 143 p.
Review by Emanuel Winternitz in *Journal of the American Musicological Society,* 19 (1966), p. 412–15.

Lief. 5: Günter Fleischhauer. *Etrurien und Rom.* 1965. 195 p.

Lief. 7: Samuel Marti. *Alt-Amerika; Musik der Indianer in präkolumbischer Zeit.* 1970. 195 p.
Review by Wolfgang Suppan in *Jahrbuch für Volksliedforschung,* 16 (1971), p. 262–64.

Lief. 8: Walter Kaufmann unter Mitarb. von Joep Bor, Wim van der Meer, und Emmie te Nijenhuis. *Altindien.* 1981. 208 p.

Lief. 9: F. M. Karomatov. *Mittelasien.* 1987.

Band III: Musik des Mittelalters und der Renaissance

Lief. 2: Henry George Farmer. *Islam.* 1966. 206 p.
Review by Emmy Wellesz in *Music and Letters,* 49 (1968), p. 73–74; by Essa Zonis in *Journal of the American Musicological Society,* 22 (1969), p. 293–96.

Lief. 3: Joseph Smits van Waesberghe. *Musikerziehung.* 1969. 214 p.
Review by Hans Oesch in *Literature, Music, Fine Arts,* 5 (1972), p. 232–33. Also cited as no. 1006.

Lief. 4: Bruno Stäblein. *Schriftbild der einstimmigen Musik.* 1975. 257 p.

Lief. 5: Heinrich Besseler und Peter Gülke. *Schriftbild der mehrstimmigen Musik.* 1973. 183 p.

Lief. 8: Edmund A. Bowles. *Musikleben im 15. Jahrhundert.* 1977. 189 p.

Lief. 9: Walter Salmen. *Musikleben im 16. Jahrhundert.* 1976. 205 p.

Band IV: Musik der Neuzeit

Lief. 1: Hellmuth Christian Wolff. *Oper, Szene und Darstellung von 1600 bis 1900.* 1968. 214 p.
Review by Karl Michael Komma in *Literature, Music, Fine Arts,* 1 (1968), p. 220–22; by Christoph-Hellmut Mahling in *Die Musikforschung,* 23 (1970), p. 97–99.

Lief. 2: Heinrich W. Schwab. *Konzert: Öffentliche Musikdarbietung vom 17. bis 19. Jahrhundert.* 1971. 230 p.

Lief. 3: Walter Salmen. *Haus- und Kammermusik zwischen 1600 und 1900.* 1969. 203 p.

115

588 Brown, Howard Mayer and Joan Lascelle. Musical iconography; a manual for cataloguing musical subjects in Western art before 1800. Cambridge, Massachusetts: Harvard University Press, 1972. 220 p.

Intends to present a workable cataloging scheme addressing problems of providing access to images on musical subjects, and to promote standardization of cataloging in an effort to increase cooperation among scholars of musical iconography. There is an introductory essay on "what works of art teach us about music." Following, there are rules and guidelines for cataloging works of art in 11 sections. Appendixes of common names for instruments with cross-references, and subject entries gathered to date. Includes bibliographical references.

589.   Cohen, H. Robert. Les gravures musicales dans *l'Illustration*. 1843–1899. Avec la collaboration de Sylvia L'Ecuyer Lacroix et Jacques Léveillé. Québec: Presses de l'Université Laval, 1983. 3 v.

Reproductions of 3,360 engravings from the important 19th-century French periodical *l'Illustration* with a thesaurus of images to direct the reader to appropriate images. A treasure of 19th-century French musical life.

590.   Collaer, Paul and Albert Van der Linden. Historical atlas of music: a comprehensive study of the world's music, past and present ... with the collaboration of F. van den Bremt. Preface by Charles van den Borren. Translated by Allan Miller. Cleveland, Ohio: World Pub. Co., 1968. 175 p.

Also published by Harrap, London and Toronto, 1968. Originally published as *Atlas Historique de la Musique* by Elsevier, Paris, 1960.

An illustrated survey of music history, with 15 full-page maps and more than 700 illustrations.

Review by Robert E. Wolf in *Musical Quarterly*, 47 (1961), p. 413–16.

591.   Crane, Frederick. A bibliography of the iconography of music. Iowa City: University of Iowa, 1971. 41 p.

Typescript bibliography of articles, catalogs, illustrated histories, and other studies distributed at the IAML meeting of 1971.

592.   Dufourcq, Norbert, ed. La musique des origines à nos jours. Préface de Claude Delvincourt. Nouv. éd., rev., augm. Paris: Larousse, 1954. 591 p.

The reprinting of a work first published in 1946 and carried through seven editions.

Richly illustrated compendium of music history and related fields, the work of 44 scholars, chiefly French. Organized in 5 books, of which the third (p. 83–431) deals with the history of Western music. Other books treat the voice and instruments, ancient and Near Eastern music, non-European music, and musical aesthetics. A series of 17 appendixes covers special topics such as notation, theory, criticism, libraries and other institutions. With 6 colored plates and numerous black-and-white illustrations.

593.   Dufourcq, Norbert. La musique, les hommes, les instruments, les œuvres. Paris: Larousse, 1965. 2 v.

Tome 1: "La musique, des origines à la mort de Rameau." Tome 2: "La musique, de l'aube du classicisme à la periode contemporaine."

This work is an expansion of the preceding. The articles are contributed by leading authorities, chiefly French. A fine, visually oriented history of music. It also serves as the basis for another Larousse publication: *Larousse Encyclopedia of Music*, ed. by Jeoffrey Hindley (New York: World Publishing Co., 1971).

594. Imago musicae: international yearbook of musical iconography. Official organ of the International Repertory of Musical Iconography. Edited by Tillman Seebass, assisted by Tilden Russell. Basel, etc.: Bärenreiter; Durham, North Carolina: Duke University Press, 1985–90. v. 1–5. Lucca: Libreria Musicale Italiana Editrice, 1991– . v. 6– .

Includes: articles on specific artistic works and collections of works; articles on cultural life, especially as concerned with music and the visual arts; catalogs and inventories of collections (real and synthetic) of art works that incorporate musical images; and a bibliography of writings on musical iconography. "Bibliografia" in vol. 1 covers 1975–81; in vol. 2 covers 1981–83.

595. Kinsky, Georg. A history of music in pictures. New York: Dutton, 1937. 363 p.

Originally published in German as *Geschicte der Musik in Bildern* in 1929; first English edition, 1930. Reprint, New York, Dover, 1951. There is also a French edition.

Pictures include musicians' portraits; music in painting, drawing, and sculpture; facsimile pages of early musical and theoretical works; early instruments. Arranged chronologically from antiquity to the early 20th century. Index to instruments, place names, and personal names.

596. Komma, Karl Michael. Musikgeschichte in Bildern. Stuttgart: Alfred Kröner, 1961. 332 p.

743 well-reproduced illustrations covering the history of music from ancient times to the present; detailed commentary on each illustration.

Review by Hans Engel in *Die Musikforschung*, 18 (1965), p. 440–41.

597. Lang, Paul Henry and Otto Bettmann. A pictorial history of music. New York: Norton, 1960. 242 p.

The text is based on Lang's *Music in Western Civilization* (no. 554) with selected illustrations. Inferior reproduction technique.

598. Leppert, Richard D. The theme of music in Flemish painting of the seventeenth century. München and Salzburg: E. Katzbichler, 1977. 2 v.

A catalog of 770 paintings with indexes to instruments and themes as well as a plethora of ancillary data.

Review by François Lesure in *Fontes Artis Musicae*, 25 (1978), p. 197.

599. Lesure, François. Musik und Gesellschaft im Bild. Zeugnisse der Malerei aus sechs Jahrhunderten.... Aus dem Französischen von Anna Martina Gottschick. Kassel: Bärenreiter, 1966. 245 p. 105 plates, 24 in color.

Skillful use of pictorial materials to illuminate the musical-social structure of European culture from the 14th through the 19th centuries.

Review by Steven J. Ledbetter in *Notes*, 24 (1968), p. 702–704.

600. Michels, Ulrich. DTV-Atlas zur Musik: Taf. u. Texte. München: Deutscher Taschenbuch-Verlag; Kassel: Bärenreiter, 1980–1985. 2 v.

Published also by Alianza, Madrid (1982–), as *Atlas de Música*.

Includes music. Includes bibliographies and indexes. Also known as *Atlas zur Musik*.

Contents: Bd. 1. Systematischer Teil. Historischer Teil: von den Anfängen bis zur Renaissance. 5. Aufl. Bd. 2. Historischer Teil: vom Barock bis zur Gegenwart.

601. Pincherle, Marc. An illustrated history of music. Edited by Georges Bernier and Rosamond Bernier. Translated by Rollo Myers. Rev. ed. New York: Reynal; London: Macmillan, 1962. 230 p.

Published in France under the title *Histoire Illustrée de la Musique* (Paris: Gallimard, 1959).

A beautifully designed volume, with 200 illustrations in black and white, 40 in full color. The text is planned as an introduction to music history but maintains a high standard of accuracy and critical comment. The work lacks a bibliography or any other documentation apart from the illustrations.

Review by Denis Stevens in *Musical Times*, 101 (Aug. 1960), p. 493; by Emanuel Winternitz in *Notes*, 18 (1960), p. 48–50; by Jack A. Westrup in *Music and Letters*, 41 (1960), p. 388.

602. Sopeña Ibáñez, Federico and Antonio Gallego Gallego. La música en el Museo del Prado. Madrid: Dirección General de Bellas Artes. Ministerio de Educación y Ciencia. Patronato Nacional de Museos, 1972. 308 p.

A splendidly illustrated book devoted to works of art in the Prado with musical symbols or interest. Bibliography.

603. Vorreiter, Leopold. "Musikikonographie des Altertums im Schrifttum 1850–1949 und 1950–1974." In *Acta Musicologica*, 46 (1974), p. 1–42.

A narrative bibliography of 532 titles devoted to writings providing information on the iconography of ancient music. Part 2 treats writings related to the iconography of ethnic music in general.

CHRONOLOGIES

604. Burbank, Richard. Twentieth century music. Introduction by Nicolas Slonimsky. New York: Facts on File, 1984. 485 p.

> The book reports and describes musical events ... between January 1900 and December 1979. It includes events in opera, dance, instrumental and vocal music, births, deaths, debuts and related events, thoughts, ideas, declarations and statements on music ... [Author's *Preface*].

> Bibliography. Index to names and titles.

605. Chailley, Jacques. Chronologie musicale en tableaux synoptiques. Paris: Centre de Documentation Universitaire et S.E.D.E.S. réunis, 1955– . 140 p.

Part I: 310 to 1600.

A workbook of musical chronology, with parallel tables of political, literary, and artistic events. Most detailed for the period prior to the 15th century.

606. Cullen, Marion Elizabeth. Memorable days in music. Metuchen, New Jersey: Scarecrow, 1970. 233 p.

A chronology of musical events by day of year with popular quotations regarding music inserted for each day. Lists important persons' birth and death days, premieres, and other significant days.

607. Detheridge, Joseph. Chronology of music composers. Birmingham, England: J. Detheridge, 1936–37. 2 v.

Reprint, 1972, by The Scholarly Press, St. Clair Shores, Michigan.

Vol. I: 820–1810. Vol. 2: 1810–1913.

More than 2,500 names of composers arranged chronologically by date of birth. Brief comments on their activity, fields of composition, nationality. Numerous inaccuracies and misleading statements, but valuable for its comprehensive coverage. Alphabetical list of names.

608. Dufourcq, Norbert, Marcelle Benoit and Bernard Gagnepain. Les grandes dates de l'histoire de la musique. 2e. éd. Paris: Presses Universitaires de France, 1976. 127 p.

Dates of events, with historical commentary, from the first century A.D. to 1960. Organized according to periods: Middle Ages, Renaissance, 17th, 18th, 19th, and 20th centuries.

609. Eisler, Paul E. World chronology of music history. Dobbs Ferry, New York: Oceana Publication, 1972– . v. 1– .

An ambitious multivolume survey of the chronology of music, projected in 8 to 10 volumes. According to the publisher it will contain, when completed, over 100,000 entries covering all significant dates in music history: composers, compositions, performers, premieres, and other pertinent dates.

Contents: vol. 1. 30,000 B.C.–A.D. 1594; vol. 2. 1594–1684; vol. 3. 1685–1735; vol. 4. Name index (vols. I–III); vol. 5. 1736–1786; vol. 6. 1771–1796.

610. Gangwere, Blanche. Music history from the late Roman through the Gothic periods, 313–1425: a documented chronology. Westport, Connecticut: Greenwood Press, 1986. 247 p. (Music reference collection, 6)

A synopsis of important topics arranged chronologically and in outline form. References from each topic are provided to sources and secondary works cited in the principal bibliography. Maps and "supplemental sources" are provided for each period. The outline for the Romanesque period, for instance, covers background, philosophy, the birth of polyphony, St. Martial period, and terms. There are appended: a general bibliography; a discography; an author-composer index; and a subject index, the last not providing any cross-references for common names of manuscripts. The bibliographies, general and supplemental, consist primarily of English-language sources.

This is an interesting, if somewhat simplistic, concept and potentially quite useful in providing an overview to nonspecialists or as a foil to specialists. The text is occasionally difficult to read because of the quality of reproduction.

In 1991, Greenwood published Gangwere's next "documented chronology," *Music history during the Renaissance period, 1425–1520* (Music reference collection, 28). 492 p.

611. Hall, Charles J. Hall's musical years; the twentieth century 1900–1979. A comprehensive, year-by-year survey of the fine arts. Northbrook, Illinois: Opus, 1980. 1 v. Unnumbered p.

Greenwood Press of New York and London published three related works as numbers 20, 21, & 25 in their *Music Reference Series: A Twentieth-Century Musical Chronicle: Events, 1900–1988*, 1989, 347 p.; *A Nineteenth-Century Musical Chronicle: Events, 1800–1899*, 1989, 375 p.; *An Eighteenth-Century Musical Chronicle: Events, 1750–1799*, 1990, 177 p.

In outline form, lists historical events, debuts, prizes, works of art, books on music and other subjects, births and deaths of musicians and others, and musical compositions for each year. A useful concatenation of facts, musical and otherwise. Derived from the author's years of compiling program notes for WAUS, one of Michigan's fine arts radio stations.

612. Hendler, Herb. Year by year in the Rock Era: events and conditions shaping the rock generations that reshaped America. Westport, Connecticut: Greenwood Press, 1983. 350 p.

Essentially a chronicle of political, social, and popular musical events. Bibliography: p. 339–50.

613. Lahee, Henry Charles. Annals of music in America; a chronological record of significant musical events from 1640 to the present day, with comments on the various periods into which the work is divided. Freeport, New York: Books for Libraries Press, 1970. 298 p.

Reprint of a work first published in 1922. Also reprinted by AMS Press, New York, 1969.

614. Manson, Adele P. Calendar of music and musicians. Metuchen, New Jersey: Scarecrow Press, 1981. 462 p.

A day-by-day list of important musical events. Indexes to personal and corporate names and to titles.

Review by Michael Ochs in *Notes*, 38 (1982), p. 612–13.

615. Mattfeld, Julius. Variety music cavalcade, 1620–1961; a chronology of vocal and instrumental music popular in the United States. Introduction by Abel Green. 3rd ed. Englewood Cliffs, New Jersey: Prentice-Hall, 1971. 766 p.

Originally appeared in a modified form as *Variety Radio Directory 1938–39*, supplemented in weekly issues of the periodical *Variety*. First issued as *Variety Music Cavalcade 1620–1950* in 1952. A revised edition appeared in 1962.

A chronological bibliography of American popular music, with parallel social, cultural, and historical events listed for each year. Index of musical works by title, with dates of first publication.

Review by Irving Lowens in *Notes*, 20 (1963), p. 233–34.

616. Mies, Paul and Norbert Schneider. Musik im Umkreis der Kulturgeschichte. Ein Tabellenwerk aus der Geschichte der Musik, Literatur, bil-
denden Künste, Philosophie und Politik Europas. Köln: P. J. Tonger, 1953.
2 v.
Vol. 1: chronological tables of musical periods and events. Vol. 2: parallel
tables of history, philosophy, literature, art, and architecture.

617. La Revue Musicale. La musique 1900–1950. Documents du demi-siècle;
tableau chronologique des principales œuvres musicales de 1900 à 1950,
établé par genre et par année. Paris: 1952. 1 v. Various pagings.

618. Saathen, Friedrich. Musik im Spiegel der Zeit: synchronoptische Taf.
zur Musikgeschichte Europas mit einem lexikalischen Personen- u. Sach-
verzeichnis. Wien: Universal Edition, 1975. 47 p. 3 tables.
Tables showing European musical events in chronological order. A brief
dictionary of persons and topics is included.

619. Schäffer, Boguslaw. Maly informator muzyki XX wieku. Wyd. 3 nowe.
Krakow: Polskie Wydaw. Muzyczne, 1975. 384 p.
A chronology of musical events of the 20th century.

620. Schering, Arnold. Tabellen zur Musikgeschichte, ein Hilfsbuch beim
Studium der Musikgeschichte. Fünfte Auflage bis zur Gegenwart ergänzt
von Hans Joachim Moser. Wiesbaden: Breitkopf & Härtel, 1962. 175 p.
First published in 1914; 3rd edition, 1921; 4th edition, 1934.
Chronological tables outlining the important events in music history
from antiquity to 1962, including birth and death dates of musicians, the
principal events of their lives, significant publications and performances,
dates marking the activity of important music centers, and stylistic developments. Parallel historical and cultural events given. The 4th edition contained a 30-page supplement giving the contents of the major *Denkmäler*
and *Gesamtausgaben* published by Breitkopf & Härtel. The 5th edition
deletes this but offers an index of names and subjects.

621. Slonimsky, Nicolas. Music since 1900. 4th ed. New York: Charles Scribner's Sons, 1971. 1,595 p.
Supplement to Music since 1900. 1986. 390 p. Includes additions, am-
plifications, and corrections. Appendix of formerly secret U.S. Army documents and documents from the Cultural Revolution of the People's Republic of China. Index.
First published by Norton, New York, 1937; 2nd edition, 1938; 3rd edition, 1949.
Contains a "Tabular view of stylistic trends in music, 1900–1969." "Descriptive chronology: 1900–1969." Letters and documents. There is an index to the descriptive chronology. The first two editions contained a "Concise biographical dictionary of 20th-century musicians," omitted in later
editions.
The chronology records significant events in the development of contemporary music: dates of composition and first performance, the founding of institutions and societies, births and deaths of contemporary musicians. International in scope, but with increased emphasis on American

music for the past two decades. An appendix quotes many of the major documents in the history of contemporary music.

The 4th edition includes a dictionary of terms (p. 1421–1502).

Review by Jack A. Westrup in *Music and Letters*, 53 (1972), p. 447–48 and by Nyal Williams in *Notes*, 30 (1973), p. 283–84.

622. Thompson, Oscar. Tabulated biographical history of music. New York: Harcourt, Brace, 1936.

13 folding charts tracing the major events in the careers of more than 100 musicians from Guido d'Arezzo (c. 995) through 1936.

Guides to Systematic and Historical Musicology

This chapter cites works intended to introduce the student to the methods, materials, and philosophy of musical research, as well as some current issues in some of the subdisciplines. These works vary widely in pattern and approach, some being concerned with the content, others with the method, of the discipline. Some emphasize the historical aspects of research, others the systematic. A few anthologies addressing the "state of the art" are included. Especially in this chapter, the compilation is *not* intended to be exhaustive. The reader will find useful bibliographies of writings on musicology in the article "Musicology" by Vincent H. Duckles *et al.* in the *New Grove* (no. 635), in Lincoln Spiess's *Historical Musicology, Appendix I*, by Ernst C. Krohn (no. 662), and in *Perspectives in Musicology*, compiled by Barry S. Brook (no. 628). A useful assemblage of articles is *Musicology in the 1980s: Methods, Goals, Opportunities* (no. 657). Perhaps the most important and stimulating book to appear recently on the subject is Joseph Kerman's *Contemplating Music: Challenges to Musicology* (no. 649).

The general discussion of musical scholarship titled "Musikwissenschaft," by Walter Wiora and Hans Albrecht in *MGG* (no. 43), with its excellent but now dated bibliography, can no longer be regarded as the single best statement of the goals, aspirations, structure, and philosophy of musical scholarship. More than ever diversity is the rule, and no single work can be said to encompass the myriad of possibilities inherent in musical scholarship. Psychohistory, semiotics, information theory, computer science, and linguistics have joined other nonmusical disciplines with influence upon the musical subjects we take up and the ways we approach and report them. A comprehensive definition of the field may not be possible and perhaps is not even desirable.

623. Adler, Guido. Methode der Musikgeschichte. Leipzig: Breitkopf & Härtel, 1919. 222 p.

Reprint by Gregg International, 1971.

This, along with the author's *Der Stil in der Musik* (1929), is a basic study of the content and method of historical musicology. Contains a bibliographical supplement, "Verzeichnis von bibliographischen Hilfswerken für musikhistorische Arbeiten," compiled by Wilhelm Fischer, now outdated but of interest as a listing of music references prior to World War I.

624. Barbag, Seweryn. Systematyka muzykologji. Lwów: "Lwowskie Wiadomości Muzyczne i Literackie," 1928. 111 p.

A Polish manual of musicological method, with bibliographical supplements: p. 56–91, general works of musicological interest; p. 91–98, Polish works of musicological interest.

625. Benestad, Finn. Musikk og tanke: Hovedretininger i musikkestetikkens historie fra antikken til vår egen tid. Oslo: H. Aschehoug, 1976. 468 p.

Subtitle is "Main currents in the history of music aesthetics from ancient times to our own."

A survey of the aesthetics of music.

Review by Sven Hansell in *Notes*, 34 (1977), p. 81–84.

626. Bengtsson, Ingmar. Musikvetenskap, en översikt. Stockholm: Esselte Studium, 1973. 448 p.

An outstanding Swedish survey of the content and methods of musicology. Bibliography.

627. Broeckx, Jan L. Methode van de muziekgeschiedenis, met een inleiding door Prof. Dr. F. Van der Mueren. Antwerpen: Metropolis, 1959. 368 p.

A comprehensive survey of the methods and content of historical musicology. The three major divisions of the work treat (1) basic concepts, (2) working procedures, and (3) terminology. Numerous bibliographical references in the text and in a bibliographical appendix, p. 329–39.

628. Brook, Barry S., Edward O. D. Downes and Sherman Van Solkema. Perspectives in musicology. The inaugural lectures of the Ph.D. program in music at the City University of New York. New York: W. W. Norton, 1972. 363 p.

Reprinted by Pendragon, New York, 1985.

15 scholars, American and European, assess the position of their discipline and project its future.

P. 335–46: "Musicology as a discipline: a selected bibliography."

629. Chailley, Jacques. Précis de musicologie. Nouvelle éd. Paris: Presses Universitaires de France, 1984. 490 p.

First published in 1958. 431 p.

A syllabus published under the auspices of the Institute of Musicology of the University of Paris. Contributions by 25 French musicologists covering varied aspects of musical research. The emphasis is historical. Main approach is chronological, but there are chapters devoted to music bibliography, ethnomusicology, instruments, dance, philosophy, and aesthetics. Bibliography is stressed throughout. Indexed.

630. Crawford, Richard. American studies and American musicology: a point of view and a case in point. Brooklyn: Institute for Studies in American Music, Brooklyn College of the City University of New York, 1975. 33 p. (Institute for Studies in American Music, I. S. A. M. monographs, 4)

Includes a second essay called "A hardening of the categories: vernacular, cultivated, and reactionary in American psalmody."

631. Current thought in musicology. Edited by John W. Grubbs, with the assistance of Rebecca A. Baltzer, Gilbert L. Blount, and Leeman Perkins. Austin: University of Texas Press, 1976. 313 p.

Contents:
"Tractatus esthetico-semioticus; model of the systems of human communication" by Charles Seeger.
"The ecstatic and the didactic; a pattern in American music" by Charles Hamm.
"Music and the time screen" by Elliott Carter.
"Instruments and voices in the fifteenth-century chanson" by Howard M. Brown.
"Nottebohm revisited" by Lewis Lockwood.
"The chanson in the humanist era" by Daniel Heartz.
"Musicology, history, and anthropology; current thoughts" by Gilbert Chase.
"The prospects for research in Medieval music in the 1970s" by Gilbert Reaney.
"The library of the mind; observations on the relationship between musical scholarship and bibliography" by Vincent H. Duckles.

632. Dahlhaus, Carl. Einführung in die systematische Musikwissenschaft. Unter Mitarbeit von Tibor Kneif, Helga de la Motte-Haber und Hans-Peter Reinecke. Köln: Musikverlag Hans Gerig, 1971. 202 p.
Chapters on "Naturwissenschaftliche Grundlagen der Musik"; "Musikpsychologie"; "Musiktheorie"; "Musikästhetik"; "Musiksoziologie." These essays introduce the subdisciplines, present some of the current thinking, problems, and situations, and conclude with bibliographies.

633. Dahlhaus, Carl. Foundations of music history. Translated by J. A. Robinson. Cambridge: Cambridge University Press, 1983. 177 p.
Translation of *Grundlagen der Musikgeschichte*, first published by Musikverlag Hans Gerig, Cologne, 1967, and subsequently by Laaber-Verlag, Laaber, 1982. Published in an Italian translation by Discanto Edizioni in Florence as *Fondamenti di Storiografia Musicale* in 1980 (212 p.).

> The following ... historiographic reflections, which were occasioned, or rather provoked, by the obvious and disproportionate lack of theory in my own discipline as compared to the veritable welter of theoretical writings in general history, sociology and epistemologically oriented philosophy, are not meant to be an introduction to the basic facts of music history. Nor are they intended as a textbook of historical method. [*Preface*]

634. Druesedow, John E., Jr. Library research guide to music; illustrated search strategy and sources. Ann Arbor, Michigan: Pierian Press, 1982. 86 p. (Library research guides series, 6)
An introductory guide for undergraduate students that includes a list of basic reference sources for courses in music.
Ann P. Basart describes this work as "the first book on library research strategy and sources specifically designed for music undergraduates," in *Cum Notis Variorum*, 63 (June 1982), p. 13.
Review by Ann P. Basart in *Notes*, 39 (1982), p. 153.

635. Duckles, Vincent H. "Musicology." In *The New Grove Dictionary of Music and Musicians*, edited by Stanley Sadie, v. 12, p. 836–63. By Vincent H. Duckles with Howard Meyer Brown, George S. Buelow, Marc Lindley, Lewis Lockwood, Miloš Velimirovic and Ian D. Bent. London: Macmillan, 1980.

An essay on the nature, disciplines, and national traditions of musicology, approached historically and systematically. Discusses the various specialties within the discipline and notes stellar achievements. Bibliography arranged in chronological order.

636. Eggebrecht, Hans Heinrich. Reflexionen über Musikwissenschaft Heute, ein Symposium. Kassel: Bärenreiter, 1972. 80 p.

First printed in the proceedings of the international congress of the Gesellschaft für Musikforschung, Bonn, 1970.

Statements by 11 musicologists on their views of the state of the discipline, with discussion from the floor.

637. Erdely, Stephen. Methods and principles of Hungarian ethnomusicology. Bloomington: Indiana University; The Hague: Mouton and Co., 1965. 150 p. (Indiana University Publications, Uralic and Altaic Series, 52)

Review by Benjamin Rajaczky in *Jahrbuch für Volksliedforschung*, 12 (1967), p. 233–34, and by John S. Weissmann in *Ethnomusicology*, 11 (1967), p. 129–31.

638. Fellerer, Karl G. Einführung in die Musikwissenschaft. 2. neubearb. und erweiterte Aufl. Münchberg: B. Hahnefeld, 1953. 190 p.

First published in 1942.

Historical musicology plays a comparatively minor role in this survey of the content of musical knowledge. Emphasis is on the systematic areas: acoustics, aesthetics, psychology, sociology, and pedagogy. Extensive bibliographies for each chapter.

Review by Glen Haydon in *Notes*, 11 (1953), p. 111–12; anon. in *Die Musikforschung*, 8 (1955), p. 96–97.

639. The Garland library of the history of Western music. General editor: Ellen Rosand. New York and London: Garland Publishing, 1985. 14 v.

Reprint of articles originally published 1940–82.

This anthology of modern musicological writings is neither history nor handbook or guide to the practice of musicology. It may serve as a convenient anthology for the practicing scholar and as a repertory of exemplars for the student of musicology.

Text chiefly in English, but also includes articles in French, German, and Italian. Includes bibliographical references.

Contents: vol. 1. *Medieval music I, monophony;* vol. 2. *Medieval music II, polyphony;* vol. 3. *Renaissance music, part I;* vol. 4. *Renaissance music, part II;* vol. 5. *Baroque music I, seventeenth century;* vol. 6. *Baroque music II, eighteenth century;* vol. 7. *Classic music;* vol. 8. *Eighteenth- and nineteenth-century source studies;* vol. 9. *Nineteenth-century music;* vol. 10. *Twentieth-century music;* vol. 11. *Opera I, up to Mozart;* vol. 12. *Opera II, Mozart and after;* vol. 13. *Criticism and analysis;* vol. 14. *Approaches to tonal analysis.*

640. Garrett, Allen M. An introduction to research in music. Washington, D.C.: Catholic University of America Press, 1958. 169 p.

A rather superficial attempt to survey the content and methods of musicology in a course intended for first-year graduate students in music.

Review by Donald J. Grout in *Notes*, 16 (1959), p. 247–49.

641. Harrison, Frank Ll., Mantle Hood and Claude V. Palisca. Musicology. Englewood Cliffs, New Jersey: Prentice-Hall, 1963. 337 p. (The Princeton studies: humanistic scholarship in America)

Reprinted by Greenwood Press, Westport, Connecticut, 1974.

Harrison writes on "American musicology and the European tradition," Palisca on "American scholarship in Western music," and Hood on "Music, the unknown." Stimulating, thoughtful statements on the place of musicology in the world of learning. The work has already exerted a wide influence on discussions of the nature and purposes of musical scholarship in America. See Joseph Kerman's paper on "A profile for American musicology," in *Journal of the American Musicological Society*, 18 (1965), p. 61–69, and the reply by Edward Lowinsky, "Character and purposes of American musicology," in the same journal, p. 222–34.

Review by Jan LaRue in *Journal of the American Musicological Society*, 17 (1964), p. 209–214; by Vincent Duckles in *Notes*, 21 (1964), p. 368–69; by Paul Henry Lang in a review editorial in *Musical Quarterly*, 50 (1964), p. 215–26. Joint review by Charles Seeger, Lincoln B. Spiess, and David McAllester in *Anuario, Inter-American Institute for Musical Research*, 1 (1965), p. 112–18.

642. Haydon, Glen. Introduction to musicology: a survey of the fields, systematic and historical, of musical knowledge and research. New York: Prentice-Hall, 1941. 329 p.

Unaltered reprint by the Univ. of North Carolina Press, Chapel Hill, 1969, and by Greenwood Press, Westport, Connecticut, 1978.

Systematic musicology (acoustics, psychology, aesthetics, theory, and pedagogy) is the major emphasis of this work. Historical musicology is treated only in the last 54 pages. Chapter bibliographies, with a general bibliography at the end, p. 301–313.

643. Helm, Eugene and Albert T. Luper. Words and music: form and procedure in theses, dissertations, research papers, book reports, programs, and theses in composition. Rev. ed. Totowa, New Jersey: European-American Music Corporation, 1982. 91 p.

First published in Hackensack, New Jersey, by Joseph Boonin, 1971, 78 p., and then in an edition with new copyright information in 1978 by the European-American Music Corporation, Clifton, New Jersey, 79 p.

A manual emphasizing the technical and mechanical aspects of academic literature.

644. Herndon, Marcia and Norma McLeod. Field manual for ethnomusicology. Norwood, Massachusetts: Norwood Editions, 1983. 137 p.

A handbook of suggestions for "minimizing the subjectivity of synchronic field investigations" and conducting ethnomusicological field work. Brief bibliography.

645. Hood, Mantle. The ethnomusicologist. New ed. Kent, Ohio: Kent State University Press, 1982. 400 p.

First published by McGraw-Hill, New York, 1971. 386 p.

A stimulating and practical exposition of what ethnomusicologists are and do. Illustrated.

Review by Willard Rhodes in *Musical Quarterly*, 58 (1972), p. 136–41.

646. Husmann, Heinrich. Einführung in die Musikwissenschaft. 3e. Aufl. Wilhelmshaven: Heinrichshofens Verlag, 1980. 291 p.
First published in Heidelberg by Quelle und Meyer, 1958. 268 p. Subsequently published in 2nd ed. by Heinrichshofen, 1975.
An introduction to systematic musicology. Much attention is given to the acoustical and psychological aspects of the subject. The approach embraces all musical phenomena in all cultures. Extensive bibliography organized by chapter headings, p. 235–55.
Review of the 1st edition by Werner Korte in *Die Musikforschung* 13 (1960), p. 340–42.

647. Irvine, Demar B. Writing about music, a style book for reports and theses. 2d ed., rev. and enl. Seattle and London: University of Washington Press, 1968. 211 p.
A much enlarged edition of a work first published in 1956.
A guide to the preparation of the research report in music, with detailed instructions regarding the preparation of the manuscript, documentation, use of illustrations, abbreviations, and the improvement of literary style.

648. Karbusicky, Vladimir. Systematische Musikwissenschaft: eine Einführung in Grundbegriffe, Methoden und Arbeitstechniken. München: W. Fink, 1979. 250 p.
An introduction to the fundamentals, methods, and working practices of musicological studies. This book is used as a text in the musicology program of the University of Hamburg.

649. Kerman, Joseph. Contemplating music; challenges to musicology. Cambridge, Massachusetts: Harvard University Press, 1985. 255 p.
Simultaneously published by Fontana, London, as *Musicology.*

This book is, ultimately, one musician's analysis of modern ideas and ideologies of music. It deals with musicology and other fields of music study mainly as he has apprehended them in the United States and Britain in the years since the Second World War. [Author's *Acknowledgments*]

One of the most important books about musicology and its relationship to other musical and nonmusical disciplines. It serves as a personal survey of the most important recent developments in Anglo-American musical scholarship and as a polemical commentary on the practice of musicology. Bibliography of main works cited.
Reviews by Erich Leinsdorf in the *New York Times Book Review* (26 May 1985), p. 19; Robert Winter in the *New York Review of Books* (18 July 1985), p. 23; by Christopher Wintle in the *Times Literary Supplement* (10 May 1985), p. 525; and by Julie E. Cumming in *Cum Notis Variorum*, 88 (December 1984), p. 7–11. Reviews also by Julian Rushton in *Music and Letters*, 67 (1985), p. 195–96; by Curtis Price in *Musical Times*, 127 (January 1986), p. 26–28; by Peter Evans in *Music Analysis*, 5 (1986), p. 97–103; by David Fallows in *Early Music*, 13 (1985), p. 573–75; and by John Harbison in *Musical Quarterly*, 72 (1986), p. 416–18.

650. Kretzschmar, Hermann. Einführung in die Musikgeschichte. Leipzig: Breitkopf & Härtel, 1920. 82 p. (Kleine Handbücher der Musikgeschichte, 7)
Reprinted by Sändig, Wiesbaden, 1970.

A brief, narrative account of the content of and sources for the historical study of music. Relevant literature is mentioned in context. Chapter 1 traces the development of music historiography through the 19th century. Also cited in no. 551.

651. Kunst, Jaap. Ethnomusicology; a study of its nature, its problems, methods and representative personalities to which is added a bibliography. 3rd much enl. ed. of *Musicologica.* The Hague: M. Nijhoff, photomechanical reprint, 1969. 303 p.

Reprint of the 1959 edition. Supplement to the 3rd edition of *Ethnomusicology;* 2nd edition published 1969. 46 p.

A fundamental work with an extensive bibliography (p. 79–215) based on Kunst's own collection of materials.

652. Lehrbuch der Musikwissenschaft. Herausgegeben von Ekkehard Kreft; Redaktion, Erhard Johannes Bücker. Düsseldorf: Schwann, 1985. 699 p.

A compendium of basic and representative facts on music, music theory, music history, and systematic musicology presented in essay form with copious musical examples. This work is intended to provide the background information useful in proceeding with a professional career in music studies or in appreciating products of such studies as an informed amateur. It is strongly slanted to a German point of view. Each section concludes with footnotes, a list of music examples, and a bibliography of relevant literature.

653. Lissa, Zofia. Wstep do muzykologii. Wyd. 1. Warszawa: Panstwowe Wyda Wnictwo Naukowe, 1974. 277 p.

Appeared first in 1970. 228 p.

A Polish guide to musicological method by one of the leading musicologists of that nation. Covers both the historical and the systematic aspects of the discipline. Extensive chapter bibliographies.

654. Machabey, Armand. La musicologie. 2. éd. Paris: Presses Universitaires de France, 1969. 128 p. (Que sais-je?, 978)

Brief, popular survey of the scope, content, and methods of musicology treated under five headings: "Sources," "Les éléments," "Les formes," "Les instruments," "Diffusion." Highly selective bibliography.

655. Madsen, Clifford K. and Charles H. Madsen, Jr. Experimental research in music. Englewood Cliffs, New Jersey: Prentice-Hall, 1970. 116 p.

Reprinted by Contemporary Publishing Co., Raleigh, 1978.

A research manual emphasizing the quantitative and descriptive aspects of musical scholarship.

656. Mixter, Keith E. General bibliography for music research. 2nd ed. Detroit, Michigan: Information Coordinators, 1975. 135 p. (Detroit studies in music bibliography, 33)

The purpose of this study is to present in an organized manner references to general bibliographical tools that may be of aid to those engaged in research in music.... The emphasis ... is on titles from North America and Europe. Coverage includes books, but is not extended to articles. [*Introduction*]

129

This is an excellent introduction to nonmusical reference works, albeit somewhat dated. Organized in chapters according to reference genres; contains indexes to names and to titles.
Brief review by Stephen M. Fry in *Notes*, 32 (1976), p. 781–82.

657. Musicology in the 1980s; methods, goals, opportunities. Edited by D. Kern Holoman and Claude V. Palisca. New York: Da Capo Press, 1982. 160 p.
Proceedings of two panel discussions held at the fall 1981 meeting of the American Musicological Society in Boston.
Contents:
Musicology I: Current Methodology, Opportunities and Limitations.
"Editor's introduction" by Claude V. Palisca.
"Reflections on musical scholarship in the 1960s" by Claude V. Palisca.
"Archival research" by Jeremy Noble.
"Applications of the history of ideas" by Maria Rika Maniates.
"Sketch studies" by Joseph Kerman.
"Structural and critical analysis" by Leo Treitler.
"Iconography" by James McKinnon.
Musicology II: The Musicologist Today and in the Future.
"Editor's introduction" by D. Kern Holoman.
"The musicologist and the performer" by Richard Taruskin.
"Publishing and/or perishing" by D. Kern Holoman.
"Teaching music history in different environments" by Anne V. Hallmark.
"Musicology and criticism" by Rose Rosengard Subotnik.
Includes bibliographical references.
Review by Christopher Hatch in *Notes*, 41 (1984), p. 51–53.

658. Pruett, James W. and Thomas P. Slavens. Research guide to musicology. Chicago, Illinois: American Library Association, 1985. 175 p. (Sources of information in the humanities, 4)
James Pruett's guide to musicology is a traditional, even conservative, exposition of the development of the discipline. Thomas Slavens' bibliography of the research literature is limited almost entirely to English-language publications and seems not to have been coordinated with the essay.
Reviews by Lenore Coral in *Notes*, 43 (1986), p. 42–44, and by James Scholter in *Music Educators Journal*, 72 (February, 1986), p. 69–71.

659. Riemann, Hugo. Grundriss der Musikwissenschaft. 4. Aufl. durchgesehen von Johannes Wolf. Leipzig: Quelle und Meyer, 1928. 160 p. (Wissenschaft und Bildung, 34)

660. Samuel, Harold. "Musicology and the music library." In *Trends in the Scholarly Use of Library Resources*, [edited by] Donald W. Krummel *et al.*, *Library Trends*, vol. 25, no. 4 (1977), p. 833–46.
An exposition on the expansion of the horizons of musicology and related disciplines with a concomitant widening of the scope of collection building and services in music libraries.

661. Schiedermair, Ludwig. Einführung in das Studium der Musikgeschichte: Leitsätze, Quellen, Übersichten und Ratschläge. 4. umbearb. und erweiterte Aufl. Bonn: F. Drummlers Verlag, 1947. 167 p.

First published in 1918.

Brief surveys, with bibliographies, of the major historical periods. Concluding chapters deal with methodology, institutions, advice to students, etc. A useful appendix lists major *Gesamtausgaben* and the contents of publishers' series devoted to early music.

662. Spiess, Lincoln B. Historical musicology, a reference manual for research in music ... with articles by Ernst C. Krohn, Lloyd Hibberd, Luther A. Dittmer, Tsang-Houei Shu, Tatsuo Minagawa, and Zdeněk Nováček. Brooklyn, New York: Institute of Medieval Music, 1963. 294 p. (Musicological studies, 4)

Reprinted by Greenwood Press, Westport, Connecticut, 1980.

A text and reference book of musical research, includes lists of suggested topics for class and seminar reports, term papers, and dissertations; with a copious bibliography, index of publishers, etc. [Publishers' *Preface*]

The bibliography consists of 1,980 numbered items, in all categories, distributed throughout the text. Ernst C. Krohn's essay, "The development of modern musicology," p. 153–72, provides a useful but dated bibliography of the history of the discipline.

Review by Vincent Duckles in *Notes*, 20 (1963), p. 469–71.

663. Stevens, Denis. Musicology: a practical guide. London: Macdonald Futura, 1980. 224 p. (Yehudi Menuhin music guides)

Also published in New York by Schirmer Books, 1981.

"This book is not for musicologists; they already know it all" (from the author's introductory remarks).

Reviews by Clifford Bartlett in *Brio*, 17 (1980), p. 67–68, and by David Fallows in *Early Music*, 9 (1981), p. 243–44.

664. Suppan, Wolfgang. Musica humana: Die anthropologische und kulturethologische Dimension der Musikwissenschaft. Wien: H. Böhlau, 1986. 121 p. (Forschen, Lehren, Verantworten, 8)

Bibliography: p. 94–115.

665. Systematische Musikwissenschaft. [Hrsg. von] Carl Dahlhaus, Helga de la Motte-Haber. Wiesbaden: Akademische Verlagsgesellschaft Athenaion; Laaber: Laaber-Verlag Müller-Buscher, 1982. 367 p. (Neues Handbuch der Musikwissenschaft, 10)

Contents:

"Umfang, Methode und Ziel der Systematischen Musikwissenschaft" by Helga de la Motte-Haber.

"Musikwissenschaft und Systematische Musikwissenschaft" by Carl Dahlhaus.

"Begründungen Musiktheoretischer Systeme" by Helga de la Motte-Haber and Peter Nitsche.

"Ästhetik und Musikästhetik" by Carl Dahlhaus.

"Musiksoziologische Reflexionen" by Carl Dahlhaus and Günter Mayer.

"Musikalische Hermeneutik und empirische Forschung" by Helga de la Motte-Haber.

"Sozialpsychologische Dimensionen des musikalischen Geschmacks" by Ekkehard Jost.

"Begabung, Lernen, Entwicklung" by Klaus-Ernst Behne, Eberhard Kötter, and Roland Meissner.

"Wissenschaft und Praxis" by Günter Kleinen and Helga de la Motte-Haber.

Series cited as no. 563.

666. Wallon, Simone. La documentation musicologique. Paris: Beauchesne, 1984. 142 p. (Guides musicologiques, 3)

A brief handbook on the practice of musicology.

667. Watanabe, Ruth T. Introduction to music research. Englewood Cliffs, New Jersey, Prentice-Hall, 1967. 237 p.

A discussion of the procedures, resources, and techniques preliminary to research activity in music. The main subdivisions are as follows: Part I, library orientation. Part II, the research paper. Part III, survey of research materials. Out of date, but useful.

Review by Donald W. Krummel in *Notes*, 24 (1968), p. 481–82.

668. Weber, Édith. La recherche musicologique: objet, méthodologie, normes de présentation. Paris: Beauchesne, 1980. 171 p. (Guides musicologiques, 1)

An introduction to the field, to the variety of methods used in pursuing musicological research, and to report writing in musicology.

669. Westrup, Jack A. An introduction to musical history. 2nd ed. London: Hutchinson University Library, 1973. 176 p.

First published in London, 1955, as a volume in the Hutchinson University Library. Subsequently in New York by Harper and Row, 1964. 174 p.

> This is not a history of music. It is simply an attempt to outline some of the problems which historians and students have to face, and to give some idea of the conditions in which music has come into existence. [Author's *Preface*]

Although intended as a layman's guide to music history, this little book is one of the few clear treatments of the problems of music historiography in English.

Review by Allen P. Britton in *Journal of Research in Music Education*, 3 (1955), p. 154.

670. Wiora, Walter. Historische und systematische Musikwissenschaft; ausgewählte Aufsätze von Walter Wiora. Hrsg. von Hellmut Kühn und Christoph-Hellmut Mahling. Tutzing: H. Schneider, 1972. 480 p.

Prof. Wiora was the leading exponent of the systematic approach to musical scholarship. This volume contains his writings on musicology and a bibliography of his later writings.

Bibliographies of Music Literature

The term "music literature" as applied here refers to writings on music as opposed to musical scores. Such writings may appear as periodical articles or monographs; they may be cited in complete, self-contained bibliographical works or in serial publications; and they can be organized in terms of a variety of subject fields. Nearly every dissertation or research study will have its appended bibliography of relevant literature, and most of the authoritative dictionaries or encyclopedias have subject bibliographies connected with their articles. It would be impossible to cite all of these resources, but the titles selected are numerous and various enough to form a substantial sample of the available titles. Following is an outline of the subdivisions employed.

Bibliographies of Music Literature
    General (nos. 671–740)
    Current or Annual (nos. 741–770)
    Indexes to Periodical Literature (nos. 771–809)
    Lists of Periodicals (nos. 810–854)

Special and Subject Bibliographies
    Contemporary Music (nos. 855–863)
    Dissertations (nos. 864–887)
    Ethnomusicology (nos. 888–930)
    Musical Instruments (nos. 931–959)
    Jazz (nos. 960–969)
    Popular Music (nos. 970–982)
    Medieval and Renaissance Music (nos. 983–992)
    Baroque and Classical Music (nos. 993–995)
    Music Education (nos. 996–1007)
    National Music (nos. 1008–1120)
    Opera and Theater Music (nos. 1121–1138)
    Primary Sources: Early Music Literature (nos. 1139–1152)
    Sacred Music (nos. 1152–1159)
    Writings on Individual Composers (nos. 1160–1189)

See also "Catalogs of Music Libraries and Collections" (nos. 1852–2494). Many of the published catalogs of major libraries contain separate volumes or sections devoted to holdings in books on music.

GENERAL

671. Aber, Adolf. Handbuch der Musikliteratur in systematisch-chronologischer Anordnung. Leipzig: Breitkopf & Härtel, 1922. 696 p. (Kleine Handbücher der Musikgeschichte nach Gattungen, 13)

Reprints by Olms, Hildesheim, and Breitkopf & Härtel, Wiesbaden, 1967.

A classified bibliography for students of music history. International coverage, although strongest in German materials. Entries from at least 13 important musicological journals are included. Subject and author indexes.

Also listed as part of the *Kretzschmar* series of music history, no. 551.

672. Adlung, Jacob. Anleitung zu der musikalischen Gelahrtheit, 1758. Faksimile-Nachdruck hrsg. von. H. J. Moser. Kassel: Bärenreiter, 1953. 814 p. (Documenta Musicologica, Erste Reihe, 4)

2nd ed., revised by J. A. Hiller, 1783.

Chronologically one of the first important critical bibliographies of music literature. The author proposed to list all works on musical subjects necessary to "educated music lovers, and particularly to lovers of keyboard music," as well as builders of organs and other instruments.

See the description of this work in Gustav Reese's *Fourscore Classics of Music Literature* (no. 1147). New York: Liberal Arts Press, 1957. p. 74–75.

673. Azhderian, Helen Wentworth. Reference works in music and music literature in five libraries of Los Angeles County. Los Angeles: Published for the Southern California Chapter of the Music Library Association by the University of Southern California, 1953. 313 p.

A Partial Supplement of Holdings in the USC Library, January 1952–June 1962. Prepared by Joan M. Meggett. 1962. 13 p.

A bibliography of musicological literature, approx. 4,500 entries. International coverage. Full bibliographical citations. Classified listing with author index. The libraries represented are the Henry E. Huntington Library, the William Andrews Clark Memorial Library, the Los Angeles Public Library, and the libraries of the University of Southern California and the University of California at Los Angeles.

Review by Otto Albrecht, in *Notes*, 11 (1954), p. 468–69; by Vincent Duckles in *Journal of the American Musicological Society*, 7 (1954), p. 242–43.

674. Baily, Dee. A checklist of music bibliographies and indexes in progress and unpublished. 4th ed. Philadelphia, Pennsylvania: Music Library Association, 1982. 104 p. (MLA index and bibliography series, 3)

1st edition, compiled by the Publications Committee MLA, 1963; 2nd, revised edition compiled by James Pruett, 1969; 3rd edition, compiled by Linda Solow, 1974.

Consists of two sections. The first is organized by name of researcher, each entry describing the work and its state of completion; addresses are provided. The second is an index to entries covering subjects, proper and place names, titles mentioned within entries. Entries are also listed under broad subjects (e.g., Renaissance era).

The results of a survey.

675. Battier, Marc and Jacques Arveiller. Documents musique et informatique: une bibliographie indexée. Réedition augmentée. Paris: Éditeur Elmeratte, 1978. 178 p.

First published in 1976.

A bibliography of computer applications to music research and practice. 1,485 numbered items, including many periodical articles. Among the tables at the end of the column are a list of sigla, a list of programs and systems, a list of computer languages, and a list of subjects.

676. Becker, Carl F. Systematisch-chronologische Darstellung der musikalischen Literatur von der frühesten bis auf die neueste Zeit.... Leipzig: R. Friese, 1836. 571 cols. and 34 p.

Nachtrag Choralsammlungen aus dem 16. 17. und 18. Jahrhundert, 1839.

Reprint by Frits A. M. Knuf, Hilversum, 1964.

Becker presents a classified bibliography of many now obscure works. His work fills the gap, chronologically, between Lichtenthal (no. 380) and Eitner's *Bücherverzeichnis,* 1885 (no. 695). Includes newspaper and periodical articles. Gives place of publication, date, pagination, with brief annotations; 33-page index by subject, author, etc.

677. Beiträge zur Musikwissenschaft. Sonderreihe: Bibliographien, musikwissenschaftliche Literatur sozialistischer Länder. Berlin: Verlag neue Musik, 1973– .

Band III: *Deutsche Demokratische Republik 1945–1970.* 334 p. A classified bibliography of 3,495 published writings on musicology by German and foreign authors. Not indexed.

Band IV: *Sowjetunion 1945–70,* 1976. 312 p. A classified bibliography, transliterated from Russian. 4,007 entries.

Band IV: *Anhang, Verzeichnis der Autoren und der publizierten Titel in russischer Sprache.* 1976. 166 p. An index of authors with titles in Cyrillic characters to Band IV.

Chief editor: Georg Knepler.

See also no. 679 and no. 1093.

678. Besterman, Theodore. Music and drama: a bibliography of bibliographies. Totowa, New Jersey: Rowman and Littlefield, 1971. 365 p.

A listing extracted by the publisher from the 4th edition of the author's *World Bibliography of Bibliographies* (1965).

Bibliography of discographies. See no. 2747.

679. Blechschmidt, Renate. "Bibliographie der Schriften über Musik aus der Deutschen Demokratischen Republik, 1945–59." In *Beiträge zur Musikwissenschaft,* Jahrg. 1 (1959), Heft 3, p. 51–75; Jahrg. 2 (1960), Heft 1, p. 50–68; Heft 2, p. 64–78.

Classified list covering the writings on music produced in East Germany for the 15-year period. Complemented by no. 677.

Block, Adrienne Fried and Carol Neuls-Bates. Women in American music; a bibliography of music and literature. See no. 2977.

680. Blom, Eric. A general index to modern musical literature in the English language, including periodicals for the years 1915–1926. London and Philadelphia: Curwen, [1927]. 159 p.

Reprint by Da Capo, New York, 1970.

Entries for books by author and for parts of books by catchword subject in one alphabet.

681. Blum, Fred. Music monographs in series: a bibliography of numbered monograph series in the field of music current since 1945. New York: Scarecrow, 1964. 197 p.

Gives contents of more than 259 monographic series originating from some 30 countries.

> Over one-third of them may best be described as broadly musicological in content, many issued under the auspices of universities or scholarly societies; others, ranging in tone from the academic to the popular, cover the gamut of musical subject matter. [*Preface*]

Review by Thomas Watkins in *Current Musicology* (Fall 1965), p. 227–29; by Richard Schaal in *Die Musikforschung*, 22 (1969), p. 521.

682. Bobillier, Marie (Michel Brenet, pseud.). "Bibliographie des bibliographies Musicales." In *L'Année Musicale*, 3 (1913), p. 1–152.

Reprint by Da Capo Press, New York, 1971. 152 p.

One of the first bibliographies of music bibliography. Outdated but still useful. Lists general works, including periodical articles, by author; individual bibliographies; catalogs of libraries; catalogs of dealers and publishers.

683. Briquet, Marie. La musique dans les congrès internationaux (1835–1939). Paris: Heugel, 1961. 124 p. (Publications de la Société Française de Musicologie, 2ème sér. Tome X)

A bibliographical survey of the contributions on music made at international congresses from 1835 to 1939. Classified listing of 164 congress reports, with papers on music itemized. Indexed by place of meeting, by chronology, by author, and by subject.

Review by Richard Schaal in *Die Musikforschung*, 17 (1964), p. 183.

Complemented by Tyrrell and Wise (no. 733).

684. Brook, Barry S. Thematic catalogues in music, an annotated bibliography, including printed, manuscript, and in-preparation catalogues; related literature and reviews; an essay on the definitions, history, functions, historiography, and future of the thematic catalogue. Hillsdale, New York: Pendragon Press, 1972. 347 p.

Published under the joint sponsorship of the Music Library Association and *RILM Abstracts of Music Literature*. This work supersedes *A checklist of thematic catalogues* edited by an MLA Committee on Thematic Indexes (1954) and its *Supplement* issued by Queens College (1966).

Indexes some 1,500 entries, including a number of 18th-century manuscript catalogs, a great many unpublished catalogs, and some large-scale national projects currently in progress.

A new edition of this bibliography is under way and publication is expected.

See also Wettstein (no. 738).

685. Büchting, Adolf. Bibliotheca musica. Verzeichnis aller in Bezug auf die Musik ... 1847–66, im deutschen Buchhandel erschienenen Bücher und Zeitschriften. Nebst Fortsetzung 1: die Jahre 1867–71 umfassend. Nordhausen: A. Büchting, 1867–72. 2 v.

A bibliography of music literature covering German publications from 1847 to 1871. The work takes its place chronologically after that of Becker (no. 676) in this history of music bibliography. The gap of eight years in coverage between Becker and Büchting has been filled by Robert Eitner (no. 695).

686. Carl Gregor, Duke of Mecklenburg. Bibliographie einiger Grenzgebiete der Musikwissenschaft. Baden-Baden: Librarie Heitz, 1962. 197 p. (Bibliotheca bibliographica Aureliana, 6)

A bibliography devoted to areas peripheral to the traditional emphasis on historical musicology. Includes books and periodical articles on aesthetics; psychology; sociology of music; relations between music and the other arts; musical interests of poets, writers, philosophers, etc. 3,519 entries, alphabetically by author, with indexes of subjects and of persons as subjects.

Review by Wolfgang Schmieder in *Die Musikforschung*, 20 (1967), p. 461–62.

687. Chicorel, Marietta. Chicorel bibliography of books on music and musicians. New York: Chicorel, 1974. 500 p.

A mechanically compiled list of currently available books.

688. Coover, James B. "Dictionaries and encyclopedias of music." In *The New Grove Dictionary of Music and Musicians*, edited by Stanley Sadie, v. 5, p. 430–59. London: Macmillan, 1980.

An extensive essay on the early history of dictionaries broken into several chronological spans, each with a bibliography of the dictionaries published in the time under examination. There is a separate section on encyclopedias, with a bibliography organized by country followed by a section on terminological dictionaries. International biographical and then national or regional biographical dictionaries are listed and discussed. Dictionaries devoted to specific topics are listed. There is a chronology titled "Landmarks in musical lexicography" and a bibliography. This article is the distillate of a lifetime of bibliographic work on the genre by the author.

Beginning with no. 115 (September 1987), *Cum Notis Variorum (CNV)* published James B. Coover's two-part essay "Lacunae in music dictionaries and encyclopedias," and from no. 117 (November 1987) *CNV* published Coover's "A non-evaluative checklist of music dictionaries and encyclopedias," a five-part classified bibliography. Together these complement the article and bibliography in the *New Grove*.

689. Coover, James B. Music lexicography, including a study of lacunae in music lexicography and a bibliography of music dictionaries. 3rd ed., rev. and enl. Carlisle, Pennsylvania: Carlisle Books, 1971. 175 p.

First published as *A Bibliography of Music Dictionaries*, Denver: Bibliographical Center for Research, 1952. 2nd edition, Denver, 1958.

The most comprehensive bibliography available of music dictionaries. 1,801 items arranged alphabetically, including all known editions of the works cited. Preceded by a general discussion of the history of music lexicography and of existing lacunae. Index to personal names, index to topics and types, and an index, by date of publication, to dictionaries before 1900.

Nyal Williams and Peggy Daub substantially increased the number of dictionaries cited in "Coover's *Music Lexicography*: two supplements" in *Notes*, 30 (1974), p. 492 ff.

Reviews of the 2nd edition by Irene Millen in *Notes*, 16 (1959), p. 383–84, and by Nyal Williams in *Notes*, 30 (1974), p. 517–18.

See also no. 688.

690. Coover, James B. Provisional checklist of priced antiquarians' catalogs containing musical materials. Buffalo: Music Library, State University of New York, 1981. 150 p. (typescript)

Organized by name of firm, then chronologically, with title or brief summary, number of lots to be sold or pages in the catalog, and location.

691. Davies, John H. Musicalia: sources of information in music. 2nd ed., rev. and enl. Oxford: Pergamon Press, 1969. 184 p. 48 facsimiles.

First published in 1966.

A practical guide to music reference materials, illustrated with facsimile pages of the major reference works.

Review by François Lesure in *Fontes Artis Musicae*, 17 (Jan.–Aug. 1970), p. 55.

692. Davis, Deta S. Computer applications in music: a bibliography. Madison, Wisconsin: A-R Editions, 1988. 537 p.

This bibliography is a comprehensive listing of works regarding applications of the computer in music. The purpose of this bibliography is to record information on publications available in the field of computer music in a form that facilitates easy reference. It has been arranged alphabetically by author in twenty-five chapters, each on a specific subject area.... Each citation lists all authors, full title, and a bibliographic description. Numbers, symbols, and wording on title pages of books and journals have been transcribed exactly when the primary source was available so that material can be located easily in library catalogs and computer databases. [from the introductory remarks]

There are 4,585 entries in 25 chapters (e.g., aesthetics, composition, music printing and transcription, musical instruments, musicology and analytic applications, sound generation for music—hardware). There is an author-title index.

693. Diamond, Harold J. Music analyses; an annotated guide to the literature. New York: Schirmer Books, 1990. 716 p.

An earlier edition published as *Music Criticism: An Annotated Guide to the Literature*, by Scarecrow Press in Metuchen, New Jersey, in 1979. 316 p.

Cites and describes analytical literature in English on Western art music. Over 4,600 citations from books, periodicals, and dissertations. Annotations indicate nature and level of analysis. In order by composer and then by work, except for general analytical works. Full citations for sources are given in each entry. For dissertations, *Dissertation Abstracts* numbers are provided. Index of distinctive titles. Classified bibliography of sources.

Review of *Music Criticism* by Barbara Henry in *Notes*, 37 (1980), p. 64–65.
See also Wenk (no. 736).

694. Duckles, Vincent H. Music reference and research materials, an annotated bibliography. 3rd ed. New York: Free Press; London: Collier Macmillan, 1974. 526 p.

First published in 1964. 2nd ed. New York: Free Press; London: Collier Macmillan, 1967. 385 p.

Review of the 1st ed. by Jan LaRue in *Journal of the American Musicological Society*, 19 (1966), p. 257–61; by Klaus Speer in *Notes*, 21 (1964), p. 375; of the 2nd ed. by William S. Newman in *Notes*, 24 (1967), p. 265–66; review of the 3rd edition in *ALA Reference and Subscription Book Reviews* (1 December 1974), p. 83–84.

695. Eitner, Robert. Bücherverzeichnis der Musikliteratur aus den Jahren 1839 bis 1846 im Anschluss an Becker und Büchting ... Leipzig: Breitkopf & Härtel, 1885. 89 p. (Monatshefte für Musikgeschichte. Beilage. 17. Jahrgang)

Intended to bridge the gap between Becker's bibliography, no. 676, and Büchting's, no. 685.

696. Elste, Martin. Verzeichnis deutschsprachiger Musiksoziologie 1848–1973. Hamburg: Verlag der Musikalienhandlung Karl Dieter Wagner, 1975. 201 p.

Part one is a classified bibliography with indexes to names and periodicals. Part two is a keyword in context index (KWIC) to titles.

697. Forkel, Johann N. Allgemeine Litteratur der Musik, oder Anleitung zur Kenntniss musikalischer Bücher, welche von den ältesten bis auf die neusten Zeiten bey den Griechen, Römern und den meisten neuern europäischen Nationen sind geschrieben worden. Leipzig: Schwickert, 1792. 540 p.

Reprint by Olms, Hildesheim, 1962.

The first comprehensive bibliography of music literature and still a work of great utility. Classified listing of some 3,000 works on all aspects of musical knowledge, with brief biographical notices on all of the authors and descriptive annotations. Complete tables of contents are given for most important books.

Forkel's classification system has served as a model for many subsequent bibliographies. See Scott Goldthwaite, "Classification problems, bibliographies of literature about music," in *Library Quarterly* (October 1948), p. 255 ff.

Forkel's work was expanded and translated into Italian by Pietro Lichtenthal in 1826 (no. 380).

698. Gardeton, César. Bibliographie musicale de la France et de l'étranger, ou Répertoire général systématique de tous les traités et œuvres de musique vocale et instrumentale, imprimés ou gravés en Europe jusqu'à ce jour avec l'indication de lieux de l'impression, des marchands et des prix.... Paris: Noigret, 1822. 608 p.

Reprinted by Minkoff, Genève, 1978 as no. 6 of the series *Archives de l'Édition Musicale Française.*

An early 19th-century bibliography of music and music literature, chiefly French, although titles from other European countries are listed. There is a section devoted to reviews, biographies, analysis, and musical news, and a directory of musicians of all kinds active in Paris.

699. Gerboth, Walter. An index to musical Festschriften and similar publications. New York: W. W. Norton, 1969. 188 p.

Expanded version of a bibliographical work first appearing in *Aspects of Medieval and Renaissance Music, a Birthday Offering to Gustave Reese* (New York: W. W. Norton, 1966), p. 183–307.

The most comprehensive treatment of music *Festchriften* available. In three parts: A. List of *Festschriften* under the name of the individual or institution honored; B. Subject listing of more than 2,700 articles; C. Author and secondary-subject index. Now out of date. *RILM* (no. 800) provides coverage of articles in musical *Festschriften* published after 1967.

Review by Donald Seibert in *Notes*, 26 (1970), p. 760–61.

700. Heaton, Wallace and Charles W. Hargens. An interdisciplinary index of studies in physics, medicine, and music related to the human voice. Bryn Mawr: T. Presser, 1968. 61 p.

Classified into 12 areas (e.g., anatomical, speech analysis, etc.). Entries provide author, title (translated to English, if necessary), source, and a fairly full abstract. Source journals are listed and are primarily Western European and North American. Indexes to institutions, to authors, and subjects provided.

The work was published as "a directory of personnel working in this research area" [laryngeal study] and so is neither an index nor a bibliography, though it has some aspects of each.

701. Heussner, Horst. Collectio musica: Musikbibliographie in Deutschland bis 1625 [von] Horst Heussner [und] Ingo Schultz. Kassel: Internationale Vereinigung der Musikbibliotheken / Internationale Gesellschaft für Musikwissenschaft, 1973. 254 p. (Catalogus musicus, 6)

A classified bibliography of music and music literature published in Germany before 1625. Arranged in two language groups, Latin and German. Indexes to: names of composers, authors of texts, editors, and collectors; printers, publishers, and dealers; names of presses; titles appearing twice. Corrigenda and addenda. Provided with a bibliography of contemporaneous bibliographies and a bibliography of modern secondary literature.

702. Honigsheim, Paul. Music and society; the later writings of Paul Honigsheim. Edited, with additional material and bibliographies, by K. Peter Etzkorn. Foreword by J. Allan Beegle. New York: J. Wiley, 1973. 327 p.

Reprinted 1979. First published as *Sociology of Music: titles selected and annotated by Paul Honigsheim* by the University of Missouri, St. Louis, 1970. 196 leaves.

"Sociology and music: additional and recent bibliographic entries," p. 299–320.

703. Iampolski, I. M. "Muzykalnoi bibliografii," in *Muzykal'naia Entsyklopedia* (no. 45).

A survey of music bibliographical works without chronological or geopolitical boundaries, but with substantial coverage of works done in socialist countries, particularly the U.S.S.R.

704. Index of music theory in the United States, 1955–1970. Richmond Browne, supervising editor. v. 3, nos. 7–11 of *In Theory Only*, journal of the Michigan Music Theory Society. Ann Arbor: Michigan Music Theory Society, 1978. 170 p.

An index of articles, books, dissertations, reviews, etc. published 1955–70 on music theory: terms and concepts, analyses, and "technical music theory" (e.g., orchestration, notation). Includes some works on ethnomusicology, musicology, aesthetics, philosophy, and theory pedagogy. Author and subject indexes. Index of musical compositions analyzed. Index of historical theorists whose work is treated as a subject.

705. Jackson, Roland. Performance practice, medieval to contemporary; a bibliographic guide. New York: Garland, 1988. 518 p.

Selective complement to Vinquist and Zaslaw (no. 734) for works published 1960–1986. 1,392 entries in order by historical periods and then by categories. There is an introductory section covering the general literature on performance practice and a concluding section titled "Reflections on performance practice." Unlike Vinquist and Zaslaw, which deals with performance practice of music composed before 1900, this work covers performance practice of 20th-century music. Works on the sociology of music performance are omitted, as are works by performers concerning their lives or interpretations of musical works.

There are indexes to theorists, authors, and subjects. Use of the indexes is particularly important, as cited works appear only once, even though some are relevant to more than one subject or period.

Reviews by Clifford Bartlet in *Brio*, 25 (1988), p. 31–32; by Pamela C. Poulin in *Notes*, 47 (1991), p. 1174; by Peter Holman in *Music and Letters*, 70 (1989), p. 245–47.

706. Kahl, Willi and Wilhelm-Martin Luther. Repertorium der Musikwissenschaft. Musikschrifttum, Denkmäler und Gesamtausgaben in Auswahl (1800–1950) mit Besitzvermerken deutscher Bibliotheken und musikwissenschaftlicher Institute. Kassel: Bärenreiter, 1951. 271 p.

A comprehensive bibliography of music literature, broadly classified, including useful lists of *Festschriften*, conference reports, and critical editions. International in scope. Prepared as a union list of musicological holdings in postwar German libraries. 2,795 items. Indexed by persons, subjects, and geographical locations.

Review by Otto Albrecht in *Notes*, 11 (1954), p. 468–69; by Vincent Duckles in *Journal of the American Musicological Society*, 7 (1954), p. 242–45.

One section cited as no. 1686.

707. Kananov, Pavel Khristoforovich and Ida Pinkhasovna Vulykh. Zarubezhnaia literatura o muzyke: referativnyi ukazatel za 1954–1958. [Foreign lit-

erature about music: annotated bibliography 1954–1958.] Moskva: Sovetskii Kompozitor, 1962.
*Zarubezhnaia Literatura o Muzyke: Referativnyi Ukazatel za 1959–
1966*, succeeding this title, was published in 1972. 604 p.
A bibliography of general literature on the methodology and history of
musical knowledge, covering both theoretical and historical disciplines.
Titles are given in Russian and in the original foreign language.

708. Keller, Michael A. "Music and dance," in *The Reader's Adviser*, p. 484–
525. New York and London: R. R. Bowker, 1986.
A briefly annotated list of currently available English-language books
intended to introduce the non-specialist to topics in music and dance.

709. Koltypina, Galina Borisovna, ed. Bibliografia muzykalnoi bibliografii.
[Bibliography of musical bibliography.] Moscow: 1963. 226 p.
An annotated bibliography of Russian music bibliographies. The work
cites bibliographies of literature on music separately published and lists
books, articles, and reviews. Designed for bibliographers and scholars.

710. Koltypina, Galina Borisovna, ed. Spravochnaia literatura po muzyke.
[Reference literature on music ... 1773–1962.] Moscow: 1964. 249 p.
A publication of the Moscow State Library.
Annotated bibliography of Russian reference literature on music, includ-
ing dictionaries, collected biography, calendars, etc., published in Russia
from 1773 to 1962. Cites reviews in Russian periodical literature.

711. Kostka, Stefan M. A bibliography of computer applications in music.
Hackensack, New Jersey: J. Boonin, 1974. 58 p. (Music indexes and bibliographies, 7)
A bibliography of writings published by mid-1973 about applications of
computers to musical problems. Covers the first 20 years of such developments. No annotations. Entries in a single alphabetical arrangement by
author. Now out of date. See nos. 692 and 716.

712. Kramer, Jonathan D. "Studies in time and music: a bibliography." In
Music Theory Spectrum, 7 (1985), p. 72–106.
A classified bibliography with articles on time in music, including relevant articles treating music from the subjects of psychology, sociology,
philosophy, criticism of other temporal arts, and anthropology. Sources
cited were published after 1900. Primarily an English-language bibliography. No index.

713. Krohn, Ernst C. The history of music: an index to the literature available in a selected group of musicological publications. St. Louis, Missouri:
Washington University, 1952. 463 p. (Washington University Library studies, 3)
Reissued by Baton Music Co., St. Louis, 1958.
Classified index of articles on music history in 39 leading musicological
publications, chiefly German and English. Chronological arrangement,
with subdivisions by subject. Includes book reviews.
Indexes a number of important music periodicals (*Musical Quarterly*,

Music and Letters, and others) from each title's first volume, providing coverage before *Music Index* began in 1949.

Review by Richard Appel in *Notes,* 10 (1952), p. 105–106; by Scott Goldthwaite in *Journal of the American Musicological Society,* 6 (1953), p. 250–51; by Wolfgang Schmieder in *Die Musikforschung,* 6 (1953), p. 278–80.

714. Krohn, Ernst C. "Musical Festschriften and related publications." In *Notes,* 21 (1964), p. 94–108.

A useful listing of *Festschriften,* cited chronologically under four headings: A. works of major musicological interest; B. works compiled in homage to individual musicians, living or in the past; C. commemorative volumes consisting of original music; and D. those celebrating a particular institution, school, society, or performing group.

For a more complete bibliography of *Festschriften,* see no. 699.

715. Laskowski, Larry. Heinrich Schenker: an annotated index to his analyses of musical works. New York: Pendragon Press, 1978. 157 p.

Lichtenthal, Pietro. Dizionario e bibliografia della musica. See no. 380.

716. Lister, Craig. The musical microcomputer: a resource guide. New York: Garland, 1988. 172 p. (Garland reference library of the humanities, 854)

This bibliography has been compiled for those interested in microcomputer applications in music. It includes annotated coverage of five types of sources: anthologies, books, dissertations, journal articles, and software. The main organization is by subject, grouped into six composite categories.... Most of the sources include an annotation, a short statement intended to be descriptive, literal, and accurate. When possible, references to reviews of the source have been included following the annotation.... The goal behind the source collection has been to establish a representative, not comprehensive, look at each subject. [from the introductory remarks]

The six "composite categories" are: bibliography, history, and criticism; composition, analysis, and notation; education and musicianship; interfaces; programming; and synthesis. There is an author index as well as a title and software index. An appendix lists journals regularly containing articles on microcomputer applications in music. A second appendix is a checklist of 20 books for the small music library.

717. Marco, Guy A. Information on music: a handbook of reference sources in European languages; with the assistance of Sharon Paugh Ferris; foreword by James Coover. Littleton, Colorado: Libraries Unlimited, 1975–84. 3 v. (to date).

Although a six-volume work was projected, the project seems to have ceased with only three volumes:

Vol. 1. *Basic and Universal Sources.* 1975. 164 p.

Vol. 2. *The Americas,* with Ann M. Garfield and Sharon Paugh Ferris. 1977. 296 p.

Vol. 3. *Europe* with Sharon Paugh Ferris and Ann G. Olszewski. 1984. 519 p.

An annotated guide to music reference works with the intention of providing comprehensive access to information about music. Each entry provides complete bibliographic information, a Library of Congress classification, and references to other guides to music reference and research materials. There are indexes to names and titles and to subjects. The index in vol. 2 covers entries in the first two volumes.

718. Marks, Martin. "Film music: the material, literature, and present state of research." In *Notes*, 36 (1980), p. 282–325.

A survey of the source material and research on it including numerous citations for secondary works and criticism. Includes "a selective bibliography of film music publications."

719. Materialy do bibliografii muzyki polskiej. [Series editor: Tadeusz Strumillo.] Kraków: Polskie Wydawnictwo Muzyczne, 1954–78. 5 v.

A series of bibliographies related to Polish music and music literature.

Vol. 1: Kornel Michalowski. *Opery Polskie.* 1954. 227 p. (Polish operas and foreign operas with Polish settings or subjects, listed by title, giving composer, librettist, date and place of first performance.)

Vol. 2: Erwin Nowaczyk. *Piésni Solowe S. Moniuszki, Katalog Tematyczny.* 1954. 332 p. (Thematic catalog of 304 songs by Moniuszki, giving authors of text, lists of editions.)

Vol. 3: Kornel Michalowski. *Bibliografia Polskiego Piśmiennictwa Muzycznego.* 1955. 280 p. (Classified bibliography of books on music in Polish. Lists of theses and dissertations, 1917–54.)

A supplement to vol. 3, published in 1964 as vol. 4, contains classified listings of new Polish books on music published between 1955 and 1963, with some addenda from earlier years. A second supplement to vol. 3, published as vol. 5, was issued in 1978 and covers the period 1964 to 1974.

720. Mathiesen, Thomas J. A bibliography of sources for the study of ancient Greek music. Hackensack, New Jersey: J. Boonin, 1974. 59 p. (Music indexes and bibliographies, 10)

"This bibliography attempts to gather together all the myriad sources dealing with ancient Greek music theory." 949 entries arranged alphabetically by author and theorist. Includes books, articles, dissertations, translations, etc. Various editions of each theorist's works are entered chronologically under the theorist's name and then the title of the work. Entries provide author's name, title, imprint information, and pagination.

721. Matthew, James E. The literature of music. London: E. Stock, 1896. 281 p.

Reprint by Da Capo, New York, 1969.

Essays on the literature of music in historical sequence to the 18th century, thereafter by topics: histories, biographies, dictionaries, sacred music, opera, instruments, music as a science, bibliography. Narrative style. Matthew, although out of date, presents a useful survey of the earlier literature of music.

722. Mrygon, Adam and Eva Mrygon. Bibliografia polskiego piśmiennictwa muzykologicznego (1945–1970). [Wyd. 1.] Warszawa: Państwowe Wydawn. Naukowe, 1972. 208 p.

Authors known also as Adam Mrygoniowie and Ewa Mrygoniowie.

A classified bibliography of 3,398 items, covering all aspects of musicology practiced in Poland.

723. Ogawa, Takashi, ed. Honpo yogaku kankei tosho mokuroku. [A list of books about foreign music in the Japanese language.] 3rd ed. Tokyo: Ongaku no Tomo Sha, 1965. 267 p.

724. Paxinos, S. "Select bibliography of harmony and counterpoint." In *Ars Nova, Magazine of the Department of Musicology, University of South Africa,* 6, 2 (August 1974), p. 3–31.
361-item bibliography arranged alphabetically in two sections: books and articles. Full bibliographical entries, but no annotations.

725. Performing arts books 1876–1981, including an international index of current serial publications. New York: R. R. Bowker, 1981. 1,656 p.
A retrospective bibliography of Library of Congress cataloged entries of works published or distributed in the U.S. Derived from the *American Book Publishing Record*. About one-third of the work is devoted to works about music. Indexes to subjects, authors, and titles for books and serials.

726. Petermann, Kurt. Tanzbibliographie. Verzeichnis der in deutscher Sprache veröffentlichten Schriften und Aufsätze zum Bühnen-, Gesellschafts-, Kinder-, Volks-, und Turniertanz sowie zur Tanzwissenschaft, Tanzmusik und zum Jazz. Hrsg. vom Institut für Volkskunstforschung beim Zentralhaus für Kulturarbeit. Leipzig: VEB Bibliographisches Institut, 1966–81. 30 *Lieferungen.*
Two *Abschluss Bänden* were published in 1981 by K. G. Saur, Munich, edited by the Akademie der Künste Tanzarchiv der DDR, Leipzig.
This is a classified bibliography of writings on the dance covering literature from the 15th century to 1979. Most of early fascicles covering much of the classification series cited works published to 1963. With the *Abschluss Bänden,* the final classes covered works published to 1979. The second *Abschluss Bände* has a table of contents for the entire publication. Cites not only secondary literature but also music for the dance. Entries provide author, title, source or imprint information, and location of the item in a library in the DDR. An index was projected but has not yet appeared.

727. Refardt, Edgar. Verzeichnis der Aufsätze zur Musik in den nicht-musikalischen Zeitschriften der Universitätsbibliothek Basel. Leipzig: Breitkopf & Härtel, 1925. 105 p.
A classified list of writings on music in over 500 nonmusical newspapers and periodicals, arranged alphabetically by author. One of the few efforts to compile a bibliography of musical literature in journals outside of the field.

728. Riemann, Hugo. Geschichte der Musiktheorie im IX.–XIX. Jahrhunderts. Dritte Auflage. Hildesheim: Olms, 1961. 541 p.
Unchanged reprint of the 2nd ed. (Berlin: Hesse, 1921). First published in Leipzig by Hesse, 1898. There is an English-language edition titled *History of Music Theory, Books 1 and 2: Polyphonic Theory to the Sixteenth*

Century, translated by Raymond H. Haggh (New York: Da Capo, 1974. 432 p.).

Includes a convenient "Alphabetisches Authoren-Register," a list of early primary sources on music theory from the 9th to the 19th century, citing author's name and brief title and giving approximate date. The Haggh translation features Riemann's bibliography of sources brought up to date with entries for modern editions, annotations (including a few references to modern secondary literature), and fuller bibliographic information.

729. Sheehy, Eugene P. "Music." In *Guide to reference books*. 10th ed. Chicago and London: American Library Association, 1986. p. 599–628.

An annotated bibliography of 353 titles most likely to be found in general libraries. Supplemented by "Music" in *Guide to reference books covering materials from 1985 to 1990: supplement to the tenth edition* (Chicago and London: American Library Association, 1992), p. 186–201.

The *Guide to reference books* is a vast annotated bibliography of basic reference tools in every discipline. Previous generations of scholars knew the work as "Mudge" and then "Winchell." Through it one is guided to literatures and reference works in unfamiliar territories. It is not comprehensive, but its coverage of subjects is very broad. There is a single index to authors and titles.

730. Sovetskaia literatura o muzyke 1918–1947. Bibliograficheskii ukazatel' knig.: Ivan I. Startsev; redaktor: S. D. Uspenskaia. Moskva: Sovetskii Kompozitor, 1963. 293 p.

A classified list of books and periodical articles in Russian.

731. Sovetskaia literatura o muzyke 1948–53. Compilers S. L. Uspenskaia and B. IAagolim. Moskva: Sovetskii Kompozitor, 1955. 343 p.

A classified list of books and periodical articles in Russian. A bibliographical series, issued irregularly; further volumes have appeared as follows:

1958, covering the years 1954–56
1959, covering the year 1957
1963, covering 1958–59
1967, covering 1960–62
1971, covering 1963–65
1974, covering 1966–67
1979–84, covering 1968–70

Title and imprint varies. Name index; list of periodicals.

732. Tripp, Wendell. "Folk song and dance." In *The Reader's Adviser*, p. 593–94. New York; London: R. R. Bowker, 1986.

A briefly annotated list of currently available English-language books intended to introduce the nonspecialist to topics within the discipline.

733. Tyrrell, John and Rosemary Wise. A guide to international congress reports in musicology, 1900–1975. New York: Garland Pub., 1979. 353 p. (Garland reference library of the humanities, 118)

A bibliographical guide to locating and identifying congress reports and an index to papers published in those reports. Covers congress published reports, so some reports for congresses held in the period 1970–75 but not yet published at the time of compilation are not included. Organized chronologically. Indexed by place, by titles, by series and sponsors, by authors and editors, and by subject.

Complemented by Briquet (no. 683).

Reviews by Walter Gerboth in *Notes*, 36 (1980), p. 902–903, and by Rita Benton in *Fontes Artis Musicae*, 27 (1980), p. 121.

734. Vinquist, Mary and Neal Zaslaw. Performance practice: a bibliography. New York: W. W. Norton, 1971. 114 p.

First appeared as issue 8 (1969) of *Current Musicology*; this issue was supplemented in issue 10 (1970).

The book is supplemented in *Current Musicology*, 12 (1971), p. 129–49, under the title "Performance practices bibliography," labeled "Second supplement" and edited by Thomas W. Baker and Robert Kline. A third supplement was published in *Current Musicology*, 15 (1973), p. 126–33, edited by Richard Koprowski and James Hines.

Not including the supplements, this is a bibliography of about 1,200 entries; includes both primary sources and secondary sources. International in scope. The index brings out writings on major subtopics. Includes, on p. 6, a bibliography of performance practice bibliographies (chiefly unpublished dissertations).

See also Jackson (no. 705).

735. Wallon, Simone. "Musicologie." In L. N. Malclès, *Les sources du travail bibliographique*. Tome II: Bibliographies spécialisées (Sciences humaines), p. 536–52. Genève: E. Droz, 1952.

Basic but highly selective list of music reference works, classified and well annotated.

736. Wenk, Arthur B. Analyses of nineteenth-century and twentieth-century music: 1940–1985. Boston: Music Library Association, 1987. 370 p. (MLA index and bibliography series, 25)

Cumulates and updates the indexes originally published as nos. 13, 14, and 15 in this series: *Analyses of Twentieth-century Music: 1940–1970*, 1975; *Analyses of Twentieth-century Music: 1970–1975*, 1975; *Analyses of Nineteenth-century Music: 1940–1980*, 1980.

"The purpose of this index is to provide rapid access to technical materials of an analytical nature contained in periodicals, monographs, *Festschriften* and dissertations."

Contains 5,664 entries by 2,400 authors arranged alphabetically by: composer; by genre or by work for composers having more than 10 entries; by author; alphabetically by title, for multiple entries of a single author. Entries contain the composer's name, the title, the author of the analysis, and the source of the analysis. The list of abbreviations is, in effect, the bibliography of sources for the analyses. Author index.

Review by Charles Lindahl in *Notes*, 47 (1990), p. 405–406.

See also Diamond (no. 693).

737. Wescott, Steven D. A comprehensive bibliography of music for film and television. Detroit, Michigan: Information Coordinators, 1985. 432 p. (Detroit studies in music bibliography, 54)

An extensive bibliography (6,340 entries) of articles and a wide variety of other sources on the subject. Filmography: p. 375–77. Discography: p. 377–79. Index to names and subjects.

Additions to Steven D. Wescott, "A Comprehensive Bibliography of Music for Film and Television," by Gillian B. Anderson, published 1986, Library of Congress, Washington. 68 p. Anderson has used Wescott's headings, numbering, and format, added substantially to Wescott's index, and provided an index to film titles.

738. Wettstein, Hermann. Bibliographie musikalischer thematischer Werkverzeichnisse. Laaber: Laaber-Verlag, 1978. 408 p.

A bibliography of thematic catalogs, alphabetical by composer. Content and organization of each catalog are described.

See also Brook (no. 684).

739. Williams, David Russell. A bibliography of the history of music theory. 2nd ed. Fairport, New York: Rochester Music Publishers, 1971. 58 p.

First printed in 1970.

A bibliography of selected theory works and writings devoted to them. Organized chronologically in study units, as in a syllabus. Indexes of treatises and names.

740. Winick, Steven. Rhythm: an annotated bibliography. Metuchen, New Jersey: Scarecrow Press, 1974. 157 p.

Lists about 500 English-language sources written in 1900–1972. Three categories: general background; psychology of rhythm; pedagogy of rhythm. Index of authors, editors, and reviewers. Focus is on music education.

CURRENT OR ANNUAL, INCLUDING PERIODICALS LISTING MUSIC LITERATURE

741. Acta musicologica. Internationale Gesellschaft für Musikwissenschaft, 1928–52. Vols. 1–24.

"Index novorum librarum," a department appearing in most issues of this journal, is one of the best sources of bibliographical information for the period between 1930 and 1950. It gives a classified listing of books on music in all languages. The department was discontinued after 1952.

See *Acta Musicologica: An Index, Fall 1928–Spring 1967,* by Cecil Adkins and Alis Dickinson. Basel: Bärenreiter, 196– . 70 p. Author and subject index.

742. African music. Journal of the African music society. Roodepoort, Transvaal, Union of South Africa: 1954– . Vols. 1– .

Each annual issue has a section of "books and pamphlets received" as well as reviews of current publications in ethnomusicology.

743. American bibliographic service. Quarterly checklist of musicology. An international index of current books, monographs, brochures, and separates. Darien, Connecticut: American Bibliographic Service, 1959–77. Vols. 1–19.

Vols. 1–10 reprinted by Johnson Reprint Corporation, 1977.

An unclassified numbered listing of current writings on music. The selection is broad and rather uncritical. Full bibliographical information, including prices. Indexed by authors, editors, and translators in the last issue of each volume.

744. Bibliographia musicologica. A bibliography of musical literature. Utrecht: Joachimsthal, 1970–77. Vols. 1–7.

An international bibliography of books about music, listed alphabetically by author, with a subject index. Vol. 1 is devoted to literature published in 1968; 2,170 items. Vol. 2, covering literature for 1969, runs to 2,057 items. Vol. 7 covers about 2,000 titles. The listings give publisher, pagination, and price and include current reprints, facsimile editions, and revised editions.

745. Bibliographic guide to music. Boston: G. K. Hall, 1975– .

The series began with the publication of the *Music Book Guide: 1974* (Boston: G. K. Hall, 1974).

An annual listing of publications cataloged each year by the Research Libraries of the New York Public Library and the Library of Congress. Also serves as an annual supplement to the *Dictionary Catalog of the Music Collection of the Research Libraries of the New York Public Library* (no. 2241). Music and works about music in all languages and all forms are included. Entries provided under personal and corporate names, titles, and subjects. This work serves as a particularly complete current listing of new editions of music and works about music.

Brief review by Stephen M. Fry in *Notes*, 33 (1976), p. 305.

746. Bibliographie des Musikschrifttums. Jahrgang 1936– . (Herausgegeben im Auftrage des Instituts für Musikforschung Preussischer Kulturbesitz, Berlin.) Leipzig; Frankfurt a. M.: F. Hofmeister, 1936– .

Editors: 1936–37, Kurt Taut; 1938–39, Georg Karstädt; (1940–49, suspended publication); 1950–59, Wolfgang Schmieder; 1960, Werner Bollet, Dieter J. Frecot, Bärbel Schleyer; 1961–64, Dieter J. Frecot, Bärbel Schleyer; 1965, Dieter J. Frecot, Heinz-Lothar Fichter; 1966–68, Dieter J. Frecot; 1969–75, Elisabeth Wilker; 1976, Claudia Wegner; 1977–78, Norbert Böker-Heil, Claudia Wegner.

A bibliography of books and an index to periodical literature in all European languages. A large number of nonmusical journals included. Classified by broad subjects with an index of names (author and subject) and places. The emphasis is on "serious" music.

This bibliography follows in a direct line of descent from the listings in the Peters *Jahrbuch* (no. 755).

Review of *Jahrgang 1950–51* by Richard Schaal in *Die Musikforschung*, 8 (1955), p. 371–72; by Richard S. Hill in *Notes*, 11 (1954), p. 555–57; by Scott Goldthwaite in *Journal of the American Musicological Society*, 8 (1955), p. 55–57. Review of *Jahrgang 1952–53* by Richard Schaal in *Die Musikforschung*, 10 (1957), p. 440.

747. Bollettino bibliografico musicale. Milan. Vol. 1, no. 1 (Sept. 1926) to vol. 8, nos. 4–5 (April–May 1933). N.s. vol. 1, no. 1 (Jan.–Feb. 1952) to vol. 1, nos. 7–8 (Aug.–Sept. 1952).

A journal devoted to matters of bibliographical interest in music; each issue customarily contains a bibliography of the works of one composer, early or contemporary, chiefly Italian. Regular departments give listings of current music publications, the contents of music journals, music and book reviews.

748. Brass quarterly. Milford, N.H.: Cabinet Press, 1957–64. Vols. 1–8.

Edited by Mary Rasmussen.

Contained in each issue review of recordings and scores of brass music as well as a section of "Current publications" classified by instrument or ensemble.

749. Bulgarski muzikalen knigopis. Trimesechen bibliografskibiuletin za novoizliazla literatura po muzika i noti. Soffia: Bulgarski Bibliografski Institut "Elin Pelin," 1958– .

Quarterly, classified list of books and periodical articles on music and publications in musical notation issued in Bulgaria. Cumulative index in the October–December issue, containing index for the entire year.

750. Cum notis variorum. Edited by Ann P. Basart. Berkeley: University of California, Music Library, 1976–89. Nos. 1–134.

One of the most distinguished of music library newsletters issued. This journal listed recent acquisitions and provided brief reviews of new reference works. There were regular features on music in the Bay Area, on conferences, on music libraries and music collections in northern California, and on news culled from journals on librarianship. By 1981, each issue contained at least one substantial article, frequently upon a subject in the sphere of music bibliography. *Cum Notis Variorum* was issued 10 times each year, but by the mid-1980s the acquisitions lists appeared less frequently and as supplements.

751. Deutsche Musikbibliographie. Leipzig: F. Hofmeister, 1829– . Jahrgang 1– .

Title varies: 1829–1942, *Hofmeisters musikalisch-literarischer Monatsbericht.*

Lists German, Swiss, and Austrian publications of music and music literature. Alphabetical by author, giving date and place of publication, pagination, and price. A monthly publication useful chiefly for its listings of music. Indexed by publisher. Entries are cumulated in Hofmeister's *Jahresverzeichnis* ... (no. 758).

752. Deutsche Staatsbibliothek (Berlin). Neuerwerbungen ausländischer Musikliteratur. Berlin: Deutsche Staatsbibliothek, 1956– . Vol. 1: Bibliographische Mitteilungen, Nr. 12, 1954–55; Nr. 16, 1956–57; Nr. 19, 1958–60.

Classified lists of books on music and foreign publications acquired by the Deutsche Staatsbibliothek (East Berlin). Issued at irregular intervals as part of the library's series of *Bibliographische Mitteilungen.* The three volumes appeared in 1956, 1958, and 1962, respectively.

753. Ethnomusicology. Journal of the Society for Ethnomusicology. Middletown, Connecticut: Wesleyan University Press, 1953– . Vol. 1– .
Title varies: 1953–57, *Ethno-Musicology Newsletter.*
Imprint varies: after January 1972, "Published by the Society for Ethnomusicology, Inc."
Each issue contains a section of "current bibliography," listing books, dissertations, films, exchange publications, and periodical articles related to the field. After January 1967 the lists include "discography," and were compiled by Joseph C. Hickerson *et al.* Organized by geographical areas and occasional topics, e.g., "dance." The journal also publishes from time to time special bibliographies devoted to the work of leading ethnomusicologists.

Fontes artis musicae. See no. 1216.

754. Hofmeisters Handbuch der Musikliteratur. Leipzig: F. Hofmeister, 1844–1943. Bd. 1–19.
Cumulation of the *Jahresverzeichnis der deutschen Musikalien und Musikschriften* (no. 758).
Preceded by a similar work compiled by C. F. Whistling and published by Anton Meysel, Leipzig, 1817, listing music and music literature through 1815, with 10 supplements (1 published by Meysel, 2–8 by Hofmeister, 9–10 by Whistling) to 1827. This initial volume, with its 10 supplements, has been reprinted by Garland in 1975 with an excellent introduction by Neil Ratliff explicating the history and relationships of these important bibliographies. There was an earlier 2-volume reprint by Vienna House, New York, 1972, under the title *Handbuch der musikalischen Litteratur.*
Title varies: Vols. 1–3 (to 1844), C. F. Whistling's *Handbuch der musikalischen Literatur.* Vols. 4–6 (1844–67), *Handbuch der musikalischen Literatur.* Vols. 4–18 (1844–1933), also called *Ergänzungsband* 1–15.
There is also an Olms reprint (1975, 1,298 p.) of the first three *Ergänzungsbande* (originally published 1828–39) of the Whistling *Handbuch* up to 1838.
Publication interrupted in Vol. 19 (1943) covering the years 1934–40, through the letter "L" in the alphabet.
The *Handbuch* is of greatest importance for its music (score) listings, but each volume contains an *Anhang* devoted to books and writings on music. The long life of the series, plus the leading position occupied by German music publishing houses during the period covered, make it one of the major reference tools, useful especially for establishing dates of publication.
For a detailed description of the organization of this complex trade bibliography, see "A survey of the music catalogues of Whistling and Hofmeister," by Rudolf Elvers and Cecil Hopkinson, in *Fontes Artis Musicae,* 19 (1972), p. 1–7.
Review of the Ratliff edition of the Whistling *Handbuch* by François Lesure in *Fontes Artis Musicae,* 24 (1977), p. 102.

Imago Musicae. International yearbook of musical iconography. See no. 594.

755. Jahrbuch der Musikbibliothek Peters. Leipzig: C. F. Peters, 1895–1941. Vols. 1–47.

Most issues contain a section entitled "Verzeichnis der in allen Kulturländern erschienenen Bücher und Schriften über Musik," edited at various times by Rudolf Schwartz, Emil Vogel, Eugen Schmitz, and Kurt Taut. Does not include periodical literature. This section, expanded to include periodical articles, has been continued as the *Bibliographie des Musikschrifttums*, published separately (no. 746).

756. Jahrbuch für Liturgik und Hymnologie. Kassel: Johannes Stauda-Verlag, 1955– . Bd. 1– .

Each volume contains an extensive "Literaturbericht," classified, frequently annotated, and covering all aspects of liturgics and hymnology.

757. Jahrbuch für Volksliedforschung. Im Auftrag des Deutschen Volksliedarchivs. Berlin and Leipzig: Walter De Gruyter, 1928– . Erster Jahrgang– .

Editors vary. The yearbook suspended publication between 1951 and 1964.

From 1965 to date it has carried an extensive section devoted to reviews ("Besprechungen") covering the important literature in the field of folk song research.

758. Jahresverzeichnis der Deutschen Musikalien und Musikschriften. Leipzig: F. Hofmeister, 1852–1985. Jahrgang 1–128.

An annual listing that cumulates the material in the *Deutsche Musikbibliographie* (no. 751) and is, in turn, cumulated in *Hofmeisters Handbuch der Musikliteratur* (no. 754).

Title varies: Vols. 1–77 (1852–1928), *Verzeichnis der im Jahre ... erschienenen Musikalien.* Vols. 78–91 (1929–42), *Hofmeisters Jahresverzeichnis.*

759. Journal of music theory. New Haven, Connecticut: Yale School of Music, 1957– . Vols. 1– .

Each issue contains a "Bibliography of current periodical literature" covering articles related to music theory.

760. Journal of the International Folk Music Council. Published with the assistance of the International Music Council under the auspices of UNESCO, 1949–68. Vols. 1–19.

Superseded by the council's *Yearbook*, 1969– . Urbana: University of Illinois Press.

Each volume of this yearly publication contains a section "Publications received," which gives a brief, authoritative survey of a wide range of publications in the field, including periodicals, recordings, and important articles.

761. Literature, music, fine arts. A review of German-language research contributions on literature, music, and fine arts. With bibliographies. Tübingen, 1968– . Vol. 1– . (German studies, Section 3)

Appears twice a year. A journal devoted to reviews and listings of cultural studies in the German language. All titles and reviews are given in English. The music section provides a useful tool for acquisition purposes.

Some 15 to 20 titles are selected for review, followed by a listing of 75 to 100 other new titles. Information includes prices.

762. Music library association notes, a magazine devoted to music and its literature. The Music Library Association, 1948– . 2nd ser. Vol. 1– .
Subsequently became *Notes*, the quarterly journal of the Music Library Association.
Notes' "Book reviews," a department compiled and edited by a variety of editors and supplemented by a list of current publications on music, offers the most comprehensive listing of books about music available. Since December 1950, the list has been international in scope; classified by language. "Music received," edited by Ruth Watanabe, is one of the most extensive lists of newly published scores.
Two ruminative surveys by Donald W. Krummel shed light on the general trends of the periodical in its first 40 years: "Twenty years of *Notes*: a retrospective," in *Notes*, 21 (1964), p. 56–82; and "The second twenty volumes of *Notes*: a retrospective re-cast," in *Notes*, 40 (1985), p. 7–25.

763. Music Teachers National Association. Committee on Literature about Music. "Report." In its *Proceedings* (annual), 1906– .
Classified lists of books on music in English, giving author, title, publisher, pagination, and price. Includes some translations, new editions, and reprints. Excellent listings of material in English; carefully selected; some annotations. Listed by authors and subjects.

764. Musica disciplina. A yearbook of the history of music. American Institute of Musicology, 1946–88. Vols. 1–42.
Title varies: Vol. 1, *Journal of Renaissance and Baroque Music.*
Until vol. 30 (1976), each volume contained a bibliography of books, periodical articles, and editions related to early music, doctoral dissertations included; compiled from 1958 to 1969 by Wolfgang Schmieder and from 1970 to 1976, the final year in which the bibliography appeared, by Keith Mixter.

765. Musica/realtà. Rivista quadrimestale. Milano: Edizioni Unicopli, 1979– . Vol. 1.
There is an annual "Supplemento libri: Libri d'interesse musicale stampati in Italia..." with brief reviews arrayed in categories ("Analisi musicale," "Cataloghi," "Musica antica," "Musica del '900," etc.). Reviews are prepared by musicologists associated with the *Dipartimento di Musica e Spettacolo dell'Università di Bologna*, principal among them Professor Mario Baroni and Laura Callegari. A list of books issued but not reviewed is appended to each category.

766. "Musical literature." In *The British Catalogue of Music.* London: Council of the British National Bibliography, 1957– .
An annual listing, broadly classified, of all books about music published in Great Britain. "Musical literature" appears first in the classified section. Scores, however, occupy the greater part of the volumes. Indexed by author and title.

153

767. The musical quarterly. New York: G. Schirmer, 1915– . Vol. 1– . Since 1989, published by Oxford University Press, New York.

The "Quarterly book-list" in each issue is a selection of books of musicological interest in all languages. Less comprehensive than the current listings in *Notes* (no. 762). Edited successively by Carroll C. Wade, Fred Blum, Frank Traficante, Jon Newsom, Carolyn Bryant.

768. Musik-Information; bibliographische Titelübersicht. Berlin: Leitstelle für Information und Dokumentation "Musik" an der Deutschen Hochschule für Musik "Hanns Eisler." 1971– . Jahrg. 1– .

An introductory number called *Jahrg. O, Heft A*, was issued in 1970.

A monthly publication covering "important international titles in the sphere of musicology in books and journals." Subject and author indexes.

769. Periodica musica. Vancouver, B.C.: Centre international de recherche sur la presse musicale; Department of Music of the University of British Columbia, 1983– . Vol. 1– .

An annual newsletter of the Répertoire international de la presse musicale du XIXe siècle, of the Centres internationaux de recherche sur la presse musicale. Covers research and publications relating to the music periodical publications of the 19th century.

The Répertoire international de la presse musicale du XIXe siècle, with headquarters in Vancouver, Canada, and Parma, Italy, has as its goal the provision of access to the enormous periodical literature about music published in the 19th century.

770. Svensk tidskrift för musikforskning. Stockholm, 1919– . Vol. 1– .

Since 1927 the *Tidskrift* has maintained an annual listing of "Svensk musikhistorisk bibliografi," compiled since 1946 by Åke Davidsson. Broadly classified. Indexes Swedish periodicals.

INDEXES OF MUSIC PERIODICALS AND TO PERIODICAL LITERATURE ABOUT MUSIC

771. Aarhus. Denmark. Statsbiblioteket. Indeks til danske periodiske musikpublicationer 1795–1841: kumulevet og annoteret indeks til *Apollo, Norden Apollo, Nye Apollo, Odeon, Musikalsk Theatre Journal* og *Vaudeville Journal* ... by Joergen Poul Erichsen. Aarhus: Statsbiblioteketforlaget, 1975. 113 p.

Bibliography: p. 129–32.

772. Anderson, Gillian B. Music in New York during the American Revolution: An inventory of musical references in *Rivington's New York Gazette*. With the editorial assistance of Neil Ratliff. Boston, Massachusetts: Music Library Association, 1987. 135 p. (MLA index and bibliography series, 24)

The inventory brings together "all references to music, musicians, musical instruments, and musical events found ... in the newspaper between 1773 and 1783." Arranged alphabetically by name, title, and subject; in-

cludes not only articles but also notices and advertisements. Extensive cross-references. Where compositions are cited, references to *RISM* are provided when possible.
Review by Karl Kroeger in *Notes*, 47 (1990), p. 384–85.

773. Anderson, Gillian B. "Unpublished periodical indexes at the Library of Congress and elsewhere in the United States of America." In *Fontes Artis Musicae*, 31 (1984), p. 54–60.
Covering the card indexes at the Library of Congress, the Works Progress Administration index now at Northwestern University, and the Boston Public Library. Lists periodicals and periods of publication indexed. Cites indexes at Washington University in St. Louis, Howard University in Washington, D.C., and at the Sibley Music Library in Rochester, New York.

774. "Articles concerning music in non-musical journals 1949–64." In *Current Musicology* (Spring 1965), p. 121–27; (Fall 1965), p. 221–26.
The first installment stresses articles on historical subjects; the second, articles under various systematic headings: acoustics, philosophy and aesthetics, music in literature, psychology, sociology, etc.

775. Artículos sobre música en revistas españolas de humanidades. Recopilados por Flora Arroyo, [*et al.*]; editor-coordinador, Jacinto Torres. Madrid: Instituto de Bibliografía Musical, 1982– . Vol. 1– .
A bibliography of articles about music appearing in major intellectual Spanish journals published from the end of the 19th century to 1980. Includes indexes.

776. Arts & humanities citation index. Philadelphia, Pennsylvania: Institute for Scientific Information, 1976– .
Issued three times each year, the third being an annual cumulation. Issued in 3 parts: pt. 1, Citation index; pt. 2, Source index/Corporate index; pt. 3, Permuterm index. Includes supplement with title "Guide & journal lists."
The "Source index" lists by author articles published during the period of coverage; the "Citation index" lists by author, composer, or artist works referred to in the source articles (whether in footnotes, endnotes, or in the body of the article); the "Permuterm index" arranges meaningful words in the titles of the source articles to allow access by pairing of such words. There is also a "Corporate index" listing source article authors by institution of affiliation.
About 60 music periodicals are regularly indexed, but numerous essays in conference reports and other anthologies are indexed as well.
This complex bibliographic tool provides a kind of access new to musical studies and is available as an on-line file through the Institute for Scientific Information in Philadelphia.
Thomas F. Heck has written an illustrated introduction to the opportunities and pitfalls of the *AHCI* as a reference work supporting musicological research: "The relevance of the *Arts and Humanities* data base to musicological research," in *Fontes Artis Musicae*, 28 (1981), p. 81–87.
Review and explanation by Michael A. Keller and Carol A. Lawrence in *Notes*, 36 (1980), p. 575–600.

777. Basart, Ann Phillips. Perspectives of new music, an index, 1962–82. With a foreword by Benjamin Boretz. Berkeley, California: Fallen Leaf Press, 1984. 127 p. (Fallen Leaf reference books in music, 1)
Review by Charles G. Eubanks in *Notes*, 41 (1984), p. 294.

778. Belknap, Sara Y. The guide to the performing arts, 1957–68. New York: Scarecrow Press, 1960–72. Vols. 1–11.
Annual periodical index to the performing arts. Began as a supplement to the compiler's *Guide to the Musical Arts*. Contains a "general" section and a "television arts" section. References to performing groups and performers as well as general subject headings.

779. "Bibliographie der Aufsätze zur Musik in aussermusikalischen Italienischen Zeitschriften." In *Analecta Musicologica*, Veröffentlichungen der Musikabteilung des Deutschen Historischen Instituts in Rom. Bd. I (1963), p. 90–112. Bd. II (1965), p. 144–228.
A bibliography of writings on music in Italian nonmusical journals. Part 1 by Paul Kast. Part 2 by Ernst-Ludwig Berz. The two installments are organized somewhat differently and indexed independently. The first contains 237 entries; the second, 1,074.

780. A bibliography of periodical literature in musicology. Washington, D.C.: American Council of Learned Societies, 1940–43. Nos. 1–2 (1938–39, 1939–40).
Indexes approximately 240 periodicals, all European languages, musical and nonmusical, from Oct. 1938 through Sept. 1940. Signed abstracts or annotations for most of the articles. Vol. 1 contains a list of graduate theses accepted in American colleges, universities, and conservatories from 1 Oct. 1939 to 1 Sept. 1939.
Vol. 1 compiled by D. H. Dougherty. Vol. 2 also compiled by Leonard Ellinwood and Richard S. Hill.

781. Brio. Journal of the United Kingdom Branch of IAML.
"Index of articles published in selected musical periodicals," compiled by Christel Wallbaum. In *Brio*, 1964–72.
A biannual subject index to articles in some 23 English-language music periodicals. The listings cover the periods January to June and July to December for each year.

782. Deutscher Büchereiverband. Arbeitsstelle für das Büchereiwesen. Zeitschriftendienst Musik. (ZD Musik.) Berlin: Deutscher Büchereiverband, 1966– . 1. Jahrgang– .
Previously (before 1977) a monthly and currently a bimonthly periodical index of articles from about 50 music periodicals, chiefly German. Approximately 3,000 articles are indexed per year. The editors are Burchard Bulling and Sibylle Schneider. The last issue of each year is a cumulative volume for the year. Titles are arranged in alphabetical order under subject headings. The listings can also be purchased in card-size format for filing.

783. Fellinger, Imogen. Periodica musicalia (1789–1830); im Auftrag des Staatlichen Instituts für Musikforschung Preussischer Kulturbesitz. Re-

gensburg: G. Bosse, 1986. 1,259 p. (Studien zur Musikgeschichte des 19. Jahrhunderts, 55)
Index to compositions appearing in periodicals from 1789 to 1830.

784. "Index to music obituaries" in *Notes.*
Formerly titled "Index to music necrology."
An index to deaths of musicians, which began with coverage of 1965 in the June 1966, vol. 22, issues of *Notes*. From 1965 through 1979, the column indexed a standard list of 16 to 18 journals. Since 1980, the current editor, Kären Nagy, has indexed as many sources as possible, while becoming somewhat more selective in the inclusion of names. Currently over 65 periodicals and newspapers are scanned for death notices of musicians. In addition, references are included to music dictionaries and encyclopedias where biographical entries may be found.
Previous editors have been Sivart Poladian, Dale L. Hudson, Patricia Matusky, Janet Rhoads Pinkowitz, Dale L. Good, Barbara Henry, and Patsy Felch Monokoski.

International inventory of musical literature. See Répertoire international de littérature musicale, no. 800.

785. Jazz index. Bibliographie unselbständiger Jazzliteratur. Bibliography of jazz literature in periodicals and collections. Compiled by Norbert Ruecker and C. Reggentin-Scheidt. Frankfurt: N. Ruecker, 1977–83. Vols. 1–7.
First volume published quarterly; subsequently published semiannually.
Indexes about 50 jazz periodicals and anthologies of essays by author and subject. Beginning in 1978 included a blues section. There is an especially useful "list of unconventional literature" at the end of each issue.
Review by Roger Cottrell in *Jazz Forum*, 12 (1978), p. 52; by Carl Gregor Herzog zu Mecklenburg in *Jazz Podium* 27 (1978), p. 44; and by Harold Rauter in *Jazzforschung*, 9 (1977), p. 183.

786. Journal of aesthetics and art criticism, 1941–1964 ... An index of articles and book reviews pertaining to music. Edited by Peter L. Ciurczak. Emporia: Kansas State Teachers College, 1965.

787. Meggett, Joan M. Music periodical literature: an annotated bibliography of indexes and bibliographies. Metuchen, New Jersey: Scarecrow Press, 1978. 116 p.
Covers more than 250 indexes to music periodicals in general works and works devoted to the subject of music. Provides a bibliography of lists of periodicals and a guide to the literature of the history of music periodicals. Index to authors, compilers, and editors. Indexes of subjects and titles.
Review by Patricia Felch in *Notes*, 35 (1979), p. 637–38, and by Rita Benton in *Fontes Artis Musicae*, 25 (1978), p. 417–18.

788. Music and Letters. Index to volumes 1–40, 1920–59. London: Oxford University Press, [1962]. 140 p.
An index compiled largely by Eric Blom and completed by Jack A. West-

rup after Blom's death in 1959. Two major sections. 1: articles (filed by author and subject in one alphabet). 2: reviews (similarly treated). Reviews of music are not indexed.

789. Music article guide. A comprehensive quarterly reference guide to significant signed feature articles in American music periodicals. Philadelphia, Pennsylvania: Music Article Guide, 1966– . Vol. 1– .

Until 1972 published a separate *Annotated Guide to Periodical Literature on Church Music.*

Indexes over 200 music periodicals, including many of local or highly specialized interest. Entries are grouped by subject and numbered consecutively within each issue. Indexed by title and author. Brief annotations. Nearly every issue until 1970 contains a "Directory of American music periodicals" listing the journals by title with their addresses.

The *Guide* changed in format after the first volume, from a small looseleafed volume to full-page typescript.

Published quarterly in 10 categories, one of which is "Musicology."

Review by Bennet Ludden in *Notes*, 24 (1967), p. 719–20, and by an anonymous reviewer in *ALA Booklist*, 65 (1969), p. 1239–41.

790. The music index; the key to current music periodical literature. Detroit, Michigan: Information Service, Inc., Jan. 1949– . Vol. 1, no. 1– .

Issued monthly with annual cumulations. Beginning with 1979, the annual cumulations are doubled up so that 1979–80 (vols. 31–32) and years following appear together in a larger format.

The founding editor was Florence Kretschmar.

The principal index to more than 500 music periodicals by subject and author. Published in 12 monthly numbers, with an annual cumulation. Reviews are indexed under "Book reviews."

Review of 1954 annual cumulation by Richard Appel in *Notes*, 14 (1957), p. 364–65; of the 1955 and 1956 cumulations by James B. Coover in *Notes*, 16 (1958), p. 45–46. Review by Richard Schaal in *Die Musikforschung*, 10 (1957), p. 442–43, and by an anonymous reviewer in *ALA Booklist*, 65 (1969), p. 123–24.

The Music Index on CD-ROM, cumulating all entries from 1981 to 1988 and eventually to be issued with annual updates, was issued by Chadwyck-Healey of Alexandria, Virginia, in 1991. The CD-ROM version for DOS computers provides vastly improved searching capabilities.

791. Music psychology index. Denton, Texas: Institute for Therapeutics Research, 1978– . Vol. 2– .

Edited by Charles T. Eagle. Successor to *Music Therapy Index.*

The "international, interdisciplinary index of the influence of music on behavior: references to the literature from the natural and behavioral sciences and the fine and therapeutic arts for the years 1976– ." Like the *Music Therapy Index*, an author and keyword index to articles from 10 primary source journals, 24 secondary source journals, and 14 secondary source indexes.

Review by Michael A. Keller and Carol A. Lawrence, "Music literature indexes in review: RILM abstracts (on-line) and the Arts and Humanities Citation Index, Music Therapy, Music Psychology, and Recording Industry Indexes," in *Notes*, 36 (1980), p. 575–600.

792. Music therapy index. Lawrence, Kansas: National Association for Music Therapy, 1976. 1v.

Edited by Charles T. Eagle. Succeeded by *Music Psychology Index.*

"An international, interdisciplinary index to the literature of the psychology, psychopsychology, psychophysics and sociology of music, contains titles of pertinent articles published ... between 1960 and 1975 inclusively." This is an author and keyword index to about 2,100 articles in six periodicals of primary importance and other articles selected from a variety of sources of secondary importance.

Review by Michael A. Keller and Carol A. Lawrence, "Music literature indexes in review: RILM abstracts (on-line) and the Arts and Humanities Citation, Music Therapy, Music Psychology, and Recording Industry Indexes," in *Notes*, 36 (1980), p. 575–600.

793. The musical quarterly. cumulative index. 1915 thru 1959 [v. 1–45]. Compiled by Herbert K. Goodkind. New York: Goodkind Indexes, [1960]. 204 p.

Cumulative Index Supplement, 1960 thru 1962. New York, 1963.

The main volume indexes by author and subject in separate alphabets, the *Supplement* in one alphabet. Indexes book reviews and "Current chronicle" as well as articles.

794. Muzykalnaia bibliografiia russkoi periodicheskoi pechati xix veka. [Bibliography of Russian music periodicals printed in the 19th century.] Sostavila Tamara Livanova [of the] Akademiia nauk SSSR Institut istorii iskusstv. Moskva: Gos. muzykalnoe izdvo, 1960– .

Vols. 4–6: published by Sovetskii kompozitor, Moskva.

Vol. 1: 1801–1825.

Vol. 2: 1826–40.

Vol. 3: 1841–50.

Vol. 4: 1851–60, 2 pts.

Vol. 5: 1861–70, with O. A. Vinogadov.

Vol. 6: 1871–80.

795. The organ. index to "The organ." A complete index to all the articles in *The Organ*, 1921–70, from the first issue to date. Compiled by Betty Matthews. Bournemouth: K. Mummery, 1970.

796. POMPI: Popular music periodicals index. Nos. 1–2, October 1984–September 1986. Compiled by Chris Clark and Andy Linehan. London: British Library National Sound Archive, 1988. 212 p.

"Devoted exclusively to the indexing of periodical articles on the performance and production of popular music and jazz."

Over 6,500 entries covering 60 periodical titles, the indexing is selective, focusing on interviews, feature articles, obituaries, and shorter informative items. No reviews of recordings, live performances, or books are indexed. Periodicals originating in the United Kingdom are especially well represented in the list of titles indexed.

Review by Linda Fidler in *Notes*, 47 (1990), p. 390–91.

797. Popular music periodicals index, 1973–1976. Edited by Dean Tudor *et al.* Metuchen, New Jersey: Scarecrow Press, 1974–77. 4 v.

Vol. 1 with Nancy Tudor; vols. 2 and 3 with Andrew D. Armitage; vol. 4 with Linda Biesenthal.

A complement to the author's *Annual Index to Popular Music Record Reviews*. Provides coverage of about 55 journals (fully indexed) and another 12 journals (partially indexed), primarily published in the U.S., Canada, and Great Britain. Subject and author sections each provide full bibliographic information for citations. Cross-references.

798. La rassegna musicale. Indice generale delle annate 1928–52. Torino: Roggero & Tortia, [1953]. Vols. 1–22. 174 p.

An index, compiled by Riccardo Allorto, of articles, musical performances reviews, book reviews, record reviews, and musical subjects.

799. Recording industry index. Cherry Hill, New Jersey: National Association of Recording Manufacturers, 1977–79. Vols. 1–3.

"A cumulative subject index of trade and consumer publications of interest, published in the United States. The main body consists of a subject index arranged alphabetically."

The 20 sources indexed complement the indexing in the *Music Index, Répertoire internationale de littérature musicale, Music Article Guide, Zeitschriftendienst Musik,* and *Popular Music Periodical Index.*

800. Répertoire international de littérature musicale. [International inventory of music literature.] *RILM* abstracts of music literature. New York: International *RILM* Center, 1967– . Vol. 1– .

An international quarterly journal devoted to abstracts of current literature on music. Published under the aegis of the International Musicological Society and the International Association of Music Libraries.

Contents are in a clear, classified arrangement. All abstracts are given in English. Foreign titles are translated, including those in the Cyrillic alphabet. Each issue contains an author index, and every fourth issue includes a name, title, and subject index to the entries for the year.

RILM is available for on-line searching for the years 1971 to the present, comprising about 56,000 abstracts, on the Dialog Information Retrieval Service. For a review of *RILM* on-line see Michael A. Keller and Carol A. Lawrence, "Music literature indexes in review: *RILM* abstracts (on-line) and the Arts and Humanities Citation Index, Music Therapy, Music Psychology, and Recording Industry indexes," in *Notes*, 36 (1980), p. 575–600. See also Naomi Steinberger in "Selected problems in searching the *RILM* database" in *Proceedings of the National Online Meeting*, 1981, p. 455–60.

The National Information Services Corporation of Baltimore, Maryland, issued in 1991 a CD-ROM version for DOS computers of *RILM* entitled *MUSE* (MUsic SEarch), containing over 100,000 entries from *RILM* for the years 1969 to the present. It offers substantially improved searching capacities.

For a full discussion of the *RILM* project and its initial implications, see Barry S. Brook, "Music literature and modern communication; revolutionary potential of the ACLS/CUNY/RILM project," in *College Music Symposium*, 9 (1969), p. 48–59.

Review in the *ALA Booklist*, 65 (1969), p. 1239–41.

RILM abstracts of music literature. See Répertoire international de littérature musicale, no. 800.

801. Rivista musicale italiana. Indici dei volumi I a XX (1894–1913). Compiled by Luigi Parigi. Torino: Fratelli Bocca, 1917. 256 p.
Indici dei Volumi XXI a XXXV (1914–28). Compiled by A. Salvatori and G. Concina. Torino, 1931. 195 p.
Indici dei Volumi XXXVI a LVII (1929–55). Compiled by Francesco Degrada. Firenze: Leo S. Olschki, 1966. 144 p. (Quaderni della Rivista Italiana di Musicologia a cura della Società Italiana di Musicologia, 1)
Review of the Degrada index by Ludwig Finscher in *Die Musikforschung*, 21 (1968), p. 365–66.

802. Royal Musical Association. Index to papers read before the members ... 1874–1944. Leeds: Printed by Whitehead & Miller for the Royal Association, 1948. 56 p.
A subject and an author index to the first 70 volumes of the *Proceedings of the Association.* Compiled by Alfred Loewenberg and Rupert Erlebach.

803. Shirley, Wayne D. *Modern music*, published by the League of Composers, 1924–1945; an analytic index. Edited by William Lichtenwanger and Carolyn Lichtenwanger. New York: AMS Press, 1976. 246 p.
Brief review by Stephen M. Fry in *Notes*, 33 (1976), p. 306–307.

804. Tilmouth, Michael. "A calendar of references to music in newspapers published in London and the provinces (1660–1719)." In *R.M.A. Research Chronicle*, 1, (1962) p. 1–107.
Index published in *R.M.A. Research Chronicle*, 2, p. 1–15.
Crucial introduction, list of titles examined. Organized chronologically. Cites advertisements, lists, notices, availability of music, concerts.

805. Vierteljahrschrift für Musikwissenschaft. Edited by Friedrich Chrysander & Philipp Spitta. Leipzig: 1885–94. Vols. 1–10.
Each volume contains a section, "Musikalische Bibliographie," compiled by F. Ascherson, which usually includes a listing of scholarly music books, critical editions, and the contents of current scholarly periodicals in all European languages.

806. Williams, Michael D. *Source: music of the avant garde*; annotated list of contents and cumulative indices. Ann Arbor, Michigan: Music Library Association, 1978. 52 p. (MLA index and bibliography series, 19)

807. Wolff, Arthur S. *Speculum*: an index of musically related articles and book reviews. 2nd ed. Philadelphia, Pennsylvania: Music Library Association, 1981. 64 p. (MLA index and bibliography series, 9)
First edition published 1970, 31 p. Originally published as *"Speculum": A Journal of Mediaeval Studies, 1926–1962 ... a Checklist of Articles and Book Reviews Pertaining to Music* in Denton, Texas, by North Texas State University in 1965.

808. Zeitschrift der Internationalen Musikgesellschaft. Leipzig: 1899/1900–1913/14. Vols. 1–15.
Most issues contain departments under the headings "Kritische Bücher-

schau" and "Zeitschriftenschau." The latter indexes approximately 84 periodicals, chiefly musical, in many languages. Vols. 1–11 by author only. Vols. 12–15 by subject with "see" references from the author.

809. Zeitschrift für Musikwissenschaft. Leipzig: 2 1918–35. v. 1–17.
Indexes annually the periodical literature on music in some 200 journals, in many languages. 1914–18 covered retrospectively in the 1918 index, thus articulating with no. 808.

Zeitschriftendienst Musik. See no. 782.

LISTS OF MUSIC PERIODICALS

One of the most comprehensive lists of music periodicals is to be found in the article "Zeitschriften" compiled by Imogen Fellinger for *MGG* (no. 826). Dr. Fellinger's bibliography of 19th-century music periodicals (no. 825) gives virtually complete coverage for the century under her consideration. Even more up-to-date and valuable is her article "Periodicals," in the *New Grove* (no. 824). The best chronological survey of the early music periodicals is offered by Wilhelm Freystätter (no. 828) but this has been supplemented and expanded in certain respects by the historical study by Eckart Rohlfs (no. 841).

Musicians should also be aware of the resources of a number of general reference works devoted to periodicals, such as Ulrich's *International Periodicals Directory* and the *Union List of Serials*.

810. Basart, Ann P. "Serials devoted to individual composers and musicians: a checklist." In *Cum Notis Variorum*, no. 83 (June 1984), p. 14–22.

811. Basart, Ann P. Writing about music: a guide to publishing opportunities for authors and reviewers. With a foreword by Joseph Kerman. Berkeley, California: Fallen Leaf Press, 1989. 588 p. (Fallen Leaf reference books in music, 11)
Substantial expansion of Basart's article, "Editorial practice and publishing opportunities in serious English-language music journals; a survey," which appeared in *Cum Notis Variorum*, 79 (January–February 1984), p. 9–51.

> This directory gives detailed information on over 430 current periodicals, from twenty-one countries, that publish serious, informative, music-related articles and/or reviews in English. Only periodicals that consider unsolicited material are included. *Writing about Music* gives a good overall picture of editorial practices in music periodicals in the late 1980s. [*Preface*]

40 monographic series in music are listed and described as well.
Extensive information from the editors of the journals and series is provided. Indexes to: titles and organizations; subjects; location; type of material reviewed. List of dropped titles.
Creative use of the indexes will reveal periodicals on subjects of interest but little visibility (e.g., reggae).

812. Bibliografia muzyczna polskich czasopism niemuzycznych. Pod redakcjá Kornela Michałowskiego. Krakow: Polskie Wydawn. Muzyczne, 1962–79. Vols. 1–5.

Contents: t. 1. *Muzyka w Polskich Czasopismach Niemuzycznych w Latach 1800–1830* opracowal Stanislaw Papierz; t. 2. *Muzyka w Polskich Czasopismach Literackich i Spolecznych, 1831–1863* opracowal Sylwester Dziki; t. 3. *Muzyka w Polskich Czasopismach Literackich i Spolecznych, 1864–1900* opracowala Elzbieta Szczawinska; t. 4. *Muzyka w Polskich Czasopismach Literackich i Artystycznych, 1901–1918* opracowala Elzbieta Szczawinska; t. 5. *Muzyka w Czasopismach Polskich, 1919–1939* opracowal Kornel Michalowski.

The several volumes in this publication are bibliographies of periodical literature about music covering the period 1880–1939. Each includes an index.

813. Blum, Fred. "East German music journals: a checklist." In *Notes*, 19 (1962), p. 399–410.

100 periodicals listed in alphabetical order (including secondary titles, former titles, and subsequent titles). Gives a critical description of a variety of East German music serials.

814. The British Union catalogue of music periodicals. Compiled by Anthony Hodges and edited by Raymond McGill. London: Library Association Publishing, 1985. 145 p.

A catalog of music periodical holdings of 292 institutions in the United Kingdom and 10 institutions in the Republic of Ireland. Periodicals are listed by title (with see references from subsequent or alternative titles). Entries give names of sponsoring organization or publisher, country and city of origin, dates of publication, miscellaneous other information, and years, volumes, and/or issues held at institutions denoted by *RISM* sigla. There is a separate list of institutions, providing full names, addresses, and telephone numbers. Titles in non-Roman alphabets are transliterated. There is an addendum to the catalog on the last page.

815. Campbell, Frank C. A critical annotated bibliography of periodicals. New York: American Choral Foundation, 1962. 14 p. (American choral foundation, Memo 33)

Evaluates 44 periodicals that treat choral music and materials, giving pertinent details (addresses, price, emphasis, etc.).

816. Canadian Library Association. Union list of music periodicals in Canadian libraries. Compiled by a committee of the Canadian Library Association. Ottawa: 1964. 32 p.

Committee chairman: Jean Lavander.

Gives data on holdings in music periodicals of 66 Canadian libraries. Brief annotations on the nature and content of each periodical listed.

817. Clough, F. F. and G. J. Cuming. "Phonographic periodicals, a survey of some issued outside the United States." In *Notes*, 15 (1958), p. 537–58.

A critical description of some 30 foreign periodicals devoted to recordings, with comments on record coverage in general periodicals.

818. Coover, James B. "A bibliography of East European music periodicals." In *Fontes Artis Musicae* 3 (1956), p. 219–26; 4 (1957), p. 97–102; 5 (1958), p. 44–45, 93–99; 6 (1959), p. 27–28; 7 (1960), p. 16–21, 69–70; 8 (1961), p. 75–90; 9 (1962), p. 78–80.

This bibliography is an attempt at a comprehensive and authoritative listing of all music periodicals which have been and which are being published in the countries of Bulgaria, Czechoslovakia, Estonia, Finland, Hungary, Latvia, Lithuania, Poland, Rumania, the U.S.S.R., and Yugoslavia. [Compiler's *Introduction*]

819. "Directory of American music periodicals." In *Music Article Guide*, vol. 1– . Philadelphia, Pennsylvania: Music Article Guide, 1966– .
Most issues of the *Guide* carry a list of periodicals indexed, with the addresses of editors or publishers given. A useful guide to current American music periodicals, but overall not as comprehensive as the *Music Index*.

820. Douglas, John R. "Publications devoted to individual musicians; a checklist." In *Bulletin of Bibliography and Magazine Notes*, 33 (1976), p. 135–39.
List of periodicals published by 52 societies, each devoted to a single musician.

821. "Europäische Musikzeitschriften 1945–48." In *Jahrbuch der Musikwelt*. Bayreuth: J. Steeger, 1949–50. p. 111–23.
A listing useful chiefly as an indication of the periodicals current during the period after World War II. Organized by country. Information brief and inconsistent, with German periodicals given most complete coverage; Russian, Czech, and others very incomplete.

822. Fairley, Lee. "A check-list of recent Latin American music periodicals." In *Notes*, 2 (1945), p. 120–23.
Treats 23 periodicals from the collections of the Library of Congress and the Pan American Union, with brief comments on each. Covers publications between 1940 and 1947.

823. Fellinger, Imogen. "List of union catalogues of (music) periodicals." In *Fontes Artis Musicae*, 28 (1981), p. 323–27.
A bibliography of 54 lists from 30 countries, arranged by country, of union lists of serials, most of them general with a music section or music entries scattered. Full bibliographic information provided.

824. Fellinger, Imogen. "Periodicals." In *The New Grove Dictionary of Music and Musicians*, edited by Stanley Sadie, v. 14, p. 407–535. London: Macmillan, 1980.

The present article provides a general account of music periodicals and their history; it is supplemented by a comprehensive list of musical periodicals (not periodic editions of music), arranged by continent and country, with an alphabetical index. [from the introductory remarks]

The "general account" is followed by an excellent bibliography which includes brief but essential annotations. Included in the bibliography are citations for indexes to periodicals.

825. Fellinger, Imogen. Verzeichnis der Musikzeitschriften des 19. Jahrhunderts. Regensburg: Gustav Bosse, 1969. 557 p. (Studien zur Musikgeschichte des 19. Jahrhunderts, 10)

Locates and lists chronologically more than 2,300 music periodicals, with a rich supply of bibliographical information. Actual coverage extends through journals established as late as 1918.

P. 10–28: historical survey of 19th-century music periodicals. P. 33–37: a bibliography of literature on periodicals. Five indexes: titles, editors, places of publication, printers and publishers, subjects.

Since the initial publication, a series of supplements have appeared in *Fontes Artis Musicae*: Nachträge, Folge 1, in vol. 17 (1970), p. 2–8; Nachträge, Folge 2, in vol. 18 (1971), p. 59–62; Nachträge, Folge 3, in vol. 19 (1972), p. 41–44; Nachträge, Folge 4, in vol. 20 (1973), p. 108–111; Nachträge, Folge 5, vol. 21 (1974), p. 36–38; Nachträge, Folge 6, vol. 23 (1976), p. 62–66.

Review by J. A. Westrup in *Music and Letters*, 50 (1969), p. 400–403; by Philip Gossett in *Notes*, 26 (1970), p. 740–41; by Willi Reich in *Literature, Music, Fine Arts*, 2 (1969), p. 200.

826. Fellinger, Imogen. "Zeitschriften." In *Die Musik in Geschichte und Gegenwart*, Band 14 (1968), cols. 1041–1188.

A comprehensive listing of music periodicals. Organized by country. Extensive bibliographies of literature on music periodicals.

827. Fredricks, Jessica M. "Music magazines of Britain and the U.S." In *Notes*, 6 (1949), p. 239–63, 457–59; 7 (1950), p. 372–76.

Lists 200 music periodicals arranged alphabetically by title, with a subject and type index. Brief descriptions of character and contents.

828. Freystätter, Wilhelm. Die musikalischen Zeitschriften seit ihrer Entstehung bis zur Gegenwart. Chronologisches Verzeichnis der periodischen Schriften über Musik. München: T. Riedel, 1884. 139 p.

Unaltered reprint of the original edition by Frits A. M. Knuf, Hilversum, 1963.

Based on E. Gregoir's *Recherches Historiques Concernant les Journaux de Musique*, Antwerp, 1872.

A chronological listing, from 1722 to 1844, with extensive annotations as to content, editors, contributors, etc. Still valuable as a convenient source of information on early music periodicals.

829. Kallmann, Helmut. "A century of musical periodicals in Canada." In *Canadian Music Journal*, vol. 1, no. 1 (1956), p. 37–43; vol. 1, no. 2 (1957), p. 25–35.

The last installment contains a section entitled: "A checklist of Canadian periodicals in the field of music," p. 30–36.

830. Malm, William P. "A bibliography of Japanese magazines and music." In *Ethnomusicology*, 3 (1959), p. 76–80.

Annotated bibliography of 25 Japanese periodicals related to music and the dance. Place, publisher, date of first issue, and price given.

831. Mekkawi, Carol Lawrence. "Music periodicals: popular and classical record reviews and indexes." In *Notes*, 34 (1978), p. 92–107.

Brief reviews of about 40 reviewing and indexing periodicals concerned with recorded music. Especially valuable for the coverage of titles devoted to popular music.

832. Michalowski, Kornel. Bibliografia polskich czasopism muzycznych. Kraków: Polskie Wydawnictwo Muzyczne, 1955– .

A bibliography of Polish music periodicals; classified listings of their contents from 1820 to 1959. 15 vols. to 1981.

833. "Music periodicals, United States." In *The Music Industry Guide, formerly the Musician's Guide*. 7th ed., p. 321–50. Chicago, Illinois: Marquis Professional Publications, 1983.

U.S., Canadian, and international periodicals are listed alphabetically within each country. Phone number, editor's name, frequency of publication, description of coverage/audience, and subscription rate are given for most publications. [from the introductory remarks]

834. Ongaku kankei chikuji kankobutsu shozai mokuroku. Union list of periodicals in music [henshu Ongaku Toshokan Kyogikai, 1979 -nenban Henshu Iinkai]. 1979-nenban. Tokyo: Do Kyogikai, 1980. 129 p.

This edition supplements the third ed. of 1969. Lists 970 periodicals in 25 Japanese music libraries in 2 sections, one for Japanese-language titles and another for Western titles. Japanese and Russian titles are romanized. Conventional entry includes location of libraries and extent of holdings.

835. Ongaku Toshokan Kyogikai. Ongaku kankei chikuji kankobutsu sōgō mokuroku. Union list of periodicals in music. 1974-ban. Tokyo: Ongaku Toshokan Kyogikai, Showa 49, 1974. 40 p.

Published in 1972 under title *Chikuji Kankobutsu Sōgō Mokuroku*.

Contents: *Wabunhen.—Obunhen*. Covers music periodical holdings in 7 Japanese music libraries. 624 titles in 2 sections, one for Japanese titles and another for Western titles.

836. Ongaku Toshokan Kyogikai. Ongaku kankei chikuji kankobutsu sōgō mokuroku. Union list of periodicals in music. 1976-ban. Tokyo: Ongaku Toshokan Kyogikai, 1976. 60 p.

Published in 1972 under title *Chikuji Kankobutsu Sōgō Mokuroku*.

Contents: *Wabunhen.—Obunhen*. A numbered list of 793 titles in 13 Japanese music libraries. Divided into Japanese- and Western-language sections.

837. "Periodicals indexed." In *The Music Index Annual Cumulation*. Detroit, Michigan: Information Service, 1949– .

Regularly indexes about 500 current periodicals. Addresses and subscription prices given. In 1949 the *Index* treated only 81 titles. Since that time there has been a constant increase in the number of periodicals covered.

838. **"Periodische Schriften."** In *Jahrbuch der Musikbibliothek Peters.* Leipzig: C. F. Peters, 1894–1941. Vols. 1–47.

A regular section of the annual "Verzeichnis ... Bücher und Schriften über Musik," listing new periodicals and other serial publications that have been issued during the year. Compiled by a variety of editors.

839. **"Revistas musicales."** In *Diccionario de la Musica Labor,* v. 2, p. 1863–70. Barcelona: Labor, 1954.

An extensive listing of music periodicals, classified by country, with a short bibliography on musical journalism.

840. **Riedel, A.** Répertoire des periodiques musicaux belges. Bruxelles: Commission belge de bibliographie, 1954. 48 p. (Bibliographia belgica)

330 items, the first 130 of which are music serials, while the remainder are periodicals in the usual sense.

841. **Rohlfs, Eckart.** Die deutschsprachigen Musikperiodica, 1945–57. Regensburg: G. Bosse, 1961. 108 p. (Forschungsbeiträge zur Musikwissenschaft, 11)

A source book of information about music periodicals, their history, coverage, distribution, and subject emphasis. Not confined to German journals as the title might suggest. The systematic bibliographic "Anhang," p. 5–64, lists 589 periodicals in 12 categories. Indexed by chronology, place, title.

Reviews by Fred Blum in *Notes,* 19 (1961), p. 77–78, and by Wolfgang Schmieder in *Die Musikforschung,* 21 (1968), p. 105–107.

842. **Savig, Norman.** A check-list of music serials in 18 libraries of the Rocky Mountain region. Greely, Colorado: Kastle Kiosk, 1970. 45 p. (typescript)

> This list includes music serials in the general sense of the word: periodicals, newspapers, annuals, proceedings, transactions of societies and some monograph series and publishers' series. [Compiler's *Introduction*]

This work supersedes a *Check-list of Music Serials in Nine Libraries of the Rocky Mountain Region,* compiled by William M. McClellan in 1963. The present work lists over 800 title entries and 250 cross-references.

843. **Solow, Linda I.** "Index to 'music periodicals' reviewed in *Notes* (1976–1982)." In *Notes,* 39 (1983), p. 585–90.

A title index to music periodicals reviewed in a regular column in *Notes,* principally by Charles Lindahl.

844. **Svobodová, Marie.** "Music journals in Bohemia and Moravia 1796–1970." In *Fontes Artis Musicae,* 19 (1972), p. 22–41.

259 journals listed alphabetically by title, with a chronological index. Most of the Czech titles are translated into English, or some indication is given of their content. Items are identified by their number in Fellinger's *Verzeichnis* (no. 825), where applicable.

845. Svobodová, Marie and Juraj Potúček. "Music journals in Slovakia, 1871–1970." In *Fontes Artis Musicae*, 21 (1974), p. 32–36.

A list of 27 titles, with a chronological index. Titles are translated into English and there is a brief description of contents.

846. Thoumin, Jean-Adrien. Bibliographie rétrospective des périodiques françaises de littérature musicale 1870–1954. Préface de Madame Elizabeth Lebeau. Paris: Éditions documentaires industrielles et techniques, 1957. 179 p.

Alphabetical listing of 594 French music periodicals. Chronological index; indexes of persons and places of publications.

847. A union list of music periodicals in the libraries of Northern California. Edited by Ann Basart, Garrett Bowles, Richard Colvig, and Harriet Nicewonger for the Northern California Chapter of the Music Library Association. 6th ed. 1979. Berkeley: Northern California Chapter of the Music Library Association, 127 p.

Covers periodicals held by 17 libraries.

848. Union list of periodicals in music in the libraries of the University of London and some other London libraries. M. A. Baird., comp. London: 1969. 56 p.

Based on the periodical holdings of 23 London libraries, excluding the British Library.

849. "Verzeichnis der Zeitschriften und Jahrbücher." In *Hofmeisters Jahresverzeichnis*, v. 100, p. 334–39. Leipzig: F. Hofmeister, 1953.

Lists more than 100 German and Austrian periodicals and yearbooks available in 1951. Since 1953, periodicals are listed in a subsection of the "Anhang: Musikschriften."

See also earlier issues of the *Jahresverzeichnis* (no. 758).

850. Weichlein, William J. A check-list of American music periodicals, 1850–1900. Detroit, Michigan: Information Coordinators, 1970. 103 p. (Detroit studies in music bibliography, 16)

Review by Dena J. Epstein in *Notes*, 27 (1971), p. 489.

851. Wunderlich, Charles. A history and bibliography of early American musical periodicals, 1782–1852. Ann Arbor, Michigan: University Microfilms, 1962. 783 leaves.

Doctoral dissertation written for University of Michigan, Ann Arbor, 1962.

A chronological and descriptive bibliography of 69 periodicals, *l.* 304–655. Variant titles, dates and numbers of publication, imprint, subscription rates, related titles, editors' names with biographical information, principal authors, notes on content, lists of music published in each periodical, and information about libraries holding copies provided. An appendix has entries on 800 publishers, printers, engravers, and others. Title and geographic indexes. List of references, *l.* 288–303.

Complements Weichlein (no. 850).

852. Zecca-Laterza, Agostina. Catalogo dei periodici musicali delle biblioteche lombarde. Milano: Biblioteca del Conservatorio Giuseppe Verdi, 1979. 50 p.

A union list of music periodicals held in libraries in Lombardy. Arranged alphabetically by title, including in each entry a list of libraries where copies are held. Periodicals published in Lombardy in a chronological index arranged in alphabetical order by city.

Review by Gisella de Caro in *Associazione Italiana Bibliotechna Bolletino*, 19 (1979), p. 234.

853. "Zeitschriften." In Mendel's *Musikalisches Conversations-Lexikon*, v. 11, p. 443–62. Berlin: Heimann, 1879.

An early listing, but still useful for its detailed descriptions of 18th- and 19th-century journals.

854. "Zeitschriften." In *Riemann Musiklexikon*. 12th ed. Band 3: *Sachteil*, p. 1073–78.

Historical introduction followed by a selective list, organized by country.

SPECIAL AND SUBJECT BIBLIOGRAPHIES

Contemporary Music

855. Basart, Ann Phillips. Serial music, a classified bibliography of writings on twelve-tone and electronic music. Berkeley and Los Angeles: Univ. of California Press, 1961. 151 p. (University of California bibliographic guides)

A classified bibliography of 823 items treating the literature of 12-tone music, electronic music, the second Viennese school (Schoenberg, Berg, and Webern), and 20 other contemporary composers using serial techniques. Author and subject indexes.

Review by Dika Newlin in *Notes*, 19 (1961), p. 256–57; by James B. Coover in *Journal of Music Theory*, 6 (1962), p. 316–17; by Donald Mitchell in *Tempo*, 63 (Winter 1962–63), p. 46–48; and by Josef Rufer in *Die Musikforschung*, 17 (1964), p. 315–16.

856. Betz, Annaliese. Auftragskompositionen im Rundfunk 1946–1975. Frankfurt am Main: Deutsches Rundfunk Archiv, 1977. 210 p.

List of works commissioned, taped, and broadcast by German radio stations. Information provided on performers, dates, and durations.

857. The Boston composers project, a bibliography of contemporary music. [Compiled by the] Boston Area Music Libraries. Editor: Linda I. Solow; associate editors: Mary Wallace Davidson, Brenda Chasen Goldman, Geraldine E. Ostrove. Cambridge, Massachusetts: MIT Press, 1983. 775 p.

Lists compositions by art music and jazz composers in the Boston area during the latter half of the 1970s. Arranged by composer. Index to names and titles.

Reviews by Margaret Jory in *Notes*, 42 (1985), p. 62–63, and by Charles Ellis in *American Music*, 3 (1985), p. 62–63.

858. Bull, Storm. Index to biographies of contemporary composers. New York and Metuchen, New Jersey: Scarecrow Press, 1964–87. 3 v.

Vol. 1 indexes 69 sources of biographical information for 5,800 composers (dictionaries, who's whos, publishers' lists, etc.) indicating whether the composer under consideration is mentioned. No page references given. Vol. 2 indexes 108 reference works for 8,000 composers, one-half of whom appeared in vol. 1. Vol. 3 indexes an additional 98 reference works and lists more than 13,500 composers, about 5,900 of whom have never been listed before.

Entries provide name of composer, country of birth or residence, year of birth, and date of death (if known or appropriate). Abbreviations indicate the source of biographical information. The list of abbreviations in each volume provides the basic bibliographical information about the sources.

859. Cross, Lowell M. A bibliography of electronic music. Toronto: University of Toronto Press, 1967. 126 p.

A bibliography of writings on electronic music. Some 1,562 articles entered covering developments in the field between 1948 and 1966. In order by author. Subject index.

Review by Otto Luening in *Notes*, 25 (1969), p. 502–503.

860. Deliè. Celestin. "Bibliographie." In *Revue Belge de Musicologie*, 13 (1959), p. 132–48.

Broadly classified bibliography of serial and experimental music with an introduction surveying the literature of the field.

861. Edmunds, John and Gordon Boelzner. Some twentieth-century American composers, a selective bibliography ... with an introductory essay by Peter Yates. New York: New York Public Library, 1959–60. 2 v.

> This bibliography has been made with the purpose of bringing together in a single body separately published writings by and about a representative group of 20th-century American composers ... conservative, moderate, dodecaphonic, and experimental. [*Preface*]

Vol. 1 includes bibliographies for 15 composers, vol. 2 for 17 (with an introductory essay by Nicolas Slonimsky). There are two appendixes, one a listing of composers cited in at least one of 21 standard reference works and the other for composers not cited but who are under 35 and merit some attention.

Both volumes are reprinted, with additions, from *The Bulletin of the New York Public Library*.

862. Tjepkema, Sandra L. A bibliography of computer music: a reference for composers. Iowa City: University of Iowa Press, 1981. 276 p.

"Intended to be a comprehensive listing of books, articles, dissertations and papers relating to the use of computers by composers." There are indexes to subjects, to names not appearing in the alphabetical array of authors' names, and to studios or centers of activity.

Review by Ann P. Basart in *Notes*, 38 (1982), p. 848–49.

863. Warfield, Gerald. Writings on contemporary music notation: an annotated bibliography. Ann Arbor, Michigan: Music Library Association, 1976. 93 p. (MLA index and bibliography series, 16)

A comprehensive bibliography of books and articles on new music published between 1950 and 1975. Selectively includes works published earlier in the century and works referring to new notation but not entirely devoted to the subject. Brief annotations and complete bibliographic information are included. Arranged alphabetically by author with a brief subject index. Includes citations of printing techniques.

Wenk, Arthur B. Analyses of nineteenth-century and twentieth-century music: 1940–1985. See no. 736.

Dissertations

Doctoral dissertations, along with articles in scholarly periodicals, represent the growing edge of research activity in any field. We are currently well supplied with bibliographies of doctoral studies in music for the United States (no. 864), for Germany (nos. 870, 884, 885, and 887), for France (no. 869), and for Great Britain (no. 883), but studies produced in other countries are less easy to locate. Included here are only those reference tools concerned exclusively with studies in music. There are a number of comprehensive national bibliographies of dissertations from which music titles can be extracted. For these, the user should consult Sheehy's *Guide to Reference Books*, 10th edition (no. 729) and Keith Mixter's *General Bibliography for Music Research* (no. 656). Chief among the general bibliographies is *Dissertation Abstracts International* (Ann Arbor, Michigan: University Microfilms, 1938–), which began as an American listing and in 1969 included dissertations from a number of European institutions.

864. Adkins, Cecil and Alis Dickinson. Doctoral dissertations in musicology. 7th North American ed. / 2nd international ed. The second combined publication of the American-Canadian *Doctoral Dissertations in Musicology* (7th cumulative ed.) and the *International Doctoral Dissertations in Musicology* (2nd cumulative ed.). Philadelphia, Pennsylvania: American Musicological Society; [Basel]: International Musicological Society, 1984. 545 p.

First published in 1951 in photo-offset from typed copy, issued jointly by a Committee of the Music Teachers' National Association and the American Musicological Society.

2nd edition, 1958; 3rd edition, 1961; 4th edition, 1965; all compiled by Helen Hewitt, who also edited supplements that appeared in *Journal of the American Musicological Society* and in the *American Music Teacher*. 5th edition, 1971, compiled by Cecil Adkins. 6th edition issued as *International Index of Dissertations and Works in Progress* compiled by Adkins and Alis Dickinson in 1977.

This edition supplemented by pamphlets covering January 1983–April 1984 (1984), May 1984–November 1985 (1986), and December 1985–November 1986 (1987).

Throughout the first four editions, entries are grouped by historical periods under the institutions where the degree was completed. The 5th and following editions abandon listings under institutions. Organized as the previous editions into broad historical periods and then classified by topic.

Covers dissertations until December 1982. Entries provide University Microfilm numbers, *Dissertation Abstracts* reference numbers, and *RILM* references.

This edition covers only dissertations, completed and in progress. *Musicological Works in Progress*, included in the 6th edition, appears annually in *Acta Musicologica*.

This list is international, covering dissertations from 30 different countries, but only those begun or completed since 1972. Earlier, non-American dissertations are covered by Schall's *Verzeichnis musikwissenschaftlicher Dissertationen* (no. 884 and 885) and annual lists in *Die Musikforschung* for German-language dissertations. For earlier British dissertations, see the lists in the Royal Musical Association's *Research Chronicle* beginning with no. 3 (1963) *et passim* (no. 883). French dissertations are covered by Gribenski's *Thèses de Doctorat* (no. 869).

865. Bradley, Ian L. A selected bibliography of musical Canadiana. Rev. ed. Victoria: University of Victoria, 1978. 177 p.

First published in 1974.

Classified contents: bibliographies, theses, biographies, compositions, education, ethnomusicology, histories, miscellaneous. The listing of theses written at Canadian academic institutions is of particular interest.

866. Comprehensive dissertation index, 1861–1972. Vol. 31: Communications and the arts. Ann Arbor, Michigan: Xerox University Microfilms, 1973. 961 p.

Includes a section covering dissertations on music. Dissertations cited in this list, with some few exceptions, can be obtained on microfilm from Xerox University Microfilms on microfilm or on paper. Includes a computer-generated index based on keywords from dissertation titles. Author index.

867. De Lerma, Dominique-René. A selective list of masters' theses in musicology. Compiled for the American Musicological Society. Bloomington, Indiana: Denia Press, 1970. 42 p.

Entries for 257 titles submitted by 36 institutions. Indexes of names, topics, and participating institutions. Entries give information as to availability by photoreproduction or interlibrary loan.

868. "Dissertations." In *Current Musicology*, no. 1– . New York: Music Department, Columbia University, 1965– .

An occasional feature printed in the journal. Offers critical reviews of selected doctoral studies and listings of current dissertations, European as well as American.

869. Dundes, Alan. Folklore theses and dissertations in the United States. Austin: Published for the American Folklore Society by the University of Texas Press, 1976. 610 p.

Even though the bulk of the dissertations listed fall outside the discipline of music, cited because access to some of these titles is difficult.

Chronological list of theses and dissertations, indexes of subjects, authors, and institutions.

Gillis, Frank and Alan P. Merriam. Ethnomusicology and folk music: an international bibliography of dissertations and theses. See no. 898.

870. Gribenski, Jean. Thèses de doctorat en langue française relatives à la musique: bibliographie commentée. [French-language dissertations in music: an annotated bibliography.] New York: Pendragon Press, 1979. 270 p. (RILM Retrospectives, 2)

Doctoral dissertations written in French between 1883 and 1976 on music and closely related disciplines, and defended in Belgian, Canadian, French, and Swiss universities are included. Arrayed on a variant of the *RILM* classification system. Each entry is extensively annotated in French. Indexes to authors, subject, dates, and universities. Addenda.

Reviewed by Geraldine Ostrove in *Notes*, 36, (1979), p. 377–78, and by François Lesure in *Fontes Artis Musicae*, 27 (1980), p. 230–31.

Hartley, Kenneth R. Bibliography of theses and dissertations in sacred music. See no. 1153.

871. "Im Jahre ... angenommene musikwissenschaftliche Dissertationen." In *Die Musikforschung*, vol. 1– . 1948– .

A listing, annual or at more frequent intervals, of doctoral dissertations completed in German, Austrian, and Swiss institutions during the current year. Beginning with vol. 18 (1965), a special section is devoted to reviews of selected dissertations.

872. International Center of Musicological Works in Progress. "Musicological works in progress." Edited by Cecil Adkins. In *Acta Musicologica*, 44 (1972), p. 146–69.

A listing of active research projects, including not only dissertations but postdoctoral studies as well. The entries are classified within major chronological divisions. In many cases the scholar's address is given to encourage communication. Subject index.

For a description of the scope of this project and the techniques employed, see Cecil Adkins' report in *Acta Musicologica*, 43 (1971), p. 103–106.

873. International directory of approved music education dissertations in progress. Richard J. Colwell, editor, and John Chenault, assistant. Urbana, Illinois: Council for Research in Music Education, 1986.

Previously published in 1984 and 1985. Successor to *Approved Doctoral Dissertations in Progress in Music Education*, which cited American dissertations in progress as of 1 January 1977.

A classified directory with entries that give name and address of candidates, institution at which enrolled, and title of dissertation. Indexes to names and to institutions.

874. Meadows, Eddie S. Theses and dissertations on Black American music. Beverly Hills, California: Theodore Front Musical Literature, 1980. 19 p.

A classified and briefly annotated bibliography of 119 doctoral, 120 master's, and a few other dissertations. Lacks references to *Dissertation Abstracts*. No author or subject indexes.

875. Melange of dissertations in music. Ann Arbor, Michigan: University Microfilms International, [1977?]. 22 p.

A listing of doctoral dissertations, written in 1974, 1975, 1976, and some from 1977. Includes a title collection of master's theses abstracted in the quarterly publication *Master's Abstracts*, vols. I–XIV, 1962–76. A list of American doctoral dissertations written 1974–77.

876. Music, a catalog of selected doctoral dissertation research. Ann Arbor, Michigan: University Microfilms International, 1984. 38 p.

Contains citations to 1,335 doctoral dissertations and 233 master's theses completed between 1978 and 1983.

877. Music: a dissertation bibliography. Edited by Kay Long. Ann Arbor, Michigan: University Microfilms, 1979. 36 p.

A list of master's theses and doctoral dissertations written between 1974 and 1978.

878. Music Educators National Conference. Bibliography of research studies in music education, 1932–48. Compiled by William S. Larson. Chicago, Illinois: Music Educators National Conference, 1949. 119 p.

An earlier edition, compiled by Arnold M. Small, appeared in 1944, State University of Iowa Press.

This, and the following five entries, provide continuing documentation for research in music education from 1932 to 1971. From 1957 on the bibliographies have appeared in issues of the *Journal of Research in Music Education*.

879. Music Educators National Conference. "Bibliography of research studies in music education, 1949–1956." Compiled by William S. Larson. In *Journal of Research in Music Education*, 5:2 (1957). 225 p.

880. Music Educators National Conference. "Doctoral dissertations in music and music education, 1963–1967." Compiled by Roderick D. Gordon. In *Journal of Research in Music Education*, 16 (Summer 1968), p. 87–218.

881. Music Educators National Conference. "Doctoral dissertations in music and music education, 1968–1971." Compiled by Roderick D. Gordon. In *Journal of Research in Music Education*, 20 (1972), p. 2–185.

In the above MENC bibliographies, coverage includes dissertations submitted for the degrees of Doctor of Philosophy, Doctor of Education, Doctor of Musical Arts, Doctor of Music Education, and Doctor of Music. No clear distinction is made between research studies in education and those engaging other research areas.

882. Music Educators National Conference. "Doctoral dissertations in music education, 1957–1963." Compiled by Roderick D. Gordon. In *Journal of Research in Music Education*, 12 (Spring 1964). 112 p.

883. "Register of theses on music in Britain and Ireland." By Nick Sandon in *R.M.A. Research Chronicle*, 15 (1979), p. 38–116.

"Supplements" in vol. 16 (p. 110–34), vol. 17 (p. 117–33), vol. 18 edited by Ian Bartlett (p. 85–118), and vol. 19, including an index (p. 59–90). Previous versions had appeared under the editorship of Paul Doe and Michael Downey.

2,155 entries arranged by period, then author. Indexed.

884. Schaal, Richard. Verzeichnis deutschsprachiger musikwissenschaftlicher Dissertationen, 1861–1960. Kassel: Bärenreiter, 1963. 167 p. (Musikwissenschaftliche Arbeiten, hrsg. von der Gesellschaft für Musikforschung, 19)

An alphabetical listing, by author, of 2,819 music dissertations in the German language. Publication data given for works in print. Subject index.

Review by Erich Schenk in *Die Musikforschung*, 17 (1964), p. 421–23, supplying numerous additional entries.

885. Schaal, Richard. Verzeichnis deutschsprachiger musikwissenschaftlicher Dissertationen, 1961–1970, mit Ergänzungen zum Verzeichnis 1861–1960. Kassel: Bärenreiter, 1974. 91 p.

A supplement of 1,271 dissertations, most written between 1961 and 1970, listed alphabetically by author. Publication dates indicated for works subsequently published. Subject index.

886. Texas Music Educators Association. A bibliography of master's theses and doctoral dissertations in music completed at Texas colleges and universities, 1919–1972. Rev. ed. Houston: Texas Music Educators Association, 1974. 152 p.

First edition published in 1964 covered only until 1962.

Listings chronological by institution. Research studies in music education completed in 14 Texas colleges or universities. Subject and author indexes.

887. "Verzeichnis der im Berichtsjahr ... bei der Deutschen Bücherei zu Leipzig registrierten musikwissenschaftlichen Dissertationen und Habilitationsschriften." Compiled by Ortrun Landmann. In *Deutsches Jahrbuch der Musikwissenschaft*. Leipzig: Peters, 1957– .

Continues a bibliography of dissertations originally published in the *Peters Jahrbuch*. Primarily those completed in East German institutions.

Ethnomusicology

Vigorous growth in the field of ethnomusicology in recent years has prompted numerous bibliographical studies. No attempt has been made to list the many useful bibliographies appended to monographs, dissertations, and periodical articles in this field. Attention has been called to the listings of current literature and recordings in *Ethnomusicology, Journal of the Society for Ethnomusicology* (no. 753). One of the most comprehensive bibliographies in this area is found in Jaap Kunst's *Ethnomusicology, a Study of Its Nature, Its Problems ...* (no. 905).

Additional references will be found under "Bibliographies of Music: Folk Song and Ballad" and under "Discographies: Ethnic and Folk Music."

888. Aning, B. A. An annotated bibliography of music and dance in English-speaking Africa. Legon: Institute of African Studies, University of Ghana, 1967. 47 p.

A bibliography of 132 items, including both books and periodical articles. Index of authors. Organized regionally.

Review by Alan P. Merriam in *Ethnomusicology*, 16 (1972), p. 544–45.

Annual bibliography of European ethnomusicology. See Musikethnologische Jahresbibliographie Europas, no. 918.

889. Baumann, Max Peter. Bibliographie zur ethnomusikologischen Literatur der Schweiz: mit einem Beitrag zu Geschichte, Gegenstand und Problemen der Volksliedforschung. Winterthur: Amadeus, 1981. 312 p.

Includes bibliographical references and indexes.

890. Bose, Fritz. Musikalische Völkerkunde. Freiburg: Atlantis-Verlag, 1953. 197 p. (Atlantis-Musikbücherei)

"Bibliographie," p. 144–63. 393 items.

891. Cavanagh, Beverly. "Annotated bibliography: Eskimo music." In *Ethnomusicology*, 16 (1972), p. 479–87.

Cites works on Eskimos in Alaska, Greenland, and the Canadian Arctic.

892. Christensen, Nerthus. Hornbostel opera omnia: Bibliographies Hornbostel opera omnia herausgegeben von Klaus P. Wachsmann, Dieter Christensen, Hans-Peter Reinecke. The Hague: Nijhoff, 1976. 114 p.

An unnumbered volume in the *Hornbostel Opera Omnia*.

Part I: Chronological bibliography of Erich Moritz von Hornbostel's published writings, p. 3–20.

Part II: Comprehensive bibliography of references, p. 23–114.

This work is included as the bibliography of references provides access to many titles encountered in the ethnomusicological guides commonly used in the U.S. This volume thus forms a bibliography of ethnomusicological writings to about 1935. In English and German.

893. Colvig, Richard. "Black music." In *Choice*, a publication of the Association of College and Research Libraries, 6 (Nov. 1969), p. 1169–79.

"A representative selection of English language monographs dealing with the contribution made to music by members of the Negro race on both sides of the Atlantic." 71 items, classified and mostly annotated.

Also published separately by the Oakland Public Library, Oakland, California, 1969, 18 p.

894. "Current Bibliography and Discography." In *Ethnomusicology*, journal of the Society for Ethnomusicology. Edited by Joseph C. Hickerson, Neil V. Rosenberg, and Frank Gillis.

Editors vary, but the above three names have been active since May 1970.

The best current listing of literature and phonorecords in the field of ethnomusicology. This excellent current listing has never been cumulated, classified, and indexed.

895. De Lerma, Dominique-René and Michael Phillips. "Entries of ethnomusicology interest in *MGG*: a preliminary listing." In *Ethnomusicology*, 13 (1969), p. 129–38.

Attention is directed to eight areas in the German reference work that contain articles of interest to ethnomusicologists: the Americas (7 entries), Africa (13), Asia and Oceania (23), Europe (33), dance (35), instruments (47), miscellaneous (24), and biographies and index of contributors (134).

896. Densmore, Frances. "The study of Indian music in the nineteenth century." In *American Anthropologist*, 29 (1927), p. 77–86.

A survey of early studies in the field of American Indian music; generally valuable, although it contains some errors.

897. Emsheimer, Ernst. "Musikethnographische Bibliographie der nichtslavischen Völker in Russland." In *Acta Musicologica*, 15 (1943), p. 34–63.

A bibliography of 433 items concerned with the music of the non-Slavic peoples of Russia. Classified according to ethnic groups. German translations for Slavic titles. Some editions of folk music cited, but chiefly concerned with periodical literature and monographs. Full bibliographical information.

898. Gaskin, Lionel. A select bibliography of music in Africa. Compiled at the International African Institute by L. J. P. Gaskin under the direction of Prof. K. P. Wachsmann. London: International African Institute, 1965. 83 pgs. (Africa bibliography series, 8)

Includes "all known works ... on music in Africa." Afro-American music in Cuba is covered as well. A classified bibliography with geographical subdivisions under each subject. Subjects are: generalities; Africa; African music; musical instruments; dance; bibliographies and catalogs. There is an author index as well as one by geography and ethnic group. List of periodicals cited. Most of the entries are for 20th-century works published before 1960.

Review by Leonard Vohs in *Die Musikforschung*, 22 (1969), p. 390–91. Review by Douglas Varley and Alan Taylor in *Ethnomusicology*, 11 (1967), p. 125–28.

899. Gillis, Frank and Alan P. Merriam. Ethnomusicology and folk music: an international bibliography of dissertations and theses. Middletown, Connecticut: Published for the Society for Ethnomusicology by the Wesleyan University Press, 1966. 148 p.

International in scope, 897 entries arranged by author, giving title, degree, granting institution, and date of dissertation. Occasional references to publications. Indexes of institutions and subjects.

900. Guèdon, Marie-Françoise. "Canadian Indian ethnomusicology: selected bibliography and discography." In *Ethnomusicology*, 16 (1972), p. 465–78.

Subdivided by five cultural areas: (1) Eastern woodlands-Great Lakes, (2) Plains, (3) Yukon-Mackenzie basins, (4) Plateau, (5) Northwest coast.

901. Haywood, Charles. A bibliography of North American folklore and folksong. 2nd rev. ed. New York: Dover Publications, [1961]. 2 v.

First published in one volume by Greenberg, New York, 1951.

Vol. 1, p. 1–748: concerned with the non-Indian Americans north of Mexico. Vol. 2, p. 749–1159: with the American Indians north of Mexico. Subdivisions in vol. 1 include general bibliography. Vol. 2 is subdivided by cultural areas. Entries for folklore and for folk music are separated under each heading; recordings included. General index. Endpapers are maps of regional and cultural areas.

Review of first edition by Duncan Emrich in *Notes*, 8 (1951), p. 700–701.

902. Henry, Mellinger Edward. A bibliography for the study of American folk songs, with many titles of folk songs (and titles that have to do with folk songs) from other lands. London: Mitre Press, [1937]. 142 p.

Studies and collections of music interfiled in one alphabet. The emphasis is on the English-Scottish ballad and its derivatives.

903. Herzog, George. Research in primitive and folk music in the U.S., a survey. Washington, D.C.: American Council of Learned Societies, 1936. 97 p.

Surveys U.S. resources for the study of primitive and folk music as of 1936. Record archives are described and their holdings tabulated; collections of primitive musical instruments listed. Bibliographies given for each of the main sections.

Huerta, Jorge A., ed. A bibliography of Chicano and Mexican dance, drama, and music. See no. 1285.

904. Kendadamath, G. C. Indian music and dance: a select bibliography. Varanasi: Indian Bibliographic Centre, 1986. 261 p.

A classified bibliography with 2,434 entries primarily published from 1970 to 1984. All sources are in English and most of the articles and books were published in India. Entries provide basic bibliographic data but are not annotated. Author and subject indexes.

905. Krader, Barbara. "Ethnomusicology." In *The New Grove Dictionary of Music and Musicians*, edited by Stanley Sadie, v. 6, p. 275–82. London: Macmillan, 1980.

After a brief historical overview, this article poses the chief problems of the field and addresses some of the approaches taken in addressing them. Classified bibliography of works on the discipline.

906. Kunst, Jaap. Ethnomusicology, a study of its nature, its problems, methods and representative personalities, to which is added a bibliography. 3rd ed. enl. The Hague: Nijhoff, 1959. 303 p.

First published in 1950 under the title *Musicologica....* The 2nd edition, 1955, contains a selective bibliography. 2nd edition reprinted in 1977 by the Scholarly Press. Reprint of the 3rd edition and its *Supplement* in 1969.

Bibliography of the 3rd edition, p. 79–215, lists 4,552 items, most of them with location symbols referring to libraries in Western Europe. Entries that contain extensive bibliographies within themselves are marked with an asterisk. Portraits of ethnomusicologists.

Supplement to the 3rd Edition, 1960, 45 p., adds some 500 items to the bibliography; new record listings through 1958, more portraits.

Review of the 3rd ed. by Bruno Nettl in *Notes*, 16 (1959), p. 560–61; of the *Supplement* by William Lichtenwanger in *Notes*, 19 (1961), p. 79.

907. Kuppuswamy, Gowri and Muthuswamy Hariharan. Indian dance and music literature. New Delhi: Biblia Impex Private Ltd., 1981. 156 p.

800 books on music and 3,000 articles are cited. Place and date of publication cited, but not publisher. Language of text indicated. Subject index.

908. Laade, Wolfgang. Gegenwartsfragen der Musik in Afrika und Asien. Eine grundlegende Bibliographie. Baden-Baden: V. Koerner, 1970. 120 p. (Sammlung musikwissenschaftlicher Abhandlungen, 51)

A regionally organized bibliography of 874 items taken chiefly from current periodical literature. This work also serves as a useful directory of institutions, societies, and broadcasting stations involved in the study of Asian-African music.

Lawless, Ray McKinley. Folksingers and folksongs in America. See no. 252.

909. Laws, George M. Native American balladry; a descriptive study and a bibliographical syllabus. Rev. ed. Philadelphia, Pennsylvania: American Folklore Society, 1964. 298 p. (Publications of the American Folklore Society. Bibliographical series, 1)

First published in 1950. 276 p.

After the study, the bibliographical portion covers "native ballads current in oral tradition: a syllabus of the ballads sung in the U.S. and Canada," p. 115–226. The syllabus is a classified bibliography (war ballads, ballads of sailors and the sea, etc.) with entries citing "usual" title and alternate titles, summaries of the ballad stories, sample stanzas, and list of printed texts of the ballads (including folk song collections). There is another section on ballads of "doubtful currency in tradition." Concludes with lists of ballad-like pieces and imported ballads and folk songs. Bibliography includes sources of ballads. Index of ballads and songs.

910. League of Nations. International Institute of Intellectual Cooperation. Folklore musical; répertoire international des collections et centres de documentation avec notices sur l'état actuel des recherches dans les différents pays et références bibliographiques. Paris: Département d'Art, d'Archéologie et d'Ethnologie, Institut International de Coopération Intellectuelle, [1939]. 332 p.

Organization similar to the following item. Special section devoted to the international phonorecord archive in Berlin, Paris, and Vienna. P. 307–322: supplement of additions and corrections to the 1934 volume (see no. 910).

911. League of Nations. International Institute of Intellectual Cooperation. Musique et chanson populaires. Paris: Institut International de Coopération Intellectuelle, 1934. 257 p.

A reference book intended to establish an international listing of museums, archives, libraries, and other institutions, public and private, concerned with research or collection in the field of popular music, with descriptions of their facilities. Contributions by leading specialists arranged alphabetically by country. Most of the essays contain bibliographies of studies and editions and a list of names and addresses of specialists.

912. Lieberman, Fredric. Chinese music, an annotated bibliography. 2nd ed., rev. and enl. New York: Garland, 1979. 257 p. (Asian music publications. Series A: Bibliographies and research aids, 1) (Garland reference library of the humanities, 75)
First edition published by the Society for Asian Music, 1970, and supplemented 1973.

> This bibliography attempts exhaustive coverage of publications in Western languages as well as critical annotation. [Author's *Preface*]

Annotated bibliography of 2,441 items arranged alphabetically by author. Index of source periodicals, of names, and of topics for selected readings. Includes discographies. Covers all aspects of Chinese music, including the emigrant Chinese. Principal sources are Chinese journals.
Reviews by Judith J. Johnson in *Notes*, 36 (1979), p. 370–71, and by François Lesure, in *Fontes Artis Musicae*, 27 (1980), p. 58–59.

913. Lomax, Alan and Sidney R. Cowell. American folksong and folklore, a regional bibliography. New York: Progressive Education Association, 1942. 59 p.
A classified bibliography with annotated entries on reference works and song and dance collections for those interested in performing or studying American folk song or folklore. Includes a bibliography and a list of periodicals. Not indexed. Dated, but still useful.

914. Marks, Paul F. Bibliography of literature concerning Yemenite-Jewish music. Detroit, Michigan: Information Coordinators, 1973. 50 p. (Detroit studies in music bibliography, 27)

915. Mattfeld, Julius. The folk music of the Western hemisphere; a list of references in the New York Public Library. New York: New York Public Library, 1925. 74 p.
Reprinted, with additions, from the *Bulletin of the New York Public Library*, November and December 1924.

916. McLean, Mervyn. An annotated bibliography of Oceanic music and dance. Wellington, New Zealand: Polynesian Society, 1977. 252 p. (Memoir of the Polynesian Society, 41)
A 74 p. supplement by the same author was issued in 1981.
In a single alphabet, with an index to areas covered by each cited work. There are area codes based on Murdoch's *Outline of World Cultures*. No subject or title index. References to books, articles, reviews, record album notes, manuscripts, and theses in commonly read western European languages are included. Trivial items, collections of songs with piano accompaniment, and publications of or about "acculturated music" are omitted.
Supplement adds 500 entries to the earlier 2,200 and brings coverage up to 1980.

917. Merriam, Alan P. "An annotated bibliography of African and African-derived music since 1936." In *Africa*, 21 (1951), p. 319–30.

918. Musikethnologische Jahresbibliographie Europas. Annual bibliography of European ethnomusicology. Hrsg. vom Slowakischen Nationalmuseum in Verbindung mit dem Institut für Musikwissenschaft der Slowakischen Akademie der Wissenschaften und dem Institut für deutsche Volkskunde der Deutschen Akademie der Wissenschaften Berlin unter Mitwirkung des International Folk Music Council durch Oskár Elschek, Erich Stockmann und Ivan Macák. Bratislava: Slovenské národné múzeum, 1967–76. 10 v.

Introduction in Czech and English. An annual bibliography of periodical articles, books, and other materials on ethnic music in Europe. Bibliographical entries are printed in the original language only.

Review of vol. 1 by Rolf W. Brednich in *Jahrbuch für Volksliedforschung*, 15 (1970), p. 182–83, and by Frank J. Gillis in *Ethnomusicology*, 16 (1972), p. 138–39.

919. Nettl, Bruno. Reference materials in ethnomusicology. 2nd ed., revised, 1967. Detroit, Michigan: Information Coordinators, 1967. 40 p. (Detroit studies in music bibliography, 1)

First published in 1961.

A narrative and critical discussion of the leading reference works in the field, organized in terms of the structure of the discipline. On p. 37–46 a list of publications is cited, with full bibliographical information.

Review by William Lichtenwanger in *Notes*, 19 (1962), p. 428–30; by Marius Schneider in *Die Musikforschung*, 19 (1964), p. 88–89.

920. Nettl, Bruno. The study of ethnomusicology; 29 issues and concepts. Urbana: University of Illinois Press, 1983. 410 p.

A discussion of issues central to the field of ethnomusicology. Each essay "deals with a concept or an aspect of theory or procedure affecting the field of ethnomusicology as a whole, and not specific to any one world area or culture." Extensive bibliography, p. 363–96.

921. Nettl, Bruno. Theory and method in ethnomusicology. New York: Free Press, 1964. 306 p.

Chapter 2 is a history of the field, focusing on bibliography. Each chapter is followed by a list of publications cited.

Review by David P. McAllester in *Musical Quarterly*, 51 (1965), p. 425–28.

922. Sandberg, Larry and Dick Weissman. The folk music source book. New York: Knopf, 1976. 260 p.

This book treats North American folk music in both the popular sense and the ethnic sense. There is information on blues as well as on North American Indian musics. Styles and genres are discussed, each with a discography. There are biographical entries, an annotated list of songbooks, and a list of reference works. There is a list of periodicals and a directory of organizations, centers, archives, and festivals.

923. Smith, Donna Ridley. Non-Western music: a selected bibliography of materials in the California State University, Sacramento, Library. 3rd ed. Sacramento: Library, California State University, 1982. 45 p.

2nd ed. by Sheila J. Johnson, 1973. 40 p.

A bibliography of works about African, Asian, and Oceanic musics held in the California State University, Sacramento, Library.

924. Song, Bang-Song. An annotated bibliography of Korean music. Providence, Rhode Island: Brown University, 1971. 250 p. (Asian music publications, ser. A, no. 2)
   A bibliography of 1,319 items. Part I cites writings on Korean music in the Korean language; Part II, writings in foreign languages. Indexes of bibliographical sources and of names and subjects. The annotations are brief but informative.

925. Stein, Evan. The use of computers in folklore and folk music: a preliminary bibliography. Washington, D.C.: Library of Congress, Archive of Folk Song, 1979. 12 p.

926. Thieme, Darius L. African music, a briefly annotated bibliography. Washington, D.C.: Library of Congress, Reference Department, Music Division, 1964. 55 p. (typescript)

   The present work lists sources discussing the music of sub-Saharan Africa. The work is divided into two main sections, the first listing periodicals and serial articles, the second listing books. [*Preface*]

   A bibliography of 597 items, with an author and linguistic area index.

927. Tsuge, Genichi. Japanese music: an annotated bibliography. New York: Garland Pub., 1986. 161 p. (Garland bibliographies on ethnomusicology, 2)

   This bibliography includes publications on Japanese music in Western languages which appeared through 1983. Although its scope is limited primarily to publications dealing with traditional Japanese music, some writings concerning dance, drama, and/or performing arts of ritualistic nature are inevitably included, as certain aspects of Japanese music are indeed inseparable from such areas. [*Introduction*]

   881 annotated entries in a single alphabet. Subject index in three sections: fields of study; genres of traditional Japanese music; Japan and the West. Name and format indexes. Indexing does not reveal the presence of reference works, especially bibliographies.

928. Varley, Douglas H. African native music: an annotated bibliography. 1st ed. reprinted; with additional note. Folkestone: Dawsons, 1970. 116 p.
   Reprint of 1st edition by the Royal Empire Society, London, 1936.
   "Confined to the Negro and Bantu cultures, roughly south of the Sahara."
   Two sections of general bibliography followed by local bibliographies relating to 30 African countries. Special sections on "African survivals in the New World" and the drum language. List of museums containing collections of African instruments. Author index. Brief but informative annotations.

929. Vetterl, Karel. A select bibliography of European folk music. Published in cooperation with the International Folk Music Council by the Institute for Ethnography and Folklore of the Czechoslovak Academy of Sciences. Prague, 1966. 144 p.

The bibliography attempts to list the most useful publications, both books and articles, and especially those of a scholarly nature, that bear on the folk music of particular European countries. [*Introduction*]

Organized alphabetically by country. Strong on East European entries, particularly Russian.

Brief review by Rolf Wilh. Brednich in *Jahrbuch für Volksliedforschung*, 14 (1969), p. 175.

Review by Ann Briegleb in *Ethnomusicology*, 12 (1968), p. 161–62.

930. Waterman, Richard. [*et al.*]"Bibliography of Asiatic musics." In *Notes*, vol. 5, no. 1 to vol. 8, no. 2 (Dec. 1947–March 1951). 181 p. in all.

A classified bibliography, published serially, of 3,488 books, monographs, articles, sections of larger works, texts, transcriptions, and recordings, arranged geographically and ethnologically. All European languages, including Russian and Romanized Turkish.

Musical Instruments

The literature on musical instruments is to be found in a variety of reference books. The reader in search of further information should look under the following additional headings: "Dictionaries of Musical Instrument Makers and Performers" (no. 270 ff.) and "Catalogs of Musical Instrument Collections" (no. 2495 ff.). Many of the reference tools contain appended bibliographies on the subject.

931. Bajzek, Dieter. Percussion: an annotated bibliography with special emphasis on contemporary notation and performance. Metuchen, New Jersey: Scarecrow, 1988. 185 p.

The bibliography centers on materials published in the English language during the last twenty years, with the exception of some earlier works of interest and some major publications in foreign languages. It covers a wide range of musical styles and techniques of the Western and Non-Western world, and is intended to be a useful tool of reference for the beginner and professional percussionist, the instrumental teacher, the academic scholar, and the contemporary composer/arranger.

The entries in this bibliography, numbering over 1400, do not refer to percussion music itself (with some exceptions), but concern themselves with journal articles, monographs, and dissertations pertaining to all aspects of percussion music, instruments, instrumental techniques and research. The majority of entries are annotated. [from the introductory remarks]

Excluded are materials that are mainly bibliographical and works on bells or other "mechanical" percussion instruments. A classified bibliography with an author index. Appendixes: a selected list of percussion music, transcriptions, and analyses; relevant bibliographies, indexes, and reviews; listing of percussion magazines and musical journals with regular features on percussion.

932. Bakus, Gerald J. The Spanish guitar: a comprehensive reference to the classical and flamenco guitar. Los Angeles: Gothic Press, 1977. 204 p.

Includes bibliography and index.

933. Blades, James. Percussion instruments and their history. Rev. ed. London: Faber, 1984. 511 p.
Previously published in 1975. 509 p.
Bibliographies and indexes.

934. Blades, James and Jeremy Montagu. Early percussion instruments: from the Middle Ages to the Baroque. London: Oxford University Press, 1976. 77 p.
Bibliography.

935. Blaetschacher, Richard. Die Lauten- und Geigenmachwerke des Füssener Landes. Hofheim am Taunus: Friedrich Hofmeister, 1978. 239 p.
Beautiful plates of instruments, chiefly viols and violins. Bibliography.

Boalch, Donald H. Makers of the harpsichord and clavichord, 1440 to 1840. See no. 277.

936. Chou, Ch'ing-yün. Ch'in shih pu. [History of the Ch'in, Supplement.] [China]: Meng-p'o shih ts'ang pan, cchi wei, [1919]. 5 v.
On double leaves, Oriental style, in case. In Chinese.
A collection of quotations from various Chinese texts in which people connected with the ch'in as musicians, ch'in makers, etc. are mentioned. Arranged chronologically by the person's name, beginning with legendary times and continuing into the 10th century, totaling over 100 names. Each person is identified briefly, the quotation is cited, and the source named.
Another two titles are included in this publication. The first is *Ch'in Shih Hsü* [*Continuation of the History of the Ch'in*], a three-volume work containing the names of another 400 people associated with the ch'in who lived from the Sung dynasty (beginning in A.D. 960) to the 19th century. There are appendixes devoted to Buddhists and women. The second is *Ch'in Shu Pieh Lu* [*Bibliography of Works on the Ch'in*], a one-volume annotated list of 200 books and manuscripts on the Ch'in from the Chou (1122 B.C.) to the Ch'ing (1644–1911) dynasties.

Coover, James B. Musical instrument collections; catalogues and cognate literature. See no. 2495.

Crane, Frederick. Extant medieval musical instruments: a provisional catalogue by types. See no. 286.

937. Evans, Tom and Mary Anne Evans. Guitars: music, history, construction, and players from the Renaissance to rock. New York: Facts On File, [1982?]. 479 p.
Previously published by Padington Press, 1977. Published in a French edition by A. Michel, Paris, 1979, as *Le Grand Livre de la Guitare, de la Renaissance au Rock.* 354 p.
A source book including biographical information.

938. Fallou, Robert and Norbert Dufourcq. Essai d'une bibliographie de l'histoire de l'orgue en France. Paris: Fischbacher, 1929. 74 p.

184

939. Graaf, G. A. C. de. Literatuur over het orgel. Literature on the organ, principally in Dutch libraries. Amsterdam: G. A. C. de Graaf; Uitgeverij, F. Knuf, 1957. 71 p. (Bibliotheca organologica, 51)

Lists over 1,250 titles of books, brochures, and reprints concerning the use, the history, and the construction of organs. Does not include books on organ playing.

Introduction and title page in Dutch, English, German, French, Spanish, and Italian.

Handbuch der europäischen Volksmusikinstrumente. See no. 293 and no. 335.

940. Hermann, Judy. "Violin makers: a selective bibliography." In *Cum Notis Variorum*, no. 96 (October 1985), p. 5–9.

Published in an abbreviated version in *Metrodata, the Newsletter of the Los Angeles Metropolitan Cooperative Library System*, November-December, 1984.

An annotated bibliography.

941. Heron-Allen, Edward. De fidiculis bibliographia: being an attempt towards a bibliography of the violin.... London: Griffith Farran, 1890–94. 2 v.

Reprint by Holland Press, 1961.

Classified bibliography of literature on the violin in all its aspects. Full bibliographical data with copious annotations. The work was issued in parts, printed on the recto only, and concludes with four supplements.

942. Hinson, Maurice. The piano teacher's source book: an annotated bibliography of books related to the piano and piano music. 2nd ed. Melville, New York: Belwin Mills Pub. Corp., 1980. 187 p.

First published in 1974 and supplemented in 1976.

A categorized bibliography of English-language books. Indexes to authors and composers.

943. Hutschenruyter, Willem. Bijdrage tot de bibliographie der muziekliteratuur. Een zooveel mogelijk aangevulde samenvatting der boek- en tijdschrift-overzichten, die sedert 1885 zijn opgenomen in het *Vierteljahrschrift für Musikwissenschaft*, het *Zeitschrift der Internationalen Musikgesellschaft*, en het *Jahrbuch der Musikbibliothek Peters*. Vol. 1: Instrumentale muziek, mechanische muziek, electrische muziek, klokken. Zeist, 1941. 513 p. (typescript)

An incomplete project, intended to be a comprehensive bibliography of music literature, but progressed only so far as to cover writings on instrumental music, electrical music, and bells.

Janson, Will. The bassoon.... See no. 1464.

944. Liebenow, Walther M. Rank on rank; a bibliography of the history and construction of organs. Minneapolis, Minnesota: Martin Press, 1973. 171 p.

Brief entries organized geographically with separate sections on history and construction. Indexed.

Review by Walter Hilse in *Notes*, 31 (1975), p. 572–74.

945. Lyons, David B. Lute, vihuela, guitar to 1800; a bibliography. Detroit, Michigan: Information Coordinators, 1978. 214 p. (Detroit studies in music bibliography, 40)

A bibliography of music for, and articles and books on, the instruments listed in the title, as well as theorbo, orpharion, bandora, and mandolin, including a list of editions featuring tablature. Organized in 28 chapters. Cross-references and author index. Addenda of 231 more sources, separately indexed.

Review by Thomas F. Heck in *Notes*, 36 (1979), p. 107–108, and by François Lesure in *Fontes Artis Musicae*, 26 (1979), p. 297.

946. Meer, John Henry van der. "Ältere und neuere Literatur zur Musikinstrumentenkunde." In *Acta Musicologica*, 51 (1979), p. 1–50.

An extensive discussion of the literature of musical instruments, citing 415 titles and ranging from important catalogs of exhibitions to monographs on the development of individual instruments. A tour de force.

947. Miller, Dayton C. Catalogue of books and literary material relating to the flute and other musical instruments, with annotations. Cleveland, Ohio: privately printed, 1935. 120 p.

Catalog of the literary portion of one of the largest collections ever assembled on the flute and related instruments. Now in the Music Division of the Library of Congress (no. 2576).

Includes material on all wind instruments, in the form of books, pamphlets, periodical articles, newspaper clippings, concert programs, makers' catalogs and price lists, etc. Brief annotations.

948. Oberkogler, Friedrich. Vom Wesen und Werden der Musikinstrumente. 2. Aufl. Schaffhausen: Novalis Verlag, 1985. 175 p.

First published in 1976.

Narrative bibliography on the nature and development of musical instruments; a well-made book.

949. Overton, Friend Robert. Der Zink: Geschichte, Bauweise und Spieltechnik eines historischen Musikinstrumentes. Mainz and New York: Schott, 1981. 260 p.

In addition to the historical study there is a valuable bibliography and list of compositions for the zink.

950. Pohlmann, Ernst von. Laute, Theorbe, Chitarrone. Die Lauten-Instrumente, ihre Musik und Literatur von 1500 bis zur Gegenwart. Zweite Auflage. Bremen: Edition Eres, 1972. 416 p.

First printed in 1968. The 2nd edition is much enlarged.

A sourcebook of information about instruments of the lute family, including sources, composers, literature, descriptions of tablatures, locations of existing instruments, makers.

Review by Stanley Buetens in *Journal of the Lute Society of America*, 5 (1972), p. 114–16.

951. Reuter, Rudolf. Bibliographie der Orgel; Literatur zur Geschichte der Orgel bis 1968. Kassel: Bärenreiter, 1973. 256 p. (Münster. Universität. Orgelwissenschaftliche Forschungsstelle. Veröffentlichungen, 3)

A bibliography of 8,574 books and articles, not including works about organists or reviews of performances. Arranged alphabetically by authors, but provided with indexes by location, names of persons, and subjects. List of periodicals devoted to literature on the organ.
Review by Walter Hilse in *Notes*, 31 (1975), p. 572–74.

952. Riley, Maurice W. "A tentative bibliography of early wind instrument tutors." In *Journal of Research in Music Education*, 6 (1958), p. 3–24.
The listing is chronological under the various instruments: flute, oboe, clarinet, bassoon, horn, trumpet, trombone, tuba, and related instruments. Annotated.

953. Schlesinger, Kathleen. A bibliography of musical instruments and archaeology. London: W. Reeves, 1912. 100 p.
Only the first 20 plates are devoted to works on musical instruments and the orchestra. Short sections on catalogs of instrument collections and general works on music. The greater part of the volume is concerned with classical and medieval antiquities.

954. Schulz, Ferdinand F. Pianographie: Klavierbibliographie der lieferbaren Bücher und Periodica sowie der Dissertationen in deutscher, englischer, französischer und italienischer Sprache. 2., verb. und erheblich erw. Aufl. Recklinghausen: Piano-Verlag, 1982. 458 p.
First published in 1978.
A classified bibliography of about 2,000 works about pianos, music for pianos, and composers of piano music. There is a short *Nachtrag*, extensive lists of addresses of publishers, libraries, piano competitions, and music societies. No title or subject index.

955. Schwarz, Werner. Guitar bibliography: an international listing of theoretical literature on classical guitar from the beginning to the present.... München: K. G. Saur, 1984. 257 p.
A classified bibliography of 4,705 entries.

956. Skei, Allen Bennet. Woodwind, brass, and percussion instruments of the orchestra, a bibliographic guide. New York: Garland, 1985. 271 p. (Garland reference library of the humanities, 458)
Selected titles on instruments annotated. Intended as a guide to research for a professional audience. A classified list of 1,195 items. Index of names and subjects.

957. Torri, Luigi. La costruzione ed i costruttori degli istrumenti ad arco. Bibliografia liutistica storico-tecnica. 2a edizione.... Padova: G. Zanibon, 1920. 43 p.
Brief critical and descriptive annotations. Alphabetically arranged, with a subject index.

958. Warman, John Watson. The organ: writings and other utterances on its structure, history, procural, capabilities, etc.: with criticisms, and depositories preceded by an analytical consideration of general bibliographical and catalogual construction. Thornton Heath, Surrey: J. W. Warman, 1898–1904. 4 pts. 287 p.

At head of title: *The Organ: A Comprehensive Treatise on its Structure.*

959. Warner, Thomas E. An annotated bibliography of woodwind instruction books, 1600–1830. Detroit, Michigan: Information Coordinators, 1967. 138 p. (Detroit studies in music bibliography, 11)

A bibliography of 450 items arranged chronologically; includes a number of unlocated titles. Contains a list of modern works cited; indexed by author and anonymous titles and by type of instrument.

Jazz

The literature of jazz continues to proliferate rapidly. Readers will find relevant information in several different sections of this book, under "Bibliographies of Music: Jazz and Popular Music," and, above all, under "Discographies: Collectors' Guides to Popular Recordings." The *Jazz Index* (no. 785) provided good coverage of the current literature of jazz but now one must depend upon *POMPI (Popular Music Periodicals Index)* (no. 796).

960. Carl Gregor, Duke of Mecklenburg. International bibliography of jazz books. Volume I: 1921–1949. Compiled with the assistance of Norbert Rücker. Baden-Baden: Valentin Koerner, 1983. 108 p. (Collections d'Etudes Musicologiques, 67) (Sammlung musikwissenschaftlicher Abhandlungen, 67)

The first of a projected four volumes intended to revise and expand the author's earlier bibliography and its two supplements (no. 961).

Arranged alphabetically including brief transcriptions of tables of contents. List of phantom titles. Indexes of collaborators; keywords and persons named in titles; subjects; collections and series; and countries of publication. Chronological survey of years of publication.

961. Carl Gregor, Duke of Mecklenburg. International jazz bibliography: jazz books from 1919 to 1968. Strasbourg: Heitz, 1969. 198 p. (Sammlung musikwissenschaftlicher Abhandlungen, 49)

1970 Supplement.... Graz: Universal Edition, 1971. 109 p. (Beiträge zur Jazzforschung, 3) *1971/72/73 Supplement....* Graz: Universal Edition, 1975. 246 p. (Beiträge zur Jazzforschung, 6)

Review of the 1969 edition by Ekkehard Jost in *Die Musikforschung*, 24 (1971), p. 330–31; by Alan P. Merriam in *Ethnomusicology*, 14 (1970), p. 177. Review of the *1970 Supplement* by James Patrick in *Notes*, 29 (1972), p. 236–39. Review of the *1971/72/73 Supplement* in *Jazz Podium*, vol. 24, no. 3 (1975), p. 34.

962. Cooper, B. Lee. The popular music handbook, a resource guide for teachers, librarians, and media specialists. Littleton, Colorado: Libraries Unlimited, 1984. 415 p.

In four parts: Part 1: Recommended teaching topics; Part 2: Print resources on popular music, a classified bibliography, occasionally anno-

188

tated; Part 3: Discographies of popular music; Part 4: A basic popular music collection for libraries.

The introductory sections to parts 2 and 3 are heavily annotated guides to the fundamental literature on the subject. Selective general bibliography. Index to artists and performers, and to subjects.

963. Haselgrove, J. R. and D. Kennington. Readers' guide to books on jazz. 2nd ed. London: Library Association, 1965. 16 p.

A popular but informed bibliography. Still valuable.

964. Hefele, Bernhard. Jazz-bibliography. Jazz-bibliographie. International literature on jazz, blues, spirituals, gospel and ragtime music with a selected list of works on the social and cultural background from the beginning to the present. München and New York: K. G. Saur, 1981. 368 p.

A superb bibliography including 6,600 entries arranged by topic, some citing reviews. Name index.

Review by Nina Davis-Millis in *Notes*, 39 (1981), p. 102–103.

965. Kennington, Donald and Danny Read. The literature of jazz, a critical guide. 2nd edition, revised. Chicago, Illinois: American Library Association, 1980. 282 p.

Nine short chapters discussing various aspects of jazz documentation, each followed by an annotated bibliography. Title index and name index.

A work first published in England, 1970, by the Library Association.

Review, unfavorable, of the first American edition by Eileen Southern in *Notes*, 29 (1972), p. 35–36.

966. Meadows, Eddie S. Jazz reference and research materials: a bibliography. New York: Garland Publishing, 1981. 300 p. (Critical studies on Black life and culture, 22) (Garland reference libraries of the humanities, 251)

Arranged in two sections: "Jazz and its genres" and "Reference materials," the latter organized by reference or research genre (e.g., bibliography, histories, discographies, etc.). Each section is separately indexed by name and subject.

967. Meeker, David. Jazz in the movies. New, enlarged edition. New York: Da Capo Press, 1981. Unnumbered pages.

Original edition published by the British Film Institute, London, 1972. Subsequent edition copublished by Talisman Books, London, and Arlington House, New Rochelle, New York, 1977.

Cites and describes 3,724 films, including television films, mentioning jazz musicians responsible for the musical elements of the sound track. Index to names.

968. Merriam, Alan P. A bibliography of jazz. With the assistance of Robert J. Benford. Philadelphia: American Folklore Society, 1954. 145 p. (Publications of the American Folklore Society, Bibliographical series, 4)

Reprint by Da Capo Press, New York, 1970.

3,324 numbered entries, arranged alphabetically by author, with subject emphasis indicated by a code system. Lists 113 jazz periodicals. Subject index.

Review by Marshall W. Stearns in *Notes*, 12 (1955), p. 436–37; of the reprint edition by Eileen Southern in *Notes*, 29 (1972), p. 34–35.

969. Reisner, Robert G. The literature of jazz; a selective bibliography. Introduction by Marshall W. Stearns. New York: New York Public Library, 1959. 63 p.

A preliminary edition appeared in the *Bulletin of the New York Public Library*, March–May 1954.

Cites some 500 books on jazz, 850 periodical articles, and 125 jazz magazines.

Review by William Lichtenwanger in *Notes*, 16 (1959), p. 398.

Popular Music

970. Booth, Mark W. American popular music: a reference guide. Westport, Connecticut: Greenwood Press, 1983. 212 p. (American popular culture series)

> This book is an inventory of resources for studying American popular music. It offers brief descriptions of books, periodicals, and special library collections where the user can seek out the many kinds of popular music, past and present, and information about that music and its makers. [*Preface*]

In six chapters Booth covers a broad range of genres and generalities through lengthy introductory essays and lists of relevant works. No articles are cited. A calendar of "significant dates in the history of American popular music" and a directory of selected reference collections precede an index of names and subjects.

Reviews by Michael Meckna in *American Music*, 4 (1986), p. 358–59, and by Diane Parr Walker in *Notes*, 41 (1985), p. 722–23.

971. Dimmick, Mary L. The Rolling Stones: an annotated bibliography. Rev. enl. ed. Pittsburgh, Pennsylvania: University of Pittsburgh, Graduate School of Library and Information Sciences, 1978. 159 p. (Pittsburgh studies in library and information sciences)

Originally issued in 1972, 73 p.

Liberal annotations, some critical, some descriptive. As a collection of documents and commentary, this is a model of its kind.

972. Hoffmann, Frank W. The literature of rock, 1954–1978. Metuchen, New Jersey: Scarecrow Press, 1981. 337 p.

Supplement issued: *The Literature of Rock, II, 1979–1983*, with additional material for the period 1954–78; by Frank Hoffmann and B. Lee Cooper, with the assistance of Lee Ann Hoffmann. 1986. 2 v.

A classified and annotated bibliography with a brief historical survey of the literature. Annotated list of popular music periodicals. Basic stock list of rock recordings. Bibliography and index to persons and groups.

The supplement is a selective bibliography arranged according to a historical outline of the genre. There are additional categories for materials not fitting into the historical framework. Includes a list of books cited in the bibliography, a basic stock list of rock recordings ordered according

to the historical outline, a list of periodicals covering the genre, and an index of artists, groups, genres, concepts and trends.
Review by Nina Davis-Millis in *Notes*, 38 (1981), p. 318–19.

973. Iwaschkin, Roman. Popular music, a reference guide. New York: Garland Pub., 1986. 658 p. (Music research and information guides, 4)
Classified and annotated bibliography of 5,276 works covering the broadest range of popular music styles and genres. Includes a bibliography of bibliographies. Lists periodicals about popular music. Index of names, groups, and some titles.

974. Kuhnke, Klaus, Manfred Miller and Peter Schulze. Schriften zur populären Musik: eine Auswahl-Bibliographie. Bremen: Archiv für Populäre Musik, 1975–77. 2 v. (Archiv für Populäre Musik. Schriften, 1–2)
Classified list of titles about a broad range of popular musics. Indexes by author and translator, subject and period.

975. Lowe, Leslie. Directory of popular music, 1900–1965. Droitwich, England: Peterson Publishing Co. Ltd, 1975. 1,034 p.
"...intended to be a standard work of reference for popular music in Great Britain." Chronological section recording information about popular songs, including citation of recordings. Following sections treat stage shows, films, music publishers, award-winning songs, and theme songs. Index to song titles.

976. Macken, Bob, Peter Fornatale and Bill Ayres. The rock music source book. Garden City, New York: Anchor Books, 1980. 644 p.
"Our main reason for writing this book was to unearth the varied treasures, of both music and meaning, that are buried in the history of rock music."
Part 1 is a subject guide to rock music using "fifty personal, social, and political themes" as the organizing headings. Within each theme is an epigrammatic definition of the theme, cross-references to other themes, and then lists of "classics," "definitive," and "reference" songs. The explanations of these characterizations are found on p. 29–33. Songs are cited with performing artist and recording company as the only identifiers.
Part 2 consists of five sections: a discography entitled "A basic rock library"; a filmography, "Rock goes to the movies"; a section on rock history (important dates and deaths); a directory of record companies; and a bibliography of rock magazines and books.

977. MacPhail, Jessica Holman Whitehead. Yesterday's papers: the Rolling Stones in print, 1963–1984. Ann Arbor, Michigan: Pierian Press, 1986. 216 p. (Rock & roll reference series, 19)
A bibliography of writings about the Rolling Stones found in newspapers and magazines published primarily in the United States from 1963 through 1984. The entries are grouped according to type—e.g., books, magazine articles, newspaper articles, reviews of recordings, etc.—with separate indexes by author, title, subject, date, and title of source publication (primarily newspapers and magazines).

Shapiro, Nat and Bruce Pollock. Popular music, 1920–1979: a revised cumulation. See no. 1529.

978. Stanley, Lana. Folk rock: a bibliography on music of the 'sixties. San Jose, California: San Jose State College Library, 1970. 80 p. (typescript) (San Jose State College Library bibliography series, 3)

Classified under topical headings and writings on particular groups or individual artists.

979. Stevenson, Gordon. "The wayward scholar: resources and research in popular culture." In *Trends in the Scholarly Use of Library Resources*, [edited by] Donald W. Krummel *et al.*, *Library Trends*, vol. 25, no. 4 (1977).

A discussion of the directions of and support for research in popular culture as an academic discipline.

980. Tamm, Eric. "Materials of rock music research." In *Cum Notis Variorum*, nos. 90–94 (March 1985–July 1985).

A thoughtful annotated bibliography arranged in classified order. Introductory comments to each section of the classified arrangement describe some of the issues and the quandries in which scholars of rock find themselves.

981. Taylor, Paul. Popular music since 1955; a critical guide to the literature. London and New York: Mansell, 1985. 533 p.

Intends "to provide a critical, bibliographical guide to the literature of popular music published in English since 1955" [*Preface*].

An annotated, categorized bibliography: generalia; social aspects; artistic aspects; business; genres; lives and works; fiction; periodicals.

982. Terry, Carol D. Here, there & everywhere: the first international Beatles bibliography, 1962–1982. Ann Arbor, Michigan: Pierian Press, 1985. 282 p. (Rock and Roll reference series, 11)

A bibliography classified by form (books, chapters, fan magazines, etc.) and including sections on reviews of books, films, and recordings. Numbered entries arranged alphabetically by author. Author, title, and subject indexes. Illustrative of the degree to which this particular group has permeated our culture.

Medieval and Renaissance Music

983. Gallo, F. Alberto. "Philological works on musical treatises of the Middle Ages: a bibliographical report." In *Acta Musicologica*, 44 (1972), p. 78–101.

A narrative bibliography treating the work recently accomplished in the editing and description of medieval treatises. The material is discussed chronologically and by country, with copious notes.

984. Gleason, Harold. Music in the Middle Ages and Renaissance. 2nd ed. Rochester, New York: Levis Music Stores, 1951. 158 p. (Music literature outlines, ser. 1)

The outline follows the organization in Reese's *Music in the Middle Ages*, but each section is accompanied by numerous bibliographical references to books, periodical articles, scores, and recordings.

985. Hughes, Andrew. Medieval music: the sixth liberal art. Rev. ed. Toronto and Buffalo, New York: University of Toronto Press, 1980. 360 p. (Toronto medieval bibliographies, 4)

First published in 1974, 326 p. Also published in London by E. Benn.

A classified, annotated bibliography of the literature on medieval music. Index of authors and editors, and a general index. Author's preface is a guide to the bibliographical conventions adopted, and a "Key to the bibliography" provides a useful guide to the subject matter.

Best exemplifies the concept of bibliography as a tool for learning. The 1980 revision consists of some alterations in the 1974 text with a supplemental section added at the end of the volume.

Review by Richard Crocker in *Cum Notis Variorum*, 66 (1982), p. 7–8.

986. Lütolf, Max. Analecta hymnica medii aevi ... Register.... Zusammenarbeit mit D. Baumann, E. Meier, M. Römer, und A. Wernli. Bern und München: Francke Verlag, 1978. 2 v. in 3. (Musikwissenschaftliches Seminar der Universität Zürich, 1)

An index to the massive *Analecta Hymnica Medii Aevi* by G. M. Dreves, Cl. Blume, and H. M. Bannister. In four sections: an index to the incipits, A–Z; and three indexes—to literary genres, to liturgical feasts, and to authors (presumed or attributed).

Review by Marie-Noëlle Colette in *Fontes Artis Musicae*, 26 (1979), p. 246–47.

987. Reese, Gustave. "Bibliography." In his *Music in the Middle Ages*, p. 425–63. New York: Norton, 1940.

Lists books, periodical articles, facsimiles, and editions. Difficult to use because the material is grouped by chapter headings. Once the most influential bibliographies available to students of early music.

988. Reese, Gustave. "Bibliography." In his *Music in the Renaissance*, rev. ed., p. 884–946. New York: Norton, 1959.

An important bibliography of monographs, editions, and periodical literature related to Renaissance music. Unclassified, alphabetical arrangement.

989. Smith, Carleton Sprague and William Dinneen. "Recent work on music in the Renaissance." In *Modern Philology*, vol. 42, no. 1 (Aug. 1944), p. 41–58.

A bibliographical article in narrative style citing and evaluating research and editorial activity in Renaissance music from about 1900 to date of publication.

990. Smits van Waesberghe, Joseph. "Das gegenwärtige Geschichtsbild der mittelalterlichen Musik." In *Kirchenmusikalisches Jahrbuch*, 46–49, 1962–65.

A narrative survey and discussion, under major topics, of the contributions on medieval music in 19 current musicological and historical journals.

For 1957–60, in Jahrgang 46 (1962), p. 61–82.
For 1960–62, in Jahrgang 47 (1963), p. 11–38.
For 1963, in Jahrgang 48 (1964), p. 1–26.
For 1964, in Jahrgang 49 (1965), p. 9–33.

991. Suñol, Grégorio María. "Bibliographie générale." In his *Introduction à la Paléographie Musicale Grégorienne*, p. 511–65. Paris: Desclée, 1935.

This bibliography first appeared in 1925 in the original edition of the author's work on Gregorian paleography. Entries are broadly classified and listed in order of publication.

992. Velimirovic, Milos. "Present status of research in Byzantine music." In *Acta Musicologica*, 43 (1971), p. 1–20.

A narrative bibliography citing the important work accomplished in this area since 1950.

Baroque and Classical Music

993. Gleason, Harold and Warren Becker. Music in the Baroque. 3rd. ed. Bloomington, Indiana: Frangipani Press, 1980. 175 p. (Music literature outlines, ser. 2)

Original published in Rochester, New York, by Levis Music Stores, 1950. A second edition appeared in 1958.

The outline is based on Bukofzer's *Music in the Baroque Era* (1947), with much additional documentation. Bibliography and index.

994. Hill, George R. A preliminary checklist of research on the classic symphony and concerto to the time of Beethoven (excluding Haydn and Mozart). Hackensack, New Jersey: Joseph Boonin, 1970. 58 p. (Music indexes and bibliographies, 2)

995. Schwartz, Judith L. and Christena L. Schlundt. French court dance and dance music: a guide to primary source writings 1643–1789. Stuyvesant, New York: Pendragon, 1987. 386 p.

> The aim of this work is to facilitate reconstruction of French court dancing in the 17th and 18th centuries in its contemporary setting.... The sources of information here described consist of printed matter issued during the reigns of Louis XIV, XV, and XVI, representing the period 1643–1789. The work focuses upon writings that bear directly or indirectly upon French court dance and its music, its practitioners in France and its imitators abroad. [*Introduction*]

In three sections: on dance and dancing in social and theatrical contexts; selected writings about music and other subjects relevant to dance music in the French style; tangentially related writings on physical, social, or cultural settings and aesthetic matters. Forewords to each section refer to modern secondary literature. There is a single short-title list in chronological order and an index to subjects, names, and titles. Each entry includes a lengthy annotation. There is a useful summary of subject headings. A ground-breaking bibliographic effort of great merit.

Music Education

996. Brookhart, Edward. Music in higher education: an annotated bibliography. Warren, Michigan: Harmonie Press for the College Music Society, 1988. 245 p. (Bibliographies in American music, 10)
 Cites 1,300 entries in classified order on the place and function of music in American institution of higher education, c. 1830 to 1985. Includes no entries for archival materials. Readers are referred to the *National Union Catalog of Manuscripts* and *Resources of American Music History* (no. 1116). There are descriptive annotations with some critical commentary. Author and subject indexes.

997. Carlsen, James C. and David Brian Williams. A computer annotated bibliography: music research in programmed instruction, 1952–1972. Reston, Virginia: Music Educators National Conference, 1978. 71 p.

998. Harris, Ernest E. Music education: a guide to information sources. Detroit, Michigan: Gale Research, 1978. 566 p. (Education information guide series, 1)
 An exemplary work, one of the best of its kind. The author extends his range to include many entries not found in ordinary bibliographies. Arranged in 74 sections, titles are divided into 5 categories: generalia, music in education, subject matter areas, uses of music, and multimedia and equipment. There are appendixes listing library holdings and music periodicals.

999. International Society for Music Education. International listing of teaching aids in music education. Edited by Egon Kraus. Cologne: International Society for Music Education (distributing agent: Möseler Verlag, Wolfenbüttel), 1959. 52 p.
 A classified bibliography of materials, since 1945, concerned with music instruction.
 Review by Theodore Normann in *Journal of Research in Music Education*, 8 (1960), p. 55–56.

1000. Modisett, Katherine C. "Bibliography of sources, 1930–1952, relating to the teaching of choral music in secondary schools." In *Journal of Research in Music Education*, 3 (1955), p. 51–60.
 A classified bibliography of 236 items, with a brief introductory survey of the field and its problems.

1001. Music Educators National Conference. Selected bibliography, music education materials. (Prepared for the U.S. Department of State by a special committee of the M.E.N.C.) Chicago, Illinois: M.E.N.C., 1952. 64 p.

Contains five bibliographies, classified, partially annotated: music education materials for elementary schools, collections for junior high, collections for senior high, instrumental music materials, textbooks on music education. The emphasis is on school music performance materials.

1002. Music Educators National Conference. Committee on Bibliography. *Music education materials, a selected bibliography.* Published as vol. 7, no. 1 of the *Journal of Research in Music Education,* 1959. 146 p.

A classified listing of materials. Major groupings are elementary music education, junior high school, choral materials, instructional materials for instrumental music, music appreciation guides and reference materials, music theory texts and workbooks, audiovisual aids, teacher training.

1003. Music Educators National Conference. Curriculum Committee. Music education source book (no. 1). Edited by Hazel N. Morgan. Chicago, Illinois: M.E.N.C., 1951. 268 p.

First printed in 1947.

Various sections contain brief bibliographies; the 1951 printing has an appendix of revisions and additions. Much of the bibliographical information in the first four printings is now out of date.

1004. Music Educators National Conference. Music in American Education Committee. Music in American education. Music education source book (no. 2). Edited by Hazel N. Morgan. Chicago, Illinois: M.E.N.C., 1955. 365 p.

Brief bibliographies to various chapters and subchapters concerned with aspects of American public school music.

1005. Phelps, Roger P. A guide to research in music education. 3rd ed. Metuchen, New Jersey: Scarecrow Press, 1986. 368 p.

First published in 1969 by W. C. Brown, Dubuque, Iowa. 2nd edition published by Scarecrow, 1980. 385 p.

Intended for the graduate student in music education. Covers bibliography and research procedures.

1006. Smits van Waesberghe, Joseph. "Chronologische Übersicht der Musiktraktate, und Literaturverzeichnis." In *Musikerziehung: Lehre und Theorie der Musik im Mittelalter,* p. 195–202. Leipzig: Deutscher Verlag für Musik, 1969. (Musikgeschichte in Bildern, III, 3)

Provides a bibliographical key to the historical study of music education. The "Chronologische Übersicht" cites the most important treatises devoted to music theory and instruction from the 5th to the 15th century. The "Verzeichnis" is an extensive bibliography of books and articles on medieval music instruction.

Also cited as part of no. 587.

1007. Sollinger, Charles. String class publications in the United States, 1851–1951. Detroit, Michigan: Information Coordinators, 1974. 71 p. (Detroit studies in music bibliography, 30)

National Musicological Trends

The entries in this section call attention to a series of articles that have appeared in *Acta Musicologica*, the journal of the International Musicological Society, since 1957. These articles survey the bibliographical and research activities in music in various countries since the end of World War II. Most of them cite major scholarly publications, dissertations, and important music reference works.

AUSTRALIA

1008. Kartomi, Margaret. "Musicological research in Australia, 1979–1984." In *Acta Musicologica*, 51 (1984), p. 109–145.

AUSTRIA

1009. Flotzinger, Rudolf. "20 Jahre Musikforschung in Österreich." In *Acta Musicologica*, 51 (1979), p. 268–78.

1010. Wessely, Othmar. "Die österreichische Musikforschung nach dem zweiten Weltkrieg." In *Acta Musicologica*, 29 (1957), p. 111–19.

BELGIUM

1011. Clercx-Lejeune, Suzanne. "La musicologie en Belgique depuis 1945." In *Acta Musicologica*, 30 (1958), p. 199–214.

CANADA

1012. Maniates, Maria Rika. "Musicology in Canada 1963–1979." In *Acta Musicologica*, 53 (1981), p. 1–14.

CZECH REPUBLIC

1013. Strakova, Theodora. "Die tschechische Musikwissenschaft in den Jahren 1945–1975." In *Acta Musicologica*, 49 (1977), p. 103–120.

DENMARK

1014. Schousboe, Torben. "Dänische musikwissenschaftliche Publikationen seit 1958." In *Acta Musicologica*, 44 (1972), p. 1–11.

FINLAND

1015. Ringbom, Nils-Eric. "Die Musikforschung in Finnland seit 1940." In *Acta Musicologica*, 31 (1959), p. 17–24.

FRANCE

1016. Lesure, François. "La musicologie française depuis 1945." In *Acta Musicologica*, 30 (1958), p. 3–17.

GERMANY

1017. Heckmann, Harald. "Musikwissenschaftliche Unternehmungen in Deutschland seit 1945." In *Acta Musicologica*, 29 (1957), p. 75–94.

GREAT BRITAIN

1018. Cooper, Barry. "Musicology in Great Britain (1982–1985)." In *Acta Musicologica*, 58 (1986), p. 1–8.

1019. Fallows, David. "Musicology in Great Britain, 1979–1982." In *Acta Musicologica*, 55 (1983), p. 244–53.

1020. Fallows, David, Nigel Fortune, Arnold Whittal and John Blacking. "Musicology in Great Britain since 1945." In *Acta Musicologica*, 52 (1980), p. 38–68.
In four parts: Introduction (Fortune); Historical musicology (Fallows); Analysis (Whittal); Ethnomusicology (Blacking).

IRAN

1021. Massoudieh, Mohammad Tagli. "Die Musikforschung in Iran." In *Acta Musicologica*, 52 (1980), p. 79–83.

IRAQ

1022. Qassim Hassan, Scheherazade. "Die Entwicklung und der gegenwärtige Stand der Musikforschung in Irak." In *Acta Musicologica*, 52 (1980), p. 148–61.

ISRAEL

1023. Gerson-Kiwi, Edith. "Musicology in Israel." In *Acta Musicologica*, 30 (1958), p. 17–26.

1024. Gerson-Kiwi, Edith and Amnon Shiloah. "Musicology in Israel, 1960–1980." In *Acta Musicologica*, 53 (1981), p, 200–216.

ITALY

1025. Allorto, Riccardo and Claudio Sartori. "La musicologia italiana dal 1945 a oggi." In *Acta Musicologica*, 31 (1959), p. 9–17.

1026. Gallo, F. Alberto, Agostino Ziino, Giulio Cattin, Lorenzo Bianconi, Elvidio Surian, Antonio Serravezza and Tullia Magrini. "Vent'anni di musicología in Italia." In *Acta Musicologica*, 54 (1982), p. 7–83.
An extensive review includes numerous bibliographical footnotes.

JAPAN

1027. Nomura, Francesco Yosio. "Musicology in Japan since 1945." In *Acta Musicologica*, 35 (1963), p. 45–53.

1028. Suppan, Wolfgang and Hachirō Sakarishi. "Musikforschung in und für Japan." In *Acta Musicologica*, 54 (1982), p. 84–123.
Includes numerous bibliographical references.

KOREA

1029. Song, Bang-Song. "Musikwissenschaft in Korea seit 1950." In *Acta Musicologica*, 57 (1985), p. 141–50.

LATIN AMERICA

1030. Devoto, Daniel. "Panorama de la musicología Latinoamericana." In *Acta Musicologica*, 31 (1959), p. 91–109.

THE NETHERLANDS

1031. Dunning, Albert. "Musikwissenschaft in Holland seit 1960." In *Acta Musicologica*, 55 (1983), p. 58–69.

1032. Reeser, Eduard. "Musikwissenschaft in Holland." In *Acta Musicologica*, 32 (1960), p. 160–74.

NORWAY

1033. Schjelderup-Ebbe, Dag. "Neuere norwegische musikwissenschaftliche Arbeiten." In *Acta Musicologica*, 44 (1972), p. 25–31.

1034. Schjelderup-Ebbe, Dag. "Norwegische musikwissenschaftliche Arbeiten." In *Acta Musicologica*, 52 (1980), p. 68–73.

199

THE PHILIPPINES

1035. Dioquino, Corazon C. "Musicology in the Philippines." In *Acta Musicologica*, 54 (1982), p. 124–47.
Includes an extensive bibliography of writings on music in the Philippines.

PORTUGAL

1036. De Brito, Manuel Carlos. "Musicology in Portugal since 1960." In *Acta Musicologica*, 51 (1984), p. 29–47.

1037. Kastner, Macario Santiago. "Veinte años de musicologia en Portugal (1940–60)." In *Acta Musicologica*, 32 (1960), p. 1–11.

RUSSIA

1038. Jarustovsky, Boris. "Soviet musicology." In *Acta Musicologica*, 46 (1974), p. 50–57.

SCANDINAVIA

1039. Rosenberg, Herbert. "Musikwissenschaftliche Bestrebungen in Dänemark, Norwegen, und Schweden in den letzten c. 15 Jahren." In *Acta Musicologica*, 30 (1958), p. 118–37.

SOUTH AFRICA

1040. Paxinos, Socrates. "Musicology in South Africa." In *Acta Musicologica*, 58 (1986), p. 9–23.
Includes a list of dissertations in order by author.

SOUTH AMERICA

1041. Bose, Fritz. "Südamerikanische Musikforschung" In *Acta Musicologica* 29 (1957), p. 43–45.

SPAIN

1042. Querol, Manuel. "Die Musikwissenschaft in Spanien (1964–1979)." In *Acta Musicologica*, 52 (1980), p. 75–78.

SWEDEN

1043. Kjellberg, Erik. "Svenska Samfundet för Musikforskning." [Swedish Society for Musicology.] In *Acta Musicologica*, 47 (1975), p. 290–92.

1044. Lönn, Anders. "Trends and tendencies in recent Swedish musicology." In *Acta Musicologica*, 44 (1972), p. 11–25.

SWITZERLAND

1045. Schanzlin, Hans Peter. "Musikwissenschaft in der Schweiz (1938–58)." In *Acta Musicologica*, 30 (1958), p. 214–24.

UNITED STATES OF AMERICA

1046. Buelow, George S. "Musicology in the United States in 1981–1982." In *Acta Musicologica*, 55 (1983), p. 253–66.

1047. Goldthwaite, Scott. "The growth and influence of musicology in the United States." In *Acta Musicologica*, 33 (1961), p. 72–79.
With a "Codetta: some details of musicology in the United States," by Jan LaRue, p. 79–83.

1048. Haar, James. "Musicology in the United States in 1979." In *Acta Musicologica*, 52 (1980), p. 84–87.

1049. Haar, James. "Musicology in the United States in 1978." In *Acta Musicologica*, 51 (1979), p. 279–82.

1050. Palisca, Claude. "Report on the musicological year 1974 in the United States." In *Acta Musicologica*, 47 (1975), p. 283–89.

1051. Steiner, Ruth. "Musicology in the United States in 1980." In *Acta Musicologica*, 53 (1981), p. 216–23.

VIETNAM

1052. Tran Van Khe. "Situation de la musique en République Socialiste du Viét-Nam." In *Acta Musicologica*, 49 (1977), p. 121–30.

YUGOSLOVIA (INCLUDING BOSNIA-HERZEGOVINA, CROATIA, AND SLOVENIA)

1053. Cvetko, Dragotin. "Der gegenwärtige Stand der jugoslawischen Musikwissenschaft." In *Acta Musicologica*, 51 (1979), p. 151–60.

1054. Cvetko, Dragotin. "Les formes et les résultats des efforts musicologiques yugoslaves." In *Acta Musicologica*, 31 (1958), p. 50–62.

National Music

ARGENTINA

1055. Suarez Urturbey, Pola. La música en revistas argentinas. Buenos Aires: Fondo Nacional de las Artes, 1969. 70 p.

A bibliography of 652 entries for articles on music in four Argentine periodicals: *La Gaceta Musical* (1874–87), *La Moda* (1837–38), *Revista de Estudios Musicales* (1949–54), and *La Revista de Musica* (1927–30). Index of names.

AUSTRALIA

1056. Murdoch, James. Australia's contemporary composers. Melbourne: Sun Books, 1975. 223 p.

Extended essays with discographies. Includes bibliography and index.

BRAZIL

1057. Correia de Azevedo, Luis H. Bibliografia musical brasileira (1820–1950). Rio de Janeiro: 1952. 252 p. (Ministerio da Eduçacao e Saude. Instituto Nacional do Livro, Col. Bl. Bibliografia 9)

1,639 titles under 13 subject sections. Includes writings by Brazilian authors on non-Brazilian music. Publications containing music only are omitted.

Review by A. Hyatt King in *Music and Letters*, 35 (1954), p. 67–68; by Charles Seeger in *Notes*, 11 (1954), p. 551–52.

CANADA

Bradley, Ian L. A selected bibliography of musical Canadiana. See no. 865.

1058. Compositeurs canadiens contemporains. Éditions français dirigée par Louise Laplante. Traduction de Véronique Robert. Montréal: Les Presses de l'Université du Québec, 1977. 382 p.

English edition published in 1975 by Oxford University Press as *Contemporary Canadian Composers* by Keith MacMillan and John Beckwith. 248 p.

A biographical work including bibliographical references and index. Analyses of most important works provided for major composers.

Lists of Canadian musical organizations of all sorts.

Review by Kathleen Toomey in *Notes*, 35 (1978), p. 86.

1059. Napier, Ronald. A guide to Canada's compsers. New, enl. and rev. ed. Ontario: Avondale Press, 1976. 56 p.

Includes a list of Canadian music publishers.

1060. Toomey, Kathleen M. and Stephen C. Willis. Musicians in Canada, a bio-bibliographical finding list. Musiciens au Canada, index bio-bibliographique. Ottawa: Canadian Association of Music Libraries, 1981. 185 p. (Canadian Association of Music Libraries, Publications, 1) (Association Canadienne des bibliothèques musicales, Publications, 1)

Previous edition published as *Bio-bibliographical Finding List of Canadian Musicians*, 1962.

An index to biographical and/or bibliographical information on over 1,700 Canadian musicians in 218 sources. Lists of musicians by specialty.

CHINA

1061. Chung-kuo ku-tai yin-yüeh shu-mu. Compiled by the Institute of Chinese Music at the Central Conservatory of Music, Pei-ching. Pei-ching: Yin yüeh ch'u pan she, 1962. 142 p.

A bibliography of works about ancient Chinese music divided into three parts: books on music commonly available; books known to be in existence but not seen by the author; known lost works. Works on histories and theory, vocal music, dance music, music to accompany storytelling, theatrical music, instruments, religious and ceremonial music, ch'in and music technique are covered. Each entry provides titles, author or editor, imprint information, and call numbers in the Library of Musical Research in the Central Music Conservatory in Pei-ching.

1062. Chung-kuo yin yüeh shu p'u chih. Pei-ching: Peoples Music Press, 1984. 200 p.

This is a union catalog of holdings of Chinese music titles in 37 Chinese libraries covering the period from 722 B.C. to 1949. It is a classified catalog in two parts, one for the period from 722 B.C. to 1911 and another for 1912–49. There is an index to all titles.

Lieberman, Fredric. Chinese music, an annotated bibliography. See no. 912.

CZECH REPUBLIC

1063. Muzíková, Ruzena. Selective bibliography of literature on Czech and Slovak music. Prague: Czechoslovak Music Information Centre, 1969. 124 p.

A useful bibliography of Czechoslovakian music literature for English readers. Czech titles are given in English translation, with brief descriptions of content and bibliographical features. Classified in nine major sections: bibliography, catalogs, dictionaries, periodical publications, history of Czech and Slovak music, monographs, anthologies, instruments, and notation.

Průvodce po pramench k dějinám hudby. Fondy a sbírky uložené v čechách. [Guide to the sources of the history of music.] See no. 1990.

1064. Vyborny, Zdeněk. "Czech music literature since World War II." In *Notes*, 16 (1959), p. 539–46.

Translated from the German by William Lichtenwanger.

A classified bibliography, each section preceded by a brief descriptive statement. Titles given in Czech and English.

EUROPE

1065. Schaal, Richard. Das Schrifttum zur musikalischen Lokalgeschichts-forschung. Kassel: Bärenreiter, 1947. 62 p.

A bibliography of studies of music in various European cities and provinces, arranged alphabetically by place. Includes articles from a few leading periodicals. Very brief citations. Much of this information is complemented by the bibliographies in articles on individual cities in *MGG* and the *New Grove*.

FRANCE

1066. Leguy, Jean. Catalogue bibliographique des livres de langue française sur la musique. Avant-propos de Norbert Dufourcq. Avec un supplément 1954–1959. Paris: E. Ploix, 1959. 59, 43 p.

Organized as the *Répertoire Bibliographique* (no. 1067).

1067. Leguy, Jean. Répertoire bibliographique des ouvrages en français sur la musique. Chambray-lès-Tours: Musica reservata, 1975. 175 p.

Supplément 1975–1978 au Répertoire Bibliographique des Ouvrages en Français sur la Musique (1975) published in Tours by Ars Musicae in 1978. 63 p.

A classified list of works about music, most of them published in France in the mid-20th century up to 1975. Arranged by author in each section. Intended as a sales catalog, but with practical bibliographic application.

GERMANY

1068. Bericht über die musikwissenschaftlichen Arbeiten in der Deutschen Demokratischen Republik 1968. Herausgegeben vom Zentralinstitut für Musikforschung beim Verband Deutscher Komponisten und Musikwissenschaftler. Berlin: Verlag Neue Musik, 1969. 150 p.

Abstracts of scholarly papers and dissertations by East German musicologists.

1069. Krautwurst, Franz. Das Schrifttum zur Musikgeschichte der Stadt Nürnberg. Hrsg. im Auftrag der Stadt Nürnberg Schul- und Kulturreferat von der Stadtbibliothek. Nürnberg: Stadtbibliothek Nürnberg, 1964. 68 p. (Veröffentlichungen der Stadtbibliothek Nürnberg, 7)

A bibliography of writings about music in the city of Nürnberg.

GREAT BRITAIN

1070. Ford, Wyn K. Music in England before 1800: a select bibliography. London: Library Association, 1967. 128 p. (Library Association bibliographies, 7)

Classified bibliography in two major divisions: Part I, music and its environment; Part II, persons. Confined to literature published in the 20th century in English, French, and German. The major critical editions of composers' works are cited in Part II.

1071. Kassler, Jamie Croy. The science of music in Britain, 1714–1830: a catalogue of writings, lectures, and inventions. New York: Garland Pub., 1979. 2 v. 1,339 p. (Garland reference library of the humanities, 74)

An extensively annotated bibliography arranged by author of English-language writings on four areas of musical knowledge: technical, mathematical, critical, and physical. Works on sacred and theatrical music, singing, and playing are omitted. Location of sources and supporting bibliography are provided for each source. Three appendixes cover genres of publication issued in Britain 1714–1830, encyclopedias and dictionaries, and musical periodicals. Indexes of names, tradesmen, places, and genres and subjects.

Review by Kerry S. Grant in *Notes*, 37 (1980), p. 43–44.

1072. Woodfill, Walter L. "Bibliography." In his *Musicians in English society*, p. 315–61. Princeton, New Jersey: Princeton University Press, 1953.

Unabridged reprint by Da Capo Press, New York, 1959.

A substantial listing of the primary and secondary sources for the study of English music of the late 16th and early 17th centuries. Separated as to works before and after 1700.

The Woodfill bibliography is a fine example of the kind of information to be found in histories of national music or monographs related to the music of a local school or development.

GREECE

1073. Michaelides, Solon. The music of ancient Greece: an encyclopaedia. London: Faber & Faber, 1978. 365 p.

Published in Greek as *Enkyklopaideia tés Archaias Hellénikés Mousikés* in Athens by Morphótiko Hidryma Ethnikés Trapezés, 1982. 364 p.

1074. Ratliff, Neil. "Resources for music research in Greece—an overview." In *Notes*, 36 (1980), p. 50–64.

HUNGARY

1075. Rajeczky, B. "Musikforschung in Ungarn 1936–1960. (Bibliographischer Bericht.)" In *Studia Musicologica*, 1 (1961), p. 225–49.

A brief survey of Hungarian musical scholarship, with a classified bibliography of music literature. Hungarian titles given with German translations. Sections on folk music, Hungarian music history, general music history, collective works.

ISRAEL AND JEWISH MUSIC

1076. Heskes, Irene. The resource book of Jewish music, a bibliographical and topical guide to the book and journal literature and program materials. Westport, Connecticut: Greenwood Press, 1985. 302 p. (Music reference collection 3)

An annotated bibliography of published English-language sources on Jewish music. Classified by type of publication, but with a topical index. Author index. Glossary of Judaica.

Sendrey, Alfred. Bibliography of Jewish music. See no. 1275.

1077. Weisser, Albert. Bibliography of publications and other resources on Jewish music. New York: National Jewish Music Council, 1969. 117 p.
"Revised and enlarged edition based in part upon *The Bibliography of Books and Articles on Jewish Music* prepared by Joseph Yasser and published in 1955."

ITALY

1078. Giovine, Alfredo. Bibliografia ed emerografia; a cura di Felice Giovine e Nicola Roncone. Bari: Edizioni F.lli Laterza, 1980. 32 p. (Biblioteca dell'archivio delle tradizioni popolari baresi. Civiltà musicale pugliese)
A bibliography, including periodical and newspaper articles, on music in the province of Bari.

JAPAN

1079. Fukuda, Naomi, ed. Bibliography of reference works for Japanese studies. Ann Arbor, Michigan: Center for Japanese Studies, University of Michigan, 1979. 210 p.
Includes on p. 48–50 annotated entries on Japanese music. Reference works, dictionaries, handbooks, directories, chronologies, annuals, and books on instruments and folk music are covered.

Kokusai Bunka Shinkokai. K.B.S. bibliography of standard reference books for Japanese studies Vol. II (B): Theatre, dance and music. See no. 1276.

1080. Nihon no Sankō Tosho Henshū Inkai. [Guide to Japanese reference works]. Chicago, Illinois: American Library Association, 1966. 303 p.
Includes 29 annotated entries on Japanese music (p. 49–52). Titles are provided in kanji, romanized and translated. Annotations are in English. Covers bibliography, dictionaries, biographies, chronology, yearbooks, illustrations, recorded music, and folk music.

LATIN AMERICA

1081. Béhague, Gérard. Music in Latin America: an introduction. Englewood Cliffs, New Jersey: Prentice-Hall, 1979. 369 p.
Translated by Miguel Castillo Didier and published in Spanish in 1983. 502 p.
"The most comprehensive and reliable general history of Latin American music written to date" [Malena Kuss]. See no. 1087.
Also cited as part of no. 570.

1082. Davis, Martha Ellen. Music and dance in Latin American urban contexts: a selective bibliography. Brockport, New York: 1973. 20 p. (Urban anthropology bibliographies, 1)

1083. Druesedow, John. "Music … Bibliography." In *Latin America and the Caribbean: A Critical Guide to Research Sources*, p. 575–88. Edited by Paula H. Covington *et al.* Westport, Connecticut: Greenwood, 1992. (Bibliographies and Indexes in Latin American and Caribbean Studies, 2)

An annotated bibliography of 151 books and articles on music of all genres and styles in Latin America and the Caribbean. The first section is devoted to works covering music of the region and is arranged by genre of publication (guides, bibliographies, biographies, catalogs, dictionaries and encyclopedias, dissertations, guides to archives, histories, and surveys). Subsequent entries are devoted to the same genres of publication, but are presented for each country, beginning with Argentina and ending with Venezuela. There are concluding sections on current periodicals and descriptions of distinguished special collections of musical materials in North American universities.

There is an excellent introductory essay by Gérard Béhague on the history of scholarship on music from Latin America and the Caribbean.

1084. Kuss, Malena. "Current state of bibliographic research in Latin American music." In *Fontes Artis Musicae*, 31 (1984), p. 206–228.

An extensive prose bibliography with bibliographical supplements. Invaluable for the information conveyed, but merely a precursor to her forthcoming book-length bibliography.

1085. "Music Section." In *Handbook of Latin American Studies*. Cambridge, Mass.: Harvard University Press, 1936–50; Gainesville: University of Florida Press, 1951–78; Austin: University of Texas Press, 1979– . Vol. 1– .

Volumes for 1936–50 reprinted by the University of Florida Press.

The first issue to include anything about music was that for 1937, in which Irma Goebel Labastille published "The music of Mexico and Central America."

In 1939, William Berrien prepared the bibliography. In 1940–42, Gilbert Chase was responsible. From 1943 to 1953, Charles Seeger prepared the section. Richard A. Waterman compiled the bibliography 1954–59. In 1959–63, Bruno Nettl was editor. Gilbert Chase returned to active duty 1964–68. Gérard Béhague took over 1970–74 and Robert Stevenson has been responsible from 1976 until the current issue.

From 1939, there has been a brief introductory essay and a classified bibliography of practically anything having to do with Latin American music. There is a section for generalia and then entries arranged by country or region. Anthologies are analyzed and periodical articles cited. Each volume indexes titles, subjects, and authors; title lists of journals indexed are supplied. Since 1965, the *Handbook* has been divided, social sciences being treated in odd-numbered years and humanities in even-numbered years.

1086. Schechter, John M. "The current state of bibliographic research in Latin American ethnomusicology." In *Latin American Masses and Minorities: Their Images and Realities*, p. 334–45 of vol. 1, edited by Dan Hazan. Madison, Wisconsin: SALALM Secretariat (University Library, University of Wisconsin–Madison), 1985.

This paper examines the current status of bibliographic research in Latin American ethnomusicology, with special attention to materials pertaining to the region's urban popular music. The discussion begins with a statement of the rationale for acquiring ethnomusicological materials, followed by a summary of major repositories of field recordings and printed sources in the United States and Latin America. The report subsequently evaluates the major bibliographic tools currently at our disposal. I make references to three bibliographic compilations: "Selected Bibliographic Sources in Latin American Ethnomusicology"; "Doctoral Dissertations in Latin American Ethnomusicology: 1965–84"; and "A Selected Bibliography on Latin American Urban Popular Music" (see Volume II, pp. 664–682). [Author's introductory paragraph]

1087. Stevenson, Robert Murrell. "The Americas in European music encyclopedias; part I: England, France, Portugal." In *Inter-American Music Review*, 3 (1981), p. 159–207.
A review of lexicographical coverage of Latin America. Extensive discussion of coverage in the *New Grove*.

1088. Thompson, Leila Fern. Selected references in English on Latin American music, a reading list. Washington, D.C.: Music Division, Pan American Union, 1944. 20 p. (Pan American Union. Music Division. Music series, 13)

MEXICO

1089. La Música de México. Julio Estrada, editor. Guía bibliográfica [por] Sylvana Young Osorio. México: Instituto de Investigaciones Estéticas, Universidad Nacional Autónoma de México, 1984– .
Part 2 of a history of music in Mexico.

POLAND

1090. Beiträge zur Musikwissenschaft. Sonderreihe: Bibliographien. I. SR Rumänien (1945–1965). II. VR Polen (1945–1965). 1966. I. 66 p. II, 192 p.
Romania and Poland are the first two countries covered in this series of bibliographies devoted to musicological literature in the East European countries. Printed in a subseries of the leading musicological journal of the German Democratic Republic (East Germany).
Subsequent volumes cited at no. 677.

1091. Lissa, Zofia. "Die Musikwissenschaft in Volkspolen (1945–56)." In *Die Musikforschung*, 10 (1957), p. 531–47.
Translated from the Polish by Werner Kaupert.
In narrative style with many titles quoted. Discusses the state and organization of Polish musicology since World War II.

Materialy do Bibliografii Muzyki Polskiej. See no. 719.

PORTUGAL

1092. Rocha da Silva Guimarãaes, Bertino D. Primeiro esboco duma bibliografia musical portuguesa, con uma breve notícia histórica de música no nosso país. Porto, 1947. 174 p.

The bibliographical section includes works on music by Portuguese authors, works on music in Portugal by native or foreign authors, old Portuguese pedagogical works, special bibliographies, and music periodicals.

ROMANIA

See no. 1090.

RUSSIA

1093.   Koltypina, Galina B. and N. G. Pavlova. Sovetskaia literatura o muzyke: bibliograficheskii ukazatel knig, zhurnalnykh statei i retsenzii za 1968–1970 gg. Moskva: Sovetskii Kompozitor, 1979–84. 2 v.
A bibliography of Soviet music literature including periodical articles.

1094.   Moldon, David. A bibliography of Russian composers. London: White Lion Publishers, 1976. 364 p.
Covers English-language books and articles on Russian music (entries 1–368 in chronological order) and Russian composers (entries on generalia and works, each in chronological order). Indexes of authors, editors, and compilers, of translators and illustrators, and of subjects.

1095.   Orlov, Georgii P. Muzykalnaia literatura; bibliograficheskii ukazatel knizhnoi i zhurnalnoi literatury o muzyke na russkom iazyke. Leningrad: Leningradskaia filarmoniia, 1935. 222 p. (Knigi o simfonicheskoi muzyke)
A bibliography of music literature in Russian.

1096.   Pavlova, N. G. Ukazatelw bibliograficeskix posobii po muzyke: annotirovannyi perecenw ukazatelei literatury, izdannyx na russkom iazyke. Moskva: Gos. biblioteka SSSR im. V.I. Lenina, Otdelnotnyx izdanii i zvukozapisei, 1978. 109 p.
This work supplements the earlier published *Bibliografii Muzykalnoi Bibliografii* compiled by G. B. Koltypinoi in 1963 and also a work of the same title compiled by N. G. Pavlova and published in 1970.

SERBIA

Dordević, Valdimir R. Ogled srpske muzicke bibliografije do 1914. [Essay on the Serbian musical bibliography until 1914.] See no. 1306.

SLOVAKIA

Muzíková, Ruzena. See no. 1063.

1097.   Potůček, Juraj. Súpis slovenských hudobnín a literatüry o hudobníkoch. [Catalog of Slovak printed music and books on musicians.] Bratislava: Slovenská akademie vëd a unmëní, 1952. 435 p.

209

Lists musicians active in Slovakia to 1949 or mentioned in Slovak periodical literature. Bibliographies of works with Slovak texts, 1881 to 1949. Chronological index, classified index, name index.

1098. Potúček, Juraj. Súpis slovenských hudobno-teoretických prác. [Catalog of Slovak musico-theoretical works.] Bratislava: Slovenská akademie věd, 1955. 467 p.

Classified bibliography of literary and theoretical works on Czech music, including periodical articles (p. 15–216). List of theoretical works in chronological order, 1519–1853 (p. 219–25). Biographical section, including, under composers' names, both publications of music and critical articles (p. 223–380). Classified list of music published 1950–52 (p. 383–403).

1099. Potúček, Juraj. Výberofá bibliografia zo slovenskej hudobnovednej literatúry 1862–1962. [Selective bibliography of Slovak musicological literature 1862–1962.] Bratislava: Slovenská akademie věd, 1963. 116 p.

SWEDEN

1100. Davidsson, Ake. Bibliografi över Svensk musiklitteratur, 1800–1945. Bibliography of Swedish music literature, 1800–1945. 2. suppl. utökad med ett suppl. Uppsala: Almqvist & Wiksell, 1980. 267 p.

First published in 1948. 215 p.

A classified bibliography of general works, general music histories, histories of music in Sweden, works on musicians of all nationalities, and theoretical works. Restricted to writings by Swedish authors except for subjects connected with Swedish music. 5,432 items in all. Index.

SWITZERLAND

1101. Nef, Karl. Schriften über Musik und Volksgesang. Bern: K. J. Wyss, 1908. 151 p. (Bibliographie der schweizerischen Landeskunde, Faszikel V)

Classified bibliography of literature on Swiss music, its history and practice. Index of names.

UNITED STATES OF AMERICA

1102. American music before 1865 in print and on records: a biblio-discography. Preface by H. Wiley Hitchcock. Brooklyn: Institute for Studies in American Music, Dept. of Music, School of Performing Arts, Brooklyn College of the City University of New York, 1976. 113 p. (I.S.A.M. monographs, no. 6)

Supplemented by *"American Music before 1865 in Print and on Records: A Biblio-discography:* supplement to music on records," by James R. Heintze in *Notes*, 34 (1978), p. 571–80, and by the same author, *"American Music before 1865 in Print and on Records: A Biblio-discography:* second supplement to music on records," in *Notes*, 37 (1981), p. 31–36.

Review by James R. Heintze in *Notes*, 33 (1977), p. 842–43.

1103. American music recordings, a discography of 20th-century U.S. composers. A project of the Institute for Studies in American Music for the Koussevitsky Music Foundation, Inc. Carol J. Oja, editor. Brooklyn, New York: Institute for Studies in American Music, 1982. 368 p.

Lists over 13,000 disc recordings of 8,000 works by almost 1,300 American composers. No jazz, folk, or popular musics are included. Bibliography. Indexes to performing groups, ensembles, vocalists and narrators, and instrumentalists.

Review by Thomas F. Heck in *Fontes Artis Musicae*, 31 (1984), p. 132–33.

1104. De Lerma, Dominique-René. Bibliography of black music. Foreword by Jessie Carney Smith. Westport, Connecticut: Greenwood Press, 1981–84. (The Greenwood encyclopedia of black music)

Vol. 1: *Reference Materials.*
Vol. 2: *Afro-American Idioms.*
Vol. 3: *Geographical Studies.*
Vol. 4: *Theory, Education, and Related Studies.*

Annotated bibliographies of books and articles, international in scope and including articles, books, graduate student papers, and journals, on many areas of black musical life. Arrangement and citations based on the *RILM* model, with coverage particularly intense up to 1975. Vol. 3 includes an extensive bibliography on acculturation and an index to authors and editors in that volume. Volume 4 has a similar index.

Review by Deane Root in *Notes*, 38 (1982), p. 832–33.

1105. De Lerma, Dominique-René. "Black music: a bibliographic essay." In *Music and Fine Arts in the General Library*, edited by Guy A. Marco and Wolfgang M. Freitag, vol. 23, no. 3 of *Library Trends* (January 1975), p. 517–32.

A bibliography citing bibliographies of black music and literature about black music and musicians, as well as discographies of black music. Organized by genre and subject.

1106. Delli, Bertrun. Music, [Section R] in vol. 3 of *Arts in America, a Bibliography*, edited by Bernard Karpel. Washington, D.C.: Smithsonian Institution, 1979. 4 v.

A 655-item classified bibliography of American musical literature. Other entries on music scattered throughout. General index in volume 4.

1107. Floyd, Samuel A. and Marsha J. Reisser. Black music in the United States: an annotated bibliography of selected reference and research materials. Millwood, New York: Kraus International Publications, 1983. 234 p.

Cites bibliographies and indexes, catalogs, discographies, biographical dictionaries, and anthologies. Includes a directory of archives holding materials relevant to the subject. Indexes to names, titles, and subjects.

1108. Heard, Priscilla S. American music, 1698–1800: an annotated bibliography. Waco, Texas: Baylor University Press, Markham Press Fund, 1975. 246 p.

"Includes all entries pertaining to music from the *American Bibliog-*

raphy by Evans and Shipton, and the supplement by the American Antiquarian Society which covers the addenda of Bristol." Arranged by imprint date. Coverage includes works about music as well as printed music. See also no. 1299.

1109. Heintze, James R. American music studies; a classified bibliography of master's theses. Detroit, Michigan: Information Coordinators, 1984. 312 p. (Bibliographies in American music, 8)
  With indexes to authors, places, and subjects.
  Review by Ann P. Basart in *Notes*, 41 (1986), p. 553–54.

1110. Horn, David. The literature of American music in books and folk music collections: a fully annotated bibliography. Metuchen, New Jersey: Scarecrow Press, 1977. 556 p.
  First published in 1972 as a catalog of holdings in the Exeter University Library. A *First Supplement* to the 1977 edition was published in 1988.
  A classified work organized on historical and cultural bases. Almost 1,400 entries. Index to names and titles. Appendix of 302 works discovered while the book was in preparation; these entries are not annotated.
  Reviews by Dan Morgenstern in *Journal of Jazz Studies*, 5 (1979), p. 93–95, by Eileen Southern in *Black Perspectives in Music*, 6 (1978), p. 94–96, and by Stephen M. Fry in *Notes*, 34 (1977), p. 89–90.

1111. Johnson, H. Earle. First performances in America to 1900. Detroit, Michigan: Information Coordinators, 1979. 470 p. (Bibliographies in American music, 4)
  A sourcebook for statistics on first performances of orchestral music. Entries in alphabetical order by composer give title and date of first performance in major cities. Choral performances with orchestra as well as some chamber music performances are included. Annotations frequently derive from contemporary reviews.
  Reviews by Mary Jane Corry in *Notes*, 36 (1980), p. 653–54, and by Himie Voxman in *Fontes Artis Musicae*, 27 (1986), p. 5657.

1112. Kinscella, Hazel G. "Americana index to *The Musical Quarterly*, 1915–57." Published as vol. 6, no. 2 (1958) of *Journal of Research in Music Education*. 144 p.
  Indexes all articles related to American music and musical events.

1113. Krummel, Donald W. Bibliographical handbook of American music. Urbana: University of Illinois Press, 1987. 269 p.
  An overview of reference sources on the subject of American music, broadly defined. Organized in four major sections: chronological perspectives; contextual perspectives; musical mediums and genres; bibliographical forms. Each chapter and most sections begin with introductory remarks, some rather long, and then follow with citations, often in a classified array, then in chronological order. Careful reading of the introduction will facilitate the fullest exploitation of this excellent resource. Name and subject indexes.
  Review by Ann P. Basart in *Cum Notis Variorum*, 126 (October 1988), p. 19–20.

1114. Maultsby, Portia K. "Selective bibliography: U.S. Black music." In *Ethnomusicology*, 19 (1975), p. 421–49.
Organized by genres and styles. Within each broad division are citations of general works, works on composers, and works on performers.

1115. Mead, Rita H. Doctoral dissertations in American music: a classified bibliography. Brooklyn: Institute for Studies in American Music, Brooklyn College of the City University of New York, 1974. 155 p. (I.S.A.M. monographs, 3)
A classified bibliography of 1,226 entries covering dissertations on American music, but in many cases written within disciplines other than music (e.g., sociology, theater, anthropology, history, American studies, theology, literature, and education). Includes University Microfilm and Library of Congress microfilm numbers and references to *Dissertation Abstracts*. Author and subject indexes.
Review by Geoffrey C. Weston in *Notes*, 32 (1976), p. 548.

1116. Resources of American music history. A directory of source materials from colonial times to World War II [by] D. W. Krummel, Jean Geil, Doris J. Dyen, [and] Deane L. Root. Urbana: University of Illinois Press, 1981. 463 p.
Geographically organized listing of source materials, including printed and manuscript music, programs and catalogs, institutional and personal papers, pictures and sound recordings. This was an American Bicentennial project with hundreds of local correspondents. There is a bibliography of reference works and an index to names, titles, and subjects.
See D. W. Krummel's "Little RAMH, who made thee?" in *Notes*, 37 (1980), p. 227–38, for an exegesis on its genesis.
Reviews by Thomas F. Heck in *Fontes Artis Musicae*, 29 (1982), p. 198–99, and by Richard Jackson in *Notes*, 38 (1982), p. 595–96.

1117. Skowronski, JoAnn. Black music in America: a bibliography. Metuchen, New Jersey: Scarecrow, 1981. 723 p.
A list of books and articles about black music and musicians in the U.S. from colonial times through 1979. Entries are listed chronologically in each section and under each musician's name. Sections are: selected musicians and singers; general references; reference works. Author index.
Reviews by Deane Root in *Notes*, 38 (1982), p. 832–35, and by Samuel A. Floyd in *American Music*, 3 (1985), p. 102–103.

1118. Stoneburner, Bryan C. Hawaiian music: an annotated bibliography. Westport, Conn.: Greenwood, 1986. 100 p. (Music reference collection, 10)

The present work, which lists and annotates writing on Hawaiian music, musicians, and music life, covers the years 1831 through 1980. It is limited to sources in English, German, French, Spanish. [from the introductory remarks]

Arranged by author, 564 historical and critical works are cited. Appendixes: glossary of Hawaiian terms, location of periodicals cited. Subject index.
Review in *Sonneck Society Bulletin for American Music*, 3 (1987), p. 75–76.

1119. Thompson, Annie Figueroa. An annotated bibliography of writings about music in Puerto Rico. Ann Arbor, Michigan: Music Library Association, 1974. 34 p. (MLA index and bibliography series, 12)

YUGOSLAVIA (INCLUDING BOSNIA-HERZEGOVINA, CROATIA, AND SLOVENIA)

1120. Pruett, Lilian. "Music research in Yugoslavia." In *Notes*, 36 (1980). p. 23–49.

Opera and Theater Music

1121. Abert, Anna Amalie. "Die Barockoper. Ein Bericht über die Forschung seit 1945." In *Acta Musicologica*, 41 (1969), p. 121–64.
A narrative account of recent research on baroque opera in its major national schools, with extensive bibliographies for each section.

1122. Abert, Anna Amalie. "Die Opera zwischen Barock und Romantik: Ein Bericht über die Forschung seit dem Zweiten Weltkrieg." In *Acta Musicologica*, 49 (1977), p. 137–93.
A study of research since 1945 on classic period opera, constructed in a similar fashion to her work *Die Barockoper*.

1123. Bustico, Guido. Bibliografia della storia e cronistorie dei teatri italiani. Milano: Bollettino bibliografici musicale, 1929. 82 p.
Subtitle: "Il teatro musicale italiano."
Part I (p. 19–27): a general bibliography of the Italian musical theater. Part II (p. 31–83): a bibliography of the musical theater in specific Italian cities, arranged alphabetically by place. Includes periodical articles. Some brief descriptive annotations.

1124. Central Opera Service. Directory of selected opera films available from American distributors. New York: Central Opera Service, 1976. 42 p. (*Central Opera Service Bulletin*, vol. 19, no. 2, Winter 1976–77)
Eleventh annual *Directory* issue.

1125. Cohen, H. Robert and Marie-Odile Gigon. Cent ans de mise en scène lyrique en France (env. 1830–1930). One hundred years of operatic staging in France. Catalogue descriptif des livrets de mise en scène, des libretti annotées et des partitions annotées dans la Bibliothèque de l'Association de la régie théâtrale (Paris). Préface de Philip Gossett. New York: Pendragon Press, 1986. 334 p. (La vie musicale en France au XIXe siècle)

> This catalogue limits itself to documents present in the central depository for Parisian staging manuals, the Bibliothèque de l'Association ... [and] it provides an indispensable base upon which later investigations of other collections can build. [from the introductory remarks]

Arranged by the title of staged work, supplies name of composers and librettists, and dates of premieres, and describes the *libret de mise en scène*. Indexes to composers, librettists, and other names and to theaters by country and city.

1126. Cowden, Robert H. Concert and opera singers; a bibliography of biographical materials. Westport, Connecticut: Greenwood Press, 1985. 278 p. (Music reference collection, 5)

An annotated bibliography treating collective works and separate monographs. Includes an index to singers in the *New Grove Dictionary of Music and Musicians*. Index of authors. Bibliography.

Review by Ann P. Basart in *Fontes Artis Musicae*, 33 (1982), p. 261–62.

1127. Farkas, Andrew. Opera and concert singers: an annotated international bibliography of books and pamphlets. With a foreword by Richard Bonynge. New York: Garland Pub., 1985. 363 p. (Garland reference library of the humanities, 466)

In two major sections: the first organized by singers, with entries of works devoted to one singer, excluding reviews and criticism; the second contains entries for works about more than one singer, organized by author or title. Most entries are annotated. There are cross-references from the first section on singers to entries in the second. International in scope, the work cites 1,850 titles in 29 languages on 796 singers from a period of 413 years ending in 1984. Comprehensiveness was an objective, but the work almost entirely excludes periodical articles.

1128. Fuld, James J. The book of world-famous libretti: the musical theater from 1598 to today. New York: Pendragon Press, 1984.

Extensive descriptions of libretti for 168 operas designated by Fuld as operas of first importance either for their places in the current world repertory or for their historical significance.

Review by Marita P. McClymonds in *Fontes Artis Musicae*, 32 (1985), p. 140–41.

1129. Giovine, Alfredo. Bibliografia di teatri musicali italiani (storia e cronologie) di Alfredo Giovine. Bari: Edizioni Fratelli Laterza, 1982. 67 p. (Biblioteca dell'Archivio delle tradizioni popolari baresi)

A bibliography of histories and chronologies of Italian theaters used for staged musical events, including opera.

1130. Grout, Donald J. "Bibliographies, lexicons, guides, histories, and other works dealing with opera...." In his *A Short History of Opera*, 2nd ed., p. 585–768. New York: Columbia University Press, 1965.

A 3rd edition appeared in 1987 with Hermine Williams as coauthor.

One of the most comprehensive bibliographies of literature on the opera. Includes both books and articles in leading European and American periodicals. Arranged alphabetically by author.

1131. Marco, Guy A. Opera: a research and information guide. New York: Garland Pub., 1984. 373 p. (Garland reference library of the humanities, 468)

A classified, annotated bibliography of 704 core titles on opera. Works about operetta and singspiel are included selectively; works on the American musical theater are omitted. All items included are in western European languages. This guide is especially good for studies of individual operas and opera in specific countries and regions. Excludes bibliographies of individuals. Includes as an appendix a checklist of opera composers and their major works. Author-title index and subject index.

1132. **"Opern-Uraufführungen in den USA und Kanada seit 1945."** In *Musik-bühne* (1975), p. 189–[242].
A list of American and Canadian opera premieres.

1133. **Quellentexte zur Konzeption der europäischen Oper im 17. Jahrhundert.** Kassel, etc.: Bärenreiter, 1981. 200 p. (Musikwissenschaftliche Arbeiten, no. 27)
Recent historians have directed their attention to source documents on which our knowledge of music is based. In this case the subject is 17th-century opera. Responsibility for its coverage is shared among Wolfgang Osthoff, Herbert Schneider, and Hellmuth Christian Wolff. Includes biblio-graphical references and indexes.

1134. **Sartori, Claudio.** I libretti italiani a stampa dalle origini al 1800: cata-logo analitico con 16 indici. Cunea: Bertola & Locatelli, 1990– . 5 v. to date.
Supersedes his photocopied *Primo Tentativo di Catalogo Unico dei Li-bretti Italiani* (Milano: Biblioteca Nazionale Braidense & Ufficio Ricerca Fondi Musicali, 1973–81), which was issued in unnumbered leaves.

> This catalogue is intended to be as complete a list as possible of Italian and Latin texts for music and any translation published up to and including the year 1800. Handwritten librettos have been omitted. [*Preface*]

A catalog of texts for operas, serenades, cantatas, prologues, choral works, intermezzi, dances, oratorios, and other forms of literary works with incidental musical settings or musical works with incidental texts set to music. Arranged alphabetically by title. Complete title page transcrip-tions with annotations and locations of extant copies. Citations of corre-sponding musical scores. Cross-references from alternate titles. Preface in Italian and English. Approximately 2,000 entries in the first volumes.

The 16 indexes include: localities and places of performances; authors of text; composers; impresarios; designers, architects, and painters; cho-reographers; costume makers; sword masters; scene shifters, property and stage managers; orchestra conductors; harpsichordists; violinists; other musicians; singers; teachers; dancers.

There are lists of bibliographical references, of principal abbreviations, and of *RISM* sigla (corresponding to those found in the last volume of *RISM A*).

1135. **Senelick, Laurence, David F. Cheshire and Ulrich Schneider.** British music-hall, 1840–1923: a bibliography and guide to sources, with a supplement on European music-hall. Hamden, Connecticut: Archon Books, 1981. 361 p.
A bibliography of 3,863 items in 12 parts.
Part 1 is a directory of collections in Ireland, the United Kingdom, and the United States with entries describing resources available on the sub-ject. There is also a bibliography of reference works.
Part 2 is a bibliography of periodicals featuring news and information on music halls and the entertainment they presented.
Part 3 is a bibliography of "general studies" on the music hall, including picture books and memoirs.

Parts 4 and 5 consist of citations of general and specific information and criticism of entertainment in particular music halls, arranged by city.

Part 6 is a bibliography on the architecture of music halls.

Part 7 considers legislation and regulation affecting music halls and their entertainments, including morality and censorship.

Part 8 presents citations concerned with performances by genre (animal acts, jugglers, etc.).

Part 9 is a bibliography of articles about individual performers.

Part 10 is a bibliography of performance materials (joke books, song books, etc.).

Part 11 is a select bibliography of literary and artistic works in which music halls or their entertainments are themes or prominent locations.

Part 12 is a discography of long-playing records of music hall entertainments.

Supplements A–F present select bibliographies on selected entertainments and music halls in European, Russian, East European, African and Asian locations. There is an addenda, an index of authors, and a cross-index of London music halls.

Contains references to publications covering virtually anything anyone would ever wish to know about the subject within its chronological limits.

1136. Surian, Elvidio. A checklist of writings on 18th-century French and Italian opera (excluding Mozart). Hackensack, New Jersey: Joseph Boonin, 1970. 121 p. (Music indexes and bibliographies, 3)

> The bibliography contained in the present volume attempts to be comprehensive in its coverage of studies on 18th-century French and Italian opera. In dealing with this genre, one must constantly remember that the literary and other extra-musical aspects play an important role. Therefore, the bibliography has been classified, and includes sections not only on the music, but also on librettos and librettists and the theatrical production (choreography, scenery, theatrical machinery, etc.). Histories of the drama and literature have been incorporated under the *General Bibliography* section. [from the introductory remarks]

There are 1,501 citations in 10 classifications on the subject, excluding anything on Mozart, on singspiel, the ballad opera, or on Russian opera in the 18th century. List of abbreviations to sources articles and books.

1137. Weaver, Robert L. and Norma W. Weaver. A chronology of music in the Florentine theater, 1590–1750; operas, prologues, finales, intermezzos, and plays with incidental music. Detroit, Michigan: Information Coordinators, 1978. 421 p. (Detroit studies in music bibliography, 38)

Of fundamental interest are chronologically ordered entries on performances or the occasions providing the reasons for performances of operas and other theatrical forms. There are indexes to: librettists; composers; singers and actors; other persons engaged in producing these events; theaters; sponsoring organizations and performing groups; and titles. There is a general index and a bibliography. Most of the sources of information are libretti, but some information is drawn from diaries and archival sources. A remarkable sourcebook on the birthplace and birth-time of opera.

Review by Thomas Walker in *Notes*, 36 (1979), p. 90–92.

1138. Wildbihler, Hubert and Sonja Völklein. The musical; an international annotated bibliography; eine internationale annotierte Bibliographie. München: K. G. Saur, 1986. 320 p.

"An overview ... of the entire theoretical literature on the stage and film musical from its beginnings to 1986," consisting of 3,629 entries arranged in a classified order. Includes sections on general references, predecessors, history and development, production, "musicals and the public," musicals outside of North America, the film musical, and people associated with musicals. Excludes citations for libretti, scores, and reviews of performances. Only citations for the most important works are annotated. Lists of sources and periodicals consulted. Author and subject index.

Primary Sources: Early Music Literature

The entries in this section are concerned with writings on music that appeared before 1800. For further listings of early music literature, one should consult the general bibliographies compiled before 1840, such as Becker (no. 676), Forkel (no. 697), and Lichtenthal (no. 380). See also the narrative bibliography by James E. Matthew (no. 721) and the catalogs of libraries with noteworthy holdings in early music theory, such as the U.S. Library of Congress (no. 2438), the library of Alfred Cortot (no. 2472), and the Paul Hirsch Library in the British Library (no. 2142). The *RISM* volume, *Écrits Imprimés Concernant la Musique*, is the international union catalog covering separate publications on music (no. 1148).

1139. Bircher, Martin. "Von Boethius bis Hindemith. Eine Züricher Sammlung von Erstausgaben zur Geschichte der Musiktheorie." In *Librarium*, 13 (1970), p. 134–61.
A description of the Erwin Jacobi collection of first editions of works on music theory.

1140. Bukofzer, Manfred F. "Check-list of Baroque books on music." In his *Music in the Baroque Era*, p. 417–31. New York: Norton, 1947.
Theory treatises, instruction books, and histories written c. 1590–1770. Modern facsimiles and reprints indicated. Arranged alphabetically by author.

1141. Cohen, Albert and Leta E. Miller. Music in the Paris Academy of Sciences, 1666–1793; a source archive in photocopy at Stanford University. Detroit, Michigan: Information Coordinators, 1979. 69 p. (Detroit studies in music bibliography, 43)
An index of proceedings of the Academie Royale des Sciences.
A study based on these documents has been published under the title *Music in the French Royal Academy of Sciences: A Study in the Evolution of Musical Thought* (Princeton, 1981).
Review by Catherine Massip in *Fontes Artis Musicae*, 29 (1982), p. 149.

1142. Coover, James B. "Music theory in translation; a bibliography." In *Journal of Music Theory*, 3 (1959), p. 70–96; and 13 (1969), p. 230–49.
Cites only English translations of early theory works. Alphabetical listing, by author, of works from antiquity to the present day.

1143. Davidsson, Ake. Bibliographie der musiktheoretischen Drucke des 16. Jahrhunderts. Baden-Baden: Heitz, 1962. 99 p. (Bibliotheca bibliographica aureliana, 9)

A bibliography of 16th-century theory works; more than 600 titles, arranged alphabetically by author, with bibliographical reference to literature on the sources. Index of persons, including printers, editors, etc. Bibliography, p. 85–88. 25 facsimile plates.

Review by Fred Blum in *Notes*, 20 (1963), p. 234.

1144. Davidsson, Ake. Catalogue critique et descriptif des ouvrages théoriques sur la musique imprimés au XVIe et XVIIe siècles et conservés dans les bibliothèques suédoises. Uppsala: Almquist & Wiksell, 1953. 83 p. (Studia musicologica upsaliensia, 2)

A union catalog of early works on music theory in Swedish libraries. 108 items, fully described, with locations and references to relevant literature. P. 77–83: bibliography of works cited.

1145. Farmer, Henry G. The sources of Arabian music: an annotated bibliography of Arabic manuscripts which deal with the theory, practice, and history of Arabian music from the eighth to the seventeenth century. Leiden: E. J. Brill, 1965. 71 p.

First issued privately by the author in 1940.

Entries arranged chronologically by century, preceded by a brief general discussion of Arabian music and its sources.

Review by Jörg Martin in *Die Musikforschung*, 25 (1972) p. 372–73.

1146. Mandyczewski, Eusebius. "Bücher und Schriften über Musik. Druckwerke und Handschriften aus der Zeit bis zum Jahre 1800." In *Geschichte der K.K. Gesellschaft der Musikfreunde in Wien...*, p. 55–84. Wien, 1912.

An extremely useful listing of the pre-1800 writings on music in the library of the Gesellschaft der Musikfreunde in Vienna.

1147. Reese, Gustave. Fourscore classics of music literature; a guide to selected original sources on theory and other writings on music not available in English, with descriptive sketches and bibliographical references. New York: Liberal Arts Press, 1957. 91 p.

Reprinted by Da Capo Press, New York, 1970.

80 works presented in chronological order, with illuminating commentary. This bibliography, sponsored by the American Council of Learned Societies, was intended to stimulate new English editions and translations of important early theory works. Index of titles.

1148. Répertoire International des Sources Musicales. Écrits imprimés concernant la musique. Ouvrage publié sous la direction de François Lesure. München: G. Henle, 1971. 2 v. (RISM B VI, 1–2)

Vol. 1: A–L. Vol. 2: M–Z.

A comprehensive bibliography of writings on music printed before 1800, comprising all theoretical, historical, aesthetic, or technical literature. Location symbols identify copies held in European and American libraries. Brief introduction; listing of the institutions that have contributed information on their holdings.

Anonymous works are listed by title in a separate section and there is an addendum. Index of printers and publishers and a chronological index.

For supplementary information see François Lesure, "*Écrits Imprimés sur la Musique;* addenda et corrigenda," in *Fontes Artis Musicae,* 26 (1979), p. 1–4.

1149. Répertoire International des Sources Musicales. Hebrew writings concerning music in manuscripts and printed books from Geonic times up to 1800 by Israel Adler. München: G. Henle, 1975. 389 p. (RISM, B IX, 2)

"This volume presents a corpus of Hebrew writings concerning music, and not only a catalogue of these sources." The entries for the 276 manuscripts and 384 books are arranged alphabetically by author. Bibliography. Indexes of quotations and references, Hebrew and Arabic titles. There is a general name, title, and subject index.

1150. Répertoire International des Sources Musicales. The theory of music from the Carolingian era up to 1400; descriptive catalogue of manuscripts. Edited by Joseph Smits van Waesberghe, with the collaboration of Peter Fischer and Christian Maas. München: G. Henle, 1961– . Vol. 1– . (RISM, B III, 1–3)

> Offers a description of all manuscripts in which are preserved Latin treatises, however small, dealing with the theory of music which was in use from the Carolingian era to 1400. [*Preface*]

Vol. 1: *Austria, Belgium, Switzerland, Denmark, France, Luxembourg, and the Netherlands.* 1961. 155 p.

Vol. 2: *Italy.* Edited by Peter Fischer. 1968, 148 p. Includes some manuscripts dating from the 15th and even the 16th century when these are sole surviving sources of the earlier tradition.

Vol. 3: *Manuscripts from the Carolingian Era up to c. 1500 in the Federal Republic of Germany.* Edited by Michel Huglo and Christian Meyer. 1986.

Each volume includes an index of libraries and an index of authors and of incipits of anonymous treatises.

Review by James B. Coover in *Journal of Music Theory,* 6 (1962), p. 314–15.

1151. Répertoire International des Sources Musicales. The theory of music in Arabic writings (c. 900–1900): descriptive catalogue of manuscripts in libraries of Europe and the U.S.A., by Amnon Shiloah. München: G. Henle, 1979. 512 p. (RISM, B X)

Preceded by a historical introduction and classification of the sources, 341 sources are arranged by author, analyzed, and described. Each entry includes an incipit, an explicit, and bibliographical references. There is a bibliography of library catalogs, a general bibliography, and an Arabic bibliography. There is a general index to names, titles, terms, and subjects.

English or Arabic; preface in English, French, and German.

1152. Vivell, Cölestin. Initia tractatuum musices ex codicibus editorum; collegit et ordine alphabetico disposuit. Genève: Minkoff Reprints, 1979. 352 p.

Reprint of the edition of J. Meyerhoff, Graz, 1912.

Indexes the first lines of each chapter in each treatise in Martin Gerbert's *Scriptores Ecclesiastici de Musica Sacra* and in Edmund de Coussemaker's *Scriptorum de Musica Medii Aevi* and to musical treatises in eleven other 19th-century collections. Includes analytical indexes to sources indexed, an index to authors of treatises (and to titles of anonymous treatises), and a chronological index to treatises.

Warner, Thomas E. An annotated bibliography of woodwind instruction books, 1600–1830. See no. 959.

Sacred Music

Bibliographies of writings on sacred music are surprisingly few. Additional references will be found in the various handbooks to hymnology (nos. 403 ff.). See also current listings in the *Jahrbuch für Liturgik und Hymnologie* (no. 756) and Gregorio Suñol's bibliography of works related to Gregorian chant (no. 991). Kenneth Hartley's *Bibliography of Theses and Dissertations in Sacred Music* (no. 1154) provides information on academic works, each with extensive bibliographies.

1153. Buszin, Walter [et al.]. A bibliography on music and the church. Prepared for the Commission on Music, Department of Worship and the Arts, National Council of Churches of Christ in the U.S.A. New York: National Council of Churches, 1958. 16 p.

1154. Hartley, Kenneth R. Bibliography of theses and dissertations in sacred music. Detroit, Michigan: Information Coordinators, Inc., 1967. 127 p. (Detroit studies in music bibliography, 9)
Listed by degree-granting institution and then alphabetically by author. Covers American master's theses and Ph.D. dissertations in the 20th century to the mid-1960s. Author and subject indexes.

1155. Jackson, Irene V. Afro-American religious music: a bibliography and catalogue of gospel music. Westport, Connecticut: Greenwood Press, 1979. 210 p.
The bibliography covers "music of the established Black churches or denominations in the United States and the Caribbean as well as Afro-American cults in the Caribbean and South America." Religious music indigenous to West Africa is covered as well. Indexed by subject.
The catalog is arranged by composer and covers music by Afro-Americans written 1938–65 and is based on the collections and catalogs of the Library of Congress.
Review in *Journal of Negro History*, 65 (1980), p. 89–90.

1156. Powell, Martha C. A selected bibliography of church music and music reference materials. Compiled and annotated by Martha C. Powell; assisted by Deborah C. Loftis. Louisville, Kentucky: Southern Baptist Theological Seminary, 1977. 95 p.
Supplement (10 p.) bound at end.
Oriented to American Protestant denominations.

1157. Szöverfly, Joseph. A guide to Byzantine hymnography: a classified bibliography of texts and studies. Brookline, Massachusetts: Classical Folia Editions; Leyden: E. J. Brill, 1978. 2 v.

An analytical guide to over 6,000 entries and 2,000 separate titles. This is a classified work with titles cited in Roman and non-Roman characters. A third volume completing the bibliography and including indexes is anticipated.

1158. Von Ende, Richard C. Church music: an international bibliography. Metuchen, New Jersey: Scarecrow Press, 1980. 453 p.

A classified list, international in scope, of 5,445 works focused almost entirely on works about Christian church music. Some anthologies of music are cited. There is an index to authors, editors, and compilers.

Review by Richard French in *Notes*, 37 (1981), p. 590–91.

1159. Yeats-Edwards, Paul. English church music; a bibliography. London: White Lion, 1975. 217 p.

A selective bibliography, the "object of which is to indicate, under subject headings, what books, pamphlets and tracts have been published in England on English church music." There is a general index to the 1,220 entries.

Individual Composers

In this section are a few representative examples of bibliographies devoted to writings about specific composers. These are to be distinguished from bibliographies made up of entries for the composer's own works, which will be found in "Bibliographies of Music" under the heading "Individual composers" (no. 1561 ff.). Two general bibliographies of composers and musicians are cited before the selected citations of bibliographies on specific composers.

1160. Adams, John L. Musicians' autobiographies; an annotated bibliography of writings available in English 1800 to 1980. Jefferson, North Carolina: McFarland, 1982. 126 p.

Arranged by author, excluding letters, histories, diaries, and articles in reference works. There are chronological, title, and subject indexes.

1161. Green, Richard D. Index to composer bibliographies. Detroit, Michigan: Information Coordinators, 1985. 86 p. (Detroit studies in music bibliography, 53)

Deals solely with bibliographies of secondary literature.

BEETHOVEN, LUDWIG VAN

1162. Gyimes, Ferenc and Veronika Vavrineca, ed. Ludwig van Beethoven; a magyar konyvtarakban es gyujtemenyekben. Bibliografia I–III. Budapest: Allami Gorkij Konyvtar, 1970–72. 3 v.

A union catalog of Beethoven documentation in Hungarian libraries.

Vol. 1: a bibliography of literature on Beethoven.

Vol. 2: a discography of 738 items, with index of performing artists and organizations.
Vol. 3: a bibliography of Beethoven compositions, 1,378 items, with indexes of titles, editors, and publishers.

1163. MacArdle, Donald W. Beethoven abstracts. Detroit, Michigan: Information Coordinators, 1973. 446 p. (Detroit studies in music bibliography, 3)
Abstracts of articles about Beethoven from the 18th century through 1964 in four sections: primary periodicals, secondary periodicals, newspapers, catalogs.
Review by Douglas Johnson in *Notes*, 30 (1974), p. 513–17.

BRAHMS, JOHANNES

1164. Bozarth, George S. "Brahms's lieder inventory of 1859–60 and other documents of his life and work." In *Fontes Artis Musicae*, 30 (1983), p. 98–117.
A catalog of documents including Brahms' index of his works and personal library, his appointment books for the last 30 years of his life, his notebooks, and some musical sketches. Discusses also an inventory of lieder in Brahms' hand from 1859–60.

BRUCKNER, ANTON

1165. Grasberger, Renate. Bruckner-Bibliographie (bis 1974). Graz: Akademische Druck- u. Verlagsanstalt, 1985. 296 p. (Anton Bruckner Dokumente und Studien, 4)

BUXTEHUDE, DIETRICH

1166. Wettstein, Hermann. Dietrich Buxtehude (1637–1707): eine Bibliographie mit einem Anhang über Nicolaus Bruhns. Freiburg i. Br.: Universtätsbibliothek, 1979. 98 p. (Schriften der Universitätsbibliothek Freiburg i. Br., 2)
Two bibliographies: one about Dietrich Buxtehude and another about Nicolaus Bruhns.

CHOPIN, FREDERIC

1167. Michalowski, Kornel. Bibliografia chopinowska. Chopin bibliography 1849–1969. Kraków: Polskie Wydawnictwo muzyczne, 1970. 268 p.
A well-organized bibliography of literature about Chopin, covering documentary evidence, life, works, interpretation, studies of Chopin's reception, and bibliographical publications.
3,970 items. Text in Polish and English. Indexes of subjects, Chopin's works, and authors.

COPLAND, AARON

1168. Skowronski, JoAnn. Aaron Copland: a bio-bibliography. Westport, Connecticut: Greenwood Press, 1985. 273 p. (Bio-bibliographies in music, 2)
Includes a discography and index.

COWELL, HENRY

1169. Manion, Martha L. Writings about Henry Cowell: an annotated bibliography. Brooklyn: Institute for Studies in American Music, Conservatory of Music, Brooklyn College of the City University of New York, 1982. 368 p. (I.S.A.M. monographs, 16)

DEBUSSY, CLAUDE

1170. Abravanel, Claude. Claude Debussy; a bibliography. Detroit, Michigan: Information Coordinators, 1974. 214 p. (Detroit studies in music bibliography, 29)
A broad survey of the literature about Debussy, listing 854 works.
Review by François Lesure in *Notes*, 31 (1975), p. 290–91.

HANDEL, GEORGE FREDERIC

1171. Sasse, Konrad. Händel Bibliographie. Zusammengestellt von Konrad Sasse unter Verwendung des im Händel-Jahrbuch 1933 von Kurt Taut veröffentlichten Verzeichnisses des Schrifttums über Georg Friedrich Händel. Abgeschlossen im Jahre 1961. Leipzig: Deutscher Verlag für Musik, 1963. 352 p.
A 2nd edition appeared in 1967. 433 p.
The expansion of a bibliography compiled by Kurt Taut for the 1933 *Händel-Jahrbuch*, with a supplement by Sasse published in the 1955 *Jahrbuch*. A highly organized work citing literature on every aspect of the composer's life and work. Author index.
Review by Willi Reich in *Literature, Music, Fine Arts*, 1 (1968), p. 87–89.

HAYDN, JOSEPH

1172. Lowens, Irving with Otto E. Albrecht. Haydn in America. Detroit, Michigan: Information Coordinators, 1979. 144 p. (Bibliographies in American Music, 5)
Documents performances and publications in America of Haydn's works. Includes Albrecht's "Haydn autographs in the United States."

JOSQUIN DES PRES

1173. Charles, Sydney Robinson. Josquin des Prez; a guide to research. New York: Garland, 1983. 235 p. (Garland composer resource manuals, 2) (Garland reference library of the humanities, 330)

This work summarizes the contemporaneous documents presenting facts of Josquin's life with references to the literature discussing each document. It provides a categorical list of works about Josquin's music with a list of compositions showing sources, bibliography, recordings, and modern editions of each work. There is a list of sources with modern editions and literature about each cited. Discography with title index. Bibliography of works cited. Index to names of persons, places, and titles. This work serves as an introduction to research on Josquin. Review by Richard Taruskin in *Notes*, 42 (1985), p. 39–41.

LISZT, FRANZ

1174. Suttoni, Charles. "Franz Liszt's published correspondence: an annotated bibliography." In *Fontes Artis Musicae*, 26 (1979), p. 191–234.
A good example of the kind of focused bibliographic research that is much needed on the letters of many important composers. Indexes of correspondents and to authors and editors.

MAHLER, GUSTAV

Vondenhoff, Brun and Eleonore Vondenhoff. Gustav Mahler Dokumentation, Sammlung Eleonore Vondenhoff: Materialien zu seinem Leben und Werk. See no. 2430.

MENDELSSOHN-BARTHOLDY, FELIX

1175. Bodleian Library. Catalogue of the Mendelssohn papers in the Bodleian Library, Oxford. [By Margaret Crum.] Tutzing: Hans Schneider, 1980– . 2 v. (Musikbibliographische Arbeiten, 7)
Contents: Vol. 1. Correspondence of Felix Mendelssohn-Bartholdy and others; Vol. 2. Music and papers.
Review by Douglass Seaton in *Notes*, 38 (1982), p. 603–604.

MOZART, WOLFGANG AMADEUS

1176. Angermüller, Rudolph and Otto Schneider. Mozart-Bibliographie (bis 1970). *Mozart-Jahrbuch* 1975. Kassel: Bärenreiter, 1976. 362 p. (Mozart-Jahrbuch 1975 des Zentralinstitutes für Mozartforschung der Internationalen Stiftung Mozarteum Salzburg)
Supplemented by *Mozart-Bibliographie 1971–1975 mit Nachträgen zur Mozart-Bibliographue bis 1970*, by the same authors, published by Bärenreiter, 1978, 175 p., and by similar titles covering 1976–1980 (Bärenreiter, 1982) and 1981–85 (Bärenreiter, 1987).
Over 6,600 entries arranged by author, but indexed by work, persons, places, and subjects. Coverage best for German-language works, adequate for works in French and Italian, but clearly less than satisfactory for works in English. The supplement adds over 2,300 entries to the bibliography.
Reviews by A. Hyatt King in *Fontes Artis Musicae*, 24 (1977), p. 101–102, and in *Fontes Artis Musicae*, 30 (1983), p. 170. Review by William P. Robinson in *Notes*, 34 (1977), p. 67–70.

RACHMANINOFF, SERGEI

1177. Palmieri, Robert. Sergei Vasilevich Rachmaninoff: a guide to research. New York: Garland, 1984. 335 p. (Garland composer resource manuals, 3) (Garland reference library of the humanities, 471)
Extensive bibliography, discography, list of compositions, and repertoire list. Indexed.

REGER, MAX

1178. Rösner, Helmut. Max-Reger-Bibliographie. Das internationale Schrifttum über Max Reger 1893–1966. Bonn, Hannover, and München: Dümmler, 1968. 138 p. (Veröffentlichungen des Max-Reger-Institutes, 5)
Review by Gerd Sievers in *Die Musikforschung*, 24 (1971), p. 93–95.

SCHOENBERG, ARNOLD

Kimmey, John A. The Arnold Schoenberg-Hans Nachod collection. See no. 1998.

1179. Satoh, Tetsuo. A bibliographic catalog with discography and a comprehensive bibliography of Arnold Schoenberg. Tokyo: Kunitachi Music College Library, 1979. 156 p.
Accompanied by an English guide to the work. 8 p.
In Japanese and English. 2,116 entries in the bibliography of writings about Schoenberg. Indexes to titles of compositions, opus numbers, subjects, places, and names. List of periodicals from which articles were drawn.

SCHUMANN, ROBERT

1180. Munte, Frank. Verzeichnis des deutschsprachigen Schrifttums über Robert Schumann 1956–1970. Hamburg: Wagner, 1972. 151 p. (Schriftenreihe zur Musik, 1)
Anhang: "Schrifttum über Clara Schumann."

SCHÜTZ, HEINRICH

1181. Skei, Allen B. Heinrich Schütz, a guide to research. New York: Garland, 1981. 186 p. (Garland composer resource manuals, 1) (Garland reference library of the humanities, 272)
Review by François Lesure in *Fontes Artis Musicae* 30 (1983), p. 223.

SIBELIUS, JEAN

1182. Blum, Fred. Jean Sibelius, an international bibliography on the occasion of the centennial celebrations, 1965. Detroit, Michigan: Information Coordinators, 1965. 114 p. (Detroit studies in music bibliography, 8)

P. 1–11: books and dissertations devoted to Sibelius; p. 13–45: books partially devoted to Sibelius; p. 47–71: music journals; p. 73–94: nonmusic journals. Index of names.
Review by Gerhard Hahne in *Die Musikforschung*, 22 (1969), p. 100; by Ruth Watanabe in *Notes*, 23 (1966), p. 279.

STRAUSS, RICHARD

1183. Ortner, Oswald and Franz Grasberger. Richard-Strauss-Bibliographie. Teil 1: 1882–1944. Wien: Georg Prachner; Kommission bei Verlag Brüer Hollinek, 1964–73. 2 v. (Museion, Veröffentlichungen der Österreichischen Nationalbibliothek, neue Folge, dritte Reihe, 2)
Vol. 1: 1882–1944; vol. 2: 1944–1964.
Vol. 2 compiled by Günther Brosche.
A bibliography organized in terms of various aspects of Strauss' career. The largest section is devoted to writings related to individual works, operas, etc.

WAGNER, RICHARD

1184. Internationale Wagner-Bibliographie 1945–1955. International Wagner bibliography 1945–1955. Bibliographie internationale de la littérature sur Wagner 1945–1955. Hrsg. von Herbert Barth. Bayreuth: Edition Musica, 1956. 56 p.
Second printing issued 1974.
Contains selective listings of German, English, and French writings on Wagner. The appendix offers an international Wagner discography, statistics of performances by major opera companies, and a survey of important Wagner collections.

1185. Internationale Wagner-Bibliographie 1956–1960. International Wagner bibliography 1956–1960. Bibliographie internationale de la littérature sur Wagner 1956–1960. Hrsg. von Herbert Barth. Bayreuth: Edition Musica, 1961. 142 p.
This volume follows the same pattern of organization as the preceding but also includes a tabulation of the casts of all the Bayreuth festivals from 1876 to 1960.

1186. Internationale Wagner-Bibliographie 1961–1966. International Wagner Bibliography 1961–1966. Bibliographie internationale de la littérature sur Wagner 1961–1966 (und Wieland-Wagner-Bibliographie). Bayreuth: Edition Musica, 1968. 99 p.
Includes a bibliography on Wieland Wagner.

1187. Internationale Wagner-Bibliographie 1967–1978. International Wagner bibliography 1967–1978. Bibliographie internationale de la littérature sur Wagner 1967–1978. Hrsg. von Herbert Barth. Bayreuth: Mühl'scher Universitätsverlag W. Fehr, 1979. 175 p.

1188. Kastner, Emerich. Wagner-Catalog. Chronologisches Verzeichniss der von und über Richard Wagner erschienenen Schriften, Musikwerke, etc., etc., nebst biographischen Notizen. Offenbach z. M.: André, 1878. 140 p.

Reprint, 1966, by Frits A. M. Knuf, Hilversum.

Chronological listing of Wagner's works and the literature about them from 1813 to 1877.

1189. Oesterlein, Nikolaus. Katalog einer Richard Wagner-Bibliothek; nach den vorliegenden Originalien systematisch-chronologisch geordnetes und mit Citaten und Anmerkungen versehenes authentisches Nachschlagebuch durch die gesammte Wagner-Literatur. Leipzig: Breitkopf & Härtel, 1882–95. 4 v.

Vols. 1 and 2 of this work consist of a bibliography of late 19th-century writings on Wagner. The remaining volumes consist of a catalog of the holdings of the Richard Wagner-Museum in Eisenach. (See also no. 2010.)

Bibliographies of Music

In this category are listed bibliographies of *musical scores* as distinct from *writings about music*. This section lends itself to fewer subdivisions than the preceding assemblage of "Bibliographies of Music Literature," the major approaches being that of the performer in search of music appropriate to his particular instrument or ensemble, on the one hand, and that of the student of early music, on the other.

Not included here, except for a token listing of some recent titles, are the numerous listings of the works of individual composers. One of the best approaches to information of this kind is through the biographical dictionaries such as Baker (no. 71) and Riemann (no. 53), or such comprehensive encyclopedias as *MGG* (no. 43) and the *New Grove* (no. 46). For thematic catalogs, a useful guide is found in Barry Brook's *Thematic Catalogues in Music; an Annotated Bibliography* (no. 684).

Two significant on-line catalogs with extensive, but not yet exhaustive, coverage of printed music are OCLC (no. 1205) and RLIN (no. 1207). These bibliographic giants usually are not available to the scholar directly but must be interrogated through intermediaries, knowledgeable music librarians and bibliographers.

This section excludes the catalogs of individual music publishing firms except where their coverage extends beyond the output of a single business house, as in the case of Hofmeister (no. 1200) or Pazdirek (no. 1208). Bibliographies of the work of early music publishers are found in the section "Histories and Bibliographies of Music Printing and Publishing."

GENERAL

1190. Aronowsky, Salomon. Performing times of orchestral works. Foreword by Percival R. Kirby. London: E. Benn, 1959. 802 p.

Covers both standard and minor composers of all countries and periods, with some emphasis on British names. Arrangements listed under both composer and arranger. Operas, orchestral versions of single songs, and opera excerpts appear frequently. No precise indication of edition or publisher, but lists of publishers and publishers' organizations are given. The work is a more lavish and expensive publication than seems warranted by its contents.

Review by Howard Mitchell in *Notes*, 17 (1960), p. 237–39.

1191. Berkowitz, Freda P. Popular titles and subtitles of musical compositions. 2nd ed. Metuchen, New Jersey: Scarecrow Press, 1975. 209 p.

Alphabetical listing of 740 works by title, with brief accounts of the origins of their popular titles. Bibliography. Composer index.
Review by Stephen M. Fry in *Notes*, 32 (1976), p. 554.

1192. Board of Music Trade of the United States of America. Complete catalog of sheet music and musical works. New York: Board of Music Trade, 1870. 575 p.
Reprinted by Da Capo, New York, 1973.
Classified catalog of music and books about music published by members of the Board of Music Trade and in print at the time of publication. Scanty bibliographic information provided and not indexed. Excludes numerous publishers who are not members of the Board.
Review by Don Hixon in *American Reference Books Annual* (1975), no. 1121.

1193. Bonner Katalog: Verzeichnis reversgebundener musikalischer Aufführungsmateriale. Bearbeitet und herausgegeben vom Deutschen Musikarchiv der Deutschen Bibliothek in Verbindung mit dem Deutschen Musikverleger-Verband e.V. 2. neubearbeitete Aufl. München and New York: K. G. Saur, 1982. 530 p.
First published in 1959.
Not a catalog of German music, strictly speaking, but a listing by composer of musical works marketed in Germany and protected by international copyright under the Bern Convention. Copyright editions of works by early composers included. Types of works indicated by symbols; duration and publishers given. Excellent source of information on published contemporary music. Entries under authors of text, editors, arrangers, and translators.

1194. Boustead, Alan. Music to Shakespeare, a practical catalogue of current incidental music, song settings and other related music.... London. Printed by Novello and Co., sole distributor. Oxford University Press, 1964. 40 p.
Shakespearean works entered alphabetically, with music given under three headings: (1) incidental music; (2) songs; (3) other music. Minimal bibliographical information. Indexes of song titles and of composers. No key to publishers.
For other listings of Shakespeare music, see nos. 1196 and 1403.

1195. British Broadcasting Corporation. Central Music Library. [Catalogues]. London: BBC, 1965–67. 13 v.
[1] *Chamber Music Catalogue:* chamber music, violin and keyboard, cello and keyboard. 1965. 1 v., various pagings.
[2] *Piano and Organ Catalogue.* 1965. 2 v., various pagings.
[3] *Song Catalogue.* 1966. 4 v. Vols. 1–2, composers; vols. 3–4, titles.
[4] *Choral and Opera Catalogue.* 1967. 2 v. Vol. 1, composers; vol. 2, titles.
[5] *Orchestral Catalogue.* Edited by Sheila Compton. 1982. 4 v.
These volumes record the holdings of one of the world's great radio libraries and are known as the *BBC Catalogues.* Each volume is devoted to a special category of materials. Entries include composer's full name, dates if known, title of the work, score or parts, duration, publisher. A

bibliography of relevant reference works and a listing of the principal music publishers are given in each volume. The chief value of this set lies in the information it offers as a reference tool. The BBC Music Library is not a lending library.

Published under the supervision of John H. Davies, former BBC Music Librarian; with an introduction by William Glock.

Review of vol. 1 (*Chamber Music Catalogue*) by Donald W. Krummel in *Notes*, 23 (1966), p. 46–48.

1196. Catalogue of musical works based on the plays and poetry of Shakespeare. In *Shakespeare in Music*, compiled by Winton Dean, Dorothy Moore, and Phyllis Hartnoll, p. 243–321. London: Macmillan, 1964.

Works listed under the titles of the plays, in three categories: opera, incidental music, song settings. Checklist of composers. The bibliography of operatic settings, by Winton Dean, is also published in *Shakespeare Survey*, 18 (1965), p. 75–93. See also nos. 1194 and 1403.

1197. Cudworth, Charles. "Thematic index of English eighteenth-century overtures and symphonies." In the Appendix to *Proceedings of the Royal Musical Association*, 78 (1953), 9 p.

Appendix to his paper entitled "The English symphonists of the eighteenth century."

1198. Cudworth, Charles. "Ye olde spuriosity shoppe, or, Put it in the Anhang." In *Notes*, 12 (1954–55), p. 25–40, 533–53.

A lively discussion of the problems of plagiarism, hoaxes, misattribution, and the use of pseudonyms in the field of music. The article contains three useful supplements: (1) spuriosities proper, listed under their supposed composers; (2) nicknames and falsely titled compositions; (3) pseudonyms, altered forms of names, and nicknames.

For a work covering similar material, see no. 2355.

1199. Documents du Demi-Siècle. Tableau chronologique des principales œuvres musicales de 1900 à 1950 établi par genre et par année. Numéro spécial. *La Revue Musicale*, no. 216 (1952), 146 p.

A listing, year by year, of the important musical works of the first half of the 20th century, together with miscellaneous information relating to music for each year. Catalogs of six publishers, with significant work issued by them between 1900 and 1950: Heugel, Costallat, Amphion, Ricordi, Choudens, Ouvrières. Minimal bibliographical information.

1200. Hofmeister, Friedrich. Verzeichnis der in Deutschland seit 1868 erschienenen Werke russischer Komponisten. Leipzig: Druck der Buchdruckerei Frankenstein, 1949. 253 p.

Alphabetical listing of composers, with their works in order of opus number. Detailed bibliographical information including price but lacking date of publication.

1201. McCarty, Clifford. Film composers in America: a check-list of their work. Foreword by Lawrence Morton. Glendale, California: John Valentine, [1953]. 193 p.

Reprint by Da Capo Press, New York, 1972.
163 names, with film scores listed by date. Index of film titles; index of orchestrators.
Review by Frederick W. Sternfeld in *Notes*, 11 (1953), p. 105.

Meggett, Joan M. Keyboard music by women composers: a catalog and bibliography. See no. 2986.

1202. Mies, Paul. Volkstümliche Namen musikalischer Werke. Bonn: Musik-handel-Verlag, [1960]. 32 p.
Nicknames and popular titles for musical compositions listed under composers, with an alphabetical index of titles. Similar compilations are cited as nos. 1191 and 1198.

1203. Music Educators National Conference. Selective music lists. Reston, Virginia: Music Educators National Conference.
From time to time, the M.E.N.C. has issued lists of compositions especially suited to meet the needs of school musical ensembles. Some of these lists cover sufficiently unusual repertories to warrant inclusion here.
Vocal Solos, Vocal Ensembles. Compiled cooperatively with the American Choral Directors Association and the Society for the Preservation and Encouragement of Barber Shop Quartet Singing in America. 1974. 86 p.
Music for Children's Choirs. Compiled under the direction of the Boy and Children's Choirs Standing Committee of the American Choral Directors Association. 1977. 44 p.

1204. Music in print series. Philadelphia, Pennsylvania: Musicdata, 1974– . 6 vol. and annual supplements (1979–).
Vol. 1: *Choral Music in Print (Sacred Choral Music).* 1st ed, 1974. 2nd ed. *Sacred Choral Music in Print* by Gary S. Eslinger and F. Mark Daugherty. 1985. 2 vol. Review by Barbara Peterson in *Notes*, 31 (1975), p. 773–75.
Vol. 2: *Choral Music in Print (Secular Choral Music).* 1974.
Supplement vol.: *Choral Music in Print: 1976 Supplement.*
Supplement vol.: *Sacred Choral Music in Print: 1981 Supplement*, by Nancy K. Nardone. 2nd ed. published 1987.
Supplement vol.: *Secular Choral Music in Print: 1982 Supplement.*
Vol. 3: *Organ Music in Print*, ed. by Thomas R. Nardone. 1st ed., 1975. 2nd ed. by Walter A. Frankel, 1984.
Vol. 4: *Classical Vocal Music in Print.* 1976.
Supplement vol.: *Classical Vocal Music in Print: 1985 Supplement*, ed. by Gary R. Eslinger.
Vol. 5: *Orchestral Music in Print*, ed. by Margaret K. Farish. 1979. Review by John D. Wiser in *Notes*, 34 (1980), p. 61.
Supplement vol.: *Orchestral Music in Print: 1983 Supplement.*
Supplement vol.: *Educational Section of Orchestral Music in Print.* 1978.
Vol. 6: *String Music in Print: 1984 Supplement*, ed. by Margaret K. Farish. 1984. Supplements no. 1412.
A master composer index was published in 1989 (824 p.) and a master title index was published in 1990 (581 p.).

Using the information supplied by cooperating publishers, the series lists specific editions which are available from a publisher ... in appropriate categories. ... The *Music-in-print series* is kept up to date by means of the ... *Annual supplements.* Each year's *Supplement* contains a separate section updating each volume already published in the series. The updates are cumulative ... [*Introduction*]

Within categories, entries are arranged by composer, then title. Instrumentation, duration, publisher, and availability of parts are indicated. Many collections are analyzed. Cross-references are provided. Each volume contains a directory of publishers. Volumes devoted to a single category include a composer-title index.

The two "master index" volumes bring together the data presented in the basic volumes and their supplements, making access to the information much easier. Because of the varying titles used and reported by publishers to Musicdata, the title index contains many entries that are difficult to interpret.

1205. OCLC. 1971– . [Online Computer Library Center, Inc.]

The first of the on-line bibliographic utilities in the United States, OCLC presently connects about 3,000 libraries, some European and the rest American, to a computer and bibliographic data base of immense size near Columbus, Ohio. Among the important music libraries that have contributed to the OCLC data base are those at the University of Illinois at Champaign/Urbana, Indiana University, the Eastman School of Music, the University of Texas at Austin, the University of California at Los Angeles, Oberlin College Conservatory, University of Wisconsin at Madison, the Newberry Library, the University of California at San Diego, the University of North Texas, Florida State University, Ohio State University, New England Conservatory of Music, Westminster Choir College, Arizona State University, the University of North Carolina at Chapel Hill, and the University of Maryland.

Although cataloging on OCLC began in 1971, numerous retrospective conversion projects have proceeded, and the data base is extraordinarily rich in music imprints of all periods. Current cataloging from the Library of Congress is loaded into the data base continuously. There are presently over 22,000,000 works represented by bibliographic records in the data base.

OCLC policy is to store a single bibliographic record and to add sigla indicating which libraries hold the item in question. Catalog records for scores, sound recordings, books, microforms, video disks and tapes, and other library materials are included in the data base. There were in 1986 over 490,000 bibliographic records for sound recordings and over 357,000 for scores.

Access to bibliographic records in the OCLC data base is accomplished through the use of "search keys," truncated versions of author or composer name and/or initial title words. Lately through a special service, one may use subject headings as access terms for the last several years' entries to the data base. Soon access by subject will be possible for the entire data base.

The fundamental basis for the OCLC data base was the creation of catalog cards for traditional North American card catalogs in libraries. For this reason, scholars generally have not been encouraged to use the data base directly for their own purposes; reference librarians usually have had to act as intermediaries between the researcher and the data base. A number of articles on the OCLC data base have been written, principal among them being "Music in the OCLC online union catalog: a review," by Richard P. Smiraglia and Ralph R. Papakhian in *Notes*, 38 (1981), p. 257–74 and p. 968. Music catalogers, reference librarians, and others who use the OCLC services have formed a "music OCLC users group," MOUG, and have published the *Music OCLC Users Group Newsletter.*

The extensive data base and telecommunications network among libraries has made interlibrary loan more efficient and effective for libraries connected to the OCLC computers, both in the United States and in Europe. In 1985 over 3 million requests were handled to the great benefit of, among others, musical scholars.

1206. Reddick, William. The standard musical repertoire, with accurate timings. Garden City, New York: Doubleday & Co., 1947. 192 p.

Reprint by the Greenwood Press, New York, 1969.

A classified list of overtures, orchestral works, works for piano and for violin, songs, and choral compositions, with timings to the nearest five seconds. Designed primarily for program directors of radio stations.

1207. Research Libraries Information Network (RLIN).

RLIN is the on-line bibliographic service of the Research Libraries Group, a partnership of about 40 American libraries, among the largest in the country. Among the important music libraries contributing to RLIN are those at the New York Public Library, Yale University, the University of California at Berkeley, Stanford University, Cornell University, Princeton University, University of Michigan, the University of Pennsylvania, Peabody Conservatory, Dartmouth College, State University of New York at Buffalo, and lately Harvard University and the Eastman School of Music. Current cataloging from the Library of Congress is loaded into the data base continuously. Numerous retrospective conversion projects have been carried out and the data base is quite rich in music imprints of all periods.

In the RLIN data base, each library's catalog records are stored uniquely, but they are clustered in most of the files around a single version of the record. The data base is segmented by form, so there are separate files for scores, sound recordings, serials, books, and so forth. There is no way of knowing how many of the 26,681,000 catalog records in the books file are related to books about music, but there are about 210,000 bibliographic records for sound recordings and 436,500 bibliographic records for scores. RLIN enumerates every repetition of a bibliographic record, so the number of unique bibliographic records is considerably smaller than the figures above suggest.

Access to the data base is possible through personal and corporate names, title phrases, words in titles, and/or subject phrases. Names, words, and phrases may be truncated. Indexes may be combined using the Boolean operators *and, or,* &, *and not.* Once a search on any of these indexes has been accomplished, it may be further modified by date or range of dates of imprint, by publisher, by language, by place of publication, by publisher, by words in subject phrases, and by the holdings of a specific library.

The RLIN data base is driven not only by the desire to share cataloging information among the partner libraries and the other libraries the network serves, but also by the programs of the various standing and special committees of the Research Libraries Group, of which the Music Program Committee was one. Among the many services offered by RLIN, as by

OCLC, interlibrary loan is a particularly effective service to users of the network.

1208. Universal-Handbuch der Musikliteratur aller Zeiten und Völker. Als Nachschlagewerk und Studienquelle der Welt-Musikliteratur. Wien: Pazdirek & Co., [1904–1910?]. 14 v.

Reprint 14 v. in 12 by Knuf, Hilversum, [1966?].

Known as *Pazdirek*, the nearest thing to a comprehensive listing of "music in print" ever published. Primarily useful for 19th-century material in establishing the existence of and dates of editions. Arrangement under composer by opus number, if known; otherwise by title.

1209. Wettstein, Hermann. Thematische Sammelverzeichnisse der Musik: ein bibliographischer Führer durch Musikbibliotheken und -archive. Laaber: Laaber-Verlag, 1982. 268 p.

A bibliography providing references to thematic indexes of collections and individual volumes in some of the major music libraries and archives. Highly selective. Names of composers whose works are to be found in the collections or volumes are listed. A brief index of composers and places is appended.

1210. Yogaku sakuin: sakkyokusha to gendai to yakudai o hikidasu tame no. Music index: for reference to original composers, foreign titles, and Japanese titles. Compiled by Takashi Ogawa. Tokyo: Min-On Music Library, 1975. 769 p.

Text in English and Japanese characters.

P. 1–294, entries by composer, alphabetically arranged. P. 297–503, entries by titles in Western languages. P. 507–765, entries by title in Japanese.

CURRENT

The current music bibliographies listed below restrict their entries to music only. For a full coverage, one should be acquainted with the various national bibliographies in which music appears in company with listings from other fields. An excellent introduction to the use of these major bibliographical tools is an article by Donald W. Krummel and James B. Coover, "Current national bibliographies, their music coverage," in *Notes*, 17 (1960), p. 375–88 (no. 1226).

See also the current listings and reviews in such periodicals as *Notes*, *Fontes Artis Musicae, Acta Musicologica*, the *Music Review*, and the *Musical Times*.

Bibliographic guide to music, 1975– . See no. 745.

1211. The British catalogue of music. London: Council of the British National Bibliography, 1957– . Vol. 1– .

Published quarterly; the last issue of each year is a cumulated annual volume. Organized in two parts: a classified and an alphabetical section. Lists of music publishers with their British agents specified.

The classification scheme used in this catalog has been published separately; see no. 3036.

1212. Brünn. Universita. Knihovna. Prírustky hudebnin v ceskoslovenských knihovnäch. Spracoval Zdeněk Zouhar. Praha: Statní Pedagogicke Nakladatelstvi, 1953– .
Joint accession list of 10 principal music libraries in Czechoslovakia, listing 2,000–3,000 items per year. Classified by medium, without index.

1213. Central opera service bulletin. Directory of operas and publishers, in two parts. New York : Central Opera Service, 1976. 2 v. in 1. 118 p.
Issued as vol. 18, nos. 2 and 3.
A bibliography of opera scores currently available.

1214. Composium directory of new music. Vol. 1– . Los Angeles, California: Crystal Record Company, 1971–1982/83.

> *Composium, a quarterly index of contemporary compositions*, is a list of recent works by living composers, and includes both published and currently unpublished compositions. The *Directory of New Music*, published annually, includes all the works that have been listed in the Quarterly during the preceding year. These are indexed here by instrumentation as well as by composer. Also included are brief biographical sketches of each of the composers listed. [From the *Preface* by Peter Christ, editor, *Composium*, and president, Crystal Record Co.]

Title and frequency vary: *Annual Index of Contemporary Compositions*. Edited by Carol Cunning. 1979.

Deutsche Musikbibliographie. See no. 751.

1215. Deutscher Büchereiverband. Arbeitsstelle für das Büchereiwesen. Musikbibliographischer Dienst (MD). 1.–13. Jahrgang. Berlin: Deutscher Büchereiverband, 1970–82.
A periodical publication that was issued six times yearly, the sixth issue being a cumulation listing all of the current publications of serious music. International in scope, but German in practice since information was reported by 12 German public libraries. The editors were Burchard Bulling and Helmut Fosner. Entries printed in catalog card format on one side of the page so that they could be cut and filed in a card tray. The publication was also available in loose sheets for this purpose.

1216. Fontes artis musicae. Review of the International Association of Music Libraries. 1954– .
Until 1976 each issue contains a "Liste internationale sélective" largely devoted to listings of current music publications by country, compiled by a series of national editors. Thereafter there is an occasional shorter, annotated list entitled "Publications à caractère bibliographique."

Hofmeisters Handbuch der Musikliteratur. See no. 754.

Jahresverzeichnis der Deutschen Musikalien und Musikschriften. See no. 758.

1217. Letopis' muzykal'noi literatury; organ gosudarstzennoi bibliografii SSSR. Izdtsia s 1931 goda; vykhodit 4 raza v god. Moskva: Izdatel'stvo vsesoiuznoi knizhnoi palaty, 1931– .

Quarterly. Organization and content vary slightly. In 1960 a classified list of publications in musical notation. Includes literary works with musical supplements or extensive musical illustrations, and music issued in periodicals. Index by composer for each issue, and separate lists of books, magazines, newspapers containing music. Annual index of vocal works by title and first line, and by language of text. Entries give full bibliographical information, including complete contents, price, size of edition.

1218. National union catalog. Music and phonorecords. 1953–57 to 1968–72. A cumulative list of works represented by Library of Congress printed cards. Ann Arbor, Michigan: J. W. Edwards, 1958–73. 11 v. (Library of Congress catalogs)

The quinquennial cumulation of Library of Congress catalog: *Music and Phonorecords.* Continued by the national union catalog: *Music, Books on Music and Sound Recordings* (no. 1219). The 1953–57 cumulation was issued as vol. 27 of the *National Union Catalog* in 1958. The 1958–62 catalog was exceptionally published by Rowman and Littlefield in 1963 as vols. 51–52 of the *National Union Catalog.* The 1963–67 cumulation (3 v.) was not issued as a volume of the *National Union Catalog,* nor was the 1968–72 cumulation (5 v.)

Current music accessions, printed or sound recordings, of the Library of Congress and of libraries participating in its cooperative cataloging program. Includes purchased current or retrospective materials and a selection of recent copyright deposits. Entries were reproduced from the library's printed cards. Name and subject index. Semiannual, with annual cumulation. Originally issued semiannually with annual cumulations. Contains entries for scores, recordings (musical and otherwise), libretti, and books about music and musicians.

See also no. 1222.

1219. National union catalog. Music, books on music, and sound recordings. Washington, D.C.: Library of Congress, 1973– . (Library of Congress catalogs)

Semiannual, with annual (the 2nd issue of each year) and quinquennial cumulations (published by Rowman and Littlefield, Totowa, New Jersey, 8 v. covering 1973–77 and 7 v. covering 1978–80).

Continues the Library of Congress catalog: *Music and Phonorecords.*

Contains bibliographic records created by the Library of Congress and by participating libraries whose collection efforts are sufficiently broad and their cataloging standards sufficiently worthy.

1220. National union catalog: pre-1956 imprints. A cumulative author list representing Library of Congress printed cards and titles reported by other American libraries. London: Mansell, 1968–81. 685 v.

A 68-v. supplement was published 1980–81, for a total of 754 v.

"A repertory of cataloged holdings of selected portions of the cataloged collections of the major research libraries of the United States and Canada, plus the more rarely held items in the collections of selected smaller and specialized libraries."

Includes over 10 million entries for materials in over 700 libraries, including books, pamphlets, maps, atlases, and music. Works in non-Roman alphabets are included only if there is a print Library of Congress card for them. Cross-references are provided sparingly and there are few added entries. The supplement includes over 3 million entries for new titles and corrected entries accumulated since the publication of the original volumes. A separate section at the end of each supplementary volume reports additional locations for items already listed.

Naturally, numerous entries are for books falling into the music literature and music theory classfications as well as for scores. However, entries representing the holdings of many of North America's most distinguished music collections are not represented for a variety of reasons. Score entries are particularly small in number relative to the great strengths of American and Canadian libraries. For the best thumbnail sketch of the situation, see entry 452 on p. 158–59 in Krummel's *Bibliographical Handbook* (no. 1113).

1221. The new music repertoire directory. New York: American Music Center and Chamber Music America, 1981– . 2 v. to date.

Second volume edited by Margaret Jory.

A list of "interesting or successful" new music solicited from a number of ensembles and composers' organizations. Each entry supplies title, instrumentation, source of score and performance materials, and the name of the ensemble recommending it. Arranged by composer with lists of participating ensembles and "resource organizations."

1222. Olmsted, Elizabeth H. Music Library Association catalog of cards for printed music, 1953–1972; a supplement to the Library of Congress catalogs. Totowa, New Jersey: Rowman and Littlefield, 1974. 2 v.

Entries for printed music reported to the *National Union Catalog* for the period 1956–72 (no. 1217). Complements cataloging in the Library of Congress catalogs treating music (nos. 1218 and 1219). Photocopies of cards supplied with attendant reproduction difficulties. Name of library holding each title not included.

1223. U.S. Copyright Office. Catalog of copyright entries ... New series, pt. 3: Musical compositions. Washington, D.C.: Government Printing Office, 1906–46. Vols. 1–41.

From 1891 to 1906, the quarterly copyright index was issued by the Treasury Department and musical compositions were included as part of the general series. From 1906 to 1945, music (published or not) was entered by title in each monthly issue, followed by renewals, with an annual index. In 1946 this arrangement was succeeded by a division into: unpublished music; published music; renewals; title index to the first two sections.

This section of the *Catalog of Copyright Entries*, including some entries covering registrations beginning in 1891, was issued in 65 reels of microfilm by the Library of Congress Photoduplication Service in 1980. Reels 1–13 consist of copy of every index, weekly, quarterly, and annual covering years 1898–1946 to facilitate copyright searches. Actual entries for 1891–1946 begin with reel 14.

1224. U.S. Copyright Office. Catalog of copyright entries. 3rd ser.: Music. Washington, D.C.: Government Printing Office, 1947–77. Vols. 1–31.

In the series from 1906 to 1946 a music catalog was published separately. In 1946 it was subdivided into separate sections: published music, unpublished music, and renewal registrations, with main entries by composer and a classified index. This arrangement was maintained until vol. 11 of the third series (1958), when the listings were grouped under "current registrations" and "renewal registrations," with the main entry under title and a name index for composers.

Cites all music deposited for copyright in the U.S. whether published in the U.S. or elsewhere. Arranged by title with index to names of composers, authors, editors, compilers, arrangers, and so forth. The *Catalog of Copyright Entries* is the most comprehensive catalog of music of its time.

In 1978, the *Catalog of Copyright Entries* went into a fourth series, issued only in microfiche (no. 1225). Music entries are included in two sections: part 3, Performing arts, issued quarterly, for scores; and part 7, Sound recordings, issued semiannually. Each part is provided with an index of names cited in it. Citations include basic bibliographic information.

1225. U.S. Copyright Office. Catalog of copyright entries ... 4th ser., pt. 3: Performing arts. Washington, D.C.: Government Printing Office, 1978– .

This new series began with the implementation of the Copyright Act of 1976. Musical works (published and otherwise) are entered by title and there is an index of authors, claimants, and other names associated with each work. Entries for sound recordings appear in part 7. This is a microfiche catalog.

NATIONAL MUSIC

In this section are to be found bibliographies of music (scores) concerned with the music of particular nations. Many of these bibliographies originate in various national music centers that exist for the purpose of promoting the works of native composers. For a survey of such organizations, their history, services, publications, see "Directory of National Music Centers" (no. 2929). A survey of the coverage of music in national bibliographies is cited first.

Several of the works cited in the section "Bibliographies of Music Literature: National Music" also include listings of composers' works.

1226. Krummel, Donald W. and James B. Coover. "Current national bibliographies, their music coverage." In *Notes*, 17 (1960), p. 375–88.

Surveys the music coverage in the national bibliographies in the Western Hemisphere, Western and Eastern Europe, Africa, Asia, and Oceania.

AUSTRALIA

1227. Australasian Performing Rights Association. Catalogue of major musical compositions by Australian and New Zealand composers. Sydney: [1967?]. 53 p.

Supplementary catalog of New Zealand composers. 9 p.

1228. Australia Music Centre. Catalogue of instrumental and chamber music. Sydney: Australia Music Centre, 1976. 142 p. (Catalogues of Australian compositions, 2)
Includes Australian music for solo instruments and chamber ensembles.

1229. Australia Music Centre. Catalogue of keyboard music. Sydney: Australia Music Centre, 1976. 90 p.
Includes Australian music for organ, harpsichord, and piano.

1230. Australia Music Centre. Catalogue of orchestral music. Sydney: Australia Music Centre, 1976. 109 p.
Listing the orchestral works of Australian composers.

1231. Australia Music Centre. Dramatic music. Edited by Suellen Burcher. Sydney: Australia Music Centre, 1977. 212 p. (Catalogues of Australian compositions, 5)
Listing of Australian operas and other staged dramatic music.

1232. Australia Music Centre. Electronic music. Sydney: Australia Music Centre, 1977. 65 p. (Catalogues of Australian compositions, 7)
Catalog of Australian electronic music.

1233. Australia Music Centre. Jazz. Sydney: Australia Music Centre, 1978. 280 p. (Catalogues of Australian compositions, 8)
Catalog of Australian jazz compositions.

1234. Australia Music Centre. Military and brass band music [in the] Australia Music Centre. Sydney: Australia Music Centre, 1977. 28 p. (Catalogues of Australian compositions, 6)
A catalog of the holdings of the Australia Music Centre in this genre.

1235. Australia Music Centre. Vocal and choral music. Sydney: Australia Music Centre, 1976. 264 p. (Catalogues of Australian compositions, 4)
Listing of music for solo voices, vocal ensembles, and choruses by Australian composers.

AUSTRIA

1236. Österreichische Musikbibliographie: Verzeichnis der österreichischen Neuerscheinungen auf der Gebiete der Musik. Vienna: Verein der österreichische Buch-, Kunst-, Musikalien- Zeitungs- und Zeitschriftenhändler, March 1949–December 1953. Jarhg. 1–5.
This publication consisted of two quarterly lists of publications newly issued in Austria, one for music literature and another for printed music. Each is arranged alphabetically by author or composer (or by title), and presents a short title, imprint information, collation, and price. The issues conclude with an index of editors and another of titles, first lines of text, and keywords.

BELGIUM

1237. Auda, Antoine. La musique et les musiciens de l'ancien pays de Liège. Essai bio-bibliographique sur la musique liégeoise depuis ses origines jusqu' à la fin de la principauté (1800). Bruxelles: Librairie Saint-Georges, [etc.], 1930. 291 p.

A study of composers active in Liège until about 1800. Works and publications are cited.

1238. Centre Belge de Documentation Musicale. Catalogus van werken van Belgische componisten. Bruxelles: Centre Belge de Documentation Musicale, 1953–57.

An irregularly published series of catalogs averaging 20 pages each, devoted to contemporary Belgian composers and their works. Some in French, others in Flemish.

CANADA

1239. Canadian Music Centre. Catalogue of Canadian choral music available for perusal from the library of the Canadian Music Centre. [3rd ed.] Toronto: Canadian Music Centre, 1978.

First issued in 1966, with an *Addendum* bringing the coverage up to 1970.

Classified listing with colored paper identifying sections devoted to mixed voices, female voices, and male voices. Composer listing and list of publishers.

Other Canadian Music Centre publications:

Canadian Music for Orchestra. 1976.
Canadian Chamber Music. 1971. *Supplement,* 1976.
Canadian Keyboard Music. 1976.
Canadian Vocal Music. 3rd ed. 1976.
List of Canadian Operas... 1978.
List of Canadian Music for Guitar. 1980.

Contemporary Canadian composers. Compositeurs Canadiens contemporaine. See no. 1058.

1240. Jarman, Lynn. Canadian music: a selected check-list 1950–73. La musique canadienne: une liste sélective 1950–73. A selective listing of Canadian music from *Fontes Artis Musicae*, 1954–73, based on the catalogued entries of *Canadiana* from 1950. Foreword by Helmut Kallmann. Toronto, Ontario, and Buffalo, New York: University of Toronto Press, 1976. 170 p.

A Canadian Association of Music Libraries bibliographical project cumulating entries for Canadian music in *Fontes Artis Musicae* in a classified arrangement. Index to composers and authors.

CHINA

Chung-kuo ku-tai yin-yüeh shu-mu. See no. 1061.

Chung-kuo yin yüeh shu p'u chih. See no. 1062.

1241. Yüan, T'ung-li. Chung-kuo yin yüeh shu p'u mu lu. [Bibliography on Chinese music.] T'ai-pei: Chung hua kuo yüeh hui, [1956]. 24, 49, 4 p.
In Chinese and English.

DENMARK

1242. Dansk Komponistførening. Danske komponister af i dag; den vaerk-førtegnelse. Danish composers of today; a catalogue of works. Dänische Komponisten von Heute; ein Werkverzeichnis. København: Dansk Komponistførening, 1980– . 2 v. (loose-leaf)
Works, including information on publisher and performing forces necessary, cited in chronological order. Includes separate list of members of the Dansk Komponistførening with addresses and telephone numbers; separate listing for music publishers. No biographies.

> The catalogue will be constantly updated with new works, and new composers. Revised and additional pages will be sent automatically to those who possess a copy of the catalogue. [*Foreword*]

1243. Dansk musikførtegnelse 1931–1979. Compiled by the Music Department of the Danish Royal Library and edited by Susanne Sugar. Copenhagen: Ballerup, the Danish Library Bureau, 1980– .
The Danish national bibliography of music. Appeared originally as monthly listings, and then published separately as an annual cumulation. Five-year cumulations will be provided with both alphabetical and classified entries.
Coverage is not only for music published in Denmark, but also music by Danish composers or edited by Danes published anywhere, music with a Danish text in Danish or in translation, and music based on Danish themes or the works of Danish authors.

1244. Samfundet Til Udgivelse af Dansk Musik 1871–1971. Society for Publishing Danish Music. Catalogue. København: Dan Fog Musikforlag, 1972. 115 p.
A similar listing was published in 1956 by Knud Larsen Musikforlag, with a *Supplement* in 1968.
The catalog is preceded by a history of the society. Contents: "An outline of Danish music history"; the composers; catalogue of publications; chronological list of publications; systematic list of publications; Samfundet's LP-Records.
P. 20–38: brief biographies of the composers; p. 39–85: the catalog, arranged alphabetically by composer. Chronological and systematic lists of publications; list of recordings issued by the society, a general index, and a 1972 price list.

FINLAND

1245. Säveltäjain Tekijänoikeustoimisto Teosto. Catalogue of Finnish orchestral and vocal compositions. Helsinki: Teosto (composers' copyright bureau), 1961. 88 p.

Lists works by 57 Finnish composers giving titles, instrumentation, timings, publishers. Brief biographical sketches. English translations of Finnish titles.

1246. Suomalaista musiikka. Suomalaista musiikkia: suomalainen orkesterimusiikki, orkesterisaestyksellinen vokaalimusiikki, oopperamusiikki, balettimusiikki. Finnish music: Finnish orchestral works, vocal works with orchestra, operas, ballets. Helsinki: Luovan Saveltaiteen Edistamissaatio, 1973. 282 p.

A bibliography of works by Finnish composers in English and Finnish.

FRANCE

1247. Le bibliograph musical. Paraissant tous les deux mois avec le concours d'une Réunion d'artistes et d'érudits. Première Année (1872)—Cinquième Année (1876), Numéro 1–29. Paris: 1872–76. 499 p. (continuous pagination)

Reprint of the complete set by Schnase, 1968.

A bibliographical journal issued bimonthly by a group of scholars, librarians, and musicians (the number varies). Contains short articles of bibliographical interest, reports of auction sales, reviews, descriptions of music institutions, etc. The most frequent contributor is Arthur Pougin.

1248. Bibliographie musicale française. Publiée par la Chambre Syndicale des Éditeurs de Musique. Année 1–26, Numéro 1–192. Paris: La Chambre Syndicale des Éditeurs de Musique, 1875–1920. 47 v. in 23.

Reprint of the original edition by Annemarie Schnase, Scarsdale, New York, 1968.

A monthly trade list of music issued by the major French publishers over a period of 45 years. The lists are classified by performing media. Some of the publishers represented are: Colombier, Choudens, Lemoine, Brandus, Durand, Gauthier, Grus, Heugel, Le Bailly, Leduc, and E. Mathieu.

Review by Rita Benton, in *Fontes Artis Musicae*, 26 (1979), p. 313.

1249. Boll, André. Répertoire analytique de la musique française des origines à nos jours. Paris: Horizons de France, 1948. 299 p.

Not as comprehensive as the title suggests. Part I: a list of composers of the French school, with dates, arranged alphabetically within historical periods. Part II: classified list of published French secular music, alphabetical by composer, followed by a similar listing of sacred music. Publishers given; indexed by works and by composers.

1250. Pierreuse, Bernard. Catalogue général de l'édition musicale en France: livres, méthodes et partitions de musique sérieuse en vente. General catalog of music publishing in France: books, methods, and scores of serious music on sale. Paris: Éditions Jobert; Distribution, Éditions musicales transatlantiques, 1984. 476 p.

A classified listing of available works arranged by composer or author in each section. Title, version, publisher, and occasionally date of composition are indicated. There is an index to composers. Coverage to 1982. For the choral and band sections, only classical works are listed.

GERMANY

1251. Bibliographie der deutschen Arbeiterliedblätter 1844–1945. Akademie der Künste der Deutschen Demokratischen Republik. Sektion Musik. Abteilung Arbeiterliedarchiv. Bearb. von e. Kollektiv d. Arbeiterliedarchivs; unter Leitung von Inge Lammel. 1. Aufl. Leipzig: Deutscher Verlag für Musik, 1975. 320 p.

A bibliography, including indexes to collections, of songs of working persons in Germany, 1844–1945.

1252. Dupont, Wilhelm. Werkausgaben Nürnberger Komponisten in Vergangenheit und Gegenwart. Nürnberg: Selbstverlag der Stadtbibliothek, 1971. 378 p. (Beiträge zur Geschichte und Kultur der Stadt Nürnberg, 18)

A list of editions of music by composers from Nürnberg.

1253. Simbriger, Heinrich. Werkkatalog zeitgenössischer Komponisten aus den deutschen Ostgebieten. Esslingen-Neckar: Künstlergilde, 1955. 203 p. *Ergänzungsband*, 1961. 151 p.

A classified bibliography of works by East German composers. Entries give title of work, instrumentation, publisher if any, and timing. A preliminary section is devoted to biographical sketches of the composers.

1254. Was Wir Singen. Katalog des in der Deutschen Demokratischen Republik erschienenen weltlichen Lied- und Chormaterials. Band I: 1945–58 Auswahl. Herausgegeben vom Zentralhaus für Volkskunst. Leipzig: Friedrich Hofmeister, 1959. 255 p.

Title listing of 6,582 entries, supplemented by lists of collections and of cantatas and oratorios. Indexed by subtitles or working titles, by voice combination and by affective theme, and by national character. Further indexes by writer of text and composer.

GREAT BRITAIN

1255. British music catalogue 1945–1981. Volume I: Works for piano [by] Paul Griffiths. London: Warwick Arts Trust, 1983. 39 p.

The first volume is a classified catalog restricted to British published music and music by British composers, some of whose works are published, including educational music.

1256. The Composers' Guild of Great Britain. British orchestral music. London: Composers' Guild, 1958; British Music Information Centre, 1970. 2 v.

Vol. I of the catalog of works by members of the Composers' Guild of Great Britain: part 1, works for full, small, or chamber orchestra; part 2, works for string orchestra. Vol. II: works by living British composers.

The listings give composer, title of work, orchestration, publisher or agent, and availability of the material. Vol. II is a sequel to the preceding catalog, adding a listing of works for brass or military bands.

1257. The Composers' Guild of Great Britain. Chamber music by living British composers. London: British Music Information Centre, 1969. 42 p.

Alphabetical listing of composers and their works for three or more instruments. Information tabulated includes instrumentation, duration, publisher or agent, and availability of the material. Unpublished works also included.

1258. The Composers' Guild of Great Britain. Instrumental solos and duos by living British composers. London: British Music Information Centre, 1972. 96 p.

Sections for solos, duos with and without keyboard, and miscellaneous solos and duos. Follows the model of the Guild's other catalogs.

1259. The Composers' Guild of Great Britain. Keyboard solos and duos by living British composers. London: British Music Information Centre, 1974. 63 p.

Two sections: one for keyboard solos for piano, organ, and other keyboards, and another for duets (one piano, two pianos, other).

1260. Hopkinson, Cecil and Cecil B. Oldman. Thomson's collections of national song: with special reference to the contributions of Haydn and Beethoven. [Edinburgh: Printed by R. & R. Clark, 1940.] 64 p. (Edinburgh Bibliographical Society; *Transactions*, vol. 2, no. 1)

Contents: Haydn thematic catalogue, p. 25–47; Beethoven thematic catalogue, p. 48–64.

1261. The music trader's guide to works by twentieth-century British composers, together with the names of their publishers; comprising instrumental works, songs, textbooks and manuals up to and including June, 1955. Compiled by L. D. Cibbin. London: Boosey and Hawkes, 1956. 132 p.

Brief entries for works by 76 composers; a listing alphabetical by title under the composers' names. Supplementary listing for "other British composers and their principal publishers."

1262. Scottish Music Archive. Catalogue of printed and manuscript music, May 1970. Glasgow: Scottish Music Archive. 74 p.

Supplement issued 1972.

A classified list of music by contemporary Scottish composers giving instrumentation, duration, publisher, and availability of the material. The archive is centered at the University of Glasgow, but its policies are dictated by a committee made up of members from a number of Scottish musical institutions.

1263. Swanekamp, Joan. English ayres: a selectively annotated bibliography and discography. Westport, Connecticut: Greenwood Press, 1984. 141 p.

In 1926 Philip Heseltine under the pseudonym of Peter Warlock, published *The English Ayre*, a slim volume with a brief two-page bibliography. Since that time articles and books focusing on the ayre composers have appeared with increasing frequency, as have editions and recordings of their works. This bibliography strives to bring these materials together as a companion volume to the Warlock book. It includes the composers mentioned by Warlock, as well as eight additional composers from E. H. Fellowes' *English*

505ool of Lutenist Song Writers and *English Lute Songs*. [from the introductory remarks]

There are 903 entries "arranged by composer and subdivided by literature, music, and recording categories. General materials are listed in the first chapter; literary works are arranged alphabetically by author." No reviews are cited. Collections are cited by title. Author and title indexes.

Review by Linda Phyllis Austern in *Notes*, 41 (1985), p. 728–29.

HUNGARY

1264. Bibliographia Hungarica 1945–1960. Catalogus systematicus notarum musicarum in Hungaria editarum. Edidit Bibliotheca Nationalis Hungariae a Francisco Széchényi fundata. Budapest: Országos Széchényi Könyvtár, 1969. 361 p.

A classified listing of all Hungarian music publications between 1945 and 1960. Indexed by composers and by first line of texts. P. 353–61: a schematic outline of the classification system. A publication of the National Szechenyi Library; the principal editors are Ivan Pethes, Veronika Vavrineca, and Jenö Vécsey.

1265. Dedinsky, Izabella K. Zenemüvek, 1936–40. Budapest: Kiadja az országos széchényi könyvtár, 1944. 286 p.

Classified bibliography of music published in Hungary, 1936–40. Includes both popular and serious music.

1266. Magyar nemzeti bibliográfia: Zenemüvek bibliográfiája. 8. évf., 3.– füzet; szept. 30, 1977– . Budapest: Országos Széchényi Könyvtár.

The current Hungarian national bibliography on music, supplement to *Magyar Nemzeti Bibliográfia: Könyvek Bibliográfiája*. Quarterly.

Continues *Magyar Zenemüvek Bibliográfiája* (no. 1267).

1267. Magyar zenemüvek bibliográfiája. 1.–8. évf., 2. füzet; júl. 15, 1970–jún. 30, 1977. Budapest: Országos Széchényi Könyvtár. 8 v.

A quarterly supplement on music to *Magyar Nemzeti Bibliográfia: Bibliográfia Hungarica*, the Hungarian national bibliography. Continued by *Magyar Nemzeti Bibliográfia: Zenemüvek Bibliográfiája* (no. 1266).

ICELAND

1268. Burt, Amanda. Iceland's twentieth-century composers and a listing of their works. Annandale, Virginia: Charles Baptie Studios, 1977. 71 p.

INDIA

1269. Kaufmann, Walter. The ragas of South India: a catalogue of scalar material. Bloomington: Indiana University Press, 1976. 723 p.

Simultaneously published in Calcutta by Oxford and IBH Publishing Co.

This is both a historical work and a thematic catalog to South Indian ragas.

1270. Kuppuswamy, Gowri and Muthuswamy Hariharan. Index of songs in south Indian music. Delhi: B. R. Pub. Corp.; New Delhi: Distributed by D. K. Publishers' Distributors, 1981. 970 p.

The general index gives, with regard to each published song, the beginning, raga, tala, language, composer and details of availability. There are separate indices for raga, tala, language and composer. [from the introductory remarks]

Cites sources of songs.

1271. Subba Rao, B. Bharatiya sangeet: raga nidhi. Encylopedia of Indian ragas, a comparative study of Hindustani and Karnatak ragas. With a foreword by M. Bhawanishankar Niyogi. Poona: V. Patwardhan, Chairman, Vishnu Digambar Smarak Samiti, 1956–66. 4 v.

Vols. 2–4 have title *Raganidhi* and imprint "Madras: Music Academy."

ISRAEL

1272. Goldberg, Ira S. Bibliography of instrumental music of Jewish interest. Part 2: Ensemble and solo. Rev. and enl. ed. New York: National Jewish Music Council, 1970. 181 p.

1273. National Jewish Welfare Board. Bibliography Committee. Bibliography of Jewish instrumental music. New York: National Jewish Music Council, 1948. 16 p.

Addenda, 1950. 7 leaves.

A selective list of the "best and most interesting works that are easily available ... either in published form or through rental." Classified according to various combinations of instruments. Publishers indicated.

1274. National Jewish Welfare Board. Bibliography Committee. Bibliography of Jewish vocal music. New York: National Jewish Music Council, 1948. 36 p.

Addenda, 1950. 15 leaves.

A selective list of available Jewish vocal music "in good taste, and suited for programming." Classified by genre. Language or languages of text; publishers indicated.

1275. Sendrey, Alfred. Bibliography of Jewish music. New York: Columbia University Press, 1951. 404 p.

Reprint by Kraus Reprint Co. in 1969.

Part I of this work is a classified bibliography of 5,854 items, writings on Jewish music and musicians. Includes periodical articles.

Part II of this work is a classified list of about 4,000 pieces of Jewish music, alphabetical by composer within classifications, giving scoring, author, and language of text. Publisher and date indicated for published works; some manuscripts also listed.

Review by Milton Feist in *Musical Quarterly*, 37 (1951), p. 432–35; by Ernst C. Krohn in *Journal of the American Musicological Society*, 7 (Summer 1954), p. 150–52.

JAPAN

1276. Kokusai Bunka Shinkokai. K. B. S. bibliography of standard reference books for Japanese studies with descriptive notes. Vol. II (B): Theatre, dance and music. Tokyo: 1960. 182 p.

A revised edition was published 1971–78. Kokusai Bunka Shinkokai is the "Society for International Cultural Relations."

Part of a multinational "annotated bibliography of standard reference works in Japanese for the use of foreign students of Japanese culture who want to get access to original sources." The music titles were selected and annotated by Kishibe Shigo. There is an appendix: "selected bibliography of works in Western languages on Japanese drama, music and dance." There are extensive annotations with titles in kanji, romanized and translated.

LATIN AMERICA

1277. Bibliografía de música latino americana. Integrada con fichas del catálogo formado por la Biblioteca Nacional "José Martí," la Biblioteca Central "Rubén Martínez Villena" de la Universidad de la Habana y la Biblioteca "José Antonio Echeverría" de la Casa de las Américas. La Habana, Cuba: Casa de las Américas, 1972. 37 leaves.

A union catalog of music from three major libraries in Cuba.

1278. Chase, Gilbert. A guide to the music of Latin America. A joint publication of the Pan American Union and the Library of Congress. 2nd ed., rev. and enl. Washington, D.C.: Pan American Union, 1962. 411 p.

First published in 1945 under the title *Guide to Latin American Music.* Reprint by AMS Press, New York, 1962 and 1972.

A general bibliography of Latin American music, followed by listings related to individual composers. Index of authors, names, and subjects.

1279. Indiana University. School of Music. Latin-American Music Center. Music from Latin America available at Indiana University: scores, tapes, and records. Edited by Juan A. Orrego-Salas. Bloomington: Latin American Music Center, School of Music, Indiana University, 1971. 412 p.

A catalog of one of the most important repositories of Latin American scores and recordings in the United States. Includes a listing of materials available at the Indiana University Archives of Traditional Music.

1280. Kuss, Malena. Latin American music in contemporary reference sources: a study session. Paramount, California: Academy Print. and Pub. Co., 1976. 19 p.

Report of a study session of the national meeting of the American Musicological Society in Washington, D.C., 1974. Bibliography: p. 10–19.

Review by Robert Stevenson in the "Music Section" of the *Handbook for Latin American Studies,* 40 (1978), p. 537.

1281. List of Latin American music—vocal, piano, instrumental, orchestral and band—which can be purchased in the United States. 2nd ed., rev. and enl. Washington, D.C.: Pan American Union, 1983. 60 leaves.

Typescript.

1282. Lotis, Howard. Latin American music materials available at the University of Pittsburgh and at Carnegie Library of Pittsburgh. Pittsburgh: Center for Latin American Studies, University of Pittsburgh, 1981. 145 p.

1283. Pan American Union, Music Section. Latin American orchestral music available in the United States. Washington, D.C.: Pan American Union, 1956. 79 p.
Supersedes a shorter list issued in 1955.
Part I: classified list of Latin American music available through publishing houses and other agencies. Part II: Latin American music in the Edwin A. Fleisher Collection in the Free Library of Philadelphia.

1284. Thompson, Leila Fern. Partial list of Latin American music obtainable in the U.S., and Supplement. 3rd ed., rev. and enl. Washington, D.C.: Pan American Union, 1948. 56 leaves.
Supplement, 17 leaves.
The first and second editions were prepared by Gilbert Chase, 1941 and 1942.
Concerned with concert music to the exclusion of popular and folk music. Classified by genre and country. Scoring, language of text, and publisher indicated. Indexed by country and by composer.

MEXICO

1285. Huerta, Jorge A. A bibliography of Chicano and Mexican dance, drama and music. Oxnard, California: Colegio Quetzalcoatl, 1972. 59 p.
The three major subdivisions of the bibliography cover dance, drama, and music subdivided to Pre-Columbian, Mexican, and Aztlan sections.

NORWAY

1286. Society of Norwegian Composers. Contemporary Norwegian orchestral and chamber music. Johan Grundt Tanam Forlag, 1970. 385 p.
Lists, with portraits, timings of the works, instrumentation.

PAPUA NEW GUINEA

1287. Gourlay, Kenneth A. A bibliography of traditional music in Papua New Guinea. Port Moresby: Institute of Papua New Guinea Studies, 1980. 176 p.
Covers Papua New Guinea, Torres Strait islands, parts of Java, and the Solomon Islands. Comprehensive index.

POLAND

1288. Hordynski, Wladyslaw. Katalog polskich druków muzycznych 1800–1863. Catalogue des imprimés musicaux polonais de 1800–1863. Krakow: Polskie Wydawnictwo Muzyczne, 1968. 1 v.

249

Contents: 1. Biblioteka Uniwersytecka w Poznaniu i Biblioteka Kórnicka Polskiej Akademii Nauk.
A catalog of Polish printed musical works for the period 1800–36.

PORTUGAL

1289. Catálogo geral da música portuguesa, repertório contemporâneo. Lisboa: Direcçao-General do Património Cultural, A Secretaria, 1978– . 1 v. (looseleaf)
Biographical sketches of contemporary Portuguese composers in English, French, and Portuguese. Also includes lists of works, bibliographies and discographies of each composer.

SPAIN

1290. Libros de música. 2. ed. Madrid: Instituto Nacional del Libro Español, Ministerio de Cultura, 1982. 327 p.
The Spanish national bibliography of music and music literature.
A classified bibliography of books in Spanish. Includes sections on pedagogy, folklore, and popular music, as well as scholarly topics. Indexes to names, subjects, and institutions.

SWEDEN

1291. Föreningen Svenska Tonsättäre. Nyare svenska orkesterverk samt instrumental- och vokalverk med orkester. Catalog of Swedish orchestral works (20th century) including instrumental soli and vocal works with orchestra. Stockholm: Society of Swedish Composers, 1956. 109 p.
Supplement, 1959. 15 p.
Earlier lists were issued in 1937 and 1944 under a slightly varied title.
Classified listings of works under composers' names. Information includes publisher, instrumentation, timings.

1292. Nordiska Musikförlaget. Swedish orchestral works. Annotated catalogue. Commentary by Edvin Kallstenius. Stockholm: Nordiska Musikförlaget, 1948. 85 p.

This catalogue is intended to guide conductors, members of programme committees and other music lovers who wish to learn something about Swedish composition. [*Foreword*]

Selected works by 25 Swedish composers. Portraits and brief biographical sketches.

SWITZERLAND

1293. Archives Musicales Suisses. (Schweizerisches Musikarchiv). Liste des œuvres. Werkverzeichnis. Zurich: Archives Musicales Suisses, 1968– . Vol. 1– .
A series of pamphlets reproduced from typescript, each devoted to the work of a contemporary Swiss composer. Information includes instrumen-

tation, timings, and availability of the works whether printed or in manuscript. Following is a list of publications through August 1985:

Adolf Brunner (1961)
Rudolf Moser (1962)
Carlo Hennerling (1963)
Will Eisenmann (1966)
Richard Flury (1966)
Georges Haenni (1966)
Henri Gagnebin (1966)
Peter Mieg (1966)
Max Kuhn (1966)
Walter Lang (1966)
Wladimir Vogel (1966)
Walther Geiser (1967)
René Matthes (1967)
Jean Daetwyler (1968)
Paul Müller-Zürich (1968)
Fernande Peyrot (1968)
Edward Staempfli (1968)
Frank Martin (1969)
Jean Binet (1970)
Luc Balmer (1970)
Richard Sturzenegger (1970)
Hans Haug (1970)
Robert Oboussier (1970)
Aloys Fornerod (1970)
Raffaele d'Alessandro (1970)
Robert Blum (1970)
Roger Vuataz (1970)
Bernard Reichel (1971)
Othmar Schoeck (1971)
Hans Vogt (1972)
Czeslaw Marek (1972)
Othmar Schoeck (1972)
Hugo Pfister (1973)
Julien-François Zbinden (1974)
Arthur Honegger (1975)
André-François Marescotti (1979)
Rudolf Kelterborn (1980)
Klaus Huber (1980)
Robert Suter (1980)
Hermann Haller (1981)
Frank Martin (1981)
Hans Ulrich Lehmann (1981)
Albert Moeschinger (1982)
Jacques Wildberger (1982)
Albert Jenny (1985)

UNITED STATES OF AMERICA

1294. American Society of Composers, Authors and Publishers. ASCAP index of performed compositions. New York: American Society of Composers, Authors and Publishers, 1978. 1,423 p.

Supplement issued in 1981. First appeared in 1942 as the *ASCAP Index* for use of radio broadcasting stations. Subsequently published in 1952, 1954, and 1963 under the present title.

An unedited alphabetical listing of compositions in the ASCAP repertory that have appeared in the society's survey of radio, television, and wired-music performances, including easy listening, soul, country, religious, children's, gospel, rock, pop, film, folk, educational, classical, jazz, and musical theater genres. Alphabetical listing by title, citing composer and publisher.

See the *ASCAP Symphonic Catalog* for more complete coverage of the ASCAP classical repertory (no. 1295).

1295. American Society of Composers, Authors and Publishers. ASCAP symphonic catalog. 3rd ed. New York: R. R. Bowker, 1977. 511 p.

Previous editions in 1959 and 1966.

Alphabetical listing, by composers and arrangers, of symphonic literature controlled by ASCAP. Entries give instrumentation, duration, publisher. List of publishers' addresses.

1296. Broadcast Music Inc. Symphonic catalogue. Rev. ed. New York: Broadcast Music Inc., 1971. 375 p.

First appeared 1963. *Supplement* to the rev. ed., 1978. 138 p.

An alphabetical listing, by composer, of symphonic works whose performing rights are controlled by Broadcast Music Inc. Entries give instrumentation, duration, and publishers of the works.

1297. De Lerma, Dominique-René. Black concert and recital music, a provisional repertoire list. Bloomington, Indiana : Afro-American Opportunities Association, 1975. 40 p.

Brief review by Stephen M. Fry in *Notes*, 32 (1975) p. 301–302.

Eagon, Angelo. Catalog of published concert music by American composers. See no. 1330.

1298. Freedom's voice in poetry and song. Compiled and edited by Gillian B. Anderson. Wilmington, Delaware: Scholarly Resources Inc., 1977. 888 p.

Contents: Pt. 1. An inventory of political and patriotic lyrics in colonial American newspapers, 1773–83; Pt. 2. Songbook.

Includes bibliographical references and indexes.

1299. Hixon, Donald L. Music in early America: a bibliography of music in Evans. Metuchen, New Jersey: Scarecrow Press, 1970. 607 p.

An index to the music published in 17th and 18th-century America as represented by Charles Evans' *American Bibliography* and the Readex Corporation's microprint edition of *Early American Imprints, 1639–1800.* [from the introductory remarks]

The major part of the work is devoted to entries for the music under composer, editor, or compiler. There is also a valuable section of biographical sketches, followed by indexes of names of composers and compilers, titles, and Evans' serial numbers. See also no. 1108.

1300. Jackson, Richard. United States music; sources of bibliography and collective biography. 2nd printing. Brooklyn: Institute for Studies in American Music, Dept. of Music, Brooklyn College of the City University of New York, 1976. 80 p. (I.S.A.M. monographs, 1)

First printing 1973.

A generic bibliography (reference works, historical studies, regional studies) with a topical section. Each entry is extensively annotated. Name index.

1301. Jackson, Richard. U.S. Bicentennial music. Brooklyn: Institute for Studies in American Music, Dept. of Music, School of Performing Arts, Brooklyn College of the City University of New York, 1977. 20 p. (I.S.A.M. special publications, 1)

470 entries for music composed or reprinted for the American Bicentennial.

1302. Lawrence, Vera Brodsky. Music for patriots, politicians, and presidents: harmonies and discords of the first hundred years. New York: Macmillan, 1975. 480 p.

A well-organized source book for information related to early American music. Numerous facsimiles of title pages and excerpts from texts. Includes bibliographical references and index.

1303. Laws, George Malcolm. American balladry from British broadsides; a guide for students and collectors of traditional song. Philadelphia, Pennsylvania: American Folklore Society, 1957. 315 p.

A discussion of the British broadside and its function as a source for American ballads precedes a bibliographic appendix of ballads in classified order giving texts and citing sources. There is a brief list of British and American printers of ballads in the 19th century and a short discography of recordings of British broadside ballads. General bibliography and an index to ballads by title.

Phemister, William. American piano concertos; a bibliography. See no. 1367.

1304. Rabson, Carolyn and Kate Van Winkle Keller. The national tune index; 18th century secular music (and user's guide). New York: University Music Editions, 1980. 80 microfiche (and 96 p.).

An extensive listing of representative sources of [American] secular music, consisting of cross-referenced indexes of source contents, sorted by text, and by music incipits represented in scale degrees, stressed notes, and interval sequences. [from the introductory remarks]

Source indexes by genre. The user's guide includes a short title index, a bibliography of sources, and an index to the various elements of the bibliography of sources.

Review by Gary W. Chapman in *Notes*, 38 (1982), p. 608.

1305. Tischler, Alice. Fifteen black American composers; a bibliography of their works. Detroit, Michigan: Information Coordinators, 1981. 328 p. (Detroit studies in music bibliography, 45)

A biographical sketch, classified works lists, and indexes for each of the composers.
Review by Deane Root in *Notes*, 38 (1982), p. 832–35.

YUGOSLAVIA

1306.   Dordevič, Vladimir R. Ogled srpske muzicke bibliografije do 1914. godine: [za shtampu priredila Ksenija B. Lazic]. [Essay on Serbian musical bibliography until 1914]. Beograd: Nolit, 1969. 281 p.
An annotated bibliography of 2,350 items in Serbo-Croatian, with separate sections for printed music, music literature, and manuscripts. Indexes of authors and titles. Summary in French and English.

1307.   Kompozitori i Muzicki Pisci Jugoslavije. (Yugoslav composers and music writers. Members of the Union of Yugoslav Composers, 1945–1967.) Catalogue. Edited by Milena Milosavljević-Pesić. Beograd: SAKOJ, 1968. 663 p.
Includes "An introduction to contemporary Yugoslav musical creation" by Krešimir Kovačević.
Contemporary Yugoslav composers and writers on music. Brief biographies; full bibliographies of works. Portraits. Addresses. Text in Serbo-Croatian and English.

MUSIC FOR INSTRUCTION AND PERFORMANCE

The reference tools listed here are designed for the musician who has a specific objective in view; namely, the selection of material for performance purposes, whether for solo or ensemble use. The need for such tools, incorporating the latest publications, is a perpetual one that has given rise to a generous number of resources. Titles are organized by instrument, although, of course, there are bibliographies principally focused on violin music including viola music, for instance. The entries are arranged in a classified order.

1308.   Brüchle, Bernhard. Musik-Bibliographien für alle Instrumente. Music bibliographies for all instruments. [English translation by Colleen Gruban.] München: Bernhard Brüchle Edition, 1976. 96 p.
In German and English. Cites some 297 bibliographies of music for instruments, both solo and in chamber ensembles. List of music publishers, followed by a list of special journals and societies devoted to instruments. Lists of bibliographic tools and music information centers. Index of instruments covered.
Review by Stephen M. Fry in *Notes*, 34 (1977), p. 87.

Bagpipes

1309.   Bagpipe Music Index. Current alphabetical tune listing. Glen Ridge, New Jersey: Bagpipe Music Index, 1966. [unpaged].
Reproduced from typescript. Contains 2,430 listings from 35 tune books.

Tunes identified by title, location in tune book, tune type, meter, and number of parts.

1310. Cannon, Roderick D. A bibliography of bagpipe music. Edinburgh: John Donald, 1980. 295 p.

A descriptive bibliography "of the music printed for each type of bagpipe played in the British Isles, to distinguish the various editions of each book, to ascertain dates and authorship, and to collect together any background information which might be of interest either to players or to music historians" (p. 1).

Treats the literature of the bagpipe in its various local styles. Four sections devoted to different pipe practices: Union pipes, Northumbrian bagpipes, Scots Highland pipes, Irish warpipes, and Brien Boru pipes. 126 titles described. Prose bibliographies of the literature on bagpipes. Contents of anthologies not analyzed.

Review by Amy Aaron in *Notes*, 37 (1980), p. 60–61.

Chamber Ensemble

1311. Altmann, Wilhelm. Handbuch für Klavierquartettspieler ... mit 237 Notenbeispielen. Wolfenbüttel: Verlag für musikalische Kultur und Wissenschaft, 1937. 147 p.

Notenbeispiele in pocket at end of *Handbuch*.

A companion to a selective list of piano quartets, arranged chronologically by birth dates of the composers. German works curtailed in an effort toward international coverage. Brief descriptive and critical commentaries. Index of composers.

1312. Altmann, Wilhelm. Handbuch für Klavierquintettspieler ... mit 343 Notenbeispielen. Wolfenbüttel: Verlag für musikalische Kultur und Wissenschaft, 1936. 178 p.

Notenbeispiele in pocket at end of *Handbuch*.

Similar to the above, with emphasis on piano quintets.

1313. Altmann, Wilhelm. Handbuch für Klaviertriospieler; Wegweiser durch die Trios für Klavier, Violine und Violoncell. Mit fast 400 Notenbeispielen. Wolfenbüttel: Verlag für musikalische Kultur und Wissenschaft, 1934. 237 p.

Similar to the above, with emphasis on piano trios.

1314. Altmann, Wilhelm. Handbuch für Streichquartettspieler.... Berlin: M. Hesse, 1928–31. 4 v. (Hesses Handbücher, 86, 87, 92, 94)

Reprinted by Heinrichshofen's Verlag, Wilhelmshaven, 1972–74, together with a vol. 5: *Ergänzungsband von 1935 bis zur Gegenwart.*

Vols. 1–2: string quartets; vol. 3: string trios, quintets, sextets, octets, addenda to quartets; vol. 4: works for strings and winds. Vol. 5 brings all sections up to date as of the year of printing.

A companion to quartet literature giving brief descriptions and analyses of works in the standard repertory as well as lesser-known works. Arrangement within each category is chronological.

See also no. 1411 (abridged version).

1315. Altmann, Wilhelm. Kammermusik-Katalog; ein Verzeichnis von seit 1841 veröffentlichten Kammermusikwerken. 6., bis August 1944 ergänzte Auflage. Leipzig: F. Hofmeister, 1945. 400 p.

Reprinted by Hofmeister, Hofheim am Taunus, 1967.

Succeeded by Richter's *Kammermusik-Katalog*.... See no. 1320.

Chamber music published since 1841, separate works or works in collections. Classified by medium, with composer indexes. International coverage.

Supplemented by no. 1421.

1316. Aulich, Bruno. Alte Musik für Liebhaber. 3. verbesserte Auflage. München: Artemis Verlag, 1981. 320 p. 17 plates.

Previously published as *Alte Musik für Hausmusikanten*, 1968.

An extensive introduction to the performance factors and genres of early instrumental music. Bio-bibliographical section listing modern editions of music originally intended or arranged to become chamber music. Index to terms and to names.

1317. Forsyth, Ella Marie. Building a chamber music collection: a descriptive guide to published scores. Metuchen, New Jersey: Scarecrow Press, 1979. 191 p.

Descriptions of formal and stylistic traits of basic chamber music repertory. Bibliography and indexes.

1318. Lemacher, Heinrich. Handbuch der Hausmusik. Graz: A. Pustet, 1948. 454 p.

The second part of the volume, p. 219 to end, lists works for solo instruments and various chamber ensembles. Many lesser-known works included. Arranged alphabetically by composer within various categories. Publisher and brief description of works given. Bibliography, p. 435–39. Index.

1319. Raaben, Lev Nikolaevich. Sovetskaia kamerno-instrumental'naia muzyka. Leningrad: Muzyka, 1963. 339 p.

History of Soviet chamber music, with bibliographical footnotes.

1320. Richter, Johannes F. Kammermusik-Katalog. Verzeichnis der von 1944 bis 1958 veröffentlichten Werke für Kammermusik und für Klavier vier- und sechshändig sowie für zwei und mehr Klaviere. Leipzig: F. Hofmeister, 1960. 318 p.

Successor to Wilhelm Altmann's work of the same title (no. 1315). Covers chamber music from 1945 through 1958. A classified bibliography, including chamber works with voice, piano four-hands, etc. Alphabetical index of composers and titles of collections. List of publishers.

1321. Saltonstall, Cecilia D. and Henry Saltonstall. List of recommended chamber music for strings, winds, and keyboard. Washington, D.C.: Amateur Chamber Players, 1984. 28 p.

Cumulates the 8 previous editions published under variant titles.

A classified list of chamber music, not including well-known composers. Cites instrumentation, editor, and publisher. Directory of publishers and index to composers.

Harpsichord

1322. Alker, Hugo. Literatur für alte Tasteninstrumente; Versuch einer Bibliographie für die Praxis. 2te verm. und erg. Aufl. Wien: Wissenschaftliches Antiquariat H. Geyer, 1967. 79 p. (Wiener Abhandlungen zur Musikwissenschaft und Instrumentenkunde, 2)

First published in 1962.

The main division is between music for harpsichord and music for organ (without pedals). Brief entries, with publishers and editors given. Collections are entered by title and filed in the same alphabet with composers. The emphasis is on music currently available in practical editions.

1323. Arneson, Arne J. and Stacie Williams. The harpsichord book: being a plaine and simple index to printed collections of musick by diffrent masters for the harpsichord, spinnet, clavichord, and virginall. Madison, Wisconsin: Index House, 1986. 119 p.

An index to multiple-composer anthologies of compositions that include early music (to 1800) for a harpsichord or its kindred instruments, excluding works for organ or pianoforte. Bibliography of anthologies. Composer, title and editor indexes.

1324. Bedford, Frances and Robert Conant. Twentieth-century harpsichord music: a classified bibliography. Hackensack, New Jersey: Joseph Boonin, 1974. 95 p. (Music indexes and bibliographies, 8)

Entries classified by ensembles: harpsichord and one stringed instrument, harpsichord and one other keyboard instrument, etc. Composer and title indexes. List of publishers.

Orchestra

1325. Altmann, Wilhelm. Orchester-Literatur-Katalog; Verzeichnis von seit 1850 erschienenen Orchester-Werken.... Leipzig: F. E. C. Leuckart, 1926–36. 2 v.

Reprinted by M. Sändig, Walluf bei Wiesbaden, 1972.

Orchestral music published since 1850, listing scores, miniature scores, parts, and arrangements. Vol. 2 gives, in addition, instrumentation and timing and contains a composer index to both volumes. Thematic quotations given for works whose serial numbers are often confused (e.g., Haydn's symphonies, Handel's concertos, etc.).

American Music Center. Library. Music for orchestra, band and large ensemble. See no. 1434.

1326. Basart, Ann P. "Finding orchestral music." In *Cum Notis Variorum*, 59 (January/February, 1982), p. 14–24.

An annotated, indexed checklist of bibliographies of orchestral music for performance. Includes a section on finding orchestral program notes.

1327. Beck, Georges H. Compositeurs contemporains: œuvres d'orchestre. Paris: Heugel & Cie, [1960]. 35 p.

A descriptive listing of recent orchestral works by 27 composers, chiefly

French. Brief biographies of the composers. Entries give instrumentation and timings. Scores and performance materials available on rental from Heugel.

Breitkopf & Härtel. Catalogo delle sinfonie.... See no. 1715.

1328. Buschkötter, Wilhelm. Handbuch der internationalen Konzertliteratur. Berlin: Walter de Gruyter & Co., 1961. 374 p.

Compiled as a successor to Theodor Müller-Reuter's *Lexikon der deutschen Konzertliteratur* (no. 1335). Works listed chronologically under composer. Information includes performance time, instrumentation, date of composition, performance, publisher.

Review by Richard Schaal in *Die Musikforschung*, 17 (1961), p. 84–85.

1329. Daniels, David. Orchestral music; a handbook. 2nd ed. Metuchen, New Jersey: Scarecrow Press, 1982. 413 p.

> The purpose of this work is to gather together in one volume the diverse information about orchestral works needed to plan programs and organize rehearsals: instrumentation, duration, and source of performance materials. [Editor's *Foreword*]

Entries arranged by composer. Particularly useful are the listing of works by performing forces, the list of orchestral works by duration, and the list of composers by nationality or ethnic group.

1330. Eagon, Angelo. Catalog of published concert music by American composers. 2nd ed. Metuchen, New Jersey: Scarecrow Press, 1969. 348 p.

This work was issued originally in 1964 as a publication of the Music Branch of the U.S. Information Agency. 175 p.

Supplement issued 1971. 150 p. *Second Supplement* issued 1974. 148 p.

Works are entered alphabetically by composer under a classified arrangement: vocal solo, instrumental solo, instrumental ensembles, concert jazz, percussion, orchestra, etc. There is a key to publishers and an author index. Information includes duration of orchestral works, author of text for vocal compositions. A useful, well-organized publication.

Review by Karl Kroeger, of the 1964 edition, in *Notes*, 22 (1966), p. 1032–33; by Richard Hunter, of the 1969 edition, in *Notes*, 26 (1970), p. 759–60.

1331. The Edwin A. Fleisher collection of orchestral music in the Free Library of Philadelphia; a cumulative catalog, 1929–1977. The Fleisher collection in the Free Library of Philadelphia. Boston, Massachusetts: G. K. Hall, 1979. 956 p.

First published in 1933–45 in 2 v., with a *Supplementary List, 1945–1955* published in 1956. Revised edition published 1965.

Catalog of a loan collection of over 13,000 pieces of orchestral music, much of the material unpublished. Classified; information includes composers' dates, title of each work in the original language with English translation, publisher, instrumentation, timing, date of composition, and information about the first performance. Occasional thematic incipits included. Indexed by performing forces needed.

Review by Joseph M. Boonin in *Notes*, 36 (1979), p. 92–93.

1332. Emery, Frederic B. The violin concerto through a period of nearly 300 years, covering about 3,300 concertos with brief biographies of 1,000 composers. Chicago, Illinois: Violin Literature Publishing Co., 1928. 615 p., with index p. i–xl.

Brief discussions of concerto composers grouped chronologically and by nationality. A mass of somewhat indiscriminate facts and information. Illustrated with portraits of musicians.

1333. International Music Council. Répertoires internationaux de musique contemporaine à l'usage des amateurs et des jeunes. I. Musique symphonique de 1880 à 1954. Frankfurt, New York: C. F. Peters, 1957– V. 1, 63 p.

A catalog of recently composed symphonic works suitable for young people's and amateur orchestras. Material listed alphabetically by country; publisher, date, and instrumentation given. Indexes of composers, types of ensemble. List of publishers.

1334. Laughlin, James E. The Alexander Broude comprehensive guide to orchestral literature: a catalogue. New York: A. Broude, 1975. 116 p.

A handy catalog of available orchestral music.

1335. Müller-Reuter, Theodor. Lexikon der deutschen Konzertliteratur; ein Ratgeber für Dirigenten, Konzertveranstalter, Musikschriftsteller und Musikfreunde. Leipzig: G. F. Kahnt nachf., 1909. V. 1, 626 p.

Nachtrag zu Band I. Leipzig, Kahnt, 1921. 238 p. Reprinted by Da Capo, New York, 1972.

The standard guide to orchestral and chamber music by the major composers of the romantic period, with detailed information as to date of composition, first performance, duration, instrumentation, and relation to the composer's other works. Band I covers the following composers: Schubert, Mendelssohn, Schumann, Berlioz, Liszt, Raff, Wagner, Dräseke, Reinecke, Bruch, Gernsheim, and Richard Strauss. The *Nachtrag* is devoted to Beethoven, Brahms, and Haydn (symphonies only).

Buschkotter's *Handbuch* ... (no. 1328) is intended to supplement Müller-Reuter and bring it up to date.

1336. Saltonstall, Cecilia Drinker and Henry Saltonstall. A new catalog of music for small orchestra. Clifton, New Jersey: European American Music Corp., 1978. 323 p. (Music Indexes and Bibliographies, 14)

Supersedes the *Catalog of Music for Small Orchestra*, Washington, D.C., 1947.

Not indexed! 6,380 compositions listed, indicating performing forces needed and duration. List of publishers.

Review by James N. Berdahl in *Notes*, 36 (1979), p. 374–75.

1337. Sartorius, Richard H. Bibliography of concertos for organ and orchestra. Evanston, Illinois: Instrumentalist Co., [1961]. 68 p.

Includes primary sources as well as modern publications. Extensive annotations, biographical and descriptive, of the music. Locations of original materials given. The list includes much material not exclusively for organ, i.e., concertos for "harpsichord or organ."

1338. Stein, Franz A. Verzeichnis der Orchestermusik von 1700 bis zur Gegenwart. Bern und München: Francke Verlag, [1963]. 126 p.

A pocket guide to orchestral literature. Selective list of composers and their principal orchestral works. Entries give title, instrumentation, date of composition, movements if a composite work. No publishers given.

1339. Svensk musik för orkester (hyresmaterial) 1985. Swedish music for orchestra (hire material) 1985. Stockholm: STIMS informationscentral för svensk musik, 1985. 150 p.

A catalog produced by the Swedish music information service covering orchestral scores and parts for hire of music written by Swedes.

1340. Tuthill, Burnet C. "The concertos for clarinet." In *Journal of Research in Music Education*, 10 (1962), p. 47–58.

Brief introduction to the history of the clarinet concerto and its literature, followed by annotated listing of such concertos from the 18th century to the present.

This list has been supplemented by Robert A. Titus in an article in the *Journal of Research in Music Education*, 13 (1965), p. 169–76.

Organ

Alker, Hugo. Literatur für alte Tasteninstrumente. See no. 1322.

1341. Arnold, Corliss Richard. Organ literature: a comprehensive survey. 2nd ed. Metuchen, New Jersey: Scarecrow Press, 1984. 2 v.

First published in 1973 with 656 p.

Part I: Historical survey with accompanying bibliographies.

Part II: Biographical catalog, providing basic information about composers and their published works.

Bibliography.

Reviews by Nathan A. Randall in *Notes*, 42 (1985), p. 58–59, and by Kurt Dorfmüller in *Fontes Artis Musicae*, 32 (1985), p. 218–20.

1342. Edson, Jean Slater. Organ preludes, an index to compositions on hymn tunes, chorales, plainsong melodies, Gregorian tunes and carols. Metuchen, New Jersey: Scarecrow Press, 1970. 2 v.

Supplement, including corrections and additions to the first volumes, published in 1974. 315 p.

Vol. I: composer index, with settings listed alphabetically under composer's name. Publishers are identified.

Vol. II: index of tune names, identified by thematic incipits. Each tune name is followed by a list of the composers who have set it.

1343. Kratzenstein, Marilou. Survey of organ literature and editions. Ames: Iowa State University Press, 1980. 246 p.

A survey of organ music arranged by country with essays on the development of the instrument, major composers, and schools for each country. Each essay precedes a bibliography of editions arranged by composer or, in the case of anthologies, by title. Originally a series of articles in the *Diapason*.

Review by Pierre Hardouin in *Fontes Artis Musicae*, 28 (1981), p. 149–50.

1344. Lohmann, Heinz. Handbuch der Orgelliteratur. Wiesbaden: Breitkopf & Härtel, 1975. 206 p.

A work in three parts: an index to settings of chorale melodies, both German and others, arranged alphabetically by the "name" of the chorale; an index of editions of works for organ; and a series of indexes to chorale tunes, melody names, and first lines. International in scope, but focused on the German Protestant tradition.

1345. Lukas, Viktor. Reclams Orgelmusikführer. 5. Aufl. Stuttgart: Philipp Reclam Jun., 1986. 461 p.

Originally published as *Orgelmusikführer* in 1963. 271 p. There is an English-language edition, *A Guide to Organ Music*, translated by Anne Wyburd with addenda by Lee Garrett, and published by Amadeus Press in Portland, Oregon, 1989. 272 p.

A listener's guide to concert organ literature, quite selective and confined to European repertory. Brief biographies of the composers; numerous thematic quotations. Contains a section on the organ with other instruments, a glossary of organ terms, and a description of the mechanics of the instrument. Index of composers and works.

1346. Münger, Fritz. Choralbearbeitungen für Orgel. Verzeichnis zu den Chorälen des Deutschen Evangelischen Kirchengesangbuches und des Gesangbuches der evang.-reform. Kirchen der deutschsprachigen Schweiz. Kassel: Bärenreiter, [1952]. 148 p.

Alphabetical listing by chorale text incipit, locating each in the German or Swiss chorale books and indicating the organ settings available in some 56 collections of chorale preludes.

1347. Opp, Walter. Verzeichnis der Orgelvorspiele zum Evangelischen Kirchengesangbuch. Berlin: Verlag Merseburger, 1974. 1 v. (loose-leaf)

An index to organ preludes by the melodies in the order of appearance in the *Evangelische Kirchengesangbuch*, giving composers and titles of the preludes based on the chorale tunes. Bibliography of publications containing the various settings of the chorale melodies.

1348. Sartoris, Richard H. Bibliography of concertos for organ and orchestra. Evanston, Illinois: Instrumentalist Co., 1961. 68 p.

1349. Spelman, Leslie. Organ plus: a catalogue of ensemble music for organ and instruments. 2nd ed. New York: American Guild of Organists, 1977. 36 p.

A classified catalog citing composer, title, collation, level of difficulty, publisher, dates of publication. Does not list music for organ with orchestra, organ with piano, organ and tape, organ with handbells, or voices with organ. No index.

Stellhorn, Martin H. Index to hymn preludes. See no. 1846.

1350. Weigl, Bruno. Handbuch der Orgelliteratur. Vollständige Umarbeitung des Führers durch die Orgelliteratur, herausgegeben von [Theophil] Kothe-Forchhammer, neubearbeitet von Otto Burkert. Leipzig: F. E. C. Leuckart, 1931. 318 p.

Classifed listing of compositions for organ solo or organ with orchestra, instruments, or voices. Original works and transcriptions listed separately. International coverage.

1351. Werning, Daniel, J. A selected source index for hymn and chorale tunes in Lutheran worship books. St. Louis, Missouri: Concordia, 1985. 234 p.

Organized alphabetically by tune name of the hymns and chorales contained in the four major Lutheran hymnals produced in the United States between 1941 and 1982. Under each tune name selected organ settings and choral settings are listed in separate sequences, by composer or by title of anthology.

Piano

1352. Altmann, Wilhelm. Verzeichnis von Werken für Klavier vier- und sechshändig, sowie für zwei und mehr Klaviere. Leipzig: F. Hofmeister, 1943. 133 p.

Classified catalog of works for piano, 4 and 6 hands, and for 2 and more pianos with and without other instruments. Original works and arrangements included. Alphabetical by composer within classification. Index.

1353. Basart, Ann P. "Guides to piano music: a check-list." In *Cum Notis Variorum*, 53 (June 1981), p. 13–21.

An annotated, indexed checklist to bibliographies providing information about piano music.

1354. Butler, Stanley. Guide to the best in contemporary piano music; an annotated list of graded solo piano music published since 1950. Metuchen, New Jersey: Scarecrow Press, 1973. 2 v.

Valuable less for the qualitative judgments than for the bibliographic citations.

1355. Chang, Frederic Ming and Albert Faurot. Team piano repertoire; a manual of music for multiple players at one or more pianos. Metuchen, New Jersey: Scarecrow Press, 1976. 184 p.

A classified, annotated list of music with cryptic bibliographical information. Lists arrangements and transcriptions as well as some recordings. Review by Stephen M. Fry in *Notes*, 34 (1977), p. 87.

1356. Fuszek, Rita M. Piano music in collections; an index. Detroit, Michigan: Information Coordinators, 1981. 895 p.

Covering 496 collections in two sections: an index to the collections by composer and a list of the contents of the collections. Title index, lists of editors, catalogs, and editions of composers' works. Review by François Lesure in *Fontes Artis Musicae*, 30 (1983), p. 78.

1357. Gillespie, John and Anna Gillespie. A bibliography of nineteenth-century American piano music with location sources and composer biography index. Westport, Connecticut: Greenwood, 1984. 358 p. (Music reference collection, 2)

A selective, classified bibliography including some music from the late 18th century and extending into the first part of the 20th century. Occasional comments on the music.

Review by John Stroud in *Notes*, 41 (1985), p. 520–21.

1358. Gratia, E. L. Répertoire pratique du pianiste.... Préface de I. Philipp. Paris: Delagrave, 1931. 117 p.

A list of 2,500 piano pieces by 271 composers arranged alphabetically by composer, with categories of varying degrees of difficulty. Four-hand pieces, p. 112–17.

1359. Hinson, Maurice. Guide to the pianist's repertoire. 2nd ed., rev. and enl. Bloomington: Indiana University Press, 1986. 856 p.

First published in 1973 and supplemented in 1979.

Lists the piano compositions of individual composers, providing brief information on publisher and occasional critical remarks. There is a classified list of major anthologies, with an annotated bibliography, and an index to editors, arrangers, and transcribers. Attempts to address three questions: "What is there?" "What is it like?" and "Where can I get it?"

There are occasional citations of literature *about* the music cited.

Indexes: composers by national designations, Black composers, women composers, compositions for tape and piano, compositions for prepared piano, titles in anthologies and collections.

First edition reviewed by Malcolm Bilson in *Notes*, 30 (1978), p. 287–88.

1360. Hinson, Maurice. Music for more than one piano: an annotated guide. Bloomington: Indiana University Press, 1983. 218 p.

Includes works originally written for piano and other forces if arranged by the composer. Includes transcriptions of important composers. Critical comments and publisher information provided. Indexes of special ensembles.

1361. Hinson, Maurice. Music for piano and orchestra: an annotated guide. Bloomington: Indiana University Press, 1981. 327 p.

Provides cryptic bibliographical information as well as more extensive analytical comments on the works cited. Includes not only the standard repertoire but also numerous contemporary works. Lists many of the cadenzas written for the Beethoven and Mozart concertos. Secondary references occasionally cited. Indexes by performing forces.

Review by Judith Kaufman in *Notes*, 38 (1982), p. 611–12.

1362. Hinson, Maurice. The piano in chamber ensemble: an annotated guide. Bloomington: Indiana University Press, 1978. 570 p.

A classified bibliography covering music from c. 1700 to the present, with considerable attention to contemporary music. There is a brief, annotated bibliography of suggested readings on the subject and an index of composers.

Reviews by Bennett Ludden in *Notes*, 35 (1979), p. 891–92, and by Peter Ward Jones in *Music and Letters*, 60 (1979), p. 335.

1363. Kennard, Daphne. "Music for one-handed pianists." In *Fontes Artis Musicae*, 30 (1983), p. 117–31.
Revision of a list published first in *Brio*, 13, 2 (1976), p. 39–42.
A comprehensive list of music for one-handed pianists. Short lists of duets for one and two pianos, references to anthologies, an article, and a thesis.

1364. McGraw, Cameron. Piano duet repertoire: music originally written for one piano, four hands. Bloomington: Indiana University Press, 1981. 334 p.

Arrangements or adaptations from other media are excluded except in rare cases where the composers themselves have made the transcriptions or where such adaptations have long been considered part of the standard four hand repertoire. [from the *General Explanation*]

Indexes of music publishers and library locations.
Review by Albert Seay in *Notes*, 38 (1981), p. 316.

1365. Moldenhauer, Hans. Duo-pianism; a dissertation. [Chicago, Illinois: Chicago Musical College Press, 1951.] 400 p.
Contains a list of original two-piano music arranged alphabetically by composer. Publishers indicated. The main part of the dissertation concerns itself with practical rather than historical aspects of the subject. Also contains a list of recorded two-piano music.

1366. Parent, Charlotte F. H. Répertoire encyclopédique du pianiste; analyse raisonnée d'œuvres choisies pour le piano, du XVIe siècle au XXe siècle, avec renseignements pratiques de degré de difficulté, nombre de pages, éditeur et prix.... Paris: Hachette et Cie, [1900–1907]. 2 v.

1367. Phemister, William. American piano concertos; a bibliography. Detroit, Michigan: Published for the College Music Society by Information Coordinators, 1986. (Bibliographies in American music, 9)
A sourcebook of information about over 1,100 concertos composed in the United States.

1368. Rezits, Joseph. The pianist's resource guide, 1978–79: piano music in print and literature on the pianistic art [by] Joseph Rezits and Gerald Deatsman. Park Ridge, Illinois: Pallma Music Co./Neil A. Kjos, 1978. 1,491 p.
First published in 1974.
Composed of three major sections: a classified and computer-generated list of music for piano with a title index; a classified list of books on the subject of pianos with an author index; a piano reader's guide consisting of reviews of 118 books and a topical index to books listed in section 2. Publisher information is provided.

1369. Rowley, Alec. Four hands—one piano. A list of works for duet players. London/New York: Oxford University Press, 1940. 38 p.

Classified list, with composer index, of original works for the medium, 1750 to date. Alphabetical arrangement within each class (the classics, the French school, etc.). Entries give composer's name and dates, title (usually in the original language), opus number, publisher.

1370. Ruthardt, Adolf. Wegweiser durch die Klavier-Literatur. 10. Aufl. Leipzig and Zürich: Hug & Co., 1925. 398 p.
First published in 1888.
Selective list of keyboard music including works for four or more hands from the Renaissance to the early 20th century. Classified according to genre and degree of difficulty. Brief descriptions of lesser-known works. Bibliography of writings on keyboard music, p. 359–76. Index.

1371. Teichmüller, Robert and Kurt Herrmann. Internationale moderne Klaviermusik, ein Wegweiser und Berater. Leipzig and Zürich: Hug & Co., 1927. 300 p.
Supplement, 1934.
Critical and selective bibliography of piano music from about 1890 to date of publication, arranged alphabetically by composer, with an index by country. Gives date of composition, opus number, title, publisher, price, grade, and critical comment.

1372. Wolters, Klaus. Handbuch der Klavierliteratur: Klaviermusik zu zwei Händen. 2., rev. und erw. Aufl. Zürich: Atlantis-Verlag, 1977. 660 p.
First published in 1967.
Intended as a guide and aid to piano teachers, this work is an extensive bibliography of editions interspersed with commentaries on the editions themselves, and upon the composers and compositions. Arrangements for piano are included, especially from earlier periods. The section on contemporary music treats, among other genres and styles, jazz, modern dance, avant-garde music, and various national musics. Index to names only.

Choral Music

1373. Burnsworth, Charles C. Choral music for women's voices: an annotated bibliography of recommended works. Metuchen, New Jersey: Scarecrow Press, 1968. 180 p.
Detailed critical and descriptive annotations given for some 135 choral works for women's voices and a like number of arrangements. Indexed by title, number of voice parts, grade of difficulty, extended compositions, and collections. The work is overloaded with apparatus and verbosity, which serve to diminish its value.

1374. Challier, Ernst. Ernst Challier's grosser Chor-Katalog, mit Nachträgen I bis III. Ein alphabetisch geordnetes Verzeichnis sämtlicher Gemischter Chöre mit und ohne Begleitung. Wiesbaden: M. Sändig, 1979. 482 p.
Reprint of the 1903 edition and its 1905–1913 supplements.

1375. Challier, Ernst. Ernst Challier's grosser Männergesang-Katalog. Ein alphabetisch geordnetes Verzeichnis sämtlicher Männer-Chöre mit und ohne Begleitung. Wiesbaden: M. Sändig, 1979.

Reprint of the 1902 edition and its six supplements through 1912. Cites over 10,000 compositions, arranged by title.

1376. DeVenney, David P. Nineteenth-century American choral music: an annotated guide. Berkeley, California: Fallen Leaf Press, 1986. 182 p. (Fallen Leaf reference books in music, 8)

Extensive bibliography: p. 97–116.

1377. Knapp, J. Merrill. Selected list of music for men's voices. Princeton, New Jersey: Princeton University Press, 1952. 165 p.

Original works and arrangements, published and unpublished. Alphabetical by composer within main classification scheme. Each entry gives birth and death dates of composer, scoring, language, publisher, and editor. Index of composers.

Review by Archibald Davison in *Notes*, 10 (1952), p. 104–105.

1378. Locke, Arthur W. and Charles K. Fassett. Selected list of choruses for women's voices. 3rd ed., rev. and enl. Northampton, Massachusetts: Smith College, 1964. 253 p.

First published in 1927; 2nd edition, 1946, edited by A. W. Locke.

Principal section is an alphabetical catalog by composers, with titles of choruses, voice combination, publishers, or source in a collection. Foreign titles usually translated. Collections listed separately and their contents given. Indexes include a chronological list of composers; compositions by categories; authors and sources of texts; and first lines and titles.

Review by Karl Kroeger in *Notes*, 23 (1966), p. 63–64.

1379. May, James D. Avant-garde choral music: an annotated selected bibliography. Metuchen, New Jersey: Scarecrow Press, 1977. 258 p.

Treats music readily available in the United States. Extensive information on musical characteristics. Indexes classified by performing forces. Composer index. Bibliography.

1380. Roberts, Kenneth C. A check-list of 20th-century choral music for male voices. Detroit, Michigan: Information Coordinators, 1970. 32 p. (Detroit studies in music bibliography, 17)

1381. Schünemann, Georg. Führer durch die deutsche Chorliteratur. Wolfenbüttel: Verlag für musikalische Kultur und Wissenschaft, 1935–36. 2 v.

Vol. 1: Männerchor. Vol. 2: Gemischter Chor.

Classified according to type of composition. Entries give composer, title, publisher, grade of difficulty, number of parts, duration. Indexed by first line of text, title, composer and arranger, author of text. Includes both secular and sacred works.

1382. Temperley, Nicholas and Charles G. Manns. Fuguing tunes in the eighteenth century. Detroit, Michigan: Information Coordinators, 1983. 504 p. (Detroit studies in music bibliography, 49)

Analytical census of fuguing tunes with indexes to texts, tune names, persons.

Reviews by Allen P. Britton in *Fontes Artis Musicae*, 32 (1985), p. 88–89, and by Karl Kroeger in *Notes*, 41 (1984), p. 58–61.

1383. Tortolano, William. Original music for men's voices: a selected bibliography. 2nd ed. Metuchen, New Jersey: Scarecrow Press, 1981. 201 p.
First published in 1973.
Arranged by composer, provides information on performing forces and duration. Section on music found in collections. There are six essays on the subject. Indexes of authors and sources of text and of first lines and titles.

1384. Vagner, Robert. "A selective list of choral and vocal music with wind and percussion accompaniments." In *Journal of Research in Music Education*, 14 (1966), p. 276–88.
"Selections are included for mixed chorus and instrumental ensemble, mixed voices and obbligato instrument, treble or male voices with obbligato instrument, men's chorus with ensemble, women's chorus with ensemble, solo voices with ensemble, solo voice with keyboard and a variety of solo instruments." A list of solo cantatas and arias by Telemann and J. S. Bach is added. Publishers' names and sometimes editors' are provided.

1385. Valentin, Erich. Handbuch der Chormusik. Hrsg. im Auftrag der Arbeitsgemeinschaft deutscher Chorverbände. Regensburg: G. Bosse, [1953–58]. 2 v.
These volumes serve as general sourcebooks of information useful to choral directors. Special sections include a discography of choral music, listings of the contents of *Denkmäler*, writings on choral conducting. Major sections devoted to classified bibliographies of choral music, with full performance details. Each volume has a composer index.

1386. White, Evelyn Davidson. Choral music by Afro-American composers; a selected, annotated bibliography. Metuchen, New Jersey: Scarecrow, 1981. 167 p.
Arranged by composer, entries cite title, copyright date, voicing, range, degree of difficulty, performing forces, publisher, and publisher's catalog number. Index to titles. There is a section of analyzed citations from collections of spirituals. Biographical sketches of composers. Appendixes: selected source readings and selected discography.
Review by Deane L. Root in *Notes*, 38 (1982), p. 832–35.

Vocal Music (Solo and Chamber)

1387. Basart, Ann P. "Finding vocal music." In *Cum Notis Variorum*, 55 (September 1981), p. 5–15, and 56 (October 1981), p. 14–22.
An annotated, indexed checklist to bibliographies providing information on vocal music and choral music for performance.

1388. Berry, Corre. Vocal chamber duets; an annotated bibliography. New York: National Association of Teachers of Singing, 1981. 71 p.
With indexes to voice combinations, poets, and titles and first lines.

Brunnings, Florence E. Folk song index; a comprehensive guide to the Florence E. Brunnings Collection. See no. 1815.

1389. Carman, Judith E., William K. Gaeddert, and Rita M. Resch. Art-song in the United States, 1801–1987; an annotated bibliography. With a special section "Art-song in the United States, 1759–1810" by Gordon Myers. 2nd ed. Jacksonville, Florida: National Association of Teachers of Singing, 1987. 371 p.

A practical tool for teachers of singing. Limited to music for a single solo voice with English text commercially available at the time of compilation. Extensive information on each publication provided. Arranged by composer. Index to broad subjects and poets. Indexes to composers and titles.

1390. Challier, Ernst. Ernst Challier's grosser Duetten-Katalog. Ein alphabetisch geordnetes Verzeichnis sämtlicher zweistimmiger Lieder mit Begleitung. Nendeln: Kraus-Thompson, 1979. 182 p.

Reprint of the the 1898 publication.

1391. Challier, Ernst. Ernst Challier's grosser Lieder-Katalog. Ein alphabetisch geordnetes Verzeichnis sämtlicher einstimmiger Lieder mit Begleitung des Pianoforte. Nendeln: Kraus-Thompson, 1979. 2,415 p.

A reprint of the 1885 publication and its 15 *Nachträge*.

1392. Coffin, Berton. Singer's repertoire. 2nd ed. New York: Scarecrow Press, 1960. 4 v.

First published in one volume, 1956.

Classified catalog of solo songs, each volume devoted to a particular voice range; information on subject, accompaniment, publisher.

Review by Arnold Caswell in *Journal of Research in Music Education*, 9 (1961), p. 76.

1393. Coffin, Berton and Werner Singer. Program notes for the singer's repertoire. Metuchen, New Jersey: Scarecrow Press, 1962. 230 p.

1394. Cushing, Helen G. Children's song index, an index to more than 22,000 songs in 189 collections comprising 222 volumes. New York: H. W. Wilson, 1936. 798 p.

A dictionary catalog of children's song literature. Main entry is by song title, with subordinate entries under composer, author of the words, and subject. References from first line to title. Foreign titles given in the original language. There is a preliminary "Catalog of collections indexed," and a "Directory of publishers" at the end of the volume.

Day, Cyrus L. and E. B. Murrie. English song-books, 1651–1702; a bibliography with a first-line index of songs. See no. 2600.

1395. De Charms, Desirée and Paul Breed. Songs in collections, an index. Detroit, Michigan: Information Service, Inc., 1966. 588 p.

Indexes 411 collections of solo songs published between 1940 and 1957. Entries for more than 9,400 songs. Composed songs entered under composer, with anonymous and folk songs entered alphabetically by title under nationality. Separate sections for carols and for sea chanties. Complete title and first line index.

This work articulates with Sears' *Song Index* (no. 1408).

Review by Donald Ivey in *Journal of Research in Music Education*, 15 (1967), p. 169–70; by Imogen Fellinger in *Die Musikforschung*, 23 (1970), p. 96–97; by Ellen Kenny in *Notes*, 23 (1966), p. 269–70.

1396. Dunlap, Kay and Barbara Winchester. Vocal chamber music; a performer's guide. New York: Garland, 1985. 140 p. (Garland reference library of the humanities, 465)

Cites music written from 1650 to 1980 for at least one voice and one instrument other than guitar and up to twelve solo voices and twelve solo instruments. Index by performing forces.

1397. Edwards, J. Michele. Literature for voices in combination with electronic and tape music: an annotated bibliography. Ann Arbor, Michigan: Music Library Association, 1977. 194 p. (MLA index and bibliography series, 7)

A historical listing to 1975 and a finding aid, with extensive information about each composition. There are appendixes covering publishers, music information centers, foreign and hard-to-find record labels, studios, and bibliography. There is also an index to the entries by medium.

Review by Peter Ward Jones in *Music and Letters*, 60 (1979), p. 229.

1398. Espina, Noni. Repertoire for the solo voice; a fully annotated guide to works for the solo voice published in modern editions and covering material from the 13th century to the present. With a foreword by Berton Coffin. Metuchen, New Jersey: Scarecrow Press, 1977. 2 v. 1,290 p.

Arranged in sections: art songs by nationality of composer; excerpts from operas; florid display songs; traditional songs. Entries provide information on source of text, degree of difficulty, accompaniment, publisher, and references to collections. Remarks are made on the general style and the musical and vocal requirements of each song. Indexes to sources of texts (poets and literary titles) and composers.

Review by Stephen M. Fry in *Notes*, 34 (1978), p. 620.

1399. Espina, Noni. Vocal solos for Christian churches; a descriptive reference of solo music for the church year including a bibliographical supplement of choral works. 3rd ed. Metuchen, New Jersey: Scarecrow Press, 1984. 241 p.

First published in 1965 and again in 1974 under the title *Vocal Solos for Protestant Services*.

Indexes to "occasions," voices, titles, and composers.

1400. Gooch, Bryan N. S. and David S. Thatcher. Musical settings of British romantic literature; a catalogue. Editorial assistant: Odean Long. New York: Garland Pub., 1982. 2 v. 1,768 p. (Garland reference library of the humanities, 326)

Lists published and unpublished compositions setting British Romantic texts by authors born after 1750 who lived to 1800 or later. Organized by author and literary title with information on composers and settings following. Bibliographical information on poetry and settings provided. Index of authors, first lines and titles, and composers.

1401. Gooch, Bryan N. S. and David S. Thatcher. Musical settings of early and mid-Victorian literature; a catalogue. Editorial assistant: Odean Long. New York: Garland Pub., 1979. 946 p. (Garland reference library of the humanities, 149)

Considers published and unpublished settings of prominent British authors born after 1800 and who lived to 1850 or later, excluding writers asssociated with the Romantic movements. Information on performing forces and publication details for both the poetry and the musical settings is provided. Listed by author, indexed by composer, title and first line.

1402. Gooch, Bryan N. S. and David S. Thatcher. Musical settings of late Victorian and modern British literature: a catalogue. Editorial assistant: Odean Long. New York: Garland Pub., 1976. 1,112p. (Garland reference library of the humanities, 3)

Review by Stephen M. Fry in *Notes*, 34 (1977), p. 88–89.

1403. Greenhill, James, William A. Harrison, and Frederick J. Furnivall. A list of all the songs and passages in Shakespeare which have been set to music. The words in old spelling, from the quartos and first folios, edited by F. J. Furnival and W. G. Stone. Folcroft, Pennsylvania: Folcroft Library Editions, 1974. 112 p.

Reprint of the 1884 edition published for the New Shakespeare Society by N. Trübner in London.

See also nos. 1194 and 1196.

Havlice, Patricia Pate. Popular song index. See no. 1519.

1404. Hovland, Michael A. Musical settings of American poetry: a bibliography. Westport, Connecticut: Greenwood Press, 1986. 531 p. (Music reference collection, 8)

Lists 5,800 musical settings of 99 American authors by 2,100 composers, providing bibliographical information as well as brief remarks on performing forces. Recordings are occasionally cited. Extensive list of works cited. Arranged by author with indexes to composers and to titles of literary works.

1405. Kagen, Sergius. Music for the voice, a descriptive list of concert and teaching material. Rev. ed. Bloomington: Indiana University Press, 1968. 780 p.

First published in 1949 by Rinehart, New York, as no. 3 in the "Field of music" series.

Songs are listed alphabetically by composer and nationality within four large categories: (1) songs and airs before the 19th century; (2) songs of the 19th and 20th centuries; (3) folk songs; (4) operatic excerpts. Each section has its own bibliography, and there are numerous biographical sketches of song writers. Data include title, compass, tessitura, and type, with descriptive remarks.

Lax, Roger and Frederic Smith. The great song thesaurus. See no. 1520.

1406. Leigh, Robert. Index to song books: a title index to over 11,000 copies of almost 6,800 songs in 111 song books published between 1933 and 1962. Stockton, California: Robert Leigh, 1964. 273 p.
   Reprint published by Da Capo Press, New York, 1973.
   Intended to supplement the Sears *Song Index*, no. 1408.

1407. Lust, Patricia D. American vocal chamber music, 1945–1980: an annotated bibliography. Foreword by Phyllis Bryn-Julson. Westport, Connecticut: Greenwood Press, 1985. 273 p. (Music reference collection, 4)
   Annotations consist of descriptions of unusual features of the music, including nontraditional notation. Appendixes classify the works by performing forces. Index to titles and to names of persons and ensembles.

1408. Sears, Minnie E. Song index: an index to more than 12,000 songs in 177 song collections.... New York: H. W. Wilson, 1926. 650 p.
   Supplement: An Index to More than 7,000 Songs in 104 Collections.... 1934. 366 p. Reprint contains original and supplement volumes. Published in Hamden, Connecticut by Shoe String Press, 1966.
   Contains titles, first lines, authors' names, and composers' names in one alphabet. Each song is cited under title, with added entry under composer and author, and cross-references for first lines and variant or translated titles. Classified and alphabetical listings of the song collections indexed.
   The work of Sears has been continued in *Songs in Collections* by De Charms and Breed (1966) (no. 1395), and by Leigh (1964) (no. 1406).

Stewart-Green, Miriam. Women composers: a check-list of works for the solo voice. See no. 2992.

1409. Swan, Alfred J. The music director's guide to musical literature (for voices and instruments). New York: Prentice-Hall, 1941. 164 p.
   P. 117–64: A selected list of works from the early Middle Ages through the 20th century. Arranged chronologically, with subdivisions by genre and country. Occasional annotations. The earlier part of the book contains brief comments on the composers represented in the bibliography.

1410. University of Tennessee, Knoxville. Song index. Compiled by Pauline S. Bayne and Patricia Barkalow. Knoxville: University of Tennessee Library, 1981. 30 microfiche and accompanying booklet.
   An index to songs in 554 anthologies with indexes to song titles, composers, genres, language of texts, authors, geographic or ethnic sources, and performance forces.

String Ensemble

1411. Altmann, Wilhelm. Kleiner Führer durch die Streichquartette für Haus und Schule.... Berlin/Halensee: Deutscher Musikliteratur-Verlag, [1950]. 166 p.

An abridgement of the author's *Handbuch für Streichquartettspieler* (no. 1314), concentrating on the classical literature for the ensemble and ignoring all post-Brahms works.

1412. Farish, Margaret K. String music in print. 2nd ed. New York: R. R. Bowker, 1973. 464 p.

First printed in 1964 by Bowker (420 p.) and supplemented in 1968 (204 p.). Reprint in 1980 for Musicdata, who published a supplement to this edition, vol. 6 in the Musicdata *Music in Print* series; see no. 1204.

The work was first published in a "preliminary" edition in 1963.

The work is

> ... a guide to published music for the violin, viola, violoncello and double-bass. It contains information on solo music, accompanied and unaccompanied; chamber music, including combinations of stringed instruments with wind instruments, keyboard instruments, harp, guitar, percussion and voice; methods and studies. [Author's *Preface*]

Arrangement is alphabetical by composer within each category; composer's dates given. Brief titles, with instrumentation. Publishers indicated by symbols, with a comprehensive list of publishers.

Review of the preliminary edition by Joel H. Berman in *Notes*, 20 (1963), p. 229; of the 1965 edition by Katherine Holum in *Journal of Research in Music Education*, 13 (1965), p. 190–91; of the *Supplement* to the 1st ed. by Dena J. Epstein in *Notes*, 25 (1969), p. 746; of the 2nd ed. (1973) by Boris Schwarz in *Notes*, 30 (1974), p. 60–61.

1413. Grünberg, Max. Führer durch die Literatur der Streichinstrumente ... Kritisches, progressiv geordnetes Repertorium von instruktiven Solo- und Ensemble-Werken.... Leipzig: Breitkopf & Härtel, 1913. 218 p. (Handbücher der Musiklehre ... hrsg. von X. Scharwenka, 10)

Reprinted by Martin Sändig, Niederwalluf bei Wiesbaden, 1971.

A listing of music for violin, viola, cello, and ensemble from the Baroque through the 19th century classified according to genre and degree of difficulty. Publishers and prices indicated. Bibliography, p. 207–209. Index.

Violin

1414. Basart, Ann P. "Finding string music." In *Cum Notis Variorum*, 57 (November 1981), p. 6–16.

An annotated, indexed checklist of bibliographies of string music for performance.

1415. Baudet-Maget, A. Guide du violoniste; œuvres choisies pour violon, ainsi que pour alto et musique de chambre, classées d'après leur degré de difficulté. Lausanne, Paris, [etc.]: Foetisch Frères, [n.d.]. 295 p.

Selective list of violin, viola, and string ensemble music from mid-17th century to the present. Classified according to genre and degree of difficulty.

Farish, Margaret K. String music in print. See no. 1412.

1416. Feinland, Alexander. The combination violin and violoncello without accompaniment. [Paramaribo, Surinam: Printed by J. H. Oliviera, 1944.] 121 p.
Classified catalog, including manuscripts, of music from the Baroque to the present. Original publisher or location given. Biographical sketches of the composers represented.
See also no. 1417.

1417. Iotti, Oscar Raoul. Violin and violoncello in duo without accompaniment based on the work by Alexander Feinland. Detroit, Michigan: Information Coordinators, 1972. 73 p. (Detroit studies in music bibliography, 25)
A bibliography based on Feinland's *The Combination Violin and Violoncello without Accompaniment* (no. 1416).

1418. Letz, Hans. Music for violin and viola. New York: Rinehart, [1948]. 107 p. (The field of music, 2)
Selective, graded list of music for unaccompanied violin, or violin and piano (p. 1–94); followed by a similar list of music for the viola (p. 96–107).

1419. Loft, Abram. Violin and keyboard: the duo repertoire. New York: Grossman, 1973. 2 v.

> This book is for players [of violin sonatas] who want to know about music that they can read, rehearse, and perform.... It is for those who want some guidance as to the type of music in question, its difficulty, what particular points of interest it has, and how it can be approached in performance. [*Preface*]

Vol. 1, from the seventeenth century to Mozart; vol. 2, from Beethoven to the present.
Not a bibliography, but extensive critical commentary on the corpus of violin sonata music. There is a bibliography at the end of vol. 1 and a list of editions used at the end of vol. 2.

1420. Toskey, Burnett R. Concertos for violin and viola, a comprehensive encyclopedia. Seattle, Washington: B. R. Toskey, 1983. 992 p.
".... a listing of more than 8,400 concertos for a solo violin or viola." In addition to information on the composer and the music, a descriptive review is provided for most works. Numerous indexes and a bibliography.

1421. Tottmann, Albert. Führer durch die Violin-Literatur.... 4. wesentlich vervollständigte, bis auf die Gegenwart seit 1901 fortgeführte und neu bearbeitete Auflage von Wilhelm Altmann. Leipzig: J. Schuberth, 1935. 472 p.
Title varies: first published as *Führer durch den Violin-Unterricht*, 1873; 2nd ed., 1886; 3rd ed., 1902.

Classified bibliography including etudes, solo or accompanied violin works, duos, trios, quartets, etc., for violins. Gives full bibliographical information and brief critical comments. Supplements Altmann's *Kammermusik-Katalog* (no. 1315) for solo works.

Viola

1422. Altmann, Wilhelm and W. Borissowsky. Literaturverzeichnis für Bratsche und Viola d'amore. Wolfenbüttel: Verlag für musikalische Kultur und Wissenschaft, 1937. 148 p.

Classified catalog, including solo works, duos, and other combinations in which the viola has the leading role. Lists some works in manuscript and all known editions of published works, with dates. Includes transcriptions as well as original works.

1423. Drüner, Ulrich. "Das Viola-Konzert vor 1840." In *Fontes Artis Musicae*, 28 (1981), p. 153–76.

A bibliography documenting the development of the viola concerto in its first stage. Works of 141 composers are listed, and locations of the sources given.

1424. Ewald, Konrad. Musik für Bratsche, Führer durch die heute Zugängliche Literatur für Viola. Liestal, Switzerland: Printed for the author, 1975. 153 p.

Arranged by composer in three broad chronological sections. Each chronological division is divided into a section in which the music is discussed and another in which it is just listed. Includes publication information. Classified index to performing forces and an index to composers.

Farish, Margaret K. String music in print. See no. 1412.

1425. Williams, Michael D. Music for viola. Detroit, Michigan: Information Coordinators, 1979. 362 p. (Detroit studies in music bibliography, 42)

A classified bibliography attempting to be comprehensive. Provides complete bibliographic information for each work cited.

Review by Ann M. Woodward in *Fontes Artis Musicae*, 27 (1980), p. 237–38.

1426. Zeyringer, Franz. Literatur für Viola: Verzeichnis der Werke für Viola-Solo, Duos mit Viola, Trios mit Viola, Viola-Solo mit Begleitung, Blockflöte mit Viola, Gesang mit Viola und der Schul- und Studienwerke für Viola. Literature for viola: catalogue of works for viola solo, duos with viola, trios with viola, solo viola with accompaniment, recorder with viola, voice with viola, and methods, etudes and exercises for viola. Neue, erw. Ausg. Hartberg, Austria: J. Schönwetter Jun., 1985. 446 p.

First published in 1963. 151 p. Supplement published in 1965. 82 p. 2nd edition published in 1976. 418 p.

Indexes of publishers and composers.

Violoncello

Farish, Margaret K. String music in print. See no. 1412.

1427. Kenneson, Claude. Bibliography of cello ensemble music. Detroit, Michigan: Information Coordinators, 1974. 59 p. (Detroit studies in music bibliography, 31)
Cites works for cello music for two cellos to orchestra works, including works with piano. Classified.

1428. Nogué, Edouard. La littérature du violoncelle ... Préface de M. Paul Bazelaire.... Paris: Delagrave, 1925. 151 p.
Lists nearly 2,000 works for violoncello, solo or with other instruments. Classified and graded, with short descriptions of most of the works. Publishers indicated.

1429. Weigl, Bruno. Handbuch der Violoncell-Literatur; systematisch geordnetes Verzeichnis der solo- und instruktiven Werke.... 3. Auflage. Wien: Universal-Edition, 1929. 357 p.
Classified listing of compositions of cello and orchestra, cello and piano, cello solo, or accompanied by other instruments. Comparable in arrangement and content to his *Handbuch der Orgelliteratur* (no. 1350).

Double Bass

Farish, Margaret K. String music in print. See no. 1412.

1430. Grodner, Murray. Comprehensive catalogue of available literature for the double bass. 3rd ed. Bloomington, Indiana: Lemur Musical Research, 1974. 169 p.
First published in 1958. 2nd edition, 1964. 84 p.
Lists works in print, 1974. Solos and ensembles for from 2 to 14 instruments, using string bass. Each entry gives composer, title, instrumentation, grade of difficulty, publisher, price, with occasional annotations as to availability. A short bibliography of works about the bass and bass playing. Index of names.
Review of the first edition by Darius Thieme in *Notes*, 16 (1969), p. 258.

1431. Planyavsky, Alfred. Geschichte des Kontrabasses. 2., wesentlich erw. Aufl. unter der Mitarbeit von Herbert Seifert. Tutzing: Hans Schneider, 1984. 917 p.
First printed in 1970. 537 p.
Primarily a historical study of the string bass from the 16th century to the present—its construction, technique, and repertoire.
P. 433–506: classified catalog of string bass music, treating the instrument as solo and in a variety of ensembles. The work also contains a bibliography of relevant literature, a discography of string bass music, and an index of names and subjects.

Viols

1432. De Smet, Robin. Published music for the viola da gamba and other viols. Detroit, Michigan: Information Coordinators, 1971. 105 p. (Detroit studies in music bibliography, 18)

Classified lists of works for viols alone and in consort, and for viols with other instruments. Entries show instrumentation, editor, publisher, and publisher's numbers. Bibliography of collected works for viols. List of publishers. Bibliography of sources consulted. Composer index.

1433. Dodd, Gordon. Thematic index of music for viols. Viola da Gamba Society of Great Britain, 1980–82. 2 v.

Third installment issued in 1984.

The intent of the index is to provide thematic incipits and locations in manuscript sources of music for viols by British composers or found mainly in British sources. Each installment includes a list of entries, a bibliography, and, for each composer, a brief essay on style. There are frequent remarks on the sources.

See the brief article by Gordon Dodd on the genesis of the *Index* in *Fontes Artis Musicae*, 25 (1978), p. 239–42.

Wind Ensemble and Band

1434. American Music Center. Library. Music for orchestra, band and large ensemble. New York: American Music Center, 1982. 196 p. (Catalog of the American Music Center Library, 3)

A catalog of the holdings of large instrumental ensemble music by American composers in the American equivalent of a national music information center.

1435. Band music guide: alphabetical listing of titles and composers of all band music. 8th ed. Evanston, Illinois: Instrumentalist Co., 1982. 408 p.

The 7th edition appeared in 1978. 367 p.

An attempt at a comprehensive listing intended to aid school band directors in the United States in program preparation.

1436. Heller, George N. Ensemble music for wind and percussion instruments: a catalog. Washington, D.C.: Music Educators' National Conference, 1970. 142 p.

1437. Helm, Sanford Marion. Catalog of chamber music for wind instruments. Revised reprint. New York: Da Capo Press, 1969. 85 p.

First printed in 1952 at Ann Arbor, Michigan.

Chamber music for from 3 to 12 instruments employing at least one wind instrument, classified according to the size of the ensemble and instrumentation. Gives publisher, date, American agent for currently available editions. Composer index.

1438. Reynolds, H. Robert. Wind ensemble literature. 2nd ed. Madison: University of Wisconsin Bands, 1975. 174 p. (various pagings)

A repertory list in four parts: compositions for wind ensemble/symphonic band; compositions for solo instruments, voice, or narrator with wind ensemble/symphonic band; chorus or choruses with wind ensemble/ symphonic band; addendum, including works for which the editors had incomplete information. Each section is organized alphabetically by composer and includes a code for instrumentation, publication information, and references to selected recorded performances.

1439. Selective music list for band. Rev. ed. Nashville, Tennessee: National Band Association, 1986. 71 p.
  A bibliography of band music.

1440. Suppan, Armin. Repertorium der Märsche für Blasorchester. Tutzing: H. Schneider, 1982. 346 p. (Alta musica, 6)
  An alphabetical listing by composer giving titles and publishers of marches. Index to titles. A second volume is projected.

1441. Wallace, David and Eugene Corporon. Wind ensemble/band repertoire. Greeley: University of Northern Colorado School of Music, 1984. 248 p. (not continuously paged)
  A broadly classified list citing composer, title, instrumentation, and, by reference, publisher. Includes work for voice and wind ensemble/band. There is a list of composers and their addresses, but no index.

1442. Whitwell, David. Band music of the French revolution. Tutzing: Schneider, 1979. 212 p. (Alta musica, 5)
  A history with an extensive bibliography and a thematic catalog.

1443. Whitwell, David. The history and literature of the wind band and wind ensemble. Northridge, California: Winds, 1982–84. 9 v.
  Contents:
  Vol. 1. *The Wind Band and Wind Ensemble before 1500.*
  Vol. 2. *The Renaissance Wind Band and Wind Ensemble.*
  Vol. 3. *The Baroque Wind Band and Wind Ensemble.*
  Vol. 4. *The Wind Band and Wind Ensemble of the Classic Period, 1750–1800.*
  Vol. 5. *The Nineteenth Century Wind Band and Wind Ensemble in Western Europe.*
  Vol. 6. *A Catalog of Multi-part Instrumental Music for Wind Instruments or for Undesignated Instrumentation before 1600.*
  Vol. 7. *A Catalog of Baroque Multi-part Instrumental Music for Wind Instruments or for Undesignated Instrumentation.*
  Vol. 8. *Wind Band and Wind Ensemble Literature of the Classic Period.*
  Vol. 9. *Wind Band and Wind Ensemble Literature of the Nineteenth Century.*
  A monumental history and bibliography.
  Review by Kerry S. Grant in *Notes*, 41 (1984), p. 61–62.

1444. Ziegenrücker, Wieland. Literaturberater Blasmusik: e. Wegweiser bei d. Repertoire- u. Programmgestaltung auf d. Grundlage d. Notenausg. d. Musikverlage d. DDR. Leipzig: Zentralhaus für Kulturarbeit der DDR, 1975. 74 p.
  A guide to the repertory and bibliography of music for bands and wind

ensembles available in the former Deutsche Demokratische Republik (East Germany).

Flute

1445. Bowers, Jane. "A catalogue of French works for the transverse flute, 1692–1761." In *Recherches sur la Musique Française Classique*, 18 (1978), p. 89–125. Paris: Éditions A. et J. Picard, 1978.

1446. Girard, Adrien. Histoire et richesse de la flûte. Paris: Libraire Gründ, 1953. 143 p.

A handsome, illustrated volume printed in an edition of 1,500 copies. Chapter IV, "Les flûtistes," lists the principal performers from the 15th to the 20th centuries, with brief comments on each. Chapter V, "Littérature," is a chronological listing of the important composers of flute music with their works, from Louis Couperin to the present, followed by an alphabetical listing, by composer, of works for solo flute accompanied by keyboard, harp, or orchestra. Manuscript works included.

Kongelige Bibliothek. Catalogue of Giedde's music collection in the Royal Library of Copenhagen. See no. 1984.

1447. Pellerite, James J. A handbook of literature for the flute (a list of graded method materials, solos, and ensemble music for the flute). Bloomington, Indiana: Zalo Publications, 1978. 408 p.

First published in 1963. 96 p.

This listing of flute literature is specifically designed to familiarize the music teachers, music educators, and students of the flute with a portion of available materials presently appearing in publishers' catalogs. [*Foreword* to the 1963 edition]

Graded and annotated.

1448. Pierreuse, Bernard. Flûte littérature; catalogue général des œuvres édités et inédités par formations instrumentales. General catalog of published and unpublished works by instrumental category. Paris: Éditions Musicales Transatlantiques, 1982. 670 p.

An international catalog with a composer index, a list of publishers, and a list of major libraries.

1449. Vester, Frans. Flute music of the 18th century, an annotated bibliography. Monteux: Musica Rara, 1985. 573 p.

Entries include information on location of works, when known. As with the *Flute Repertoire Catalogue* (1967) (no. 1450), there are indexes to the composer listing arranged by performing forces. This work omits music including voice, studies, method and instruction books, literature about the flute, and a list of publishers.

1450. Vester, Frans. Flute repertoire catalogue. 10,000 titles. London: Musica Rara, 1967. 383 p.

Lists music for flute alphabetically under composer, with indexes directing the user to music for flute in combination with other instruments and with orchestra and voice. There is a short bibliography of literature on the flute and a listing of publishers of flute music.

1451. Wilkins, Wayne. The index of flute music including the index of Baroque trio sonatas. Magnolia, Arkansas: Music Register, 1974. 131 p.
Supplements issued in 1975 (25 p.) and 1978 (14 p.).
Classified lists of works citing composer and publisher.

Oboe

1452. Bigotti, Giovanni. Storia dell'oboe e sua letteratura. Padova: G. Zanibon, 1974. 77 p.
Historical survey of the instrument in its varied forms. Brief entries, alphabetical by composer, classified by instrumentation.

1453. Gifford, Virginia Snodgrass. Music for oboe, oboe d'amore, and English horn; a bibliography of materials in the Library of Congress. Westport, Connecticut: Greenwood, 1983. 431 p. (Music reference collection, 1)
A bibliography of cataloged and uncataloged holdings at the Library of Congress. Essentially a locating device for the Library's holdings in specified classes. Includes a detailed table of contents, an index of publishers, an index of instruments, and an index of composers.

1454. Haynes, Bruce. Music for oboe, 1650–1800: a bibliography. Berkeley, California: Fallen Leaf Press, 1985. 394 p. (Fallen Leaf reference books in music, 4)
"This book is a complete revision of Music for oboe to 1800 (interim edition, June 1982) published privately by the author" in The Hague, 1980. 65 p.
Covers over 9,400 pieces for oboe, oboe d'amore, and F-oboe in printed and manuscript editions. Also lists chamber music up to eight parts, concertos with up to three solo parts, vocal music with obbligato oboe parts, and oboe method books containing music. Cites lost works.
Arranged by composer, each entry includes title, key, opus and/or thematic index information, instrumentation, imprint, location of source, modern edition, and occasionally notes.

1455. Hošek, Miroslav. Katalog der Oboenliteratur tschechischer und slowakischer Autoren. Praha: Tschechoslowakischen Musikinformationszentrum, 1969. 89 p.
Alphabetical listing by composer of chamber works for oboe and as many as 13 other instruments. Concertos and other orchestral works featuring the oboe are also included. Indexes of libraries, publishers, and instrumental combinations.

1456. Hošek, Miroslav. Oboen-Bibliographie. 2. Aufl. bearb. von Rudolf H. Führer. Wilhelmshaven: Heinrichshofen, 1984. 403 p.
Essentially a reprint of the edition of 1975.

A bibliography of modern, published oboe music, international in scope. Includes a separate bibliography of oboe methods. Arranged alphabetically by composer, with an index by instrumentation, a list of publishers, and a short bibliography of works about the oboe.

1457. Wilkins, Wayne. The index of oboe music including the index of Baroque trio sonatas. Magnolia, Arkansas: Music Register, 1976. 96, 11 p.
Supplement issued in 1977 and 1978.
Classified lists of works for solo oboe and oboe in ensemble citing composer and publisher.

Clarinet

1458. Brixel, Eugen. Klarinetten-Bibliographie. 2. Aufl. Wilhelmshaven: Heinrichshofens Verlag, 1978. 493 p.
A classified listing, international in scope, citing composer, title, and publisher of music for solo clarinet and for clarinet as a member of an ensemble. There is a short bibliography of literature about the clarinet and an index to composers listed.

1459. Gee, Harry. Clarinet solos de concours, 1897–1980: an annotated bibliography. Bloomington: Indiana University Press, 1981. 118 p.
A bibliography of clarinet music approved by the Paris Conservatoire.

1460. Gillespie, James E., Jr. Solos for unaccompanied clarinet; an annotated bibliography of published works. Detroit, Michigan: Information Coordinators, 1973. 79 p. (Detroit studies in music bibliography, 28)
The annotations feature composers' comments on performance and include biographical information.

1461. Kroll, Oskar. The clarinet. Revised, and with a repertory by Diethard Riehm. Translated by Hilda Morris. New York: Taplinger Pub. Co., 1968. 183 p.
Translation of *Die Klarinette; ihre Geschichte, ihre Literatur, ihre grossen Meister.*
Bibliography: p. 133–35. "Repertory of the clarinet": p. 136–75.

1462. Opperman, Kalmen. Repertory of the clarinet. New York: Ricordi, [1960]. 140 p.
Classified index of music for the clarinet, including methods, etudes, and music for the instrument as solo and in combination with other instruments. List of publishers and a short bibliography of books on the clarinet.
Review by Roger P. Phelps in *Notes*, 18 (1960), p. 63–64.

1463. Tuthill, Burnet C. "The sonatas for clarinet and piano." In *Journal of Research in Music Education*, 14 (1966), p. 197–212.
An annotated listing of sonatas from the 18th century to the present. A few transcriptions and works in manuscript are included.

Bassoon

1464. Jansen, Will. The bassoon: its history, construction, makers, players, and music. Buren, The Netherlands: F. Knuf, 1978. 5 v.

An extensive work on all aspects of the bassoon, including a dictionary of bassoon makers, a chapter on the principal modern firm, Heckel, bibliographic studies of bassoon literature, bibliographical data on lesser-known composers for the instrument, and lists of music for bassoon in order by composer. There is a biographical dictionary of bassoonists of the past and present. Discography. The table of contents appears in vol. 2 and there is an index to names in vol. 4. Although there is an enormous quantity of information in this work, it is difficult to locate. Most of the text does not cite sources. Vol. 5 is devoted entirely to illustrations.

1465. Langwill, Lyndesay Graham. The bassoon and the contrabassoon. London: E. Benn; New York: W. W. Norton, [1965]. 269 p.

A history of the development of the bassoon and contrabassoon with a list of solo music for each and a discography. Numerous bibliographical footnotes.

1466. Risdon, Howard. Musical literature for the bassoon; a compilation of music for the bassoon as an instrument in ensemble. Seattle, Washington: Berdon, [1963]. 24 p.

1467. Wilkins, Wayne. The index of bassoon music including the index of Baroque trio sonatas. Magnolia, Arkansas: Music Register, 1976. 76, 11 p.

Supplements published in 1976–77 and 1978.

Classified lists of works citing composer and publisher.

Horn

1468. Brüchle, Bernhard. Horn Bibliographie. Wilhelmshaven: Heinrichshofen, 1970–83. 3 v.

First volume published with a 14-page supplement of plates.

Entries classified according to ensembles: horn solo, horn and keyboard, various duo combinations, trios, quartets, etc. The work contains a bibliography of literature on the instrument, list of publishers, and index of names.

1469. Gregory, Robin. The horn, a comprehensive guide to the modern instrument and its music. New York: Praeger, 1969. 410 p.

First printed in 1961 in London.

P. 181–393: Appendix C. A list of music for the horn. A classified list of music for horn solo or in combination with various ensembles, instrumental or vocal. Entries give composer, title, ensemble, and publisher.

Recorder

1470. Alker, Hugo. Blockflöten-Bibliographie. Neuausgabe. Wilhelmshaven: Heinrichshofen's Verlag, 1984. 2 v.

1st edition published 1960 with a supplement appearing in 1961. 2nd edition appeared in 1966 and was supplemented in 1969.

Band I: Systematischer Teil.

Band II: Alphabetischer Teil.

Band I includes a classified listing by composer and title with imprint of music for recorder. There is a section devoted to articles about performance practice and other works relating to the recorder.

Band II contains an alphabetical index to composers in Band I and a list of publishers' names and addresses.

1471. McCowan, Richard A. Italian Baroque solo sonatas for the recorder and the flute. Detroit, Michigan: Information Coordinators, 1978. 70 p. (Detroit studies in music bibliography, 37)

In two sections, the first listing and describing 18th-century manuscripts and editions and the second containing modern editions.

1472. Winterfeld, Linde H. von and Harald Kunz. Handbuch der Blockflöten-Literatur. Berlin and Wiesbaden: Bote & Bock, 1959. 139 p.

Listings of music for recorder: solo, ensemble, and in combination with other instruments. Publisher and price given. Composer and title index, and a short list of books on the recorder.

Saxophone

1473. Londeix, Jean-Marie. 125 ans de musique pour saxophone. Répertoire général des œuvres et des ouvrages d'enseignement pour le saxophone. 125 years of music for the saxophone. General repertory of pieces and educational literature for the saxophone. Paris: Alphonse Leduc, 1971. 398 p.

A general listing of works involving saxophone by composer, followed by indexes under individual instruments (soprano, alto, tenor, baritone) and by ensembles. Composers are identified, and rather full biographical information, with critical quotations, is given for major composers. Supplementary lists of addresses for composers and publishers of saxophone music.

1474. Wilkins, Wayne. The index of saxophone music. Magnolia, Arkansas: Music Register, 1979. 59 p.

Classified lists of works for saxophone and for saxophone in ensembles citing composer and publisher.

Brass Instruments (Solo and Chamber)

1475. Anderson, Paul G. Brass ensemble music guide. Evanston, Illinois: Instrumentalist Co., 1978. 259 p.

Classified lists with brief titles and publisher codes. Composer index.

1476. Anderson, Paul G. and Larry Bruce Campbell. Brass music guide: solo and study guide material in print. 1985 edition. Northfield, Illinois: Instrumentalist Co., 1984. 294 p.

First published as *Brass Solo and Study Material Music Guide*, 1976. There is a 1987 edition with 345 p.
Classified lists with brief titles and publisher codes. Composer index.

1477. Arling, Harry J. Trombone chamber music; an annotated bibliography. 2nd ed., rev. and enl. Nashville, Tennessee: Brass Press, 1983. 43 p.
First published in 1978.
The majority of works cited in this guide were composed in the 20th century. Most of the works cited involve trombone as the only brass instrument.
Reviewed by Peter B. Brown in *Notes*, 36 (1979), p. 103–104.

1478. Bell, William J. and R. Winston Morris. Encyclopedia of literature for the tuba. New York: C. Colin, 1967. 161 p.
A bibliography of tuba music and music for the tuba.

1479. Cansler, Philip T. Twentieth century music for trumpet and organ: an annotated bibliography. Nashville, Tennessee: Brass Press, 1984. 46 p. (Brass research series, 11)
Catalog and description of 83 compositions. Each entry gives a short biography of the composer and a critical interpretation of the work. Lists of pieces by nationality of composer. Bibliography of sources consulted.

1480. Carnovale, Norbert. Twentieth-century music for trumpet and orchestra; an annotated bibliography. Nashville, Tennessee: Brass Press, 1975. 55 p. (Brass research series, 3)
A guide to 179 works with imprint information, duration, range, and reviews cited.
Briefly reviewed by Stephen M. Fry in *Notes*, 32 (1976), p. 780.

1481. Decker, Richard G. A bibliography of music for three heterogeneous brass instruments alone and in chamber ensembles. Oneonta, New York: Swift-Dorr Publications, 1976. 82 p.

1482. Devol, John. Brass music for the church; a bibliography of music appropriate for church use. New York: H. Branch, 1974. 102 p.
Lists "a total of 1,309 works, including brass parts for one trumpet up to a twenty-piece brass choir."

1483. Everett, Thomas G. Annotated guide to bass trombone literature. 3rd ed., rev. and enl. Nashville, Tennessee: Brass Press, 1985. 94 p. (Brass research series, 6)
1st edition published in 1973; 2nd edition, 1978.
726 entries of published and manuscript music. Bibliography, list of recordings, index to composers.
Review by Peter B. Brown in *Notes*, 36 (1979), p. 103–104.

1484. Morris, R. Winston. Tuba music guide. Evanston, Illinois: Instrumentalist Co., 1973. 60 p.
A classified and annotated bibliography of solo and chamber music for the tuba.

Electronic and Computer Music

1485. Davies, Hugh. Répertoire international des musiques electroacous-tiques. International electronic music catalog. A cooperative publication of le Groupe de recherches musicales de l'O.R.T.F., Paris, and the Independent Electronic Music Center, New York. Cambridge, Mass.: distributed by M.I.T. Press, 1968. 330 p. (*Electronic Music Review,* nos. 2/3, April/July 1967)
Text in French and English.

> The aim of this new catalog is to document all the electronic music ever composed in the almost 20 years since composers first began to work in this media. [from the introductory remarks]

Main alphabet is by country, subdivided by city (and state, if in U.S.A.). Gives data on composers, titles of work, functions, dates of composition, duration, and number of tape tracks involved.
Some 5,000 compositions listed. Appendixes include a discography, a directory of permanent studies, and an index of composers.
Review by Jon Appleton in *Notes,* 25 (1968), p. 34–35.

1486. Melby, Carol, comp. Computer music compositions of the United States, 1976. Prepared for the first International Conference on Computer Music, 28–31 October 1976, Massachusetts Institute of Technology. 2nd ed. Urbana, Illinois: 1976. 28 p.
First ed. prepared for the Music Computation Conference II, held at the University of Illinois at Urbana-Champaign, 7–9 November 1975. 42 p.

1487. Storey, Cheryl Ewing. A bibliography of computer music. Denton, Texas: North Texas State University Music Library, 1981. 41 p.
"Compiled for the North Texas State University Music Library and the International Computer Music conference held at NTSU November 5–8, 1981." Includes a discography.

Wind Instruments (Chamber)

1488. Basart, Ann P. "Bibliographies of wind music: a check-list." In *Cum Notis Variorum,* 37 (November 1979), p. 10–13, and 39 (February 1980), p. 9–13.
An annotated checklist to bibliographies providing information on music for wind instruments.

1489. Chapman, James, Sheldon Fine and Mary Rasmussen. "Music for wind instruments in historical editions, collected works, and numbered series: a bibliography." In *Brass and Woodwind Quarterly,* 1 (1968), p. 115–49, and 2 (1969), p. 17–58.
Part I: Music, without voices, for specified instrumentations with basso continuo.
Part II: Music with voices, for specified instrumentation.
Part III: Music without voices, for unspecified instrumentation.
Part IV: Music with voices, for unspecified instrumentation.
Indexes 42 collected editions of early music and series.

1490. Gillespie, James E. The reed trio: an annotated bibliography of original published works. Detroit, Michigan: Information Coordinators, 1971. 84 p. (Detroit studies in music bibliography, 20)

1491. Hošek, Miroslav. Das Bläserquintett. The woodwind quintet [Englisch von Colleen Gruban]. Grünwald: B. Brüchle, 1979. 234 p.
Bibliography of woodwind quintets by categories. Essays on origin, acoustics, and performance practice. Bibliography. Lists of personnel in professional woodwind quintets.

1492. Houser, Roy. Catalogue of chamber music for woodwind instruments. 2nd ed. Bloomington: Indiana University, 1960. 158 leaves (typescript).
Reprinted by Da Capo, 1973.
Supplement: *Woodwind Ensembles Bibliography.*
Material for from 3 to 10 instruments, classified according to ensemble. P. 147–48: a list of woodwind music found in the Moravian archives at Winston-Salem, North Carolina, and at Bethlehem, Pennsylvania. p. 152–55: selected publications from the catalog of the Donemus Foundation, Amsterdam.

1493. National Association of Schools of Music. Solo literature for the wind instruments. *Bulletin of the National Association of Schools of Music*, 31 (1951). 32 p.
Lists of solos, including concertos, for flute, oboe, clarinet, bassoon, French horn, cornet and trumpet, trombone. Graded as to difficulty; brief critical or descriptive annotations. Publishers indicated.

1494. Peters, Harry B. The literature of the woodwind quintet. Metuchen, New Jersey: Scarecrow Press, 1971. 174 p.
A basic listing of woodwind quintet music, followed by a section on the quintet with one, two, three, four, or five additional performers.

1495. Rasmussen, Mary. A teacher's guide to the literature of brass instruments. Durham, New Hampshire: Brass Quarterly, 1964. 84 p.
General discussion of music available for brass ensembles and solos, followed by extensive listings giving publisher, price, instrumentation, and grade level of the works cited.

1496. Rasmussen, Mary and Donald Mattran. A teacher's guide to the literature of woodwind instruments. Durham, New Hampshire: Brass and Woodwind Quarterly, 1966. 226 p.
Bibliographies of woodwind music for solos or ensembles.

1497. Voxman, Himie and Lyle Merriman. Woodwind music guide, solo and study material in print. 1984 ed. Evanston, Illinois: Instrumentalist Co., 1984. 499 p. (Music guide series, 3)
Updated edition of *Woodwind Solo and Study Material Music Guide,* 1975.
Classified list with brief titles and publisher codes.

Percussion

Bajzek, Dieter. Percussion: an annotated bibliography. See no. 931.

1498. Combs, F. Michael. Solo and ensemble literature for percussion. Knoxville, Tennessee: Percussive Arts Society, 1978. 93 leaves.

Originally published in 1967, reissued in enlarged form in 1972, and supplemented in 1976.

A classified list of music for various percussion instruments. Includes information on publishers and sources.

Lute, Vihuella, Guitar, and Other Plectoral

1499. Gilmore, George and Mark Pereira. Guitar music index: a cross-indexed and graded listing of music in print for classical guitar and lute. Honolulu, Hawaii: Galliard Press, 1976–81. 2 v.

1500. International Music Service. A catalog of music for the harp.... New York: International Music Service, 1981. 1 v. (unpaged loose-leaf)

A distributor's catalog.

1501. Moser, Wolf. Gitarre-Musik; ein internationaler Katalog. Hamburg: Joachim Trekel-Der Volksmusikverlag, 1974–77. 2 v.

A classified list by performing forces, with separate sectors for etudes, collections, books about the guitar, and Flamenco guitar music. There is a composer index. Vol. 2 supplements vol. 1.

1502. Ragossnig, Konrad. Handbuch der Gitarre und Laute. Mainz: Schott, 1978. 256 p.

A brief and superficial bibliography appended to a work intended to inform students of the instruments. Valuable comments upon editions of music.

Review by Thomas F. Heck in *Notes*, 36 (1979), p. 107–108.

1503. Rensch, Roslyn. The harp; its history, technique and repertoire. New York: Praeger Publishers, 1969. 246 p.

A historical monograph with discographies and bibliographies.

1504. Rezits, Joseph. The guitarist's resource guide: guitar music in print and books on the art of guitar. San Diego: Pallma Music Co., distributed by N. A. Kjos Music Co., 1983. 574 p.

Includes sections on lute, mandolin, and vihuela music. Each section has a composer and title index. The guitar section is further subdivided by performing forces.

1505. Rudén, Jan Olof. Music in tablature: a thematic index with source descriptions of music in tablature notation in Sweden. Stockholm: Svenskt musikhistoriskt arkiv, 1981. 257 p. (Musik i Sverige, 5. Music in Sweden, 5)

One of the first national catalogs of music in tablature. Includes bibliographical references and index.

1506. Zingel, Hans Joachim. Harfenmusik; Verzeichnis der gedruckten und zur Zeit greifbaren Literatur für Pedalharfe. Harp music. Musique de la harpe. Harp muziek. Musica per arpa. Hofheim am Taunus: F. Hofmeister, 1965. 35 p.

1507. Zingel, Hans Joachim. Harfenmusik im 19. Jahrhundert: Versuch einer historischen Darstellung. Wilhelmshaven: Heinrichshofen, 1976. 95 p. (Veröffentlichungen zur Musikforschung, 2)

A historical monograph with bibliographical references.
362

JAZZ AND POPULAR MUSIC

The study of jazz and popular music (including film music) as well as popular culture is beginning to permeate academic curricula. There is an international scholarly society devoted to it, the International Association for the Study of Popular Music, and that society produces a journal, *Popular Music Perspectives*. Still, popular music reference works by and large continue to be the product of the work of dedicated amateurs. Roger Kinkle's *Complete Encyclopedia of Popular Music and Jazz* (no. 250) and the *Encyclopedia of the Musical Theatre* (no. 466) by Stanley Green are good examples what is being produced. In the 20th century, popular music has come to mean "mass-disseminated music" and is really distinct from "folk music" and other "music of the people."

Jazz has become a fully accepted scholarly specialty and bibliographical resources have expanded concomitantly. Some of the principal items in this area are listed below. Others will be found in the section on "Dictionaries and Encyclopedias," e.g., Leonard Feather's *The Encyclopedia of Jazz* (nos. 240, 241, and 242) and *The New Grove Dictionary of Jazz* (no. 253). Others are cited under "Collectors' Guides to Jazz Recordings" (nos. 2803 ff.).

1508. Anderson, Gillian B. Music for silent films, 1894–1929: a guide. With a foreword by Eileen Bowser. Washington, D.C.: Library of Congress, 1988. 182 p.

> The purpose of this work is to provide a guide for locating scores and musical cue sheets made for films of the silent era, 1894–1929. An essay about the nature, history, and presentation of the musical accompaniments for silent films provides the context for these artifacts. The guide follows the introductory essay. All the entries are for microfilmed items found in the Library of Congress (LC) and the Museum of Modern Art (MOMA) music collections. MOMA's collection is on permanent loan to the Library's Music Division. [from the introductory remarks]

The guide is organized alphabetically by film title. Entries include information on the author and/or literary source, producer, director, film company, composer, publisher and imprint of music, instrumentation, copyright data, projection time and film footage, LC or MOMA call number, collation, and microfilm and item numbers. Appendixes list materials found at the Kleiner Collection at the University of Minnesota, the Eastman House in Rochester, New York, and the Fédération International des Archives du Film in Brussels, Belgium. "The index is to names and titles found on the LC and MOMA scores and cue sheets, and consequently in the guide as well." There is an extensive bibliography and there are a number of illustrations.

See also Wescott (no. 737) for a bibliography on film music.

1509. Brooks, Elston. I've heard those songs before; the weekly top ten tunes for the past 50 years. New York: Morrow Quill, 1981. 444 p.

Titles of the most played popular songs on American radio in chronological order with an index to titles cited.

1510. Burton, Jack. The blue book of Tin Pan Alley, a human interest encyclopedia of American popular music. Expanded new edition. Vol. 1: 1776–1860–1910; Vol 2: 1910–1960, with a 1950–1965 supplement by Larry Freeman. Watkins Glen, New York: Century House, 1962–65. 2 v.

First published in 1951.

The approach is chronological, with detailed listings of songs by the principal popular composers. Covers jazz and its musicians as well as popular music.

See also nos. 449 and 450.

1511. Burton, Jack. The index of American popular music; thousands of titles cross-referenced to our basic anthologies of popular songs. Watkins Glen, New York: Century House, 1957. 1 v.

Titles indexed: 1. *Blue Book of Tin Pan Alley.* 2. *Blue Book of Broadway Musicals.* 3. *Blue Book of Hollywood Musicals.* 4. *The Melodies Linger on.* This work brings together the song indexes from the several "Blue Books."

1512. Chipman, John H. Index to top-hit tunes (1900–1950) ... with a foreword by Arthur Fiedler. Boston, Massachusetts: Bruce Humphries, [1962]. 249 p.

An alphabetical index, by title, of the most popular American songs of the first half of the 20th century. Gives key, composer and author, publisher and original publication date, source in film or musical comedy. Chronological index, short bibliography.

Cooper, B. Lee, Resource guide to themes in contemporary American song lyrics. See no. 2823.

1513. 80 years of American song hits 1892–1972. A comprehensive yearly reference book listing America's major hit songs and their writers. Chappel, 1973. 106 p.

A chronological list of song hits as determined by radio "play." Cites authors and composers or performers.

1514. Ewen, David. American popular songs: from the Revolutionary War to the present. New York: Random House, 1966. 507 p.

Provides information on more than 3,600 songs popular in America from

1775 to 1966. Cites composer, lyricist, place, medium, and date, including the performer who made the song popular.
Review by Ruth Hilton in *Notes*, 24 (1968), p. 501.

1515. Folio-Dex II: choral, orchestral, band. Loomis, California: Folio-Dex Co., 1980– . 1 v. (loose-leaf)
"Index of all types of music (popular, classical, sacred, etc.) ... listing ... those songs that are published for choral, band and orchestra music." Updated by revised and new loose-leaf pages.

1516. Fuld, James J. American popular music (reference book) 1875–1950. Philadelphia, Pennsylvania: Musical Americana, 1955. 94 p.
Supplement.... 1956. 9 p.
A bibliography of some 250 selected American popular songs. Detailed information as to first printing, copyright date, description of cover. 20 plates of song covers. An interesting attempt to approach American popular song with the methods of descriptive bibliography.

1517. Fuld, James J. The book of world-famous music; classical, popular and folk. 3rd ed., rev. and enlarged. New York: Dover, 1985. 714 p.
First published in 1966; 2nd edition published in 1971.
Considerable new information has been incorporated in this new edition of a work that traces the lineage, in printing or manuscript, of the most familiar ("world-famous") compositions of the Western world. A thematic index with detailed commentary on sources, composers, history. An admirable exercise in bibliography.
Not all of the author's revisions could be incorporated in the main body of the text, so there is a supplement section beginning on p. 669 keyed by symbols to the main text. Index to names and titles.
Review of the 1966 edition by Ruth Hilton in *Notes*, 23 (1966), p. 56–57.
Review of the 1971 edition by Nyal Williams in *Notes*, 29 (1973), p. 448–49.

1518. Gargan, William and Sue Sharma. Find that tune; an index to rock, folk-rock, disco and soul in collections. New York: Neal-Shumann, 1984. 303 p.
A second volume was published in 1988. 387 p.
An index to over 4,000 songs in 203 published collections of rock, folk-rock, soul, and disco music from 1950–81. List of collections indexed. Title index including information on composer and lyricist, performers, publisher, and copyright date. Index to first lines. Index to composers and lyricists. Index to performers.
Review by Norma Jean Lamb in *Notes*, 41 (1984), p. 286–87.

1519. Havlice, Patricia Pate. Popular song index. Metuchen, New Jersey: Scarecrow Press, 1978. 933 p.
First supplement, indexing collections appearing 1970–75, published 1978. 386 p. Second supplement, indexing collections appearing 1974–81, published 1984. 530 p. Third supplement, indexing collections appearing 1979–87, published in 1989. 875 p.
Indexes to folk songs, pop tunes, spirituals, children's songs, sea chanties, and blues in almost 1,000 song anthologies published since 1940. Bibliography of sources. Indexes of titles, first lines, first lines of choruses, and composers and lyricists.

Brief review by Stephen M. Fry in *Notes*, 32 (1976), p. 781. Review of the first supplement by Patricia Felch in *Notes*, 35 (1979), p. 637–38.

1520. Lax, Roger and Frederic Smith. The great song thesaurus. New York: Oxford University Press, 1984. 665 p.

A 2nd edition, revised and expanded, was published in 1989. 774 p.

The intent was to select, from all divisions of song literature, the 10,000 best-known popular and/or significant songs in English-speaking countries and to cross index the pertinent data. [from the introductory remarks]

One section organized chronologically beginning with 1926. Second section devoted to listing award-winning songs by year beginning with 1932. Third section lists "trademark" songs, theme and signature songs. Fourth section lists songs based on preexisting musical sources. Fifth section provides complete title listing citing composers, dates, and sources (if from a show). Sixth section lists British titles. Indexes to composers' and lyricists' names and to sources (including film, radio, and television). Thesaurus of song titles by subject, keyword, and category.

To be used in tandem with Havlice (no. 1519) and Gargan and Sharma (no. 1518). Shapiro and Pollock (no. 1529) provide the most comprehensive references.

Review by Norma Jean Lamb in *Notes*, 41 (1985), p. 709–711. Review of the 2nd ed. by David Dodd in *Notes*, 47 (1990), p. 389–80.

1521. Lewine, Richard and Alfred Simon. Songs of the theater. New York: H. W. Wilson, 1984. 897 p.

A title listing of songs from virtually all the shows appearing on- and off-Broadway from 1891 to 1983. Each entry includes names of composer(s) and lyricist(s), author(s), and name and dates of the show. Indexes to names, titles of shows, and film and television productions. Chronological list of shows citing all songs with references to sources and adaptations.

This work based on and largely superseding the authors' *Encyclopedia of Theater Music* (1961) and *Songs of the American Theater* (1973).

Review by Ed Glazier in *Notes*, 43 (1986), p. 301–303.

1522. Limbacher, James L. Film music: from violins to video. Metuchen, New Jersey: Scarecrow Press, 1974. 835 p.

Part one is an anthology of essays on the subject, with a bibliography. Part two is divided into four sections: film titles and dates; films and their composers; composers and their films; discography of recorded movie music. Name and title index to part one.

Review by Clifford McCarty in *Notes*, 31 (1974), p. 48–50.

1523. Limbacher, James L. Keeping score, film music 1972–1979. Metuchen, New Jersey: Scarecrow Press, 1981. 510 p.

Continues *Film Music: From Violins to Video* (no. 1522), superseding individual entries with corrected information. This is a book of lists: winners of Academy Awards for best original film scores, 1935–79; a necrology of film music composers; a bibliography of recent books on the subject of film music; film music titles and dates; films and their composers/adapters; composers and their films; and recorded musical scores.

Review by Gillian B. Anderson in *American Music*, 3 (1985), p. 354–55.

1524. Lynch, Richard Chigley. Musicals! a directory of musical properties available for production. Chicago, Illinois: American Library Association, 1984. 197 p.

Lists 400 titles and supplies vital information: title, date of original production, author, composer, lyricist, plot, cast requirements, licensing agent, recordings available.

Mattfeld, Julius. Variety music cavalcade, 1620–1961. See no. 615.

1525. Naha, Ed. Lillian Roxon's rock encyclopedia. Rev. ed. New York: Grosset & Dunlap, 1978. 565 p.

An updated version of Lillian Roxon's *Rock Encyclopedia* covering the growth of the industry and the eclectic branching of the genre. Lists of albums and single titles. Index.

1526. Ragtime, its history, composers, and music. Edited by John Edward Hasse. New York: Schirmer Books, 1985. 400 p.

Brief history of the genre. Biographical essays on principal figures (e.g., Scott Joplin, James Scott). Essay on use of ragtime elements in other genres. Checklist of compositions; bibliography; list of ragtime music folios and method books; discography; list of ragtime compositions by women.

1527. Rapee, Erno. Encyclopedia of music for pictures. New York: Arno Press, 1970. 510 p. (The literature of cinema)

Reprint of the 1925 edition.

An anthology of music.

1528. Rapee, Erno. Motion picture moods for pianists and organists. New York: Arno Press, 1970. 678 p.

Reprint of the 1925 edition.

This and the preceding volume are reference works that were designed to assist musicians of the 1920s and early 1930s to select the appropriate musical themes, or moods, to accompany motion pictures.

1529. Shapiro, Nat and Bruce Pollock. Popular music, 1920–1979: a revised cumulation. Detroit, Michigan: Gale Research Co., 1985. 3 v.

Supersedes *Popular Music: An Annotated Index of American Popular Songs* by Shapiro alone, an eight-volume 1st edition published 1964–79 by the Adrian Press in New York. Supplemented by volumes for 1980–84, 1985, 1986, and 1987, designated vols. 9, 10, 11, and 12.

> An annotated index of over 18,000 American popular songs, cumulating and updating eight volumes of *Popular music* and including introductory essays, lyricists and composers index, important performances index, award index, and list of publishers. [Author's *Preface*]

A series that aims "to set down in permanent and practical form a selective annotated list of the significant popular songs of the 20th century" [Author's *Preface*].

In the 1st edition, songs are listed alphabetically by title under each year of the decade. Each volume has its own index of titles and list of publishers.

Review of the 1st edition by Ruth Hilton in *Notes*, 25 (1968), p. 247–48, and 27 (1970), p. 60–61. Review of vol. 6 of the 1st edition by Michael D. Williams in *Notes*, 31 (1971), p. 307–308.

1530. Stecheson, Anthony and Anne Stecheson. The Stecheson classified song directory. Hollywood, California: Music Industry Press, 1961. 503 p.

Supplement issued 1978. 69 p.

About 100,000 songs popular in the U.S. are arranged under 400 topics or catchwords. Composers, titles, publishers, and sometimes dates are cited. There is no title index.

1531. Swanekamp, Joan. Diamonds & rust: a bibliography and discography on Joan Baez. Ann Arbor, Michigan: Pierian Press, 1980. 75 p.

1532. Voigt, John. Jazz music in print and jazz books in print. 3rd ed. Boston, Massachusetts: Hornpipe Music Pub. Co., 1982. 195 p.

Revised edition of *Jazz Music in Print*, 2nd ed., 1978. 1st ed., 1975.

Organized by individual artist. Contents of anthologies provided. Publisher and catalog distribution numbers cited. List of publishers.

Reviews of 2nd ed. by Lewis Porter in *Black Perspective in Music*, 7 (1979), p. 121–23, and by Dan Morgenstern in *Journal of Jazz Studies*, 5 (1979), p. 97–98.

1533. Woll, Allen L. Songs from Hollywood musical comedies, 1927 to the present: a dictionary. New York: Garland Pub., 1976. 251 p. (Garland reference library of the humanities, 44)

Contents: the songs; the films; a chronology of the Hollywood musical; composers and lyricists.

Covers American musicals and foreign films of musicals that had appeared on Broadway. There is an alphabetical list of song titles with references to the films for which they were written. Only musicals produced after 1950 with soundtrack recordings are included. Chronological list of shows. Index of composers and lyricists. No single entry presents all information about a particular film.

REGIONAL AND LOCAL OPERA REPERTOIRES

A useful type of reference work is that which traces the chronology of opera as it has been performed in a particular region, place, or theater: New York, Milan, Rome, Paris, Bologna, etc. Many of the leading opera companies of the world have been provided with such chronicles, which often include valuable data about first productions, the original cast of singers and dancers, the frequency of performance, etc.

These works are, strictly speaking, bibliographies of music, and they can be distinguished from other reference tools devoted to the musical theater; namely, dictionaries of opera and theater music and bibliographies of music literature devoted to the same subject.

1534. Allacci, Leone. Drammaturgia di Lione Allacci, accresciuta e continuata fino all'anno MDCCLV. Venezia: Presso G. Pasquali, 1755. 1,016 cols.
First edition, Rome, 1666. Revised and continued by Giovanni Cendoni, Apostolo Zeno, and others. Reprint of the 1755 edition by Bottega d'Erasmo, Torino, 1966.
A listing, alphabetical by title, of dramatic works produced in the Italian theater from the late 15th century to 1755. Not restricted to music but includes many operas and oratorios. See introduction to the facsimile reprint by Francesco Bernardelli.

1535. Bauer, Anton. Opern und Operetten in Wien; Verzeichnis ihrer Erstaufführungen in der Zeit von 1629 bis zur Gegenwart. Graz-Köln: Hermann Böhlaus Nachf., 1955. 156 p. (Wiener musikwissenschaftliche Beiträge, 2)
4,856 stage works, listed by title, with indexes by composer, author, and chronology.

1536. Bignami, Luigi. Cronologia di tutti gli spettacoli rappresentati al Teatro Comunale di Bologna della sua apertura 14 maggio 1763 a tutto l'autunno 1881. Bologna: Mattiuzzi, 1882. 248 p.
The entries consist of transcriptions of theater bills for the period under consideration. All types of dramatic works are included, but by far the largest part of the repertory is opera. Numerous indexes of performers, composers, authors, and other categories of theater personnel.

1537. Bolongaro-Crevenna, Hubertus. L'Arpa festante; die Münchner Oper 1651–1825, von den Anfängen bis zum *Freyschützen.* München: Callwey, 1963. 272 p.
A cultural history of the Munich opera from its beginnings to 1825. P. 209–272: a chronological listing of the repertory, with factual information drawn from the Munich theater archives.

1538. Brenner, Clarence D. A bibliographical list of plays in the French language 1700–1789, with a new foreword and an index by Michael A. Keller and Neal Zaslaw. New York: AMS Press, 1979. 229 p.; index, 43 unnumbered pages.
Reprint of the first edition published by the University of California, Berkeley, in 1947.
Brenner construed "play" to mean all stage works, including operas, ballets, and divertissements as well as *opéras-comique.* He provided in the *List* of 1947 all the information on his sources' title pages, libretti in Parisian libraries, archives, and published collections. The names of composers responsible for the continuous and incidental music mentioned on the title pages were thus provided in the original publication but not indexed. This reprint edition indexes composers' names.
The entries preceded with asterisks in the *List* are those for which Brenner could not verify attributions conclusively.

1539. Falk, Marguerite. Les parodies du Nouveau Théâtre Italien (1731); répertoire systématique des timbres. Bilthoven: A. B. Creyghton, [1974?]. 213 p.
An index to vocal music in the 25 vaudevilles in the source volumes and

a concordance to nine other 18th-century collections. Arranged by first line of text with an alphabetical representation of the melody, followed by a thematic index to the music arranged as in Barlow and Morgenstern (nos. 499 and 500). Appendixes of extracts of the "Parodies" showing the placement of the airs and of the musical incipits in order of appearance.

1540. Filippis, Felice de and R. Arnese. Cronache del Teatro di S. Carlo (1737–1960). Napoli: Edizioni Politica Popolare, 1961. 466 p.

P. 25–112: chronological listing, by year, of first performances of operas given at the San Carlo Opera in Naples from 1737 to 1960.

P. 113–304: a biographical dictionary of opera composers, with lists of their major works.

Indexes of librettists and singers; a summary of the seasons in which each work was performed. 76 full-page illustrations.

1541. Florimo, Francesco. La scuola musicale di Napoli e i suoi conservatorii, con uno sguardo sulla storia della musica in Italia. Bologna: Forni editore, 1969. 4 v. (Bibliotheca musica Bononiensis, III, 9)

Reprint of the edition of Stabilimento Tipografico di Vinc. Moreno, Naples, 1881–83. First appeared in 1869–71 in 2 vols. as *Cenno Storico Sulla Scuola Musicale di Napoli.*

Contents: vol. I. *Come venne la musica in Italia;* vol. II–III. *Cenno storico sulla scuola musicale di Napoli e suoi conservatorii, con le biografie dei maestri useiti dai medesimi;* vol. IV. *Elenco di tutte le opere in musica rappresentate nei teatri di Napoli.*

In vol. 4, information is organized under the name of the individual theater, citing title of opera, poet, composer, performers, and general observations.

1542. Fog, Dan. The Royal Danish Ballet, 1760–1958, and August Bournonville. A chronological catalogue of the ballets and ballet-divertissements performed at the Royal Theatres of Copenhagen, and a catalogue of August Bournonville's works. Copenhagen: Dan Fog, 1961. 79 p.

Lists 516 ballet works performed by the Royal Danish Ballet, citing the choreographer, composer, and publisher of the music if available. Index of titles and of persons. Facsimile plates of music title pages.

1543. Gatti, Carlo. Il teatro alla Scala, nella storia e nell'arte (1778–1963). Milano: Ricordi, 1964. 2 v.

A handsome set, the second volume of which contains the chronicles of La Scala—complete inventories of the opera, ballet, and concert performances from 1778 to the present, with an analytical index. The chronologies were compiled by Giampiero Tintori.

1544. Groppo, Antonio. "Catalogo di tutti i drammi per musica recitati ne' Teatri di Venezia dall'anno 1637, in cui ebbere principio le pubbliche rappresentazioni de' medesimi fin all'anno presente 1745." In *Bollettino Bibliografico Musicale*, Nuova serie. Milano, 1952.

Published serially in four installments.

Lists 811 operas performed in Venice between 1637 and 1745, in chronological order, with title, librettist, composer, theater, and date of performance. Index of titles.

1545. La Vallière, Louis César de la Baume Le Blanc, duc de. Ballets, opera, et autres ouvrages lyriques, par ordre chronologique depuis leur origine; avec une table alphabetique des ouvrages et des auteurs. Paris: Cl. J. Baptiste Bauche, 1760.
Unaltered reprint by H. Baron, 1967.
The chronological list is preceded by catalogs of poets and composers.

1546. Lajarte, Théodore de. Bibliothèque musicale du Théâtre de l'Opéra. Paris: Libr. des Bibliophiles, 1878. 2 v.
Reprint by Olms, Hildesheim, 1969.
Descriptive list of 594 stage works arranged in order of first production at the Paris Opera, 1671–1876. Classified by period. Each period concludes with a biographical section listing composers and librettists alphabetically. Composer and title index to works in the repertoire.

1547. Mattfeld, Julius. A handbook of American operatic premieres, 1731–1962. Detroit, Michigan: Information Service, Inc., 1963. 142 p. (Detroit studies in music bibliography, 5)

This guide to operatic performances in the United States attempts to present a record of the premieres of nearly 2,000 operas and related works from 1731 to the end of 1962.... Included are operas by native and naturalized composers, which have been performed outside the country. [*Preface*]

Works listed alphabetically by title, with a composer index.

1548. Mooser, Robert-Aloys. Opéras, intermezzos, ballets, cantates, oratorios joués en Russie durant le XVIIIe siècle.... Essai d'un répertoire alphabétique et chronologique. 3e édition revue et complétée. Bâle: Bärenreiter, 1964. 177 p.
First published in 1945; 2nd edition, 1955.
Gives librettist, translators of work, date and place of first performance, language of performance, date of publication of the libretto, etc. Sources of information are well documented. Indexes.
Review of the 2nd edition by Anna A. Abert in *Die Musikforschung*, 9 (1956), p. 106.

1549. Pitou, Spire. The Paris Opéra: an encyclopedia of operas, ballets, composers, and performers. Westport, Connecticut: Greenwood Press, 1983– . 2 v. to date.
Vol. 1, subtitled "Genesis and glory, 1671–1715," lists the repertory from 1671 to 1715 and includes a list of leading singers and dancers from 1671 to 1982. Entries for the productions have a plot synopsis in the case of staged works. Many entries have abbreviated bibliographic references leading the reader to the general bibliography cited in the list of abbreviations on p. 133–35. There is a repertory list in chronological order and a general index.
Vol. 2, subtitled "Rococo and romantic, 1715–1815," published 1985, is similar to the first. The abbreviations (p. xiii–xviii) provide full bibliographic citations for works cited in the entries.

1550. Radiciotti, Giuseppe. "Teatro e musica in Roma nel secondo quarto del secolo XIX (1825–50)." In *Storia dell'Arte Musicale e Drammatica*. Sezione 4, p. 157–318. Roma: Tip. della R. Academia dei Lincei, 1906.

Parte seconda: A chronicle of the musical-dramatic productions given in the three major theaters in Rome during the early 19th century: Teatro Valle, Teatro Argentina, and Teatro Apollo.

1551. Salvioli, Giovanni. I teatri musicali di Venezia nel secolo XVII (1637–1700). Memorie storiche e bibliografiche di Livio Niso Galvani [pseud. for Giovanni Salvioli]. Milano: Ricordi, 1878. 193 p.

Reprint by A. Forni, Bologna, 1969, in the series Biblioteca musica bononiensis (III, 32).

Operas performed in Venice during the 17th century, listed chronologically under 16 different theaters or opera houses. Entries listed by title, with composer, librettist, publication data of libretti, dedicatee, and much useful information. Indexes of names, titles, librettists, and composers.

1552. Salvioli, Giovanni and Carlo Salvioli. Bibliografia universale del teatro drammatico italiano con particolare riguardo alla storia della musica italiana ... Volume primo. Venezia: C. Ferrari, 1903. 932 cols.

Issued in parts, 1894–1903. Only vol. 1 was published.

"Contenente i titoli e l'analisi di tutte le produzioni drammatiche publicate per la stampa in lingua italiana e nei vari dialetti in Italia ed all'estero dalle origini del teatro italiano e del dramma musicale sino ai nostri giorni, con note illustrative, indici copiosi, appendici e supplementi periodici per mantenere quest' opera nello stato di attualità."

Contents: vol. 1. A–C. Aggiunte e rettifiche.

1553. Seltsam, William H. Metropolitan Opera annals. New York: H. W. Wilson Co., 1947. 751 p.

Chronological listing of Metropolitan Opera performances, with casts, from the initial season (1883–84) through 1946–47. Coverage for each season includes a roster and excerpts from press reviews of noteworthy performances. Indexed by artist and opera.

Supplements issued annually in the final issue of each volume of the periodical *Opera News. First Supplement, 1957,* cumulates information for 1945–57. *Second Supplement: 1957–1966—A Chronicle of Artists and Performers.* Foreword by Francis Robinson. New York, H. W. Wilson, 1968. 126 p. *Third Supplement, 1966–76,* edited by Mary Ellen Peltz and Gerald Fitzgerald.

1554. Shteinpress, Boris S. Opernye premiery XX veka 1901–1940: slovar'. Moskva: Sovetskii Kompozitor, 1983. 469 p.

A listing of first performances of 20th-century operas in the Soviet Union. Includes index.

1555. Strohm, Reinhard. Die italienische Oper im 18. Jahrhundert. Wilhelmshaven: Heinrichshofen, 1979. 398 p. (Taschenbücher zur Musikwissenschaft, 25)

Like the following study, this one includes a very useful index and bibliography.

1556. Strohm, Reinhard. Italienische Opernarien des frühen Settecento (1720–1730). Köln: Volk, 1976. 2 v. (Analecta musicologica, 16)

Attached to this study of the Italian opera aria is an index to the genre for the period. Vol. 1. Studien; vol. 2. Notenbeispiele und Verzeichnisse.

1557. Trezzini, Lamberto. Due secoli di vita musicale. Storia del Teatro Comunale di Bologna. Bologna: Edizioni ALFA, 1966. 2 v.

Vol. 1 contains a series of essays on the history of various aspects of musical life in Bologna, chiefly related to the theater.

Vol. 2 consists of a *Repertorio Critico degli Spettacoli e delle Esecuzioni Musicali dal 1763 al 1966*, by Sergio Paganelli. This is a chronological listing of opera, oratorio, and symphony productions, giving the names of members of the casts, soloists, and conductors represented.

1558. Wiel, Taddeo. I teatri musicali veneziani del settecento. Catalogo delle opere in musica rappresentate nel secolo XVIII in Venezia (1701–1800). Venezia: Fratelli Visentini, 1897. 600 p.

Reprinted by A. Forni, Bologna, 1978, as part of Biblioteca musica bononiensis (III, 51). New edition with an introduction and updated bibliography by Reinhard Strohm published by Peters, Leipzig, 1979. 635 p.

Chronological listing of operas performed in Venice during the 18th century. 1,274 items. Entries give librettist, composer, place of performance, cast if known, ballet if included. Indexes of titles, librettists, composers, singers, dancers, etc. Introductory essay of 80 pages on the Venetian musical theater.

1559. Wolff, Stéphane. Un demi-siècle d'opéra comique (1900–50): les œuvres, les interprètes. Paris: Éditions André Bonne, 1953. 339 p.

I. p. 15–231: the works arranged alphabetically by title, with much detailed information as to cast, production, etc. II. p. 233–339: the interpreters and their roles, a series of biographical sections treating the singers, dancers, conductors, and other personnel involved in *opéra-comique* productions.

1560. Wolff, Stéphane. L'Opéra au Palais Garnier, 1875–1962: les œuvres, les interprètes. Paris: "L'Entr'acte," [1963]. 565 p.

Reprint by Slatkine, 1983.

A book of facts related to the Paris opera and its productions from 1875 to the present.

I, p. 23–378: productions listed in several alphabets according to type ("œuvres lyriques et oratories, œuvres chorégraphiques, œuvres dramatiques," etc.). II, p. 379–552: persons affiliated with the opera (singers, conductors, dancers, composers, administrative personnel).

MUSIC OF INDIVIDUAL COMPOSERS

A large number of bibliographical tools have been created to serve as guides to the music of individual composers; work lists and thematic catalogs exist in abundance. To cite them all would extend the present work beyond reasonable limits, but a few are cited here as exemplars. For an exhaustive listing of thematic catalogs and reviews of them, the reader can be referred to Barry Brook's compilation (no. 684). Important nonthematic inventories are to be found in the major encyclopedias, such as the *New Grove*, *MGG*, and *La Musica*. Often important information about catalogs of music of individual composers can be found in the bibliographies of literature *about* individual composers (nos. 1160–1189).

The entries in the following section have been selected primarily as representative of recent compilations of composers' work lists.

1561. Composers' collected editions from Europe. 7th rev. ed. Wiesbaden: Otto Harrassowitz, 1992. 295 p., 25 p. (Special music catalog, 15)

A dealer's catalog of composers' complete works, ranging from Albinoni to Zajc, valuable for its currency and completeness of coverage.

ABEL, KARL FRIEDRICH

1562. Knape, Walter. Bibliographisch-thematisches Verzeichnis der Kompositionen von Karl Friedrich Abel (1723–1787). Cuxhaven: W. Knape, [1972?]. 299 p.

ARNE, THOMAS AUGUSTINE

1563. Parkinson, John A. An index to the vocal works of Thomas Augustine Arne and Michael Arne. Detroit, Michigan: Information Coordinators, 1972. 82 p. (Detroit studies in music bibliography, 21)

BACH, JOHANN SEBASTIAN

1564. Schmieder, Wolfgang. Thematisch-systematisches Verzeichnis der musikalischen Werke von Johann Sebastian Bach; Bach-Werke-Verzeichnis; (BWV). Wiesbaden: Breitkopf & Härtel, 1990. 1,014 p.

First edition published in 1950. 747 p. Numerous unaltered reprints 1958–80.

The essential reference for Bach scholars and students, this is a classified thematic catalog providing information on sources of text, instrumentation, early and authoritative publications of the music, manuscript sources, and secondary literature. Each entry is provided with extensive thematic quotations. The prefaces and remarks are in German and English and are essential aids to proper use of the catalog. Among the useful appendixes are a chronology of the creation of the compositions, a calendar for the cantatas arranged by church year, a thematic index to the instrumental works, an index to first lines of text, and an index to names and terms.

1565. Schulze, Hans-Joachim and Christoph Wolff. Bach Compendium. Analytisch-bibliographisches Repertorium der Werke Johann Sebastian Bachs. Frankfurt: C. F. Peters, 1985– . Vols. I/1–I/4 to date.

Projected to appear in three parts: vocal works, instrumental works, and miscellanea. The first part is complete and further volumes are expected.

The purpose of the *Bach Compendium* is to provide reliable information, both bibliographical and analytical, on Bach's entire output. The present work incorporates substantial quantities of new research, together with a thorough re-examination of all relevant sources. [There is a] detailed presentation of all essential facts pertaining to each individual composition, including citations to both primary and secondary sources, as well as important editions and secondary literature. The *Bach Compendium* cannot nor is intended to re- place the *Bach-Werke-Verzeichnis*. The *Bach Compendium* is intentionally limited to authentic and first editions, and its citations to secondary literature are both selective and topically arranged.

The *Bach Compendium* offers a systematic overview of Bach's works in all their authentic versions, arranged primarily according to genre. It also in- cludes sketches and drafts, lost works, compositions of doubtful and spurious authenticity, and works from Bach's musical library written by other compos- ers. [*Foreword*]

Entries in the *Bach Compendium* vary in order from those in the *Bach- Werke-Verzeichnis (BWV)* for a variety of reasons. For instance, cantatas are arranged in order of the church year. There are "see" references to *BWV* entries. In the *Bach Compendium*, thematic incipits appear separate from the entries for each work; "see" references direct one to the appro- priate pages. Each entry includes a section on the early history of the work, a particularly clear statement of the sources and important early editions, and a classified bibliography of secondary sources.

Each volume includes a concordance to the *BWV* and from the *BWV*. It is extremely important for the reader to be familiar with the abbreviations and preliminary remarks in each volume.

Reviewed by Lothar Hoffman-Erbrecht in *Die Musikforschung*, 41 (1988), p. 175–76; by Stephen Dow in *Music and Letters*, 69 (1988), p. 254– 55; by Joshua Rifkin in *Early Music*, 17 (1989), p. 79–88; by John Butt in *Notes*, 47 (1990), p. 361–68.

1566. Whaples, Miriam K. Bach aria index. Ann Arbor, Michigan: Music Li- brary Association, 1971. (MLA index series, 11)

The main index classifies the arias by performing forces. Works are iden- tified by text incipit, location in the Bach *Thematisch-systematisches Ver- zeichnis*, and in the principal editions. Alphabetical index of first lines and of instruments.

BANCHIERI, ADRIANO

1567. Mischiati, Oscar. "Adriano Banchieri (1568–1634): Profilo biografico e bibliografia delle opere." In *Annuario* (1965–1970), Conservatorio di Mu- sica "G. B. Martini." Bologna: 1971. p. 39–201.

Also printed as a separate work by Casa Editrice Patron, Bologna, 1971.

A model bibliographical study of one of the most versatile composers and theorists of the Bolognese school of the early 17th century. Prelimi- nary biographical essay followed by a systematic bibliography of Ban- chieri's sacred music, instrumental music, secular music, music theory, and literary writings. Copies of the works are located in major European li- braries and the Library of Congress. Facsimile plates.

BARBER, SAMUEL

1568. Hennessee, Don A. Samuel Barber, a bio-bibliography. Westport, Con- necticut: Greenwood Press, 1985. 404 p. (Bio-bibliographies in music, 3)

This book is cited as an exemplar of a new and numerous series of works bringing together short biographies and long catalogs and bibliographies of and about works by 20th-century composers under the editorship of Don Hixon. The work is in four sections: a brief biography; a complete list of works and performances classified by genre and arranged alphabetically by title with annotations on each work, on the location of manuscripts, sketches, etc.; a discography; an annotated bibliography of writings by and about Barber. Appendixes include an alphabetical list of compositions and a list of compositions in opus-number order. There is a general index.

BEETHOVEN, LUDWIG VAN

1569. Dorfmüller, Kurt. Beiträge zur Beethoven Bibliographie. Studien und Materialen zum Werkverzeichnis von Kinsky-Halm. München: G. Henle Verlag, 1978. 452 p.

An indispensable adjunct to the Kinsky-Halm *Verzeichnis* (no. 1570), bringing entries on each opus and without opus (WoO) number up to date.

Review by Lewis Lockwood in *Fontes Artis Musicae*, 28 (1981), p. 22–53.

1570. Hess, Willy. Verzeichnis der nicht in der Gesamtausgabe veröffentlichten Werke Ludwig van Beethovens. Wiesbaden: Breitkopf & Härtel, 1957. 116 p.

Cites 335 works not included in the complete edition, plus 66 doubtful works.

1571. Kinsky, Georg and Hans Halm. Das Werk Beethovens thematisch-bibliographisches Verzeichnis seiner sämtlichen vollendeten Kompositionen. München-Duisburg: G. Henle Verlag, 1955. 808 p.

Divided into three major sections: works with opus numbers; works without opus numbers (WoO numbers); and works of doubtful or false attribution. Each entry provides a thematic incipit(s), location in the *Gesamtausgabe*, information on the creation of the work, manuscript sources, early printed versions, information on the sources and version of the text (if any), and references to discussions of the work in the standard Beethoven biographies and to other secondary literature. Numerous appendixes: a classified index to the compositions; a calendar of composition; a calendar of early publication of Beethoven's works; an index to early publishers; a table of equivalents for the varying use of opus numbers among the early publishers; a list of dedicatees; a directory of libraries holding Beethoven manuscripts; an index of titles and first lines of Beethoven's vocal or choral works; and a general index.

Supplemented by Dorfmüller (no. 1569) and Hess (no. 1570).

BERLIOZ, HECTOR

1572. Bibliography Committee, New York Chapter, MLA. An alphabetical index to Hector Berlioz: *Werke*. Ann Arbor, Michigan: Music Library Association, 1963. (MLA Index series, 2)

300

1573. Holoman D. Kern. Catalogue of the works of Hector Berlioz. Kassel: Bärenreiter, 1987. 527 p. (Hector Berlioz new edition of the complete works, 25)

This catalogue attempts to present a complete survey of Berlioz's music and writings, and to furnish fundamental documentary information concerning each of his works.... [It also] attempts to clarify such problems of title and version ... to show how works evolved in the composer's mind, and to develop a chronology of composition that explains titles or works as Berlioz saw them at any given time. Its fundamental purpose is to list all known sources—autograph manuscripts, and printed—for the works of Berlioz and to summarize what they show about each individual composition. [*Foreword*]

Arranged in several sections: catalog of musical works; catalog of works contemplated but not composed; catalog of prose works. There is a table of works by *œuvre* numbers. Berlioz's own catalog of his works is included. There are indexes of names, and of titles and first lines. Entries provide references to the *Hector Berlioz New Edition of the Complete Works* and to selected secondary sources. A model of clarity, completeness, and simplicity.

1574. Hopkinson, Cecil. A bibliography of the musical and literary works of Hector Berlioz, 1803–1869: with histories of the French music publishers concerned. 2nd ed. edited by Richard Macnutt; with a new foreword by Alec Hyatt King. Royal Tunbridge Wells, England: R. Macnutt, 1980. 230 p.

First published in Edinburgh by the Edinburgh Bibliographical Society, 1951. 205 p. The 2nd edition incorporates the author's corrections and additions.

Review by Christopher Rouse in *Notes*, 37 (1981), p. 849–50.

BILLINGS, WILLIAM

1575. Nathan, Hans. William Billings; data and documents. Detroit, Michigan: Information Coordinators, 1976. 69 p. (Bibliographies in American Music, 2)

A bio-bibliographical study covering Billings' life and his musical and literary works.

BLOCH, ERNEST

1576. Ernest Bloch: creative spirit. A program source book prepared by Suzanne Bloch, in collaboration with Irene Heskes. New York: Jewish Music Council of the National Jewish Welfare Board, 1976. 146 p.

A sourcebook of information related to Ernest Bloch and his music. Contains a brief biography, reviews and descriptions of his works, a discography, and a bibliography.

BOCCHERINI, LUIGI

1577. Gérard, Yves. Thematic, bibliographical, and critical catalogue of the works of Luigi Boccherini. Translated by Andreas Mayor. London: Oxford University Press, 1969. 716 p.

Review by Ellen Amsterdam in *Journal of the American Musicological Society*, 24 (1971), p. 131–33.

BRAHMS, JOHANNES

1578. Bozarth, George S. "The first generation of Brahms manuscript collections." In *Notes*, 40 (1984), p. 239–62.
A bibliographical study intended to

> reassemble ... sources (at least in catalogue format and on microfilm), to establish the 'source situations' of individual compositions, and to ascertain the value of the various manuscripts in source-critical studies ... The Appendix to this article details the contents of these large collections, as well as many of the smaller private holdings. [from the introductory remarks]

1579. Dedel, Peter. Johannes Brahms: a guide to his autographs in facsimile. Ann Arbor, Michigan: Music Library Association, 1978. 86 p. (MLA index and bibliography series, 18)
Review by Otto E. Albrecht in *Notes*, 35 (1979), p. 892.

1580. Deutsch, Otto Erich. "The first editions of Brahms." In *Music Review*, 1 (1940), p. 123–43; 255–278.

1581. Hofmann, Kurt. Die Erstdrucke der Werke von Johannes Brahms: Bibliographie mit Wiedergabe von 209 Titelblättern. Tutzing: Schneider, 1975. 414 p. (Musikbibliographische Arbeiten, 2)
Review by Donald M. McCorkle in *Notes*, 32 (1976), p. 528–30.

1582. McCorkle, Margit and Donald M. McCorkle. Johannes Brahms thematisch-bibliographisches Werkverzeichnis. München: G. Henle Verlag, 1984. 841 p.
Similar in intent and content to the Bach (no. 1564) and Beethoven (no. 1571) thematic catalogs, but with several additional objectives:

> 1. The complete listing of Brahms's extant orignal compositions with and without opus number in *all* versions, and by his extant arrangements, transcriptions, and editions of works by other composers; for the latter group and for the works without opus number, the establishment of a conclusive order and identification.
> 2. The listing of all now-lost original works, earlier versions, and arrangements of works by other composers, which are known to have once existed.
> 3. The listing and description of all music manuscripts, both extant and missing (that is, lost or destroyed).
> 4. The listing and description of all editions and successive issues to have appeared in Brahms's lifetime, as well as posthumously published first editions.
> The compilation of important facts for each work, with documentation, about the circumstances of compositions, first performance, and first publication. [from the introductory remarks]

The documentation in each entry is based on primary sources and important secondary sources. In cases where sources contradict one another, all are cited, including recent scholarly researches bearing upon the problem. There are six appendixes: works of other composers arranged by Brahms; lost works and arrangements by Brahms; varia, fragments, and sketches; unauthenticated and misattributed works; holograph collections and copies; works of other composers edited by Brahms. There is a substantial bibliography. There are 10 indexes: classified list of Brahms' works; list of titles and text incipits; list of literary text sources; chronology of dates of composition; list of arrangers; list of dedicatees; list of publishers; list of copyists; list of manuscript repositories; general index. The introduction is presented in German and English and must be comprehended to make best use of this substantial work of scholarship.

Review by Karl Geiringer in *Notes*, 42 (1985), p. 289–90.

BRITTEN, BENJAMIN

1583. Benjamin Britten: a complete catalogue of his published works. London: Boosey & Hawkes, 1973. 52 p.

A "Supplement to a complete catalogue of his published works, 1978," 2 leaves, was issued.

The catalog produced by his major publisher. Indexed.

BRUCKNER, ANTON

1584. Grasberger, Renate. Werkverzeichnis Anton Bruckner. Tutzing: Schneider, 1977. 309 p. (Institut für Österreichische Musikdokumentation. Publikation, 7)

Review by Robert Winter in *Notes*, 35 (1979), p. 640–41.

BUXTEHUDE, DIETRICH

1585. Karstädt, Georg. Thematisch-Systematisches Verzeichnis der musikalischen Werke von Dietrich Buxtehude: Buxtehude-Werke-Verzeichnis (BuxWV). 2., erweiterte und verbesserte Auflage. Wiesbaden: Breitkopf & Härtel, 1985. 246 p.

First ed. published in 1974.

Review by Kerala J. Snyder in *Fontes Artis Musicae*, 23 (1976), p. 148–49.

CARISSIMI, GIACOMO

1586. Buff, Iva M. A thematic catalog of the sacred works of Giacomo Carissimi. Clifton, New Jersey: European American Music Corp., 1979. 159 p. (Music indexes and bibliographies, 15)

Review by Andrew V. Jones in *Notes*, 38 (1981), p. 66–67.

1587. Sartori, Claudio. Giacomo Carissimi, catalogo delle opere attribuite. Milano: Finarte, 1975. 143 p.

Review by Iva M. Buff in *Notes*, 33 (1977), p. 584–86.

CEBALLOS, RODRIGO DE

1588. Snow, Robert J. The extant music of Rodrigo de Ceballos and its sources. Detroit, Michigan: Information Coordinators, 1980. 155 p. (Detroit studies in music bibliography, 44)

CHOPIN, FRÉDÉRIC

1589. Kobylańsk, Krystyna. Frédéric Chopin. Thematisch-bibliographisches Werkverzeichnis. Munich: G. Henle Verlag, 1979. 362 p.

Published previously in Polish as *Rękopisy Utworów Chopina; Katalog* [*Manuscripts of Chopin's Works; Catalogue*] by Polskie Wydawnictwo Muzyczne, Cracovia, 1977. 2 v.

Reviewed by Jean-Jacques Eigeldinger in *Fontes Artis Musicae*, 29 (1982), p. 142–45; this review includes a bibliographic addendum to the Chopin thematic catalog. Another review by Eigeldinger in *Fontes Artis Musicae*, 26 (1979), p. 142–44.

Review by Jeffrey Kallberg in *Journal of the American Musicological Society*, 34 (1981), p. 357–65. Review by L. Michael Griffel in *Notes*, 37 (1981), p. 847–49.

CLARKE, JEREMIAH

1590. Taylor, Thomas. Thematic catalog of the works of Jeremiah Clarke. Detroit, Michigan: Information Coordinators, 1977. 134 p. (Detroit studies in music bibliography, 35)

CLEMENTI, MUZIO

1591. Tyson, Alan. Thematic catalogue of the works of Muzio Clementi. Tutzing: Hans Schneider, 1967. 136 p.

Review by Donald W. Krummel in *Notes*, 25 (1969), p. 725–26.

COPLAND, AARON

Skowronski, JoAnn. Aaron Copland: a bio-bibliography. See no. 1168.

DEBUSSY, CLAUDE

1592. Lesure, François. Catalogue de l'œuvre Claude Debussy. Genève: Minkoff, 1977. 168 p. (Publication du Centre de documentation Claude Debussy, 3)

A *catalogue raisonné* in chronological order. No thematic incipits. Cites dates of composition, provides poet and source of texts, references to standard secondary literature, and various remarks. Appendixes: pieces composed during Debussy's education; works with domestic character or for friends; editions, transcriptions, and orchestrations; compositions not

completed; index to dedicatees; classified index; index to text incipits; index to titles.
Review by James R. Briscoe in *Notes*, 34 (1978), p. 862–65.

DELIUS, FREDERICK

1593. Lowe, Rachel. A descriptive catalogue with checklists of the letters and related documents in the Delius collection of the Grainger Museum, University of Melbourne, Australia. London: Delius Trust, 1981. 233 p.
Review by Harold J. Diamond in *Notes*, 38 (1981), p. 317–18.

1594. Lowe, Rachel. Frederick Delius, 1862–1934: a reprint of the catalogue of the music archive of the Delius Trust, 1974, with minor corrections. London: Delius Trust and Boosey & Hawkes Music Publishers [distributors], 1986. 183 p.
First published in 1974.
"List of printed music held by the Delius Trust as part of the original accession": p. 177–79.
Review of the 1974 edition by Don C. Gillespie in *Notes*, 32 (1976), p. 547–58.

D'ORDOÑEZ, CARLO

1595. Brown, A. Peter. Carlo d'Ordoñez, 1734–1786; a thematic catalog. Detroit, Michigan: Information Coordinators, 1978. 234 p. (Detroit studies in music bibliography, 39)
Includes watermark and copyist indexes.
Review by Catherine Massip in *Fontes Artis Musicae*, 29 (1982), p. 148–49.

EISLER, HANNS

1596. Notowicz, Nathan and Jürgen Elsner. Hanns Eisler Quellennachweise. Hrsg. im Auftrag des Hanns-Eisler Archives bei der Deutschen Akademie der Künste zu Berlin. Leipzig: Deutscher Verlag für Musik, 1966. 174 p.
A bibliographical source book of the work of Hanns Eisler (1898–1962) based on the holdings of an archive in East Berlin. Coverage includes a listing of his compositions, an annotated bibliography of his literary work, and a discography of his music.

FARWELL, ARTHUR

1597. A guide to the music of Arthur Farwell and to the microfilm collection of his work. Prepared by his children; Brice Farwell, editor. Limited edition. Briarcliff Manor, New York: Issued by B. Farwell for the estate of Arthur Farwell, 1972. 138 p.
First issued 1971. 130 p.
Bibliography: p. 108–111. Music supplement.

FIELD, JOHN

1598. Hopkinson, Cecil. A bibliographical thematic catalogue of the works of John Field, 1782–1837. London: Printed for the author, 1961. 175 p.

FRANZ, ROBERT

1599. Boonin, Joseph M. An index to the solo songs of Robert Franz. Hackensack, New Jersey: Joseph Boonin, Inc., 1970. 19 p. (Music indexes and bibliographies, 4)
A listing of Franz's songs by opus numbers; a brief survey of their publishing history, including the various collections issued in the late 19th century; title and first-line index and a listing of the poets whose work was set to music by the composer.

FRESCOBALDI, GIROLAMO

1600. Mischiati, Oscar. "Catalogo delle Edizioni Originali delle Opere di Girolamo Frescobaldi." In *Frescobaldi e il suo tempo*, p. 45–72. Venezia: Marsilio, 1983.
First systematic bibliographic descriptions of the early printed editions of Frescobaldi. Includes transcriptions of title pages, dedications, and notices to the reader. There are lists of contents for each publication. Organized chronologically.

GASSMANN, FLORIAN LEOPOLD

1601. Hill, George R. A thematic catalog of the instrumental music of Florian Leopold Gassmann. Hackensack, New Jersey: J. Boonin, 1976. 171 p. (Music indexes and bibliographies, 12)
Review by Malcolm S. Cole in *Notes*, 34 (1977), p. 596–97.

GERSHWIN, GEORGE

1602. Schwartz, Charles. George Gershwin; a selective bibliography and discography. Detroit, Michigan: Information Coordinators for the College Music Society, 1974. 118 p. (Bibliographies in American music, 1)
Includes a chronology. The discography covers concert and operatic works, song collections, and musicals.

GLUCK, CHRISTOPH WILLIBALD

1603. Hopkinson, Cecil. A bibliography of the printed works of C. W. von Gluck, 1714–1787. 2nd ed., rev. and enl. New York: Broude Bros., 1967. 96 p.
First published in 1959. 79 p.

GOTTSCHALK, LOUIS MOREAU

1604. Doyle, John G. Louis Moreau Gottschalk, 1829–1869. Detroit, Michigan: Information Coordinators, 1983. 396 p. (Bibliographies in American music, 7)

Lists works by Gottschalk. Extensive bibliography of literature about the composer.

Review by H. Wiley Hitchcock in *Fontes Artis Musicae*, 30 (1983), p. 168–70.

1605. Offergeld, Robert. The centennial catalogue of the published and unpublished compositions of Louis Moreau Gottschalk. Prepared for *Stereo Review*. New York: Ziff-Davis Pub. Co., 1970. 34 p.

The introduction discusses Gottschalk's output and the state of research based on the source materials. This is followed by an annotated listing of 298 compositions. The annotations are entertaining and informative; a model of bibliographical technique.

GRIFFES, CHARLES T.

1606. Anderson, Donna K. Charles T. Griffes; an annotated bibliography-discography. Detroit, Michigan: Information Coordinators, 1977. 255 p. (Bibliographies in American music, 3)

Includes chronologies of Griffes' life and works.

HANDEL, GEORGE FREDERIC

1607. Bell, A. Craig. Handel: a chronological thematic catalogue. Darley, England: Grian-Aig Press, 1972. 452 p.

First published as *Chronological Catalogue of Handel's Work* in 1969. 68 p.

Contains some 3,000 thematic incipits. Appendixes list spurious and doubtful works, unpublished and lost works, and works with opus numbers. Indexed by librettists, instrumental and vocal titles, instrumental interludes. Classified index and first-line index.

1608. Händel-Handbuch in 4 Bd., gleichzeitig Suppl. zu Hallische Händel-Ausgabe (Kritische Gesamtausgabe). Hrsg. vom Kuratorium d. Georg-Friedrich-Händel-Stiftung von Walter Eisen u. Margret Eisen. Kassel, etc.: Bärenreiter, 1978–86. 4 v.

Contents:

Bd. 1. Siegfried Flesch. *Lebens- und Schaffensdaten.* Bernd Baselt. *Thematisch-systematisches Verzeichnis, Bühnenwerke.*

Bd. 2. Bernd Baselt. *Thematisch-systematisches Verzeichnis, oratorische Werke, vokale Kammermusik, Kirchenmusik.*

Bd. 3. Bernd Baselt. *Thematisch-systematisches Verzeichnis, Instrumentalmusik, Pasticci und Fragmente.*

Bd. 4. Otto Erich Deutsch. *Dokumente zu Leben und Schaffen.*

Review by Hugh Cobbe in *Notes*, 36 (1980), p. 883–84.

1609. Kinnear, Betty and Robert Illing. An illustrated catalogue of the early editions of Handel in Australia. Adelaide: Published by the authors, 1976. 255 p.
A first supplement was issued in 1986. 33 p.

1610. Smith, William Charles. Handel: a descriptive catalogue of the early editions. 2nd ed. with suppl. Oxford: B. Blackwell, 1970. 378 p.
First published in 1960 by Cassell, London.
The *Supplement*, p. 331–40, serves to bring the 1960 work up to date.

HARTMANN, KARL AMADEUS

1611. McCredie, Andrew D. Karl Amadeus Hartmann, thematic catalogue of his works. Wilhelmshaven; New York: Edition Heinrichshofen; New York: C. F. Peters, 1982. 227 p. (Catalogues of musical sources, 18) (Quellen-kataloge zur Musikgeschichte, 18)

HASSE, JOHANN ADOLF

1612. Hansell, Sven Hostrup. Works for solo voice of Johann Adolf Hasse (1699–1783). Detroit, Michigan: Information Coordinators, 1968. 110 p. (Detroit studies in music bibliography, 12)
Review by Robert L. Marshall in *Die Musikforschung*, 24 (1971), p. 463–64; by Owen Jander in *Notes*, 25 (1969), p. 722–23.

HAYDN, JOSEPH

1613. Bryant, Stephen C. and Gary W. Chapman. Melodic index to Haydn's instrumental music: a thematic locator for Anthony van Hoboken's Thematisch-bibliographisches Werkverzeichnis, volumes I and III. New York: Pendragon Press, 1982. 100 p. (Thematic catalogues, 8)
Reviews by Catherine Massip in *Fontes Artis Musicae*, 31 (1984), p. 134, and by Karl Geiringer in *Notes*, 41 (1984), p. 70–71.

1614. Haydn, Joseph. Thematisches Verzeichnis sämtlichen Kompositionen ... zusammengestellt von Aloys Fuchs 1839. Facsimile-Ausgabe. Hrsg. von Richard Schaal. Wilhelmshaven: Heinrichshofen's Verlag, 1968. 204 p. (Quellen-Kataloge zur Musikgeschichte, 2)
Thematic catalog of Haydn's works compiled by the Viennese collector Aloys Fuchs in 1839. Reproduced in facsimile.
Review by H. C. Robbins Landon in *Haydn Yearbook*, 6 (1969), p. 217–18.

1615. Hoboken, Anthony van. Joseph Haydn; thematisch-bibliographisches Werkverzeichnis. Mainz: B. Schott's Söhne, 1957–78. 3 v.
The standard thematic catalog to the works of Joseph Haydn.
Beilage zu Band I. Beilage zu Band I und II.
Contents: Bd. 1. Instrumentalwerke. Bd. 2. Vokalwerke. Bd. 3. Register; Addenda und Corrigenda.

A classified thematic catalog with information on authographs, manu-scripts, and early printed editions. Extensive appendixes: analysis of early printed collections and "complete" works; a concordance from the opus numbering scheme to the Hoboken *Gruppe* and item numbers; an index to publishers; an index to common or local names for various of Haydn's works; a list of institutions holding manuscripts; a list by *Gruppe* and item number to the autographs; a title and text incipit index to vocal music; and an index to persons, institutions, and works.

Reviews of vol. 1 by Otto Erich Deutsch in *Music Review*, 18 (1957), p. 330–36; by Karl Geiringer in *Notes*, 14 (1957), p. 565–66; by Willi Kahl in *Die Musikforschung*, 11 (1958), p. 525–29; and by Rosemary Hughes in *Music and Letters*, 39 (1958), p. 86–90. Reviews of vol. 2 by H. C. Robbins-Landon in *Haydn Yearbook*, 9 (1975), p. 361–64; by Karl Geiringer in *Journal of the American Musicological Society*, 25 (1972), p. 471–73; by James Webster in *Notes*, 29 (1972), p. 234–36; and by Alan Tyson in *Musical Times*, 115 (1974), p. 657–58. Reviews of vol. 3 by George Hill in *Notes*, 36 (1979), p. 102–103; by Hubert Unverricht in *Die Musikforschung*, 32 (1979), p. 331–34; and by David Wyn Jones in *Haydn Yearbook*, 11 (1980), p. 199–204.

1616. Holm, Anna-Lena, comp. Index of titles and text incipits to Anthony Van Hoboken *Joseph Haydn, Thematisch-bibliographisches Werkver-zeichnis, [Bd.] 2, Vokalwerke* (Mainz 1971). Stockholm: Swedish Music History Archive, 1978. 53 leaves.

HENZE, HANS WERNER

1617. Hans Werner Henze: list of works. Mainz and New York: Schott, 1983. 64 p.

Bibliographical sketch of Henze by Gerhard R. Koch.

1618. Der Komponist Hans Werner Henze: ein Buch der Alten Oper Frankfurt, Frankfurt Feste '86, herausgegeben von Dieter Rexroth. Mainz and New York: Schott, 1986. 382 p.

"Hans Werner Henze Werkverzeichnis," p. [341]–382.

This work includes material by Henze and bibliographical references.

HEWITT, JOHN HILL

1619. Hoogerwerf, Frank W. John Hill Hewitt: sources and bibliography. At-lanta, Georgia: Emory General Libraries, 1981. 42 p.

A 19th-century composer of songs and ballads. Active in all aspects of the popular theater. This work is a guide to a special collection in the Emory University Woodruff Library.

HOLST, GUSTAV

1620. Holst, Imogen. A thematic catalogue of Gustav Holst's music. London: Faber Music Ltd. in association with G. and I. Holst Ltd., 1974. 285 p.

IVES, CHARLES

1621. De Lerma, Dominique-René. Charles Edward Ives, 1874–1954: a bibliography of his music. Kent, Ohio: Kent State University Press, 1970. 212 p.
Works listed alphabetically by title, with indexes of publishers, medium, chronology, arrangers, poets and librettists, phonorecords, and performers.

JIRÁK, KAREL BOLESLAV

1622. Tischler, Alice. Karel Boleslav Jirák; a catalog of his works. Detroit, Michigan: Information Coordinators, 1975. 85 p. (Detroit studies in music bibliography, 32)
Brief review by Stephen M. Fry in *Notes*, 36 (1975), p. 303.

KUHLAU, FRIEDRICH

1623. Fog, Dan. Kompositionen von Friedrich Kuhlau. Thematisch- Bibliographischer Katalog. Copenhagen: Dan Fog Musikforlag, 1977. 203 p.
233 numbered items. Index of titles and text incipits. Index to persons cited.
Review by June C. Ottenberg in *Notes*, 35 (1978), p. 85–86.

LISZT, FRANZ

1624. Eckhardt, Mária P. Franz Liszt's music manuscripts in the national Széchényi Library, Budapest. [Translated by Erzsébet Mészáros; translation revised by Rena Mueller.] Budapest: Akadémiai Kiadó; Stuyvesant, New York: Pendragon Press, 1986. 252 p. (Studies in Central and Eastern European music, 2)

LOCKE, MATTHEW

1625. Harding, Rosamund. A thematic catalogue of the works of Matthew Locke; with a calendar of the main events of his life. Oxford: R. E. M. Harding; distributed by Blackwell, 1971. 177 p.
Review by Jack A. Westrup in *Music and Letters*, 53 (1972), p. 442–44; an anonymous review in *Times Literary Supplement*, no. 3,658 (April 1972), p. 387; by Michael Tilmouth in *Musical Times*, 113 (1972), p. 561–62; by Gloria Rose in *Notes*, 29 (1973), p. 457.

LULLY, JEAN-BAPTISTE

1626. Schneider, Herbert. Chronologisch-thematisches Verzeichnis sämtlicher Werke von Jean-Baptiste Lully (LWV). Tutzing: Schneider, 1981. 570 p. (Mainzer Studien zur Musikwissenschaft, 14)
Covers printed and manuscript sources. False attributions and lost copies are identified. Musical incipits are provided in treble and bass parts. A splendid thematic catalog.
See "The Lully labyrinth: cross-references and misattributions in the

Lully Werke-Verzeichnis," by Bruce Gustafson in *Notes*, 44 (1987), p. 33–39.

MARCELLO, BENEDETTO

1627. Fruchtman, Caroline S. Checklist of vocal chamber works by Benedetto Marcello. Detroit, Michigan: Information Coordinators, 1967. 37 p. (Detroit studies in music bibliography, 10)
Review by Owen Jander in *Notes*, 24 (1968), p. 491–92.

MIGOT, GEORGES

1628. Honegger, Marc. Catalogue des œuvres musicales de Georges Migot. Strasbourg: Amis de l'œuvre et de la pensée de Georges Migot, Institut de musicologie, 1977. 126 p.

MONTEVERDI, CLAUDIO

1629. Bibliography Committee, New York Chapter, MLA. An alphabetical index to Claudio Monteverdi: Tutte le opere. Ann Arbor, Michigan: Music Library Association, 1963. (MLA index series, 1)

MOSCHELES, IGNAZ

1630. Kistner, Friedrich (Leipzig firm). Thematisches Verzeichnis im Druck erschienener Compositionen von Ignaz Moscheles. London: H. Baron, 1966. 66 p.

MOZART, WOLFGANG AMADEUS

1631. Haberkamp, Gertraut. Die Erstdrucke der Werke von Wolfgang Amadeus Mozart, Bibliographie. Tutzing: H. Schneider, 1986. 2 v. (Musikbibliographische Arbeiten, 10/11)
Vol. 1. Textband; Vol. 2. Bildband.

1632. Hill, George R. and Murray Gould, *et al.* A thematic locator for Mozart's works as listed in Köchel's *Chronologisch-thematisches Verzeichnis*, 6th edition. Hackensack, New Jersey: Joseph Boonin, 1970. 76 p. (Music indexes and bibliographies, 1)

> The thematic locator contained in this volume presents the incipits of Mozart's musical works systematically, enabling the user to determine quickly the Köchel number and movement of any piece by Mozart. [*Preface*]

In two sections, one arranging the themes by interval size, the other arranging them by pitch name.

1633. Köchel, Ludwig, Ritter von. Chronologisch-thematisches Verzeichnis sämtlicher Tonwerke Wolfgang Amadé Mozarts. Sechste Auflage bearbeitet von Franz Giegling, Alexander Weinmann, Gerd Sievers. Wiesbaden: Breitkopf & Härtel, 1964. 1,024 p.

First published in Leipzig, 1862. 2nd edition prepared by Paul Graf von Waldersee and published in 1905. 3rd edition, edited by Alfred Einstein, was published in 1937 and reissued with a supplement in 1947 by Edwards Brothers in Ann Arbor, Michigan. The 4th and 5th editions were unaltered reprints of the 4th, but did not include the Einstein supplement of 1947.

The monumental thematic catalog of Mozart's works, edited and brought up to modern standards by Alfred Einstein in the 3rd edition (1946), and then for the 6th edition made the beneficiary of more recent scholarship by Giegling, Weinmann, and Sievers.

Presented in chronological order, entries cite references to manuscripts, early editions, and to the modern complete works (the *Sämtliche Werke* of Breitkopf & Härtel as well as the *Neue Ausgabe Sämtlicher Werke* of Bärenreiter, the volumes of the latter issued until about 1964). Köchel provides a classified catalog with brief thematic incipits as an overview of the main chronological catalog.

There are numerous appendixes providing information on early "complete" editions and the Hoboken *Photogram-Archive* in Vienna (no. 2431). There is an index to vocal titles and first lines and a general index. This is a tour de force of scholarship and a brilliant example of the accretion of musico-bibliographical knowledge by generations of researchers.

1634. Schlager, Karl-Heinz. Wolfgang Amadeus Mozart, Verzeichnis von Erst- und Frühdrucken bis etwa 1800. Kassel: Bärenreiter, 1978. 2 v. (RISM, ser. A, pt. I, supplement)

"Sonderdruck aus Répertoire International des Sources Musicales A/I, Einzeldruck vor 1800. Redaktion Karlheinz Schlager. Bd. 6: Montalbano-Pleyel." The second volume includes the directory of sigla of libraries contributing to the catalog.

MUSGRAVE, THEA

1635. Hixon, Donald L. Thea Musgrave, a bio-bibliography. Westport, Connecticut: Greenwood Press, 1984. 187 p. (Bio-bibliographies in music, 1)

First number of a series, each devoted to a single composer. There is a lengthy biographical section followed by a critical bibliography of the composer's works and a discography.

NICHELMANN, CHRISTOPH

1636. Lee, Douglas A. The works of Christoph Nichelmann: a thematic index. Detroit, Michigan: Information Coordinators, 1971. 100 p. (Detroit studies in music bibliography, 19)

PALESTRINA, GIOVANNI PIERLUIGI DA

1637. Hall, Alison. Palestrina: an index to the Casimiri, Kalmus, and Haberl editions. Philadelphia, Pennsylvania: Music Library Association, 1980. 82 p. (MLA index and bibliography series, 22)

PALLAVICINO, BENEDETTO

1638. Flanders, Peter. A thematic index to the works of Benedetto Pallavicino. Hackensack, New Jersey: J. Boonin, 1974. 85 p. (Music indexes and bibliographies, 11)

PERGOLESI, GIOVANNI BATTISTA

1639. Paymer, Marvin E. Giovanni Battista Pergolesi, 1710–1736; a thematic catalogue of the opera omnia with an appendix listing omitted compositions. New York: Pendragon Press, 1977. 99 p. (Thematic catalogues, 1)

PEZEL, JOHANN

1640. Weinandt, Elwyn. Johann Pezel (1639–1694): a thematic catalogue of his instrumental works. New York: Pendragon Press, 1983. 102 p. (Thematic catalogues, 9)

PLEYEL, IGNACE

1641. Benton, Rita. Ignace Pleyel: a thematic catalogue of his compositions. New York: Pendragon Press, 1977. 482 p. (Thematic catalogues, 2)
Exhaustive coverage of the voluminous works of a popular composer of the late 18th and early 19th centuries.
Reviews by Floyd K. Grove in the *Journal of the American Musicological Society*, 33 (1980), p. 204–210, by Lenore Coral in *Notes*, 35 (1978), p. 75–76, and by Alan Tyson in *Fontes Artis Musicae*, 26 (1979), p. 139–41.

PUCCINI, GIACOMO

1642. Hopkinson, Cecil. A bibliography of the works of Giacomo Puccini, 1858–1924. New York: Broude Bros., 1968. 77 p.
An analytical bibliography.

REGNART, JACOB

1643. Pass, Walter. Thematischer Katalog sämtlicher Werke Jacob Regnarts [c. 1540–1599]. Wien, Köln, and Graz: Böhlau in Komm., 1969. 244 p. (Tabulae musicae Austriacae, 5)
Review by John Graziano in *Notes*, 27 (1971), p. 493–94; by Wilhelm Schepping in *Jahrbuch für Volksliedforschung*, 16 (1971), p. 186; by Jürgen Kindermann in *Die Musikforschung*, 25 (1972), p. 371–72.

ROSETTI, ANTON

1644. Kaul, Oskar. Thematisches Verzeichnis der Instrumentalwerke von Anton Rosetti. Wiesbaden: Breitkopf & Härtel, [1968]. 27 p.

ROSSI, SALAMONE

1645. Newman, Joel and Fritz Rikko. A thematic index to the works of Salamone Rossi. Hackensack, New Jersey: J. Boonin, 1972. 143 p. (Music indexes and bibliographies, 6)
Review by Neal Zaslaw in *Notes*, 31 (1975), p. 577.

SAMMARTINI, GIOVANNI BATTISTA

1646. Jenkins, Newell and Bathia Churgin. Thematic catalogue of the works of Giovanni Battista Sammartini: orchestral and vocal music. Cambridge, Massachusetts: Published for the American Musicological Society by Harvard University Press, 1976. 315 p.
Review by Eugene K. Wolf in *Notes*, 34 (1978), p. 850–52, and by Howard Brofsky in *Journal of the American Musicological Society*, 32 (1978), p. 365–67.

SCHUBERT, FRANZ

1647. Deutsch, Otto Erich. Franz Schubert: Thematisches Verzeichnis seiner Werke in chronologischer Folge. Neuausgabe in deutscher Sprache bearbeitet und herausgegeben von der Editionsleitung der Neuen Schubert-Ausgabe und Werner Aderhold. Kassel: Bärenreiter, 1978. 712 p. (Neue Schubert Ausgabe, Serie VIII, Bd. 4)
Review by L. Michael Griffel in *Notes*, 36 (1979), p. 83–86.

1648. Deutsch, Otto Erich. Die Originalausgaben von Schuberts Goethe-Liedern; Ein musikbibliographischer Versuch. Wien: Antiquariat V. A. Heck, 1926. 23 p.
A pamphlet distributed to the participants in the Jubelfeier der Nationalbibliothek (25–29 May 1926).
Precise bibliographical descriptions of 26 Goethe settings by Franz Schubert.

1649. Hilmar, Ernst. Verzeichnis der Schubert-Handschriften in der Musiksammlung der WienerStadt-und Landesbibliothek. Kassel: Bärenreiter, 1978. 144 p. (Catalogus musicus, 8)
Review by Michael Griffel in *Notes*, 36 (1979), p. 83–86.

SCHUMANN, ROBERT

1650. Hofmann, Kurt. Die Erstdrucke der Werke von Robert Schumann: Bibliographie mit Wiedergabe von 234 Titelblättern. Tutzing: H. Schneider, 1979. 464 p. (Musikbibliographische Arbeiten, 6)
Review by Susan T. Sommer in *Notes*, 37 (1980), p. 322–23.

1651. Ochs, Michael. Schumann index, part 1: an alphabetical index to Robert Schumann: *Werke*. Ann Arbor, Michigan: Music Library Association, 1967. 26 p. (MLA index series, 6)

1652. Weichlein, William. Schumann index, part 2: an alphabetical index to the solo songs of Robert Schumann. Ann Arbor, Michigan: Music Library Association, 1967. 35 p. (MLA index series, 7)

SCHÜTZ, HEINRICH

1653. Miller, D. Douglas and Anne L. Highsmith. Heinrich Schütz: a bibliography of the collected works and performing editions. New York: Greenwood Press, 1986. 278 p. (Music reference collection, 9)

This is an annotated guide to the very complex bibliography of modern editions of the works of Schütz. Source and title indexes. Index to performing forces.

SEEGER, RUTH CRAWFORD

1654. Graume, Matilda. "Ruth Crawford Seeger." In *Women Making Music; the Western Art Tradition, 1150–1950*, p. 370–88. Edited by Jane Bowers and Judith Tick. Urbana: University of Illinois Press, 1986.

Includes a list of compositions by Seeger and a discography of those works.

SHOSTAKOVICH, DMITRI

1655. MacDonald, Malcolm. Dmitri Shostakovich; a complete catalogue, revised edition. London: Boosey & Hawkes, 1985. 56 p.

Contains a chronological listing of works, with a classified index and alphabetical index.

STRADELLA, ALESSANDRO

1656. Jander, Owen H. A catalogue of the manuscripts of compositions by Alessandro Stradella found in European and American libraries. Wellesley, Massachusetts: Wellesley College, 1962. 72 leaves (typescript).

First issued in 1960.

A classified catalog of Stradella's works with locations of the manuscript sources. The principal divisions are instrumental music, vocal music with sacred texts, vocal music with secular texts.

STRAUSS, RICHARD

1657. Mueller von Asow, Erich Hermann. Richard Strauss; thematisches Verzeichnis. Wien: L. Doblinger, 1955–74. 3 v. 1,688 p.

Vol. 3: "Nach dem Tode des Verfassers vollendet und hrsg. von Alfons Ott und Franz Trenner."

Contents: Bd. 1. Opus 1–59; Bd. 2. Opus 60–86; Bd. 3. Werke ohne Opuszahlen.

Review by Neal Zaslaw in *Notes*, 31 (1975), p. 772–73.

1658. Trenner, Franz. Richard Strauss: Werkverzeichnis. Wien: Doblinger, 1985. 153 p.

This is a revised works list to be used in conjunction with the Mueller von Asow thematic catalog (no. 1657).

Review by Scott Warfield in *Notes*, 42 (1985), p. 292–93.

STRAVINSKY, IGOR

1659. De Lerma, Dominique-René and Thomas J. Ahrens. Igor Fedorovitch Stravinsky, 1882–1971; a practical guide to publications of his music. Kent, Ohio: Kent State University Press, 1974. 158 p.

1660. Shepard, John. "The Stravinsky *Nachlass*: a provisional checklist of music manuscripts." In *Notes*, 40 (1984), p. 719–50.

An inventory including extensive descriptions of "223 music manuscript items for 98 works by Stravinsky," including arrangements and copies of the works of other composers.

1661. White, Eric Walter. Stravinsky, the composer and his works. London: Faber and Faber, 1979. 656 p.

First edition, 1966. 608 p.

Review by François Lesure in *Fontes Artis Musicae*, 27 (1980), p. 121–22.

SULLIVAN, ARTHUR

1662. Poladian, Sirvart. Sir Arthur Sullivan: an index to the texts of his vocal works. Detroit, Michigan: Information Coordinators, 1961. 91 p. (Detroit studies in music bibliography, 2)

A comprehensive index of first lines, titles, and refrains to the composer's vocal works, sacred and secular.

Review by William Lichtenwanger in *Notes*, 19 (1962), p. 428–30.

1663. Presenting in word and song, score and deed, the life and work of Sir Arthur Sullivan. Composer for Victorian England from *Onward, Christian Soldiers* to Gilbert and Sullivan opera. Compiled by Reginald Allen in collaboration with Gale R. d'Luhy. New York: Pierpont Morgan Library, 1975. 215 p.

Also published in Boston by D. R. Godine, 1975.

Catalog of an exhibition of some of the extensive Gilbert and Sullivan collection at the Pierpont Morgan Library.

Variant edition of no. 2252.

TELEMANN, GEORG PHILIPP

1664. Menke, Werner. Thematisches Verzeichnis der Vokalwerke von Georg Philipp Telemann. Frankfurt am Main: V. Klostermann, 1982–83. 2 v.

Contents: Bd. 1. *Cantaten zum gottesdienstlichen Gebrauch*; Bd. 2. *Thematisches Werkverzeichnis*.

THOMSON, VIRGIL

1665. Meckna, Michael. Virgil Thomson, a bio-bibliography. New York: Greenwood Press, 1986. 203 p. (Bio-bibliographies in music, 4)

VERDI, GIUSEPPE

1666. Chusid, Martin. A catalog of Verdi's operas. Hackensack, New Jersey: Joseph Boonin, 1973. 125 p. (Music indexes and bibliographies, 5)

1667. Hopkinson, Cecil. A bibliography of the works of Giuseppe Verdi, 1813–1901. New York: Broude Bros., 1973–78. 2 v.
Contents: vol. 1. Vocal and instrumental works; vol. 2. Operatic works.
Review of vol. 1 by David Rosen in *Notes*, 31 (1975), p. 570–72. Reviews of vol. 2 by James J. Fuld in *Notes*, 35 (1979), p. 626, and by Andrew Porter in *Fontes Artis Musicae*, 27 (1980), p. 55–56.

VICTORIA, TOMAS LUIS DE

1668. Bibliography Committee, New York Chapter, MLA. An alphabetical index to Tomas Luis de Victoria: *Opera omnia.* Ann Arbor, Michigan: Music Library Association, 1966. 26 p. (MLA index series, 5)

VIVALDI, ANTONIO

1669. Coral, Lenore. A concordance of the thematic indexes to the instrumental works of Antonio Vivaldi. Ann Arbor, Michigan: Music Library Association, 1965. 32 p. (MLA index series, 4)
2nd edition, Ann Arbor, 1972. 40 p.

1670. Fanna, Antonio. Opere strumentali di Antonio Vivaldi (1678–1741); catalogo numerico-tematico. Secondo la catalogazione Fanna. 2a edizione riveduta e ampliata. Milano: Ricordi, 1986. 185 p.
Introductory material in Italian and English.

1671. Martin, Arlan Stone. Vivaldi violin concertos; a handbook. Metuchen, New Jersey: Scarecrow Press, 1972. 278 p.
A thematic catalog of the Vivaldi concertos with indexes coordinating various numbering systems: Fanna, Ricordi, Pincherle, Rinaldi. Appendix E lists recorded versions of the works.
Review by John Hill in *Notes*, 31 (1975), p. 577.

1672. Ohmura, Noriko. A reference concordance table of Vivaldi's instrumental works. Tokyo: Academia Music, 1972. 267 p.
Reviews by Seymour Kesten in *Journal of the American Musicological Society*, 28 (1975), p. 153–56, and by Lenore Coral in *Notes*, 30 (1974), p. 533–34.

1673. Ryom, Peter. Répertoire des œuvres d'Antonio Vivaldi: les compositions instrumentale. Copenhague: Engstrom & Sødring, 1986. 726 p.

Based on recent scholarship, this catalog provides the best and latest information on the instrumental works of Vivaldi, a complex repertory with numerous identification systems provided by publishers from Vivaldi's time to the present. These entries give substantial descriptions of autograph sources, references to preceding thematic catalogs, references to the Ricordi edition of the complete instrumental works, and various historical or bibliographical remarks. This is a classified catalog, with tables of concordances to the Rinaldi *Catalogo*, the Pincherle *Inventaire Thématique*, and the Fanna *Catalogo*. Exhaustive lists of known copies of early printed sources are not provided; readers are referred to RISM series A, part I, vol. 9 (no. 1781). The introduction, essay on bibliographic research, and key to the repertoire are essential aids to using the Ryom *Répertoire*. Indexes of names, titles of vocal works cited, and titles.

Refer to the Ryom *Verzeichnis* for entries on music including voices (no. 1674).

1674. Ryom, Peter. Verzeichnis der Werke Antonio Vivaldis (RV) Kleine Ausg., 2., verb. und erw. Aufl. Leipzig: Deutscher Verlag für Musik, 1977. 226 p.

First printed in 1974.

Erratum slip inserted. "Chronologische Übersicht der Vivaldi-Werkverzeichnisse," p. [213]–17.

WAGENSEIL, GEORG

1675. Scholz-Michelitsch, Helga. Das Orchester- und Kammermusikwerk von Georg Christoph Wagenseil. Thematischer Katalog. Wien: Hermann Böhlaus Nachf., 1972. 228 p.

The incipits reflect all parts and movements in the works. Sources are located in libraries throughout the world. Bibliographical references.

WAGNER, RICHARD

1676. Hopkinson, Cecil. Tannhäuser. An examination of 36 editions. Tutzing: H. Schneider, 1973. 48 p. (Musikbibliographische Arbeiten, 1)

1677. Klein, Horst F. G. Erst- und Frühdrucke der Textbücher von Richard Wagner: Bibliographie. Tutzing: Schneider, 1979. 63 p. (Musikbibliographische Arbeiten, 4)

1678. Klein, Horst F. G. Erstdrucke der musikalischen Werke von Richard Wagner: Bibliographie. Tutzing: H. Schneider, 1983. 236 p. (Musikbibliographische Arbeiten, 5)

Review by James J. Fuld in *Notes*, 41 (1984), p. 284–85.

WEBERN, ANTON VON

1679. Roman, Zotán. Anton Webern; an annotated bibliography. Detroit, Michigan: Information Coordinators, 1983. 219 p. (Detroit studies in music bibliography, 48)

Covers over 100 journals in numerous languages.

EARLY MUSIC IN MODERN EDITIONS
(Including Collections and Monuments)

The purpose of the bibliographies listed in this category is to direct the user to new editions of old music — one of the most pressing needs of the performer, the teacher, and the music historian. Some of the items listed below are focused on the contents of the major critical editions (*Denkmäler, Gesamtausgaben*); others emphasize the more practical, performing editions of early music. In either case, listings of this kind are soon out of date. To keep abreast of new publications in this area, one should consult the music review sections of a variety of current periodicals: *Notes, Music and Letters, Die Musikforschung*, and *Journal of the American Musicological Society*, as well as such regular listings as may be found in *Fontes Artis Musicae*. See also the entries in this volume under "Guides to Systematic and Historical Musicology." Many of the works listed there have bibliographical supplements that cite and evaluate historical editions and monuments.

By far the most useful guide to the contents of the historical sets and critical editions is Heyer (no. 1691 below).

1680. Basso, Alberto. "Repertorio generale dei 'monumenta musicae,' delle antologie, raccolte e pubblicazioni di musica antica sino a tutto il 1970." In *Rivista Italiana di Musicologia*, 6 (1972), p. 3–135.

Introduction treats the history of the publication of monumental sets, providing inventories of the contents of 33 sets of anthologies published before 1850. There follows a description with a listing of contents of 61 international sets, then national sets grouped alphabetically by country. The last section is devoted to minor collections or single-volume anthologies, also organized by country.

1681. Bennwitz, Hanspeter, ed. Musikalisches Erbe und Gegenwart: Musiker-Gesamtausgaben in der Bundes-Republik Deutschland. Im Auftrag der Stiftung Volkswagenwerk herausgegeben von Hanspeter Bennwitz, Georg Feder, Ludwig Finscher, und Wolfgang Rehm. Kassel: Bärenreiter, 1975. 147 p.

A survey of 11 complete editions in progress in Germany. Contents of each set are given along with sample pages illustrating the editorial process.

1682. Bukofzer, Manfred. "List of editions [of Baroque music]." In his *Music in the Baroque Era*, p. 461–69. New York: Norton, 1947.

A selective, but dated, list organized under four main headings: (1) general anthologies; (2) historical collections; (3) smaller collections and performing editions; and (4) complete or collected editions of individual composers. Minimum bibliographical information.

Chapman, James, Sheldon Fine and Mary Rasmussen. "Music for wind instruments in historical editions...." See no. 1489.

1683. Charles, Sydney Robinson. "Editions, historical." In *The New Grove Dictionary of Music and Musicians*, edited by Stanley Sadie, vol. 5, p. 848–69. Julie Woodward assisted with the bibliography. London: Macmillan, 1980.

Extensive bibliographies of single-composer complete editions, other collected editions, editions of theoretical works, anthologies (extended, small vocal, small instrumental, small general), and a short bibliography on the subject.

1684. Charles, Sydney Robinson. A handbook of music and music literature in sets and series. New York: Free Press, 1972. 497 p.

Useful, but dated, guide to the contents of critical editions, both collective and devoted to the works of individual composers. Two further sections treat (1) monographs and facsimile series, and (2) music periodicals and yearbooks.

Review by Dale Good in *Notes*, 30 (1974), p. 789–90.

1685. Coover, James B. Gesamtausgaben: a checklist. Distant Press, 1970. 27 leaves.

A practical listing, alphabetical by composer, of 376 *Gesamtausgaben*. The list was designed to help with acquisitions in a college or university music library. Includes all works "for which completeness was the professed goal, disregarding failure to accomplish it."

1686. "Denkmäler und Gesamtausgaben. " In *Repertorium der Musikwissenschaft*.... bearb. von Willi Kahl und Wilhelm-Martin Luther, p. 232–43. Kassel & Basel: Bärenreiter, 1953.

140 entries for major historical sets. Full bibliographical information, but no listing of contents.

The *Repertorium* cited as no. 706.

1687. "Éditions et Rééditions de Musique Ancienne (avant 1800)." In *Fontes Artis Musicae*, no. 1–22. Paris: Assoc. Internationale des Bibliothèques Musicales, 1954–75.

One of the few listings of new editions of early music. International coverage. Full bibliographical information, including price.

1688. Eitner, Robert. Verzeichniss neuer Ausgaben alter Musikwerke aus der frühesten Zeit bis zum Jahre 1800. Berlin: Trautwein, 1871. 208 p. (Monatshefte für Musikgeschichte. Beilage. 1871)

Nachträgen, published in *Monatshefte*, 9 (1877); "Register zu den Nächtragen" as its *Beilage, 1877*; and 10 (1878).

Reprint published by Anne-marie Schnase, Scarsdale, New York, in 1960.

Still useful as a guide to the contents of early historical collections, including music in histories. *Abtheilung I*: annotated list of collections and literary works containing music; *Abtheilung II*: index of composers and their works, with separate listings of anonymous works and of German secular song through the 16th century.

1689. Hagopian, Viola L. Italian ars nova music, a bibliographic guide to modern editions and related literature. 2nd ed., revised and expanded. Berkeley and Los Angeles: University of California Press, 1973. 175 p.

First printed in 1964.

An organized, annotated bibliography treating the work done by scholars in the field of 14th-century Italian music.

Review of the first edition by Ursula Günther in *Die Musikforschung*, 20 (1967), p. 83–84.

1690. Hall, Alison. E. H. Fellowes, an index to the *English Madrigalists* and the *English School of Lutenist Song Writers*. Boston, Massachusetts: Music Library Association, 1984. 100 p. (MLA index and bibliography series, 23)

An analytic index to the *English Madrigalists* and the *English School of Lutenist Song Writers*.

1691. Heyer, Anna Harriet. Historical sets, collected editions, and monuments of music; a guide to their contents. 3rd ed. Chicago, Illinois: American Library Association, 1980. 2 v.

First published in 1957. 2nd edition published in 1969. 563 p.

An indispensable guide to the contents of the principal anthologies of music. Cites approximately 1,300 anthologies, ranging from one-volume publications to the extended national monuments series and complete works of prolific composers. Detailed listings of the contents of sets, including important publisher's series (e.g., Bärenreiter's *Hortus musicus*, Nagel's *Musik-Archiv*, Kistner und Siegel's *Organum*, etc.). Without recourse to Heyer, access to tens of thousands of works would be tedious at best and in the worst cases impossible.

Entries provide full bibliographic information and list contents of individual volumes. Numerous cross-references. A comprehensive index of composers, editors, and titles provides access to the contents of the anthologies.

A team of scholar-bibliographers under the direction of George Hill is preparing a continuation of this work using computers; distribution of this new work is expected to take place in one of the newer electronic forms, perhaps CD-ROM, in the foreseeable future.

Review of the 1st edition by Irene Millen in *Notes*, 15 (1958), p. 390–91; by Harriet Nicewonger in *Library Journal* (Sept. 1958), p. 2380. Of the 2nd edition by Lenore Coral in *Journal of the American Musicological Society*, 24 (1971), p. 308–309; by Richard H. Hunter in *Notes*, 26 (1969), p. 275–77. Of the 3rd edition by George R. Hill in *Notes*, 38 (1982), p. 594.

1692. Hilton, Ruth B. An index to early music in selected anthologies. Clifton, New Jersey: European American Music Corporation, 1978. 127 p. (Music indexes and bibliographies, 13)

An index to 1,633 pieces of music in anthologies of music from antiquity to the end of the baroque period. Part 1 cites entries for composers and titles; each entry providing information about the type of work, the country of origin, date of composition or first publication, performing medium, texts, source "school," and thematic catalog number. Chants and anonymous works are entered by title, except for dances, which are entered by form (e.g., estampie). Part 2 is a subject (i.e., form and genre) index. There is a list of thematic catalogs employed in the index and another list of the 19 anthologies treated.

Review by Susan T. Sommer in *Notes*, 35 (1979), p. 641–42.

1693. Hirsch, Paul and Kathi Meyer. "Sammelwerke und Gesamtausgaben." In their *Katalog der Musikbibliothek Paul Hirsch*, Bd. IV. Cambridge: Cambridge University Press, 1947. p. 331–409.

Lists 90 complete editions and collections, with a detailed survey of their contents.

1694. "Novae editiones musicae classicae." In *Acta Musicologica*, vols. 3–24. Leipzig and Copenhagen: Internationale Gesellschaft für Musikwissenschaft, Jan. 1931–52.

Regular listing of the new editions of early music arranged alphabetically by composer, giving title, scoring, editor, place, publisher, date, and price. Discontinued after 1952.

1695. Ochs, Michael. An index to *Das Chorwerk*, vols. 1–110. Ann Arbor, Michigan: Music Library Association, 1970. 38 p. (MLA index series, 10)

Composer index and title index. Information includes volume, page, type of composition and vocal ensemble.

1696. Petrov, Stoian V. and Khristo Kodov. Starobulgarski muzikalni pametnitsi. [Old Bulgarian musical documents.] Sofia: Nauka i izkustvo, 1973. 360 p.

Facsimiles of most of the musical notation preserved in Bulgarian manuscripts.

Review by Miloš Velimirovic in *Notes*, 32 (1976), p. 531–33.

1697. Sakkyokuka zenshu, gakufu sosho shozai mokuroku. Union check list of collected editions, historical sets, and monuments of music in Japanese music libraries. Sakkyokuka Zenshu Gakufu Sosho Shozai Mokuroku Henshu Iinkai hen. Zoho kaiteiban. Tokyo: Ongaku Toshokan Kyogikai & Sohatsubaimoto Akademia Myujikku, 1983. 2 v.

Compiled by the Working Group of Union Checklist in Music Library Association of Japan.

First published in 1975, indexes holdings of 25 music libraries in Japan.

1698. Samuel, Harold E. "Editions, historical." In *The New Harvard Dictionary of Music*, edited by Don M. Randel, p. 264–76. Cambridge, Massachusetts: Harvard University Press, 1986.

Lists 427 important serial publications of early music, from plainsong through the 18th century. Organized in three checklists: Collected works; *Denkmäler*; Series of performing editions.

1699. Schering, Arnold. "Übersicht über die musikgeschichtlichen Sammel-werke und kritische Gesamtausgaben der Werke der grossen Meister der Musik aus dem Verlage von Breitkopf & Härtel." In his *Tabellen zur Musikgeschichte. Anhang*, 30 p. Leipzig: Breitkopf & Härtel, 1934.

A useful breakdown of the contents of the critical editions published by Breitkopf & Härtel. This supplement is omitted from the 1962 edition of the *Tabellen* (no. 620).

1700. Schiedermair, Ludwig. "Gesamtausgaben und Publikationsreihen in Übersichten." In his *Einführung in das Studium der Musikgeschichte. Anhang*, p. 104–161. Bonn: F. Bummlers Verlag, 1947.

Surveys the contents of the major sets and publishers' series.

1701. Schmieder, Wolfgang. "Denkmäler der Tonkunst." In *MGG*, v. 3, cols. 164–92.

Lists 213 major editions, practical and scholarly, with contents given in considerable detail. Classified as to national or international coverage.

1702. Schmieder, Wolfgang. "Gesamtausgaben." In *MGG*, v. 4, cols. 1850–76.

A valuable discussion of the historical development of critical editions of the work of individual composers followed by entries for 84 such editions, with detailed listings of contents.

1703. The symphony, 1720–1840: a comprehensive collection of full scores in sixty volumes: reference volume, contents of the set and collected thematic indexes. Preface by Barry S. Brook. New York: Garland Publishing, 1986. 627 p.

A thematic catalog of the 549 works of 244 composers in the collection *The Symphony, 1720–1840*, including 13 thematic indexes not included in the individual volumes when originally published. Includes thousands of incipits with copious information on each symphony and its sources. Organized by composer, but not indexed. Bibliography of catalog references.

1704. Verzeichnis der Neudrucke alter Musik. Herausgegeben im Auftrage des Staatlichen Instituts für deutsche Musikforschung von Walter Lott. Leipzig: F. Hofmeister, 1937–43. 7 v.

An annual bibliography of new editions of music composed before 1800, covering the years of publication 1936–42. Includes separate works and contents of collections. German publications emphasized. Works listed by composer; medium and title index.

PRIMARY SOURCES OF EARLY MUSIC: MANUSCRIPTS AND PRINTED BOOKS

This section will direct users to bibliographies of original source materials, chiefly those prior to 1800. The list is highly selective. Nearly every dissertation or research study devoted to early music contains its bibliography of primary sources. Some of these bibliographies are of great value, but any attempt to cite them all would extend far beyond the scope of the present work. The user should be reminded that the major reference works such as the *New Grove, MGG,* or Riemann's *Lexikon* contain abundant listings of primary sources. See, for example, the *MGG* articles under "Ars antiqua," "Ars nova," or "Chanson" and the "Sources" article in the *New Grove.*

Since the third edition of the present work was published, several important volumes in the *Repertoire International des Sources Musicales* (*International Inventory of Musical Sources*) have made their appearance (see nos. 1148–1151, 1781–1790, 1853). In fact, the characteristics of the various RISM series have become well-defined and important progress has been made in each series toward the goal of providing international union catalogs of the primary and early secondary sources for the study of music written before 1800. RISM series A part I concerns the works of individual composers; the *Einzeldrucke* volumes (nos. 1781 and 1782) provide citations of editions of printed music by individual composers. RISM series A, part II, the music manuscripts 1600–1800 (no. 1786), is underway in its mission to prepare an international union list of manuscripts of music attributable to single composers. RISM series B (nos. 1148–1151, 1781–1785, and 1841) concerns a variety of collective works, including a two-volume bibliography of writings about music published before 1800. RISM series C (no. 1853) is a multivolume international directory of music research libraries and collections.

It should be obvious that one of the most direct approaches to primary sources will be found in the section entitled "Catalogs of Music Libraries and Collections." Another useful approach, although not employed here apart from one or two exceptions, is through the catalogs of antiquarian music and book dealers such as Lisa Cox, J. & J. Lubrano, etc.

See also the section "Histories and Bibliographies of Music Printing and Publishing" for bibliographies of the output of some of the major music publishing houses from the 16th through the 18th centuries.

1705. Abravanel, Claude. "A checklist of music manuscripts in facsimile edition." In *Notes,* 34 (1978), p. 557–70.

A selected bibliography of facsimiles of entire works.

Substantially supplemented by James B. Coover in "Music manuscripts in facsimile edition: supplement" in *Notes,* 37 (1981), p. 533–56. Coover's bibliography includes a helpful section on facsimiles appearing in series included in the bibliography.

See also no. 1723 for a bibliography of composite music manuscripts in facsimile.

1706. Anderson, Gordon A. "Notre Dame and related conductus: a catalogue raisonné." In *Miscellanea Musicologica. Adelaide Studies in Musicology,* 6 (1972), p. 153–229; 7 (1975), p. 1–81.

A "work in progress" designed to give "systematic coverage to all pieces which may be designated conductus and which issue from c. 1170 to the close of the 13th century." Sources are identified and bibliographical references cited.

1707. Becker, Carl Ferdinand. Die Tonwerke des XVI. und XVII. Jahrhunderts, oder systematisch-chronologische Zusammenstellung der in diesen zwei Jahrhunderten gedruckten Musikalien. Zweite Ausgabe. Leipzig: E. Fleischer, 1855. 358 cols.

First published in 1847. Reprint of the 2nd ed. by Olms, Hildesheim, 1969.

An early classified bibliography of musical source materials, chronologically arranged under categories, with an index of composers and a general index to the whole. Attempts to list all musical compositions published in the 16th and 17th centuries to which actual or approximate dates could be assigned. An abridgment of Rimbault's *Bibliotheca Madrigaliana* (no. 1792) is included as a supplement.

1708. Besseler, Heinrich. "Studien zur Musik des Mittelalters: 1. Neue Quellen des 14. und beginnenden 15. Jahrhunderts. 2. Die Motette von Franko von Köln bis Philipp von Vitry." In *Archiv für Musikwissenschaft*, 7 (1925), p. 167–252, and 9 (1927), p. 137–258.

Two articles that are basic source studies for the music of the late medieval period, containing numerous inventories and descriptions of *ars nova* manuscripts. They supplement the work of Friedrich Ludwig covering the *ars antiqua* sources (no. 1764).

1709. Bibliotheca Musico-Liturgica. A descriptive handlist of the musical and Latin-Liturgical mss. of the Middle Ages preserved in the libraries of Great Britain and Ireland. Drawn up by W. H. Frere ... and printed for the members of the Plainsong and Mediaeval Music Society.... London: Quaritch, 1901–1932. 2 v.

Reprinted by Georg Olms, Hildesheim, 1967.

A union list of manuscript sources of early music in Great Britain. Vol. 1 (nos. 1–545): manuscripts at Lambeth and Oxford. Vol. 2 (nos. 546–1,031): manuscripts in cathedral chapter libraries and at Manchester, Dublin, Cambridge, etc. Full descriptions of the manuscripts; 17 plates. Indexes of service books, places, persons, and of Oxford Bodleian and Cambridge University Library manuscripts.

1710. Bohn, Emil. "Bibliothek des gedruckten mehrstimmigen weltlichen deutschen Liedes vom Anfange des 16. Jahrhunderts bis c. 1640." In the author's *Fünfzig historische Concerte in Breslau, 1881–1892*, p. 77–188. Breslau: Hainauer, 1893.

A bibliography of German printed secular polyphonic song. The collections are listed chronologically to 1625; the volumes containing works by individual composers are listed alphabetically. Detailed bibliographical information, but contents not given. A useful guide to the printed sources of early German song.

1711. Bolle, Wilhelm. Die gedruckten englischen Liederbücher in der Zeit Shakespeares. Mit Abdruck aller Texte aus den bisher noch nicht neugedruckten Liederbüchern und den zeitgenössischen deutschen Übertragungen. Berlin: Mayer und Müller, 1903. cxxvi, 283 p. (Palestra, 29)

Reprint by Johnson Reprint Co., 1969.

There are short biographies of the principal composers of English songs 1530–1600 (e.g., William Byrd, Thomas Weelkes, Thomas Morley, John

Dowland), followed by a monograph on the content and form of Morley's lyrics. The principal portion of the book reproduces the poetry of the songs. Each songbook is related to other sources, printed and manuscript, and the whole of the front matter and dedication is presented. In all, the lyrics of 26 books are included and 4 are included by reference. There is a text incipit index.

1712. Boorman, Stanley. "Sources, MS." In *The New Grove Dictionary of Music and Musicians,* edited by Stanley Sadie, v. 17, p. 590–702, by Stanley Boorman, John A. Emerson, David Fallows, David Hiley, Ernest H. Sanders, Ursula Günther, Gilbert Reaney, Kurt von Fischer, Charles Hamm, Jerry Call, and Herbert Kellman. London: Macmillan, 1980.

After an introduction to the nature, function, preparation, history, and study of musical manuscripts, there follow eight extensive bibliographies of manuscript sources of Western music: Western plainchant; Secular monody; Organum and discant; Early motet; English polyphony 1270–1400; French polyphony 1300–1400; Italian polyphony c. 1325–c. 1430; and Renaissance polyphony.

Each section presents and describes manuscripts, citing modern editions and secondary literature for each source. The introductory sections are followed by a brief bibliography.

Ann P. Basart is responsible for an "Index to the manuscripts in the *New Grove* articles on 'Sources,'" in *Cum Notis Variorum,* nos. 117–134 (November 1987 to July–August 1989). The index covers citations of manuscripts in the articles "Sources, manuscripts," "Sources of instrumental ensemble music to 1630," "Sources of keyboard music to 1660," and "Sources of late music" in the *New Grove.* Arranged alphabetically with entries and cross-references in one alphabet, the filing is word by word, not letter by letter. Entries are arranged by country, city, library or archive, name of collection, and manuscript shelfmark. This is a substantial aid to readers of the *New Grove* seeking information on a specific manuscript. Entries also mention topics within "Source..." articles where the citation is located and there are explanatory notes.

1713. Borren, Charles van den. "Inventaire des manuscrits de musique polyphonique qui se trouvent en Belgique." In *Acta Musicologica,* 5 (1933); p. 66–71, 120–27, 177–83; 6 (1934), p. 23–29, 65–73, 116–21.

An inventory of the manuscript sources of early polyphony in Belgian libraries. Detailed descriptions, with listing of contents, of manuscripts in the libraries in Brussels, Ghent, Liège, Louvain, Malines, and Tournai.

1714. Bowers, Jane. "A catalogue of French works for the transverse flute, 1692–1761." In *Recherches sur la Musique Française Classique,* XVIII (1978), p. 89–125. Paris: Éditions A. et J. Picard, 1978.

1715. The Breitkopf thematic catalogue. The six parts and sixteen supplements, 1762–1787. Edited and with an introduction and indexes by Barry S. Brook. New York: Dover, 1966. 888 p.

First published as *Catalogo delle Sinfonie, Partite, Overture, Soli, Trii, Quattri e Concerti per il Violino, Flauto Traverso, Cembalo ed Altri Stromenti, che si Trovano in Manuscritto nella Officina Musica di Giovanni Gottlob Breitkopf in Lipsia* (Leipzig: Breitkopf & Härtel, 1762–65), and *Supplementi* I–XVI (1766–87).

Facsimile reproduction of the major 18th-century thematic catalog, giving almost 15,000 musical incipits and 1,300 first lines of texts representing over 1,000 composers. Preceded by an informative essay and an outline of the contents. Chiefly instrumental music, but some vocal, from the archives of Breitkopf & Härtel. Useful in tracing or identifying works of the period. Index of first lines of texts and a general index of names and topics.

Review by Bernard E. Wilson in *Journal of the American Musicological Society*, 21 (1968), p. 400–404; by Donald W. Krummel in *Notes*, 24 (1968), p. 697–700; by H. C. Robbins Landon in the *Haydn Yearbook*, 6 (1969), p. 218.

1716. Breslauer, Martin. Das deutsche Lied, geistlich und weltlich bis zum 18. Jahrhundert. Berlin: M. Breslauer, 1908. 304 p. (Documente frühen deutschen Lebens, Reihe 1)
Reprint by Olms, Hildesheim, 1966.

An important music dealer's catalogue listing 556 items in the field of early German song. Full bibliographical entries with descriptive annotations. Numerous facsimiles of title pages. Prices given. Index of first lines of song texts, melodies, persons.

1717. Bridgman, Nanie. "Musique profane italienne des 16e et 17e siècles dans les bibliothèques françaises." In *Fontes Artis Musicae*, 2 (1955), p. 40–59.

Full bibliographical descriptions of 32 16th- and 17th-century prints of Italian secular music in branch libraries.

British Library. Department of Printed Books. Hand-list of music published in some British and foreign periodicals between 1787 and 1848. See no. 2141.

1718. The British-Union-catalogue of early music printed before the year 1801.
A record of the holdings of over 100 libraries throughout the British Isles. Edited by Edith B. Schnapper. London: Butterworths Scientific Publications, 1957. 2 v.

A major reference tool for work with early printed sources of music. These volumes provide the key to sources in British libraries. Brief bibliographical entries; locations established in more than 100 libraries in England, Wales, Scotland, and Ireland.

Review by A. Hyatt King in *Music and Letters*, 39 (1958), p. 77–79; by Richard S. Hill in *Notes*, 15 (1958), p. 565–68; by Richard Schaal in *Die Musikforschung*, 12 (1959), p. 367–69.

1719. Brook, Barry S. La symphonie française dans la seconde moitié du XVIIIe siècle. Paris: Publications de l'Institut de Musicologie de l'Université de Paris, 1962. 3 v.

Vol. 1 is a study of the French symphony of the latter half of the 18th century, with important bibliographical supplements: Annexe IV, "Index thématique arrangé par tonalités et temps" (p. 511–73); Annexe V, "Index alphabetique des incipits transposés en do majeur ou do mineur et indiqués par les lettres" (p. 574–84); Annexe VI, "Inventaire sommaire de la symphonie et de la symphonie concertante françaises" (p. 585–633); Annexe VII, "Rééditions et enregistrements" (p. 634–39). Bibliography (p. 643–65); general index.

Vol. 2: "Catalogue thématique et bibliographique." Full descriptions of the works, location of sources, short biographies of each composer.
Vol. 3: Scores of 6 previously unedited symphonies.
The work treats some 1,200 symphonies by 150 composers.
Review by Marc Pincherle in *Revue de Musicologie*, 49 (1963), p. 131–33; by H. C. Robbins Landon in *Die Musikforschung*, 17 (1964), p. 435–39; by Jan LaRue in *Musical Quarterly* (1963), p. 384–88.

1720. Brown, Howard M. Instrumental music printed before 1600; a bibliography. Cambridge, Massachusetts: Harvard University Press, 1965. 559 p.
A bibliography of the greatest importance for students of early instrumental music. Chronologically arranged beginning with Michel de Toulouze's *L'Art et Instruction de Bien Dancer* (148?) and ending with works printed in 1599. Full bibliographical descriptions incorporating much valuable commentary. Includes references to works now lost.
P. 441–69: list of works cited. Indexes: (1) list of libraries and their holdings; (2) volumes described, arranged by type of notation; (3) volumes described, arranged by performing medium; (4) names; (5) first lines and titles.
Review by Claudio Sartori in *Notes*, 22 (1966), p. 1209–1212; by Jack A. Westrup in *Music and Letters*, 47 (1966), p. 354–55; by Jeremy Noble in *Journal of the American Musicological Society*, 19 (1966), p. 415–17; by Ingrid Brainard in *Die Musikforschung*, 20 (1967), p. 465–70; by Martin Picker in *Musical Quarterly*, 28 (1967), p. 136–39; by A. Hyatt King in *Library*, ser. 5, 22 (June 1969), p. 154–58.

1721. Bryden, John R. and David G. Hughes. An index of Gregorian chant. Cambridge, Massachusetts: Harvard University Press, 1969. 2 v.
An index of chants found chiefly in modern service books. Vol. 1 gives text incipits; vol. 2, melodic incipits in number notation. A useful tool for identifying the chants used in polyphonic composition.
Review by Don M. Randel in *Notes*, 27 (1971), p. 477–78; by Andrew Hughes in *Music and Letters*, 51 (1970), p. 317–19.

1722. Caldwell, John. "Sources of keyboard music to 1660." In *The New Grove Dictionary of Music and Musicians*, edited by Stanley Sadie, v. 17, p. 717–33. London: Macmillan, 1980.
Includes "sources up to 1660, divided into broad geographical areas, and further divided within those areas into manuscript and printed sources arranged geographically." Sources are described and contents are incompletely analyzed; modern editions and secondary literature are cited.

Census catalogue of manuscript sources of polyphonic music 1450–1550. See no. 2387.

1723. Coover, James B. "Composite music manuscripts in facsimile." In *Notes*, 38 (1981), p. 275–95.
"This list comprises only complete manuscripts, mostly medieval and renaissance, reproduced in facsimile." Arranged by location, with cross-references from names of manuscripts. Index to personal names. Identifies *RISM* items in the list. Index to items in series.

1724. Corbin, Solange. Répertoire de manuscrits médievaux contenant des notations musicales. Paris: Éditions du Centre National de la Recherche Scientifique, 1965– . Vol. 1– .
Vol. 1: Bibliothèque Sainte-Geneviève. 1965.
Vol. 2: Bibliothèque Mazarine, par Madeleine Bernard. 1966.
Vol. 3: Bibliothèque Parisiennes—Arsenal, Nationale (Musique), Universitaire, École des Beaux-Arts, et Fonds Privés, par Madeleine Bernard. 1974.
This series promises to provide descriptions and inventories of all the manuscripts containing medieval chant notation. Each volume includes bibliographies and facsimiles.
Vol. 1 includes tables of origins of notation (describing types of books and their notations), of the provenance of each manuscript, of the contents of the manuscripts by musico-liturgical genres, of neumes, and of pictorial images of instruments. Map of notational styles in northern France. Plates. Extensive tables in other volumes. Vol. 3 includes a table of text incipits.
Review by John A. Emerson in *Journal of the American Musicological Society*, 22 (1969), p. 119–22; by Ewald Jammers in *Die Musikforschung*, 21 (1968), p. 103–104.

1725. Crane, Frederick. Materials for the study of the 15th-century Basse danse. New York: Institute of Medieval Music, 1968. 131 p. (Wissenschaftliche Abhandlungen, 16)
Review by Peter Gülke in *Die Musikforschung*, 24 (1971), p. 339–40.

1726. Daniel, Ralph T. and Peter Le Huray. The sources of English church music 1549–1660. London: Published for the British Academy by Stainer and Bell, 1972. 2 v. (Early English church music, supplementary volume 1)

This is the first attempt to compile a complete inventory of sacred music in English covering the period from the early years of the Reformation to the mid-17th century. [*Preface*]

Part I is a listing of the sources, printed or in manuscript, a thematic catalog of all anonymous works, and a first-line index of anthems. Part II: services and anthems arranged in alphabetical order by composer, with all the data as to sources and locations of sources.
Review by Bradford R. DeVos in *Notes*, 31 (1974), p. 305–307.

1727. Danner, Peter. "Bibliography of guitar tablatures, 1546–1764." In *Journal of the Lute Society of America*, 5 (1972), p. 40–51.
A bibliography of 165 printed and 50 manuscript sources. Brief descriptive annotations.

1728. Dart, Thurston. "A hand-list of English instrumental music printed before 1681." In *Galpin Society Journal*, 1955, p. 13–26.

1729. Daschner, Hubert. Die gedruckten mehrstimmigen Chansons von 1500–1600. Bonn: Rheinische Friedrich-Wilhelms-Universität, 1962. 195 p.
A dissertation the greater part of which consists of a first-line index of polyphonic chansons from the printed collections of the 16th century. 4,273 chansons entered.
P. 175–82: "Verzeichnis der Musikdrucke"; p. 184–86: "Verzeichnis der anonymen Gedichtsammlungen"; p. 187–95; "Literaturverzeichnis."

1730.   Davidsson, Ake. Catalogue critique et descriptif des imprimés de musique des XVIe et XVIIe siècles conservés dans les bibliothèques suédoises (excepté la Bibliothèque de l'Université Royale d'Upsala). Upsala: Almquist et Wiksells, 1952. 471 p. (Studia musicologica upsaliensia, 1)
   A union catalogue of early music in 18 Swedish libraries, excluding the University of Uppsala, which is treated elsewhere (nos. 2384–2386). Full descriptions, contents, references; p. 455–71: bibliography of works cited.

1731.   Deakin, Andrew. Outlines of musical bibliography: a catalogue of early music and musical works printed or otherwise produced in the British Isles; the whole chronologically arranged with descriptive and critical notes on the principal works. Birmingham: A. Deakin, 1899. 112 p.
   Reprint by Olms, Hildesheim, c. 1971.
   A work projected on a much larger scale, but not completed. P. 5–18: a listing of manuscript sources. P. 19–96: chiefly printed music of the 16th and 17th centuries, but with a few manuscripts included. The entries are not precise, and the locations given are indefinite. Indexed by composer and title.

1732.   Dichter, Harry. Handbook of American sheet music ... first annual issue, 1947. Philadelphia, Pennsylvania: H. Dichter, 1947. 100 p.
   Second Series, with Bernice Larrabee. Philadelphia, 1953.
   Catalogs of early American sheet music for sale by the author. Full of useful bibliographical data. Classified under selected headings: topic, author, title. Prices given. No index. The 1947 volume lists over 2,000 items.

1733.   Dichter, Harry and Elliott Shapiro. Early American sheet music, its lure and its lore, 1768–1889 ... including a directory of early American music publishers.... New York: R. R. Bowker, 1941. 287 p.
   A cross-section of early American sheet music, classified as to subject content. Composer, main title, publisher, and date included. The directory of publishers is an alphabetical listing of firms active from 1768 to 1899 and carries their histories to 1940. Additional lists of lithographers and artists active before 1870. Plates of illustrated title pages. Index.

1734.   Draudius, Georg. Verzeichnisse deutscher musikalischer Bücher, 1611–1625. In originalgetreuem Nachdruck herausgegeben von Konrad Ameln. p. 545–63; 733–69. Bonn: Deutscher Musikverleger-Verband, 1957.
   Facsimile reprint of the music sections from the 1611 and 1625 editions of Draudius's *Bibliotheca Librorum Germanicorum Classica*, an early document in the history of music bibliography. ("Musikalische Bücher" here means "scores.") Classified according to type of composition. Primarily of historical interest.

1735.   Duckles, Vincent H. "The music for the lyrics in early seventeenth-century English drama: a bibliography of the primary sources." In *Music in English Renaissance Drama*, p. 117–60. Edited by John H. Long. Lexington: University of Kentucky Press, 1968.
   Directs the reader to manuscript and early printed sources for the songs introduced into English drama from 1603 to 1642. Modern editions of these songs are cited when available.

1736. Duyse, Florimond van. Het oude Nederlandsche lied; wereldlijke en geestelijke liederen uit vroegeren tijd, teksten en melodieën, verzameld en toegelicht door Fl. van Duyse. 's-Gravenhage: M. Nijhoff, 1903–1908. 4 v.

First issued in parts, 1900–1908; unaltered reprint by Frits A. M. Knuf, Hilversum, 1965.

The standard reference book for the study of early Dutch song. Actually an edition of 714 melodies given with their variants and with an abundance of related information on texts and music. Sacred song is treated in vol. 3; vol. 4 contains indexes of names, of song titles, and of first lines of texts.

1737. Edwards, Warwick. "Sources of instrumental ensemble music to 1630." In *The New Grove Dictionary of Music and Musicians*, edited by Stanley Sadie, v. 17, p. 702–717. London: Macmillan, 1980.

"Concerned with ... music for two or more instruments (excluding ... keyboards, lutes and other chordal instruments) to play together without the voice.... An attempt has been made to identify music originally conceived for instruments." Organized geographically, entries give locations, manuscript numbers or titles (and if titles, then imprint information), and a description of contents, citing any modern editions or secondary literature. See no. 1712 for citation of Ann P. Basart's index to sources mentioned in this article.

1738. Eitner, Robert. Bibliographie der Musik-Sammelwerke des XVI. und XVII. Jahrhunderts. Im Vereine mit Frz. Xav. Haberl, A. Lagerberg und C. F. Pohl. Berlin: L. Liepmannssohn, 1877. 964 p.

Supplemented by additions and corrections published in Eitner's *Monatshefte für Musikgeschichte*, 14 (1882), p. 152–55, 161–64.

Reprint of the original edition by Olms, Hildesheim, 1963.

Chronological bibliography of some 795 collections of music published between 1501 and 1700, with full descriptions, summary of contents, lists of composers represented, and library locations of individual copies. The second part of the work, p. 297–938, is a first-line index of the vocal texts, arranged alphabetically by composer.

Eitner's *Sammelwerke* is one of the major bibliographical tools for historical research in music, although it has been superseded, in part, by the first volume to appear of the *International Inventory of Musical Sources* (no. 1788).

1739. Eitner, Robert. Biographisch-bibliographisches Quellen-Lexikon der Musiker und Musikgelehrten der christlichen Zeitrechnung bis zur Mitte des 19. Jahrhunderts.... Leipzig: Breitkopf & Härtel, 1898–1904. 10 v.

Supplemented by the *Miscellanea Musicae Bio-bibliographica* (no. 1766), and by G. Radiciotti's "Aggiunte e correzioni ai dizionari biografici dei musicisti" (no. 1777).

Reprinted with the supplements by Musurgia, New York, 1947. Neuauflage published by Breitkopf & Härtel, Wiesbaden, 1959–60. "2. verbesserte Auflage," Graz, Akademische Druck- und Verlagsanstalt, 1959–60.

Eitner's *Quellen-Lexikon* was the basic tool for locating primary sources of music before 1800. Both printed music and manuscripts are included, with their locations in European libraries. The work is badly out of date; much of the information, particularly as regards locations, is no longer correct. The *International Inventory of Musical Sources* has replaced Eitner as a key to the sources of early music (nos. 1148–1151, 1781–1790, 1841 and 1853). Eitner is still valuable, especially to identify works no longer extant, as it precedes the two major multinational conflagrations that resulted in so much damage to European library collections.

Stephen A. Willier's article "The present location of libraries listed in Robert Eitner's Biographisch-bibliographisches Quellen-Lexikon," in *Fontes Artis Musicae*, 28 (1981), p. 220–39, documents the present location of most of the collections mentioned in the *Verzeichnis der Bibliotheks-Abkürzungen* in the first volume of the *Quellen-Lexikon*.

Also cited as no. 79.

1740. Fernández De La Cuesta, Ismael. Manuscritos y fuentes musicales en España: Edad media. Madrid: Editorial Apluerto, 1980. 397 p.

An international inventory of medieval Spanish musical manuscripts and other sources arranged in order of collection. Annotations include physical description, notational style, contents analytics, references to related manuscripts, and bibliographical references. General bibliography. Indexes of first lines of Visigothic and Mozarabic chants, Gregorian chants, Latin monody, polyphony, and romances. Index of locations.

1741. Fischer, Kurt von. Studien zur italienischen Musik des Trecento und frühen Quattrocento. Bern: P. Haupt, 1956. 132 p. (Publikationen der Schweizerischen Musikforschenden Gesellschaft, ser. 2, v. 5)

A bibliography of Italian secular music of the 14th and early 15th centuries. Text incipits, arranged alphabetically, for 177 madrigals, 25 caccie, and 423 ballate, with information as to sources and modern editions.

Review by Hans Tischler in *Notes*, 15 (1958), p. 405–406.

1742. Ford, Terence. "Index to the facsimiles of polyphonic music before 1600 published in *Die Musik in Geschichte und Gegenwart*." In *Notes*, 39 (1983), p. 283–315.

Providing access to about 400 facsimiles by four indexes: informal name of the manuscript; titles of prints; first line and/or title of compositions; and personal names.

1743. Fortune, Nigel. "A handlist of printed Italian secular monody books, 1602–1635." In *R.M.A. Research Chronicle*, no. 3, p. 27–50. Published for the Royal Musical Association, 1963.

A list of all Italian publications from 1602 to 1635 containing at least one secular monody. Location symbols given for the scarcer volumes. The notes indicate contemporary reprints and modern editions where they exist. By far the most comprehensive listing of Italian monody books available.

1744. Friedlaender, Max. Das deutsche Lied im 18. Jahrhundert, Quellen und Studien.... Stuttgart and Berlin: Cotta, 1902. 2 v. in 3.

Reprinted by Georg Olms, Hildesheim, 1962.

Vol. 1:1, p. 1–62: a chronological listing of 798 German songbooks of the 18th century (1689–1799), followed by a detailed commentary on the most important examples. Vol. 1:2, a collection of musical examples. Vol. 2: discussion of the poets, with indexes of names, text incipits.

1745. Fuld, James J. and Mary Wallace Davidson. 18th-century American secular music manuscripts: an inventory. Philadelphia, Pennsylvania: Music Library Association, 1980. 225 p. (MLA index and bibliography series, 20)

Included are eighty-five secular musical manuscripts held by twenty libraries and private individuals. The manuscripts vary from one piece to collections of about four hundred pieces, and include a variety of types: keyboard sonatas, suites, variations, and other classical forms, military marches and bugle calls, ballroom dances, ballads, children's songs, folk songs, and theater music. [Authors' *Preface*]

The manuscripts are fully described, analyzed, and indexed.

Review by Geraldine Ostrove in *Fontes Artis Musicae*, 28 (1981), p. 195; by Irving Lowens, in *Notes*, 37 (1981), p. 594–95.

1746. Geck, Martin. Deutsche Oratorien, 1800 bis 1840. Verzeichnis der Quellen und Aufführungen. Wilhelmshaven: Heinrichshofen's Verlag, 1971. 105 p. (Quellen-Kataloge zur Musikgeschichte, 4)

The bibliography has three major parts: (1) an alphabetical listing of the oratorios under composer; (2) a listing of performances by place; and (3) a listing by chronology. Some reviews and notices in contemporary periodicals are indicated. Oratorios by some 100 composers are cited.

1747. Geering, Arnold. Die Organa und mehrstimmigen Conductus in den Handschriften des deutschen Sprachgebietes vom 13. bis 16. Jahrhundert. Bern: P. Haupt, 1952. 99 p. (Publikationen der Schweizerischen Musikforschenden Gesellschaft, ser. 2:1)

A study concerned with the sources of early polyphony in the German-speaking countries, with a listing of the relevant manuscripts and an inventory of the organum and conductus settings they contain.

1748. Gennrich, Friedrich. Bibliographie der ältesten französischen und lateinischen Motetten. Darmstadt: Selbstverlag, 1957. 124 p. (Summa musicae medii aevi, 2)

A bibliography of the 13th-century motet, serving also as a guide to the manuscript sources and a record of scholarly work done in this field. Gennrich expands the work begun by Friedrich Ludwig in his *Repertorium* (no. 1764). Motets are grouped under their respective tenors, with references to all known concordances and modern editions. Supplementary bibliographies of literature and of scripts, indexes of Latin and French tenors, and incipits to motettus and triplum parts.

Review by Hans Tischler in *Notes*, 16 (1959), p. 561–62.

1749. Gennrich, Friedrich. Der musikalische Nachlass der Troubadours. Kommentar. Darmstadt: Selbstverlag, 1960. 176 p. (Summa musicae medii aevi, 4)

A complete bibliography of the surviving musical settings of troubadour song, 302 entries in all, with information as to source, editions of text and music, verse forms, and use of the melody as a contrafactum. Songs are numbered consecutively but grouped under composer, with bibliographical references to work done on the individual musicians. 25 manuscript sources are described and discussed.

Vol. 3 of the series *Summa Musicae Medii Aevi* (1958) is a musical edition of the surviving troubadour melodies.

1750. Göhler, Albert. Verzeichnis der in den Frankfurter und Leipziger Messkatalogen der Jahre 1564 bis 1759 angezeigten Musikalien.... Leipzig: C. F. Kahnt Nachf., 1902. 4 parts in 1 v.
Unaltered reprint by Frits A. M. Knuf, Hilversum, 1965.
A bibliography of the music listed in the Frankfurt and Leipzig trade catalogs from 1564 to 1759. Works separately listed by century, under composer. Works identified by type.

1751. Gröninger, Eduard. Repertoire-Untersuchungen zum mehrstimmigen Notre-Dame-Conductus. Regensburg: Bosse, 1939. 163 p. (Kölner Beiträge zur Musikforschung, 2)
An introductory essay of 59 pages, followed by tabulations, with concordances, of the polyphonic conductus compositions found in the four major Notre Dame sources.

1752. Gustafson, Bruce. French harpsichord music of the 17th century; a thematic catalog of the sources with commentary. Ann Arbor, Michigan: UMI Research Press, 1979. 3 v.
Volume 1 presents descriptions and commentary on each manuscript arranged by present location. Volumes 2 and 3 provide detailed bibliographic description, thematic entries, and concordances to other manuscripts. The complex thematic catalog and the index to all three volumes are not well explained, but once understood are quite useful. A monumental bibliographic feat.

1753. Haberkamp, Gertraut. "Text- und Musikincipit-Register zu den Anhängen 1 und 2 in RISM A/1 Band 9," zusammengestellt von Gertraut Haberkamp und Helmut Rösing. In *Fontes Artis Musicae*, 28 (1981), p. 48 ff. and p. 259–306.
Indexes to first lines of text and musical incipits in the first and second supplements in vol. 9 of *Einzeldrucke vor 1800 (RISM A/1)*.

Hixon, Donald L. Music in early America: a bibliography of music in Evans. See no. 1299.

1754. Hughes, Andrew. Medieval manuscripts for mass and office: a guide to their organization and terminology. Toronto and Buffalo, New York: University of Toronto Press, 1982. 470 p.

> This book originated ... to introduce students of the later Middle Ages to the manuscripts of the liturgy.... My purpose here is to show the reader how liturgical books are organized and how they may be used for research. [Author's *Preface*]

After an extensive introduction concerning the history and context, music, order and content of services in general terms, and terminology of the liturgies and source manuscripts, there are chapters on liturgical time, on textual and musical form, on Offices and the mass, and on the content and form of liturgical books. There are then specific sections on individual feasts and rites appropriate for them. The book provides instruction on reading and using texts and chants in liturgical manuscripts dating from c. 1300 to c. 1600.
The extensive outline of the book printed on the recto of the frontispiece should be consulted. There are many appendixes, including facsim-

iles of manuscript pages, a bibliography of secondary sources, and a list of primary sources. Indexes of sources and other manuscripts, manuscripts by location, and incipits. There is a general index. A useful key to symbols employed is printed on the flyleaves.

Reviews by David G. Hughes in the *Journal of the American Musicological Society*, 37 (1984), p. 412–15, and by Anne Walters Robertson in the *Journal of Musicology*, 4 (1985–86), p. 350–54.

1755. Huglo, Michel. Les tonaires; inventaire, analyse, comparison. Paris: Société française de musicologie, 1971. 487 p.

This is an extended bibliographic and historical work on the medieval tonaries. Huglo describes and discusses the significance of each manuscript, analyzes its contents, and compares it to others. The manuscripts are classed by date, by region, by musical and liturgical characteristics. There is an index of books discussed arranged by city, library, and manuscript name and number. Bibliography of printed tonaries (facsimiles and originals). There is a bibliography of secondary literature. Table of incipits and mnemonic formulas. A magisterial work.

1756. Index to early American periodicals to 1850. E. Songs. (Cards E1 to E11). New York: Readex Microfilm Corp., [1965]. (Bibliographic aids in microprint)

Microprint edition of the entries under "Songs" from an index of some 650,000 cards compiled by members of the English department of Washington Square College, New York University, with the aid of the Work Projects Administration. Indexes some 340 early American magazines by authors, composers, anonymous titles, first lines.

1757. International Association of Music Libraries. Radio Commission. Catalogue of rare materials, and first supplement. Edited by Folke Lindberg. Stockholm: 1959. 185 leaves.

Supplement I: leaves 175–85.

A list designed for the use of radio librarians in locating copies of rare material that can be used for performance purposes.

International inventory of musical sources. See Répertoire International des Sources Musicales, nos. 1148–1151, 1781–1790, 1841 and 1853.

Internationales Quellenlexikon der Musik. See Répertoire International des Sources Musicales, nos. 1148–1151, 1781–1790, 1841 and 1853.

1758. Keller, Kate Van Winkle. Popular secular music in America through 1800: a preliminary checklist of manuscripts in North American collections. Philadelphia, Pennsylvania: Music Library Association, 1981. 140 p. (MLA index and bibliography series, 21)

Explores a little-known area of scholarship.

1759. Kreider, J. Evan. "Austrian graduals, antiphoners, and noted missales on microfilm in the Hill Monastic Manuscript Library, St. John's Abbey and University." In *Notes*, 36 (1980), p. 849–63.

1760. Kreider, J. Evan. "A checklist of Spanish chant sources at the Hill Monastic Manuscript Library, St. John's Abbey and University." In *Notes*, 40 (1984), p. 7–29.

A tabulation of resources gathered from Spain and elsewhere at the Hill Monastic Manuscript Library.

1761. Linker, Robert W. Music of the Minnesinger and early Meistersinger, a bibliography. Chapel Hill: University of North Carolina Press, [1961]. 79 p.

A bibliography of German medieval song arranged alphabetically under the composers' names. A preliminary list gives 40 manuscript sources and 41 modern publications of literary history, music, and text editions.

Review by Walter Salmen in *Die Musikforschung*, 17 (1964), p. 432.

Loewenberg, Alfred. Annals of opera, 1597–1940.... See no. 474.

1762. Lowens, Irving. A bibliography of songsters printed in America before 1821. Worcester, Mass.: American Antiquarian Society, 1976. 229 p.

A bibliography of collections of secular poems or song lyrics intended to be sung. Introductory essay on the songster. Detailed bibliographical descriptions with extensive annotations in chronological order. Geographical directory of printers, publishers, booksellers, engravers, etc. Index of compilers, editors, proprietors, and authors. Index to titles of songsters.

1763. Ludwig, Friedrich. "Die Quellen der Motetten ältesten Stils." In *Archiv für Musikwissenschaft*, 5 (1923), p. 185–222, 273–315.

A basic source study of medieval polyphony, in which the author gives complete or partial inventories for some 50 manuscripts containing motets of the *ars antiqua* period.

This study has been reprinted as a supplement to Gennrich's edition of Ludwig's *Repertorium, Abteilung 2.* (no. 1764). Supplemented by no. 1708.

1764. Ludwig, Friedrich. Repertorium organorum recentioris et motetorum vetustissimi stili. Band 1: Catalogue raisonné der Quellen. Abteilung 1: Handschriften in Quadrat-Notation. Halle: Niemeyer, 1910. 344 p.

Ludwig's *Repertorium*, although incomplete, is the starting point for all studies in the music of the *ars antiqua* period. It is essentially an inventory, with concordances, of the contents of the major manuscripts of the Notre Dame repertory.

Band 1, Abteilung 2: *Handschriften in Mensuralnotation.* Besorgt von Friedrich Gennrich. Langen bei Frankfurt, 1961. (Summa musicae medii aevi, 7)

This portion of the *Repertorium* appeared in proof copy but was never published in Ludwig's lifetime. It consists chiefly of inventories of two major sources of the 13th-century motet, the *Montpellier Codex* and the *Clayette MS*. Included as a supplement to this volume is a reprint of Ludwig's study, "Die Quellen der Motetten ältesten Stils," which appeared in the *Archiv für Musikwissenschaft*, 5 (1925). See no. 1763.

A 2. erweiterte Auflage edited by Luther A. Dittmer, appeared 1964–78 as a joint publication of the Institute of Mediaeval Music, New York, and Georg Olms, Hildesheim. 2 v. in 3. Includes Band 1, Abteilung 1: *Handschriften in Quadrat-Notation.* (Wissenschaftliche Abhandlungen, Bd. 7, 17, 26)

Band 2: *Musikalisches Anfangs-Verzeichnis des nach Tenores geord-neten Repertorium.* Besorgt von Friedrich Gennrich. Langen bei Frank-furt, 1962. 71 p. (Summa musicae medii aevi, 8) Reprinted in a new edition by Luther A. Dittmer by the Institute of Mediaeval Music and Olms, Hil-desheim, 1983.

A thematic catalog of 515 motets based on 50 tenors taken from liturgy of the mass. Reprinted, incomplete, from Ludwig's unpublished proof copy. Expanded by Gennrich (no. 1748).

1765. Meyer, Ernst H. "Quellennachweise." In his *Die mehrstimmige Spiel musik des 17. Jahrhunderts in Nord- und Mittel-Europa*, p. 128–258. Kas-sel: Bärenreiter, 1934.

A bibliography of the sources of 17th-century chamber music of the North European school. Partially thematic for the English sources.

1766. Miscellanea musicae bio-bibliographica.... Hrsg. von H. Springer, M. Schneider, und W. Wolffheim. 2., um einen Anhang vermehrte Auflage. New York: Musurgia, 1947. 435 p.

Originally published by Breitkopf & Härtel in quarterly issues, 1912–16, with annual index for each of the years covered. Provides corrections and additions to all the kinds of information in Eitner's *Quellen-Lexikon* (no. 1738).

Reprinted in vol. 11 of the Akademische Druck- und Verlagsanstalt, *2. verbesserte Auflage* of the *Quellen-Lexikon*, which also contains marginal, numerical references to the *Miscellanea*.

1767. Mischiati, Oscar. Bibliografia delle opere dei musicisti bresciani pub-blicate a stampa dal 1497 al 1740. Editio minor. Brescia: Centro di studi musicali 'Luca Marenzio,' 1982. 205 p. (Pubblicazioni del Centro di studi musicali "Luca Marenzio," presso la Civica biblioteca queriniana di Bres-cia)

Also known as the *Bibliografia dei Musicisti Bresciani.*

Including 7 titles in the addenda, a bibliography of 817 works written by Brescian composers, entered under composer and then chronologically. There are title page transcriptions, references to RISM, to Eitner, and to *Il Nuovo Vogel*, and libraries holding the title described. Lists of holding li-braries and private collections cited. There is a section describing anthol-ogies in which Brescian composers' music appears, with references from the main bibliography. There is a classified index.

1768. Mischiati, Oscar. La prassi musicale presso i Canonici regolari del Ss. Salvatore: nei secoli XVI e XVII e i manoscritti polifonici della Biblioteca musicale "G. B. Martini" di Bologna. Roma: Edizioni Torre d'Orfeo, 1985. 157 p. (Documenti. Istituto di paleografia musicale; 1)

A study of musical practices with bibliographic references.

1769. Monumenta monodica medii aevi. Band I– . Herausgegeben im Auftrag des Musikwissenschaftlichen Seminars der Universität Erlangen-Nürnberg von Bruno Stäblein. Kassel: Bärenreiter, 1956– .

Band I: *Hymnen* (1956). 724 p.

Band II: *Die Gesänge des altrömischen Graduale. Vat. lat. 5319* (1970). 724 p.

Band III: *Introitus-Tropen 1. Das Repertoire der südfranzösischen Tro-pare des 10. und 11. Jahrhunderts* (1970). 470 p.
Band VII: *Alleluia-Melodien I, bis 1100* (1968). 682 p.
A series devoted to the publication of medieval monody, chiefly sacred. The music is organized liturgically and given in neume notation, with copious documentation. A basic tool for research in medieval music.
Band XI: Trouvères-Melodien I (1977). 598 p. Hrsg. von Hendrik van der Werf.
Band XII: Trouvères-Melodien II (1979). 727 p. Hrsg. von Hendrik van der Werf.

1770. Musiker Handschriften ... Composers' autographs. Translated from the German with a new preface by Ernst Roth. London: Cassell, 1968. 2 v.
Published in the U.S.A. under the imprint of Fairleigh Dickinson University Press, Madison, New Jersey.
Translation of *Musikerhandschriften von Palestrina bis Beethoven*, edited by W. Gerstenberg, and *Musikhandschriften von Schubert bis Strawinsky*, edited by M. Hürlimann, both of which are based on *Musiker-handschriften von Bach bis Schumann*, by G. Schünemann (1936).
Two handsome volumes of facsimiles made chiefly from composers' autographs in the Berlin State Library. Vol. 1 contains 159 plates; vol. 2, 140 plates, with brief descriptive commentaries and identification of the sources.
Review by Werner Neumann in *Die Musikforschung*, 17 (1964), p. 454–55.

1771. Ness, Arthur J. "Sources of lute music." In *The New Grove Dictionary of Music and Musicians*, edited by Stanley Sadie, v. 17, p. 733–53. London: Macmillan, 1980.
An introduction to the sources with descriptions and analysis of each source. Arranged by zones of origin and chronologically. Modern editions and secondary literature cited with each source.

1772. Newman, Joel. An index to capoversi and titles cited in Einstein's *The Italian Madrigal*. New York: Publications of the Renaissance Society of America, 1967. 39 p. (Indexes and bibliographies, 3)
Incorporated in the 1971 edition of *The Italian Madrigal*.
Indexes more than 2,000 madrigal titles cited in Einstein's work. Composer and poet are cited where known. Those with musical settings in the Einstein book are identified.

1773. Nisser, Carl M. Svensk instrumentalkomposition, 1770-1830. Nomin-alkatalog. Stockholm: Bökforlaget Gothia, [1943]. 467 p.
Swedish instrumental music, native composers or composers living in Sweden. Alphabetical listing by composer, with detailed bibliographical and analytical descriptions, including key, movements, time signature, measure count. Bibliographical references, index of names and places.

1774. Page, Christopher. "A catalogue and bibliography of English song from its beginnings to c. 1300." In *R.M.A. Research Chronicle*, 13 (197?), p. 67–83.

"This catalogue lists all the twelfth- and thirteenth-century songs with English words known to exist." 19 items arranged in chronological order, indicating first line and source, with extensive descriptions and lists of modern editions.

1775. Pillet, Alfred. Bibliographie der Troubadours. Erg., weitergeführt und herausgegeben von Dr. Henry Carstens. Halle: Niemeyer, [1933]. 518 p. (Schriften der Königsberger Gelehrten Gesellschaft. Sonderreihe, 2)
Reprinted by B. Franklin, New York, 1968.
Based on a bibliography of troubadour songs compiled by Karl Bartsch in 1872. Songs arranged alphabetically by first word of text, with inclusive numeration and subseries of numbers for works by individual authors. The emphasis is directed toward literary rather than musical scholarship.

1776. Preston, Michael J. A complete concordance to the songs of the early Tudor court. Leeds: W. S. Maney and Son, 1972. 433 p. (Compendia; computer-generated aids to literary and linguistic research, 4)
An index and concordance to the poetry in the three British Library manuscripts containing virtually all that is known of early Tudor song: BL Add. Ms. 5665 (Ritson's ms.); BL Add. Ms. 5465 (The Fayrfax ms.); and BL Add. Ms. 31922 (Henry VIII's ms.). This concordance treats the works edited by John Stevens in *Music and Poetry of the Early Tudor Court* (London: Methuen, 1961).
In addition to a first-line index are keyword out of context concordances for English and foreign words, reverse indexes to English and foreign words, index to rhymes, and ranking lists of the frequency of appearance of English words and foreign words.

1777. Radiciotti, Giuseppe. "Aggiunte e correzioni ai dizionari biografici dei musicisti." In *Sammelbände der Internationalen Musikgesellschaft*, 14 (1914), p. 551–67; 15 (1915), p. 566–86.
Corrections and additions to Eitner's *Quellen-Lexikon* (no. 1738) with special attention to Italian composers.
Reprinted in the Musurgia edition of the *Quellen-Lexikon*, and as vol. 11 of the Akademische Druck- und Verlagsanstalt, *2. verbesserte Auflage*, 1960.

1778. Randel, Don M. An index to the chants of the Mozarabic rite. Princeton, New Jersey: Princeton University Press, 1973. 670 p.
A comprehensive bibliography of the manuscript sources of Mozarabic chant, indicating the parts of the Office for which each chant would have been used.

1779. Raynaud, Gaston. Bibliographie des altfranzösischen Liedes. Neu bearbeitet und ergänzt von Hans Spanke. Erster Teil. Leiden: E. J. Brill, 1955. 386 p.
Reprinted by Brill in 1980 with a discography and index to chansons by A. Bahat. 348 p.
The first part of a projected revision of Raynaud's *Bibliographie des Chansonniers Français des XIIIe et XIVe Siècles*. Paris, 1884. 2 v. This work serves as a guide to trouvère songs, similar to that offered by the

Pillet (no. 1775) or the Gennrich (no. 1748) for the troubadour repertory. Lists more than 2,130 songs, arranged according to the rhyme word of the first stanza, with references to the manuscript source and to literary and musical studies concerned with the item. P. 1–32: a bibliography of the manuscript sources and of modern editions and studies.

1780. Reich, Wolfgang. Threnodiae sacrae. Katalog der gedruckten Kompositionen des 16.–18. Jahrhunderts in Leichenpredigtsammlungen innerhalb der Deutschen Demokratischen Republik. Dresden: 1966. 75 p. (Veröffentlichungen der Sächsischen Landesbibliothek, 7)

A catalog of 434 funereal compositions of the 16th through the 18th centuries found in East German collections, chiefly, Gotha, Dresden, East Berlin, and Zwickau.

Review by Martin Geck in *Die Musikforschung*, 22 (1969), p. 389–90.

1781. Répertoire International des Sources Musicales. Einzeldrucke vor 1800. Redaktion Karlheinz Schlager. Kassel: Bärenreiter, 1971–81. Vols. 1–9. (RISM A I, 1–9)

These volumes are the first part of the Series A of *RISM*, which are intended to supersede the list of works in Eitner's *Quellenlexikon*. This part, A/I, is an alphabetical catalog covering individual editions of music printed between 1500 and 1800 under the name of a single composer. The ninth volume includes an appendix devoted to printed editions with composers' attributions by initial and another appendix including anonymous printed editions. The *Anhänge* exclude entries in the *British Union Catalogue of Early Music* and *Das Deutsche Kirchenlied* (RISM B. VIII "DKL").

Each entry includes as much of the title as is needed to distinguish the edition, imprint, a unique *RISM* identifier, and the location of each surviving exemplar known. Each volume contains a list of contributing libraries ordered by country and city.

Karlheinz Schlager was responsible for vols. 1–7 (Aarts–Schreyer). Otto Albrecht joined Schlager for vols. 8 and 9 (Schrijer–Zwingmann).

Gertraut Haberkamp and Helmut Rösing were responsible for *Anhänge* 1 and 2. Rösing and Haberkamp prepared "Text- und Musikincipit-Register zu den Anhängen 1 und 2 in RISM A/I Band 9," for *Fontes Artis Musicae*, 28 (1981), 48 p. This is an index to the text incipits appearing as part of a title in either of the appendixes and an index to the music incipits cited in the appendixes. In the brief explanation of the two indexes, the use of asterisks is identified as denotations of the existence of music incipits.

For documentation concerning series A, see "*RISM*: zur Katalogisierung von Musikdrucken und Musikhandschriften der Serie A," by Karlheinz Schlager, Jürgen Kindermann, and Helmut Rösing in *Acta Musicologica*, 51 (1979), p. 173–92.

Vols. 1–2 reviewed by Neal Zaslaw in *Notes*, 31 (1974), p. 42–45. Vol. 7 reviewed by Richard Schaal in *Die Musikforschung*, 32 (1979), p. 86–87; and by François Lesure in *Fontes Artis Musicae*, 26 (1979), p. 145. Vol. 8 reviewed by A. Hyatt King in *Fontes Artis Musicae*, 30 (1983), p. 78–80.

1782. Répertoire International des Sources Musicales. Einzeldrucke vor 1800; Addenda et Corrigenda. Bd. 11– . Redaktion Ilse Kindermann und Jürgen Kindermann. Kassel: Bärenreiter, 1986– . (RISM, A I,11.2 v. to date–)

Incorporating new rules for inclusion allowing entries for all editions by composers born before 1770, published before 1830; and by composers born after 1770 but who died before 1810. "Works by these composers published by 1830 and 1850 (the final terminus) are also included if no earlier editions of these works are recorded." Volumes issued to date cover entries A–F, G–L.

1783. Répertoire International des Sources Musicales. Handschriften mit mehrstimmiger Musik des 14., 15. und 16. Jahrhunderts. Mehrstimmige Musik in italienischen, polnischen, und tschechischen Quellen des 14. Jahrhunderts. Mehrstimmige Stücke in Handschriften aller Länder aus der Zeit um 1400-1425/30. Originale Sätze im älteren Stil und mehrstimmige Stücke in Choralhandschriften des 15. und 16. Jahrhunderts. Beschrieben und inventarisiert von Kurt von Fischer und herausgegeben in Zusammenarbeit mit Max Lutolf. München-Duisburg: G. Henle, 1972. 2 v. (RISM B IV, 3–4)

Group one, the manuscripts of polyphonic music of the 14th, 15th, and 16th centuries follows *RISM* volumes B/IV/1 and B/IV/2. It covers sources of the Italian Trecento and Polish and Czech sources of the 14th century.

Group two, the sources of 14th-century polyphonic music in manuscripts from all countries and dating from 1400 to 1425 links *RISM* volume B/IV/2 to the present volume.

"Group 3 consists of sources of organ polyphony of the 15th and 16th centuries and of choral manuscripts of these centuries in which polyphonic pieces in black notation occur next to liturgical, monodic ones."

The manuscripts are arranged by country, city, and library in each of the groups described above. Indexes of text incipits and composers.

1784. Répertoire International des Sources Musicales. Handschriftlich überlieferte Lauten- und Gitarrentabulaturen des 15. bis 18. Jahrhunderts: beschreibender Katalog von Wolfgang Boetticher. München: Henle, 1978. 82, 374 p. (RISM, B, 7)

A descriptive catalog of 726 manuscripts containing lute and guitar music in tablature within the *RISM* time span (until c. 1820). Includes manuscripts containing music for other plectoral instruments (e.g., theorbo, chitarrone). Organized by country, city, and library. *RISM* issued a separate supplement by Christian Meyer, *Register der Tabulaturgattungen und Namen zusammengestellt*, a classified register of the tablatures and an index to names in the catalogs.

Supplemental information in "Zur inhaltlichen Bestimmung des für Laute intavolierten Handschriftenbestands," by Wolfgang Boetticher in *Acta Musicologica*, 51 (1979), p. 193–203. Dinko Fabris provides a supplement of 18 previously unknown lute tablatures from 11 Italian cities in "Prime aggiunte Italiane al volume RISM B/VII" in *Fontes Artis Musicae*, 29 (1982), p. 103–121.

Review by Hans Lenneberg in *Notes*, 36 (1979), p. 108; by Jörg Wagner in *Musica*, 33 (1979), p. 74–75; and by Arthur Ness in *Journal of the American Musicological Society*, 34 (1981), p. 339–45.

1785. Répertoire International des Sources Musicales. Manuscripts of polyphonic music (c. 1320–1400). Edited by Gilbert Reaney. München-Duisburg: G. Henle, 1969. 427 p. (RISM, B IV, 2)

Organized as in the preceding volume. Indexes of composers and text incipits. Includes *Supplement of manuscripts to RISM B/IV/1* in alphabetical order by country, town, and library with its own indexes to composers and text incipits.
Review by Ernest Sanders in *Music and Letters*, 51 (1970), p. 458–59.

1786. Répertoire International des Sources Musicales. Manuscripts of polyphonic music, 11th–early 14th century. Edited by Gilbert Reaney. München-Duisburg: G. Henle, 1969. 876 p. (RISM, B IV, 1)
The manuscripts are grouped by nationality of location; described individually with detailed bibliographical references. Thematic incipits in square notation.

1787. Répertoire International des Sources Musicales. Musikhandschriften 1600–1800: Datenbank-Index. Music manuscripts 1600-1800: database index. Manuscrits musicaux 1600–1800: banque de données, index. [1986 ed.] Kassel: Bärenreiter, 1986. 2 microfiches and a 16-p. pamphlet. (RISM, A II)
First issued in 1983, also in microfiche.

> Series A/II ... could not be published in book form as originally planned, and indeed could never be published in its entirety as a self-contained catalogue, because of the enormous number of items in it. The Commission Mixte and The Advisory Research Committee accordingly decided on publication in a new form: that of indices only, on microfiche. [pamphlet, p. 5]

RISM A/II is the part of the international union catalog of music devoted to music attributable to a single composer and preserved in manuscripts dating between 1580 and 1850. The bibliographic approach here is based on individual musical works, rather than bibliographic entities or documents; this means that there will be a principal entry describing each manuscript and then as many analytical entries as are needed to describe the individual works in each manuscript.

RISM A/II is a database and the microfiche indexes distributed by the *RISM* Sekretariat in Frankfurt are intended to provide the most commonly needed access points to fuller information in the data base. It is possible, however, to query the data base by other access points and to combine searches. Among the available possibilities are names (composer, librettist, former owners, dedicatee, copyist), musical information (instrumentation, key or mode, genre, musical incipits), text (title, text incipit, text language), physical attributes (type of manuscript, size, format, collation, watermark), provenance, dates, and opus or thematic catalog number. For example, it should be possible to extract entries for works involving a single librettist from a particular geographical region or location; it should be equally possible to discover what works there are written in the 18th century for flute in the key of B minor. Indeed, it is the specific intention of the *RISM* Commission Mixte that national organizing bodies will produce catalogs of holdings based on the *RISM* data base. One such is *Die Musikhandschriften der Benediktiner-Abtei Ottobeuren: Thematischer Katalog* by Gertraut Haberkamp (no. 2256).

Almost 300,000 European worksheets had been provided by 1986 to the *RISM* Sekretariat, but only 48,000 of these had been entered in the data base. The U.S. Music Manuscript Inventory based in the Isham Memorial Library of the Loeb Music Library at Harvard University is midway in the cataloging and analysis of the nearly 12,000 manuscripts in America qualifying for inclusion in *RISM* A/II. Queries are accepted by the staffs of the *RISM* Sekretariat in Kassel and the United States for interrogations of the files in their hands. Remote access by Internet to the U.S. file is projected for the near future.

The microfiche index provides access by composers' names, uniform title, medium of performance, thematic catalog number, opus number, key, location and shelf mark, and *RISM* control number. Entries in the microfiche index do not include music or text incipits.

The following articles describe the development and principles of the *RISM* A/II enterprise:

"Computer-Einsatz bei der Serie A/II RISM: Möglichkeiten, Bedingungen, Vorschläge" by Norbert Böker-Heil in *Fontes Artis Musicae* 22 (1975), p. 86–89;

"The changing face of RISM" by Kurt Dorfmüller in *Fontes Artis Musicae*, 25 (1978), p. 285–89;

"RISM-Handschriftenkatalogisierung und elektronische Datenverarbeitung (EDV)" by Helmut Rösing in *Fontes Artis Musicae*, 26 (1979), p. 107–109;

"Zur Katalogisierung von Musikdrucken und Musikhandschriften der Serie A: Konzept und Realisation der Serie A/II des Internationalen Quellenlexikon der Musik" by Helmut Rösing in *Acta Musicologica*, 51 (1979), p. 184;

"Sinn und Nutzen des Versuchs einer weltweiten Erfassung von Quellen zur Musik" by Helmut Rösing in *Quellenforschung in der Musikwissenschaft*, ed. by Georg Feder (no. 15 in the series *Wolfenbütteler Forschungen*, published 1982).

1788. Répertoire International des Sources Musicales. Recueils imprimés XVIe–XVIIe siècles. Ouvrage publié sous la direction de François Lesure. I. Liste chronologique. München-Duisburg: G. Henle, [1960–]. 639 p. (RISM, B 1)

This volume is Part I of the systematic-chronological section of a comprehensive bibliography of musical sources currently being compiled under the joint auspices of the International Musicological Society and the International Association of Music Libraries. The present volume supersedes Eitner's *Bibliographie der Musik-Sammelwerke* (no. 1738) and, when completed, the entire *RISM* project will replace his *Quellen-Lexikon* (no. 1739) as a modern, comprehensive reference tool for locating primary source materials for musical research.

This volume lists collections of music published between 1501 and 1700, with a summary of their contents and with the locations of copies in major European and American libraries. Index of editors and printers and of titles and authors.

Review by Vincent H. Duckles in *Notes*, 18 (1961), p. 225–27; by Jack A. Westrup in *Music and Letters*, 42 (1961), p. 76; by Daniel Heartz in *Journal of the American Musicological Society*, 14 (1961), p. 268–73; by Gustave Reese in *Fontes Artis Musicae*, 8 (1961), p. 4–7.

For documentation on U.S. response to *RISM*, see "RISM: a report on U.S. activities," by Wayne D. Shirley in *Notes*, 23 (1967), p. 477–97.

1789. Répertoire International des Sources Musicales. Recueils imprimés XVIIIe siècle. Ouvrage publié sous la direction de François Lesure. München-Duisburg: G. Henle, [1964]. 461 p. (RISM, B II)

Cites about 1,800 collections printed between 1701 and 1801, giving basic bibliographic descriptions, composers represented, and locations of copies throughout the world. This volume is organized alphabetically by title rather than chronologically as in the preceding entry. Indexes of publishers and printers, and composers' names.

1790. Répertoire International des Sources Musicales. Tropen- und Sequenzenhandschriften. Von Heinrich Husmann. München-Duisburg: G. Henle, [1964]. 236 p. (RISM, B V, 1)
A volume of the RISM set devoted to the manuscript sources of tropes and sequences. Sources grouped by country. Each entry gives information as to the signature, provenance, type of liturgical book, notation, structure of the source, contents, and related literature. Indexes of manuscripts arranged by libraries and by places of origin. Further indexes of places and subjects, names of saints, names of persons. Bibliography.
Review by Edward H. Roesner in *Journal of the American Musicological Society*, 21 (1968), p. 212–15.

1791. Riedel, Friedrich W. Quellenkundliche Beiträge zur Geschichte der Musik für Tasteninstrumente in der zweiten Hälfte des 17. Jahrhunderts (vornehmlich in Deutschland). Kassel and Basel: Bärenreiter, 1960. 224 p. (Schriften des Landesinstituts für Musikforschung Kiel, 10)
A "source study" concerned with late 17th-century prints and manuscripts of keyboard music, with emphasis on the German school. Numerous useful lists and inventories incorporated into the work, e.g., "Verzeichnis der 1648–1700 im Druck veröffentlichten Musik für Tasteninstrumente" (p. 57–72); "Quellenregister" [Handschriften], p. 219–24.

1792. Rimbault, Edward F. Bibliotheca madrigaliana; a bibliographical account of the musical and poetical works published in England during the 16th and 17th centuries under the titles of madrigals, ballets, ayres, canzonets, etc. London: J. Smith, 1847. 88 p.
Reprint by B. Franklin, New York, [196–?].
An early, and rather faulty, chronological list of vocal music published in England, 1588–1638, giving bibliographical descriptions and contents, source references. First-line index of madrigals and songs, and composer index.
An abridgment is included as a supplement in Becker's *Tonwerke* (no. 1707).

1793. Samuel, Harold E. "Sources, musical (pre-1500)." In *The New Harvard Dictionary of Music*, edited by Don M. Randel, p. 773–78. Cambridge, Massachusetts: Harvard University Press, 1986.
A brief but useful listing of some of the major sources of Gregorian chant and secular monophonic and polyphonic music to 1500. Each entry includes citation of more recent literature about the source. Locations of the sources are given with references to modern editions, if any.

1794. Sartori, Claudio. Bibliografia della musica strumentale italiana stampata in Italia fino al 1700. Firenze: L. Olschki, 1952–68. 2 v. (Biblioteca di bibliografia italiana, 23)
Chronological list of instrumental music, collections of vocal music containing one or more instrumental pieces or vocal music with one or more instrumental parts, published in Italy to 1700. Includes a few works by Italian composers published outside Italy. Excludes lute music and dra-

matic music. Complete bibliographical data, including dedications, prefaces, tables of contents. Composer index.

Review by Dragan Plamenac in *Notes*, 10 (1953), p. 616–19; by Harvey Olnick in *Musical Quarterly*, 40 (1954), p. 98–102; by Willi Apel in *Journal of the American Musicological Society*, 7 (1954), p. 84–86; by Richard Schaal in *Die Musikforschung*, 7 (1954), p. 342.

Vol. II. (Volume secondo di aggiunte e correzioni con indici.) Firenze: Leo S. Olschki, 1968. 216 p. (Biblioteca di bibliografia italiana, 56)

Review by Owen Jander in *Notes*, 26 (1970), p. 738–39, and by Howard M. Brown in *Journal of the American Musicological Society*, 23 (1970), p. 531–33.

1795. Sartori, Claudio. "Finalmente svelati i misteri delle biblioteche italiane." In *Fontes Artis Musicae*, 2 (1955), p. 15–37; 3 (1956), p. 192–202.

A product of the work on *RISM* in Italy, this article contains a summary report of the holdings of 40 Italian libraries and an alphabetical listing of early printed music newly discovered in these collections.

1796. Schanzlin, Hans Peter. "Musik-Sammeldrucke des 16. und 17. Jahrhunderts in schweizerischen Bibliotheken." In *Fontes Artis Musicae*, 4 (1957), p. 38–42.

1797. Schanzlin, Hans Peter. "Musik-Sammeldrucke des 18. Jahrhunderts in schweizerischen Bibliotheken (I)." In *Fontes Artis Musicae*, 6 (1959), p. 20–26; (II), ibid., 8 (1961), p. 26–29.

Preliminary reports prepared by the Swiss office of RISM.

1798. Scheurleer, Daniel F. Nederlandsche liedboeken; lijst der in Nederland tot het jaar 1800 uitgegevan liedboeken.... s'Gravenhage: M. Nijhoff, 1912. 321 p.

Erstes Supplement, 1923.

A bibliography of songbooks published in the Netherlands from 1487 to 1800, with or without music, arranged chronologically under main headings of sacred and secular music, with index by author, editor, publisher, main word of title. 3,887 titles in the main work, 660 in the supplement.

1799. Schierning, Lydia. Die Überlieferung der deutschen Orgel- und Klaviermusik aus der 1. Hälfte des 17. Jahrhunderts. Eine quellenkundliche Studie. Kassel: Bärenreiter, 1961. 147 p. (Schriften des Landesinstituts für Musikforschung Kiel, 12)

A source study devoted to the manuscripts of German organ and keyboard music of the first half of the 17th century. Each manuscript is described and the contents inventoried.

1800. Silbiger, Alexander. Italian manuscript sources of 17th-century keyboard music. Ann Arbor, Michigan: UMI Research Press, 1980. 219 p. (Studies in musicology, 18)

Inter alia an annotated catalog of about 75 manuscripts. Each manuscript is described, but individual works are not listed. Extensive bibliography, an extended essay on the sources, and short studies on seven of the most important composers.

Review by Georgie Durosoir in *Fontes Artis Musicae*, 28 (1981), p. 330.

1801. Smith, Carleton. "Music manuscripts lost during World War II." In *Book Collector*, 17 (1968), p. 26–36.

Deals with holographs by Bach, Beethoven, Haydn, Mozart, *et al.* stored in Silesia and now presumably in Wroclaw (formerly Breslau), Poland. See no. 1902.

1802. Sonneck, Oscar G. T. A bibliography of early secular American music (18th century) ... rev. and enl. by W. T. Upton. [Washington, D.C.]: Library of Congress, Music Division, 1945. 617 p.

First published in 1905. Reprinted, with a new preface by Irving Lowens, by Da Capo Press, New York, 1964.

A title list, with full bibliographical descriptions, including first lines of texts. Completely indexed, with lists of composers, first lines, publishers, etc.

Review by Harry Eskew of the 1964 reprint in *Anuario, Inter-American Institute for Musical Research*, 1 (1965), p. 134.

1803. Stevenson, Robert. Renaissance and Baroque musical sources in the Americas. Washington, D.C.: Organization of American States, 1970. 346 p.

Typescript catalog of printed and manuscript works seen in Bogotá, Cuzco, Guatemala City, La Paz, Lima, Mexico City, Montevideo, Morelia, Oaxaca, Puebla Sucre, Buenos Aires, Rio de Janeiro, and Santiago. Music cited from the last three locations exceeds the chronological limits into the 20th century. Almost completely lacking in description, although each source is analyzed and many individual works are described. Not indexed or cross-referenced. Some of the commentary is idiosyncratic. Corrigenda provided on a separate page.

Review by Samuel Claro Valdédes in *Revista Musical Chilena*, 31 (1977), p. 123–24.

1804. Stevenson, Robert M. "Sixteenth and seventeenth century resources in Mexico." In *Fontes Artis Musicae*, 1 (1954), p. 69–78; 2 (1955), p. 10–15.

The first installment is concerned with the manuscript resources of the Puebla Cathedral music archive, comprising some 365 sacred works by 36 composers. Arranged alphabetically by composer. The second part is a description of a 16th-century manuscript of sacred music in the library of Canon Octaviano Valdes of Mexico City. Continued by no. 2308.

1805. Das Tenorlied: mehrstimmige Lieder in deutschen Quellen 1450–1580. Hrsg. vom Deutschen Musikgeschichtlichen Archiv Kassel und vom Staatlichen Institut für Musikforschung Preussischer Kulturbesitz Berlin. Zusammengestellt und bearbeitet von Norbert Böker-Heil, Harald Heckmann, und Ilse Kindermann. Kassel: Bärenreiter, 1979. 3 v. (Catalogus Musicus, 9) (RISM Sonderband)

A thematic catalog with incipits for each voice, arranged by source (both printed and manuscript) with indexes to text incipits and musical incipits. A most significant achievement made possible through the application of automated data processing techniques.

1806. Thibault, Geneviève, and Louis Perceau. Bibliographie des poésies de P. de Ronsard mises en musique au XVIe siècle. Paris: E. Droz, 1941. 121 p. (Publications de la Société Française de Musicologie, 2 ser., t. 8)

Chronological bibliography, 1552–1629, of some 148 collections containing musical settings of lyrics by Ronsard. Full bibliographical citations of the collections, with Ronsard settings listed for each. Index of text incipits and of collections and names.

1807. Vogel, Emil, Alfred Einstein, François Lesure and Claudio Sartori. Bibliografia della musica italiana vocale profana pubblicata dal 1500 al 1700. Nuova edizione interamente rifatta e aumenta con gli indici dei musicisti, poeti, contanti, dedicatori, e dei capoversi dei testi letterari. Il nuovo Vogel. Pomezia: Staderini-Minkoff, 1977. 3 v.

First published in Berlin by A. Haazk, 1892, with Vogel as sole author and entitled *Bibliothek der gedruckten weltlichen Vocalmusik Italiens aus den Jahren 1500–1700*. Subsequently issued in a partially revised and enlarged edition including Alfred Einstein's corrections and additions originally published in *Notes*, 2–5 (1945–48), by Olms, in Hildesheim, 1962, in 2 v.

This work is the basic source of information concerning early printed secular vocal music in Italy appearing in editions attributed to a single composer between 1500 and 1700. The new edition does not cite anthologies, referring readers to appropriate RISM volumes. The editors claim that this edition supersedes information present in the *Einzeldrucke* volumes issued prior to it (no. 1781). Of course, some editions published with the name of a single composer on the title page in fact include works by other composers. These are included in this bibliography.

Arranged alphabetically by composer, each entry gives full title-page transcription, describes the publication, and lists the works in the order of the original edition. Poets are suggested when such attribution is possible. Locations for each publication or part books from it are cited. Reissued editions are cross-referenced. There is an appendix of five additional publications at the end of vol. 2, and after the indexes in vol. 3 are more additions and corrections. Cross-references are provided for alternate forms of composers' names.

The preface discusses the need for a new Vogel-Einstein and cites the many editions, revisions, and contributing articles that have supplemented the original edition of 1892 and Alfred Einstein's own considerable revisions.

The indexes to composers not cited on title pages, to poets, to singers cited on the title pages or in the dedications, to other persons cited in the publications, and most especially to the capoversi of each work make the vast body of information in this work accessible. The index to capoversi includes numerous and invaluable see references, but the reader must understand that the Italian language was by no means standardized in the period during which these works were written. Thus, for instance, seeking first lines beginning with 'Lacrime' as well as 'Lagrime' is necessary.

Reviews by Don Harran in *Fontes Artis Musicae*, 26 (1979), p. 67–69; by Francesco Luisi in *Nuova Rivista Musicale Italiana*, 13 (1979), p. 703–705; by Andrea Wernli in *Die Musikforschung*, 31 (1981), p. 342; and by Howard Mayer Brown in the *Journal of the American Musicological Society*, 36 (1983), p. 142–50.

1808. Walther, Hans. Initia carminum ac versuum medii aevi posterioris latinorum. Alphabetisches Verzeichnis der Versanfänge mittellateinischer Dichtungen. Göttingen: Vandenhoeck & Ruprecht, 1959. 1,186 p. (Carmina medii aevi posterioris latina, 1)

Not a music bibliography but a most valuable reference tool for musicologists working in the field of medieval studies. An alphabetical index of text incipits for more than 20,000 medieval Latin lyrics, with references to manuscript sources and modern editions. Bibliography of literature; index of names and subjects.

1809. Ward, Tom R. The polyphonic Office hymn 1450–1520; a descriptive catalogue. Neuhausen-Stuttgart: American Institute of Musicology and Hänssler-Verlag, 1980. 315 p.

This book is primarily an annotated catalogue of a small segment of the repertory of a polyphonic liturgical music of the early Renaissance.... The information given here will provide bibliographic control over the polyphonic Office hymns.... New sources and new examination of already known ones may increase the size of the repertory, but the inventory will provide a context in which to view these works. Finally, this inventory removes 755 works from that vague category "motet."

Musical incipits are given for each voice in every composition. Entries are in order by first line of text. Sources for each incipit are cited and there are comments on stylistic aspects, especially the presence of cantus firmi. Indexes are provided to texts found in settings in the inventory, to cantus firmi used in settings in the inventory, to settings by composer, to sources for the repertory, and to inventory entries for all compositions in each source.

Review by Giulio Cattin in *Rivista Italiana di Musicologia*, 15 (1980), p. 276–85.

1810. Winternitz, Emanuel. Musical autographs from Monteverdi to Hindemith. Princeton, New Jersey: Princeton University Press, 1955. 2 v.

Reissued by Dover Publications, New York, paperbound edition, 1965. 2 v.

Vol. 1 is devoted to commentary on the plates, with two introductory chapters: "The written sign" and "The writing act." Vol. 2 contains 196 full-page plates of autographs.

1811. Wolf, Johannes. Handbuch der Notationskunde. I. Teil: Tonschriften des Altertums und des Mittelalters. II. Teil: Tonschriften der Neuzeit, Tabulaturen, Partitur, Generalbass und Reformversuche. Leipzig: Breitkopf & Härtel, 1913–19. 2 v. (Kleine Handbücher der Musikgeschichte, 8)

Reprinted by Olms, Hildesheim, 1963.

The Wolf Handbuch is cited here on the strength of its useful listings of early manuscript sources connected with the author's discussion of notational practices. For example: "Quellen der *Ars antiqua*" (vol. 1, p. 258–63); "Die *Ars nova*" (vol. 1, p. 351–54); "Handschriftliche Quellen des 15. und 16. Jahrhunderts" (vol. 1, p. 444–65); "Verzeichnis einiger wichtigen deutschen Lautentabulaturen" (vol. 2, p. 47–59); "Italienische Lautentabulaturen" (vol. 2, p. 66–71); "Quellen französischer Lautentabulatur" (vol. 2, p. 95–106); "Guitarretabulaturen" (vol. 2, p. 209–218).

Also listed in no. 551.

1812. Wolfe, Richard J. Secular music in America, 1801–1825. A bibliography. Introduction by Carleton Sprague Smith. New York: New York Public Library; Astor, Lenox and Tilden Foundations, 1964. 3 v.

A major work of bibliography in the field of early American music. Prepared as a continuation of the Sonneck-Upton *Bibliography* (no. 1802). The arrangement is alphabetical by composer. Brief biographies. Full bibliographical descriptions and locations of copies in American libraries and private collections.

Appendixes: (1) "Unrecorded 18th-century imprints located during the course of this work." (2) "A list of works in the Sonneck-Upton Bibliography which have been redated into 19th-century." (3)"Locations of newly discovered copies of works in the Sonneck-Upton Bibliography." Index of titles; of first lines; of publishers, engravers, and printers; of numbering systems. General index.

Complemented by Fuld and Davidson, *18th-century American Secular Music Manuscripts* (no. 1745).

Review by James C. Downey in *Anuario, Inter-American Institute for Musical Research*, 1 (1965), p. 122–24.

1813. Wotquenne, Alfred. Table alphabétique des morceaux mesurés contenus dans les œuvres dramatiques de Zeno, Metastasio, et Goldoni. Leipzig: Breitkopf & Härtel, 1905. 77 p.

An alphabetical first-line index of aria and ensemble texts by Zeno, Metastasio, and Goldoni, citing volume and page numbers in the standard editions of their works and title of the work from which the incipit is derived. Table of librettos by the three authors.

FOLK SONG AND BALLAD

This section should be used in conjunction with the section "Bibliographies of Music Literature: Ethnomusicology," which lists studies and monographs pertaining to folk song and ballad. Here, the emphasis is on the music itself. The user should bear in mind, however, that a work such as Haywood's *Bibliography of North American Folklore and Folksong* (no. 800) contains numerous entries for music, both printed and on sound recordings. Also relevant in certain respects are such bibliographies as Sears' *Song Index* (no. 1408), Fuld's *American Popular Music* (no. 1516), and the bibliographies by Sonneck-Upton (no. 1802) and by Wolfe (no. 1812), which serve to bridge the uncertain gap between folk and popular song.

1814. Bronson, Bertrand H. The traditional tunes of the Child ballads, with their texts, according to the extant records of Great Britain and America. Princeton, New Jersey: Princeton University Press, 1959–1972. 4 v.

Vol. 1: ballads 1–53; vol. 2: ballads 54–113; vol. 3: ballads 114–243; vol. 4: includes addenda and various bibliographies and indexes.

A monumental work of scholarship in the field of English-Scottish ballads. Based on the work of Francis J. Child, but far exceeding it in scope and authority. The literary and musical traditions of each ballad are discussed, together with a printing of all the known variants, both literary and musical.

Review by Klaus Roth in *Jahrbuch für Volksliedforschung*, 13 (1968), p. 228–29.

1815. Brunnings, Florence E. Folk song index; a comprehensive guide to the Florence E. Brunnings Collection. New York: Garland Publishing, 1981. 357 p. (Garland reference library of the humanities, 252)

A title index to the 49,399 songs in the printed and recorded anthologies of folk songs in the Brunnings Collection (located in North Weymouth, Massachusetts) with references from first lines to titles. There is a list of the 1,305 anthologies indexed.

1816. Chappell, William. Popular music of the olden time. A history of the ancient songs, ballads, and of the dance tunes of England.... Reprint by Dover Publications, Inc., of the original London publication of 1855–59. New York: Dover, 1965. 2 v.

A revision of this work, by H. Ellis Wooldridge, appeared in 1893. This edition was, in turn, reprinted by Jack Brussel, New York, 1961.

Chappell is the classic work on English popular song. It is the basis for the expanded work by Claude Simpson on *The British Broadside Ballad* (no. 1819).

1817. Dean-Smith, Margaret. A guide to English folk song collections.... Liverpool: University Press of Liverpool, in association with the English Folk Dance and Song Society, 1954. 120 p.

Foreword by Gerald Abraham.

Indexes approximately 62 collections of English folk song, 1822–1952. Main entry is by song title, with cross-references from text incipit. Chronological list of collections. Detailed annotations.

Review by Bertrand H. Bronson in *Journal of the American Musicological Society*, 8 (1955), p. 57–58.

Gesellschaft der Musikfreunde (Vienna). Volksmusiksammlung Die. See no. 2411.

1818. Sidel'nikov, Viktor M. Russkaia narodnaia pesnia: bibliograficheskii ukazatel' 1735–1945. Moskva: Izd. Akademii Nauk SSSR, 1962. 169 p.

At head of title: *Akademia Nauk SSSR, Institut Mirovoi Literatury im. A. M. Gor'kogo.*

Part I: texts of folk poetry and folk songs, published in journals, newspapers, etc., with or without music. Part II: books, articles, etc., about Russian folk song. Index of names.

1819. Simpson, Claude M. The British broadside ballad and its music. New Brunswick, New Jersey: Rutgers University Press, 1966. 919 p.

An indispensable reference tool for students of English popular song from the 16th through the 18th centuries. Gives music for 540 broadside ballads and traces each melody from its earliest printed and manuscript sources. No ballad texts printed. The work takes its point of departure from William Chappell's *Popular Music of the Olden Time* (1855–59, 2 v.; no. 1816) but far exceeds Chappell in coverage.

Review by Bertrand H. Bronson in *Musical Quarterly*, 52 (1966), p. 384–87; by John Ward in *Journal of the American Musicological Society*, 20 (1967), p. 131–34 (see also Ward's extended commentary, "Apropos the British broadside ballad and its music," in the same issue of *Journal of the*

American Musicological Society, p. 28–86); by Walter Woodfill in *Journal of Research in Music Education*, 14 (1955), p. 238–39; by Walter Suppan in *Jahrbuch für Volksliedforschung*, 13 (1968), p. 229–31; by Charles Heywood in *Ethnomusicology*, 11 (1967), p. 133–34.

1820. Sonkin, Annabelle B. Jewish folk-song resources; an annotated bibliography. New York National Jewish Music Council, 1957. 24 leaves.
  Somewhat dated, but still useful.

1821. University of California. Department of Music. Check list of California songs. Archive of California folk music. Part I: texts in print. Berkeley: University of California, 1940. 160 leaves (typescript).
  Published in connection with a Work Projects Administration project supervised by Sidney H. Robertson.
  A list, alphabetical by title, of more than 2,500 songs from texts either published or known to have circulated in California, with an index of first lines. P. 157–60: bibliography of songsters and broadsides.

1822. Van der Merwe, F. Z. Suid-Afrikaanse musiekbibliografie 1787–1952. Pretoria: J. L. Van Schaik, 1958. 410 p.
  Supplemented by *En 1953–1972 bygewerk vir die Raad vir Geesteswetenskaplike Navorsing deur Jan van de Graaf.* (Kaapstad: Tafelberg-uitgewers vir die Instituut vir Taal. Lettere en Kuns. Raad vir Geesteswetenskaplike Navorsing, 1974. 297 p.)
  A comprehensive bibliography of music related to South Africa (works by South African composers, wherever published, and writings on South African themes or subject matter). The largest part of the citations refer to songs, marches, or dance music of a popular nature, although a few studies and monographs are interfiled. Entries are unclassified, arranged alphabetically by composer or author. Index of South African composers and musicians. The language is Afrikaans.

SACRED MUSIC

Many of the items entered in this section are actually editions of Protestant or Catholic liturgical music. At the same time, they qualify as reference books because of the scope and authority of their documentation.

1823. Bäumker, Wilhelm. Das katholische deutsche Kirchenlied in seinen Singweisen, von den frühesten Zeiten bis gegen Ende des 17. Jahrhunderts. Freiburg: Herder'sche Verlagshandlung, 1883–1911. 4 v.
  Reprinted from the original by Georg Olms, Hildesheim, 1962.
  Bäumker's work is the basic study of the German Catholic church song. The main body of the work consists of quotations and discussion of the individual melodies, classified according to the church year or liturgical use. Each volume contains an extensive bibliography, arranged chronologically, of early printed song collections. Entries cover the period from 1470 to 1800. Transcriptions from the prefaces of early song collections are given.

1824. Becker, Carl F. Die Choralsammlungen der verschiedenen christlichen Kirchen. Hildesheim: H. A. Gerstenberg, 1972. 220 p.

Reprint of the edition of F. Fleischer, Leipzig, 1845 ed.

A bibliography of sources for sacred choral music in collections classified by a variety of Christian denominations. Within each section, chronologically arranged, are entries outlining the contents of each title cited, and there are references to related works and modern sources. For some, locations of copies are shown in public and private libraries. There is a section on manuscripts showing no locations. Indexes to the collections in chronological order and to names.

1825. Chevalier, Ulysse. Repertorium hymnologicum. Catalogue des chants, hymnes, proses, séquences, tropes en usage dans l'église latine depuis les origines jusqu'à nos jours. Louvain: Société des Bollandistes, 1892–1920. 6 v.

The standard bibliography of Latin rhymed poetic texts for liturgical use, identifying saints and feasts with which each incipit is associated. There are references to author (if known), to dates of composition, and to sources. A 315-p. volume of additions and emendations was prepared by Clemens Blume under the title *Repertorium Repertorii*, Leipzig, 1901.

The *Repertorium* has been reprinted by Bollandistes, 1959; the Blume supplement by Olms, Hildesheim, 1971.

Corrected and supplemented by no. 1847.

1826. Cunningham, W. Patrick. The music locator. Saratoga, New York: Resource Publications, 1976. 187 p.

A computer-generated index to over 12,800 songs usable in Christian worship by title and composer. The main list is classified and entries in it supply information on year of publication, format, style, and publisher.

1827. Diehl, Katharine S. Hymns and tunes—an index. Metuchen, New Jersey: Scarecrow Press, 1966. 1,242 p.

A comprehensive finding tool for anyone interested in locating or identifying a Protestant hymn or hymn tune. Approach offered through first lines of text, authors, tune names, composers, and melodies given in alphabetical notation. The texts are almost exclusively English. Appendixes include a glossary and a chronological list of hymnals indexed.

See also nos. 420 and 1838 for other indexes to hymnbooks.

1828. Ellinwood, Leonard W. Bibliography of American hymnals compiled from the files of the *Dictionary of American Hymnology*, a project of the Hymn Society of America. Elizabeth Lockwood, associate editor. New York: University Music Editions, 1983. 27 microfiche.

Lists 7,500 entries for hymnals in all languages using the Roman alphabet; includes nondenominational collections. Eye-readable contents guides on sheets in pockets with microfiches in binder.

1829. Ellinwood, Leonard W. Dictionary of American hymnology; first line index. A project of the Hymn Society of America. New York: University Music Editions, 1984. 179 reels.

Accompanied by printed guide consisting of the front matter and pages

1–26 of the introduction (reel 001). These pages provide the useful detail needed in using the first-line index. There are "Essays on hymns with confused authorship" on p. 27–118 on reel 001.

1830. Foster, Myles B. Anthems and anthem composers, an essay upon the development of the anthem from the time of the Reformation to the end of the 19th century; with a complete list of anthems (in alphabetical order) belonging to each of the four centuries. London: Novello, 1901. 225 p.

Reprint by Da Capo Press, New York, 1970.

1831. Frost, Maurice. English and Scottish psalm and hymn tunes, c. 1543–1677. London: Oxford University Press, 1953. 531 p.

P. 3–50: a bibliography of English-Scottish "Old Version" psalters from 1556 to 1677, with full descriptions and lists of contents. The main body of the work is an edition of 457 psalm tunes or harmonized versions thereof.

For an index to this work, see Kirby Rogers' *Index to Maurice Frost's English and Scottish Psalm and Hymns Tunes* (no. 8 in the MLA index series).

1832. Higginson, J. Vincent. Handbook for American Catholic hymnals. New York: Hymn Society of America, 1976. 334 p.

A complex work presenting information (text, themes, sources, composers, authors, and bibiliography) in several sections arranged by use in the church year. There are indexes to composers, authors, tune names, and first lines.

1833. Kirsch, Winfried. Die Quellen der mehrstimmigen Magnificat- und Te-Deum-Vertonungen bis zur Mitte des 16. Jahrhunderts. Tutzing: Hans Schneider, 1966. 588 p.

Review by James Erb in *Journal of the American Musicological Society*, 22 (1969), p. 122–25; by Martin Just in *Die Musikforschung*, 21 (1968), p. 523–24.

1834. Laster, James H. Catalogue of choral music arranged in biblical order. Metuchen, New Jersey: Scarecrow Press, 1983. 261 p.

Anthems arranged in order from Genesis to Revelation according to biblical passage, including those with texts from the Apocrypha. Citations include information about performing forces necessary, publisher, and date of publication. There is a short addendum and a composer index.

1835. Laster, James H. Catalogue of vocal solos and duets arranged in biblical order. Metuchen, New Jersey: Scarecrow Press, 1984. 204 p.

Works arranged in order from Genesis to Revelation.

1836. Mason, Henry L. Hymn-tunes of Lowell Mason: a bibliography. New York: AMS Press, 1976. 118 p.

Reprint of the 1944 ed. published by University Press, Cambridge, Mass.

A bibliography of the hymn tunes of the prolific 19th-century American composer.

1837. Metcalf, Frank Johnson. American psalmody; or titles of books containing tunes printed in America from 1721 to 1820. New introduction by Harry Eskew. New York: Da Capo Press, 1968.

An unabridged republication of the first edition published in New York in 1917.

A checklist of: psalm, hymn, and anthem collections; psalm and hymn collections for children; single hymns and anthems; musical collections; and prose tracts on hymnody and sacred music. Each entry identifies first and successive imprints as well as libraries holding copies. There is a key to the location of collections.

Review by Richard A. Crawford in *Notes*, 26 (1969), p. 42–43.

1838. Parks, Edna D. Early English hymns: an index. Metuchen, New Jersey: Scarecrow Press, 1972. 168 p.

Lists 1,157 hymns from some 51 hymnals and psalters and other sources. No music is given, but the tune names are identified and metrical structure is given.

See also nos. 420 and 1827 for other indexes to hymnbooks.

1839. Protestant Episcopal Church in the U.S.A. Joint Commission on Church Music. Service music and anthems for the nonprofessional choir. Greenwich, Connecticut: Seabury Press, 1955. 56 p.

Service music classified by liturgical use; anthems by the church year. Information includes degree of difficulty, number of parts, presence of solos, type of accompaniment, publisher, and number in series.

1840. Rado Polykarpe. Répertoire hymnologique des manuscrits liturgiques dans les bibliothèques publiques de Hongrie. Budapest: Stephaneum Nyomda, 1945. 59 p. (Az országos széchenyi könyvtár kiadványai, 20)

Alphabetical listing of 727 hymns found in 146 liturgical manuscripts in libraries in Hungary.

1841. Répertoire International des Sources Musicales. Das Deutsche Kirchenlied, DKL: kritische Gesamtausgabe der Melodien herausgegeben von Konrad Ameln, Markus Jenny und Walther Lipphardt. Kassel: Bärenreiter, 1975–80. 2 v. (RISM, B VIII, 1–2)

Contents: Bd. 1, T. 1. Verzeichnis der Drucke. Bd. 1, T. 2. Register.

"This volume comprises the catalog of traceable printed sources of German hymns, of all denominations, that contain at least one melody in musical notation." The entries are arranged in chronological order and consist of title page transcriptions including imprint, format and dimensions, and bibliographical references when necessary. The second part includes indexes to titles, names of persons, place names, printers and publishers, and the *DKL* symbols. There is also an afterword and corrigenda.

Review in *Die Musikforschung*, 30 (1977), p. 83–84.

1842. Rogal, Samuel J. "A bibliographical survey of American hymnody, 1640–1800." In *Bulletin of the New York Public Library* (Winter 1975), p. 231–52.

Rogal, Samuel J. Sisters of sacred song See no. 2987.

1843. Schreiber, Max. Kirchenmusik von 1500-1600, Originaldrucke und Manuskripte chronologisch zusammengestellt.... [Regensburg]: Druckerei St. Georgsheim Birkeneck, 1932. 88 p.

Chronological list of 16th-century sacred music, printed and manuscript sources. Entered alphabetically by composer under year of issue. Brief titles, and locations in British and continental libraries. Index of composers and classified index of forms.

1844. Schreiber, Max. Kirchenmusik von 1600–1700, Originaldrucke und Manuskripte chronologisch zusammengestellt.... [Regensburg]: Druckerei St. Georgsheim Birkeneck, 1934. 184 p.

Treats 17th-century sacred music as in the entry above.

1845. Spencer, Donald Amos. Hymn and Scripture selection guide: a cross-reference of scripture and hymns with over 12,000 references for 380 hymns and gospel songs. Valley Forge, Pa.: Judson Press, 1977. 176 p.

An index relating biblical text to hymns.

1846. Stellhorn, Martin H. Index to hymn preludes ... and other organ compositions, based on hymns, chorales, and carols. A listing of 2,200 selections of various publishers according to key, difficulty, and length. St. Louis, Missouri: Concordia Publishing House, [1948]. 151 p.

1847. Szövérffy, Joseph. Repertorium hymnologicum novum. Berlin: Classical Folia Editions, 1983– . (Publications of the archives for medieval poetry; v. 1, etc.)

"Das Repertorium novum will Chevaliers altes Werk (Repertorium hymnologicum) ersetzen und mit neuem Material bereichern" (from the introduction). This work corrects and supplements Chevalier's *Repertorium Hymnologicum* and Blume's *Repertorium* (no. 1825).

Contents: T. 1, Bd. 1. Einführung und alphabetisches Verzeichnis. Religiöse Dichtung als Kulturphänomen und Kulturleistung.

1848. Thuner, O. E. Dansk Salme-Leksikon: Haandbog i dansk Salmesang. En hymnologisk Sammenstilling af Ord og Toner med historiske og bibliografiske Oplysninger. København: O. Lohse, 1930. 592 p.

Lists 1,108 Danish psalm settings, with detailed information as to sources of texts and music. Index of melody groups, personal names, first lines of texts.

1849. Wackernagel, Philipp. Bibliographie zur Geschichte des deutschen Kirchenliedes im XVI. Jahrhundert. Frankfurt am Main: 1855. 718 p.

Unaltered reprint of the original edition by Georg Olms, Hildesheim, 1961.

A chronological listing of 1,050 editions of German sacred song published during the 16th century. Detailed bibliographical descriptions, with annotations. Transcriptions given of the introductions to 110 of the collections.

1850. Wackernagel, Philipp. Das deutsche Kirchenlied von der ältesten Zeit bis zu Anfang des 17. Jahrhunderts. Mit Berücksichtigung der deutschen kirchlichen Liederdichtung im weiteren Sinne und der lateinischen von Hilarius bis Georg Fabricius und Wolfgang Ammonius. Leipzig: Teubner, 1864–1877. 5 v.

Reprinted by Olms, Hildesheim 1964.

Vol. 1 provides in chronological order the full texts of Latin hymns and sequences from sources ranging from Hilarius of Poitiers to 1579. There is an alphabetical index to the hymns and sequences in mid-volume. The second half of the volume is an extensive bibliography of German sources of hymns and sequences with complete, almost diplomatic, transcriptions of title pages and analytic annotations. There is an index to hymn incipits.

Vol. 2 provides texts of German hymns from the time Otfrid to that of Hans Sachs (roughly to the beginnings of the Reformation). Manuscript and printed sources are cited. Indexes to text incipits and to authors of the texts.

Vol. 3 concerns hymns from the genesis of the Reformation, from Martin Luther to Nicholas Herman (1523–53). Author and text incipit indexes as well as an index to the sources of the themes in the texts.

Vol. 4 presents texts from the later Reformation, from Paulus Eber to Bartolomäus Ringwaldt (1554–84). The apparatus is as in vol. 3.

Vol. 5 contains texts from the time of Bartolomäus Ringwaldt to the beginning of the 17th century. In this volume, the foreword is signed by Otto Wackernagel and Ernst Wackernagel. The apparatus is as in vol. 3.

Wackernagel is the fundamental research tool for the sources of the texts to German church music.

Includes bibliographical references.

1851. Zahn, Johannes. Die Melodien der deutschen evangelischen Kirchenlieder aus den Quellen geschöpft und mitgeteilt.... Gütersloh: Bertelsmann, 1889–93. 6 v.

Reprint of the original edition by Olms, Hildesheim, 1963.

Zahn is primarily an edition presenting 8,806 melodies, derived from the earliest sources, for the German Protestant liturgy. Classified according to metrical form.

Vol. 5, p. 307–494: biographical notices of 463 chorale composers or editors of chorale collections. Index of composers; first-line index of texts.

Vol. 6: a bibliography of 1,408 items listing the sources of the melodies and arranged chronologically from 1507 to 1892, with locations of copies in the principal European libraries. Further supplements give non-German sources and manuscript sources.

Catalogs of Music Libraries and Collections

A knowledge of the published catalogs of the major music libraries and collections is essential for locating source materials for study or research. Access to this information has been made immeasurably easier by the *Directory of Music Research Libraries*, published under the auspices of the International Association of Music Libraries (no. 1853) as series C of *RISM*. This work supplies international coverage for music libraries in Europe, North America, and other parts of the world. Substantial lists of libraries are found in *MGG* (by Alfons Ott) and in the *New Grove*, although the former is out of date. The German music libraries are separately described and their catalogs cited in Richard Schaal's *Führer durch deutsche Musikbibliotheken*, 1971 (no. 2036), and Claudio Sartori has done likewise for the Italian institutions in a 1971 issue of *Fontes Artis Musicae* (no. 2082).

The following section covers the catalogs of the principal music libraries of the world and also includes a number of important exhibition catalogs, although we have made no effort to be comprehensive in the latter category. Excluded are the auction or sale catalogs of music collections that have been dispersed—with a few exceptions such as the famous Wolffheim catalog (no. 2494), which is itself a bibliographical tool of first importance.

It goes without saying that a great many musical source materials have never been cited in special music catalogs. Information must be sought in general library catalogs of early printed books and manuscripts. Descriptions of the music manuscripts in the Bodleian Library at Oxford, for example, must be extracted from the seven volumes of Madan's *Summary Catalogue of Western Manuscripts in the Bodleian Library* ... (1895–1953). Likewise, Cambridge University music manuscripts are fully described in the series of college library catalogs compiled by Montague Rhodes James. No attempt has been made here to cite general catalogues of this kind, but the reader's attention may be called to the invaluable guide to Latin manuscript books before 1600, a list of the printed catalogues and unpublished inventories of extant collections by Paul Kristeller, *Latin Manuscript Books before 1600* (rev. ed., Fordham University Press, 1960). The search for sources has, of course, been greatly facilitated by the continuing appearance of volumes in the series *Répertoire International des Sources Musicales* and related volumes deriving from the large store of information in the offices of the RISM-Sekretariat in Frankfurt.

In the present list the catalogs have been grouped, as far as is possible, by place. Place is ordinarily designated as a city followed by the appropriate country (or state in the case of the United States). Certain national union catalogs or descriptions of the holdings of several libraries within a country are entered under the name of the country.

There are a few catalogs of important collections that remain in private hands or that have been dispersed or changed their locations in recent years: the Hirsch, Cortot, and Wolffheim collections are examples. These catalogs are grouped in a special category at the end of this section; see nos. 2467–2494.

The first two entries of this chapter, nos. 1852 and 1853, provide substantial information about research music libraries, their holdings, and their catalogs. The second entry is for an international directory of music research libraries issued under the auspices of the International Association of Music Libraries and issued as series C of *RISM*. The first entry supplements the second.

1852. "Libraries." In *The New Grove Dictionary of Music and Musicians*, edited by Stanley Sadie, v. 10, p. 719–821, by Rita Benton, Mary Wallace Davidson, Samuel Claro, Catherine Dower, José Ignacio Perdomo Escobar, Norma González, Francesco Curt Lange, Mercedes Resi Pequeno, Robert Stevenson, Pola Suárez Urturbey, Dorothy Freed, Werner Gallusser, Don Harran, Katharine A. Haslam, James Siddons. London: Macmillan, 1980.

After a discussion of the history and various functions and types of music libraries, there follows a geographically organized survey of music libraries. There is an introductory paragraph on each country's music libraries that occasionally cites the principal means of access to music bibliographic records for that country. Each entry in the survey describes the library's history and holdings as well as citing any literature about the library, including catalogs. This survey supplements the *RISM* series C directories (no. 1853) and provides information to libraries in countries not yet covered by those directories. The article covers only institutional libraries.

Includes a directory of national music information centers.

1853. Répertoire International des Sources Musicales. Directory of music research libraries. Rita Benton, general editor. Kassel and New York: Bärenreiter, 1970– . (RISM, C)

Parts II and III issued by the Commission on Research Libraries of the International Association of Music Libraries. Remaining volumes issued as numbers in *RISM*, series C.

Contents:

Volume 1: *Canada*, [edited by] Marian Kahn and Helmut Kallmann. *United States*, [edited by] Charles Lindahl. 2nd rev. ed. Kassel, etc.: Bärenreiter, 1983. 253 p.

Supersedes Part I: *Canada and the United States*, edited by Rita Benton. Iowa City: University of Iowa, 1967. 70 p.

Includes music collections in general, special, and private libraries. Entries arranged alphabetically by name of city and then by institution. Addresses, telephone numbers, services offered, nature of catalogs, size of collection, and ordinary hours open to readers are listed. Significant special collections are described. Literature pertinent to each collection cited. References to more extensive or more specific descriptions in the works cited in the initial bibliography of general literature are provided. There are indexes to host institutions, to personal and corporate names of collections, and to archives within host institutions. Includes a bibliography of general literature concerning library collections in the U.S. and Canada. The introduction to the U.S. section contains valuable information on the revision and the guidelines for including libraries in it.

The *RISM* sigla for each library is provided in parentheses immediately after the number of the entry; page headings show country codes in the same fashion. The U.S. section entries include references to entries in *Resources of American Music History* (no. 1116).

Review by Geraldine Ostrove in *Fontes Artis Musicae*, 331 (1984), p. 134–35.

Part II: *Thirteen European Countries* (preliminary edition). Rita Benton, editor. Iowa City: University of Iowa, 1970. 235 p.

The directory is arranged by country (Austria, Belgium, Switzerland, Federal Republic of Germany, German Democratic Republic, Denmark, Ireland, Great Britain, Luxemburg, Norway, The Netherlands, Sweden, Finland), and within each country by city, and then by institution.

There is a short bibliography of general literature and at the beginning of each country's section there is a bibliography of works concerning libraries and collections in that country. For some cities there is also a bibliography of works as well (e.g., Köln, p. 79). Libraries cited are primarily those reporting holdings to RISM, though some others are included. For the most part, the entries include the same kind of information provided in vol. 1, although some entries are quite brief. The bibliographies of literature concerning works and collections in each institution are invaluable. The index cites present and former names of libraries and their host institutions and is arranged also by country.

Reviews by Jack A. Westrup in *Music and Letters*, 52 (1971), p. 316; by Vincent H. Duckles in *Journal of Research in Music Education*, 20 (1972), p. 293–94; by Susan T. Sommer in *Notes*, 29 (1972), p. 259–60; and by François Lesure in *Fontes Artis Musicae*, 18 (1971), p. 129.

Part III: *Spain, France, Italy, Portugal* (preliminary edition). Rita Benton, editor. Iowa City: University of Iowa, 1972. 342 p.

4 p. errata bound in after p. 342.

The organization and content is very similar to that of vol. 1 and part II.

One should note that some entries contain references to published catalogs of individual collections that are continuously updated and annotated by hand in the home institution (see entry no. 118 in part III for the Biblioteca Communale Ariostea in Ferrara, Italy, for instance).

See Maurice Esses, "New information concerning some music research libraries in Spain," in *Fontes Artis Musicae*, 26 (1979), p. 189–91, which serves as an addenda, corrigenda, and supplement to the volume including Spain, and Eugene Casjen Cramer, "New information concerning some music libraries and archives in Spain and Portugal," in *Notes*, 40 (1984), p. 30–40, which is a second update to the volume.

Reviews of parts I–III by Eugene K. Wolf in the *Journal of the American Musicological Society*, 29 (1976), p. 484–86, by Jörg Martin in *Die Musikforschung*, 30 (1977), p. 526, and by Imogen Fellinger in *Melos/Neue Zeitschrift für Musik*, 4 (1978), p. 167–68.

Volume 4: *Australia*, [edited by] Cecil Hill. *Israel*, [edited by] Katya Manor. *Japan*, [edited by] James Siddons. *New Zealand*, [edited by] Dorothy Freed. Kassel: Bärenreiter, 1979. 177 p.

Organized as in vols. 1–3. Japanese place names transliterated; city names also show prefecture.

Reviews by Harold J. Diamond in *Notes*, 36 (1980), p. 660–61, and by Wolfgang Kruger in *Fontes Artis Musicae*, 27 (1980), p. 223–24.

Volume 5: *Czechoslovakia; Hungary; Poland*, [edited by] James B. Moldovan. *Yugoslavia*, [edited by] Lilian Pruett. Kassel: Bärenreiter, 1985. 267 p.
Organized as in vols. 1–4.

AARHUS, DENMARK

1854. Clausen, Per Groth. Dansk Musik; Katalog øver Statsbibliothek samling af trykte musikalier. Danish music; a catalog of printed music in the State and University Library, Aarhus. Aarhus: Universitetsførlaget, 1977. 316 p.
A classified catalog of the Danish printed music in the Aarhus collections as of 1975. Entries give publisher, opus number, and number of pages. Index to names cited in the classified catalog. There is an alphabetical list of composers and titles not listed in the classified catalog but available at the university in an "unbound" collection.

1855. Statsbiblioteket. Fagkataloger (redigeret af Erling Winkel og Ingeborg Heilmann). 2. førøgede udg. Aarhus: Aarhus Stiftsbogtrykkerie, 1946–57. 4 v.
Three volumes cover scores; one, music literature. Entries for scores include collections and separate publications, with contents given for collections.

1856. Statsbibliotek. Musikalier. Udenlandsk musik. 2. udg. Aarhus: Aarhus Statsbiblioteketsførlaget, 1951–1970. 4 v.
Volume 1 covers collections and music for one instrument. Volume 2 covers chamber music and orchestral music. Volume 3 covers vocal music, dramatic music, and folk music. Volume 4 is a supplement to the first three and contains an index to composers.

ABERDEEN, SCOTLAND

1857. Cooper, B. A. R. "Catalogue of early printed music in Aberdeen libraries." In *R.M.A. Research Chronicle*, 14 (1978), p. 2–138.
Covers holdings of the University Library, the Library of the University Music Department, and the Aberdeen City Public Library. Updates the *British Union Catalogue of Early Music* and *RISM*; provides 800 entries, of which 100 seem to be unique. Arranged alphabetically by main entry (author or title). Entries occasionally provide annotations. Appendixes: writings on music; volumes containing plainsong; private collections; chronological index. Index to genres. Index of publishers.

ADRIA, ITALY

1858. Cattedrale, Archivio, Fondo Musicale. "Il fondo musicale dell'Archivio della Chiesa Cattedrale di Adria: Elenco." By Ivano Cavallini. In *Fontes Artis Musicae*, 27 (1980), p. 84–91.
An inventory of early printed editions and manuscripts, most of the 19th century.

AGEN, FRANCE

1859. Archives Communales. Inventaire sommaire des Archives communales antérieures à 1790. Lot-et-Garonne. Supplement à la série II: Bibliothèque d'ouvrages de musique provenant du château des ducs d'Aiguillon.
[Rédigé par MM. M. Bosvieux et G. Tholin]. Paris: P. Dupont, 1884. 26 p.
(Collection des inventaires sommaire des archives départementales antérieures à 1790)

AMSTERDAM, HOLLAND

1860. Toonkunst-Bibliotheek. Catalogus van de uitleen-afdeling. Amster-
dam-Zuid: Toonkunst-Bibliotheek, 1968. 43 p.
    Catalog of a loan collection of music for performance in the Amsterdam
municipal library. Classified by performance forces. Index of names.

1861. Vereniging Voor Nederlandse Muziekgeschiedenis. Bibliotheek. Catalogus van de bibliotheek der Vereniging voor Nederlandse Muziekgeschiedenis. Amsterdam: G. Alsbach, 1919. 274 p.
    Classified catalog, including both early and recent works. Contains a
special section of manuscripts. Index of names and titles.

ANN ARBOR, MICHIGAN

1862. University of Michigan. "The University of Michigan's purchase of the
Stellfeld music library." By Louise E. Cuyler, Gordon A. Sutherland, and
Hans T. David. In *Notes*, 12 (1954), p. 41–57.
    Describes Michigan's acquisition of the collection of the jurist, musicol-
ogist, and collector Dr. J. A. Stellfeld of Antwerp. Hans David gives a brief
summary of some of the important holdings of the library. 8 facsimile
plates.

AOSTA, ITALY

1863. Cattedrale. Biblioteca Capitolare. Il fondo musicale della Biblioteca
Capitolare di Aosta [di] Giorgio Chatrian. Torino: Centro Studi Piemontesi,
Fondo "Carlo Felice Bona," 1985. 252 p.
    A classified catalog of manuscripts and printed works. Dedications are
transcribed in full and anthologies are analyzed. Extensive introductory
essay on the cathedral and the collection. Name index.

ARLINGTON, TEXAS

1864. University of Texas. Garrett Library. "Sheet music related to the United
States war with Mexico (1846–1848) in the Jenkins Garrett Library, University of Texas at Arlington." By Elise K. Kirk. In *Notes*, 37 (1981), p. 15–
30.
    An inventory arranged by composer, providing information on other
copies at the Beinecke Library of Yale University, the Lilly Library of Indiana University, and the Library of Congress.

ASSISI, ITALY

1865. La Cappella della Basilica di S. Francesco. Biblioteca. Catalogo del fondo musicale nella Biblioteca Comunale di Assisi, a cura di Claudio Sartori. Milano: Istituto Editoriale Italiano, 1962. 449 p. (Bibliotheca musicae, 1)
Expands the work of Francesco Pennacchi published in the series *Associazione dei Musicologi Italiani* (no. 2077). Lists early printed music, books, and manuscripts separately. Most of the material is pre-1800, but a few 19th-century manuscripts are included. Entries give contents of early items, locations for rarities. Descriptive annotations.
Review by Walther Dürr in *Die Musikforschung*, 18 (1965), p. 83–84.

ATLANTA, GEORGIA

1866. Emory University. Woodruff Library. "Confederate sheet music at Robert W. Woodruff Library, Emory University." By Frank W. Hoogerwerf. In *Notes*, 34 (1978), p. 7–26.
A checklist of Emory's collection of Confederate sheet music arranged by title.

AUGSBURG, GERMANY

1867. Schaal, Richard. Das Inventar der Kantorei St. Anna in Augsburg. Ein Beitrag zur protestantischen Musikpflege im 16. und beginnenden 17. Jahrhundert. Kassel: Bärenreiter, 1965. 107 p. (Catalogus Musicus, 3)
Transcription of an inventory compiled in the early 17th century of the music collection of the Lutheran church and school of St. Anna in Augsburg. The collection itself is no longer intact.

1868. Schletterer, Hans M. Katalog der in der Kreis- und Stadtbibliothek der Städtischen Archive und der Bibliothek des Historischen Vereins zu Augsburg befindlichen Musikwerke. Augsburg: Fidelis Butsch Sohn, 1879. 138 p. (Monatsheft für Musikgeschichte, Beilage, Jahrgang 10–11, 1878–79)
Essentially a classified inventory of the holdings of 43 manuscripts and several hundred printed works, including 29 early books on music. Entries provide title page transcriptions and information on part books. Name and subject index. Index of publishers and booksellers.

1869. Staats- und Stadtbibliothek. Handschriften der Staats- und Stadtbibliothek Augsburg. Band I: Die Musikhandschriften der Staats- und Stadtbibliothek Augsburg (einschliesslich der Liturgica mit Notation). Beschrieben von Clytus Gottwald. Wiesbaden: Otto Harrassowitz, 1974. 328 p.
A catalog providing extensive descriptions and full analytical entries of musical manuscripts in the state and city library of Augsburg. Index to names, places, and things. Index of first lines and titles. List of prior owners. Facsimile pages.

AUSTIN, TEXAS

1870. University of Texas at Austin. Harry Ransom Humanities Research Center. *Library Chronicle*, 25/26 (1984).

Eight articles provide information on French music manuscripts (including Ravel's *Daphnis et Chloé*, *Rapsodie Espagnole*, and *Ma Mère l'Oye*, works by Debussy, Fauré, Roussel, and Dukas), the Bachmann Collection of 19th-century first and early editions, sacred vocal music from the Cortot Collection, various settings by William Walton of *Façade*, and the Ross Russell Collection of materials on Charlie "Bird" Parker and Dial Records.

BAD TÖLZ

1871. Pfarrkirchen Indersdorf. Thematischer Katalog der Musikhandschriften der Benediktinerinnenabtei Frauenwörth und der Pfarrkirchen Indersdorf, Wasserburg am Inn und Bad Tölz. Unter d. Leitung von Robert Münster, bearb. von Ursula Bockholdt, Robert Machold u. Lisbet Thew. München: G. Henle, 1975. 211 p. (Kataloge bayerischer Musiksammlungen)
Thematic catalogs of musical manuscripts at the Benedictine abbey Frauenwörth at Wasserburg-St. Jakob and the Pfarrkirchen Indersdorf at Bad Tölz. Mostly 18th-century sacred music. Full descriptions of sources. Indexes to copyists and watermarks. Includes an index to early printed music in the abbeys of Indersdorf and Wasserburg. Bibliography of works consulted. Index to titles and first lines. Name index.

BADAJOZ, SPAIN

1872. Monasterio de Guadalupe. Catálogo del archivo musical del Monasterio de Guadalupe, por El. P. Dr. Archangel Barrado, O.F.M., Bibliotecario y maestro de capilla. Badajoz: 1945. 181 p.
Catalog of a collection of accompanied sacred vocal music, chiefly late 18th century. 947 items, preceded by a historical study of the archive. Indexes of composers and of musical forms.

BALTIMORE, MARYLAND

1873. Milton S. Eisenhower Library. Guide to the Lester S. Levy collection of sheet music. Baltimore: Milton S. Eisenhower Library, Johns Hopkins University, 1984. 40 p.
An introduction to one of the most extensive collections of sheet music in the United States.

BARCELONA, SPAIN

1874. Diputación Provincial. Biblioteca Central. Catàlech de la Biblioteca Musical ... per en Filipe Pedrell. Barcelona: Palau de la Diputació, 1908–1909. 2 v.
Classified catalog of 1,271 entries, including theory, history, practical music. Full bibliographical entries, collations, extensive notes, facsimiles, and musical quotations. Items listed by signature number, with an alphabetical index in vol. 2.

1875. Diputación Provincial. Biblioteca Central. La música española desde la edad media hasta nuestros días; catálogo de la exposición histórica ... por Higinio Anglés. Barcelona: Diputación Provincial de Barcelona, Biblioteca Central, 1941. 82 p.

Exhibition catalog commemorating the centennial of the birth of Filipe Pedrell. 171 items, manuscripts and printed books, associated with the history of Spanish music, assembled from a number of collections. Chronological arrangement, full entries, 52 facsimiles.

BASEL, SWITZERLAND

1876. Kunstmuseum. Strawinsky: Sein Nachlass. Sein Bild. Kunstmuseum Basel in Zusammenarbeit mit der Paul Sacher Stiftung Basel. Basel: Kunstmuseum, 1984. 386 p.

Publication on the occasion of the 1st exhibition of the Stravinsky collection after it was acquired by the Paul Sacher Stiftung in 1983. Includes a list of manuscripts by Igor Stravinsky in the Sacher Stiftung (p. 33–42), facsimiles, and photographs. Essays by Hans Jörg Jans, Albi Rosenthal, Jacques Handschin, Leo Schrade, Hans Oesch, Christian Geelhaar, Hugo Wagner, and James Lord.

Some copies have been tipped in: *Strawinsky: Sein Nachlass. Sein Bild. — Katalog der ausgestellten Bildnisse und Entwürfe für die Ausstattung seiner Bühnenwerke* (which cites the 272 items displayed in the exhibit); and *Programm und Ansprachen des Eröffnungsaktes im Stadttheater Basel 5. June 1984, 17.00 Uhr* (which includes the remarks of Christian Geelhaar, Theodore Stravinsky, Albi Rosenthal, and Paul Sacher).

Albi Rosenthal's essay in this volume, "Der Strawinsky-*Nachlass* in der Paul Sacher Stiftung," is complemented by an excellent article by John Shepard, "The Stravinsky *Nachlass*: a provisional checklist of music manuscripts," which appeared in *Notes*, 40 (1984), p. 719–50. Shepard provides a brief introduction to the collection of sketches, scores, clippings, letters, and many other documents as well as a very useful checklist of music manuscripts in the Stravinsky *Nachlass*. Each entry in the checklist provides reasonably full description of the various versions of the work in the collection.

1877. Öffentliche Kunstsammlung. Musikhandschriften in Basel: aus verschiedenen Sammlungen: Ausstellung im Kunstmuseum Basel vom 31. Mai bis zum 13. Juli 1975. Veranstaltet vom Kunstmuseum Basel in Verbindung mit einer ad hoc gebildeten Ausstellungskommission; Katalog, Tilman Seebass; Ausstellung, Yvonne Boerlin-Brodbeck und Tilman Seebass. Basel: Kunstmuseum, 1975. 99 p.

193 items from Praetorius to Stockhausen with informative descriptions. Numerous facsimiles.

1878. Paul Sacher Stiftung. Komponisten des 20. Jahrhunderts in der Paul Sacher Stiftung. Basel: Paul Sacher Stiftung, 1986. 462 p.

Diese Publikation erscheint aus Anlass der Eröffnung der damit verbundenen Austellung *"Die Musik des 20. Jahrhunderts in der Paul Sacher Stiftung"* im Kunstmuseum Basel. 25. April bis 20. Juli 1986.

[This publication appears on the occasion of the opening of the exhibit "The music of the 20th-century in the Paul Sacher Archive" in the Basel Museum of Art, 25 April through 20 July 1986.] [from the introductory remarks]

"Vorrede" by Paul Sacher. "Die Paul Sacher Stiftung in der Öffentlichkeit zur Ausstellung und Publikation" by Hans Jörg Jans. "Enstehung und Ziele der Paul Sacher Stiftung" by Albi Rosenthal.

The exhibition included not only 20th-century manuscripts, but also Bach and Handel autographs.

The book consists of 47 essays on composers and works displayed; there are English summaries of each article. Includes "Die Genere des Webern-Archivs" by Hans Moldenhauer, "Komponisten des 20. Jahrhunderts in der Paul Sacher Stiftung; Katalog in alphabetischer Reihenfolge" by Felix Myer and Sabine Stumpfl, which includes entries for individual manuscripts and for entire collections. The collection of the Sacher Stiftung includes autograph compositions, sketches, photographs, letters, essays, and other documentation. There are important collections of the following composers: Conrad Beck, Luciano Berio, Pierre Boulez, Bruno Maderna, Frank Martin, Igor Stravinsky, and Anton Webern.

1879. Paul Sacher Stiftung. Musikhandschriften aus der Sammlung Paul Sacher; Festschrift zu Paul Sachers siebzigstem Geburtstag. In Verbindung mit Ernst Lichtenhahn und Tilman Seebass von F. Hoffmann–La Roche & Co. Basel: Éditions Roche, 1976. 197 p.

In addition to a number of facsimiles of manuscripts in the Sammlung Sacher, there is a "Katalog sämtlicher Musikhandschriften der Sammlung Paul Sacher," p. 47–79.

1880. Universität. Bibliothek. Katalog der Musik-Sammlung auf der Universitäts-Bibliothek in Basel (Schweiz) ... von Julius Richter. Leipzig: Breitkopf & Härtel, 1892. 104 p. (Beilage. Monatshefte für Musikgeschichte. Jahrgang 23–24)

Full descriptions, contents, musical quotations for manuscripts, and early printed music in the university library.

1881. Universität. Bibliothek. Katalog der Musikabteilung der Öffentlichen Bibliothek der Universität Basel und in ihr enthaltenen Schweizerischen Musikbibliothek. Band I: Musikalische Kompositionen. Hrsg. von Edgar Refardt. Basel: Universitäts-Bibliothek, 1925. 141 p.

Works listed in alphabetical order by composer; important collections analyzed. Separate listing of collections, followed by a summary of the contents of several manuscript collections of music by Swiss composers. Index of editors, arrangers, librettists.

1882. Universität. Bibliothek. Katalog der Schweizerischen Musikbibliothek. Hrsg. von der Öffentlichen Bibliothek der Universität Basel. I. Musikgeschichtliche und theoretische Werke. Basel: E. Birkhauser, 1906. 39 p.

A collection of music literature. The catalog of music that was to form vol. 2 was issued as vol. 1 of the library's *Katalog der Musikabteilung der Öffentlichen Bibliothek* ... (no. 1881).

1883. Universität. Bibliothek. Thematischer Katalog der Instrumentalmusik des 18. Jahrhunderts in den Handschriften der Universitätsbibliothek Basel. Von Edgar Refardt. Bern: P. Haupt, 1957. 59 p. (Publikationen der Schweizerischen Musikforschenden Gesellschaft, ser. 2, v. 6)

The major part of this collection was assembled by the Basel silk manufacturer Lucas Sarasin (1730–1802). Some 473 of the works cited were once part of his library. With these are incorporated the collection of the Basel *Collegium Musicum* and that of the de Pury family. References are made to 18th-century printings of the works here found in manuscript.

BATH, ENGLAND

1884. Holburne of Menstrie Museum. Science and music in eighteenth century Bath: an exhibition in the Holburne of Menstrie Museum, Bath, 22 September 1977–29 December 1977; catalogue by Anthony J. Turner, with the assistance of I. D. Woodfield (section III) and contributions by H. S. Torrens. Bath: University of Bath, 1977. 131 p.
  Covering 212 items relating to the 18th-century astronomer and musician Sir William Herschel. Bibliography.

BAVARIA

1885. Kataloge Bayerischer Musiksammlungen. Hrsg. von der Generaldirektion der Bayerischen staatlichen Bibliotheken. Thematischer Katalog der Musikhandschriften der ehemaligen Klosterkirchen Weyarn, Tegernsee, und Benediktbeuern. Hrsg. von Robert Münster und Robert Machold. München: Henle, 1971. 196 p.
  Records the holdings of Bavarian cloisters and abbeys, catalogs of which are maintained in the Bavarian State Library in Munich.

1886. Münster, Robert. "Die Erfassung von Musikhandschriften aus nichtstaatlichem Besitz in Bayern." In *Mitteilungen für die Archivpflege in Bayern*, 12 (1966) Heft 2, p. 45 ff.
  Describes the seizing of privately owned collections of musical autographs.

1887. Musik in Bayern. I. Bayerische Musikgeschichte, Überblick und Einzeldarstellungen. Hrsg. von Robert Münster und Hans Schmid. II. Ausstellungskatalog Augsburg, Juli bis Oktober 1972. Hrsg. von Folker Göthel. Tutzing: Hans Schneider, 1972. 2 v.
  Vol. I is a collection of essays on various aspects of Bavarian music history; vol. II is an exhibition catalog of 850 items illustrative of Bavarian musical history and culture. Numerous facsimile plates.

BELGIUM

Borren, Charles van den. "Inventaire des manuscrits de musique polyphonique qui se trouve en Belgique." See no. 1713.

BEREA, OHIO

1888. Balwin-Wallace College. Riemenschneider Memorial Bach Library. Catalog of the Emilie and Karl Riemenschneider Memorial Bach Library. Ed. by Sylvia W. Kenney. New York: Columbia Univ. Press, 1960. 295 p.

A numbered catalog of 2,537 items, of which the first 520 are writings on Bach and his time. Nos. 521–31: music of Bach's sons and contemporaries. No. 532 to end: music of J. S. Bach. The principal grouping is by musical forms; manuscripts listed separately. Index of cantatas and general index.

13 *Supplemental Catalogs*, the first 4 compiled by J. B. Winzenburger, have been issued to members of the Riemenschneider Bach Institute (1970–84). Current acquisitions reported in the periodical *Bach*, 1970– .

Review by Walter Emery in *Music and Letters*, 42 (1961), p. 376–77.

BERGAMO, ITALY

1889. Biblioteca Civica. Il fondo musicale Mayr della Biblioteca Civica di Bergamo, nel secondo centenario della nascita di Giovanni Simone Mayr (1763–1963). Ed. Arrigo Gazzaniga. Bergamo: Edizioni "Monumenta Bergomensia," 1963. 149 p. (Monumenta bergomensia, 11)

A classified catalog of works by Simone Mayr and his contemporaries in the Biblioteca Civica in Bergamo. Chiefly manuscripts, including many autographs. 24 p. of facsimiles.

1890. Il Museo Donizettiano. Catalogo. Bergamo: Centro di Studi Donizettiani, 1970. 273 p.

First published in 1936.

The present edition gives a brief historical introduction, followed by a tabulation of important Donizetti performances between 1946 and 1969.

The *Catalogo* (p. 53–273) is subdivided into six sections: (1) autographs and manuscripts, (2) musical publications, (3) theatrical publications, (4) letters and documents, (5) iconography, and (6) artifacts.

BERKELEY, CALIFORNIA

1891. University of California. Music Library. Autograph manuscripts of Ernest Bloch at the University of California. Berkeley: University of California, 1962. 20 p.

Describes 35 autograph manuscripts bequeathed to the University of California Music Library from the estate of Ernest Bloch. The catalog was compiled by Minnie Elmer.

1892. University of California. Music Library. Catalog of the opera collections in the Music Libraries: University of California, Berkeley [and] University of California, Los Angeles. Boston: G. K. Hall, 1983. 697 p.

Photo-offset duplication of the main entry cards in each library representing substantial collections of opera scores. Divided into sections for each library; the Berkeley portion is further sub-divided into operas and dramatic music for children. Cataloging for the Berkeley collection was subsequently entirely revised to meet contemporary cataloging standards and entered into the scores file of the Research Libraries Information Network (RLIN) of the Research Libraries Group (RLG) in the period 1984–1986.

1893. **University of California. Music Library.** Early music printing in the Music Library of the University of California, Berkeley. An exhibition in honor of the 12th Congress of the International Musicological Society. Compiled by Mary Kay Duggan. Foreword by Vincent H. Duckles. Berkeley: General Library of the University of California, 1977. 32 p.
78 numbered items; 9 facsimile plates.

1894. **University of California. Music Library.** "Ernest Bloch manuscripts at the University of California." By David L. Sills. In *Notes*, 42 (1986), p. 7–21.
A new catalog that corrects and expands the one prepared by Minnie Elmer (no. 1891) and that is supplemented by the one the author prepared on the Bloch holdings of the Library of Congress (no. 2437).

1895. **University of California.** Music Library. "Musique classique française à Berkeley: pièces inédites de Louis Couperin, Lebègue, La Barre, etc." By Alan Curtis. In *Revue de Musicologie*, 55 (1969), p. 123–64.
Describes and inventories 14 manuscripts of French music, chiefly keyboard, of the late 17th and early 18th centuries in the Music Library of the University of California at Berkeley.

1896. **University of California. Music Library.** Thematic catalog of a manuscript collection of 18th-century Italian instrumental music in the University of California, Berkeley, Music Library. By Vincent Duckles and Minnie Elmer. Berkeley and Los Angeles: Univ. of California Press, 1963. 403 p.
A collection comprising some 990 manuscripts containing works by 82 composers of the Tartini school at Padua. The central figures are Giuseppe Tartini and Michele Stratico. Preliminary chapters discuss the historical background of the collection and tabulate the handwritings and the watermarks represented. A revision of the catalog has been completed by Gloria Eive to accompany a microfiche edition of the manuscripts in the collection that has not yet appeared.
Review by Charles Cudworth in *Galpin Society Journal*, 18 (March 1965), p. 140–41; by Denis Stevens in *Musical Times*, 105 (July 1964), p. 513–14; by Donald Krummel in *Notes*, 22 (1966), p. 1025–1026.

BERLIN, GERMANY

1897. **Die Amalien-Bibliothek.** Musikbibliothek der Prinzessin Anna Amalia von Preussen (1732–1787). Historische Einordnung und Katalog mit Hinweisen auf die Schreiber der Handschriften. Von Eva Renate Blechschmidt. Berlin: Merseburger, 1965. 346 p. (Berliner Studien zur Musikwissenschaft, 8)
Reconstruction of the catalog of an important 18th-century music collection formed by the youngest sister of Friedrich the Great. The bulk of the collection was acquired by the Joachimsthalsche Gymnasium in the late 18th century. The collection was dispersed for safekeeping in World War II, and since then parts of it have found their way to libraries in Tübingen, Marburg, and the Deutsche Staatsbibliothek in Berlin. Blechschmidt's study treats the history of the collection and describes each item in detail, including both printed music and manuscripts. Special attention is given to the identification of the scribes responsible for the manuscript copies.

1898. Deutsche Staatsbibliothek. Die Bach-Handschriften der Berliner Staatsbibliothek, von Paul Kast. Trossingen: Hohner-Verlag, 1958. 150 p. (Tübinger Bach-Studien, 2/3)

A catalog of manuscripts of music by members of the Bach family, once a part of the collection of the Prussian State Library, now distributed between the two Deutsche Staatsbibliotheken (West and East) and the University Library at Tübingen. Essentially a finding list for one of the world's great collections of Bach sources now dispersed. Brief entries; indexes of composers, scribes, and former owners of the manuscripts.

1899. Deutsche Staatsbibliothek. Die Beethoven-Sammlung in der Musikabteilung der Deutschen Staatsbibliothek. Verzeichnis: Autographe, Abschriften, Dokumente, Briefe. Aufgenommen und zusammengestellt von Eveline Bartlitz. Berlin: Deutsche Staatsbibliothek, 1970. 229 p.

A well-organized bibliography of all types of materials in the extensive Beethoven collections of the former East German State Library. Includes manuscripts, sketches, first editions, letters, items from Beethoven's library, etc. Numerous bibliographical references.

Review by William Drabkin in *Notes*, 28 (1972), p. 692–94.

1900. Deutsche Staatsbibliothek. "Die Musikabteilung." By Karl-Heinz Köhler. In *Deutsche Staatsbibliothek, 1661–1961*. Redaktion Horst Kunze, Werner Dube, Günter Fröschner. Band I: Geschichte und Gegenwart, p. 241–74. Leipzig: VEB Verlag für Buch- und Bibliothekswesen, 1961. 2 v.

A narrative account of the founding of the music division of the Berlin State Library, the work of its successive directors, and the growth of its collections up to the restoration of the music room after its destruction in World War II. The riches of the collection are summarized, particularly the Bach, Mozart, and Beethoven holdings. The author is director of the Music Division.

1901. Deutsche Staatsbibliothek. Paperchase: Mozart, Beethoven, Bach ... the search for their lost music. By Nigel Lewis. London: Hamish Hamilton, 1981. 246 p.

Recounts in exposé style the history of the evacuation—from the Preussische Staatsbibliothek to Schloss Fürstenstein, thereafter to the Benedictine monastery in Grüssen, and eventually to Kraków at the end of the Second World War—of almost 200 manuscripts by more than 20 composers, among them J. S. Bach, W. A. Mozart, Beethoven, Mendelssohn, Schumann, J. Haydn, Brahms, Schubert, C. P. E. Bach, Telemann, E. T. A. Hoffmann, Paganini, and Hugo Wolf. Provides details, without citing sources or providing footnotes, of the discovery and recovery of some of these works. There are some references in the story to verify the main points. Makes clear the involvement of Robert Carleton Smith (Dr. Carleton Smith) and the key role of Peter Whitehead in the affair. Seven of the manuscripts, including Beethoven's Ninth Symphony and Mozart's *The Magic Flute*, have been returned to the Deutsche Staatsbibliothek in Berlin. The remainder are in the Jagiellonian Library in Kraków. See nos. 1801 and 1902.

1902. Deutsche Staatsbibliothek. "Return of treasures to the Deutsche Staatsbibliothek." By Karl-Heinz Köhler. In *Fontes Artis Musicae*, 26 (1979), p. 86–87.

A report on the location of manuscripts moved from Berlin in the closing days of the Second World War. Revises information in no. 1801. See no. 1901.

1903. Internationale Musikleihbibliothek. Katalog. Berlin: 1952. 276 p.
Classified catalog of an international lending library of instrumental, vocal, and choral works. Includes parts for orchestral music. Strong in works by Soviet composers, but other countries are also well represented. Composer index.

1904. Joachimsthalsches Gymnasium. Bibliothek. Katalog der Musikaliensammlung des Joachimsthal'schen Gymnasiums zu Berlin. Verfasst von Robert Eitner. Berlin: T. Trautwein, 1884. 106 p. (Beilage, Monatshefte für Musikgeschichte. Jahrgang 16)
This collection incorporates the library of Princess Anna Amalie, sister of Friedrich the Great (see also no. 1897). Strong in 18th-century music of the North German school. 627 numbered items. Author-composer index. The collection was partially dispersed and destroyed in World War II.

1905. Joachimsthalsches Gymnasium. Bibliothek. Thematischer Katalog der Von Thulemeir'schen Musikalien-Sammlung in der Bibliothek des Joachimsthal'schen Gymnasiums zu Berlin. Hrsg. von Robert Eitner. Leipzig: Breitkopf & Härtel, 1899. 110 p. (Beilage, Monatshefte für Musikgeschichte. Jahrgang 30–31)
The collection covers the period 1700–1800.

1906. Königliche Hausbibliothek. Katalog der Musiksammlung aus der Königlichen Hausbibliothek im Schlosse zu Berlin. Verfasst und erläutert von Georg Thouret.... Leipzig: Breitkopf & Härtel, 1895. 356 p.
Supplemented by *Neue Erwerbungen der Königlichen Hausbibliothek zu Berlin* (Beilage, Monatshefte ... Jahrgang 35, 1903).
Brief entries, alphabetical by composer. 6,836 items, printed and manuscript, with a special section of works dedicated to members of the royal family and a supplementary section for military music.

1907. Staatsbibliothek der Stiftung Preussischer Kulturbesitz. Die Handschrift Johann Sebastian Bachs: Musikautographe aus der Musikabteilung der Staatsbibliothek Preussischer Kulturbesitz Berlin, Ausstellung zum 300. Geburtstag von J. S. Bach 22. März bis 13. Juli 1985; [Hrsg. von Rudolf Elvers ... et al.]. Wiesbaden: Reichert, 1985. 148 p.
Catalog of an exhibition of autographs from one of the largest collections of Bach sources.

1908. Staatsbibliothek der Stiftung Preussischer Kulturbesitz. Katalog der Sammlung Bokemeyer, [von] Harald Kümmerling. Kassel: Bärenreiter, 1970. 423 p. (Kieler Schriften zur Musikwissenschaft, 18)
Reconstruction of an important 18th-century private music library of more than 3,000 manuscripts, printed music, and theoretical works. Partially dispersed. Parts of the collection surviving in the West Berlin State Library have been identified by Kümmerling and the rest reconstructed. Review by Richard H. Hunter in *Notes*, 28 (1971), p. 57–58.

1909. Staatsbibliothek der Stiftung Preussischer Kulturbesitz. Ludwig van Beethoven, Autographe und Abschriften: Katalog bearbeitet von Hans-Günter Klein. Berlin: Merseburger, 1975. 344 p. (Kataloge der Musikabteilung. Erste Reihe, Handschriften. Staatsbibliothek Preussischer Kulturbesitz, 2)
A catalog of Beethoven autographs (including sketches and sketchbooks) and copyists' manuscripts in opus-number order with extensive descriptions. Indexes to copyists, to names. List of works appearing in the eight sketchbooks. Bibliography of works consulted.

1910. Staatsbibliothek der Stiftung Preussischer Kulturbesitz. Ludwig van Beethoven 1770–1970. Autographe aus der Musikabteilung der Staatsbibliothek Preussischer Kulturbesitz. [Ausstellung 1.-30. Dez. 1970 im Mendelssohn-Archiv der Staatsbibliothek. Bearbeitet von Rudolf Elvers und Hans-Günter Klein]. Berlin-Dahlem: Staatsbibliothek Preussischer Kulturbesitz, 1970. 32 p.
Exhibition catalog of one of the most important collections of Beethoven sources, by the curator of the collection and one of the outstanding Beethoven scholars.

1911. Staatsbibliothek der Stiftung Preussischer Kulturbesitz. Mendelssohn-Archiv. Felix Mendelssohn-Bartholdy. Dokumente s. Lebens. Ausstellung. zum 125. Todestag im Mendelssohn-Archiv d. Staatsbibliothek Preuss. Kulturbesitz, Berlin-Dahlem. 1.-30. Nov. 1972. [Bearb. von Rudolf Elvers.] Berlin: Staatsbibliothek Preussischer Kulturbesitz, 1972. 23 p.
An exhibition of important Mendelssohn holdings.

1912. Staatsbibliothek der Stiftung Preussischer Kulturbesitz. Wolfgang Amadeus Mozart Autographe und Abschriften: Katalog; bearbeitet von Hans-Günter Klein. Kassel: Merseburger, 1982. 542 p. (Kataloge der Musikabteilung. Erste Reihe, Handschriften. Staatsbibliothek Preussischer Kulturbesitz, 6)
Catalog of the rich holdings of Mozart manuscripts and correspondence.

BERN, SWITZERLAND

1913. Schweizerische Landesbibliothek. Katalog der Schweizerischen Landesbibliothek. Musik-Werke der Mitglieder des Schweizerischen Tonkünstlervereins veröffentlicht von 1848–1925.... Hrsg. von K. Joss. Bern-Bumpliz: Buchdruckerei Benteli, 1927. 152 p.
About 5,000 titles, abridged to essential information, in a classified arrangement.

BETHLEHEM, PENNSYLVANIA

1914. Archives of the Moravian Church. A catalogue of music by American Moravians, 1724–1842, from the Archives of the Moravian Church at Bethlehem, Pennsylvania. Bethlehem, Pa.: Moravian Seminary and College for Women, 1938. 118 p.
Reprint by AMS Press, New York, 1970.
Short biographies and lists of compositions by 17 Moravian-American

composers. Appendix of 24 plates of selected compositions and sample pages from the original manuscripts.

1915. Lititz Congregation Collection. Catalog of the Lititz Congregation collection. By Robert Steelman. Chapel Hill: University of North Carolina Press, 1981. 488 p.

"The Lititz Congregation collection is housed at The Moravian Archives in Bethlehem, Pennsylvania. Access to and use of the collection is controlled by the Moravian Church Music Foundation."

The collection consists of manuscripts of music for Moravian worship and devotional gatherings. Entries for over 500 manuscripts, each identifying composer when known and including musical incipits, information on the composition(s), an inventory of parts or scoring, and cross-references. Indexes of composers and of titles and first lines.

BIRMINGHAM, ENGLAND

1916. University of Birmingham. Barber Institute of Fine Arts. Catalogue of the printed music and music manuscripts before 1801 in the Music Library of the University of Birmingham, Barber Institute of Fine Arts. Edited by Ian Fenlon. London: Mansell; München: Verlag Dokumentation, 1976. 140 p. 7 microfiche.

Catalog of printed music provides complete title page transcription and physical description. Catalog of manuscript music describes and analyzes more fully each manuscript. Facsimiles of interesting pages. Indexes to booksellers, printers, and publishers, to artists, designers, and engravers, and to previous owners. Microfiche of Barber MS 5001: "Autograph anthems by English composers c. 1665–85."

BLOOMINGTON, INDIANA

1917. Indiana University. Archives of Traditional Music. Catalog of the Terence R. Bech Nepal Music Research Collection. Compiled by Anne Helen Ross, supported by a Research Collections Grant from the National Endowment for the Humanities; project coordinator, Terence R. Bech; project librarian, Anne H. Ross; project director, Frank J. Gillis. Bloomington: Archives of Traditional Music, Folklore Institute, Indiana University, 1978. 435 p.

Catalog of a collection of materials, including musical instruments, on musical culture in Nepal.

1918. Indiana University. Lilly Library. The Fritz Busch collection. Compiled by Dominique-René De Lerma. Bloomington: Indiana University Libraries, 1972. 52 p.

1919. Indiana University. School of Music. Latin-American Music Center. Music from Latin America available at Indiana University: scores, tapes, and records. Edited by Juan A. Orrego-Salas. Bloomington: Latin American Music Center, School of Music, Indiana University, 1971. 412 p.

A catalog of one of the most important repositories of Latin American scores and recordings in the United States. Includes a listing of materials available at the Indiana University Archives of Traditional Music.

BOGOTÁ, COLOMBIA

1920. Catedral de Bogotá. El Archivio Musical de la Catedral de Bogotá. [By] Jose Ignacio Perdomo Escobar. Bogotá: Instituto Caro y Cuervo, 1976. 818 p.

Includes a dictionary catalog of the archive and a bibliography.
Review by Catherine Massip in *Fontes Artis Musicae*, 26 (1979), p. 61.

BOLOGNA, ITALY

1921. Accademia Filarmonica. Catalogo descrittivo degli autografi e ritratti di musicisti lasciati alla Reale Accademia Filarmonica di Bologna dall'Abb. Dott. Masseangelo Masseangeli. Compilato a cura degli Accademici Prof. Cav. Federico Parisini e Maestro Ernesto Colombani. Bologna: Regia Tipografia, 1896. 435 p.

This catalog first appeared, under a slightly different title, in 1881. Reprint of the 1881 edition by Forni, Bologna, 1969.

1922. Accademia Filarmonica. Mostra internazionale di musica in Bologna 1888. Catalogo con brevi cenni biografici e succinte discrizioni degli autografi e documenti de' celebri o distinti musicisti posseduti da Emilia Succi. Accademia Filarmonica di Bologna. Bologna: Società Tipografica giã Compositori, 1888. 179 p.

A collection of 886 items, chiefly letters of musicians of the 18th and 19th centuries, mostly autographs. Arranged alphabetically, with brief biographical notices and descriptions of the items.

Accademia Filarmonica. Archivio. See no. 2065.

Archivio di S. Petronio. See no. 2065.

Biblioteca Ambrosini. See no. 2065.

1923. Biblioteca Universitaria. "Codici musicali della R. Biblioteca Universitaria di Bologna." By Lodovico Frati. In *Rivista Musicale Italiana*, 23 (1916), p. 219–42.

A general description of the resources of the music collection in the library of the University of Bologna, drawing attention to major holdings in plainchant, early theory, and polyphony.

1924. Civico Museo Bibliografico Musicale. (Formerly Conservatorio di Musica "G. B. Martini.") Catalogo della biblioteca del Liceo Musicale di Bologna, compilato da Gaetano Gaspari, compiuto e pubblicato da Federico Parisini per cura del municipio.... Bologna: Libreria Romagnoli dall'Acqua, 1890–1943. 5 v.

Vols. 1–4 reissued in photo-offset by Arnaldo Forni (Bologna, 1961) with corrections by Napoleone Fanti, Oscar Mischiati, and Luigi Ferdinando Tagliavini.

Vol. 1: music theory. Vol. 2: sacred vocal music (ed. Luigi Torchi). Vol. 3: secular vocal music and opera (ed. Luigi Torchi). Vol. 4: instrumental music and pedagogy (ed. Raffaele Caldolini). Vol. 5: Libretti (ed. Ugo Sesini).

373

This catalog provides access to one of the richest collections of early music in the world, incorporating the library of the 18th-century scholar Padre Giambattista Martini. Full bibliographical descriptions; contents given for collections; transcriptions of numerous prefaces and dedications. Entries are alphabetical within each category. General index of names.

1925. Civico Museo Bibliografico Musicale. Padre Martini's collection of letters in the Civico Museo Bibliografico Musicale in Bologna: an annotated index by Anne Schnoebelen. New York: Pendragon Press, 1979. 721 p. (Annotated reference tools in music, 2)

Covers 5,876 letters written by or to 670 correspondents of Giovanni Battista Martini during his 45 years at the monastery of San Francesco, 1730–84. For each letter, the incipit in the original language is supplied along with names of persons and pieces of music cited in the letter. The content of each letter is summarized. Index to names and subjects.

Review by John W. Hill in *Notes*, 36 (1980), p. 893–94; by Vincent H. Duckles in *Music and Letters*, 61 (1980), p. 376–77; and by Pierluigi Petrobelli, with additions, in *Fontes Artis Musicae*, 27 (1980), p. 225–27.

1926. Il Convento di San Francesco. Catalogo del fondo musicale. By Gino Zanotti. Bologna: Forni, 1970. 2 v. (Bibliotheca musica bononiensis, VI, 3)

Vol. I: *Le edizioni*. 324 p. Vol. II: *I manoscritti*. 393 p.

Catalogs the music collection of the Franciscan church where Padre Martini lived and worked during the 18th century. The collection includes a considerable amount of his music.

1927. Enrico, Eugene. The orchestra at San Petronio in the Baroque era. Washington, D.C.: Smithsonian Institution Press, 1976. 64 p. (Smithsonian studies in history and technology, 35)

P. 45–60: "A catalogue of manuscripts at San Petronio, the sources of Torelli's festival compositions with trumpet."

BOLZANO, ITALY

1928. Palazzo Toggenburg. La raccoltá di manoscritti e stampe musicali "Toggenburg" di Bolzano (secc. XVIII–XIX) [di] Tarcisio Chini, Giuliano Tonini. Torino: EDT/Musica, 1986. 307 p. (Cataloghi di fondi musicali italiani, 5)

Catalog of a collection gathered by a merchant from Menz, containing prints and manuscripts from the last quarter of the 18th century and through the first half of the 19th. The libretto collection is cataloged as well.

BONN, GERMANY

1929. Beethoven-Haus. "Die Beethovenhandschriften des Beethovenhauses in Bonn." By Hans Schmidt. In *Beethoven-Jahrbuch*, p. 1–443. Jahrgang 1969–70. Bonn: Beethovenhaus, 1971.

A catalog of 776 items. Major sections are letters (489 items), documents partially or wholly in Beethoven's hand (29 items), works (76 items), copies by Beethoven of other composers' works (9 items), sketches (106 items), copyists' work (31 items), and early printed music with annotations by the composer (11 items). Detailed indexes.

1930. Beethoven-Haus. Eine Schweizer Beethovensammlung. Von Max Unger. Zürich: Verlag der Corona, 1939. 235 p. (Schriften der Corona, 24)

Catalog of the Bodmer collection, perhaps the world's greatest accumulation of Beethoven documents, once in private hands but now part of the archive of the Beethoven Haus in Bonn. The catalog is organized in 12 categories, the most important of which are 389 letters, including those of the composer's contemporaries; 108 manuscripts of music; 43 early or first editions; 17 pictures; 16 facsimile plates; index of names.

1931. Friedrich-Wilhelms-Universität. Bibliothek. "Die musikalischen Autographen der Universitäts-Bibliothek Bonn." By Theo Clasen. In *Festschrift Joseph Schmidt-Görg zum 60. Geburtstag,* p. 26–65. Bonn: Beethoven-Haus, 1957.

567 autographs by 245 musicians, extracted from bequests or autograph books. Wide representation of musicians and musical scholars of the early 19th century.

1932. Friedrich-Wilhelms-Universität. Musikwissenschaftliches Seminar. Katalog der Musikhandschriften im Besitz des Musikwissenschaftlichen Seminars der Rheinischen Friedrich-Wilhelms-Universität zu Bonn. By Magda Marx-Weber. Köln: Arno Volk-Verlag, 1971. 138 p. (Beiträge zur Rheinischen Musikgeschichte, 89)

A collection of 595 manuscripts, some 550 of which were assembled by the organist-cantor Christian Benjamin Klein (1754–1825). Prominent among the composers represented are Benda, Bernabei, Homilius, Reichardt, Weinlig, Wirbach, and Zumsteeg.

BORDEAUX, FRANCE

1933. Galerie des Beaux-Arts. L'art et la musique dix-neuvième. Exposition du Mai organisée à l'initiative de Monsieur Jacques Chaban-Delmas, Maire de Bordeaux.... Bordeaux: Galerie des Beaux-Arts, 1969. 119 p.

Catalog for an exhibition held in Bordeaux from 30 May to 30 September 1969.

206 items, including 30 instruments. 81 plates. Brief descriptions including bibliographies and some information as to provenance.

BOSTON, MASSACHUSETTS

1934. Boston Public Library. Catalogue of the Allen A. Brown collection of music. Boston: Boston Public Library, 1910–16. 4 v.

Originally issued in 13 parts, 1908–1916, by the Trustees of the Library. Reprint of 1919 edition by G. K. Hall, 1970.

A dictionary catalog of composers, titles, subjects, with explicit contents and analytics given for all collections. One of the first of such catalogs, and one of the few printed catalogs for a major American music collection. Rich in opera and in orchestral scores, primarily 19th-century editions.

1935. Boston Public Library. Dictionary catalog of the music collection of the Boston Public Library. Boston, Mass.: G. K. Hall and Co., 1972. 20 v. *First Supplement* of 4 volumes published by G. K. Hall in 1977.
Photo-offset publication of the dictionary catalog for a collection of some 80,000 volumes covering music, biography, history and criticism, theory and composition, music education, collected editions and monuments, bibliographical works, libretti, and periodicals. This catalog incorporates the Allen A. Brown music collection, but excludes sheet music, clippings and programs, and recordings.

BRANDENBURG, GERMANY

1936. St. Katharinenkirche. Bibliothek. Die musikalischen Schätze der St. Katherinenkirche zu Brandenburg a.d. Havel. Ein Beitrag zur musikalischen Literatur des 16. und 17. Jahrhunderts. By Johann F. Täglichsbeck. Brandenburg: A. Müller, 1857. 50 p.
Manuscripts and printed works, 1564–1671, chronologically arranged, with full bibliographical information and descriptive notes.

BRASOV, ROMANIA

1937. Honterusgymnasium. Bibliothek. Die Musiksammlung der Bibliothek zu Kronstadt, von Erich H. Müller. Kronstadt: J. Gött's Sohn, 1930. 176 p.
Manuscripts, printed music and books. Brief biographical sketches of authors or composers. Publication dates, plate numbers.

BRESCIA, ITALY

1938. Archivio Capitolare del Duomo. Catalogo del fondo musicale dell'Archivio Capitolare del Duomo di Brescia. Compiled by Mariella Sala. Torino: E.D.T./Musica, 1984. 288 p. (Cataloghi di Fondi Musicali Italiani, 3)
A catalog of printed and manuscript music, mostly from the 16th–18th centuries, including anthologies. Indexed by composer, by text incipits, and by musical genre. Useful histories of the Cappella and the Archivio.

BRESLAU, GERMANY and BRIEG, GERMANY
See WROCLAW, POLAND

BRNO, SLOVAKIA

1939. Moravskŕ Muzeum. Průvodce po archívních fondech ústavu dějin hudby Moravského musea v Brně. Zprac. Theodora Straková, *et al.* 1. vyd. Brno, ústav dějin hudby: Mor. musea, rozmn., 1971. 256 p. 22 plates.
Summary in Russian, German, and English.
Catalog of the music holdings of the Moravian Museum in Brno (Brünn).

1940. Universitätsbibliothek. Alte Drucke der Werke von tschechischen Komponisten des 18. Jahrhunderts in der Universitätsbibliothek in Brno. Von Vladimír Telec. Praha: Státní Pedagogické Nakladatelství, 1969. 163 p.

Cites 1,278 works by 42 Czech composers; a total of 522 bibliographical units. 278 of the items are on microfilm. Full bibliographical descriptions, including tempo and metrical indications for the movements of composite works. Introduction in German and Czech. Eight plates.

BRUSSELS, BELGIUM

1941. Bibliothèque Royale Albert Ier. "De Afdeling Muziek (van de Koninklijke Bibliotheek van België)." [By] Bernard Huys. In *Koninklijke Bibliotheek. Liber memorialis 1559–1969*, p. 311–34. Brussels: 1969.

A history of the music collection of the Royal Library at Brussels, including the establishment of a new Music Division in that library.

1942. Bibliothèque Royale Albert Ier. Catalogue de la bibliothèque de F. J. Fétis, acquisé par l'État belge. Bruxelles: C. Muquardt, 1877. 946 p.

The Fétis library was acquired by the Bibliothèque Royale in 1872 and contains many rarities. 7,325 items classified under two main headings: (1) "Bibliothèque générale" and (2) "Bibliothèque musicale."

1943. Bibliothèque Royale Albert Ier. Catalogue des imprimés musicaux des XVe, XVIe et XVIIe siècles. Fonds général. Par Bernard Huys. Bruxelles: Bibliothèque Royale de Belgique, 1965. 422 p.

446 numbered items. The catalog lists those works not part of the Fétis collection (no. 1942), although if another copy or a more complete copy is found in Fétis, this information is given. Contents listed for each item. Of particular interest is the listing of music excerpted from theoretical works such as those of Kircher, Glareanus, Zarlino, etc.

Fonds Général Supplement published in 1974, by Bernard Huys.

Review by François Lesure in *Revue de Musicologie*, 51 (1965), p. 102; by Ute Schwab in *Die Musikforschung*, 21 (1968), p. 104–105.

1944. Bibliothèque Royale Albert Ier. Catalogue des imprimés musicaux du XVIIIe siècle. Fonds général. Catalogus van de muziek drukken van de XVIIIde eeuw. Algemene verzameling Bernard Huys. Bruxelles: Bibliothèque Royale Albert Ier, 1974. 519 p.

The catalog presents all the musical works and writings about music printed in the 18th century possessed by the Bibliothèque Royale *not* in the Fétis collection (no. 1942). Complete title page transcriptions, physical descriptions, provenance, references in other catalogs, cross-references, and analysis of collections are provided. There are indexes to authors, composers, and translators, to printers and booksellers, to persons and institutions formerly owning the works, to engravers of music, and to musical genres. A masterful catalog.

1945. Bibliothèque Royale Albert Ier. Catalogue des partitions musicales éditées en Belgique et acquisés par la Bibliothèque royale Albert Ier; fascicule spécial de la Bibliographie de Belgique [par] Bernard Huys [chef de la Section de la musique]. Bruxelles: La Bibliothèque, 1976– 2 v.

Published with an added title page: *Catalogus van de Muziekpartituren in België Uitgegeven en Verworven door de Koninklijke Bibliotheek Albert I. Speciale Aflevering van de Belgische Bibliografie.*
Serves as a catalog of music published in Belgium and acquired by the library; contents: [1] 1966–75; [2] 1976–80.

1946. Bibliothèque Royale Albert Ier. De Grégoire le Grand à Stockhausen. Douze siècles de notation musicale. Catalogue de l'exposition rédigé par Bernard Huys. Bruxelles: Bibliothèque Royale, 1966. 169 p.
Catalog of a well-organized exposition of 100 items tracing the history of musical notation. 16 facsimile plates and 48 illustrations in the text. Each entry is fully described, with bibliographical references.

1947. Bibliothèque Royale Albert Ier. François-Joseph Fétis et la vie musicale de son temps, 1784–1871. Bruxelles: Bibliothèque Royale, 1972. 254 p. 64 plates.
"Exposition organisée à l'occasion du centième anniversaire de l'achat de la collection Fétis," 27 May to 26 August 1972.
An admirably documented exhibition catalog treating the multiple interests and activities of Fétis as a musicologist, historian, composer, and collector.

1948. Bibliothèque Royale Albert Ier. Trésors musicaux de la Bibliothèque royale Albert Ier, 1220–1800; [exposition, Bibliothèque royale Albert Ier du 6 au 27 septembre 1975]; catalogue de l'exposition rédigé par Bernard Huys. Bruxelles: Bibliothèque royale Albert Ier, 1975. 49 p.
Simultaneously published as *Muzikale Schatten uit de Koninklijke Bibliotheek Albert I, 1220–1800.*
A splendid catalog of an exposition of some of the early sources in this important collection.

1949. Conservatoire Royal de Musique. Bibliothèque. Catalogue de la bibliothèque ... par A. Wotquenne. Bruxelles: Coosemans, 1898–1912. 4 v.
Annexe I: Libretti d'Opéras et d'Oratorios Italiens du XVIIe Siècle. Bruxelles: O. Schepens, 1901.
An unaltered reprint was published in 1980 by Éditions Culture et Civilization, Brussels.
A classified catalog to one of the richest European music collections. Printed scores and manuscripts interfiled.

BUDAPEST, HUNGARY

1950. Országos Széchényi Könyvtár. "Catalogue raisonné der Esterházy Opernsammlung, in chronologischer Ordnung der Premièren." In *Haydn als Opernkapellmeister; die Haydn-Dokumente der Esterházy Opernsammlung,* bearbeitet von Dénes Bartha und László Somfai, p. 179–403. Budapest: Verlag der Ungarischen Akademie der Wissenschaften, 1960.
Chronological listing of the operatic works preserved in the Esterházy archive in the National Széchényi Library. Each work is fully described, with special attention given to Haydn's annotations on works performed under his direction. An important approach to Haydn research.

1951. Országos Széchényi Könyvtár. "Die Musikalien der Pfarrkirche zu St. Aegidi in Bartfa." By Otto Gombosi. In *Festschrift für Johannes Wolf*, p. 38–47. Berlin, 1929.

The collection described here is now in the National Széchényi Library at Budapest. Gombosi discusses some 20 music prints of the 16th century and a number of important 16th- and 17th-century manuscripts.

1952. Országos Széchényi Könyvtár. Haydn compositions in the music collection of the National Széchényi Library, Budapest. Published on the occasion of the 150th anniversary of Haydn's death (1809–1959). Edited by Jeno Vecsey. Budapest: Publishing House of the Hungarian Academy of Sciences, 1960. 167 p.

Also published in Hungarian and German.

A classified listing of 372 items, 72 of which are Haydn autographs. 42 facsimiles of manuscripts, prints, and other documents related to the composer's career.

1953. Országos Széchényi Könyvtár. Zenei kéziratok jégyzeke. Budapest: Kiadja a Magyar Nemzeti Múzeum Országos Széchényi Könyvtár, 1921–40. 2 v. (Catalogus bibliothecae musaei nat. hungarici. Musica, I, II)

Vol. 1 (391 p.): editor, Isoz Kálmán. Catalog of 1,449 autograph letters of musicians, including some of Haydn and Liszt. Vol. 2 (237 p.): editor, Lavotta Rezso. Catalog of music manuscripts.

CAMBRAI, FRANCE

1954. Coussemaker, Edmond de. Notice sur les collections musicales de la Bibliothèque de Cambrai et des autres villes du Department du Nord.... Paris: Techener, 1843. 180, 40 p.

Concerned chiefly with 16 manuscripts and 4 printed collections in the Cambrai library. The descriptions are brief, faulty, and outdated.

CAMBRIDGE, ENGLAND

1955. Cambridge University. Fitzwilliam Museum. Catalogue of the music in the Fitzwilliam Museum, Cambridge. By A. J. Fuller-Maitland and A. H. Mann. London: C. J. Clay and Sons, 1893. 298 p.

209 manuscripts, 196 printed books, and an important collection of Handel materials.

1956. Peterhouse College. Catalogue of the musical manuscripts at Peterhouse, Cambridge. Compiled by Anselm Hughes. Cambridge: Cambridge University Press, 1953. 75 p.

Important source materials for the study of English church music of the 16th and 17th centuries comprising four Latin part books c. 1540 and two sets of English part books c. 1630–40.

1957. University Library. Cambridge music manuscripts, 900–1700. Edited by Iain Fenlon. Cambridge: Cambridge University Press, 1982. 174 p.

A catalog of music manuscripts in the various libraries at Cambridge. Published to coincide with an exhibition in the Fitzwilliam Museum, July–August 1982. Bibliographical references.

Review by Christian Meyer in *Fontes Artis Musicae*, 31 (1984), p. 133–34.

CAMBRIDGE, MASSACHUSETTS

1958. Harvard University. Houghton Library. Music in Harvard libraries; a catalogue of early printed music and books on music in the Houghton Library and the Eda Kuhn Loeb Music Library. By David F. Wood. Cambridge, Massachusetts: Houghton Library of the Harvard College Library and Harvard University Department of Music, 1980. 306 p.

> The catalogue describes the music and books on music [1,628 titles] printed before 1801, which had been added to the Harvard Libraries by 1967. [from the introductory remarks]

Arrangement by author and composer. References to principal bibliographic tools. Index to names, including names of printers, booksellers, and editors. Bibliography. Additions and corrections cited on p. 282.

Review by Donald W. Krummel in *Notes*, 37 (1981), p. 852–54.

1959. Harvard University. Isham Memorial Library. "The collection of photographic reproductions at the Isham Memorial Library, Harvard University." By Willi Apel. In *Musica Disciplina*, 1 (1946), p. 68–73.

Describes the first stages of the Isham collection of microfilms of musical source materials and other holdings.

1960. Harvard University. Isham Memorial Library. "The Isham Memorial Library of Harvard University." By Archibald T. Davison. In *Organ Institute Quarterly*, 3 (1953), p. 13–16.

Describes the holdings of the Isham collection particularly of interest to historians of keyboard music.

1961. Harvard University. Loeb Music Library. A catalogue of books relating to music in the library of Richard Aldrich. New York: Printed at the Plimpton Press, Norwood, Massachusetts, 1931. 435 p.

A classified catalog of music literature, primarily of the 19th and 20th centuries, with a small collection of books printed before 1800 (p. 35–55). This library has been incorporated into the Harvard University music collection.

1962. Harvard University. Loeb Music Library. "The Eda Kuhn Loeb Music Library." By Nino Pirotta. In *Harvard Library Bulletin* 12, (1958), p. 410–17.

Describes the development and holdings of the library.

1963. Harvard University. University Library. Card catalog of the Harvard University Music Library to 1985. New York: Saur, 1985. 224 negative microfiche.

Catalog of one of the great American collections supporting musical research; part one is the dictionary catalog of the book and score holdings of the collections of the Loeb Music Library, the Isham Memorial Library of microforms, the hymnbook collection at the Andover-Harvard Divinity Library, the rare materials in the Houghton Library, and relevant materials from the Widener Library. In part 1 there are entries of composers, authors, subjects, and series. Part 2 is a shelf list of the Loeb Music Library, providing classified access to the collection as well.

1964. Harvard University. University Library. "Rare music manuscripts at Harvard." By Craig Wright. In *Current Musicology*, (1970), p. 25–33.
Describes the holdings of the Loeb Library, the Houghton Library, and the Isham Library at Harvard.

CARPENTRAS, FRANCE

1965. Bibliothèque d'Inguimbert. Catalogue de la collection musicale J. B. Laurens donnée à la ville de Carpentras pour la Bibliothèque d'Inguimbert. Carpentra: J. Seguin, 1901. 151 p.
Classified catalog of music books and scores; a 19th-century scholar's library. Preceded by a biography of the donor, J. B. Laurens, archeologist, painter, writer, organist, composer, and musicologist.

CARRIBBEAN ISLANDS

1966. Dower, Catherine A. "Libraries with music collections in the Carribbean Islands." In *Notes*, 34 (1978), p. 27–38.
Descriptions of music collections in Aruba, Barbados, Bermuda, Cuba, Curaçao, Haiti, Jamaica, Martinique, Puerto Rico, Trinidad, and the Virgin Islands.

CASALE MONFERRATO, ITALY

1967. Archivio Capitolare. Sixteenth-century choirbooks in the Archivio Capitolare at Casale Monferrato. By David Crawford. American Institute of Musicology, 1975. 207 p. (Renaissance manuscript studies, 2)
A catalog of seven manuscripts of polyphonic sacred music copied between 1508 and 1518. There are extensive introductory and descriptive remarks, followed by an incipit catalog for each manuscript, in order as the works appear in each manuscript. Citations for modern editions and secondary literature for all but 90 *unica* are provided. There is a catalog of compositions (masses, magnificats, hymns, miscellaneous liturgical genres, and motets). There is a list of manuscripts cited in the catalog but located elsewhere, as well as a list of early printed music editions containing works in this repertory. There is a similar list of modern editions. There is a list of liturgical sources quoted and a general index.
Reviews by Nicholas Sandon in *Early Music*, 5 (1977), p. 225–29; by William F. Prizer in *Notes*, 34 (1977), p. 327–29; and by Mary S. Lewis in the *Journal of the American Musicological Society*, 31 (1978), p. 521–29.

CESENA, ITALY

1968. Biblioteca Comunale. "Catalogo delle opere musicali a stampa dal '500 al '700 conservate presso la Biblioteca Comunale di Cesena." By Sergio Paganelli. In *Collectanea Historiae Musicae*, 2 (1957), p. 311–38.
95 early editions of vocal and instrumental music; 6 theory works.

CHARLOTTESVILLE, VIRGINIA

1969. University of Virginia. Alderman Library. Computer catalog of nineteenth-century American-imprint sheet music; compiled by Lynn T. McRae. Charlottesville: University of Virginia, 1977. 12 p., 8 microfiche.
Catalog of a collection in the Rare Book Room, Alderman Library, University of Virginia. Indexes about 7,700 pieces of American sheet music.

CHICAGO, ILLINOIS

1970. Newberry Library. Bibliographical inventory to the early music in the Newberry Library, Chicago, Illinois. Edited by D. W. Krummel. Boston, Massachusetts: G. K. Hall, 1977. 587 p.
Photo-offset duplication of cards from the Newberry Library representing musical items published before 1860 and manuscripts dating from before 1860. These cards had been arranged in a classified order for the catalog.

> The Newberry Library has what is considered to be one of the most important music collections in the United States, particularly rich in the fields of Renaissance music, early theory, and Americana. [*Foreword*]

Comprehending the introduction is of crucial importance to the efficient use of this work. Addenda and corrigenda, p. 527–532. Index to composers, editors, and musical subjects. Index to printers, engravers, artists, copyists, and publishers.

1971. Newberry Library. The Newberry Library catalog of early American printed sheet music. Compiled by Bernard E. Wilson. Boston, Massachusetts: G. K. Hall, 1983. 3 v.
Photo-offset duplication of cards representing about 6,300 pieces of early American sheet music, including the James Francis Driscoll collection. The catalog covers works printed before 1871. There are sections devoted to main entries, added entries, chronological entries, places, and titles. Approximately 90,000 pieces of American sheet music held by the Newberry are not included in this catalog.

1972. Newberry Library. "The Newberry Library, Chicago." By Donald W. Krummel. In *Fontes Artis Musicae* (July–December 1969), p. 119–24.
A narrative account of the music resources of the Newberry Library in the areas of medieval music, Renaissance and baroque music, music of the 18th and 19th centuries, music of master composers, and Americana.

COIMBRA, PORTUGAL

1973. Universidade. Biblioteca. Inventário dos inéditos e impressos musicais (subsídios par um catálogo). Fasc. I. Prefaciado por Santiago Kastner. Coimbra: Impresso nas oficinas da "Atlântida," 1937. 47, 55 p.
Separate alphabets and pagination for manuscripts and early printed works. Full descriptions.

1974. Universidade. Biblioteca. Os manuscritos musicais nos. 6 e 12 da Biblioteca Geral da Universidade de Coimbra (Contribuïçãao para um catálogo definitivo). Por Mário de Sampayo Ribeiro. Coimbra: 1941. 112 p.
A detailed study of two manuscripts of polyphonic music in the university library at Coimbra.

COLLEGE PARK, MARYLAND

1975. University of Maryland at College Park. Music Library. A guide to the Jacob Coopersmith Collection of Handeliana at the University of Maryland at College Park; compiled by Richard Brundage and Neil Ratliff. College Park: Music Library, University of Maryland, 1986. 18 p.

COLLEGEVILLE, MINNESOTA

1976. St. John's Abbey and University. Hill Monastic Microfilm Library. "Music manuscripts on microfilm in the Hill Monastic Manuscript Library at St. John's Abbey and University." By Peter Jeffrey. In *Notes*, 35 (1978), p. 7–30.
A survey of the entire collection of microfilms gathered from a large number of Roman Catholic repositories in Europe.

1977. St. John's University. Alcuin Library. "The monastic manuscript microfilm library." By Julian G. Plante, in *Notes*, 25 (1968), p. 12–14.
The article describes a microfilm library of nearly 11,000 codices filmed from the monastic libraries in Europe (Göttweig, Heiligenkreuz, Herzogenburg, Klosterneuburg, Kremsmünster, Lambach, Lilienfeld, Melk, etc.). The author cites 27 manuscripts of early music theory available for study in the collection at Collegeville.

1978. St. John's University. Alcuin Library and Hill Monastic Manuscript Library. A bibliography for medieval and renaissance musical manuscript research; secondary materials at the Alcuin Library and the Hill Monastic Manuscript Library ... By Peter Jeffrey. Collegeville, Minnesota: St. John's University Press for the Hill Monastic Manuscript Library, 1980. 68 p.
A very handy, pocket-size, annotated bibliography with sections on musical paleography, musical iconography, catalogs, music texts and studies, and reference materials. Index to names and titles.

COLOGNE, GERMANY

1979. Domcapelle. Die Leiblsche Sammlung. Katalog der Musikalien der Kölner Domcapelle. Von Gottfried Göller. Köln: Arno Volk-Verlag, 1964. 133 p. (Beiträge zur rheinischen Musikgeschichte, 57)

Thematic catalog of 291 sacred choral works, chiefly early 19th century, formerly in the chapel of Cologne Cathedral. The collection is now in the Diözesanbibliothek of the Archbishopric of Cologne. A former owner was Carl Leibl, Kapellmeister.

Review by Winfried Kirsch in *Die Musikforschung*, 20 (1967), p. 95.

1980. Universitäts- und Stadtbibliothek. Katalog der in der Universitäts- und Stadtbibliothek Köln vorhandenen Musikdrucke des 16., 17., und 18. Jahrhunderts. By Willi Kahl. Köln: 1958. 20 p.

118 items. Bibliographical references.

CONSTANCE, SWITZERLAND

1981. Kollegiat- und Pfarrkirche St. Stephan. "Das Noteninventar der Kollegiat- und Pfarrkirche St. Stephan." By Manfred Schuler. In *Kirchenmusikalisches Jahrbuch*, 58/59 (1974/75), p. 85–103.

COPENHAGEN, DENMARK

1982. Kommunebiblioteker. Katalog øver dansk og udenlandsk musik og musiklitteratur. 2. udgåave. København: B. Lunos Bogtrykkeri, 1932. 157 p.

First published in 1921.

Tilvaext (supplement), 1932–39. København: B. Lunos, 1939.

1983. Kommunebiblioteker. Katalog øver musik og musiklitteratur. København: Nordlunde, 1954–58. 4 v.

Vol. 1: *Orkestermusik, Kammermusik, Enkelte Instrumenter.* 1956. 72 p.

Vol. 2: *Klaver, Orgel, Harmonium.* 1954. 65 p.

Vol. 3: *Vokalmusik.* 1958. 118 p.

Vol. 4: *Operaer, Operetter, Balletter.* 1955. 46 p.

A fifth volume devoted to books on music was never published.

1984. Kongelige Bibliothek. Catalogue of Giedde's music collection in the Royal Library of Copenhagen. Compiled by Inge Bittmann. Copenhagen: Edition Egtved, 1976. 198 p.

A catalog of "a fairly comprehensive collection, mostly of flute music from the second half of the 18th century" [*Preface*].

Arranged alphabetically by composer with thematic incipits. There is a classified list of titles, a list of publishers, and a bibliography.

CREMONA, ITALY

1985. Biblioteca Governativa e Libreria Civica. Mostra bibliografica dei musicisti cremonesi: catalogo storico-critico degli autori a cura di Raffaello

Monterosso. Catalogo bibliografico. Cremona: Biblioteca Governativa e Libreria Civica, 1951. 149 p. (Annali della Biblioteca governativa e libreria civica di Cremona, 2)

Catalog of an exhibition held in 1949. P. 1–106: biographical notices of Cremonese musicians; p. 107–145: exhibition catalog, arranged chronologically; about 140 items related to the history of music in Cremona.

CRESPANO VENETO, ITALY

1986. Biblioteca Musicale del Prof. Pietro Canal in Crespano Veneto. Bassano: Prem. Stabilimento Tipogr. Sante Pezzato, 1885. 104 p.

A scholar's library of 1,152 items, of which the first 1,034 are books on music. Contains many rarities. The owner was a professor at the University of Padua and wrote studies of music in Mantua and Venice.

CUENCA, SPAIN

1987. Catedral. Archivo. Catálogo musical del Archivo de la Santa Iglesia Catedral Basilica de Cuenca. Recogido por Restituto Navarro Gonzalo. Revisado por Jesús López-Cobos. Dirigido por Antonio Iglesias. 2nd ed., revised and corrected. Cuenca: Ediciones del Instituto de Música Religiosa, 1973. 376 p. (Instituto de música religiosa, Publicaciones, 9)

1st edition published as vol. 1 of the series in 1965. 372 p.

Contains extensive holdings of sacred and secular music. Indexes by composer and by century.

CZECH REPUBLIC AND SLOVAKIA

1988. Fischer, Kurt von. "Repertorium der Quellen tschechischer Mehrstimmigkeit des 14. bis 16. Jahrhunderts." In *Essays in Musicology in Honor of Dragan Plamenac on his 70th Birthday*, p. 49–60. Pittsburgh, Pennsylvania: University of Pittsburgh Press, 1969.

Identifies 73 manuscript sources of early Czech polyphony in 23 institutions, chiefly in Czechoslovakia but including the Austrian National Library at Vienna.

1989. Plamenac, Dragan. "Music libraries in Eastern Europe, a visit in the summer of 1961." In *Notes*, 19 (1962), p. 217–34; 411–20; 584–98.

An illuminating account of conditions in some of the major East European music libraries, including those in the former Czechoslovakia. Locations of important bodies of source materials are indicated.

1990. Průvodce po pramenech k dějinám Hudby. Fondy a sbírky uložené v. čechách. [Music collections and archives in the CSSR.] Zpracovali: Jaroslav Bužga, Jan Kouba, Eva Mikanová a Tomislav Volek. Redigoval: Jan Kouba. Praha: Československá Akademie Ved, 1969. 323 p.

An annotated bibliography of music history for Bohemia. General descriptions of the music resources of Czech museums, libraries, and archives. Name index.

1991. Svobodová, Maria. "Musikbüchereien, Archive und Museen in der CSSR." In *AIBM, Ländergruppe Deutsche Demokratische Republik. Internationaler Sommerkurs für Musikbibliothekare*, 1964, p. 48–69. Berlin, 1965.

A descriptive account of the major music archives, libraries, and museums in Czechoslovakia.

1992. Terrayová, Maria J. "Súpis archívnych hudobných fondov na Slovensku." In *Hudobnovedné Studié*. VI, p. 197–328. Bratislava: Vydavatel'stvo Slovenskej Akadémie, Vied, 1960.

Thematic catalog of the music manuscripts in two hitherto undescribed Czech archives: the archive of the Pfarrkirche of Púchov (on deposit in the Musicological Institute of the Slovakian Academy of Sciences) and the archive of the Príleský Ostrolucky family (on deposit in the Slovakian National Museum in Martin). The manuscripts are chiefly of late 18th-century instrumental and vocal music by Italianate Czech composers of the period.

DAGENHAM, ENGLAND

1993. Public Libraries. Catalogue of music; a complete catalogue of the scores, miniature scores, recorded music and books ... in the Dagenham Public Libraries. [2nd ed.] Compiled by W. C. Pugsley, G. Atkinson and C. Tripp. Dagenham (Essex): Valence House, 1964. 515 p.

First edition published 1958. 299 p.

DANZIG
See GDANSK, POLAND.

DARMSTADT, GERMANY

1994. Hofbibliothek. "Musik-Handschriften der Darmstädter Hofbibliothek." Beschrieben von F. W. E. Roth. In *Monatshefte für Musikgeschichte*, 20 (1888), p. 64–73; 82–92.

117 items, 10th to 19th centuries. Brief descriptions.

1995. Hofbibliothek. "Zur Bibliographie der Musikdrucke des XV. bis XVII. Jahrhunderts in der Darmstädter Hofbibliothek." By F. W. E. Roth. In *Monatshefte für Musikgeschichte*, 20 (1888), p. 118–25; 134–41; 154–61.

75 items, fully described.

1996. Internationales Musikinstitut Darmstadt. Informationszentrum für zeitgenössische Musik. Katalog der Abteilung Noten. Darmstadt: Internationales Musikinstitut, 1966. 293 p.

Title varies, began as *Kranichsteiner Musikinstitut*.

Supplements published for 1967, 1968, 1969–70, 1971–73, 1974–75 and 1976–77. In 1970, a supplement covering books and periodicals was published.

An international lending library established in 1948 to further the study

and performance of contemporary music. Classified catalog, chiefly scores but including a small collection of books.
Review by Karl Kroeger in *Notes*, 23 (1967), p. 531–32.

DENTON, TEXAS

1997. **North Texas State College. Music Library.** A bibliography of contemporary music in the Music Library of North Texas State College, March 1955. Compiled by Anna Harriet Heyer. Denton, Texas: 1955. 128 leaves (typescript).
Alphabetical listing by composer and by title under composer. Chiefly scores and chamber music with parts. No index.
Review by Dorothy A. Linder in *Notes*, 13 (1956), p. 656–57.

1998. **North Texas State University. Hans Nachod Collection.** The Arnold Schoenberg–Hans Nachod Collection. By John A. Kimmey. Detroit, Michigan: Information Coordinators, 1979. 119 p. (Detroit studies in music bibliography, 41)
Annotated catalog of the collection of correspondence, proof sheets, and holographs in the Music Library of North Texas State University, Denton, Texas.
Review by Alexander L. Ringer in *Fontes Artis Musicae*, 27 (1980), p. 224–35.

DETROIT, MICHIGAN

1999. **Detroit Public Library. Hackley Collection.** Catalog of the E. Azalia Hackley Memorial Collection of Negro music, dance and drama [in the] Detroit Public Library. Boston, Massachusetts: G. K. Hall, 1979. 510 p.
Photo-offset duplication of cards representing books, scores, sheet music, broadsides, posters, and photographs in the Hackley Collection.

DRESDEN, GERMANY

2000. **Sächsische Landesbibliothek.** Katalog der Musiksammlung der Kgl. öffentlichen Bibliothek zu Dresden (im Japanischen Palais). Robert Eitner und Otto Kade, bearb. Leipzig: Breitkopf & Härtel, 1890. 150 p. (Monatshefte für Musikgeschichte. Beilage. Jahrgang 21–22)
Music manuscripts to the date of compilation; printed music and books on music to 1700.

2001. **Sächsische Landesbibliothek.** Klaviermusik der sozialistischen Länder aus der Sächsischen Landesbibliothek. Bestandsverzeichnis zusammengestellt von Wolfgang Reich. Dresden: Sächsische Landesbibliothek, 1962. 79 p.
A list, grouped alphabetically by country, of keyboard music by East European composers. Date, publisher, and pagination given for each entry.

2002. **Sächsische Landesbibliothek.** Die Musiksammelhandschriften des 16. und 17. Jahrhunderts in der Sächsischen Landesbibliothek zu Dresden. Unter Verwendung von Vorarbeiten Harald Kümmerling im Auftrag der Sächsischen Landesbibliothek beschrieben von Wolfgang Steude. Wilhelmshaven: Heinrichshofen, 1974. 315 p. (Quellenkataloge zur Musikgeschichte, 6)

Fully describes and analyzes 112 manuscripts. Indexes of persons, Latin titles and first lines, and German titles and first lines.

Sächsische Landesbibliothek. See no. 2046.

DUBLIN, IRELAND

2003. Archbishop Marsh's Library. A catalogue of the printed books on music, printed music, and music manuscripts in Archbishop Marsh's Library, Dublin. By Richard Charteris. Clifden, Ireland: Boethius Press, 1982. 142 p.

Arranged in three sections, each presenting bibliographic entries for works printed or written before 1800 held by the Archbishop Marsh Library. Includes a page of supplementary references extending the information provided in the catalog. Appendix of books and manuscripts missing from the library. Name index to collections.

Reviews by John D. Arnn in *Notes*, 39 (1983), p. 605–606, and by R. Gordon Dodd in *Chelys*, 12 (1983), p. 79–80.

2004. Trinity College Library. "The lute books of Trinity College, Dublin." By John Ward. In *Lute Society Journal*, 9 (1967), p. 17–40; 10 (1968), p. 15–32.

DURANGO, MEXICO

2005. Catedral. Capilla de música. La capilla de música de la Catedral de Durango, México, siglos XVII y XVIII. [Por Francisco Antúnez.] Aguascalientes: 1970. 47 p.

Includes a short catalog of the music manuscript holdings of the cathedral.

DURHAM, ENGLAND

2006. Durham Cathedral Library. A catalogue of Durham Cathedral music manuscripts, compiled by Brian Crosby. Oxford: Oxford University Press for the Dean and Chapter of Durham Cathedral, 1986. 271 p.

Includes descriptions of manuscripts from the monastery, the cathedral, and Bamburgh Castle. Indexes of composers, dates, dated signatures (for liturgical manuscripts only), copyists, musical genres, titles and first lines (for Bamburgh Castle manuscripts). The manuscripts are described, but no title analytics are included in the descriptions. The indexes provide the analysis of contents.

2007. Durham Cathedral Library. A catalogue of the printed music and books on music in Durham Cathedral Library. By Alec Harman. London, New York, and Toronto: Oxford University Press, 1968. 136 p.

Review by Imogen Fellinger in *Die Musikforschung*, 25 (1972), p. 99–100; by Henry Leland Clarke in *Notes*, 25 (1969), p. 501–502.

EDINBURGH, SCOTLAND

2008. L'Institut Français d'Ecosse. Hector Berlioz (1803–1869), an exhibition at l'Institut Français d'Ecosse on the occasion of the 1963 Edinburgh International Festival. Edinburgh: Institut Français d'Ecosse, 1963. 40 p.

An exhibition catalog compiled by Richard Macnutt. 127 items, arranged chronologically with respect to the composer's career. Fully annotated with connecting commentary.

2009. University. Reid Library. Catalogue of manuscripts, printed music, and books on music up to 1850 in the library of the Music Department of the University of Edinburgh.... Edited by Hans Gal. Edinburgh: Oliver and Boyd, 1941. 78 p.

Important for its holdings in 18th-century music, printed and in manuscript, from the private collection of John Reid, 1721–1807. Brief entries.

EISENACH, GERMANY

2010. Richard Wagner-Museum. Katalog einer Richard Wagner Bibliothek; nach den vorliegenden Originalien systematisch-chronologisch geordnetes und mit Citaten und Anmerkungen versehenes authentisches Nachschlagebuch durch die gesammte Wagner-Literatur. Von Nikolaus Oesterlein. Leipzig: Breitkopf & Härtel, 1882–95. 4 v.

Apart from the bibliography of Wagner literature (vols. 1–2), this work provides a catalog of a collection of Wagner documents, formerly in Vienna but purchased by the city of Eisenach in 1895 (vols. 3–4).

ENGLAND

See under GREAT BRITAIN.

ESCORIAL, SPAIN

2011. Monasterio de San Lorenzo El Real. Catálogo del Archivio de Música del Monasterio de San Lorenzo El Real de El Escorial. [By] Samuel Rubio. Préambulo de Antonio Iglesias. Cuenca: Instituto de Música Religiosa, 1976–82. 2 v. (Instituto de Música Religiosa. Ediciones, 12 and 18)

Vol. 2 gives the incipits of the works listed in vol. 1 and has title: *Catálogo del Archivo de Música de San Lorenzo El Real de El Escorial* [por Samuel Rubio y J. Sierra; presentación Pablo López de Osaba].

A catalog of manuscript choirbooks, scores, part books, and unbound sets of parts from the 16th to the 19th century, with descriptions and analyzed contents. There is an appendix of brief biographies of the principal composers and an index of names.

ESSEN, GERMANY

2012. Essen Stadtbibliothek. Systematischer Katalog der Musikbibliothek. Verzeichnis des Gesamtbestandes 1973. Bearbeitet von Manfred Willfort. Essen: Stadtbibliothek, 1974. 372 p.

Teil 1: Bücher.
A classified catalog of books on music.

FERRARA, ITALY

Biblioteca Comunale. See no. 2074.

FLORENCE, ITALY

2013. Biblioteca Nazionale Centrale. Catalogo dei manoscritti musicali della Biblioteca Nazionale di Firenze di Bianca Becherini. Kassel: Bärenreiter, 1959. 178 p.
144 numbered items; detailed descriptions, contents of collections. Indexes of text incipits, musicians, poets, and names mentioned in the descriptive notes.
Review by Frank Ll. Harrison in *Music and Letters*, 42 (1961), p. 281; by Nanie Bridgman in *Fontes Artis Musicae*, 8 (1961), p. 31–33; by Walther Durr in *Die Musikforschung*, 14 (1961), p. 234–35.

2014. Biblioteca Nazionale Centrale. Mostra bibliografica di musica italiana dalle origini alla fine del secolo XVIII. Firenze: L. S. Olschki, 1937. 102 p.
An exhibition catalog. Preface signed by Anita Mondolfo.

Conservatorio di Musica "Luigi Cherubini" (formerly cited as R. Istituto Musicale). See also no. 2067.

2015. Conservatorio di Musica "Luigi Cherubini." Catalogo delle opere musicali teoriche e pratiche di autori vissuti sino ai primi decenni del secolo XIX [nella] Biblioteca del Conservatorio di Musica di Firenze, per R. Gondolfi, C. Cordara, ed A. Bonaventura. Bologna: Forni, 1977. 321 p. (Bibliotheca musica bononiensis, I, 11)
A reprint of the 1929 edition, published in Parma, which was itself a slightly altered version of the corresponding volume (IV, 1) in the Associazione dei Musicologi Italiani *Catalogo Generale* ... (see no. 2067).

2016. Conservatorio di Musica "Luigi Cherubini." Esposizione nazionale dei Conservatori Musicali e delle Bibliotheche. Palazzo Davanzati, 27 ottobre 1949–8 gennaio 1950. Firenze: G. Barbera, 1950. 121 p.
Exposition catalog celebrating the 100th anniversary of the founding of the conservatory. Includes manuscripts, printed music, and some musical instruments.

2017. Conservatorio di Musica "Luigi Cherubini." Indice di alcuni cimeli esposti appartenenti alla Biblioteca del R. Istituto di Riccardo Gandolfi. Firenze: Tipografia Galletti e Cocci, 1911. 32 p.
At head of title: "Nella commemorazione cinquantenaria dalla fondazione del R. Istituto Musicale 'Luigi Cherubini' di Firenze."
Brief descriptive entries for 30 manuscripts and 37 early printed books, 32 theory works, and 4 "curiosita diversi."

2018. Conservatorio di Musica "Luigi Cherubini." "I manoscritti e le stampe rare della Biblioteca del Conservatorio 'L. Cherubini' di Firenze" di Bianca Becherini. In *La Bibliofilia*, 66 (1964), p. 255–99.

20 manuscripts and 21 early printed books "nuova catalogazione e reintegrazione."

A catalog compiled for the purpose of giving full descriptions of those items in the collection that are most rare and most interesting to foreign scholars.

2019. Conservatorio di Musica "Luigi Cherubini." Basevi Collection. "The 'Basevi' collection in the Library of Cherubini Conservatory, Florence." By Anna Maria Trivisonno. In *Fontes Artis Musicae*, 32 (1985), p. 114–16.

A very brief introduction to the collection of Abramo Basevi, who was a composer, musicologist, and editor for the publishing house of Guidi and of the journals *L'Armonia* (1856–59) and *Il Boccherini*. A book-length catalog is anticipated.

2020. Galleria degli Uffizi. I disegni musicali del Gabinetto degli "Uffizi" e delle minori collezioni pubbliche a Firenze di Luigi Parigi. Firenze: L. S. Olschki, 1951. 233 p.

A catalog of prints and drawings with musical content or subject matter: musicians, musical instruments, performance practice, etc. Indexed by instruments and by subjects.

2021. Galleria degli Uffizi. Mostra di strumenti musicali in disegni degli "Uffizi." Catalogo a cura di Luisa Marcucci con prefazione di Luigi Parigi. Firenze: L. S. Olschki, 1952. 47 p.

An exhibition of 65 items from the Uffizi print collection; 25 plates.

2022. Galleria degli Uffizi. Gli strumenti musicali nei dipinti della Galleria degli Uffizi di Marziano Bernardi e Andrea Della Corte. Torino: Edizioni Radio Italiana, 1952. 177 p. 51 plates.

A handsome volume devoted to representations of musical activity in paintings in the Uffizi gallery. Index of artists and of instruments depicted.

2023. Gandolfi, Riccardo. Illustrazioni di Alcuni Cimeli Concernenti l'Arte Musicale in Firenze ... di Riccardo Gandolfi. In Firenze, a cura della Commissione per la Esposizione di Vienna, 1892.

A lavish, illustrated catalog prepared for the Vienna exposition of 1892. Limited edition, elephant folio, 39 facsimile plates of Italian musical documents from the 11th to the 19th centuries. Historical introduction and notes on the plates.

FRANCE

2024. Bridgman, Nanie. "Musique profane italienne des 16e et 17e siècles dans les bibliothèques françaises." In *Fontes Artis Musicae*, 2 (1955), p. 40–59.

Precise description of 32 rarities of the 16th and 17th centuries found in five public or private libraries in France.

2025. Chaillon, Paule. "Les fonds musicaux de quelques bibliothèques de province." In *Fontes Artis Musicae* 2, (1955), p. 151–63.

Describes a group of source materials found in 24 French provincial libraries, sources that came to light in connection with work done in preparation for the RISM volumes.

FRANKFURT AM MAIN, GERMANY

2026. Deutsches Rundfunkarchiv. Die ersten vier Jahrzehnte unseres Jahrhunderts im Spiegel einer Berliner Schallplattensammlung. Verzeichnis von Musik- und Sprechschallplatten aus der Sammlung des Berliner Theaterwissenschaftlers Martin Günther Sarneck. Frankfurt am Main: Deutsches Rundfunkarchiv, 1966. 2 v.

Preface signed by Hans-Joachim Weinbrenner.

Bd 1: Sänger und Sängerinnen A–S. Nr. 1–1278.

Bd 2: Sänger und Sängerinnen T–Z; Instrumentalmusik. Wortaufnahmen. Nr. 1279–2312.

A catalog of the Sarneck Collection in the Deutsches Rundfunkarchiv. Vol. 2 contains indexes of persons by profession. Separate composer index.

2027. International Exhibition "Music in the Life of the People." Katalog der Internationalen Austellung "Musik im Leben der Völker" von Kathi Meyer. Frankfurt am Main: Hauserpresse Werner U. Winter, 1927. 340 p.

Catalog of the large international music exhibition held 11 June to 28 August 1927. Organized according to the systematic arrangement of the exhibition halls. Includes printed books, manuscripts, instruments, pictures, and other artifacts. 49 plates.

A separate catalog of the Italian section was printed in Rome, 1927. 161 p.

2028. Lessing-Gymnasium. Bibliothek. Die musikalischen Schätze der Gymnasialbibliothek und der Peterskirche zu Frankfurt a. M. von Carl Israël. Frankfurt a. M.: Mahlau und Waldschmidt, 1872. 118 p.

Covers the period to about 1800; full bibliographical data.

2029. Stadt- und Universitätsbibliothek. Thematischer Katalog der kirchlichen Musikhandschriften des 17. und 18. Jahrhunderts in der Stadt- und Universitätsbibliothek Frankfurt am Main: (Signaturengruppe Ms. Ff. Mus.); bearb. u. beschrieben von Joachim Schlichte; [hrsg. von d. Stadt- u. Univ.-Bibliothek Frankfurt am Main]. Frankfurt am Main: Klostermann, 1979. 500 p. (Kataloge der Stadt- und Universitätsbibliothek Frankfurt am Main, 8)

A catalog focusing mainly on the Telemann holdings (p. 187–384), but with anonymi and other composers represented. Telemann works divided into sacred and secular sections, each organized by *Werke* numbers. Descriptions include information about copyists and watermarks. Indexes to names, and to titles and text incipits. Bibliography of works on watermarks and a general bibliography.

2030. Stadtbibliothek. Kirchliche Musikhandschriften des XVII. und XVIII. Jahrhunderts; Katalog von Carl Süss, im Auftrage der Gesellschaft der

Freunde der Stadtbibliothek, bearb. und hrsg. von Peter Epstein. Berlin: Frankfurter Verlags-Anstalt, 1926. 224 p.
Chiefly cantatas arranged alphabetically under composer, with a separate section of 834 works by G. P. Telemann. Entries give date if known, title, instrumentation.

FREIBERG, GERMANY

2031. Gamber, Klaus. Codices liturgici latini antiquiores. Freiberg: Universitätsverlag, 1963. 334 p. (Spicilegii friburgensis subsidia, 1)
Liturgical music manuscripts in the library of the University at Freiberg.

2032. Kade, Otto. Die älteren Musikalien der Stadt Freiberg in Sachsen. Leipzig: Breitkopf & Härtel, 1888. 32 p. (Beilage. Monatshefte für Musikgeschichte. Jahrgang 20)

FREIBURG IM BREISGAU, GERMANY

2033. Universität Freiburg im Breisgau. Bibliothek. Die Musikhandschriften der Universitätsbibliothek und anderer öffentlicher Sammlungen in Freiburg im Breisgau und Umgebung. Beschrieben von Clytus Gottwald. Wiesbaden: Otto Harrassowitz, 1979. 224 p.
Covers music manuscripts in seven institutions, most of them churches or seminaries, in the vicinity of Freiburg im Breisgau. Each manuscript is described and analyzed fully. Some descriptions include thematic incipits. Indexes to text incipits and to persons, places, and things.

GDANSK, POLAND (formerly DANZIG)

2034. Stadtbibliothek. Die musikalischen Handschriften der Stadtbibliothek und in ihrer Verwaltung befindlichen Kirchenbibliotheken von St. Katharinen und St. Johann in Danzig von Otto Günther. Danzig: Saunier 1911. 188 p. (Katalog der Handschriften der Danziger Stadtbibliothek, Bd. 4: Handschriften, Teil 4)
The surviving music manuscripts and early printed books of the Danzig Stadtbibliothek have been filmed and are listed in the catalog of music sources published by the Polish National Library in Warsaw (no. 2433). Professor Plamenac in his articles on East European music libraries (no. 1989) has given a summary listing of the major holdings of this collection.

GENOA, ITALY

2035. Biblioteca dell'Istituto Musicale "Nicolo Paganini." Catalogo del fondo antico a cura di Salvatore Pintacuda. Milano: Istituto Editoriale Italiano, 1966. 489 p. (Bibliotheca musicae, 4)
A catalog of printed and manuscript music, music literature, vocal anthologies, and the rarities in the Istituto Paganini. Vocal anthologies are analyzed. Supplies information on instrumentation. Composer index.
Review by Frank A. D'Accone in *Notes*, 23 (1967), p. 530–31.

Biblioteca Universitaria. See no. 2072.

Biblioteca Universitaria. See no. 2069.

GERMANY (See also BAVARIA)

Kahl, Willi und Wilhelm-Martin Luther. Repertorium der Musikwissenschaft.... See no. 706.

2036. Schaal, Richard. Führer durch deutsche Musikbibliotheken. Wilhelmshaven: Heinrichshofen's Verlag, 1971. 163 p. (Taschenbücher zur Musikwissenschaft, 7)
German libraries are listed alphabetically by place, covering all of Germany. For the major libraries there are descriptions given of the collection, with some historical information. Bibliographies include catalogs and other publications related to the libraries under consideration.

GERMANY (Formerly DEUTSCHE DEMOKRATISCHE REPUBLIK)

2037. Deutscher Bibliotheksverband. Sektion Musikbibliotheken. Musikbibliotheken und Musikaliensammlungen in der Deutschen Demokratischen Republik. Red. Peter Thuringer. Mitarb. Jutta Theurich und Rose Hebenstreit. Halle: Internat. Vereinigung d. Musikbibliotheken, Ländergruppe DDR, 1969. 62 p.
A publication sponsored by the East German section of the International Association of Music Libraries.
91 institutions are described, with pertinent data concerning their resources and services. Catalogs and other publications cited.

GLASGOW, SCOTLAND

2038. Anderson's College. Library. Euing Collection. The Euing musical library. Catalogue of the musical library of the late Wm. Euing, Esq., bequeathed to Anderson's University, Glasgow.... Glasgow: Printed by W. M. Ferguson, 1878. 256 p.
Classified catalog. The collection is strong in theoretical works from 1487 and liturgical music of the Church of England, 16th to 19th centuries.

GÖTTINGEN, GERMANY

2039. Niedersächsische Staats- und Universitäts-Bibliothek. Die Musikwerke der Kgl. Universitäts-Bibliothek in Göttingen. Verzeichnet von Albert Quantz. Berlin: T. Trautwein, 1883. 45 p. (Monatshefte für Musikgeschichte. Beilage, Jahrgang 15)
45 theoretical works and some 100 music editions of the 16th and 17th centuries. Good representation of German composers of the period.

2040. Niedersächsische Staats- und Universitäts-Bibliothek. Johann Sebastian Bach Documenta. Hrsg. von Wilhelm-Martin Luther zum Bachfest 1950 in Göttingen. Kassel: Bärenreiter, 1950. 148 p.

545 numbered items from an exhibition illustrating J. S. Bach's influence from his own time to the present day. Covers a wide area of documentation. 54 plates.

GÖTTWEIG (BENEDICTINE ABBEY), AUSTRIA

2041. Graphisches Kabinett. Musik, Theater, Tanz vom 16. Jahrhundert bis zum 19. Jahrhundert in ihren Beziehungen zur Gesellschaft. Ausstellung Stift Göttweig, Niederösterreich, 28. Mai–23. Okt. 1966. 86 p.

This library has been enriched by materials from the collection of the Viennese collector Aloys Fuchs.

2042. Wondratsch, Heinrich. Der Göttweiger thematische Katalog von 1830 hrsg., kommentiert und mit Registern versehen von Friedrich W. Riedel. München: E. Katzbichler, 1979. 2 v. (Studien zur Landes- und Sozialgeschichte der Musik, Bd. 2–3)

Edition of a thematic catalog originating in 1830 of a collection of music in the Benedictine Abbey of Göttweig in Austria.

Original manuscript title page reads: *Katalogus operum musicalium in choro musicali monasterii O.S.P.B. Gottwicensis, R.R.D.D. Altmanno abbate, per R.D. Henricum Wondratsch, p.t. chori regentem, conscriptus. Anno MDCCCXXX. Tom. 1.*

Contents: 1. Faksimile der Originalhandschrift; 2. Historisch-quellenkundliche Bemerkungen, Kommentar und Register.

GRANADA, SPAIN

2043. Capilla Real. Archivo. "El Archivo de música de la Capilla Real de Grenada." By José López Calo. In *Anuario Musical*, 13 (1958), p. 103–128.

A small collection of manuscripts, early printed books, and documents. Lists full contents for polyphonic sources.

GRAZ, AUSTRIA

2044. Neue Galerie. Bilder aus Beethovens Leben, aus der Beethoven Sammlung G. L. de Baranyai. Ausstellung des Landes Steiermark und der Stadt Graz. Graz: 1962. 77 p.

GREAT BRITAIN

Bibliotheca Musico-Liturgica. A descriptive handlist of the musical and Latin-liturgical mss. of the Middle Ages preserved in the libraries of Great Britain and Ireland. See no. 1709.

Penney, Barbara. Music in British libraries: a directory of resources. See no. 2965.

Schnapper, Edith B., ed. The British Union-catalogue of early music printed before the year 1801. See no. 1718.

GREENSBORO, NORTH CAROLINA

2045. University. Walter Clinton Jackson Library. Cello music collections in the Jackson Library, University of North Carolina at Greensboro. Part I: The Luigi Silva Collection. Compiled by Barbara B. Cassell and Clifton E. Karnes III. Greensboro: Walter Clinton Jackson Library, 1978. 20 p.

Photocopies of catalog cards. The library is made chiefly of 20th-century compositions and editions.

GRIMMA, GERMANY

2046. Königliche Landesschule. Bibliothek. Verzeichniss der in der Bibliothek der Königl. Landesschule zu Grimma vorhandenen Musikalien aus dem 16. und 17. Jahrhundert, von N. M. Petersen. Grimma: G. Gensel, 1861. 24 p.

The greater part of this collection is now in the Sächsische Landes-bibliothek in Dresden.

GROTTAFERRATA, ITALY

2047. Biblioteca della Badia di Grottaferrata. "La musica bizantina e i codici di melurgia della biblioteca di Grottaferrata." By D. Lorenzo Tardo Iero-monaco. In *Accademie e Biblioteche d'Italia*, 4 (1930–31), p. 355–69.

Library of the principal center of Byzantine musical studies in Italy. De-scribes 54 codices.

THE HAGUE, THE NETHERLANDS

2048. Gemeentemuseum. Catalogus van de musiekbibliotheek. Amsterdam: F. Knuf, 1969– . 2 v. (Catalogi van de muziekbibliotheek en de collectie muziekinstrumenten)

Simultaneously published by Da Capo, New York, 1969–73.

Deel I: *Historische en Theoretische Werken tot 1800*, door Marie H. Charbon.

Deel II: *Vocale Muziek van 1512 tot ca 1650*, door Marie H. Charbon.

The first two volumes in a series of catalogs projected to cover the re-sources, printed and in manuscript, of the Music Library of the Gemeen-temuseum at The Hague. These catalogs will incorporate the holdings of the Scheurleer collection. A parallel series is devoted to the musical in-struments in the Gemeentemuseum (nos. 2524–2527).

Deel II covers a cappella and accompanied works. Provides entries for new acquisitions and analyzes contents more extensively than the Scheur-leer *Catalogus* (no. 2050) and this supplements it. Index of text incipits, names and publishers.

2049. Gemeentemuseum. Nederlandsch muziekleven 1600–1800. 's-Grav-enhage: Gemeentemuseum, 6 Juni–6 September, 1936. 124 p.

Catalog of an exhibition on Dutch musical life of the 17th and 18th centuries. Includes printed books, manuscripts, musical instruments, and paintings with musical subjects. Illustrated. Introduction by D. J. Balfoort.

2050. Muziekhistorisch Museum van Dr. D. F. Scheurleer. Catalogus van de muziek-werken en de boeken oven muziek. 's-Gravenhage: M. Nijhoff, 1923–25. 3 v.

The catalog was preceded by two earlier compilations, one in two volumes, 1885–87, and one in three volumes, 1893–1910.

A classified catalog; volume 3 is a general index. Numerous facsimiles of early title pages. The Scheurleer collection is an outstanding working library of musicology as well as a repository of many rarities. It is now the property of the city of The Hague.

HALLE, GERMANY

2051. Händel-Haus. Katalog zu den Sammlungen des Händel-Hauses in Halle. Halle an der Saale: Händel-Haus, 1961– . Vol. 1– .

Teil 1: *Handschriftensammlung* (1961). Teil 2: *Bildsammlung, Porträts* (1962). Teil 3: *Bildsammlung, Städte- und Gebäudedarstellung* (1964). Teil 5: *Musikinstrumentensammlung, Besaitete Tasteninstrumente* (1966). Teil 6: *Musikinstrumentensammlung, Streich- und Zupfinstrumente* (1972). Teil 7: *Musikinstrumentensammlung, Blasinstrumente, Orgeln, Harmoniums* (1979). See no. 2528.

A growing series of catalogs concerned not only with Handel documents but with material on early 19th-century German song, iconography, and musical instruments. Numerous plates.

HAMBURG, GERMANY

2052. Gesellschaft der Freunde des vaterländischen Schul- und Erziehungswesens, Hamburg. Ausschuss für Musik. Musikalisches Schaffen und Wirken aus drei Jahrhunderten. Sein Fortleben in der Gegenwart. Ausstellung musikgeschichtlicher Drucke, Handschriften und alter Musikinstrumente. Staats- und Universitätsbibliothek. Museum für hamburgische Geschichte. Hamburg: Staats- und Universitätsbibliothek. Museum für hamburgische Geschichte, 1925. 89 p.

An exhibition catalog covering manuscripts, early printed editions, and instruments in the Hamburg City and University Library and the Museum für hamburgische Geschichte.

Contents: Aufsätze 1. *Kurzer Abriss der Musikgeschichte Hamburgs*, von Dr. Hans Schröder; 2. *Alte Musikinstrumente im Museum für hamburgische Geschichte*, von Dr. Hans Schröder.

Katalog I. T. *Musikalisches Schaffen aus drei Jahrhunderten*. Einführung von Philip Thorn. II. T. *Alte Quellen neuer Musikübung*. Einführung von Armin Ciasen.

2053. Hamburger Musikbücherei. Oper, Operette, Singspiel. Ein Katalog der Hamburger Musikbücherei, 1965. Hrsg von Annemarie Eckhoff. Hamburg: Hamburger Öffentliche Bücherhallen, 1965. 207 p.

A catalog of the theater holdings of the Hamburg Musikbücherei comprising some 3,198 volumes, 1,590 titles. Full scores and vocal scores are indicated, with publishers and plate numbers. Chiefly 19th- and 20th-century works, but with some early items. Arranged alphabetically by composer, with indexes of singspiel, of full scores, of titles.
Review by Klaus Hortschansky in *Die Musikforschung*, 22 (1969), p. 521–22.

HARBURG, GERMANY

2054. Wallerstein'sche Bibliothek. Thematischer Katalog der Musikhandschriften der Fürstlich Oettingen-Wallerstein'schen Bibliothek Schloss Harburg [von] Gertraut Haberkamp; mit einer Geschichte des Musikalienbestandes, von Volker von Volckamer. München: G. Henle, 1976. 298 p. (Kataloge bayerischer Musiksammlungen)
Review by Stephen M. Fry in *Notes*, 34 (1977), p. 89.

HEILBRONN, GERMANY

2055. Gymnasium. Bibliothek. Alter Musikschatz, geordnet und beschrieben von Edwin Mayers. Heilbronn: C. F. Schmidt, 1893. 82 p. (Mitteilungen aus der Bibliothek des Heilbronner Gymnasiums, 2)

2056. Stadtarchiv. Die Musiksammlung der Stadt Heilbronn. Katalog mit Beiträgen zur Geschichte der Sammlung und zur Quellenkunde des XVI. Jahrhunderts. Von Ulrich Siegele. Heilbronn: Stadtarchiv, 1967. 323 p. (Veröff. des Archivs der Stadt Heilbronn, 13)
Gives full bibliographical descriptions with contents of collections. *RISM* items are identified. 16 plates of early manuscripts, bindings, and editions. First-line index; index of names and subjects.

HRADEC KRÄLOVÉ (KÖNIGGRÄTZ), CZECH REPUBLIC

2057. Černý, Jaromir. Soupis hudeních rukopisů muzea v. Hraci Králové. [Catalog of music manuscripts in the Museum at Hradec Králové]. Praha: Universita Karlova, 1966. 240 p. (Miscellanea musicologica, 19)
Catalog of 56 items, chiefly manuscripts of liturgical music. Copiously indexed by form, texts indexed by language, with a bibliography of relevant literature; 16 facsimile plates.

HUNGARY

Rado, Polykarpe. Répertoire hymnologique.... See no. 1840.

2058. Pethas, Iván. "Musikbibliotheken in Ungarn." In *Fontes Artis Musicae*, 15 (May–December 1968), p. 114–18.
Describes 15 current Hungarian music libraries, with a table giving comparative statistics on their holdings and services.

IOWA CITY, IOWA

2059. University Library. An annotated catalog of rare musical items in the libraries of the University of Iowa. Additions: 1963–72. Compiled by Gordon S. Rowley, with a preface by Rita Benton. Iowa City: University of Iowa, 1973. 121 p.

A catalog of 278 items, articulating with the volume entered below. Extended annotations, descriptive and biographical. *RISM* items identified. Bibliography (p. 107–116). Index of names.

2060. University Library. An exhibit of music and materials on music, early and rare. Preface by Albert T. Luper. Iowa City: Graduate College and University Libraries, State University of Iowa, April 1953. 39 p.

An annotated exhibition catalog of materials on loan from the Library of Congress, the Newberry Library, the University of Illinois, the Sibley Music Library, and private sources. Part I: autograph scores (13 items). Part II: early music editions and manuscripts. Part III: books on music (45 items).

2061. University Library. Rare musical items in the libraries of Iowa. By Frederick K. Gable. Foreword by Albert T. Luper. Iowa City: University of Iowa, 1963. 130 p.

A carefully annotated catalog of 275 items. Part I: books on music. Part II: music scores. Index of names and of selected subjects. Selected bibliography.

For an account of the history, resources, and services of this music library, see Rita Benton, "The music library of the University of Iowa," in *Fontes Artis Musicae*, 16 (July–December 1969), p. 124–29.

ITALY

2062. Associazione dei Musicologi Italiani. Catalogo generale delle opere musicali, teoriche o pratiche, manoscritti o stampate, di autori vissuti fino ai primi decenni del XIX secolo, esistenti nelle biblioteche e negli archivi d'Italia.... Parma: Freschig, 1911–38. 14 v.

The *Associazione* catalogs are of mixed quality and completeness, but in many cases they represented the best available listings of the holdings of important Italian libraries. Their coverage is confined to music and theoretical works written or published before 1810. *RISM* should be consulted before these catalogs are approached.

2063. Associazione dei Musicologi Italiani. Catalogo generale delle opere musicali ... Vol. 1/1. Città di Parma. (Compilatori: Guido Gasperini e Nestore Pellicelli.) 1909–11. 295 p.

Reprint by Forni, Bologna, 1970.

2064. Associazione dei Musicologi Italiani. Catalogo generale delle opere musicali ... Vol. 1/2. Città di Reggio-Emilia. (Compilatori: Guido Gasperini e Nestore Pellicelli.) 1911. 24 p.

Reprint by Forni, Bologna, 1970.

2065. Associazione dei Musicologi Italiani. Catalogo generale delle opere musicali ... Vol. 2/1. Città di Bologna. (Compilatori: Alfredo Bonora e Emilio Giani.) 1910–38. 159 p.
Archivio della R. Accademia Filarmonica (p. 1–43).
Biblioteca dell'Avv. Raimondo Ambrosini (p. 47–66).
Archivio di S. Petronio (p. 71–159).

2066. Associazione dei Musicologi Italiani. Catalogo generale delle opere musicali ... Vol. 3. Città di Milano. Biblioteca Ambrosiana. (Compilatore: Gaetano Cesari.) 1910–11. 20 p. (incomplete)

2067. Associazione dei Musicologi Italiani. Catalogo generale delle opere musicali ... Vol. 4/1. Città di Firenze. Biblioteca del R. Istituto Musicale. (Compilatori: Riccardo Gandolfi, Carlo Cordara.) 1910–11. 321 p.

2068. Associazione dei Musicologi Italiani. Catalogo generale delle opere musicali ... Vol. 4/2. Città di Pistoia. Archivio capitolare della cattedrale. (Compilatore: Umberto de Laugier.) 1936–37. 106 p.

2069. Associazione dei Musicologi Italiani. Catalogo generale delle opere musicali ... Vol. 5. Città di Roma. Biblioteca della R. Accademia di S. Cecilia. (Compilatore: Otello Andolfi.) 1912–13 (incomplete).

2070. Associazione dei Musicologi Italiani. Catalogo generale delle opere musicali ... Vol. 6/1. Città di Venezia. (Compilatore: Giovanni Concina.) 1913–18. 382 p.
Reprint by Forni, Bologna, 1983.
Biblioteca Querini Stampalia (p. 1–25).
Museo Correr (p. 29–113).
Pia Casa di Ricovero (p. 117–61).
R. Biblioteca di S. Marco (compilatori: Taddeo Wiel, A. d'Este, R. Faustini) (p. 169–382).

2071. Associazione dei Musicologi Italiani. Catalogo generale delle opere musicali ... Vol. 6/2. Città di Vicenza. Biblioteca bertoliana ... ; Archivio della cattedrale. (Compilatore: Primo Zanini.) 1923. 48 p.

2072. Associazione dei Musicologi Italiani. Catalogo generale delle opere musicali ... Vol. 7. Città di Genova. R. Biblioteca Universitaria. (Schedatore: Raffaele Bresciano.) n.d. 21 p.

2073. Associazione dei Musicologi Italiani. Catalogo generale delle opere musicali ... Vol. 8. Città di Modena. R. Biblioteca Estense. (Compilatore: Pio Lodi.) 1916–24. 561 p.
Reprint by Forni, Bologna, 1967.

2074. Associazione dei Musicologi Italiani. Catalogo generale delle opere musicali ... Vol. 9. Città di Ferrara. Biblioteca Comunale. (Compilatori: Emmannuele Davia e Alessandro Lombardi.) 1917. 40 p.
Reprint by Forni, Bologna, 1978.

2075. Associazione dei Musicologi Italiani. Catalogo generale delle opere musicali ... Vol. 10/1. Città di Napoli. Archivio dell'Oratorio dei Filippini. (Compilatore: Salvatore di Giacomo.) 1918. 108 p.

2076. Associazione dei Musicologi Italiani. Catalogo generale delle opere musicali ... Vol. 10/2. Città di Napoli. Biblioteca del R. Conservatorio di S. Pietro a Majella. (Compilatori: Guido Gasperini e Franca Gallo.) 1918–34. 696 p.
Reprint by Forni, Bologna, 1988.

2077. Associazione dei Musicologi Italiani. Catalogo generale delle opere musicali ... Vol. 11. Città di Assisi. Biblioteca Comunale. (Compilatore: Francesco Pennacchi.) 1921. 45 p.

2078. Associazione dei Musicologi Italiani. Catalogo generale delle opere musicali ... Vol. 12. Città di Torino. R. Biblioteca Nazionale. (Compilatori: Attilo Cimbro e Alberto Gentili.) 1928. 38 p.
Reprint by Forni, Bologna, 1978.

2079. Associazione dei Musicologi Italiani. Catalogo generale delle opere musicali ... Vol. 13. Biblioteche e archivi della Città di Pisa. (Compilatore: Pietro Pecchiai.) 1932–35. 90 p.
Reprint by Forni, Bologna, 1979

2080. Associazione dei Musicologi Italiani. Catalogo generale delle opere musicali ... Vol 14. Città di Verona. Biblioteca della Soc. Accademica Filarmonica di Verona. Fondo musicale antico. (Compilatore: Giuseppe Turrini.) 1935–36. 54 p.
Reprint by Forni, Bologna, 1983.

2081. Rubsamen, Walter H. "Music research in Italian libraries." In *Notes*, 6 (1948–49), p. 220–33, 543–69; 8 (1950–51), p. 70–89, 513.
A narrative account of the author's experiences working in Italian libraries shortly after World War II. Contains useful inventories, partially thematic, of manuscripts of early music in Italian libraries. Many of the difficulties described in this article have long since disappeared.

2082. Sartori, Claudio. "Italian music libraries." In *Fontes Artis Musicae*, 18 (1971), p. 93–157.
An issue of *Fontes* devoted primarily to the description of Italian music libraries and their resources; preceded by an illuminating discussion, in Italian, English, and German, of the general situation.

2083. Smijers, Albert. "Vijftiende en zestiende eeuwsche muziek handschriften in Italie met werken van Nederlandsche componisten." In *Tijdschrift der Vereeniging voor Nederlandsche Muziekgeschiedenis*, 14 (1935), p. 165–81.
Describes a card file of compositions by Netherland composers of the 15th and 16th centuries in 50 manuscripts in Italian libraries. By means of collation, the author has been able to clarify numerous misattributions and

identify anonymous works in these sources. Compositions by non-Netherlands composers in the mss. are not listed.

JENA, GERMANY

2084. Universitätsbibliothek. Die geistlichen Musikhandschriften der Universitätsbibliothek Jena, von Karl Erich Roediger. Jena: Frommansche Buchhandlung Walter Biedermann, 1935. 2 v. Vol. 1: *Textband.* Vol. 2: *Notenverzeichnis.* Reprinted by Olms, Hildesheim, 1985.

Primarily a source study with inventories of 18 choirbooks containing music of the Burgundian-Netherland repertory in the University Library at Jena. Vol. 1 treats the sources and their contents, with indexes of liturgical settings, of cantus firmi, of composers. Vol. 2 is a thematic catalog of the choirbooks. Vol. 1, p. 111–14: a listing of 63 16th-century prints in the Jena library.

JERUSALEM, ISRAEL

2085. Jewish National and University Library, A. Z. Idelsohn Archives. A. Z. Idelsohn archives at the Jewish National and University Libary, Catalogue. Jerusalem: Magnes Press, Hebrew University, 1976. 134 p. (Yuval monograph series, 4)

A guide to the *Nachlass* of one of the founders of historical and ethnic studies on Jewish music.

Reviewed by Simha Arom in *Fontes Artis Musicae*, 24 (1977), p. 103.

JONKÖPING, SWEDEN

2086. Ruuth, Gustaf. Katalog över äldere musikalier i Per Brahegymnasiet i Jonköping (Catalog of the music collection in Per Brahegymnasiet, Jonköping). Stockholm: Svenskt Musikhistoriskt Archiv, 1971. 131 p. (Musik i Sverige, 2)

A collection of 18th- and 19th-century music reflecting the repertoires of local musicians.

KALININGRAD, RUSSIA (formerly KÖNIGSBERG, GERMANY)

2087. Staats- und Universitäts-Bibliothek. Bibliotheca Gottholdiana. Die musikalischen Schätze der Königlichen- und Universitäts-Bibliothek zu Königsberg in Preussen. Aus dem Nachlasse Friedrich August Gottholds. Ein Beitrag zur Geschichte und Theorie der Tonkunst, von Joseph Müller. Im Anhang: Joseph Müller-Blattau, "Die musikalischen Schätze der Staats- und Universitäts-Bibliothek zu Königsberg in Preussen." Hildesheim and New York: Georg Olms, 1971. 731 p.

Reprint of the edition originally published by Adolph Marcus, Bonn, 1870. The article by Müller-Blattau was published in the *Zeitschrift für Musikwissenschaft*, 6 (1924), p. 215–39.

An important collection of 55,000 volumes, strong in 17th-century church music, in print and in manuscript; also vocal music from the 16th to the 19th centuries. Works by various Königsberger Kapellmeistern such as Eccard, Stobaeus, Sebastini. Also numerous first editions of Beethoven, Haydn, Mozart.

KASSEL, GERMANY

2088. Deutsches Musikgeschichtliches Archiv. Katalog der Filmsammlung. Zusammengestellt und bearbeitet von Harald Heckmann [und Jurgen Kindermann]. Kassel: Bärenreiter, 1955– . Band I, Nr. 1– .
Title varies: Nr. 1, *Mitteilungen und Katalog.* . . .
A series of lists documenting the holdings of a microfilm archive of primary source materials for the study of German music history. Includes manuscripts and early printed books. For a description of this project and its catalogs, see Harald Heckmann, "Archive of German music history," in *Notes*, 16 (1958), p. 35–39.
Brief review by Stephen M. Fry in *Notes*, 32 (1976), p. 781.

2089. Landesbibliothek. Katalog der Musikalien der Landesbibliothek, Kassel. Durchgearbeitet und abgeschrieben von Wilhelm Lange. Kassel: 1920. 1 v. (various pagings)
An unpublished catalog, available on microfilm from the *Deutsches Musikgeschichtliches Archiv*, which supplements the printed catalog by Carl Israël, (no. 2088), extending the coverage to 18th- and 19th-century materials. The Lange catalog describes 438 folio volumes, 247 quartos, 53 octavos, and a supplement of 32 items.

2090. Landesbibliothek. Übersichtlicher Katalog der ständischen Landesbibliothek zu Cassel. Bearbeitet von Carl Israel. Cassel: A. Freyschmidt, 1881. 78 p.
Works from the 16th and 17th centuries, both manuscripts and printed books. Rich in German and Italian church and chamber music. An unpublished catalog by Wilhelm Lange, available in Kassel, supplements the coverage supplied by Israel's work.

KIEL, GERMANY

2091. Hortschansky, Klaus. Katalog der Kieler Musiksammlungen: die Notendrucke, Handschriften, Libretti und Bücher über Musik aus der Zeit bis 1830. Kassel: Bärenreiter, 1963. 270 p. (Kieler Schriften zur Musikwissenschaft, 14)
A catalog of the music in three libraries in Kiel: the Schleswig-Holsteinische Landesbibliothek; Bibliothek des Musikwissenschaftlichen Instituts der Universität; Universitätsbibliothek.

KNOXVILLE, TENNESSEE

2092. University of Tennessee Library. The Gottfried Galston Music Collection and the Galston-Busoni Archive. By Pauline Shaw Bayne. Knoxville: University of Tennessee Library, 1978. 297 p.
1,490 numbered items. Multiple indexes: class index, title index, index

of arrangers, editors, transcribers. Describes a collection of miniature scores, books on music, and archival materials.

KÖNIGSBERG, GERMANY
See KALININGRAD, RUSSIA.

KRAKOW, POLAND

2093. Uniwersytet Jagielloński. Bibljoteka. Ksiazki o muzyce w Bibljotece Jagielloński. Krakow: 1924–38. 3 v.
At head of the title: Jósef Reiss.

KREMSMÜNSTER, AUSTRIA

2094. Benediktiner-Stift Kremsmünster. Bibliothek. Die Lautentabulaturen des Stiftes Kremsmünster. Thematischer Katalog. Wien: Hermann Böhlau, 1965. 274 p. (Tabulae musicae austriacae, 2)
Describes and inventories a group of nine manuscripts and two early prints of lute music in the library of the Benedictine abbey at Kremsmünster.
Review by Hans Radke in *Die Musikforschung*, 21 (1968), p. 242–44.

LANCASTER, ENGLAND

2095. University of Lancaster. Library. Catalogue of the Hans Ferdinand Redlich Collection of musical books and scores, including material on the Second Viennese School. Cataloging by Graham Royds. Lancaster: University of Lancaster, 1976. 117 p.

LAŃCUT, POLAND

2096. Biblioteka Muzyczna Zamku w Lancucie. Katalog. By Krzyztof Bieganski. Kraków: Polske Wydawnictwo Muzyczne, 1968. 430 p.
A library of some 2,637 items, strong in late 18th- and early 19th-century music. Broadly classified as to vocal and instrumental music, theory and didactic works, with very specific subdivisions. Index of composers, arrangers, publishers (listed by place), ballets, and operas; first-line index of texts.

LANGENBURG, GERMANY

2097. Fürstlich Hohenlohe-Langenburg'sche Schlossbibliothek. "Fürstlich Hohenlohe-Langenburg'sche Schlossbibliothek. Katalog der Musikhandschriften." [Hrsg. von] Norbert Böker-Heil, Ursula Böker-Heil, Gertraut Haberkamp, und Helmut Rösing. In *Fontes Artis Musicae*, 25 (1978) p. 205–411.

An experimental printed form of part of the RISM A/II data base covering 249 manuscripts with thematic incipits and brief descriptions. Indexes to text incipits, to titles, to genres, to names, and to the musical incipits.

LAUSANNE, SWITZERLAND

2098. Vaud. Bibliothèque Cantonale et Universitaire. Département de la Musique. Catalogue de l'œuvre de Hans Haug par Jean-Louis Matthey et Louis-Daniel Perret. Lausanne: Bibliothèque cantonale et universitaire, 1971. 83 p. (Inventaire des fonds manuscrits, 1)

2099. Vaud. Bibliothèque Cantonale et Universitaire. Département de la Musique. Inventaire du fonds musical Adrien Bovy par Micheline Demont. Lausanne: Bibliothèque cantonale et universitaire, 1980. 63 leaves. (Inventaire des fonds manuscrits, 11)

2100. Vaud. Bibliothèque Cantonale et Universitaire. Département de la Musique. Inventaire du fonds musical Alfred Pochon par Jean-Louis Matthey. Lausanne: Bibliothèque cantonale et universitaire, 1979. 51 p. (Inventaire des fonds manuscrits, 9)

2101. Vaud. Bibliothèque Cantonale et Universitaire. Département de la Musique. Inventaire du fonds musical Auguste Sérieyx par Jean-Louis Matthey. Lausanne: Bibliothèque cantonale et universitaire, 1974. 124 p. (Inventaire des fonds manuscrits, 4)

2102. Vaud. Bibliothèque Cantonale et Universitaire. Département de la Musique. Inventaire du fonds musical Bernard Reichel par Jean-Louis Matthey. Lausanne: Bibliothèque cantonale et universitaire, 1974. 101 p. (Inventaire des fonds manuscripts, 5)

2103. Vaud. Bibliothèque Cantonale et Universitaire. Département de la Musique. Inventaire du fonds musical Carlo Hemmerling par Jean-Louis Matthey, avec la collaboration de Rose Hemmerling-Dumur. Lausanne: Bibliothèque cantonale et universitaire, 1976. 77 p. (Inventaire des fonds manuscrits, 7)

2104. Vaud. Bibliothèque Cantonale et Universitaire. Département de la Musique. Inventaire du fonds musical Émile-Robert Blanchet par Jean-Louis Matthey, avec la collaboration de Germaine Schmidt. Lausanne: Bibliothèque cantonale et universitaire, Département de la musique, 1975. 71 p. (Inventaire des fonds manuscrits 6)

2105. Vaud. Bibliothèque cantonale et universitaire. Département de la Musique. Inventaire du fonds musical Ferenc Farkas: catalogue des œuvres Jean-Louis Matthey et András Farkas; avec la collab. de Ferenc Farkas. Lausanne: Bibliothèque cantonale et universitaire, 1979. 49 p.

2106. Vaud. Bibliothèque Cantonale et Universitaire. Département de la Musique. Inventaire du fonds musical François Olivier, par Jean-Louis Matthey. Lausanne: Bibliothèque cantonale et universitaire, 1971. 69 p. (Inventaire des fonds manuscrits, 2)

2107. Vaud. Bibliothèque cantonale et universitaire. Département de la Musique. Inventaire du fonds musical George Templeton Strong, par Jean-Louis Matthey. Lausanne: Bibliothèque cantonale et universitaire, Département de la musique, 1973. 134 p. (Inventaire des fonds manuscrits, 3)

2108. Vaud. Bibliothèque cantonale et universitaire. Département de la Musique. Inventaire du fonds musical Jean Apothéloz par Jean-Louis Matthey. Lausanne: Bibliothèque cantonale et universitaire, 1977. 35 p. (Inventaire des fonds manuscrits, 8)

2109. Vaud. Bibliothèque cantonale et universitaire. Département de la Musique. Inventaire du fonds Paul Budry (1883–1949) par Marianne Perrenoud. Lausanne: Bibliothèque cantonale et universitaire, 1970. 36 leaves. (Inventaire des fonds manuscrits, 8)

LEGNICA, POLAND (formerly LIEGNITZ, GERMANY)

2110. Ritter-Akademie. "Katalog der in der Kgl. Ritter-Akademie zu Liegnitz gedruckten und handschriftlichen Musikalien nebst den hymnologischen und musikalisch-theoretischen Werken." By Robert Eitner. In *Monatshefte für Musikgeschichte*, 1 (1869), p. 25–39, 50–56, 70–76 (incomplete).

2111. Ritter-Akademie. Die Musik-Handschriften der Königl. Ritter-Akademie zu Liegnitz. Verzeichnet von Ernst Pfudel. Leipzig: Breitkopf & Härtel, 1886–89. 74 p. (Monatshefte für Musikgeschichte. Beilage. Jahrgang 18 u. 21)

LEIPZIG, GERMANY

2112. Breitkopf & Härtel. Katalog des Archivs von Breitkopf & Härtel, Leipzig, im Auftrag der Firma. Hrsg. von Wilhelm Hitzig. Leipzig: Breitkopf & Härtel, 1925–26. 2 v. in 1.
1. Musik-Autographe. 2. Briefe.
348 autograph scores from Handel to Hindemith, fully described, with a composer index. Autograph letters are limited to persons born before 1780. Separate index to letters.

2113. Musikbibliothek der Stadt Leipzig. Erst- und Frühdrucke von Robert Schumann in der Musikbibliothek Leipzig. Leipzig: 1960. 64 p. (Bibliographische Veröffentlichungen der Musikbibliothek der Stadt Leipzig)
The exhibition also included pictures, autographs, and literature on Robert Schumann.

2114. Musikbibliothek der Stadt Leipzig. Handschriften der Werke Johann Sebastian Bachs in der Musikbibliothek der Stadt Leipzig. Bearb. von Peter Krause. Leipzig: 1964. 62 p.

2115. Musikbibliothek der Stadt Leipzig. Katalog der vor 1800 gedruckten Opernlibretti der Musikbibliothek der Stadt Leipzig bearbeitet von Cornelia Krumbiegel und Peter Krause. Leipzig: Musikbibliothek der Stadt Leipzig, 1981–82. 2 v.

Catalog of an extensive collection, brought together in part from the collection of Carl Ferdinand Becker and the music library of the publishing firm Peters.

Review by Claudio Sartori in *Fontes Artis Musicae*, 30 (1983), p. 225.

2116. Musikbibliothek der Stadt Leipzig. Quellenwerke zur Händelforschung: Katalog. Hrsg. anlässlich der wissenschaftlichen Konferenz zur Händel-Ehrung der D.D.R., 11–19 April 1959, in Halle. Leipzig: 1959. 29 p.

2117. Musikbibliothek Peters. Katalog der Musikbibliothek Peters, neu bearb. von Rudolf Schwartz. Band I: Bücher und Schriften. Leipzig: C. F. Peters, 1910. 227 p.

An earlier edition by Emil Vogel (1894) included both books and music.

Classified catalog of a large reference library of music literature maintained by C. F. Peters before the first World War. All publishers represented. Many early works, although the chief strength is in 19th-century literature. Entries give place and date of publication but not publisher. Major classes: dictionaries, periodicals, music history, biographies and monographs, instruction, instruments, aesthetics, etc.

LENINGRAD, RUSSIA
See ST. PETERSBURG, RUSSIA

LEXINGTON, KENTUCKY

2118. University of Kentucky. Library. "The Alfred Cortot collection at the University of Kentucky Libraries." By Frank Traficante. In University of Kentucky Library *Library Notes*, v. 1, no. 3 (1970), p. 1–18.

An account of that portion of the Cortot collection now resident at the University of Kentucky. Well illustrated with facsimiles. An alphabetical listing of all the Cortot materials. A shorter version appears in *Notes*, 26 (1970), p. 713–17.

LIÈGE, BELGIUM

2119. Conservatoire Royal de Musique. Bibliothèque. Inventaire général des manuscrits anciens du Conservatoire royal de musique de Liège [par] Maurice Barthélemy, bibliothécaire. Liège: DUP, 1977. 128 leaves.

Lists manuscripts in the general collection, the Debroux collection, and the Terry collection. Addenda on p. 119. Index.

2120. Conservatoire Royal de Musique. Fonds Terry. Catalogue de la Bibliothèque du Conservatoire Royal de Musique de Liège. Fonds Terry: Musique dramatique. Liège: Conservatoire Royal, 1960. 75 p.

A second volume covers "Musique instrumentale." 51 p.

The Terry collection was acquired by the Liège Conservatory in 1882. The dramatic works stem chiefly from the period 1780 to 1880. Broadly classified as to full or vocal scores and by language of the libretto: French or foreign. The instrumental music is late 18th- or early 19th-century material, both printed and in manuscript.

LIEGNITZ, GERMANY
See LEGNICA, POLAND.

LILLE, FRANCE

2121. Bibliothèque de Lille. Catalogue des ouvrages sur la musique et des compositions musicales de la Bibliothèque de Lille. Lille: Imprimerie de Lefebvre-Ducrocq, 1879. 752 p.

2,721 items. The collection is particularly rich in late 18th- and early 19th-century French operas, which exist here in complete sets of performance materials. Also a large collection of symphonies, overtures, chamber music.

LINZ, AUSTRIA

2122. Bundesstaatliche Studienbibliothek. "An inventory of pre-1600 manuscripts pertaining to music, in the Bundesstaatliche Studienbibliothek (Linz, Austria)." By William Liddel Smith. In *Fontes Artis Musicae*, 27 (1980), p. 162–71.

Includes a list of liturgical documents. Based on the microfilm holdings of the Hill Monastic Microfilm Library at St. John's Abbey and University, Collegeville, Minnesota.

LISBON, PORTUGAL

2123. Biblioteca da Ajuda. Catálogo de música manuscrita ... Elaborado sob a direcção de Mariana Amelia Machado-Santos, directora da biblioteca. Lisboa: 1958–69. 9 v.

A collection of manuscripts, 5,382 items, entered alphabetically by composer and running consecutively through the first six volumes, with two appendixes in vols. 7–8 and an index in vol. 9. The collection is strong in 18th- and early 19th-century music, particularly opera.

2124. Biblioteca da Ajuda. Flores de música da Ajuda: exposição de raridades musicais manuscritas e impressas dos séculos XI a XX. Lisboa: Ministério da Educação Nacional, Biblioteca da Ajuda, 1973. 63 p.

Catalog of an exhibition of 390 rare and unusual items from the collection.

2125. Library of João IV, King of Portugal. Primeira parte do index de livraria de musica do muyto alto, e poderoso Rey Dom João o IV ... Por ordem de sua Mag. por Paulo Crasbeck. Anno 1649. (Edited by J. de Vasconcellos.) Porto: 1874–76. 525 p.

Reprinting of a catalog, compiled in 1649 by Paul Crasbeck, for the royal library in Lisbon, which was destroyed in the earthquake of 1755. The catalog, although of a collection now destroyed, remains an important bibliographical tool for the study of early Spanish and Portuguese music.

LIVERPOOL, ENGLAND

2126. Public Library. Catalogue of the music library. Liverpool: Central Public Libraries, 1954. 572 p.

Supersedes an earlier catalog of the same type, 1933.

About 45,000 entries for books and music published for the most part after 1800.

LÓDŹ, POLAND

2127. Biblioteka Uniwersytecka w Lodzi. Muzykalia. Opracowala Krystyna Biélska. Lódź: Uniwersytecka Lódzki, 1975–84. 3 v.

A catalog of the music holdings of the University Library. Vol. 1 is a catalog of scores in anthologies, collected works, and series published between 1801 and 1945. Vol. 2 is a catalog of opera scores and a discography of operas. Vol. 3 is a catalog of opera libretti; for this volume there was an additional editor, Jerzy K. Andrzejewski.

LONDON, ENGLAND

British Broadcasting Corporation. Central Music Library. See no. 1195.

2128. British Library. Beethoven and England: an account of sources in the British Museum. By Pamela J. Willetts. London: Trustees of the British Museum, 1970. 76 p. 16 plates.

Review by William Drabkin in *Notes*, 28 (1972), p. 692–94.

2129. British Library. The British Library Music Manuscript Collection; a listing and guide to [parts one through ten] of the Harvester microfilm collection; compiled by Professor Roger Bray. Brighton: Harvester Press Microform Publications, 1983–86. 4 v.

As in the other Harvester guides, there is a list of the contents of each reel in each part and a listing of the manuscripts in each part followed by a unified index of names and composers for each volume. Vol. 3 includes a separate index of works by Handel.

2130. British Library. "Early Dutch librettos and plays with music in the British Museum." By Alfred Loewenberg. In *The Journal of Documentation*, 2 (March 1947), p. 210–37.

Subsequently published as a separate pamphlet by Aslib, London, 1947. 30 p.

Catalog of 97 Dutch librettos of the 17th and 18th centuries. The list was projected as the first installment of a complete bibliography of librettos in the British Library, a project never carried out.

British Library. Four hundred years of music printing. See no. 2643.

2131. British Library. Henry Purcell, 1659–1695; George Fredric Handel, 1685–1759; catalogue of a commemorative exhibition, May–August 1959. London: Published by the Trustees, 1959. 47 p.

66 items related to Purcell, 180 to Handel. Introduction; annotations; 8 full-page plates.

2132. British Library. Mozart in the British Museum. London: Published for the Trustees, 1956. 27 p. 12 plates.

Catalog of an exhibition of 196 prints, autographs, early editions, etc. drawn from various collections in the British Museum, including the Department of Prints and Drawings, the Burney collection, and the Maps, Hirsch, and Zweig collections.

2133. British Library. Printed music before 1800, collection one of the Music Collection of the British Library, London. Series I: British printed music; Period A: Music before 1650; Part one: Individual composers; [and] Part two: Anthologies and tract volumes. Introduction by William Pidduck. General editor Roger Bray, Consultant editor Oliver Neighbour. Brighton: Harvester Press Microform Publications, 1983–86. 108 p.

As in the other Harvester guides, there is a list of the contents of each reel in each part and a listing of the manuscripts in each part followed by an index to names and composers in anthologies.

2134. British Library. Printed music in the British Museum: an account of the collections, the catalogues, and their formation, up to 1920; by Alexander Hyatt King. London: C. Bingley; Munich: K. G. Saur, 1979. 210 p.

A descriptive, historical work of particular use to those making intense use of the collections of printed music in the British Library.

Review by Rita Benton in *Fontes Artis Musicae*, 27 (1980), p. 57–58.

2135. British Library. Department of Manuscripts. Catalogue of manuscript music in the British Museum, by A. Hughes-Hughes. London: 1906–1909. 3 v.

Reprint of the first edition, London, 1964.

Vol. 1: sacred vocal music. Vol. 2: secular vocal music. Vol. 3: instrumental music, treatises, etc.

Entries are classified by genre or form, which means that the contents of the manuscripts are often separated and distributed through the three volumes. Author indexes; title, first-line index of songs.

2136. British Library. Department of Manuscripts. Handlist of music manuscripts acquired 1908–67. By Pamela J. Willetts, Assistant Keeper, Department of Manuscripts. London: Trustees of the British Museum, 1970. 112 p.

This handlist supplements the Hughes-Hughes *Catalogue of Manuscript Music* (no. 2135).

Covers Additional manuscripts, Egerton manuscripts, music manuscripts on loan to the Department of Manuscripts, and music manuscripts preserved with printed collections in the Department of Printed Books. Index of names.

Review by Gordon Dodd in *Chelys, Journal of the Viola da Gamba Society,* 2 (1970), p. 41–42; by Jack A. Westrup in *Music and Letters,* 52 (1971), p. 184–85.

2137. British Library. Department of Printed Books. Catalogue of music. Accessions. London: British Museum, 1884– . Vol. 1– .

An annual publication compiled from the printing catalog slips. It is ordinarily reserved for departmental use in the British Museum, but there are copies in the New York Public Library and the Library of Congress. Occasional volumes of special bibliographical interest, like the Paul Hirsch collection, have been given wider distribution. See nos. 2141 and 2142.

2138. British Library. Department of Printed Books. The catalogue of printed music in the British Library to 1980; [editor Laureen Baillie]. Preface to vol. 1 by Oliver W. Neighbour. London; New York: K. G. Saur, 1981–87. 62 v.

"The collection of printed music up to 1980 listed in the present catalogue forms part of the Department of Printed Books...."

Editor: vols. 21–62, Robert Balchin.

A bibliographical tool of the first rank. Estimated at more than 1 million entries.

The introductory "Guide to the arrangement of entries" is the essential tool for understanding and using the catalog. A work may appear under the name of the person or body primarily responsible for it, by name of compiler, or by title (if anonymous). There are a variety of cross-references leading the reader to the principal entry. The arrangement of headings is basically alphabetical, but there is a guide to the arrangement of entries within a heading. Because the catalog was assembled over a long period, entries vary in fullness of information and, in particular, rules for entering works in series have varied. Supersedes nos. 2137 and 2139.

2139. British Library. Department of Printed Books. Catalogue of printed music published between 1487 and 1800 now in the British Museum, by W. Barclay Squire. London: Printed by order of the Trustees, 1912. 2 v.

Reprint by Kraus, 1969.

First Supplement, 34 p., bound in. *Second Supplement,* by W. C. Smith. Cambridge University Press, 1940. 85 p.

Includes early music of all countries, but particularly rich in British sources. Early theory and some literary works on music included. Brief entries with dates, or estimated dates, of publication.

2140. British Library. Department of Printed Books. Hand-list of music published in some British and foreign periodicals between 1787 and 1848, now in the British Museum. London: Trustees of the British Museum, 1962. 80 p.

Indexes the music, chiefly songs, in 12 periodicals. 1,855 entries arranged by composer. Printed from slips prepared for entry in the British Museum catalog.

Review by Richard Schaal in *Die Musikforschung*, 17 (1964), p. 423.

2141. British Library. Department of Printed Books. Hirsch Music Library. Books in the Hirsch Library, with supplementary list of music. London: Trustees of the British Museum, 1959. 542 p. (Catalogue of printed books in the British Museum. Accessions, 3rd ser., pt. 291B)

A catalog of over 11,500 books on music, acquired by the British Museum in 1946 as part of the Paul Hirsch library. Brief entries printed from slips prepared for the British Museum catalog.

Review by Richard S. Hill in *Notes*, 17 (1960), p. 225–27.

See also no. 2479 under "Catalogs of Private Collections."

2142. British Library. Department of Printed Books. Hirsch Music Library. Music in the Hirsch Library. London: Trustees of the British Museum, 1951. 438 p. (Catalogue of printed music in the British Museum. Accessions, pt. 53)

About 9,000 entries listed in two sections: "Music printed before 1800," p. 1–112; "Music printed since 1800," p. 113 to end.

See also the "Supplementary list of music" printed in the catalog *Books in the Hirsch Library* (no. 2139).

Review by Vincent H. Duckles in *Notes*, 10 (1952), p. 281–82.

See also no. 2479 under "Catalogs of Private Collections."

2143. British Library. King's Music Library. Catalogue of an exhibition of music held in the King's Library, October 1953. London: 1953.

2144. British Library. King's Music Library. Catalogue of the King's Music Library, by William Barclay Squire and Hilda Andrews. London: Printed by order of the Trustees, 1927–29. 3 v.

Part I: *The Handel Manuscripts*, by William Barclay Squire. 143 p. 5 facsimile plates. Part II: *The Miscellaneous Manuscripts*, by Hilda Andrews. 277 p. Part III: *Printed Music and Musical Literature*, by William Barclay Squire. 383 p.

The King's Music Library, once on loan, is now part of the permanent collection of the British Museum. It is now generally referred to as the Royal Music Library.

2145. British Library. Reference Division. "The music collections of the British Library Reference Division." By Malcolm Turner and Arthur Searle. In *Notes*, 38 (1981), p. 499–549.

An historical resume of the situation with a description of the services and catalogs of the British Library, followed by descriptions of the Royal Music Library, the Hirsch Library, the general collections of printed music, music in the Department of Manuscripts, and the Music Library in the Department of Printed Books. There is a chronological survey of music manuscripts in the collections and a bibliography of works about the music holdings in the British Library. A most helpful summary.

2146. British Library. Royal Music Library. A list of manuscript and printed music available on positive microfilm. London: British Museum Photographic Service, 1968. 17 p.

A useful listing of primary source material on positive microfilm. Lengths of film strips are noted so that estimates can be made.

2147. English Folk Dance and Song Society. Cecil Sharp House. Vaughan Williams Memorial Library. The Vaughan Williams Memorial Library catalog of the English Folk Dance and Song Society; acquisitions to the library of books, pamphlets, periodicals, sheet music, and manuscripts, from its inception to 1971. London: Mansell, 1973. 769 p.

Located at Cecil Sharp House, the collection focuses primarily, but not exclusively, on folk song and dance of the British Isles. There is an author catalog, a classified subject catalog, and an index to subjects.

2148. Guildhall Library. Gresham Music Library. A catalogue of the printed books and manuscripts deposited in Guildhall Library. London: Corporation of London. Printed by authority of the Library Committee, 1965. 93 p.

A collection made up chiefly of late 18th-century materials reflecting the collecting activity of Edward Taylor, Gresham Professor from 1837 to 1883.

The section on manuscripts was prepared by Margery Anthea Baird. Index of names.

2149. Historical Music Loan Exhibition, 1885 ... A descriptive catalogue of rare manuscripts and printed books, chiefly liturgical ... by W. H. James Weale. London: B. Quaritch, 1886. 191 p.

An exhibition held at Albert Hall, London, June–October 1885.

Full bibliographical citations, with descriptive annotations, for 23 liturgical manuscripts, 73 liturgical books, 46 theoretical works, and some 56 items of early music. 14 plates.

2150. Musicians' Company. An illustrated catalogue of the music loan exhibition held ... by the Worshipful Company of Musicians at Fishmongers' Hall, June and July 1904. London: Novello, 1909. 353 p.

Includes early printed music, manuscripts, instruments, portraits, concert and theater bills, etc. Descriptive annotations; numerous plates and facsimiles.

See the article by Donald W. Krummel, "An Edwardian gentlemen's music exhibition," in *Notes*, 32 (1976), p. 711–18. The article concerns the music exhibition celebrating the 300th anniversary of the royal charter of the Worshipful Company of Musicians.

2151. Plainsong and Mediaeval Music Society. Catalogue of the Society's library. Nashdom Abbey, Burnham, Buckinghamshire.: 1928. 39 p.

A short-title catalog. 4 facsimile plates. The collection is now on deposit in the Music Library of the University of London.

2152. Royal College of Music. Catalogue of the manuscripts in the Royal College of Music, by William Barclay Squire, with additions by Rupert Erlebach.... London: 1931. 568, 216 leaves (typescript).

This catalog was never published. Typewritten copies are available in the major British libraries, and the catalog may be obtained on microfilm.

2153. Royal College of Music. Catalogue of the printed music in the library of the Royal College of Music by William Barclay Squire ... London: Printed by order of the Council..., 1909. 368 p.

This collection, rich in sources of early English music, incorporates the holdings of the Sacred Harmonic Society (no. 2156) and the library of Sir George Grove.

2154. Royal College of Music. The music collection of the Royal College of Music, London; a listing and guide to parts [one through nine] of the Harvester microfilm collection. Compiled by Roger Bray. Brighton: Harvester Press Microform Publications, 1983–85. 3 v.

As in the other Harvester guides, there is a list of the contents of each reel in each part and a listing of the manuscripts in each part followed by a unified index of names and composers for each volume.

2155. Sacred Harmonic Society. Catalogue of the library ... new edition, revised and augmented. London: Published by the Society, 1872. 399 p.

First printed in 1862, with a *Supplement* in 1882.

Classified catalog of printed music, manuscript music, and musical literature. 2,923 numbered items. General index.

2156. Westminster Abbey. Musik-Katalog der Bibliothek der Westminster-Abtei in London. Angefertigt von William Barclay Squire. Leipzig: Breitkopf & Härtel, 1903. 45 p. (Monatshefte für Musikgeschichte, Beilage. Jahrgang 35)

Broadly classified catalog, including both printed and manuscript music, sacred and secular.

LONDON (ONTARIO), CANADA

2157. University of Western Ontario. Music Library. Opera I. Being the catalogue of the collection: *Opera 1600–1750 in contemporary editions and manuscripts* now in the holdings of the Music Library of the University of Western Ontario. Don J. Neville, editor. In *Studies in Music*, 4 (1979), p. 1–487.

A collection of 220 opera editions and manuscripts sold by Richard Macnutt in 1974. Includes transcriptions of title pages, bibliographic descriptions, and historical notes.

Opera II covers 1751–1800 and comprises a reprint of Macnutt's *Music Catalogue 103* with the library's call numbers added. It appeared as the fourth issue of *Studies in Music*, 4 (1979).

LORETO, ITALY

2158. Santa Casa di Loreto. Archivio Musicale. L'Archivio musicale della Cappella Lauretana. Catalogo storico-critico. By Giovanni Tebaldini. Loreto: A cura dell'Amminstrazione di S. Casa, 1921. 198 p.

Printed music, 16th–18th centuries; manuscripts of the same period; an archive of manuscript scores by the Maestri della Cappella, anonymous works, etc. Full descriptions. Detailed history of the chapel. Index of composers.

LOS ANGELES, CALIFORNIA

University of California, Los Angeles. Music Library. See no. 1892.

2159. University of California, Los Angeles. Music Library. European folk music: a century of systematic scholarship. Catalog of the exhibition at the Music Library and the Foyer of Schoenberg Hall. Los Angeles: UCLA Music Library, 1978. 31 p.
Exhibit coordinated by Stephen M. Fry.
95 items, each copiously annotated.

2160. University of California, Los Angeles. Music Library. The George Pullen Jackson collection of southern hymnody: a bibliography by Paul Joseph Revitt. Los Angeles: UCLA Library, 1964. 26 p. (UCLA Library Occasional Papers, 13)
Review by Harry Eskew in *Anuario* of the Inter-American Institute for Musical Research, 1 (1965), p. 135.

LÜBECK, GERMANY

2161. Stadtbibliothek. Die Musikabteilung der Lübecker Stadtbibliothek in ihren älteren Beständen: Noten und Bücher aus der Zeit vom 12. bis zum Anfang des 19. Jahrhunderts, verzeichnet von Wilhelm Stahl. Lübeck: Verlag der Lübecker Stadtbibliothek, 1931. 61 p.
A classified author catalog of music literature in Lübeck. Name and subject index.

2162. Stadtbibliothek. Katalog der Musik-Sammlung aus der Stadtbibliothek zu Lübeck. Verzeichnet von Carl Stiehl. Lübeck: Druck von Gebrüder Borchers, [1893]. 59 p.

2163. Stadtbibliothek. Musik-Bücher der Lübecker Stadtbibliothek, verzeichnet von Prof. Wilhelm Stahl. Lübeck: Verlag der Lübecker Stadtbibliothek, 1927. 42 p.
Classified catalog of 19th- and 20th-century music literature.

LUCCA, ITALY

2164. Biblioteca del Seminario. Catalogo delle musiche stampate e manoscritte del fondo antico. Edited by Emilio Maggini. Milano: Istituto Editoriale Italiano, 1965. 405 p. (Bibliotheca musicae, 3)
Early printed music and manuscripts from the 16th to the early 19th centuries, with a small collection of writings on music. Contents of collec-

tions and locations of other copies listed. The collection is rich in early 17th-century prints of sacred music.

2165. Biblioteca del Seminario. "Il fondo di musiche a stampa della Biblioteca del Seminario di Lucca." By Claudio Sartori. In *Fontes Artis Musicae* (1955, no. 2), p. 134–47.

A listing, alphabetically by composer, of the early music editions in the seminary library, including, at the end of the list, five anthologies and three manuscripts.

2166. Bonaccorsi, Alfredo. "Catalogo con notizie biografiche delle musiche dei maestri lucchesi esistenti nelle biblioteche di Lucca." In *Collectanea Historiae Musicae*, 2 (1957), p. 73–95.

Sources listed from three libraries in Lucca: the Seminario Arcivescovile; the Istituto Musicale "L. Boccherini"; and the Biblioteca Governativa.

2167. Lucca all'Esposizione della Musica e del Teatro in Vienna nel 1892. Lucca: Dalla Tipografia Giusti, 1892. 50 p.

A rare exposition catalog of music from Lucca displayed at the exposition in Vienna in 1892. 37 facsimile plates, with detailed discussions, and a brief introduction on the history of music in Lucca.

2168. Paoli, Marco. I corali della biblioteca statale di Lucca. Firenze: L. S. Olschki, 1977. 143 p. (Biblioteca di bibliografia italiana, 83)

Catalog of choirbooks and other manuscripts of choral music in the city library at Lucca. Includes bibliographical references and indexes.

LUND, SWEDEN

2169. Universitetsbibliotek. Die Handschriften und Varia der Schubertiana-Sammlung Taussig in der Universitätsbibliothek Lund [von] Siegfried Mühlhauser. Wilhelmshaven: Heinrichshofen, 1981. 203 p. (Quellenkataloge zur Musikgeschichte, 17)

A richly illustrated catalog with facsimile pages of the Taussig collection of Schubertiana in Lund, Sweden. Includes bibliographical references and index.

LÜNEBURG, GERMANY

2170. Ratsbücherei. Katalog der Musikalien der Ratsbücherei Lüneburg, von Friedrich Welter. Lippstadt: Kistner & Siegel, 1950. 332 p.

Music imprints and manuscripts, theoretical and practical music to 1850, and holdings in 17th- and 18th-century instrumental music, particularly in the manuscript collections, which are listed separately. Numerous thematic incipits given.

LUZERN, SWITZERLAND

2171. Theater- und Musik-Liebhabergesellschaft. Die Haydndrucke aus dem Archiv der "Theater- und Musik-Liebhabergesellschaft zu Luzern," nebst

Materialien zum Musikleben in Luzern um 1800. Von Wilhelm Jerger. Freiburg in der Schweiz: Universitätsverlag, 1959. 45 p. (Freiburger Studien zur Musikwissenschaft, 7)

Entries for 64 early Haydn editions, with a table of concordances with the Hoboken *Thematisch-bibliographisches Werkverzeichnis* of Haydn's compositions (no. 1615).

MACERATA, ITALY

2172. Biblioteca Comunale. Studi sulla Biblioteca Comunale e sui tipografi di Macerata. Miscellanea a cura di Aldo Adversi. Casa di Risparmio della Provincia di Macerata, 1966.

P. 63–77: "La raccolta musicale ed in particolare gli spartiti autografi della Cappella del Duomo di Macerata nella Biblioteca Comunale Mozzi-Borgetti," by Lepanto de Angelis.

P. 79–122: "Catalogo del fondo musicale fino all'anno 1800 della Biblioteca Comunale di Macerata," by Antoni Garbelatto.

A small collection comprising 22 items of early printed music, 24 items of music literature, and 23 music manuscripts.

MADRID, SPAIN

2173. Ayuntamiento. Biblioteca Musical Circulante. Catálogo. Ed. ilus. Madrid: Ayuntamiento, Seccion de Cultura e Informacion, 1946. 610 p.

Apéndice 1, 1954. 213 p.

Music arranged in 16 classes, by instrument and form. Class T, "Bibliografia," contains books on music almost exclusively in Spanish. No publishers or dates given for entries. Many light and popular works. No index.

2174. Biblioteca Medinaceli. "Catalogue of the music in the Biblioteca Medinaceli, Madrid." By J. B. Trend. In *Revue Hispanique*, 71 (1927), p. 485–554.

"The Medinaceli library is notable for possessing almost the entire corpus of Spanish (Castilian) madrigals." 34 items fully described, with inventories of contents and biographical sketches of the composers. Appendix: musical settings of famous poets.

2175. Biblioteca Municipal. Catálogo de la sección de música de la Biblioteca Municipal de Madrid. By José Subirá. Tomo primero: Teatro Menor tonadillas y sainetes. Madrid: Sección de Cultura Artes Gráficas Municipales, 1965. 394 p.

A collection of Spanish popular drama. Works are identified by text incipits.

2176. Biblioteca Nacional. Catálogo músical de la Biblioteca Nacional de Madrid, por Higinio Anglés y José Subirá. Barcelona: Consejo Superior de Investigaciones Científicas, Instituto Español de Musicología, 1946–51. 3 v. (Catálogos de la música antigua conservada in España, 1–3)

Vol. 1: Manuscritos (490 p., 27 facsimile plates). Vol. 2: Impresos: Libros litúrgicos y teóricos musicales (292 p., 12 facsimile plates). Vol. 3: Impresos: Música práctica (410 p., 13 facsimile plates).

Entries for 234 manuscripts, 285 liturgical and theoretical prints, 337 music prints. Full descriptions with bibliographical references, lists of contents.

2177. Biblioteca Nacional. Esposicion de música sagrada española. Catalog de los codices, manuscritos y libros musicales expuestos por Jaime Moll-Requeta. Madrid: 1954. 41 p.

120 items. 12 facsimile plates.

2178. La Casa de Alba. La música en la Casa de Alba; estudios históricos y biográficos, por José Subirá. Madrid: [Establecimiento tipográfico "Sucesores de Rivadeneyra"], 1927. 374 p.

Not a catalog, but a mine of bibliographical information concerning the early music and books on music in the library of the Casa de Alba. Numerous early prints and manuscripts cited and described; 60 plates, chiefly facsimiles of bibliographical interest.

2179. La Casa de Alba. "La musique de chambre espagnole et française du XVIIIe siècle dans la bibliothèque du Duc d'Alba." By José Subirá. In *Revue de Musicologie*, 7 (1926), p. 78–82.

2180. Palacio Nacional. Capilla. Archivo de Música. Catálogo del Archivo de Música de la Real Capilla del Palacio, por Jose Garcia Marcellan. Madrid: Editorial del Patrimonio Nacional, [1938]. 361 p.

P. 13–142: listing of works by composer. P. 151–247: brief biographies of the composers represented. P. 249–361: classified listing of works.

MAINZ, GERMANY

2181. Gutenberg-Museum. Tausend Jahre Mainzer Musik; Katalog der Ausstellung, 1957 [Text: Adam Gottron]. Mainz: 1957. 32 p. (Kleiner Druck der Gutenberg-Gesellschaft, 63)

An illustrated exhibition catalog of 138 items related to the history of music in Mainz.

2182. Stadtbibliothek. "Zur Bibliographie der Musikdrucke des XV.–XVIII. Jahrhunderts der Mainzer Stadtbibliothek." By F. W. E. Roth. In *Monatshefte für Musikgeschichte*, 21 (1889), p. 25–33.

A catalog of 45 early music editions, including both theoretical works and practical music. Full bibliographical citations for some items; otherwise, references to citations in the catalogs of other collections.

MANCHESTER, ENGLAND

2183. Henry Watson Music Library. George Frideric Handel. The Newman Flower collection in the Henry Watson Music Library. A catalogue compiled by Arthur D. Walker, with a foreword by Winton Dean. Manchester: Manchester Public Libraries, 1972. 134 p.

2184. Henry Watson Music Library. List of glees, madrigals, part-songs, etc. in the Henry Watson Music Library. Compiled by J. A. Cartledge. New York: B. Franklin, 1970. 197 p.
Reprint of the original edition issued by the library in 1913.

MANNHEIM, GERMANY

2185. Hof- und Nationaltheater. Archiv und Bibliothek des Grossh. Hof- und Nationaltheaters in Mannheim, 1779–1839 ... von Dr. Friedrich Walter. Leipzig: S. Hirzel, 1899. 2 v.
Band I: Das Theater-Archiv ... Repertorium mit vielen Auszügen aus den Akten und Briefen, Inhalts-Ausgaben, usw.
Band II: Die Theater-Bibliothek ... Katalog der gedruckten Bücher, Manuskripte und Musikalien der älteren Periode nebst einem Repertoire der Dalbergschen Zeit.
An important collection of theater history, in which music is well represented.

MECKLENBURG-SCHWERIN
See SCHWERIN, GERMANY.

MEXICO, D.F.

2186. Spiess, Lincoln and Thomas Stanford. An introduction to certain Mexican musical archives. Detroit, Michigan: Information Coordinators, 1969. 185 p. (Detroit studies in music bibliography, 15)
Catalog of musical materials in the archives of the Metropolitan Cathedral of Mexico, the Museo de Virreinato of Tepotzotlán, the Metropolitan Cathedral of Pueblo, the Sánchez Collection in Mexico City now held by the Instituto Nacional de Bellas Artes, the Museo Bello of Puebla, the Colegio de Las Vizcainas in Mexico, D.F., the Chapultepec Castle in Mexico, D.F., Huamelula in Oaxaca, the Cathedral of Morelia in Michoacán, and parts of the Biblioteca Nacional in Mexico, D.F. Bibliography of reference works. Index of composers. A 95-p. musical supplement is appended. References to a fuller and as yet unpublished catalog of these collections.
Review by Henry Cobos in *Notes*, 27 (1971), p. 491–92.

MILAN, ITALY

Biblioteca Ambrosiana. See no. 2066.

2187. Biblioteca Nazionale Braidense. La musica nelle biblioteche milanesi. Mostra di libri e documenti, Milano, 28 maggio-8 giugno 1963.... Milano: U. Allegretto di Campi, 1963. 55 p.
An exhibition catalog compiled by Mariangela Donà.

2188. Biblioteca Nazionale Braidense. "Musiche a stampa nella Biblioteca Braidense di Milano." By Mariangela Donà. In *Fontes Artis Musicae*, 7 (1960), p. 66–69.

Although it does not have a music collection as such, the National Library at Milan has a number of important items cataloged under "music." This article describes some 30 such items.

2189. Biblioteca Trivulziana. Civica Raccolta delle Stampe. Ritratti di musicisti ed artisti di teatro conservati nella raccolta delle stampe e dei disegni. Catalogo descrittivo. By Paolo Arrigoni and Achille Bertarelli. Milano: Tipografia del "Popolo d'Italia," 1934. 454 p. 30 plates.

Catalog of the Bertarelli collection of portraits of musicians, singers, comedians, dancers, and persons connected with the theater. Separate sections for acrobats, extemporaneous poets, child prodigies, etc. Entries give full names of subjects, descriptions of pictures, biographical information. Numerous indexes: names, places, theatrical performances, etc.

2190. Cappella del Duomo. Archivio. La Cappella del Duomo di Milano. Catalogo delle musiche dell'archivio. By Claudio Sartori. Milano: A cura della Ven. Fabbrica del Duomo, 1957. 366 p.

The archive, established in 1394, contains important manuscript holdings of the 15th century and sacred vocal works to the 19th. Separate section for manuscripts and printed music. Brief entries; contents for anthologies.

2191. Conservatorio di Musica "Giuseppe Verdi." Catalogo della biblioteca ... Fondi speciali I: Musiche della Cappella di Santa Barbara in Mantova. Schede compilate da Gilda Grigolato. Prefazione di Guglielmo Barblan. Indici a cura di Agostina Zecca-Laterza. Firenze: L. S. Olschki, 1972. 527 p. (Biblioteca di bibliografia italiana, 68)

This and the following entry are part of a series of catalogs devoted to the holdings of the library of the Milan conservatory, edited under the supervision of Guglielmo Barblan.

The collection of the Cappella di Santa Barbara in Mantua has been incorporated into the collection of the Milan conservatory.

2192. Conservatorio di Musica "Giuseppe Verdi." Catalogo della biblioteca. Letteratura musicale e opere teoriche. Parte prima: Manoscritti e stampe fino al 1899. Milan: Distributed by Casa Editrice Leo S. Olschki, Florence, 1969. 151 p.

This volume lists 2,458 writings on music published before 1900. Indexes of subjects and of editors, compilers, and translators.

Review by Susan Sommer in *Notes*, 27 (1971), p. 730–31.

2193. Conservatorio di Musica "Giuseppe Verdi." Indice generale dell' Archivio Musicale Noseda; compilato dal Prof. Eugenio de' Guarinoni ... con una breve biografia del fondatore e con alcuni cenni intorno all'archivio stesso ed alla Biblioteca del R. Conservatorio di musica di Milano. Milano: E. Reggiani, 1898. 419 p.

First published in the *Anuario* of the Milan conservatory, 1889–96. 10,253 titles.

The strength of the collection is centered in late 18th- and early 19th-century music. Preceded by a brief historical introduction. Index of composers represented in autographs, and index of operas in full score.

2194. Museo Teatrale alla Scala. Catalogo del Museo teatrale alla Scala. Edito a cura del consiglio direttivo; compilato da Stefano Vittadini.... Milano: E. Bestetti, 1940. 401 p.
An illustrated catalog of the musical-theatrical collection at La Scala. Bibliography: p. 375–93.

2195. Parigi, Luigi. La musica nelle gallerie di Milano. Con 21 illustrazioni in tavole fuori testo. Milano: Perrella, 1935. 71 p.
Paintings with musical subjects in the art galleries of Milan. Descriptions of each work and its subject matter. 21 plates.

MODENA, ITALY

2196. Archivio di Stato. "Repertorio dei libri musicali di S. A. S. Francesco II d'Este nell'Archivio di Stato di Modena." By E. J. Luin. In *La Bibliofilia*, 38 (1936), p. 419–45.
A catalog compiled in the late 17th century of the holdings of the music library of Francesco II d'Este. Much of the material has been incorporated into the collection of the Biblioteca Estense in Modena. Rich in late 17th-century opera, oratorios, cantatas, etc. Both manuscripts and printed editions.

2197. Biblioteca Estense. "Bibliografia delle stampe musicali della R. Biblioteca Estense." By Vittorio Finzi. In *Rivista delle Biblioteche* (1892–95): vol. 3, p. 77–89, 107–114, 162–76; vol. 4, p. 16–28, 174–85; vol. 5, p. 48–64, 89–142.
Full descriptions of 321 works. Index.

Biblioteca Estense. See also no. 2073.

MONTECASSINO, ITALY

2198. Archivio Musicale. "L'Archivio Musicale di Montecassino." By Eduardo Dagnino. In *Casinensia*: miscellanea di studi Cassinesi publicati in occasione del XIV centenario della fondazione della Badia di Montecassino. Vol. 1 (1929), p. 273–96.
A summary account of the music holdings of the Montecassino archive, a collection of some 1,100 items, including more than 100 full scores of 18th-century operas, oratorios, etc. 4 plates illustrating rarities from the collection.

2199. Archivio Musicale. "I manoscritti musicali gregoriani dell'archivio di Montecassino." By Paolo M. Ferretti. In *Casinensia*: miscellanea di studi Cassinesi.... Vol. 1 (1929), p. 187–203.
Detailed descriptions of 11 manuscripts of Gregorian chant in the Montecassino archive. The 11th consists of a group of fragments from various sources. 2 facsimile plates.

MONTECATINI-TERME, ITALY

Biblioteca Antonio Venturi.... See no. 2298.

MONTSERRAT, SPAIN

2200. Lenaerts, Rene B. "Niederländische polyphone Musik in der Bibliothek von Montserrat." In *Festschrift Joseph Schmidt-Görg zum 60. Geburtstag*, p. 196–201. Bonn: Beethoven-Haus, 1957.
Describes six manuscripts containing Netherlands polyphony: manuscript numbers 765, 766, 769, 771, 772, 778.

MONZA, ITALY

2201. Duomo. Catalogo musicale del Duomo di Monza, per Rossana Dalmonte. Bologna: Forni, 1969. 219 p. (Bibliotheca musica Bononiensis, 6:2)

MOSCOW, RUSSIA

2202. Lenin State Library. Notnye izdaniia v. fondakh Gosudarstvennoi biblioteki SSSR imeni V. I. Lenina. Katalog. [Music editions in the collections of the Lenin State Library. Catalog.] Moscow: Gosudarstvennaia Biblioteka SSR imeni V. I. Lenin, 1976– .
Catalog of a collection of over 300,000 titles in the music collections of the Lenin Library in Moscow. Detailed entries for printed music. There are indexes in all parts. Introductions to these catalogs are in Russian. Entries are in the language of the original.
Part 1. Monuments of musical art: Publications of the 18th century from the homeland. 1979. 100 p.
Part 2. Monuments of musical art: Foreign publications of the 16th–19th centuries and individually published works for composers (including volumes on Haydn and Mozart scores). 1982–91. 5 v.
Part 3. Russian musical folklore collection, 1917–55, 1956–75. 1980–85. 2 v.
Part 4. Soviet editions for accordion, 1956–75. 1978. 4 v.
Part 5. Soviet editions for bajan, concertina, 1956–75. 1978. 4 v.
Part 6. Soviet editions for classical guitar, 1930–75. 1978.
Part 7. Soviet editions for Russian (seven-string) guitar, 1923–55, 1956–75. 1979. 159 p.
Part 8. Foreign publications of music written for the theater. 1976. Soviet editions of opera, ballet, operetta. 1978.
Part 9. Soviet editions of string music. 1982. 315 p.
Part 10. Works by Haydn. 1984. 66 p.
Part 11. Piano pedagogical repertoire, Soviet scores 1970–80. 1983.
Part 12. Scores (including string music) in the collection of V. V. Borisovskii. 1982.

2203. Publichnaia Biblioteka. Otdel Rukopisei. Sobraniia D. V. Razumovskogo i V. F. Odoevskogo. Arkhiv D. V. Razumovskogo. Opisaniia pod redaktsiei I. M. Kudriavtseva. Moskva: 1960. 261 p.

Catalog of manuscripts, 15th–19th centuries, primarily of church music in various notations. The Razumovskii collection contains 135 manuscripts, the Odoevskii, 35. Description of biographical material, papers, letters, etc. in the Razumovskii archive. Chronological index; index of names and titles.

MOUNT ATHOS, GREECE

2204. Stathēs, Grēgorios Th. Ta cheirographa vyzantinēs mousikēs. Hagion Oros: Katalogos perigraphikos tōn cheirographōn Kōdikōn vyzantinēs mousikēs tōn apokeimenon en tais vivliothēkais tōn hierōn monōn Kai sketon tou Hagiou Orous. [The Byzantine musical manuscripts of the Athos monasteries.] Athēnai: Hidryma Byzantines Mousikologias, 1975–76. 2 v.

Added title page in French: *Les manuscrits de musique byzantine.* Projected to 7 v.

Covers manuscripts in the monasteries Eisagōgē, Xeropotamou, Docheiariou, Kōnstamonitou, Xenophōntos, Panteleēmonos, Simōnos Petras, Grēgoriou, Dionysiou.

MUNICH, GERMANY

2205. Bayerische Staatsbibliothek. "Die Augsburger Bibliothek Herwart und ihre Lautentabulaturen. Ein Musikbestand der Bayerischen Staatsbibliothek aus dem 16. Jahrhundert." By Marie Louise Martinez-Göllner. In *Fontes Artis Musicae* (January–June 1969), p. 29–48.

A study focused primarily on 15 manuscripts of lute tablature acquired in 1586 by the Bavarian State Library with the purchase of the private library of Johann Heinrich Herwart of Augsburg. The article includes publication of a 16th-century catalog of printed instrumental music in the Herwart collection.

2206. Bayerische Staatsbibliothek. Carl Orff. Das Bühnenwerk. Mit einem Vorwort von Wolfgang Schadewaldt und einem chronologischen Werkverzeichnis. Ausstellung anlässlich des 75. Geburtstags, 10. Juni bis 31. Juli 1970. [Ausstellung und Katalog von Robert Münster]. München: Bayerische Staatsbibliothek, 1970. 58 p.

An exhibition on Orff's operatic works in honor of the composer's 75th birthday. Includes bibliography and index.

2207. Bayerische Staatsbibliothek. La finta giardiniera; Mozarts Münchener Aufenthalt, 1774/75: Bayerische Staatsbibliothek, 13. Januar bis 28. Februar 1975. [Text und Ausstellung, Robert Münster]. München: Bayerische Staatsbibliothek, 1975. 45 p.

Catalog of an exhibition of 119 items relating to Mozart's stay in Munich. Includes bibliography and index.

2208. Bayerische Staatsbibliothek. Katalog der Musikhandschriften; Bayerische Staatsbibliothek. München: G. Henle, 1979– . 2 v. (Kataloge bayerischer Musiksammlungen, 5)

Contents:
Bd. 2: Marie Louise Göllner. *Tabulaturen und Stimmbücher bis zur Mitte des 17. Jahrhunderts.*
Bd. 3: Bettina Wackernagel. *Collectio Musicalis Maximilianea.*

2209. Bayerische Staatsbibliothek. Die musikalischen Handschriften der K. Hof- und Staatsbibliothek in München beschrieben von Jul. Jos. Maier. Erster Theil: Die Handschriften bis zum Ende des XVII. Jahrhunderts. München, in Commission der Palm'schen Hofbuchhandlung, 1879. 176 p.
278 items, chiefly anthologies, containing about 6,380 pieces of music. One of the richest collections of 16th-century music. A notable collection of 74 choirbooks belonging to the original Bavarian court chapel. "Inhalts-Verzeichnis" of anonymous and attributed works.

2210. Bayerische Staatsbibliothek. Das Orff-Schulwerk: Ausstellung, Bayerische Staatsbibliothek, 27. Oktober 1978 bis 20. Januar 1979. [Ausstellung und Katalog, Robert Münster und Renata Wagner]. Tutzing: H. Schneider, 1978. 139 p.
An exhibition on the Orff-Schulwerk materials and method. Includes bibliography and index.

2211. Bayerische Staatsbibliothek. Volksmusik in Bayern: ausgewählte Quellen und Dokumente aus sechs Jahrhunderten. Ausstellung, München 8.5–31.7. 1985. [Ausstellung und Katalogredaktion, Robert Münster; Mitarbeit, Margot Attenkofer]. München: Ehrenwirth, 1985. 207 p.
Catalog of an exhibition on folk music in Bavaria. Includes bibliography and index.

2212. Bayerische Staatsbibliothek. Wolfgang Amadeus Mozart, Idomeneo: 1781–1981: Essays, Forschungsberichte, Katalog mit der Rede zur Eröffnung der Ausstellung von Wolfgang Hildesheimer. Ausstellung, 27. Mai bis 31. Juli 1981. Bayerische Staatsbibliothek; [Ausstellung und Katalog, Robert Münster, Mitarbeit, Margot Attenkofer]. München and Zürich: Piper, 1981. 328 p.
Catalog of an exhibition on Mozart's *Idomeneo*. Includes bibliography and index.

2213. Hofkapelle Musikhandschriftensammlungen. Die ehemaligen Musikhandschriftensammlungen der Königlichen Hofkapelle und der Kurfürstin Maria Anna in München: thematischer Katalog. By Gertraut Haberkamp and Robert Münster. München: G. Henle, 1982. 251 p. (Kataloge bayerischer Musiksammlungen, 9)

2214. St. Michaelskirche. Die Musikhandschriften der St. Michaelskirche in München: thematischer Katalog. By Hildegard Herrmann-Schneider. München: G. Henle, 1985. 392 p. (Kataloge bayerischer Musiksammlungen, 7)

2215. Städtische Musikbücherei. Kataloge der städtischen Musikbücherei München ... Erster Band: Klavier. Bearbeitet von Bibliotheksrat Dr. Willy Krienitz. München: 1931. 407 p.

Catalog of the holdings in keyboard music of one of the major public music libraries in Germany. Some 40,000 items, classified. Includes works for piano solo, duet, and two pianos. Index of names.

2216. Theatermuseum. "Die vor 1801 gedruckten Libretti des Theatermuseums München." By Richard Schaal. In *Die Musikforschung*, 10 (1957), p. 388–96, 487–94; 11 (1958), p. 54–69, 168–77, 321–36, 462–77; 12 (1959), p. 60–75, 161–77, 299–306, 454–61; 13 (1960), p. 38–46, 164–72, 299–306, 441–48; 14 (1961), p. 36–43, 166–83.

Also published separately by Bärenreiter, Kassel, 1962.

983 librettos listed alphabetically by title, with date and place of first performance, name of composer, etc.

2217. Theatinerkirche Sankt Kajetan. Die Musikhandschriften in der Theatinerkirche St. Kajetan in München, thematischer Katalog. By Siegfried Gmeinwieser. München: Henle, 1979. 208 p. (Kataloge bayerischer Musiksammlungen, 4)

2218. Universitätsbibliothek. Die Musikhandschriften der Universitätsbibliothek München. Beschrieben von Clytus Gottwald. Wiesbaden: Harrassowitz, 1968. 127 p. (Die Handschriften der Universitätsbibliothek München, 2)

MÜNSTER, GERMANY

2219. Bischöfliches Priesterseminar. Santini Bibliothek. Kirchenmusikalische Schätze der Bibliothek des Abbate Fortunato Santini, ein Beitrag zur Geschichte der katholischen Kirchenmusik in Italien. By Joseph Killing. Düsseldorf: L. Schwann, 1910. 516 p.

A study based on the material in the Santini collection, a library of early music scored from the original part books by Fortunato Santini (1778–1862) and acquired about 1856 by the University Library at Münster.

P. 455–67: "Verzeichnis der in der Bibliothek Santini enthaltenen Druckwerke." P. 469–516: "Verzeichnis von Musikwerken die in der Santinischen Bibliothek als Handschriften enthalten sind."

2220. Bischöfliches Priesterseminar. Santini Bibliothek. "Verzeichnis der italienischen Messkompositionen aus der Bibliothek des Abbate Fortunato Santini, 18. Jahrhundert," p. 45–58, in *Studien über Gebrauch der Instrumente in dem italienischen Kirchenorchester des 18. Jahrhunderts.* Ein Beitrag zur Geschichte der instrumental begleiteten Messe in Italien. (Auf Grund des Materials in der Santini-Bibliothek zu Münster i. W.). Quakenbrück: Robert Kleinert, 1929.

Lists 450 18th-century masses in the Santini library, alphabetically by composer, with descriptions of their instrumentation.

2221. Bischöfliches Priesterseminar. Santini Bibliothek. "Verzeichnis der kirchenmusikalischen Werke der Santinischen Sammlung." In *Kirchenmusikalisches Jahrbuch*, 1931–38.

Published in annual installments between 1931 and 1938.

An incomplete inventory of the sacred music in the Santini collection.

2222. Universitätsbibliothek. Die musikalischen Schätze der Santinischen Sammlung. Führer durch die Ausstellung der Universitäts-Bibliothek.... Münster: Westfälische Vereinsdruckerei, 1929. 32 p.
Exhibition catalog prepared by K. G. Fellerer.

NAPLES, ITALY

2223. Biblioteca Nazionale. I codici notati della Biblioteca Nazionale di Napoli. By Raffaele Arnese. Firenze: Leo S. Olschki, 1967. 257 p. (Biblioteca di bibliografia italiano, 47)
Concerned chiefly with liturgical manuscripts in which musical notation is present, but also including a few sources in mensural notation. Indexes of types of notation, types of script, chronological arrangement, titles, and names. Bibliography, p. 127–47.
Review by Ewald Jammers in *Die Musikforschung*, 21 (1968), p. 504–506.

2224. Biblioteca Nazionale. "Il fondo musicale cinquecentesco della Biblioteca Nazionale di Napoli." By Anna Mondolfo. In *Collectanea Historiae Musicae*, 2 (1957), p. 277–90.
Describes 51 16th-century works.

Conservatorio di Musica San Pietro a Majella. See also no. 2076.

2225. Conservatorio di Musica San Pietro a Majella. "La biblioteca del Conservatorio di Napoli." By Anna Bossarelli Mondolfi. In *Accademie e Biblioteche d'Italia*, 38 (1970), p. 286–92.
A brief narrative account stressing the important holdings of the library, particularly works related to the opera and cantata and documents of the Bellini-Donizetti period.

2226. Conservatorio di Musica San Pietro a Majella. Catalogo dei libretti d'opera in musica dei secoli XVII e XVIII, a cura di Francesco Melisi. Naples: Conservatorio di Musica "San Pietro a Majella," 1985. 295 p.
Covers about 1,500 libretti in the Conservatory.

2227. Conservatorio di Musica San Pietro a Majella. Mostra autografi musicali della scuola napoletana ... settembre–ottobre 1936. Napoli: Confederazione Fascista dei Professionisti e degli Artisti, 1936. 58 p.
An exhibition catalog of musical autographs and portraits of musicians of the Neapolitan school.

2228. Conservatorio di Musica San Pietro a Majella. "Mozart alla Biblioteca del Conservatorio di Napoli." By Francesco Bossarelli. In *Analecta Musicologica*, 5 (1968), p. 248–66; 7 (1969), p. 190–212.
A bibliography of the Mozart holdings of the Naples conservatory.

2229. Conservatorio di Musica San Pietro a Majella. Il Museo storico musicale di S. Pietro a Majella. Napoli: R. Stabilimento Tipografico Francesco Giannini e Figli, 1930. 153 p.

A collection of musicians' portraits, busts, autographs, musical instruments, medals, and photographs. 734 items. Special archives of materials related to Vincenzo Bellini and Giuseppe Martucci.

Oratorio dei Filippini. Archivio. See no. 2075.

THE NETHERLANDS

2230. Nederlands Bibliotheek- en Lektuurcentrum. Sektie Muziekbibliotheken en Fonotheken. Standaardkatalogus van boeken over muziek samengesteld in opdracht van de Sektie Muziekbibliotheken en Fonotheken. 2e, herz. dr. 's-Gravenhage: Nederlands Bibliotheek en Lektuur Centrum, 1977. 43 p.

NEW HAVEN, CONNECTICUT

2231 Yale University. Beinecke Rare Book and Manuscript Library. "Manuscript music in the James Marshall and Marie-Louise Osborn Collection." By Diane Boito. In *Notes*, 27 (1970), p. 237–44.
    Describes each musical manuscript in the Osborn Collection: 4 from the 16th and 17th centuries; 20 from the 18th century, including 2 Alessandro Scarlatti manuscripts; 14 from the 20th century, including important works by Britten, Dohnányi, Holst, Mahler, and Vaughan Williams.

2232. Yale University. Beinecke Rare Book and Manuscript Library. Music, printed and manuscript, in the James Weldon Johnson Memorial Collection of Negro Arts and Letters: an annotated catalog. By Rae Linda Brown. New York: Garland Pub., 1982. 322 p. (Garland reference library of the humanities, 277)
    A catalog of the 1,057 musical works in the collection established by Carl van Vechten.

2233. Yale University. Jackson Music Library. "The Filmer manuscripts: a handlist." By Robert Ford. In *Notes*, 40, (1978), p. 814–25.
    An inventory of 37 manuscripts of English music from the late 16th through the early 18th centuries.

2234. Yale University. Jackson Music Library. A temporary mimeographed catalog of the music manuscripts and related materials of Charles Edward Ives.... Compiled by John Kirkpatrick in 1954–60. New Haven: Yale School of Music, 1960. 279 p. (typescript)

2235. Yale University. Jackson Music Library. Horatio Parker Archives. "The Horatio Parker Archives in the Yale University Music Library." By William C. Rorick. In *Fontes Artis Musicae*, 26 (1979), p. 298–304.
    A description of the papers left by a prominent member of the "Second New England School."

NEW YORK, NEW YORK

2236. American Music Center. Library. Catalog of the American Music Center Library. New York: American Music Center, 1975–83. 4 v.

Volume 1, edited by Judith Greenberg Finnell, covers choral and vocal works and is arranged by composer and title.

Volume 2, edited by Karen McNerney Famera, covers chamber music and is classified; there is a composer index.

Volume 3, edited by Karen Famera *et al.*, covers music for orchestra, band, and large ensembles and is composed of bibliographic entries drawn from the New York Public Library's data base; the catalog is in a single alphabetical sequence with composer, title, and subject entries as well as cross-references.

Volume 4, edited by Eero Richmond, covers opera and music theater works.

The American Music Center Library collects printed and manuscript works of contemporary American composers and disseminates information about those works.

2237. American Music Center. Library. The National Endowment for the Arts: Composer/librettist program collection at the American Music Center. New York: American Music Center, 1979. 304 p.

"In the spring of 1978 a brochure was distributed by AMC under the title: *Compositions, libretto and translations; supported by the National Endowment for the Arts: Composer/librettist program.*"

2238. Bartók Archives. The Béla Bartók Archives, history and catalogue. By Victor Bator. New York: Bartók Archives Publication, 1963. 39 p.

Description of the Archives and of their founding, with summary inventories of materials in such categories as letters, books, articles, clippings, concert programs, printed music, photographs, and recordings as well as autograph manuscripts.

This collection has been virtually inaccessible because of legal complications involving its ownership. Two reports by Fritz A. Kuttner, published in *Die Musikforschung*, will help to clarify its status: "Der Katalog des Bartók-Archives in New York City," 21 (1969), p. 61–63; and "Das Bartók-Archiv in New York City, ein Nachtrag," 22 (1969), p. 75–76. Further information on access is available in entry no. 215 in the RISM Series C directory to music research libraries in the United States (no. 1853).

2239. New York Public Library. Music Division. Catalogue of Jos. W. Drexel's musical library. Part I: Musical writings. Philadelphia, Pennsylvania: King and Baird, 1869. 48 p.

This catalog contains only 1,536 of the more than 6,000 items in the Drexel collection. Especially rich in English printed music and manuscripts in the 16th, 17th, and 18th centuries. The collection contains numerous items from the library of Edward F. Rimbault, English antiquarian and collector.

2240. New York Public Library. Music Division. Dictionary catalog of the music collection, New York Public Library. 2nd ed. Boston, Massachusetts: G. K. Hall, 1982. 44 v.

First published in 1965 in 33 v. Supplemented 1973 and 1976.

Duplication by photo-offset of a catalog of the holdings of the Music Division of the New York Public Library. Books, pamphlets, and musical scores in one alphabet. The catalog includes numerous analytics for articles in Festschriften, periodicals, etc. A comprehensive reference tool based on the resources of one of the great music libraries of the United States.

Kept current by the *Bibliographic Guide to Music* (no. 745), an annual supplement published by G. K. Hall beginning in 1976. These volumes include all publications cataloged by the New York Public Library and entries from the Library of Congress MARC (Machine-readable cataloging) tapes of current cataloging.

2241. New York Public Library. Music Division. Elliott Carter: sketches and scores in manuscript; a selection of manuscripts and other pertinent material from the Americana Collection of the Music Division, the New York Public Library, on exhibition December 1973 through February 1974 in the Vincent Astor Gallery, Library & Museum of the Performing Arts, the New York Public Library at Lincoln Center. New York: New York Public Library; Astor, Lenox and Tilden Foundations, 1973. 64 p.

Includes an extensive bibliography on Elliott Carter.

2242. New York Public Library. Music Division. "The Music Division of the New York Public Library." [By Frank C. Campbell.] In *Fontes Artis Musicae* (July–December 1969), p. 112–19.

General account of the history, holdings, special indexes, and collections of one of America's richest music libraries.

2243. New York Public Library. Music Division. "Musicalia in der New York Public Library, mitgeteilt von Hugo Botstiber." In *Sammelbände der Internationalen Musikgesellschaft*, 4 (1902–1903), p. 738–50.

A summary account of some of the more interesting and important items in the Drexel collection. Gives a full inventory of the "Sambrook MS," with brief entries for other manuscripts and early printed books. Includes a listing of musicians' autographs.

2244. New York Public Library. Vincent Astor Gallery. Musical treasures in American libraries. An exhibition in the Vincent Astor Gallery. Reprinted from the *Bulletin of the New York Public Library*, vol. 72 (Spring 1968). 16 p.

33 items fully described, illustrated in 4 full-page plates.

2245. Pierpont Morgan Library. The Dannie and Hettie Heineman Collection. Compiled by Herbert Cahoon and others. New York: Pierpont Morgan Library, 1978.

A description of the entire Heineman collection, of which music manuscripts are only a part.

2246. Pierpont Morgan Library. Four centuries of opera: manuscripts and printed editions in the Pierpont Morgan Library. Compiled by J. Rigbie Turner, Tobert Kendall, and James Parsons. New York: Pierpont Morgan Library and Dover, 1983. 132 p.

"This volume illustrates the history of opera through slightly more than 50 examples, from the earliest known opera to one first performed in the last five years." All items described are from the Morgan Library's collections or from collections on deposit there. Each description is extensive and is accompanied by a facsimile of a page from the work in question. There is a selective checklist of opera manuscripts in the Morgan Library and another of printed operas and opera libretti at the Morgan.

Review by Robert Winter in *Notes*, 39 (1983), p. 851–53.

2247. Pierpont Morgan Library. The Mary Flager Cary music collection: printed books and music, manuscripts, autograph letters, documents, portraits. New York: Pierpont Morgan Library, 1970. 108 p. 49 plates.

Introduction signed by Charles Ryskamp, Director.

Collection comprises 64 printed books and 216 manuscripts as well as a large list of autograph letters and 18 items under "portraits and miscellany."

Compiled by Otto E. Albrecht (manuscripts), Herbert Cahoon (autograph letters and documents), and Douglas C. Ewing (printed books, portraits, and memorabilia).

Review by Susan T. Sommer in *Notes*, 28 (1972), p. 681–82.

2248. Pierpont Morgan Library. "Musical treasures in the Morgan Library." By Otto E. Albrecht. In *Notes*, 28 (1972), p. 643–51.

A tantalizing introduction to the music collections of the Morgan Library.

2249. Pierpont Morgan Library. Nineteenth-century autograph music manuscripts in the Pierpont Morgan Library: a checklist [by] J. Rigbie Turner. New York: Pierpont Morgan Library, 1982. 53 p. 17 facsimile plates.

First appeared as an article in *19th-century Music*, 2 (1980).

Brief descriptive entries on manuscripts dating from 1791 to 1911 given to the Morgan Library (including the Heineman Collection and the Mary Flagler Carey Collection), deposited in the Morgan Library by Robert Owen Lehman and Margaret G. Cobb, or purchased by the Morgan Library. Describes briefly the large number of autograph letters in the Morgan collection. Entries include references to sources of further information on the collections and collectors.

2250. Pierpont Morgan Library. "ROLF." By Robert O. Lehman. In *Notes*, 21 (1963), p. 83–93.

Describes the development of the Robert Owen Lehman Collection on deposit in the Morgan Library. Appended list of manuscripts no longer accurate as some have been removed from the collection and many others added.

2251. Pierpont Morgan Library. Sir Arthur Sullivan; composer and personage, by Reginald Allen in collaboration with Gale R. D'Luhy. New York: Pierpont Morgan Library, 1975. 215 p.

This volume presents the life of Sir Arthur Sullivan as seen in the archive formed first of all by his mother, and then by Sir Arthur himself. The original archive has been supplemented with dozens of autograph manuscripts and letters, printed scores, librettos, posters, drawings, prints, photographs, and memorabilia which came to the Pierpont Morgan Library before the acquisition of the papers of Sir Arthur Sullivan, and afterward, and which today form the Gilbert and Sullivan Collection in the Library. [*Introduction*]

An exhibition catalog of heroic scope. Includes items associated with Sir William Gilbert and Richard D'Oyly Carte.
Variant edition cited as no. 1663.

NUREMBERG, GERMANY
See no. 1069.

OBERLIN, OHIO

2252. Oberlin College. Conservatory of Music. Mary M. Vial Music Library. Mr. and Mrs. C. W. Best collection of autographs in the Mary M. Vial Music Library of the Oberlin College Conservatory of Music. Oberlin: Oberlin College Library, 1967. 55 p.
A collection of 110 autograph letters, signed photographs, etc., chiefly related to 19th- and early 20th-century musicians. Partial translations given for many of the documents. 10 facsimile plates.

OSTIGLIA, ITALY

2253. Biblioteca Greggiati. "Nascita, letargo e risveglio della Biblioteca Greggiati." By Claudio Sartori. In *Fontes Artis Musicae*, 24 (1977), p. 126–38.
Describes a large and rich collection of music, including much by Mantuan composers, gathered by Giuseppe Greggiati in the mid-19th century.

2254. Biblioteca Greggiati. Ostiglia, biblioteca dell'opera Pia Greggiati: catalogo del fondo musicale. A cura di Claudio Sartori. Milano: Nuovo Istituto Editoriale Italiano, 1983. 655 p. (Bibliotheca musicae, 7)
A catalog of the printed works of music and music literature gathered from the mid-18th century to the late 19th century by members of the Greggiati family. Entries arranged in alphabetical order within each section. Another volume covering the manuscripts in the collection is projected. No indexes in this volume.

OTTOBEUREN, GERMANY

2255. Benediktiner-Abtei. Die Musikhandschriften der Benediktiner-Abtei Ottobeuren: thematischer Katalog. [By] Gertraut Haberkamp. München: G. Henle, 1986. 299 p. (Kataloge bayerischer Musiksammlungen, 12)

OXFORD, ENGLAND

2256. University. Bodleian Library. "American sheet music in the Walter N. H. Harding Collection at the Bodleian Library, Oxford University." By Jean Geil. In *Notes*, 34 (1978), p. 805–813.

A description of the collection of 60,000 to 70,000 pieces of American sheet music donated to the Bodleian Library.

2257. University. Bodleian Library. The Bodleian Library Music Collection; a listing and guide to part two, part three, part four, and part five [and part six] of the Harvester Microfilm Collection. Compiled by Professor Roger Bray. Brighton: Harvester Press Microform Publications, 1984–86. 2 v.

Each volume lists the contents of the reels in each part of the collection and then lists the manuscripts in each part. There is a unified index of names and composers in each volume.

2258. University. Bodleian Library. [Catalog, in manuscript, of the music manuscripts in the Bodleian Library, with a list of books given to the University by Dr. Heather.]1 v. (unpaged)

An unpublished, handwritten catalog made in the early 19th century, available for study in the Bodleian Library. Gives contents for some 303 "Music School" manuscripts dating from the early 17th century.

2259. University. Bodleian Library. English music, guide to an exhibition held in 1955. Oxford: Bodleian Library, 1955. 40 p.

An exhibition catalog of 101 items, well annotated. 8 full-page plates. Informative introduction, unsigned. The exhibition covers English music from the 11th to the 20th century, although early music is stressed.

2260. University. Bodleian Library. Manuscripts of Byzantine chant in Oxford, by N. G. Wilson and D. I. Stefanovic. Oxford: Bodleian Library, 1963. 56 p.

An exhibition catalog. Facsimiles. Bibliography, p. 5–6.

2261. University. Bodleian Library. Medieval polyphony in the Bodleian Library, by Dom Anselm Hughes. Oxford: Bodleian Library, 1951. 63 p.

Descriptions and inventories of contents for 51 manuscripts and fragments in the Bodleian. Index of text incipits and of composers and places of origin.

Review by Manfred Bukofzer in *Journal of the American Musicological Society*, 5 (1952), p. 53–65.

2362. University. Bodleian Library. The Oxford Music School collection at the Bodleian Library, Oxford; a guide and index to the Harvester microfilm collection. With an introduction by Margaret Crum. Brighton: Harvester Press Microform Publications, 1979. 41 p.

Contains a guide to the contents of the 19 reels in the collection, an excellent introduction, and an index of composers and their works. This is a finding aid to a commercial microfilm collection and forms in effect part one of the Harvester Bodleian Library Music Collection.

2263. University. Bodleian Library. "Seventeenth-century Italian instrumental music in the Bodleian Library." By Denis Stevens. In *Acta Musicologica*, 26 (1954), p. 67–74.

The author lists some 85 sets of parts of early Italian instrumental music in the Bodleian, by composer in alphabetical order, with essential bibliographical information. In an article in *Collectanea Historiae Musicae*, 2 (1957), p. 401–412, he discusses nine unica from the above collection.

2264. University. Christ Church Library. Catalogue of music [manuscripts] in the Library of Christ Church, Oxford, by G. E. P. Arkwright. London: Oxford University Press, 1915–23.

Part I: works of ascertained authorship, 1915. 128 p. Reprint of the 1915 volume by S. R. Publishers, East Ardsley, England, 1971, with a preface by T. B. Strong. Part II:1: manuscript works of unknown authorship. Vocal. 1923. 182 p. Part II:2: [manuscripts of instrumental music of unknown authorship]. An unpublished catalog, completed in 1935, available for examination in the Christ Church College library.

2265. University. Christ Church Library. Catalogue of printed music published prior to 1801, now in the Library of Christ Church, Oxford. Edited by Aloys Hiff. London: Oxford University Press, 1919. 76 p.

A collection rich in Italian and English music of the 16th and 17th centuries. Alphabetical arrangement by composer, with analytics for collections.

2266. University. Christ Church Library. The music collection of Christ Church, Oxford; a listing and guide to [parts one through three] of the Harvester microfilm collection. Compiled by Professor Roger Bray and [the guide for part three] by Professor Tim Carter. Brighton: Harvester Press Microform Publications, 1981–82. 3 v.

As in the other Harvester guides, there is a list of the contents of each reel in each part and a listing of the manuscripts in each part.

PADUA, ITALY

2267. Basilica di San'Antonio. Archivio Musicale. L'Archivio musicale della Cappella Antoniana in Padova; illustrazione storico-critico, con cinque eliotipie. Padova: Tipografia e Libreria Antoniana, 1895. 175 p.

Compiled by Giovanni Tebaldini.

P. 1–92: Historical essay on the chapel of St. Anthony. P. 93–149: Partial catalog of manuscripts and printed editions. Complete lists of works for Vallotti, Sabbatini; thematic incipits for Tartini concertos.

2268. Biblioteca Capitolare. "Codici musici della Biblioteca Capitolare di Padova." [By Antonio Garbelotti.] In *Revista Musicale Italiana*, 53 (1951), p. 289–314; 54 (1952), p. 218–30.

A summary description of the manuscript holdings of the Biblioteca Capitolare in Padua. Sources discussed chronologically by centuries. Both plainchant and polyphonic manuscripts considered.

2269. Conservatorio "Cesare Pollini." Catalogo dei manoscritti musicali dei Conservatorio "Cesare Pollini" di Padova. Torino: Edizione di Torino, 1982. 159 p.

Nineteenth-century opera and dance music manuscripts primarily from the archives of the Teatro Nuovo, *olim* Teatro Verdi.

PARIS, FRANCE

2270. Archives Nationales. Archives du Théâtre Nationale de l'Opéra (AJ13 à 1466). Inventaire par Brigitte Labat-Poussin. Paris: Archives Nationales, 1977. 677 p.

In addition to the archives of the Opéra, the archives of the Théâtre Italien, the Opéra Comique, and the Théâtre Lyrique are described. There is an index to personnel who served in the Théâtre Nationale de l'Opéra and a general index.

Review by François Lesure in *Fontes Artis Musicae*, 25 (1978), p. 195–96.

2271. Archives Nationales. Minutier Central. Documents du Minutier Central concernant l'histoire de la musique (1600–1650). Comp. by Madelaine Jurgens. Préface de François Lesure. Paris: S.E.V.P.E.N., 1966–74. 2 v. (Ministère des Affaires Culturelles. Direction des Archives de France. Archives Nationales)

An organized presentation of documents related to musicians of the first half of the 17th century in the French national archives. Musicians are grouped according to their occupations: musicians of the court, of the city, instrument makers, music printers, etc. Tome I, general index, p. 895–1038.

Tome II presents records of contracts and depositions, giving names and monetary values. The material is arranged chronologically within social categories, as in Tome I, dealing with the Parisian cultural milieu of the first half of the 17th century. Lists instrument collections. Useful introduction of 90 p. Extensive index, p. 911–1085.

Review of Tome I by Albert Cohen in *Journal of the American Musicological Society*, 22 (1969), p. 126–29; by James R. Anthony in *Notes*, 26 (1970), p. 511–13.

Review of Tome II by Margaret Murata in *Notes*, 35 (1978), p. 310.

2272. Bibliothèque de l'Arsenal. Catalogue des livres de musique (manuscrits et imprimés) de la Bibliothèque de l'Arsenal à Paris. Par L. de La Laurencie ... et A. Gastoué. Paris: E. Droz, 1936. 184 p. (Publications de la Société française de musicologie, 2. ser., t. 7)

Manuscripts and printed music arranged alphabetically by composer, or catchword of title if anonymous, under main divisions of sacred and secular. Manuscripts from the 10th century; printed works of the 16th–18th centuries. Exceptionally rich in editions of little-known French composers of the 18th century.

2273. Bibliothèque Nationale. Claude Debussy. Paris: Bibliothèque Nationale, 1962. 73 p.

An exposition catalog of 335 items celebrating the centennial of Debussy's birth. Arranged chronologically. 8 plates.

2274. Bibliothèque Nationale. Frédéric Chopin. Exposition du centenaire. Paris: [Bibliothèque Nationale], 1949. 82 p.

234 items, 8 plates; documents arranged to parallel the chronology of the composer's life.

2275. Bibliothèque Nationale. Gabriel Fauré. Paris: [Bibliothèque Nationale], 1963. 16 p.
An exhibition catalog of 100 items, with a chronology of the composer's life and work.

2276. Bibliothèque Nationale. Introduction à la paléographie musicale byzantine; catalogue des manuscrits de musique byzantine de la Bibliothèque Nationale de Paris et des bibliothèques publiques de France. [Paris: Impressions artistiques L. M. Fortin, 1928.] 99 p. (Publications de la Société internationale de musique. Section de Paris)
Compiled by Amédée Gastoué.

2277. Bibliothèque Nationale. Jean-Philippe Rameau, 1683–1764. Paris: [Bibliothèque Nationale], 1964. 100 p.
Illustrated exhibition catalog celebrating the 200th anniversary of the death of Rameau.

2278. Bibliothèque Nationale. Mozart en France. Paris: [Bibliothèque Nationale], 1956. 76 p.
Illustrated exhibition catalog of 234 items related to Mozart's life in France. P. 67–76: a bibliography of early French editions of Mozart's music.

2279. Bibliothèque Nationale. La musique française du moyen âge à la revolution, catalogue rédigé. Par Amédée Gastoué, Abbé V. Leroquais, André Pirro, Henry Expert, Henry Prunières, et Emile Dacie. Paris: Édition des Bibliothèques Nationales de France, 1934. 196 p.
Illustrated catalog of 660 manuscripts, books, and works of art from major French public and private collections, displayed at the "Exposition de la musique française," 1933, in the Galerie Mazarine of the Bibliothèque Nationale.

2280. Bibliothèque Nationale. Collection Toulouse-Philidor. "La collection musicale Toulouse-Philidor à la Bibliothèque nationale." By Catherine Massip. In *Fontes Artis Musicae*, 30 (1983), p. 184–207.
Following the sale of the bulk of the collection by St. Michael's College, Tenbury, in 1978, this article provides an inventory of the collection and a concordance to earlier catalogs.

2281. Bibliothèque Nationale. Département de la Musique. Lettres autographes conservées au Département de la Musique: catalogue sommaire par Antoine Bloch-Michel. Paris: Bibliothèque Nationale, 1984. 404 p.
A summary description of the collection of 30,000 letters by and to musicians in the Département de la Musique. The majority of these letters came from the collection in the Bibliothèque du Conservatoire. In alphabetical order by author, showing name of addressee and date(s). Other documents are listed as well in a separate section under author. There is a supplement of letters entered between 1978 and 1981. Index of addressees.

2282. Bibliothèque Nationale. Département des Imprimés. Catalogue du fonds de musique ancienne de la Bibliothèque Nationale. [By Jules Ecorcheville.] Paris: 1910–14. 8 v.

Reprint by Da Capo Press, New York, 1972.

Manuscripts, printed music, and theoretical and literary works on music not included in the general catalog of the library, to 1750. Partially thematic. Arranged alphabetically by composer, with collections analyzed. Brief bibliographical descriptions.

2283. Bibliothèque Sainte-Geneviève. Catalogue du fonds musical de la Bibliothèque Sainte-Geneviève de Paris. Manuscrits et imprimés. Par Madeleine Garros and Simone Wallon. Kassel: Internationale Vereinigung der Musikbibliotheken; Internationale Gesellschaft für Musikwissenschaft, 1967. 156 p. (Catalogus musicus, 4)

2284. Bibljoteka Polska. Frédéric Chopin, George Sand et leurs amis. Exposition à la Bibliothèque Polonaise. Paris: 1937. 63 p.

An exposition of 638 items related to Chopin, George Sand, and their circle. Includes manuscripts, letters, portraits. Illustrated.

2285. Catalogue de la musique imprimée avant 1800 conservée dans les Bibliothèques Publique de Paris. Edited by François Lesure. Paris: Bibliothèque Nationale, 1981. 708 p.

The majority of works catalogued in this source are contained in the Département de la Musique (established in 1942) and in the collections of the Bibliothèques du Conservatoire brought into the Bibliothèque Nationale in 1964.

A catalog by composer generally showing genre or performing forces, imprint, and location, including shelf marks. Unattributed works appear in a separate listing by title at the end of the catalog. RISM numbers, when appropriate, are supplied. First lines are provided for vocal works. When known, bibliographic announcements in contemporaneous French publications are cited.

2286. Conservatoire National de Musique et de Déclamation. Catalogue bibliographique. Par J. B. Weckerlin, bibliothécaire. Paris: Firmin-Didot et Cie, 1885. 512 p.

Covers the period to about 1800. Includes only part of the early materials in the collection. Following a prefatory history of the library, three sections are given: early treatises, vocal music, and early instrumental music of the French school.

2287. Conservatoire National de Musique et de Déclamation. Fonds Blancheton. Inventaire critique du Fonds Blancheton. Paris: E. Droz, 1930–31. 2 v. (Publications de la Société française de musicologie, 2 ser., 2:1–2)

Compiled by Lionel de La Laurencie.

The Blancheton collection consists of 27 volumes containing some 330 instrumental compositions by 104 composers. It was assembled before 1750. Important source materials for the history of the symphony. Full descriptions, with critical and biographical notes, on the composers.

2288. Opéra. Bibliothèque, Archives et Musée. Bibliothèque musicale du Thé-âtre de l'Opéra. Catalogue historique, chronologique, anecdotique.... Ré-digé par Théodore De Lajarte. Paris: Librairie des Bibliophiles, 1878. 2 v. Reprint by Olms, Hildesheim, 1969.

A descriptive list of 594 stage works arranged in order of their first pro-duction at the Paris Opera, 1671–1876. Classified by periods. Each period is included with a biographical section which lists composers and librettists alphabetically. Composer and title index to works in the repertoire.

PARMA, ITALY

Città di Parma. See no. 2063.

2289. Conservatorio di Musica "Arrigo Boito." "Biblioteche musicali in Italia: La Biblioteca del Conservatorio di Parma e un fondo di edizioni dei sec. XVI e XVII non comprese nel catalogo a stampa." [By Riccardo Allorto.] In *Fontes Artis Musicae*, 2 (1955), p. 147–51.

Describes a collection of 31 sets of 16th- and 17th-century part books acquired by the library in 1925.

2290. Conservatorio di Musica "Arrigo Boito." "Osservazioni sulla Biblioteca Musicale di Parma." [By Mario Medici.] In *Avrea Parma*, 48 (May–August 1964), p. 3–49.

Provides copious data on the library of the Conservatorio. Many of the rare manuscripts and printed books are cited in full, along with an account of the history of the institution and its administrative structure.

PHILADELPHIA, PENNSYLVANIA

2291. Curtis Institute of Music. Catalogue of the Burrell Collection of Wagner documents, letters, and bibliographical material. London: Nonpareil Press, 1929. 99 p.

Dispersed by sale at an auction in the late 1970s. See no. 2471.

2292. Free Library. Drinker Library of Choral Music. Catalog. [By Henry R. Drinker.] Philadelphia: 1957. 116 p.

First published in 1947 by the Association of American Choruses, Princeton, New Jersey, with a *Supplement*, July 1948.

Catalog of a lending library of choral materials, made available to mem-bers of the Association of American Choruses.

Free Library. Edwin A. Fleisher Collection of Orchestral Music. See no. 1331.

2293. Library Company. American song sheets, slip ballads and poetical broadsides, 1850–1970; a catalogue of the collection of the Library Com-pany of Philadelphia. By Edwin Wolf 2nd. Philadelphia: Library Company of Philadelphia, 1963. 205 p.

A listing, alphabetical by title, of 2,722 American song sheets, ballads, and broadsides, with information as to author, composer, format, cover design, etc. Separate listing of 194 Confederate songs. Index of printers and publishers, of authors and composers, of singers. Reproduction of pictorial covers.

2294. The Musical Fund Society. Catalog of orchestral and choral compositions published and in manuscript between 1790 and 1840 from the library of the Musical Fund Society of Philadelphia. Philadelphia: Musical Fund Society, 1974. 81 p.

Listing of 299 scores now in the custody of the Music Department of the Free Library of Philadelphia.

PIACENZA, ITALY

2295. Archivio del Duomo. "L'Archivio del Duomo di Piacenza e il Liber XIII di Costanzo Antegnati." [By Claudio Sartori.] In *Fontes Artis Musicae*, 4 (1957), p. 28–37.

Description of the collection and catalog of its early printed music. Special attention given to a unique copy of the *Liber XIII*, a collection of sacred and secular vocal music by C. Antegnati.

2296. Archivio del Duomo. Catalogo del fondo musicale a cura di Francesco Bussi. Milano: Istituto editoriale italiano, 1967. 209 p.

A catalog in four parts: (1) printed music, chiefly of the 16th and 17th centuries; (2) music manuscripts, including anthologies; (3) manuscript and printed liturgical books; and (4) a small collection of books on music. Index of names.

PIRNA, GERMANY

2297. Hoffmann-Erbrecht, Lothar. "Die Chorbücher der Stadtkirche zu Pirna." In *Acta Musicologica*, 27 (1955), p. 121–37.

Detailed description of eight choirbooks of polyphonic music of the mid-16th century. Partially thematic; summary inventories; 2 facsimile plates. These manuscripts are now in the Sächsische Landesbibliothek in Dresden.

PISA, ITALY

Biblioteche e Archivi.... See no. 2079.

PISTOIA, ITALY

Archivio Capitolare della Cattedrale. See no. 2068.

2298. Biblioteca Antonio Venturi. "La collection Antonio Venturi, Montecatini-Terme (Pistoia), Italie." [By Raymond Meylan.] In *Fontes Artis Musicae*, 5 (1958), p. 21–44.

A private collection of late 18th-century vocal and instrumental music.

PITTSBURGH, PENNSYLVANIA

2299. Finney, Theodore M. A union catalogue of music and books on music printed before 1801 in Pittsburgh libraries. 2nd ed. Pittsburgh: University of Pittsburgh, 1963. 106 leaves (typescript).
First published in 1959. Second edition supplement, 1964. 42 leaves.
Lists the holdings in early music in four Pittsburgh-area libraries: the Carnegie Library, the University of Pittsburgh library, St. Vincent's College library, and the private library of the compiler. There is a strong emphasis on early English music.
Review by Donald W. Krummel in *Notes*, 21 (1963–64), p. 129–31.

2300. University. Music Library. "A group of English manuscript volumes at the University of Pittsburgh." By Theodore M. Finney. In *Essays in Musicology in Honor of Dragan Plamenac on His 70th Birthday*, p. 21–48. Pittsburgh: University of Pittsburgh Press, 1969.
Describes the contents of a collection of 12 17th- and 18th-century manuscripts of English provenance, formerly privately owned but now owned by the Music Library of the University of Pittsburgh. The study incorporates two indexes, one of composers and the other of initial words and titles.

PLASENCIA, SPAIN

2301. Catedral. Archivo. "El Archivo de musica en la catedral de Plasencia." By Samuel Rubio. In *Anuario Musical*, 5 (1950), p. 147–68.
A small collection of early manuscripts and printed music, fully described and contents listed.

POLAND

2302. Music libraries of the Polish People's Republic. "Traditions and achievements of music libraries and library science in the Polish People's Republic." By Maria Prokopowicz. In *Fontes Artis Musicae*, 26 (1979), p. 36–43.
A brief resume of activities in Poland since the Second World War, including a bibliography of pertinent articles on libraries, catalogs of collections, works on music publishing and printing, and works on music bibliography and librarianship.

2303. Musicalia vetera: katalog tematyczny rekopismiennych zabytkow dawnej muzyki w Polsce redakcja Zygmunt M. Szweykowski; thematic catalogue of early musical manuscripts in Poland. Warsaw: Polskie Wydawnictwo Muzyczne, 1969– .

> The edition will consist of a number of volumes constituting thematic catalogues of individual early manuscripts or their groups.... The first volumes will be devoted to the collections copied for use at Wawel, the following to the collections from Sandomierz and Lowicz regions and from the surroundings of Cracow. [Editor's *Introduction*]

T. 1, zesz. 6. *Zbiory muzyczne proweniencji wawelskiej.* [Collections of music copied for use at Wawel.] Edited by Elzbieta Gluszcz-Zwolińska. 1969.

T. 2, zesz. 1. *Zbiory muzyczne proweniencji podkrakowskiej.* [Collections of music from the surroundings of Cracow.] Edited by Zofia Surowiak. 1972.

See also WARSAW, POLAND. **Biblioteka Narodowa.** No. 2433.

See also Dragan Plamenac's article in *Notes*, 19 (1962), no. 1989.

PORTUGAL

For information about Portuguese music libraries, see no. 1853.

PRAGUE, CZECH REPUBLIC

2304. Cathedral. Catalogus collectionis operum artis musicae quae in bibliotheca capituli metropolitani pragensis asservantur. Composuit DR. Antonius Podlaha. Prague: Metropolitan Capitulary of Prague, 1926. 87 p.

2305. National Museum. Hudební sbírka Emiliána Troldy (The music library of Emilián Trolda). By Alexander Buchner. Prague: Národní Museum, 1954. 132 p.
Thematic catalog of the Trolda music collection deposited in the Music Department of the National Museum. The collection contains music c. 1550–1820 scored by Trolda from numerous archives, native and foreign.

2306. University Library. Catalogus codicum notis musicis instructorum qui in bibliotheca publica rei publicae bohemiae socialisticae—in Bibliotheca Universitatis Pragensis servantur. (Catalog of Latin musical manuscripts in the state Library of the CSSR.) Prague: University Library, 1971. 830 p. in 2 v.
Edited by Václav Plocek.

PUEBLA, MEXICO

2307. Catedral. "Sixteenth- through eighteenth-century resources in Mexico: part III." By Robert M. Stevenson. In *Fontes Artis Musicae*, 25 (1978), p. 156–87.
A continuation of Stevenson's earlier articles on sources in Mexico (no. 1804).
A catalog of 130 sources, arranged by composer.

PULLMAN, WASHINGTON

2308. Washington State University. Rosbaud Library. "The Hans Rosbaud Library at Washington State University, Pullman, Washington, U.S.A." By Joan Evans. In *Notes*, 41 (1985), p. 26–40.
A description of an extensive collection of correspondence between

Rosbaud, a conductor who championed the cause of new music, and composers, performers, conductors, and other persons significant in the history of 20th-century music.

QUÉBEC, CANADA

2309. Hôtel-Dieu and the Ursuline Convent. "The motet in New France: some 17th- and 18th-century manuscripts in Quebec." By Erich Schwandt. In *Fontes Artis Musicae*, 28 (1981), p. 194–219.

Presents thematic entries for 128 pieces found in 6 manuscript anthologies in the two convents. Index to titles.

REGENSBURG, GERMANY

2310. Fürst Thurn und Taxis Hofbibliothek. Die Musikhandschriften der Fürst Thurn und Taxis Hofbibliothek Regensburg: thematischer Katalog. [Von] Gertraut Haberkamp; mit einer Geschichte des Musikalienbestandes von Hugo Angerer. München: Henle, 1981. 500 p. (Kataloge bayerischer Musiksammlungen, 6)

2311. Fürst Thurn und Taxis Hofbibliothek. "Verzeichnis der vollständigen Opern, Melodramen und Ballette, wie auch der Operntextbücher der Fürstlich Thurn und Taxisschen Hofbibliothek, Regensburg." By Dr. Sigfrid Färber. In *Verhandlungen des Historischen Vereins von Oberpfalz und Regensburg*, 86 (1936). 30 p.

Part of the author's inaugural dissertation, Munich, issued under title: *Das Regensburger Fürstlich Thurn und Taxissche Hoftheater und seine Oper, 1760–1786* (Regensburg, 1936).

"Opern, Melodramen und Ballette aus dem 18. Jahrhundert" (from the Vorbemerkung).

REGGIO-EMILIA, ITALY

Città di Reggio-Emilia. See no. 2064.

RIO DE JANEIRO, BRAZIL

2312. Biblioteca Nacional. "Estudio Brasilenos I. Manuscritos musicales en la Biblioteca Nacional de Rio de Janeiro." By Francesco Curt Lange. In *Revista de Estudios Musicales*, 1 (April 1950), p. 98–194.

Chiefly 19th-century composers. A: works by European composers. B: works by Brazilian composers or Europeans active in Brazil.

2313. Biblioteca Nacional. Música no Rio de Janeiro imperial 1822–1870. Rio de Janeiro: Biblioteca Nacional, 1962. 100 p.

At head of title: "Exposiçio comemorativa do primeiro decénio da seçao de música e arquivo sonore."

391 items, chiefly Brazilian imprints of the period.

2314. Biblioteca Nacional. Rio musical; crônica de uma cidade. Rio de Janeiro: Biblioteca Nacional, 1965. 51 p.
At head of title: "Exposiçao comemorativa do IV centenário da cidade
do Rio de Janeiro."

RIVER FOREST, ILLINOIS

2315. Concordia Teachers College. Klinck Memorial Library. Hymnals and cho-
rale books of the Klinck Memorial Library, compiled by Carl Schalk. River
Forest: Concordia Teachers College, 1975. 89 p.
A catalog of the holdings of the Concordia Teachers College Library.

RÖ, SWEDEN

**2316. "The Silverstolpe music collection in Rö, Uppland, Sweden: a preliminary
catalogue."** By Bertil van Boer, Jr. and Leif Jonsson. In *Fontes Artis Musicae*, 29 (1982), p. 93–103.
Introducing an extensive collection of 19th-century music in manuscript
and printed editions gathered by a family of Swedish nobility and diplo-
mats.

ROME, ITALY

For catalogs of music collections in the Vatican, see under VATICAN CITY.

2317. Accademia di Santa Cecilia. Biblioteca. "Cantata and aria manuscripts
in the Santa Cecilia Library." By John Glenn Paton. In *Notes*, 36 (1980),
p. 563–74.
An inventory of 36 manuscripts of the 17th and 18th centuries. Not indexed, but analyzed. Cites modern editions.

2318. Basilica of Santa Maria in Trastevere. "Music in the archives of the Basilica of Santa Maria in Trastevere." By Beekman C. Cannon. In *Acta Musicologica*, 41 (1969), p. 199–212.
Description and inventory of the music in one of the most renowned
Roman churches. Most of the material comes from the latter half of the
17th century. The collection is rich in music by Angelo Berardi, who became Maestro di Cappella in 1693.

2319. Biblioteca Casanatense. "Cantata manuscripts in the Casanatense Library." By John Glenn Paton. In *Notes*, 40, (1988), p. 826–35.
An analyzed inventory of 32 manuscripts each consisting mostly of Italian cantatas of the 17th century.

2320. Biblioteca Corsiniana. Biblioteca corsiniana e dell'Accademia Nazionale dei Lincei; catalogo dei fondi musicali Chiti e Corsiniano. Ed. Argia
Bertini. Milano: Istituto editoriale italiano, 1964. 109 p. (Bibliotheca musicae, 2)

Catalog covering printed music, theoretical works, and manuscripts. 17th- and early 18th-century vocal and instrumental music.

2321. Biblioteca Corsiniana. "La collezione Corsini di antichi codici musicali e Girolamo Chiti." By Vito Reali. In *Rivista Musicale Italiana*, 25 (1918–20).
Describes the founding of the Corsini library and the role played by the early 18th-century church musician Girolamo Chiti, friend of Padre Martini.

Biblioteca della R. Accademia di Santa Cecilia. See no. 2069.

2322. Biblioteca Doria Pamphilj. "L'Archivio musicale Doria Pamphilj: saggio sulla cultura aristocratica a Roma fra il 16o e 19o secolo." By Claudio Annibaldi. In *Studi Musicali*, 11 (1982), p. 91–120.
Discusses the origin and organization of the archive. Cites and describes the catalogs of manuscripts and printed materials, the subject catalog, and the author catalog.

2323. Biblioteca Doria-Pamphilj. "Die Musiksammlung der Fürsten Doria-Pamphilj in Rom." By Andreas Holschneider. In *Archiv für Musikwissenschaft*, 18 (1961), p. 248–64.
Description of the collection and inventory of its contents, classified under five main headings: (1) collections, 16th and 17th centuries; (2) sacred music; (3) oratorios (early manuscripts); (4) operas, early manuscripts; (5) German instrumental music, chiefly 18th century.

2324. Biblioteca Doria-Pamphilj. "Die Sinfonien-Manuskripte der Bibliothek Doria-Pamphilj in Rom." By Friedrich Lippmann. In *Analecta Musicologica*, 5 (1968), p. 201–47.
Thematic catalog of some 119 symphonies by 36 composers. Many of the works are not known from other sources.

2325. Biblioteca Doria-Pamphilj. "Die Streichquartettmanuskripte der Bibliothek Doria-Pamphilj in Rom." By Friedrich Lippmann with Ludwig Finscher. In *Analecta Musicologica*, 7 (1969), p. 120–44.
Thematic catalog of the string quartet repertory in the library.

2326. Biblioteca Doria-Pamphilj. "Die Streichtriomanuskripte der Bibliothek Doria-Pamphilj in Rom." By Friedrich Lippmann with Hubert Unverricht. In *Analecta Musicologica*, 9 (1970), p. 299–335.
Thematic catalog of string trios in the Doria-Pamphilj collection.

2327. Congregazione dell'Oratorio di Roma. Inventario del fondo musicale dell'Oratorio. A cura di Argia Bertini. Roma: 1968–71. 4 fascicles.

2328. Deutsches Historische Institut in Rom. "Die Musikgeschichtliche Abteilung des Deutschen Historischen Instituts in Rom." By Karl Gustav Fellerer. In *Die Musikforschung*, 20 (1967), p. 410–13.

Brief description of the leading musicological reference library in Italy, calling attention to its major areas of interest, special files, and indexes.

2329. Kast, Paul. "Römische Handschriften." In *MGG*, 11 (1963), cols. 750–61.
A narrative account citing and describing the principal manuscripts, chiefly polyphonic, in Rome. Much attention given to sources in the Vatican Library. Bibliography of writings on Roman libraries and their manuscript sources.

2330. San Pantaleo, Archivio dei Padri Scolopi. Fondo musicale: (manoscritti, stampe, copie fotostatiche e dattiloscritte). Ed. by Argia Bertini. Roma: Archivio dei padri Scolopi a San Pantaleo, [1981?].

ROME, ITALY

Vatican Library. See under VATICAN CITY, ROME.

ST. PETERSBURG, RUSSIA

2331. Golubovskii, I. V. Muzykal'nyi Leningrad. Leningrad: Gosudarstvennoe Muzykalnoe Izdatel'stvo, 1958. 526 p.
"Biblioteki i muzei," p. 351–411.
Describes in general terms the musical content of 14 libraries, 2 record libraries, and 12 museums. Lists manuscripts of Russian composers and mentions a few examples of Western manuscripts and early books in various collections. Details as to organization, cataloging, circulation, etc.

SALAMANCA, SPAIN

2332. Catedral. Archivo de Música. Catálogo archivo de música de la catedral de Salamanca. Por Dámaso García Fraile. Cuenca: Instituto Música Religiosa de la Diputación Provincial, D.L. 1981. 626 p. (Instituto de Música Religiosa. Ediciones)
This is a collection of sacred music in manuscript gathered during the course of events in one of the great cathedrals in Spain. It is rich in manuscripts of music from the 13th to the 18th centuries, particularly in the latter part of that period. There are 10 manuscripts of early polyphony. Entries give titles or first lines, description of the source, dates of copying, key (if relevant), shelf marks, composer (in known), and thematic incipit. Works are arranged by composer after anonymous works and anthologies. There are many indexes: first lines; by composer and then title under composer; works with various instrumental accompaniments; authors showing numbers of works in the catalog.

SALT LAKE CITY, UTAH

2333. University of Utah. Library. A catalogue of books and music acquired from the library of Hugo Leichtentritt. Edited by Carol E. Selby. Salt

Lake City: Univ. of Utah, 1954. 106 p. (Bulletin of the University of Utah, 45:10)

A scholar's working library of music books and scores; a few early editions, but centered in the 19th and 20th centuries. The catalog is divided in two sections: books (p. 9–46) and music (p. 49–106).

SALZBURG, AUSTRIA

2334. Mozart-Museum. Katalog des Mozart-Museums im Geburts- und Wohnzimmer Mozarts zu Salzburg ... 4. Aufl. Salzburg: Im Selbstverlage der obengenannten Stiftung, 1906. 62 p.

Describes a collection of Mozart memorabilia maintained in the composer's birthplace. The collection includes portraits, medals, letters, and music.

2335. Museum Carolino Augusteum. Die Musikaliensammlung im Salzburger Museum Carolino Augusteum. By Josef Gassner. Salzburg: 1962. 247 p.

Originally published in the Museum's *Jahresschrift*, 1961. Salzburg, 1962, p. 119–325.

The collection, founded in 1834, is rich in 19th-century editions. Manuscripts and printed music interfiled. Full bibliographical citations, with publishers' plate numbers given. Facsimile plates.

2336. Die Musikaliensammlung der Erzabtei St. Peter in Salzburg. Katalog. Erster Teil. Leopold und Wolfgang Amadeus Mozart, Joseph und Michael Haydn. Mit einer Einführung in die Geschichte der Sammlung vorgelegt von Manfred Hermann Schmid. Salzburg: 1970. 300 p. (Schriftenreihe der Internationalen Stiftung Mozarteum, Band 3/4. Zugleich Band I der Publikationen des Instituts für Musikwissenschaft der Universität Salzburg)

Review by Susan T. Sommer in *Notes*, 29 (1972), p. 258.

SAN FRANCISCO, CALIFORNIA

2337. San Francisco State University. Frank V. De Bellis Collection. The Frank V. De Bellis Collection: San Francisco State University (RISM siglum, US-SFsc), bound music manuscript miscellanies, preliminary survey of contents with index of names. San Francisco State University, 1975. 92 leaves.

Typescript (photocopy), "Introductory note" signed by James L. Jackman.

2338. San Francisco State University. Frank V. De Bellis Collection. Orchestra scores and parts in the Frank V. De Bellis Collection of the California State Colleges. San Francisco State College, 1964. 24 unnumbered leaves (typescript).

A preliminary catalog of the orchestral portion of the De Bellis collection, a collection devoted exclusively to Italian music. Entries listed alphabetically by composer, with early and modern editions interfiled. Parts specified.

SAN MARINO, CALIFORNIA

2339. Henry E. Huntington Library and Art Gallery. Catalogue of music in the Huntington Library printed before 1801. Compiled by E. N. Backus. San Marino, Calif.: Henry E. Huntington Library, 1949. 773 p.

"Music publications and publications without music notation but of distinct interest to musicians and musicologists...." Excluded are manuscripts, song texts, opera librettos. Includes music published in periodicals. Entry is under composer, with anonymous works under title. Index to composers and editors, chronological index, first-line index of songs. The collection is strong in 17th- and 18th-century English music.

Review by Cyrus L. Day in *Notes*, 6 (1949), p. 609–610; by Harold Spivacke in *Musical Quarterly*, 35 (1949), p. 640–42.

SANTIAGO, CHILE

2340. Catedral. Archivo de Música. Catalogo del Archivo musical de la Catedral de Santiago de Chile [por] Samuel Claro. Santiago de Chile: Editorial del Instituto de Extensión Musical, Universidad de Chile, 1974. 67 p.

SANTIAGO, CUBA

2341. Hernandez Balaguer, Pablo. Catalogo de musica de los archivos de la catedral de Santiago de Cuba y del Museo Bacardi. La Habana: Biblioteca Nacional "Jose Marti," 1961. 59 p.

Catalog of works by Cuban composers in the archives of the cathedral at Santiago and in the Bacardi Museum in the same city.

SANTIAGO, SPAIN

2342. Catedral. Archivo. Catalogo musical del Archivo de Santa Iglesia Catedral de Santiago, edited by José López-Calo. Cuenca: Ediciones del Instituto de Música Religiosa, 1972. 386 p. (Instituto de música religiosa, Publicaciones, 8)

Catalog of 2,292 items from one of the richest musical traditions of Spanish cathedrals. Arranged by century and then by composer. Appendix of documents. Index and bibliography.

SCHOTTEN, GERMANY

2343. Liebfrauenkirche. Thematischer Katalog der kirchlichen Musikhandschriften in der Liebfrauenkirche zu Schotten; von Joachim Schlichte; mit einer Geschichte der Kirchenmusik und ihren Notenbeständen von Peter Albrecht. Tutzing: H. Schneider, 1985. 375 p. (Frankfurter Beiträge zur Musikwissenschaft, 19)

SCHWERIN, GERMANY

2344. Grossherzogliche Regierungsbibliothek. Die Musikalien-Sammlung des grossherzoglich Mecklenburg-Schweriner Fürstenhauses aus den letzten zwei Jahrhunderten. Schwerin: Druck der Sandmeyerschen Hofbuchdruckerei, 1893. 2 v.
Reprinted by Olms, Hildesheim, 1974.
Compiled by Otto Kade.
Primarily 18th- and 19th-century manuscripts and printed music. Part I is a thematic catalog, alphabetical by composer, with a classified section under "Anonyma." Part II: librettos. Part III: index of dedications, autographs, etc.

2345. Grossherzogliche Regierungsbibliothek. Der musikalische Nachlass der Frau Erbgrossherzogin Auguste von Mecklenburg-Schwerin ... von Otto Kade. Schwerin: Druck der Sandmeyerschen Hofbuchdruckerei, 1899. 142 p.
Reprinted by Olms, Hildesheim, 1974.

SEVILLE, SPAIN

2346. Biblioteca Colombina. "La musica conservada en la Biblioteca Colombina y en la Catedral de Sevilla." By Higinio Anglés. In *Anuario Musical*, 2 (1947), p. 3–39.
88 manuscripts and printed editions from the Colombina library; 9 manuscripts and 22 printed editions from the cathedral archives. Bibliographical references and notes on all the items.

2347. Biblioteca Colombina. "Printed collections of polyphonic music owned by Ferdinand Columbus." By Catherine Weeks Chapman. In *Journal of the American Musicological Society*, 21 (1968), p. 34–84.
Reconstruction of the 16th-century library of the son of Christopher Columbus, based on a manuscript catalog preserved in that library. The catalog makes reference to a number of editions now lost.

SITTEN, SWITZERLAND (VALAIS)

2348. Stenzl, Jürg. Repertorium der liturgischen Musikhandschriften der Diozesen Sitten, Lausanne und Genf. Band I: Diozese Sitten. Freiburg: Universitätsverlag, 1972– . Vol. 1– . (Veröffentlichungen der Gregorianischen Akademie zu Freiburg in der Schweiz. Neue Folge, Band I)
The first volume of a series devoted to the liturgical music manuscripts in the dioceses of Sitten, Lausanne, and Geneva. Band I has 383 pages, 100 illustrations, 60 facsimiles, and 72 pages of edited music.

SLOVAKIA
See CZECH REPUBLIC AND SLOVAKIA

SLOVENIA

2349.   Glasbeni Rokopisi in Tiski na Slovenskem do Leta 1800. Music manuscripts and printed music in Slovenia before 1800. Catalogue. [Compiled by J. Höfler and I. Klemencic.] Ljubljani: Narodna in Univerzitetna knjiznica v Ljubljani, 1967. 105 p.

> The present catalogue is an attempt to catalogue all surviving early musical material in libraries and archives throughout Slovenia. [Editors' *Introduction*]

The material comprises 32 chant manuscripts, 343 general manuscripts, chiefly 18th- and early 19th-century, and an unnumbered section devoted to printed music. Items are located in 17 Slovenian libraries or collections.

SORAU, GERMANY
See ZARY, POLAND.

SPAIN

2350.   Aubry, Pierre. "Iter Hispanicum: notices et extraits de manuscrits ancienne conservés dans les bibliothèques d'Espagne." In *Sammelbände der Internationalen Musikgesellschaft*, vols. 8 and 9 (1907–1908). Also issued separately.

A series of essays treating early Spanish sources of polyphony, Mozarabic chant, the "Cantigas de Santa Maria," and folk music.

2351.   Riaño, Juan F. Critical and bibliographical notes on early Spanish music. London: B. Quaritch, 1887. 154 p.

Reprint by the Da Capo Press, New York, 1971.

Manuscripts and printed music to 1600, classified, giving descriptions and library locations of manuscripts. Numerous facsimile plates.

SPRINGFIELD, OHIO

2352.   Wittenberg University. Hamma School of Theology. School of Music. Hymnbooks at Wittenberg: a classified catalog of the collections of Hamma School of Theology, Wittenberg School of Music, Thomas Library, by Louis Voigt with the collaboration of Darlene Kalke [*et al.*]. Springfield, Ohio: Chantry Music Press, 1975. [96 unnumbered p.]

Lists 1084 hymnbooks, principally Lutheran. Index of names.

STANFORD, CALIFORNIA

2353.   Stanford University. Library. Catalogue of the Memorial Library of Music, Stanford University, by Nathan van Patten. Stanford, Calif.: Stanford University Press, 1950. 310 p.

A collection of manuscripts, printed editions, inscribed copies of books and scores; the emphasis is on "association items." 1,226 entries.

Review by Otto E. Albrecht in *Notes*, 8 (1951), p. 706–709.

STOCKHOLM, SWEDEN

2354. J. H. Roman-samling i Kungl. Musikaliska Adademien. Handstilar och notpikturer i Kungl. Musikaliska akademiens Roman-samling. Handwriting and musical calligraphy in the J. H. Roman collection of the Swedish Royal Academy of Music. Av Ingmar Bengtsson och Ruben Danielson. With an English summary. Uppsala: AlMusical Quarterlyvist & Wiksells, 1955. 74 p. (Studia musicologica Upsaliensia, 3)

A brief guide to the collection with some facsimiles.

2355. Musikaliska Akademiens Bibliotek. Mr. Roman's spuriosity shop; a thematic catalogue of 503 works from c. 1680 to 1750 by more than sixty composers. Compiled and presented by Ingmar Bengtsson. Stockholm: Swedish Music History Archive, 1976.

A catalog of more than 1,200 works composed and gathered by Johann Helmich Roman, of which only 250 have supportable attributions.

For a work also covering spurious attributions, see no. 1198.

2356. Stiftelsen Musikkulturens Framjande [Foundation for the Promotion of Musical Culture]. Förtekning över musikhandskrifter: musikalier, brev och biografica [Catalog of music manuscripts, letters and biographical documents]. Stockholm: Svenskt Musikhistoriskt Arkiv, 1972. 51 p. (Bulletin, 8)

A preliminary catalog, or checklist, of the manuscript collection of Rudolf Nydahl, Stockholm, now owned by the Foundation for Furthering Musical Culture. About 4,500 items in all, including some 1,200 autographs, correspondence, and other documents. The catalog is in two parts: (1) music manuscripts, (2) letters and other documents. The collection is strong in the work of 19th-century musicians.

STRASBOURG, FRANCE

2357. Archives de la Ville. "Aperçu général sur les sources dans les Archives de la Ville de Strasbourg." By René Kopff. In *Fontes Artis Musicae*, 26 (1979), p. 47–54.

An inventory of musical documents in the city archives as well as the archives of St. Thomas Church, the Cathedral, and the musicologist Eugène Wagner.

STUTTGART, GERMANY

2358. Württembergische Landesbibliothek. Die Handschriften der Württembergischen Landesbibliothek Stuttgart. Erste Reihe, erster Band: Codices musici (Cod. Mus. fol. I 1–71). Beschrieben von Clytus Gottwald. Wiesbaden: Otto Harrassowitz, 1964. 184 p.

Describes 53 manuscripts in mensural notation and 18 plainchant sources, giving concordances for texts and music, index of text incipits, thematic catalog for anonymous works, with full bibliographical apparatus. An exemplary catalog.

Review by Franz Krautwurst in *Die Musikforschung*, 21 (1968), p. 233–37.

2359. Württembergische Landesbibliothek. Die Handschriften der Württembergischen Landesbibliothek Stuttgart. Zweite Reihe: Die Handschriften der ehemaligen königlichen Hofbibliothek. Sechster Band: Codices musici. Erster Teil ... Beschrieben von Clytus Gottwald. Wiesbaden: Otto Harrassowitz, 1965. 66 p.

Continues the cataloging begun in the preceding volume, covering a different series of manuscripts.

Review by Ute Schwab in *Die Musikforschung*, 24 (1971), p. 210–12.

2360. Württembergische Landesbibliothek. Katalog über die Musik-Codices des 16. und 17. Jahrhunderts auf der K. Landesbibliothek in Stuttgart. Angefertigt von A. Halm. Langensalza: Beyer, 1902–1903. 58 p. (Monatshefte für Musikgeschichte. Beilage. Jahrgang 34–35)

Cites 70 manuscripts with listings of contents for each. Index to text incipits under individual composers.

SUCRE, BOLIVIA

2361. Catedral Platense. Un archivo musical americano. [By] Carmen García Muñoz and Waldemar Axel Roldán. Buenos Aires: Editorial Universitaria de Buenos Aires, 1972. 166 p.

Catálogo de los manuscritos, p. 51–96.

183 numbered items.

SWEDEN

The Swedish bibliographer Åke Davidsson has prepared union catalogs of early printed music and of music theory works in Swedish libraries. See his *Catalogue Critique et Descriptif des Ouvrages Théoriques sur la Musique Imprimés au XVIe et au XVIIe Siècles et Conservés dans les Bibliothèques Suédoises* (no. 1144) and his *Bibliographie der Musiktheoretischen Drucke des 16. Jahrhunderts* (no. 1143).

SYDNEY, AUSTRALIA

Australia Music Centre. Catalogs. See nos. 1228–1235.

SYRACUSE, NEW YORK

2362. University Libraries. Sources for the study of 19th-century opera in the Syracuse University Libraries; an annotated libretti list by Aubry S. Garlington. Syracuse: Syracuse University Libraries, 1976. 563 p.

A catalogue of libretti indexed by composer, librettist, choreographers, etc. Addenda, p. 445–70.

TENBURY WELLS, ENGLAND

2363. St. Michael's College (Tenbury). Library. Auction catalogues of the Toulouse-Philidor collection, the late property of St. Michael's College,

Tenbury, Eng.; sold by auction by Sotheby Parke Bernet & Co., London 26 June 1978 and Pierre Berès, Paris 30 Nov. 1978. London and Paris: Sotheby Parke Bernet, 1978. 2 v.

Pre-auction catalog of a sale that resulted in the dissolution of part of one of England's most distinguished collections. Materials from St. Michael's College Toulouse-Philidor collection found new homes in the British Library, the Bibliothèque Nationale, Paris, and the University of North Carolina at Chapel Hill, etc. For further information about the holdings that were acquired by the Bibliothèque Nationale, see no. 2280.

2364. St. Michael's College (Tenbury). Library. The catalogue of manuscripts in the library of St. Michael's College, Tenbury. Compiled by E. H. Fellowes. Paris: Éditions de l'Oiseau-Lyre, 1934. 319 p.

Manuscripts in the library bequeathed to the College by Sir Frederick Ouseley. 1,386 items; rich in early English music. The "Toulouse-Philidor collection," consisting of 290 volumes of manuscripts and 67 printed books devoted to the repertory of early 18th-century French opera, was sold in 1978. (See no. 2363.) The other manuscripts are now at the Bodleian Library, Oxford. Composer index.

2365. St. Michael's College (Tenbury). Library. The music collection of St Michael's College, Tenbury; a listing and guide to parts one to five. Compiled by Professor Roger Bray. Brighton: Harvester Press Microform Publications, 1983–86. 98 p.

The *Catalogue of Manuscripts in the Library of St. Michael's College* compiled by E. H. Fellowes "has been completely revised" and has been reproduced in full on the first reel.

As in the other Harvester guides, there is a list of the contents of each reel in each part and a listing of the manuscripts in each part followed by a unified index of names and composers in the volume. There is also a numerical index to the manuscript volumes in the collection.

2366. St. Michael's College (Tenbury). Library. A summary catalogue of the printed books and music in the library of St. Michael's College, Tenbury. Compiled by E. H. Fellowes, 1934. 143 leaves (unpublished manuscript).

An unpublished catalog of the printed books and music in the library of St. Michael's College. Intended as a companion volume to the manuscript catalog above (no. 2364), but never printed. The collection of printed materials is now at the Bodleian Library, Oxford, except for duplicates which have been sold.

TOKYO, JAPAN

2367. Musashino Academia Musicae. Biblioteca. List of acquisitions. Tokyo: Musashino Academia Musicae, 1957– . No. 1– .

Text in Japanese and English.

An annual volume listing materials acquired from April of one year to March of the next. Classified listing of both books and scores. The first section of each issue is devoted to rare materials.

2368. Musashino Academia Musicae. Biblioteca. Litterae rarae. Tokyo: Musashino Academia Musicae, 1962– . Liber primus– .

A catalog of rare music materials added to the collection. Published irregularly; *Liber Secundus* appeared in 1969. A library rich in first or early editions of music and music literature from the 16th through the 19th centuries.
Liber Primus, 1962. 141 p. *Liber Secundus,* 1969. 276 p.

2369. Nanki Music Library. Catalogue of rare books and notes: the Ohki Collection, Nanki Music Library. Tokyo: 1970. 60 p.

2370. Nanki Music Library. Catalogue of the Nanki Music Library. Part I: Musicology. Tokyo: 1929. 372 p.
A reference library for the historical study of Western music. Much of the material came from the collection of W. H. Cummings, an English collector, whose library was sold at auction in 1918.

2371. Nanki Music Library. Catalogue of the W. H. Cummings collection in the Nanki Music Library. Tokyo: 1925. 70 p.
A catalog focused on the rare materials acquired in the Cummings sale. About 450 items, including much important early English music.

TOLEDO, OHIO

2372. Museum of Art. The printed note, 500 years of music printing and engraving, January 1957. Toledo: Museum of Art, 1957. 144 p.
Foreword by A. Beverly Barksdale.
Catalog of an exhibition devoted to the history of music printing and engraving. Splendidly illustrated, 188 items, on loan from major public and private collections throughout the country. Informative annotations; bibliography of 67 items.

TOLEDO, SPAIN

2373. Biblioteca Capitolar. "Les manuscrits polyphoniques de la Bibliothèque Capitulaire de Tolede." By René Lenaerts. In *International Society for Musical Research, Fifth Congress, Utrecht, 1952,* p. 267–81.
Brief descriptions and discussion of about 30 sources of early polyphonic music in the Toledo library.

TORONTO, CANADA

2374. University of Toronto. Thomas Fisher Rarebook Library. "A collection of oratorio libretti, 1700–1800 in the Thomas Fisher Rarebook Library, University of Toronto." By Robert Elliott and Harry M. White. In *Fontes Artis Musicae,* 32 (1985) p. 102–113.
The collection includes opera libretti that are not included in this inventory but are included in Beatrice Corrigan's *Catalogue of Italian Plays, 1500–1700, in the University of Toronto* (Toronto: University of Toronto Press, 1961). Arranged in chronological order in chart form with indexes to librettists and composers.

TREVISO, ITALY

2375. Archivio Musicale del Duomo. La Cappella Musicale del Duomo di Treviso (1300–1633). By Giovanni d'Alessi. Vedelago: Tipografia "Ars et Religio," 1954. 272 p.

Historical study of the musical establishment of the cathedral at Treviso. Chapter 15, p. 169–218, deals with the musical archive and its resources. Manuscripts are listed briefly; printed works in greater detail.

TULLN, AUSTRIA

2376. Pfarrkirche St. Stephan. Das alte Musikarchiv der Pfarrkirche St. Stephan in Tulln. By Karl Schnürl. Wien: Böhlau, 1964. 88 p. (Tabulae musicae austriacae, 1)

The catalog is chiefly concerned with manuscripts, although a short section of printed editions is included. Partially thematic. The principal composers represented are Albrechtsberger, Diabelli, Eybler, Joseph and Michael Haydn, Krottendorfer, Mozart, Schneider, Schubert, Winter, etc.

Review by Imogene Horsley in *Notes*, 24 (1967), p. 52–53.

TURIN, ITALY

2377. Biblioteca Nazionale. "L'Intavolatura d'organo tedesca della Biblioteca Nazionale di Torino. Catalogo ragionato." By Oscar Mischiati. In *L'Organo, rivista di cultura organaria e organistica*, 4 (1963), p. 1–154.

An inventory of the contents of 16 volumes of German organ tablature in the National Library in Turin, the largest body of source material for German organ music known. The manuscripts contain 1,770 compositions on 2,703 written folios, compiled between 1637 and 1640. Appendixes include paleographical descriptions of the volumes, author lists added by later hands, watermarks, concordant printed editions, manuscripts and modern editions, and an index of composers.

2378. Biblioteca Nazionale. Manoscritti e libri a stampa musicali esposti dalla Biblioteca Nazionale di Torino. Firenze: L. Franceschini, 1898. 24 p.

Exposition catalog of 20 manuscripts and 36 printed editions of the 16th–18th centuries.

2379. Biblioteca Nazionale. "La raccolta di antiche musiche 'Renzo Giordano' alla Biblioteca Nazionale di Torino." By Alberto Gentili. In *Accademie e Biblioteche d'Italia*, 4 (1930–31), p. 117–25.

A description of the collection of manuscripts of sacred music, instrumental works of Vivaldi and Vanhall, vocal music of Corelli, among others, and opera by Traetta and Vivaldi, among others.

2380. Biblioteca Nazionale. "La raccolta di rarità musicali "Mauro Foà" alla Biblioteca Nazionale di Torino." By Alberto Gentili. In *Accademie e Biblioteche d'Italia*, 1 (1927), p. 36–50.

Descriptive account of a collection of 95 volumes, manuscripts, and prints founded by Count Giacomo Durazzo, Genoan Ambassador to Venice in 1765. Includes autographs of Vivaldi and Stradella, as well as the organ tablatures mentioned in no. 2377.

2381. Biblioteca Nazionale. Raccolta Mauro Foà, Raccolta Renzo Giordano. By Isabella Fragalà Data and Annarita Colturato. Roma: Edizioni Torre d'Orfeo, 1987. 613 p. (Cataloghi di fondi musicali italiani, a cura della Società Italiana di Musicologia in collaborazione con il Répertoire International des Sources Musicales, 7. Biblioteca Nazionale Universitaria di Torino, I)

Catalogs of two collections containing many Vivaldi, Stradella, Pallavicino, Legrenzi, Giovanni Gabrieli, and Merulo sources. Incipits for works not otherwise cataloged in other reference works are supplied. No incipits for Vivaldi instrumental works are provided. Instead, there are references to Ryom (no. 1673). There is an index to text incipits.

Biblioteca Nazionale. See also no. 2078.

UNITED STATES OF AMERICA

2382. Albrecht, Otto E. A census of autograph music manuscripts of European composers in American libraries. Philadelphia: University of Pennsylvania Press, 1953. 331 p.

Lists 2,017 manuscripts now in America, representing 571 European composers, giving title, pagination, dimensions, and descriptive notes. Current and former owners indicated. Organized alphabetically by composer. Index of owners.

Review by Jack A. Westrup in *Music Review*, 16 (1955), p. 84–85.

2383. Seaton, Douglass, ed. "Important library holdings at forty-one North American universities." In *Current Musicology*, 17 (1974), p. 7–68.

Brief accounts by domestic corresponding editors of the musical rarities in the university libraries of the following institutions:

Boston University	University of Chicago
Bryn Mawr College	University of Colorado
Catholic University of America	University of Illinois
City University of New York	University of Iowa
CUNY Hunter College	University of Kansas
CUNY Queens College	University of Maryland
Columbia University	University of Miami
Cornell University	University of Michigan
Harvard University	University of Minnesota
Indiana University	University of North Carolina
Juilliard School	University of Oregon
Memphis State University	University of Pennsylvania
New York University	University of Pittsburgh
Northwestern University	University of Rochester (Eastman)
Princeton University	University of Texas
Rutgers University	University of Washington
Stanford University	University of Western Ontario
University of California, Berkeley	University of Wyoming
University of California, Los Angeles	West Virginia University
University of California, Riverside	Yale University
University of California, Santa Barbara	

UPPSALA, SWEDEN

2384. Universitetsbiblioteket. Catalogue critique et descriptif des imprimés de musique des XVIe et XVIIe siècles, conservés à la Bibliothèque de l'Université Royale d'Upsala. Par Rafael Mitjana avec une introduction bibliographique par Isak Collijn.... Upsala: Almqvist et Wiksell, 1911–1951. 3 v.
Vol. 1: Musique religieuse, I, par Rafael Mitjana (1911). Vol. 2: Musique religieuse, II; musique profane, musique dramatique, musique instrumentale; additions au Tome I par Åke Davidsson (1951). Vol. 3: Recueils de musique religieuse et profane, par Åke Davidsson (1951).
Entries in vols. 1 and 2 are arranged alphabetically within each category; vol. 3 is chronological, with an index of the contents of the collections under composer. Index of printers and publishers and a bibliography of works cited. Full bibliographical entries, with locations of copies in other libraries.

2385. Universitetsbiblioteket. Catalogue of the Gimo collection of Italian manuscript music in the University Library of Uppsala. By Åke Davidsson. Uppsala: 1963. 101 p. (Acta Bibliothecae R. Universitatis Upsaliensis, 14)
A catalog of 360 items, comprising both vocal and instrumental music of the 18th century. An introduction relates the history of the collection. Useful bibliography of sources and related literature.
Review by Minnie Elmer in *Notes*, 22 (1965), p. 715–16; by R. Thurston Dart in *Library*, ser. 5, 20 (June 1965), p. 166–67.

2386. Universitetsbiblioteket. Düben Samling. "Die Dübensammlung. Ein Versuch ihrer chronologischen Ordnung." By Bruno Grusnick. In *Svensk Tidskrift för Musikforskning*, 46 (1964), p. 27–82; 48 (1966), p. 63–186.
Concerning the collection of music gathered mostly by Gustaf Düben, an organist and composer in Stockholm 1648–90. The collection consists of approximately 1,500 manuscripts of vocal sacred music, 300 manuscripts of instrumental music, and some printed works. One of the largest collections of 17th-century music extant, it contains many *unica* and a Buxtehude autograph, as well as numerous contemporaneous copies. The article cites copyists, displays watermarks, and shows the development of the collection chronologically.

URBANA, ILLINOIS

2387. University of Illinois. Musicological Archives for Renaissance Studies. Census-catalogue of manuscript sources of polyphonic music 1450–1550. Compiled by Jerry Call, and edited by Herbert Kellman and Charles Hamm. Neuhausen-Stuttgart: American Institute of Musicology and Hänssler-Verlag, 1979–88. 5 v. (Renaissance manuscript studies, 1)
An exceptional catalog presenting extensive descriptions and analyses of sources of Renaissance polyphony; virtually all sources have been gathered in microfilm copies in the Illinois Archives. It is called a *Census-Catalog* because the intention of the compiler and editors has been to gather in one publication information on all sources whether obtainable by the archive or not.
The entries are presented in order of the location of the institution holding the original. Each entry provides a summary of the source's contents,

a list of the contents in order of appearance, an extensive description of the source including information on provenance, and citations of literature about the manuscript. There is an extended bibliography of secondary sources cited, an index of composers, and a general index of persons, places, RISM numbers, and watermarks in each of volumes one through three. Each volume also includes an index of informal names and designations for manuscripts and a key to sigla. Volume 4 lacks these indexes and lists, but describes additional A–U manuscripts in a 263-p. supplement. The supplement also includes revisions for previously described manuscripts.

Volume 5 consists of a cumulative bibliography and cumulative indexes as well as statistics on distribution of manuscripts by country, city, and library. There is also an index to provenance by country and period of origin. Finally, there is a general index.

Charles Hamm and Herbert Kellman present their vision of the archive in the article "The Musicological Archive for Renaissance Manuscript Studies" in *Fontes Artis Musicae*, 16 (1969), p. 148–49. Reviews of vol. 1 by John Caldwell in *Music and Letters*, 61 (1980), p. 394–95, and by Thomas Noblitt in *Tijdschrift van der Vereniging voor Nederlandse Muziekgeschiedenis*, 42 (1982), p. 156–65. Review of vols. 4 and 5 by David Fallows in *Early Music*, 12 (1989), p. 89–90.

VALENCIA (REGION), SPAIN

2388. Fondos musicale de la región Valenciana. By José Climent. Valencia: Istituto de musicología; Institución Alfonso el Magnánimo; Diputación Provincial de Valencia, 1979– . 2 v.

Vol. 1 covers the holdings of the Catedral Metropolitana de Valencia (1979, 471 p.). It is a catalog of the manuscript and printed works in this very large collection. Biographical notes on composers are provided, but only brief bibliographical descriptions of the sources. Index to names.

Vol. 2 covers the holdings of the Archivio Musical of the Real Colegio de Corpus Christi Patriarca (1984, 849 p.). It is a catalog of manuscripts and printed works in what was an extraordinary musical establishment. Index to names.

VALLADOLID, SPAIN

2389. Catedral. Archivo Musical. "El Archivo Musical de la Catedral de Valladolid." By Higinio Anglés. In *Anuario Musical*, 3 (1948), p. 59–108.

20 manuscripts and 97 early printed books. Inventories given for the contents of the manuscripts and full bibliographical citations for the prints, with references to Eitner (no. 1739) and other bibliographies.

VATICAN CITY, ROME

2390. Biblioteca Apostolica Vaticana. Libretti di melodrammi e balli del secolo XVIII [nella] Fondo Ferraioli della Biblioteca Apostolica Vaticana [per] Elisabetta Mori. Firenze: L. Olschki, 1984.

A catalog of the libretti in the Ferraioli collection. Indexes.

2391. Biblioteca Apostolica Vaticana. Monumenti vaticani di paleografia musicale latina. By H. M. Bannister. Lipsia: O. Harrassowitz, 1913. 2 v. 130 plates. (Codices e vaticanis selecti, 12)

Reprint by the Gregg Press, 1969.

A volume of commentary and a volume of plates containing excerpts from Vatican manuscripts, assembled for the purposes of paleographical study. Contains a vast amount of information on the manuscript sources of plainchant in the Vatican Library.

2392. Biblioteca Apostolica Vaticana. "Die Sammlungen der Oratorienlibretti (1679–1725) und dem restlichen Musikbestand der Fondo San Marcello der Biblioteca Vaticano in Rom." By Andreas Liess. In *Acta Musicologica*, 31 (1959), p. 63–80.

Cites 106 oratorio libretti in the Fondo San Marcello of the Biblioteca Vaticano. References to whether or not the works were cited in Eitner (no. 1739).

2393. Biblioteca Apostolica Vaticana. Cappella Giulia. Le opere musicali della Cappella Giulia. I. Manoscritti e edizioni fino al '700. By José M. Llorens. Città del Vaticano: Biblioteca Apostolica Vaticana, 1971. 412 p. (Studi e testi, 265)

Review by Samuel F. Pogue in *Notes*, 29 (1973), p. 445–48.

2394. Biblioteca Apostolica Vaticana. Cappella Sistina. Bibliographischer und thematischer Musikkatalog des Päpstlichen Kapellarchives im Vatikan zu Rom ... von Fr. X. Haberl. Leipzig: Breitkopf & Härtel, 1888. 183 p. (Monatshefte für Musikgeschichte. Beilage. Jahrgang 19/20)

Descriptions of 269 items, manuscripts and early printed works, with a thematic catalog, by composer, of the early polyphonic sources. Considerable documentation on the Cappella Sistina and the musicians employed there. The Haberl catalog represents only a small part of the Cappella Sistina collection. See no. 2395.

2395. Biblioteca Apostolica Vaticana. Cappella Sistina. Capellae Sixtinae codices musicis notis instructi sive manuscripti sive praelo excussi. Rec. José M. Llorens. Città del Vaticano: Biblioteca Apostolica Vaticana, 1960. 555 p. 10 facsimile plates.

A catalog of the collection treated by F. X. Haberl (no. 2394) but much more thoroughly, since Haberl covered only 269 of the 660 manuscripts and printed volumes present. Volumes listed by number, with detailed inventories of contents. Descriptive annotations in Latin. Thematic catalog of anonymous works.

Review by Dragan Plamenac in *Notes*, 19 (1961), p. 251–52; by Peter Peacock in *Music and Letters*, 42 (1961), p. 168–69; by Glen Haydon in *Musical Quarterly*, 48 (1962), p. 127–29.

VENICE, ITALY

2396. Biblioteca del Palazzo Giustinian Lolin. Stampe e manoscritti preziosi e rari della Biblioteca del Palazzo Giustinian Lolin a San Vidal. By Siro Cisilino. Venezia: A cura del fondatore Dott. Ugo Levi sotto gli auspici dell'Ateneo Veneto, 1966. 55 p.

At head of title: Fondazione Ugo e Olga Levi, Centro di Cultura Musicale Superiore.
Catalog of the library of a musical foundation in Venice. 70 items listed, including printed books and manuscripts from the 16th to the early 19th centuries. Many of the manuscripts are composite in content. The collection contains important source materials for the study of 18th-century instrumental music.

2397. Biblioteca Nazionale Marciana. I codici musicali contariniani del secolo XVII nella R. Biblioteca di San Marco in Venezia. Illustrati dal Dr. Taddeo Wiel. Venezia: F. Ongania, 1888. 121 p.
Reprinted by Forni, Bologna, 1969.
The Contarini collection is a special library of manuscript scores of 17th-century Venetian opera, by such composers as Cesti, Cavalli, Pallavicino, Ziani, etc. 120 numbered items. Entries give information as to date of first performance, librettist, cast, general description of the work. Composer index.

Biblioteca Nazionale Marciana. (R. Biblioteca di San Marco) See also no. 2070.

Biblioteca Querini Stampalia. See no. 2070.

2398. Conservatorio di Musica Benedetto Marcello. Il Conservatorio di musica Benedetto Marcello di Venezia, 1876–1976: centenario della fondazione: Palazzo Pisani, Venezia [un'exposizione a cura di] Pietro Verardo. Venezia: Stamperia di Venezia, 1977. 299 p.
A catalog of the exposition including a description of the conservatory's holdings of research materials. Almost 50 pages of "documenti" are included.

2399. Conservatorio di Musica Benedetto Marcello. Biblioteca. I manoscritti del Fondo Torrefranca del Conservatorio Benedetto Marcello: catalogo per autori [di] Franco Rossi. Firenze: Leo S. Olschki, 1986. 357 p. (Biblioteca "Historiae musicae cultores," 45) (Catalogo dei fonti storici della biblioteca del Conservatorio di musica Benedetto Marcello, Venezia, I)
This is an alphabetically ordered catalog of manuscripts in the Torrefranca collection, but the catalog also includes anthologies, libretti, treatises, and nonmusical manuscripts. Includes some thematic incipits.

2400. Fondazione Cini. La raccoltà di libretti d'opera. Catalogo e indici a cura di Anna Laura Bellina, Bruno Brizi, e Maria Grazia Pensa. Roma: Istituto della Enciclopedia Italiana fondata da Giovanni Treccani, 1986. 185 p.
There are approximately 40,000 libretti in the Rolandi collection. This volume provides numerous indexes to the multivolume catalog of the collection, which has been in preparation for some time.

2401. Fondazione Levi di Venezia. Catalogo del fondo musicale. Venezia: Edizioni Fondazione Levi, 1986. 347 p. (Studi musicologici, cataloghi e bibliografia)

Classified catalog of the substantial collection developed since 1965, covering manuscripts, pictures of musicians, printed music (many already cited in RISM), writings about music, and libretti of operas and oratorios. Entries provide full descriptions, contents analysis, medium of performance, composer and title, author and title. Libretti are entered by title. Indexes to titles and text incipits, to characters in staged works, and to names.

Museo Correr. See no. 2070.

Pia Casa di Ricovero. See no. 2070.

VERCELLI, ITALY

2402. Archivio della Cattedrale. "Il fondo musicale dell'archivio della Cattedrale di Vercelli." By Claudio Sartori. In *Fontes Artis Musicae*, 5 (1958), p. 24–31.

VERONA, ITALY

2403. Accademia Filarmonica. L'Accademia Filarmonica di Verona, dalla fondazione (Maggio 1543) al 1600 e il suo patrimonio musicale antico. By Giuseppe Turrini. Verona: La Tipografica Veronese, 1941. 346 p.

A detailed history of the Accademia Filarmonica from its beginnings to 1600. Chapter 16 discusses the holdings of the library on the basis of early inventories. Chapter 17 continues the discussion to the first half of the 19th century. Chapter 18 includes a catalog of the existing materials in the "Fondo Musicale Antico," some 217 prints and 21 manuscripts.

Accademia Filarmonica. See also no. 2080.

2404. Biblioteca Capitolare. Mille anni di musica nella Biblioteca Capitolare di Verona. By A. Piazzi, E. Paganuzzi, V. Donella, and G. Zivelonghi. Verona: Stimmatini, 1985. 127 p.

Articles on medieval, Renaissance, and modern period holdings, lists of items in the Fondi Musicali, and descriptions of the instruments in the Biblioteca Capitolare. Color facsimiles of manuscript pages. Bibliography of writings about music in Verona.

2405. Biblioteca Capitolare. Il patrimonio musicale della Biblioteca Capitolare di Verona dal sec. XV al XIX. By Giuseppe Turrini. Verona: "La Tipografica Veronese," 1953. 83 p. (Estratto dagli Atti dell'Academia di Agricoltura, Scienze e Lettere di Verona, ser. 6, vol. 2, p. 95–176)

VICENZA, ITALY

2406. Archivio Capitolare del Duomo. Il fondo musicale dell'Archivio Capitolare del Duomo di Vicenza [di] Vittorio Bolcato, Alberto Zanotelli. Torino: E.D.T./Musica, 1986. 514 p. (Cataloghi di fondi musicali Italiani, 4)

A result of collaboration between the Società Italiana di Musicologia and RISM, this catalog treats a corpus of manuscripts and printed music from the 18th century, 15th- and 16th-century printed music, choir and liturgical books, and a few theoretical works. Includes an index.

Archivio della Cattedrale. See no. 2071.

Biblioteca Bertoliana. See no. 2071.

VIENNA, AUSTRIA

2407. Beethoven-Zentenarausstellung. Führer durch die Beethoven-Zentenarausstellung der Stadt Wien: "Beethoven und die Wiener Kultur seiner Zeit." Wien: Selbstverlag der Gemeinde Wien, 1927. 248 p.

An exhibition catalog of 1,070 items, including letters, documents, pictures, musical instruments, scores, and prints related to Beethoven and his circle.

2408. Gesellschaft der Musikfreunde. Geschichte der Gesellschaft der Musikfreunde in Wien, 1912–1927. (Fortsetzung der Festschrift zur Jahrhundertfeier vom Jahre 1912.) Wien: Gesellschaft der Musikfreunde, 1937.

Continues the documentation given in the next item. Of particular interest is the account by Hedwig Kraus of "Die Sammlungen der Gesellschaft der Musikfreunde, 1912–1937," p. 1–42.

2409. Gesellschaft der Musikfreunde. Geschichte der K. K. Gesellschaft der Musikfreunde in Wien.... In einem Zusatzbande: "Die Sammlungen und Statuten," von Dr. Eusebius Mandyczewski. Wien: Adolf Holzhausen, 1912. 2 v.

Vol. 1 is a history of the Gesellschaft from 1812 to 1870 and from 1870 to 1912. Vol. 2, "Zusatz-Band," is not a true catalog but a summary listing of the holdings of the archive, library, and museum. Of particular value is Mandyczewski's listing of "Bücher und Schriften über Musik. Druckwerke und Handschriften aus der Zeit bis zum Jahre 1800," p. 55–84. Also "Musik-Autographe," p. 85–123.

2410. Gesellschaft der Musikfreunde. "Sources of Brahms's manuscript copies of early music in the Archiv der Gesellschaft der Musikfreunde in Wien." By Virginia L. Hancock. In *Fontes Artis Musicae*, 24 (1977), p. 113–21.

2411. Gesellschaft der Musikfreunde. Die Volksmusiksammlung der Gesellschaft der Musikfreunde in Wien (Sonnleithner-Sammlung). 1. Teil, bearbeitet von Walther Deutsch und Gerlinde Hofer, mit einem Beitrag von Leopold Schmidt. Wien: A. Schendl, 1969. 186 p. (Schriften zur Volksmusik, 2)

Catalog of a collection of folk music, chiefly Austrian, begun in 1818. Entries are grouped by genre and by region. First-line index of songs; indexes of places and names. 29 plates duplicating pages from the collection. Review by Hartmut Braun in *Jahrbuch für Volksliedforschung*, 15 (1970), p. 159–60.

2412. Hoftheater. Katalog der Portrait-Sammlung der K. V. K. Generalintendanz der K. K. Hoftheater. Zugleich ein biographisches Hilfsbuch auf dem Gebiet von Theater und Musik. Wien: Adolph W. Kunast, 1892–94. 3 v.

Catalogs a large collection of portraits and other graphic materials related to the theater; classified according to type of theater or kind of entertainment. Gruppe III, Vol. 1, p. 119–264, is concerned with pictorial documents on musicians: composers, librettists, concert singers, writers on music, etc.

2413. Internationale Ausstellung für Musik- und Theaterwesen. Fach-Katalog der Musikhistorischen Abteilung von Deutschland und Österreich-Ungarn.... Wien: 1892. 591 p.

Catalog for a large and varied music exhibition held in Vienna in 1892. Includes prints, manuscripts, instruments, portraits, letters, and other documents arranged roughly in chronological order from ancient times to the end of the 19th century.

2414. Künstlerhaus. Katalog der Ausstellung anlässlich der Centenarfeier Domenico Cimarosas. Wien: Verlag des Comites, 1901. 163 p.

Exhibition catalog of 524 items related to Cimarosa and his contemporaries; includes scores, portraits, medals, etc.

2415. Minoritenkonvent. Das Musikarchiv im Minoritenkonvent zu Wien (Katalog des älteren Bestandes vor 1784). By Friedrich Wilhelm Riedel. Kassel: Bärenreiter, 1963. 139 p. (Catalogus musicus, 1)

Broadly classified catalog of manuscripts and printed music, chiefly 17th and 18th centuries. Strong in early keyboard music. Indexes of composers, copyists, and former owners.

Review by Othmar Wessely in *Die Musikforschung*, 18 (1965), p. 204–206.

2416. Museum des 20. Jahrhunderts. Schönberg—Webern—Berg: Bilder—Partituren—Dokumente. (Catalog of an exhibition at the Museum des 20. Jahrhunderts, Vienna, 17 May–20 July 1969.) Wien: Museum des 20. Jahrhunderts, 1969. 118 p.

Review by Dika Newlin in *Notes*, 27 (1971), p. 488–89.

2417. Österreichische Nationalbibliothek. Die Estensischen Musikalien; thematisches Verzeichnis mit Einleitung von Robert Haas. Regensburg: G. Bosse, 1927. 232 p.

Reissued in 1957 as Bd. VII of *Forschungsbeiträge zur Musikwissenschaft*. Regensburg, G. Bosse.

Catalog, largely thematic, of an important collection of 18th-century instrumental music originating in northern Italy. Includes a small group of cantatas and other vocal works. Classified with major sections of printed editions and manuscripts. Index of names, text incipits.

2418. Österreichische Nationalbibliothek. Die Lautentabulaturhandschriften der Österreichischen Nationalbibliothek (17. und 18. Jahrhundert). Von Elizabeth Maier. Wien: Verlag der Österreichischen Akademie der Wissenschaften, 1974. 131 p. (Tabulae musicae Austriacae, 8)
A thematic catalog to the contents of nine manuscripts with references to modern editions and an extensive introduction. Index of names and titles or captions.

2419. Österreichische Nationalbibliothek. "Die Musikbibliothek von Raimund Fugger d.J.: ein Beitrag zur Musiküberlieferung des 16. Jahrhunderts." By Richard Schaal. In *Acta Musicologica*, 29 (1957), p. 126–37.
Catalog of the Fugger library, from a 16th-century manuscript in the Staatsbibliothek, Munich. The bulk of the Fugger family music collection is now in the National Library.

2420. Österreichische Nationalbibliothek. "Die Musiksammlung." By Leopold Nowak. In *Die Österreichische Nationalbibliothek. Festschrift herausgegeben zum 25. jährigen Dienstjubiläum des Generaldirektors Prof. Dr. Josef Bick*, p. 119–38. Wien: H. Bauer-Verlag, 1948.

2421. Österreichische Nationalbibliothek. "Die Musiksammlung der Nationalbibliothek." By Robert Haas. In *Jahrbuch der Musikbibliothek Peters*, 37 (1930), p. 48–62.

2422. Österreichische Nationalbibliothek. Richard Strauss Ausstellung zum 100. Geburtstag. Bearbeitet von Franz Grasberger und Franz Hadamowsky. Wien: Österreichische Nationalbibliothek, 1964. 360 p.
Exhibition catalog of a rich collection of documents related to Richard Strauss. Illustrated.

2423. Österreichische Nationalbibliothek. Tabulae codicum manuscriptorum praeter graecos et orientales in Bibliotheca Palatina Vindobonensi asservatorum ... x. IX–X: Codicum musicorum, Pars I–II. Vindobonae: venum dat. Geroldi filius, 1897–99. 2 v. in 1.
Catalog, compiled by Joseph Mantuani, of the manuscripts numbered 15,501–19,500 comprising the music holdings of the Austrian National Library. Introduction and descriptive notes in Latin. Each volume has an index of names, of subjects, and of text incipits.

2424. Österreichische Nationalbibliothek. Musiksammlung. Der Franz-SchrekerFonds in der Musiksammlung der Österreichischen Nationalbibliothek: Katalog bearb. v. Friedrich C. Heller, unter Mitarb. v. Hans Jancik und Lucia Vogel. Wien: Hollinek in Komm., 1975. 70 p. (Museion; Veröffentlichungen der Österreichischen Nationalbibliothek, Neue Folge, Reihe 3, 4)
A description of the Schreker collection with a brief bibliography of his works.

2425. Österreichische Nationalbibliothek. Musiksammlung. Katalog der Handschriften Österreichische Nationalbibliothek, Wien, Musiksammlung. Vienna: Olms Microform, 1983. 106 microfiches with 29-p. booklet. (Die Europäische Musik. I, Kataloge, 1)

Booklet *Die Musiksammlung der Österreichischen Nationalbibliothek und ihr Handschriftenkatalog* by Günther Brosche.
Photographic reproduction of the music manuscript catalog.

2426. Österreichische Nationalbibliothek. Musiksammlung. The music collection of the Austrian National Library by Franz Grasberger. (Translator: Hans Suesserott.) Vienna: Federal Chancellery, Federal Press and Information Dept., 1972. 32 p.
Translation of the 1970 edition of *Die Musiksammlung der Österreichischen Nationalbibliothek.*

2427. Österreichische Nationalbibliothek. Musiksammlung. Die Musiksammlung der Österreichischen Nationalbibliothek, Funktion und Benützung von Franz Grasberger. Wien: Österreichische Nationalbibliothek, 1980. 100 p.
Includes bibliographical references and index.

2428. Österreichische Nationalbibliothek. Musiksammlung. Die österreichische Nachfolge der Wiener Schule. Musiksammlung d. Österr. Nationalbibliothek, Inst. f. Österr. Musikdokumentation. Sonderausstellung, 2.–21. Mai 1974. (Ausarb. des Ausstellungskataloges: Lieselotte Theiner [und] Lucia Vogel.) Wien: Musiksammlung d. Österr. Nationalbibliothek, 1974. 44 p.
Catalog of an exhibition of holdings of the Viennese School.

2429. Österreichische Nationalbibliothek. Musiksammlung. Österreichische Spätromantiker: Studien zu Emil Nikolaus von Reznicek, Joseph Marx, Franz Schmidt und Egon Kornauth: mit einer Dokumentation der handschriftlichen Quellen in der Musiksammlung der Österreichischen Nationalbibliothek [von] Thomas Leibnitz. Tutzing: H. Schneider, 1986. 182 p. (Institut für Österreichische Musikdokumentation, 11)
Monograph on some early 20th-century Viennese composers with a catalog of the manuscript sources.

Österreichische Nationalbibliothek. Musiksammlung. Richard-Strauss-Bibliographie. See no. 1183.

2430. Österreichische Nationalbibliothek. Musiksammlung. Sammlung Eleonore Vondenhoff. Gustav Mahler Dokumentation, Sammlung Eleonore Vondenhoff: Materialien zu seinem Leben und Werk; hrsg. von Bruno Vondenhoff und Eleonore Vondenhoff. Tutzing: Schneider, 1978. 676 p. (Institut für Österreichische Musikdokumentation, 4)
A 4-p. "Ergänzung des Nachtrags" was issued and has been inserted in many copies.
Catalog of the Vondenhoff collection of documents on the life and works of Gustav Mahler.

2431. Österreichische Nationalbibliothek. Photogrammarchiv. Katalog des Archivs für Photogramme musikalischer Meisterhandschriften, Widmung Anthony van Hoboken. Bearb. von Agnes Ziffer. Wien: Prachner, 1967– . 482 p.

(Museion; Veröffentlichungen der Österreichischen Nationalbibliothek, neue Folge. 3. Reihe, 3)

An archive of photocopies of the autographs of a selected group of great composers, chiefly Viennese, founded in 1927 by Anthony van Hoboken and Heinrich Schenker. 2,684 entries; many references to related literature.

2432. Österreichische Nationalbibliothek. Sammlung Anthony van Hoboken. Katalog der Sammlung Anthony van Hoboken in der Musiksammlung der Österreichischen Nationalbibliothek: musikalische Erst- und Frühdrucke. Herausgegeben vom Institut für österreichische Musikdokumentation, unter der Leitung von Günther Brosche. Tutzing: H. Schneider, 1982–86. 5 v.

A catalog of the first and early imprints in the Hoboken collection. Contents:

Bd. 1. *Johann Sebastian Bach und seine Söhne,* bearbeitet von Thomas Leibnitz. Reviewed by Christoph Wolff in *Notes,* 41 (1984), p. 281–83.

Bd. 2. *Ludwig van Beethoven,* bearbeitet von Karin Breitner und Thomas Leibnitz.

Bd. 3. *Ludwig van Beethoven, Werke ohne Opuszahl und Sammelausgaben,* bearbeitet von Thomas Leibnitz.

Bd. 4. *Johannes Brahms, Frédéric Chopin,* bearbeitet von Karin Breitner und Thomas Leibnitz.

Bd. 5. *Christoph Willibald Gluck, Georg Friedrich Händel,* bearbeitet von Karin Breitner.

Bd. 6. *Joseph Haydn, Symphonien (Hob. I, Ia),* bearbeitet von Karin Breitner.

Bd. 7 & 8. *Joseph Haydn, Instrumentalmusic (Bd. 7: Hob. II bis XI; Bd. 8: Hob. XIV-XX/1),* bearbeitet von Karin Breitner.

Bd. 9. *Joseph Haydn, Vokalmusik (Hob. XX/2-XXXI),* bearbeitet von Karin Breitner.

Bd. 11. *Wolfgang Amadeus Mozart, Werke KV 6-581,* bearbeitet von Karin Breitner.

Catalogs of the contents of the collection of manuscripts, first and early editions of Anthony van Hoboken.

WARSAW, POLAND

2433. Biblioteka Narodowa. Katalog mikrofilmów muzycznych (Catalog of musical microfilms). Warszawa: Biblioteka Narodowa, 1956– . Vol. 1– .

A series of catalogs originating in the microfilm archive of the National Library at Warsaw. Three volumes—volumes 8, 9, and 10—of a larger series (Katalog mikrofilmow) are concerned with music. The holdings of numerous Polish libraries are represented.

Vol. 1 (1956): chiefly manuscripts and printed materials of the 19th century. Vol. 2 (1962): musical documents of the 17th and 18th centuries. Vol. 3 (1965): historical source materials related to Polish music.

2434. University Library. Katalog druków muzycznych XVI, XVII e XVIII w. Biblioteki Uniwersytetu warszawskiego. Tom I: Wiek XVI. Warszawa: Wydawn. Uniwers. warszawsk, 1970. 380 p. (Acta bibliothecae universitatis varsoviensis, 7)

Catalog of printed music of the 16th–18th centuries in the University Library at Warsaw.

This work is highly praised in a brief description in *Fontes Artis Musicae*, 19 (1972), p. 46.

WASHINGTON, DISTRICT OF COLUMBIA

2435. Copyright Office. Dramatic compositions copyrighted in the United States, 1870–1916. Washington, D.C.: Government Printing Office, 1918. 2 v.

Unaltered reprint by Johnson Reprint Corp., New York, 1968.
Review by Lenore Coral in *Notes*, 26 (1969), p. 52–53.

2436. Library of Congress. M, ML & MT shelflist. Ann Arbor, Michigan: University Microfilms International, 1979. 218 microfiche.

A microfiche edition of the shelf lists of classified materials in the Music Division of the Library of Congress; thus a classified catalog.

A study of the L.C. shelf list was prepared by Michael A. Keller and Holly Rowe and published as "An analysis of the L.C. music shelflist on microfiche" in *Cum Notis Variorum*, 78 (December 1983), p. 11–18. Additional information on the L.C. shelf list and its relationship to the actual content of the shelves at the Library of Congress was provided by Robert J. Palian in "Discrepancies between the Keller shelflist count and the contents of the shelves in the Music Division of the Library of Congress" in *Cum Notis Variorum*, no. 83 (June 1984), p. 43–46.

2437. Library of Congress. Music Division. "Bloch manuscripts at the Library of Congress." By David L. Sills. In *Notes*, 42 (1986), p. 727–53.

A survey of the collection of music manuscripts, complementing the author's catalog of the Bloch music manuscripts at the Berkeley Music Library (no. 1894).

2438. Library of Congress. Music Division. Catalogue of early books on music (before 1800). By Julia Gregory. Washington, D.C.: Government Printing Office, 1913. 312 p.

Supplement (Books acquired by the Library, 1913–42) by Hazel Bartlett ... with a list of books on music in Chinese and Japanese. 1944. 143 p.

Republication in one volume of the original catalog and its supplement by the Da Capo Press, New York, 1969.

The Library of Congress has one of the richest collections of early music theory in the world. The entries conform to the Library's printed catalog cards.

Review by Ruth Watanabe in *Notes*, 26 (1970), p. 521–24.

2439. Library of Congress. Music Division. Catalogue of first editions of Edward MacDowell (1861–1908). By O. G. Sonneck. Washington, D.C.: Government Printing Office, 1917. 89 p.

Includes works with and without opus numbers, compositions written under pseudonyms, and works edited by the composer. Index of titles, first line of texts, authors and translators, publishers.

2440. Library of Congress. Music Division. Catalogue of first editions of Stephen C. Foster (1826–1864). By Walter R. Whittlesey and O. G. Sonneck. Washington, D.C.: Government Printing Office, 1915. 79 p.

Works arranged by title; indexed by authors of text, publishers, first lines. Detailed annotations.

2441. Library of Congress. Music Division. Catalogue of opera librettos printed before 1800. Prepared by O. G. T. Sonneck. Washington, D.C.: Government Printing Office, 1914. 2 v.

Reprint by Johnson Reprint Corp., New York, 1970; and by Burt Franklin, New York, 1967.

The library's collection of librettos began in 1909 with the purchase of the Schatz collection. By 1914 it contained 17,000 items and was particularly strong in first editions of 17th- and 18th-century works. Vol. 1 is a title listing, with notes giving date of first performance, place, and name of composer, if known. Vol. 2 is an index by composers, by librettists, and of titles of specific arias mentioned.

2442. Library of Congress. Music Division. Dramatic music. Catalogue of full scores. Compiled by O. G. T. Sonneck. Washington, D.C.: Government Printing Office, 1908. 170 p.

Reprint by Da Capo Press, New York, 1969.

Full scores of operas in original editions, some manuscript copies included, and some photocopies. Arranged alphabetically by composer.

Review by Ruth Watanabe in *Notes*, 26 (1970), p. 521–24.

2443. Library of Congress. Music Division. The Music Division, a guide to its collections and services. Washington, D.C.: Government Printing Office, 1972. 22 p.

Published in 1960 under the title *The Music Division in the Library of Congress.*

A brief descriptive account of the work and resources of the Music Division, with illustrations.

2444. Library of Congress. Music Division. The music manuscripts, first editions, and correspondence of Franz Liszt (1811–1886) in the collections of the Music Division, Library of Congress. Compiled by Elizabeth H. Auman, Gail L. Freunsch, and Robert J. Palian. Washington, D.C.: Library of Congress, 1991. 126 p.

2445. Library of Congress. Music Division. The musical manuscripts and letters of Johannes Brahms (1833–1897) in the collections of the Music Division, Library of Congress. Prepared by George S. Bozarth with the assistance of Elizabeth H. Auman and William C. Parsons. Washington, D.C.: Library of Congress, 1983. 22 p.

2446. Library of Congress. Music Division. Orchestral music ... catalogue. Scores. Prepared under the direction of O. G. T. Sonneck. Washington, D.C.: Government Printing Office, 1912. 663 p.

Reprint by Da Capo Press, New York, 1969.

Orchestra scores from about 1830 to 1912.

Review by Ruth Watanabe in *Notes*, 26 (1970), p. 521–24.

2447. Library of Congress. Music Division. Elizabeth Sprague Coolidge Foundation. Coolidge Foundation program for contemporary chamber music; preliminary checklist of works available for loan (November 1961). Compiled by Frances G. Gewehr. Washington, D.C.: Library of Congress, 1961. 38 p. (typescript)
Supplement, April 1963.
A classified list of contemporary chamber music scores and parts that may be borrowed by qualified ensembles for study purposes. Entries give publisher and price; recordings if available are also cited.

2448. Library of Congress. Music Division. Gertrude Clarke Whittall Foundation. Autograph musical scores and autograph letters in the Whittall Foundation collection. Prepared by Edward N. Waters. Washington, D.C.: Gertrude Clarke Whittall Foundation, 1953. 18 p.

2449. Washington Cathedral. Library. "The Douglas collection in the Washington Cathedral Library." In *The life and work of Charles Winfred Douglas,* by Leonard Ellinwood and Anne Woodward, p. 36–72. New York: Hymn Society of America, 1958. (Hymn Society of America, Papers, no. 23)
A library of hymnology and liturgical music formed by one of the leading authorities in the field.

WASSERBURG AM INN, GERMANY

Benediktinerinnenabtei Frauenwörth. Thematischer Katalog der Musikhandschriften der Benediktinerinnenabtei Frauenwörth und der Pfarrkirchen Indersdorf, Wasserburg am Inn und Bad Tölz. See no. 1871.

WINDSOR, ENGLAND

2450. Windsor Castle. St. George's Chapel. The musical manuscripts of St. George's Chapel, Windsor Castle: a descriptive catalogue. By Clifford Mould. Windsor: Oxley and Son (Windsor) Ltd. for the Dean and Canons of St. George's Chapel in Windsor Castle, 1973. 76 p. (Historical monographs relating to St. George's Chapel, Windsor Castle, 14)
An index to composers in the 93 manuscripts followed by a table of descriptions and then descriptions of individual manuscripts and groups of manuscripts. Thematic incipits for anonymous music. Appendix listing additional early printed music in the collection.

WINSTON-SALEM, NORTH CAROLINA

2451. Collegium Musicum. "Repertory and resources of the Salem Collegium Musicum, 1780–1790." By Jeannine S. Ingram. In *Fontes Artis Musicae,* 26 (1979), p. 267–81.
A survey of the 100 pieces in printed editions and manuscripts remaining in the Moravian community's musical establishment.

2452. Moravian Church. Catalog of the Salem congregation music. Edited by Frances Cumnock. Chapel Hill: University of North Carolina Press, 1980. 682 p.

There is a lengthy introduction to the 18th- and 19th-century music of the Salem Congregation of the Moravian Church. Thematic catalog entries include attributions to composer, location within the collection, key, and instrumentation and voices required. Organized in three sections for individual collections within the congregation. Indexes of composers and text incipits.

Review by Karl Kroeger in *Notes*, 37 (1981), p. 854–55.

2453. Moravian Music Foundation. Catalog of the Johannes Herbst collection. Edited by Marilyn Gombosi. Chapel Hill: University of North Carolina Press, 1970. 255 p.

A thematic catalog of some 500 manuscripts of sacred music for use in the Moravian service. There are about 1,000 anthems and arias in the collection. The catalog is preceded by a historical introduction describing the musical practices of the 18th-century Moravian church. Index of composers and titles.

Review by Susan T. Sommer in *Notes*, 29 (1972), p. 258–59.

WOLFENBÜTTEL, GERMANY

2454. Herzog-August-Bibliothek. Die Handschriften nebst den älteren Druckwerken der Musikabteilung ... Beschrieben von Emil Vogel. Wolfenbüttel: J. Zwissler, 1890. 280 p. (Die Handschriften der Herzoglichen Bibliothek zu Wolfenbüttel ... 8)

A catalog in two sections, one on music manuscripts and another on printed music, each divided into three subsections—works by a single author, works by anonymous authors, and collections, the latter two organized by title. The collection is especially rich in 17th- and 18th-century music. No indexes, although anthologies are analyzed.

2455. Herzog-August-Bibliothek. Libretti: Verzeichnis der bis 1800 erschienenen Textbücher. Hrsg. von Eberhard Theil und Gisela Rohr. Frankfurt am Main: Klostermann, 1970. 395 p. (Katalog der Herzog-August-Bibliothek Wolfenbüttel, 14)

The entire collection, 1,742 listings, of pre-1800 libretti of operas, interludes, operettas, musical comedies, burlesques, and ballets was available for purchase on microfiche from Kraus-Thomson, Nendeln, Liechtenstein.

Review by Susan T. Sommer in *Notes*, 29 (1972), p. 259.

2456. Herzog-August-Bibliothek. Musik: Alte Drucke bis etwa 1750. Beschrieben von Wolfgang Schmieder. Mitarbeit von Gisela Hartwieg. Text- und Registerband. Frankfurt am Main: V. Klostermann, 1967. 2 v. (Kataloge der Herzog-August-Bibliothek Wolfenbüttel, 12 u. 13)

Vol. I: Textband. 764 p. Vol. II: Registerband. 310 p.

A splendid catalog of 1,334 entries, representing the resources of one of the great German libraries. Early printed music and theoretical treatises.

Review by Harald Heckmann in *Die Musikforschung*, 23 (1970), p. 207–209; by Donald W. Krummel in *Notes*, 26 (1969), p. 39–40.

WROCLAW, POLAND (formerly BRESLAU, GERMANY)

2457. Bohn, Emil. Bibliographie der Musik-Druckwerke bis 1700 welche in der Stadtbibliothek, der Bibliothek des Acad. Inst. für Kirchenmusik, und der K. und Universitäts-Bibliothek zu Breslau aufbewahrt werden.... Berlin: A. Cohn, 1883. 450 p.

Reprint by Georg Olms, Hildesheim, 1969.

The three collections cataloged here are outstanding for their 16th- and 17th-century manuscripts and printed editions, particularly of liturgical and vocal music. P. 1–31: theoretical works; p. 32–351: practical works (music); p. 371–74: collections in chronological order; p. 374–400: continuation of practical works. Full bibliographical descriptions.

2458. Staats- und Universitäts-Bibliothek. Beschreibendes Verzeichnis der alten Musikalien-Handschriften und Druckwerke des Königlichen Gymnasiums zu Brieg. Bearbeitet von Friedrich Kuhn. Leipzig: Breitkopf & Härtel, 1897. 98 p. (Monatshefte für Musikgeschichte. Beilage, Jahrgang 29)

A collection placed in the library of Breslau University in 1890. 54 manuscripts and some 110 printed books, chiefly 16th-century. Contents given for manuscript anthologies; full bibliographical description for printed works. Index.

2459. Stadtbibliothek. Die musikalischen Handschriften des XVI. und XVII. Jahrhunderts in der Stadtbibliothek zu Breslau ... von Emil Bohn. Breslau: Commissions-Verlag von J. Hainauer, 1890. 423 p.

Reprint by Georg Olms, Hildesheim, 1970.

356 items, with full inventories of contents. Numerous indexes and supplementary lists; first-line incipits of vocal texts, anonymous compositions, composer index, etc.

2460. Uniwersytet Wroclawski. Katalog muzycznych dziel teoretycznych XVI i XVII wieku. [Catalog of music theory works of the 16th and 17th centuries.] Compiled by Aniela Kolbuszewska. Wroclaw: Biblioteka Uniwersytecka, 1973. 67 p.

A catalog of 102 numbered theoretical works. Precise bibliographical descriptions with references to descriptive literature. Information as to provenance. Call numbers given. Index of printers and publishers, by place. Index of names.

Review by Fred Pajerski in *Notes*, 31 (1975), p. 785–86.

YORK, GREAT BRITAIN

2461. York Minster. Library. A catalogue of the music manuscripts in York Minster Library. Compiled by David Griffiths. York: University of York Library, 1981. 266 p.

A catalog of 218 manuscripts in the collection, each described and analyzed. Indexes to composers, first lines and titles, copyists, previous owners, genres and performing forces, and to other names and places.

2462. York Minster. Library. A catalogue of the printed music published before 1850 in York Minster Library. Compiled by David Griffiths. York: University of York Library, 1977. 118 p.

A catalog arranged by composer with brief bibliographic information, references to RISM and to other catalogues. Collection of sacred music mainly from the 17th and 18th centuries. Extract from the account books in an appendix. Indexes to: publishers, engravers, music sellers; owners, donors, other associations; names, including dedicatees.

ZARY, POLAND (formerly SORAU, GERMANY)

2463. Hauptkirche. Musikalienkatalog der Hauptkirche zu Sorau N. L. Hergestellt von G. Tischler und K. Burchard. [Langensalza: H. Beyer & Söhne, 1902.] 24 p. (Monatshefte für Musikgeschichte. Beilage. Jahrgang 34)
  The collection contains 33 printed editions, chiefly 17th-century, and a small group of manuscripts in which Telemann, Petri, and C. G. Tag are well represented.

ZÜRICH, SWITZERLAND

2464. Allgemeine Musikgesellschaft. Katalog der gedruckten und handschriftlichen Musikalien des 17. bis 19. Jahrhunderts im Besitze der Allgemeinen Musikgesellschaft Zürich. Red. von Georg Walter. Zürich: Hug, 1960. 145 p.
  A collection rich in 17th- and 18th-century instrumental music. Thematic incipits for works in manuscript.
  Review by Donald W. Krummel in *Notes*, 19 (1961), p. 77; by Willi Kahl in *Die Musikforschung*, 16 (1963), p. 284.

2465. Zentralbibliothek. "Die Österreichische Musiküberlieferung der Züricher Zentralbibliothek." [By Erich Schenk.] In *Die Österreichische Nationalbibliothek. Festschrift hrsg. zum 25. jährigen Dienstjubiläum des Generaldirektors Prof. Dr. Josef Bick*, p. 576–81. Wien: H. Bauer-Verlag, 1948.
  Consists chiefly of a listing of works by Austrian composers in the Zürich library, giving place, publisher, and library signature. Special attention given to works not mentioned in Eitner.

ZWICKAU, GERMANY

2466. Ratsschulbibliothek. Bibliographie der Musikwerke in der Ratsschulbibliothek zu Zwickau, bearb.... von Reinhard Vollhardt. Leipzig: Breitkopf & Härtel, 1893–96. 299 p. (Monatshefte für Musikgeschichte. Beilage. Jahrgang 25–28)
  764 numbered items, manuscripts and printed books, including liturgical works, theoretical works, instrumental and vocal music. Chiefly 16th- and 17th-century materials.

CATALOGS OF PRIVATE COLLECTIONS

In this section some of the catalogs of major private music collections are cited. Few of these remain intact. Some, like the Cortot or the Wolffheim collections, have been dispersed; others have changed location in recent years. No attempt has been made here to list the numerous catalogs issued in connection with auction sales, although some of these are of great bibliographical interest. Some indication of the information to be gained from the study of early music auction catalogs, a field very little explored as yet, can be found in A. Hyatt King's book *Some British Collectors of Music, c. 1600–1960,* Cambridge University Press, 1963 (no. 2468) and in Otto E. Albrecht's article "Collections, private" in the *New Grove Dictionary of Music and Musicians.* James B. Coover's *Provisional Checklist of Priced Antiquarians' Catalogues Containing Musical Materials* (no. 690) and the bibliography of literature about private collections of books and scores he announced as forthcoming in his *Musical Instrument Collections; Catalogues and Cognate Literature* (no. 2495) will be of use to those interested in private collections. Lenore Coral's work on British book sale catalogs (her thesis, *Music in English Auction Sales, 1676–1750* [University of London, 1974] and with A. N. L. Munby, *British Book Sale Catalogues, 1676–1800; a Union List* [London: Mansell, 1977]) sheds some light on this subject as well.

Frits Knuf, Amsterdam, has published a series of reprints of important auction catalogs of music from the collections of Selhof, Burney, Turk, Coussemaker, Novello, and Rimbault. Numerous entries in the preceding section refer to private collections now in institutional custody; there are entries in the subject index in the names of the previous, private owners of these collections.

Siegrun Folter's *Private Libraries of Musicians and Musicologists* and A. Hyatt King's *Some British Collectors of Music* are cited first in this section because they cover numerous collectors.

2467. Folter, Siegrun H. Private libraries of musicians and musicologists: a bibliography of catalogs with introduction and notes. Buren: Frits Knuf, 1987. 261 p. (Auction catalogs of music, 7)

> The present bibliography concentrates on catalogs of private collectors who were or are known to be musicians (composers, performers) or musicologists. Music publishers and dealers as collectors are omitted unless they were active as musicians beyond their professional trade. [*Introduction*]

Arranged by name of collector and then chronologically, there are annotated citations of auction and dealers' catalogs, exhibition catalogs, privately printed and institutional catalogs, as well as those published in monographs and articles. Catalogs listed in King's *Some British Collectors of Music* are omitted, but are cited. Pattick & Simpson catalogs are omitted also, because of the pending publication of a study on the subject by James B. Coover. Citations provide locations of known copies. Chronological index and dealers index.

Reviewed by Lenore Coral in *Fontes Artis Musicae,* 36 (1989), p. 333–34, and by Ann P. Basart in *Cum Notis Variorum,* 128 (December 1988), p. 7–8.

2468. King, A. Hyatt. Some British collectors of music. Cambridge: Cambridge University Press, 1963. 178 p. (The Sandars Lectures for 1961)

A pioneer study of the activity of private collectors of music in England, with an appendix containing classified lists of collectors from the mid-17th century to 1960.

Aldrich, Richard. A catalogue of books.... See no. 1961.

2469. Bokemeyer, Heinrich. Collection.
An important 18th-century music library assembled by the theorist Heinrich Bokemeyer (1679–1751). Harald Kümmerling has reconstructed the collection and identified its surviving elements now in the Stiftung Preussischer Kulturbesitz in Berlin. See no. 1908.

2470. Burney, Charles. Catalogue of the music library of Charles Burney, sold in London, 8 August 1814. With an introduction by A. Hyatt King. Amsterdam: Frits Knuf, 1973. (Auction catalogues of music, no. 2)
A facsimile list of the music collection Burney gathered on his travels and in response to his need for sources while writing *A General History of Music* (no. 526).
Review by Kerry S. Grant in *Notes*, 31 (1974), p. 45–58.

2471. Burrell, Mary. The Richard Wagner collection formed by ... Mary Burrell. The property of The Curtis Institute of Music, Philadelphia; which will be sold on Friday, October 27, 1978. New York: Christie, Manson & Woods, International, 1978. 172 p.
One of the most distinguished collections of Wagneriana ever in private hands, the collection was sold and largely dispersed. See the earlier catalog of the collection (no. 2291).

2472. Cortot, Alfred. Bibliothèque Alfred Cortot.... v. 1. Catalogue établi par Alfred Cortot et rédigé par Frederik Goldbeck, avec la collaboration de A. Fehr. Préface de Henry Prunières. [Argentueil: Sur les presses de R. Coulouma, 1936.] 221 p.
Premiere Partie (all published): Traités et autres ouvrages théoriques des XVe, XVIe, XVIIe, & XVIIIe siècles.
The music holdings in the library of Alfred Cortot. Cortot's interests as a collector extended over a wide area of musical practice. The collection passed into the hands of a dealer at the owner's death in 1962.
Portions of the Cortot library have since been acquired by the British Library, the Newberry Library in Chicago, the University of California Music Library at Berkeley, the University of Texas at Austin, and the University of Kentucky at Lexington. For an account of this dispersal, and a complete list of Kentucky's acquisition of 290 treatises, see Frank Traficante, "The Alfred Cortot collection at the University of Kentucky Libraries," in *University of Kentucky Library Notes*, vol. 1, no. 3 (Spring 1970), 19 p. (no. 2118). A shorter version of the same paper is printed in *Notes*, 26 (1970), p. 713–17. The Cortot materials in the British Library are described by A. Hyatt King and O. W. Neighbour in *British Museum Quarterly*, 31 (1966), p. 8–16. The Cortot materials at the Harry Ransom Humanities Research Center, University of Texas at Austin, are described in *Library Chronicle*, 25/26 (1984), p. 24–49.

2473. Coussemaker, Charles Edmond Henri de. Catalogue of the music library of Charles Edmond Henri de Coussemaker, sold at Brussels 1877. With an introduction by A. Hyatt King. Buren: Frits Knuf, 1977. (Auction catalogues in music, no. 4)

A facsimile of the classified catalog of the holdings of the pioneering musicologist. Portions of the Coussemaker collection were acquired by Vander Straeten, Weckerlin, the Bibliothèque Royale of Brussels, and the Bibliothèque de Douai.

2474. The Dickinson Collection. "New Schumann materials in upstate New York: a first report on the Dickinson Collection, with catalogues of its manuscript holdings." By Ralph P. Locke and Jurgen Thym. In *Fontes Artis Musicae*, 27 (1980), p. 137–61.

An inventory of manuscripts, letters, printed music, books, and miscellaneous items in the collection gathered by Edward and June Dickinson and kept in Livona, New York.

2475. Feininger, Laurence. Repertorium cantus plani. Tridenti: Societas Universalis Sanctae Ceciliae, 1969. 2 v.

Catalog of a private collection of liturgical manuscripts. Vol. I: Antiphonaria. Vol. II: Gradualia.

Each volume treats 24 manuscripts. Descriptions are followed by complete inventories of the contents of each source. Indexes of liturgical incipits conclude each volume.

2476. Fuchs, Aloys. "The autographs of the Viennese music collections of Aloys Fuchs, using the original catalogues." Edited by Richard Schaal. In *Haydn Yearbook*, vol. VI (1969), p. 3–191.

The autographs are listed alphabetically by composer, with information as to provenance and destination if known. Introduction in German and English.

Fuchs (1799–1853) was the first great collector of musical autographs. His collection was dispersed, but portions of it can be found in the Berlin Staatsbibliothek, the Staatsbibliothek der Stiftung Preussischer Kulturbesitz, and the Benedictine abbey at Gottweig.

See also no. 2477.

2477. Fuchs, Aloys. Quellen und Forschungen zur Wiener Musiksammlung von Aloys Fuchs von Richard Schaal. Wien: H. Böhlaus Nachf., 1966. 151 p. (Veröffentlichungen der Kommission für Musikforschung, 5)

A report on the contents of the Fuchs collection. Bibliography: p. 135–151.

2478. Gehring, Franz Eduard. Katalog der musikalischen Bibliothek des Herrn Dr. F. Gehring ... die Versteigerung ... findet am Montag dem 29. November 1880 ... im Kunst-Auctions-Hause, Berlin. Berlin: A. Cohn, 1880. 143 p.

The sale catalog for a collection of 1,671 titles: 317 early works on music history and theory; 191 pieces of instrumental music; 583 opera scores; and other vocal scores. This was a very carefully chosen collection of the most important works available of the time; apparently some of the manuscripts and early printed works came from Otto Jahn. Entries are brief, but some additional information on degree of rarity is provided. Manuscripts are mixed in with printed works and can be discovered only by careful reading of the annotations.

2479. Heyer, Wilhelm. Musikhistorisches Museum von Wilhelm Heyer in Köln. Katalog von George Kinsky. Band 4: Musik-Autographen. Leipzig: Breitkopf & Härtel, 1916. 870 p.

1,673 items; one of the finest collections of musical autographs ever assembled. Dispersed and sold at auction in 1926 by the firm of Henrici and Liepmannssohn. Kinsky's catalogs of the Heyer collection are models of music bibliography, full of biographical and descriptive detail. 64 facsimile plates.

For other volumes of the Heyer Katalog, see nos. 2531 and 2532.

2480. Hirsch, Paul. Katalog der Musikbibliothek Paul Hirsch ... Frankfurt am Main, hrsg. von K. Meyer und P. Hirsch. Berlin: M. Breslauer, 1928–47. 4 v. (Vol. 4 has imprint of Cambridge University Press.)

Vol. 1: Theoretische Drucke bis 1800. Vol. 2: Opern-Partituren. Vol. 3: Instrumental- und Vokalmusik bis etwa 1830. Vol. 4: Erstausgaben, Chorwerke in Partitur, Gesamtausgaben, Nachschlagewerke, etc. Ergänzungen zu Bd. I–III.

The Paul Hirsch Library, one of the great private music collections of the world, was removed from Frankfurt to Cambridge, England, just prior to World War II and was acquired by the British Museum in 1946.

See the brief article, "The Hirsch catalog," by P. H. Muir in *Music Review*, 9 (1948), p. 102–107.

See also nos. 2141 and 2142.

2481. Jacobi, Erwin R. Musikbibliothek Erwin R. Jacobi. Seltene Ausgaben und Manuskripte. Katalog. The music library of Erwin R. Jacobi. Rare editions and manuscripts. Compiled by Regula Puskás. [Hrsg.:] Allgemeine Musikgesellschaft Zürich. 3., erg. und rev. Aufl. Zürich: Hug, 1973. 84 p.

Second ed. published in 1970 titled *Seltene Originalausgaben von Musica Practica und Musica Theoretica aus dem 15.–20. Jahrhundert.*

A private collection of 514 items. 11 plates. Preface in English and German. Errata slip inserted.

2482. Koch, Louis. Collection. Katalog der Musikautographen Sammlung Koch ... Manuskripte, Briefe, Dokumente, von Scarlatti bis Stravinsky. Beschrieben und erläutert von Georg Kinsky. Stuttgart: Hoffmannsche Buchdruckerei F. Krais, 1953. 360 p.

An important collection of musical autographs. Strong in German music of the classic and romantic periods. 21 facsimile plates.

Review by Richard S. Hill in *Notes*, 11 (1953), p. 119–20.

Levy, Lester S., Collection. See no. 1873.

2483. Meyer, André. Collection musicale André Meyer: manuscrits, autographes, musique imprimée et manuscrite, ouvrages théoriques, historiques et pédagogiques, livrets, iconographie, instruments de musique. Abbeville: F. Paillart, [1960]. 118 p.

Catalog compiled by François Lesure and Nanie Bridgman. A collection of manuscripts and early printed music, particularly noteworthy for its holdings in iconography. Beautifully illustrated by 292 plates. Review by Hans Halm in *Die Musikforschung*, 17 (1964), p. 83–84.

2484. Die Musikalien der Grafen von Schönborn-Wiesentheid. Thematisch-bibliographischer Katalog. Bearbeitet von Fritz Zobeley. I. Theil: Das Repertoire des Grafen Rudolf Franz Erwein von Schönborn (1677–1754). Tutzing: Hans Schneider, 1967–82. 2 v. (Veröffentlichungen der Gesellschaft für bayerische Musikgeschichte e.V.)

Band I: Drucke aus den Jahren 1676 bis 1738; Band II: Handschriften.

Thematic catalog of a private collection of early vocal and instrumental music assembled by the Counts von Schönborn-Wiesentheid in Schloss Weiler bei Aschaffenburg. 149 items, with full bibliographical descriptions and inventories of contents. Informative introductory chapters on the history of the collection and its composition. Further catalogs of the MSS and archive materials projected.

Review by W. Gordon Marigold in *Notes*, 24 (1968), p. 715–16.

2485. Novello, Vincent. Catalogue of the music library of Vincent Novello, sold in London 25 June 1852 and 3 September 1862. With an introduction by A. Hyatt King. Buren: Frits Knuf, 1975. (Auction catalogues in music, no. 5)

A facsimile of the listing of the collection of Vincent Novello, who had "a remarkable grasp of the functions of a music librarian."

2486. Pretlack, Ludwig, Freiherr von. Die Musikbibliothek des Ludwig Freiherrn von Pretlack (1716–1781). [Hrsg. von] Joachim Jaenecke. Wiesbaden: Breitkopf & Härtel, 1973. 330 p. (Neue musikgeschichtliche Forschungen, 8)

The Pretlack collection is now in the Staatsbibliothek der Stiftung Preussischer Kulturbesitz, Berlin.

2487. Rimbault, Edward Francis. Catalogue of the music library of Edward Francis Rimbault, sold at London 31 July–7 August 1877. With the Library of Dr. Rainbeau. With an introduction by A. Hyatt King. Buren: Frits Knuf, 1975. (Auction catalogues of music, no. 6)

A facsimile of the list of music and books that supported various of Rimbault's musical studies, such as *Bibliotheca Madrigaliana* (no. 1792). Many of the more valuable titles went to Joseph Drexel and thereafter to the New York Public Library (no. 2239).

With the actual sale catalog is published the satirical *Catalogue of the Extensive Library of Doctor Rainbeau*, which was previously published as a separate facsimile with an introduction by James B. Coover (Distant Press, 1962).

2488. Scheide, William. Selections from the library of William H. Scheide. New York: Grolier Club, 1967. 11 p.

Catalog of the exhibition of selections from Mr. Scheide's collection, known to be rich in manuscripts and early prints. The exhibit occurred in March 1967.

2489. Selhof, Nicholas. Catalogue of the music library, instruments and other property of Nicholas Selhof, sold in The Hague, 1759. With an introduction by A. Hyatt King. Amsterdam: Frits Knuf, 1973. (Auction catalogues of music, no. 1)

A facsimile listing about 2,940 works, published and in manuscript.

2490. Stainer, John, Sir. Catalogue of English song books: forming a portion of the library of Sir John Stainer. Boston, Massachusetts: Longwood Press, 1977. 107 p.

Reprint of the Novello, Ewer edition of 1889.

A catalog prepared by Stainer's children on not only songbooks but also books about bells in Stainer's library.

2491. Türk, Daniel Gottlob. Catalogue of the music library of Daniel Gottlob Türk, sold in Halle, 13 January 1817. With an introduction by A. Hyatt King. Amsterdam: Frits Knuf, 1973. (Auction catalogues in music, no. 3)

A facsimile of the catalog of music and books about music auctioned posthumously. Includes references to works not sold but in Türk's collection.

2492. Weckerlin, Jean Baptiste Théodore. Katalog der Musikbibliothek des Herrn J. B. Weckerlin. Music — Tanz — Theater. Versteigerung, 10. bis 12. März 1910. Leipzig: C. G. Boerner, 1910. 172 p.

Auction catalog of the private library of Weckerlin, distinguished French music librarian and musicologist of the 19th century. Illustrated with facsimile pages. Extensive holdings of vocal music. Foreword in French and German by C. G. Boerner. Catalog has descriptive notes mainly in French.

2493. Wittgenstein Collection. "Ursprung und Geschichte der Sammlung Wittgenstein im 19. Jahrhundert." By E. Fred Flindell. In *Die Musikforschung*, 22 (1969), p. 298–314.

A 19th-century collection of musical autographs including works of Mendelssohn, Brahms, Joachim, Grillparzer, Beethoven, Schubert, etc. Now largely dispersed, a part is in the Library of Congress.

2494. Wolffheim, Werner J. Versteigerung der Musikbibliothek des Herrn Dr. Werner Wolffheim ... durch die Firmen: M. Breslauer & L. Liepmannssohn.... Berlin: 1928–29. 2 v. in 4.

> One of the finest collections ever brought together by a private person ... the 2-volume catalog compiled at the time of its sale will always rank as an indispensable work of reference. [*Grove's*, 5th ed.]

Classified catalog of a library that included not only rarities but the standard reference books and editions as well. Full descriptions with copious notes. Numerous facsimile plates.

Catalogs of Musical Instrument Collections

Collections of musical instruments are frequently annexed to music libraries. The reader will note that a number of the catalogs in the preceding section are concerned, in part, with Western or Asian instruments. In the section that follows, the catalogs of some of the major specialized collections of musical instruments are listed along with a number of exhibition catalogs emphasizing this area of collecting activity.

For a comprehensive and historical view of instrument collections, see Alfred Berner's article, "Instrumentensammlungen," in *MGG*, vol. 6, cols. 1295–1310. There is also an illuminating paper by Georg Kinsky entitled "Musikinstrumentensammlungen in Vergangenheit und Gegenwart," in the *Jahrbuch Peters*, 27 (1920), p. 47–60.

Three surveys, listed first, provide a broad, if somewhat dated, overview of the potential sources for literature in this chapter. One is that of the Music Library Association, *A Survey of Musical Instrument Collections in the United States and Canada* (no. 2496), and a second is James B. Coover's *Musical Instrument Collections; Catalogues and Cognate Literature* (no. 2495), which cites 2,418 catalogs published up to the late 1970s. Philip T. Young's inventory of historical woodwind instruments (no. 2497) is the third survey cited before catalogs of individual collections. In the main, new entries to this chapter have been important titles published after Coover's bibliography appeared.

2495. Coover, James B. Musical instrument collections; catalogues and cognate literature. Detroit, Michigan: Information Coordinators, 1981. 464 p. (Detroit studies in music bibliography, 47)

An annotated bibliography of 2,418 titles arranged in section one by name of institutions or exposition and in section two by name of private collectors. Appendixes list chronologically some early inventories, expositions, and exhibitions. General index and index to auctioneers, antiquarians, and firms.

Review by Paula Morgan in *Notes*, 39 (1982), p. 198. Review by Jeremy Montagu in *Early Music*, 11 (1983), p. 100–102.

2496. A survey of musical instrument collections in the United States and Canada. Conducted by a committee of the Music Library Association: William Lichtenwanger, chairman and compiler; Dale Higbee, Cynthia Adams Hoover, Phillip T. Young. Ann Arbor, Michigan: Music Library Association, 1974. 137 p.

Details on 572 collections in institutions. Information on collections of historical instruments, modern replicas, ethnic instruments, toy instruments, etc. Directory with addresses, personnel, hours of service, catalogs, and bibliography. Index of instruments and classes of instruments; of cultural, geographical, and historical origins.
Review by Laurence Libin in *Notes*, 33 (1976), p. 57–59.

2497. Young, Philip T. 2,500 historical woodwind instruments; an inventory of major collections. New York: Pendragon Press, 1982. 155 p.
Organized alphabetically by makers' last name. Instruments listed in orchestral score order: flutes, oboes, clarinets, bassoons, etc. Bibliography. Appendixes of museums and collections represented and bibliography of sources of illustrations.
Review by Malou Haine in *Fontes Artis Musicae*, 30 (1983), p. 225–27.

ANN ARBOR, MICHIGAN

2498. University of Michigan. Stearns Collection of Musical Instruments. Catalog of the Stearns collection of musical instruments. By Albert A. Stanley. 2nd ed. Ann Arbor: University of Michigan, 1921. 276 p.
First published in 1918. A supplement, *Stearns Collection of Musical Instruments—1965*, by Robert Austin Warner was published in 1965. 10 p.

A catalog of 1,464 instruments, Western and Asian. 13 plates, descriptive annotations. Bibliography and indexes of makers, geographical distribution, names of instruments.
A brief, informative survey of the history of the collection, its character, and its present condition. 3 plates.

ANTWERP, BELGIUM

2499. Museum Vleeshuis. Catalogus van de muziekinstrumenten uit de verzameling van het Museum Vleeshuis. Antwerpen: Ruckers Genootschap, 1981. 189 p.
An illustrated, classified catalog of the 475 early musical instruments in the museum, with references to maker, city of manufacture, gross measurements, and references to fuller descriptions for each. Index to names of makers with brief biographical data. Classified bibliography of works consulted.

BASEL, SWITZERLAND

2500. Historisches Museum. Katalog der Musikinstrumente im Historischen Museum zu Basel. Von Dr. Karl Nef. Basel: Universitäts-Buchdruckerei von Friedrich Reinhardt, 1906. 74 p.
Bound with *Festschrift zum zweiten Kongress der Internationalen Musikgesellschaft*, Basel, 1906. 294 instruments listed and described. 12 plates.

BERKELEY, CALIFORNIA

2501. University of California. Department of Music. Catalogue of the collection of musical instruments in the Department of Music, University of California, Berkeley. Part I. Edited by David Boyden.... Berkeley, Calif.: 1972. 104 p.

An unpublished catalog.

A collection of 88 instruments, including early originals and modern replicas. Short essays on the principal instrument forms. Each instrument is introduced historically, followed by its precise dimensions. A second part is projected.

BERLIN, GERMANY

2502. Institut für Musikforschung. Die Berliner Musikinstrumentensammlung; Einführung mit historischen und technischen Erläuterungen von Alfred Berner. Berlin: 1952. 58 p.

Not strictly a catalog, but a guide to the principal types of instruments with reference to examples in the Berlin collection. 11 plates.

2503. Staatliche Akademische Hochschule für Musik. Führer durch die Sammlung alter Musik-Instrumente, von Dr. Oskar Fleischer. Berlin: A. Haack, 1892. 145 p.

Classified catalog, chiefly early Western instruments, with a few Asian.

2504. Staatliche Akademische Hochschule für Musik. Sammlung alter Musikinstrumente bei der Staatlichen Hochschule für Musik zur Berlin; beschreibender Katalog von Curt Sachs. Berlin: J. Bard, 1922. 384 cols. 30 plates.

The collection contains some 3,200 items, of which about 250 are non-European instruments. Classified catalog. Entries give descriptions of instrument, maker, date and place of manufacture. Index of instruments, places, makers, etc.

2505. Staatliches Institut für Musikforschung. Das Musikinstrumenten-Museum Berlin. Eine Einführung in Wort und Bild. Berlin: 1968. 70 p.

Historical essay: "75 Jahre Musikinstrumenten-Sammlung" by Irmgard Otto; 56 photo plates of instruments.

2506. Staatliches Institut für Musikforschung. Musikinstrumenten-Museum Berlin. Ausstellungsverzeichnis mit Personen- und Sachregistern. Bearbeitet von Irmgard Otto. Berlin: 1965. 144 p.

A guide to the Berlin musical instrument collection, with a diagram of the exposition halls, index of donors, a list of catalog numbers, and 12 pages of photo plates of instruments.

BOLOGNA, ITALY

2507. Tagliavini Collezione. Clavicembali e spinette dal XVI al XIX secolo: collezione L. F. Tagliavini a cura di Luigi Ferdinando Tagliavini e John

Henry van der Meer; con i contributi di Wanda Bergamini e Friedemann Hellwig. Casalecchio di Reno and Bologna: Grafis, 1986. 243 p.

At head of title: Cassa di risparmio in Bologna; Collezioni d'arte e di documentazione storica. Catalog of an exhibition held at Chiesa di San Giorgio in Poggiale, 1 Nov.–21 Dec. 1986.

Catalog of a remarkable private collection gathered by the distinguished musicologist, organologist, and organist. The collection was exhibited while the 1987 Congress of the International Musicological Society was held in Bologna.

BOSTON, MASSACHUSETTS

2508. Museum of Fine Arts. Leslie Lindsey Mason Collection. Ancient European musical instruments ... By N. Bessaraboff. Cambridge, Massachusetts: Published for the Museum ... by the Harvard University Press, 1941. 503 p.

An authoritative, well-illustrated catalog, 213 items. Provides a wealth of background information for the historical study of instruments. Bibliography, p. 453–69. Indexes of names and subjects. 16 plates and 72 illustrations in text. The collection of Canon Francis W. Galpin forms the basis of the Mason collection.

Review by Curt Sachs in *Musical Quarterly*, (July 1942), p. 380–83.

For an evaluation of the book, and a tribute to its author, see David Boyden's article "Nicholas Bessaraboff's *Ancient European Musical Instruments*," in *Notes*, 28 (1971), p. 21–27.

BRAUNSCHWEIG, GERMANY

2509. Städtisches Museum. Verzeichnis der Sammlung alter Musikinstrumente im Städtischen Museum Braunschweig ... Instrumente, Instrumentenmacher und Instrumentisten in Braunschweig.... Braunschweig: E. Appelhans, 1928. 124 p. (Werkstücke aus Museum, Archiv und Bibliothek der Stadt Braunschweig, 3)

The catalog occupies p. 5–34; lists 113 items, all European. The remainder of the volume is devoted to studies of local instrument makers and performers.

BRUGES, BELGIUM

2510. Gruuthusemuseum. Catalogus van de muziekinstrumenten. [Prepared by] M. Awouters, I. De Keyser, [and] S. Vandenberghe. Brugge: Brugge Gruuthusemuseum, 1985. 120 p.

BRUSSELS, BELGIUM

2511. Conservatoire Royal de Musique. Musée Instrumental. Catalogue descriptif et analytique du Musée par Victor-Charles Mahillon, conservateur.... 2e ed. Gand: A. Hoste, 1893–1922. 5 v.

One of the great instrument collections of the world. More than 3,000 instruments of all cultures. Classified catalog. The descriptions include precise indications of each instrument's pitch, tuning, and range.

BUSSUM, THE NETHERLANDS

2512. Leeuwen Boomkamp, C. van and J. H. Van der Meer. The Carel van Leeuwen Boomkamp collection of musical instruments. Amsterdam: Frits Knuf, 1971. 188 p. 80 plates.

A private collection of 112 items, expertly described and illustrated in photographs. The collection is strongest in its stringed instruments (57) and its bows (32).

Review by Anthony Baines in *Galpin Society Journal*, 25 (1972), p. 123–35.

CAIRO, EGYPT

2513. Museum of Egyptian Antiquitiés. Catalogue général des antiquités égyptiennes du Musée du Caire. Nos. 69201–69852: Instruments de musique, par Hans Hickmann. Le Caire: Imprimerie de l'Institut français d'archéologie orientale, 1949. 216 p. 116 plates.

Classified catalog of 651 ancient Egyptian instruments, or fragments thereof, with detailed descriptions and photo reproductions.

CAMBRIDGE, MASSACHUSETTS

2514. Eddy Collection. The Eddy Collection of Musical Instruments: a checklist. By Edwin M. Good. Berkeley, California: Fallen Leaf Press, 1985. 91 p. (Fallen Leaf reference books in music, 3)

A classified catalog of a private collection of over 300 European and American instruments from the late 18th to the 20th centuries, principally of woodwind instruments and pianos. Each entry provides information on maker, place of manufacture, material, shape, and approximate date of construction. There is a list of manufacturers and dealers with cross-references to entries, but no other indexes as this is a provisional checklist appearing before a fuller catalog of the collection.

CINCINNATI, OHIO

2515. Art Museum. Musical instruments. [Collection of the Cincinnati Art Museum.] Cincinnati: Cincinnati Art Museum 1949. 23 p.

An illustrated brochure listing 110 instruments, 60 European, 50 non-European.

COPENHAGEN, DENMARK

2516. Carl Claudius Collection. Carl Claudius' Samling af gamle musikinstrumenter. København: Levin og Munskgaard, 1931. 423 p.

A rich private collection of musical instruments, now administered by the University of Copenhagen. The catalog describes 757 items.

2517. Musikhistorisk Museum. Das Musikhistorische Museum zu Kopenhagen: beschreibender Katalog von Angul Hammerich; deutsch von Erna

Bobe. Mit 179 Illustrationen. Kopenhagen: G. E. C. Gad, 1909; Leipzig: Kommissionsverlag von Breitkopf & Härtel, 1911. 172 p.

Classified catalog of 631 items, 582 of which are instruments, Western and Asian, followed by a short listing of liturgical manuscripts, printed editions, and miscellany.

EDINBURGH, SCOTLAND

2518. University. Dept. of Early Keyboard Instruments. The Russell collection and other early keyboard instruments in Saint Cecilia's Hall, Edinburgh. [Compiled by Sidney Newman and Peter Williams.] Edinburgh: Edinburgh University Press, 1968. 79 p.

2519. University. Galpin Society Exhibition. An exhibition of European musical instruments. Edinburgh International Festival, 18 Aug.–7 Sept. 1968, Reid School of Music, Edinburgh University. Edinburgh: 1968. 99 p. 40 plates.

The 21st anniversary exhibition of the Galpin Society.

An exhibition catalog of 716 items, including bibliography. Instruments described, dimensions given. The introductory paragraphs for each group of instruments are supplied by specialists. The editor of the catalog is Graham Melville-Mason.

See also the Galpin Society exhibition catalog, London, 1951 (no. 2539).

EISENACH, GERMANY

2520. Bachmuseum. Verzeichnis der Sammlung alter Musikinstrumente im Bachhaus zu Eisenach, hrsg. von der Neuen Bach Gesellschaft. 4., erweiterte Aufl. Leipzig: Breitkopf & Härtel, 1964. 97 p. (Veröffentlichungen der Neuen Bachgesellschaft. Vereinsjahr 50, 1962)

First issued in 1913.

Classified catalog of more than 230 items. Illustrated with line drawings.

FLORENCE, ITALY

2521. Conservatorio di Musica "Luigi Cherubini." Gli strumenti musicali raccolti nel Museo del R. Istituto L. Cherubini a Firenze. [By Leto Bargagna.] [Firenze: G. Ceccherini, 1911.] 70 p.

A catalog of 146 instruments; 12 plates.

2522. Museo del Conservatorio "Luigi Cherubini." Gli strumenti musicali della corte medicea e il Museo del Conservatorio "Luigi Cherubini" di Firenze. Cenni storici e catalogo descrittivo. [By] Vincio Gai. Firenze: LICOSA, 1969. 286 p.

The instruments are illustrated by line drawings with precise measurements. P. 255–71: "Bibliografia." Preceded by an introduction relating the history of the collection.

GIJÓN, SPAIN

2523. Museo Internacional de la Gaita. Catalogo. Gijón: Asturias (España), 1970. 152 p.
Catalog of a museum devoted to the bagpipe, its history and distribution. Organized by country, with numerous color plates and black-and-white illustrations.

THE HAGUE, THE NETHERLANDS

2524. Gemeentemuseum. Catalogi van de muziekbibliotheek en de collectie muziekinstrumenten onder redactie van dr. C. C. J. von Gleich. Catalogus van de muziekinstrumenten. Deel I: Hoorn- en trompetachtige blaasinstrumenten door Leo J. Plenckers. Amsterdam: Frits Knuf, 1970. 85 p.
The first of a series of catalogs projected to cover the musical instrument collections at the Gemeentemuseum. Describes 136 instruments of the horn and trumpet type. 8 plates. A classified grouping of instrument types, and a glossary. Index of names.
This series is paralleled by another devoted to the holdings of the museum's music library (no. 2048).

2525. Gemeentemuseum. Europese muziekinstrumenten in het Haagse Gemeentemuseum. [By A. W. Ligtvoet and W. Lievense.] 's-Gravenhage: Gemeentemuseum, 1965. 160 p.
With 64 full-page illustrations.

2526. Gemeentemuseum. Exotische en oude Europese muziekinstrumenten, in de muziekafdeling van het Haagse Gemeentemuseum; 25 afbeeldingen toegelicht. [By A. W. Ligtvoet.] s'-Gravenhage: Nijgh & Van Ditmar, [1955]. 51 p.
A general, popular introduction to the collection. 25 plates. Text in Dutch and English.

2527. Gemeentemuseum. Pianofortes from the Low Countries. Pianofortes uit de Lage Landen. [Text, Dr. Clemens von Gleich; translation: Delboy & Behnsen; photographs: B. Frequin *et al.*] Buren: Haags Gemeentemuseum; F. Knuf, 1980. 55 p.
Pianofortes from the 18th and 19th centuries by Dutch makers from the instrument collection of the Haags Gemeentemuseum. In English and Dutch.

HALLE, GERMANY

2528. Händel-Haus. Katalog zu den Sammlungen des Händel-Hauses in Halle. 5. Teil: Musikinstrumentensammlung. Besaitete Tasteninstrumente. By Konrad Sasse. 6. Teil: Musikinstrumentensammlung, Streich- und Zupfinstrumente (1972). 7. Teil: Musikinstrumentensammlung, Blasinstrumente, Orgeln, Harmoniums (1979). Halle: Händel-Haus, 1966–79. 7 vol.
One of the largest collections of keyboard instruments in Europe, comprising some 115 items. Founded on the collection of J. C. Neupert of Nu-

remberg, acquired in the 1930s. These are classified catalogs with extensive descriptions, often with photographs of the instruments. Indexes to makers. Bibliographies of works cited. Index to catalogs by identification number of each instrument. There is an outline to the cataloging scheme employed.

Review by Friedrich Ernst in *Die Musikforschung*, 21 (1968), p. 506–507.

For a catalog of the complete holdings of the Handel House in Halle, see nos. 2051.

HOLYOKE, MASSACHUSETTS

2529. Mount Holyoke College. The Belle Skinner collection of old musical instruments.... A descriptive catalogue. Compiled under the direction of William Skinner. [Philadelphia, New York, etc.: Printed by the Beck Engraving Co.], 1933. 210 p.

Illustrated catalog of 89 instruments, including some particularly fine examples of keyboard instruments. Colored plates.

Since 1959 this collection has been on loan to Yale University.

JOHANNESBURG, SOUTH AFRICA

2530. Kirby, Percival Robson. Catalogue of the musical instruments in the collection of Percival R. Kirby. Compiled by Margareet M. de Lange. Johannesburg: Africana Museum, 1967. 155 p.

LEIPZIG, GERMANY

2531. Heyer Collection. Kleiner Katalog der Sammlung alter Musikinstrumente, verfasst von Georg Kinsky. Köln: 1913. 250 p.

An abridgment of the material in the following catalog; valuable because it contains entries for the wind instruments in the Heyer collection, not included in the larger catalog.

2532. Heyer Collection. Musikhistorisches Museum von Wilhelm Heyer in Köln. Katalog von Georg Kinsky. Leipzig: Breitkopf & Härtel, 1910–16. 2 v.

The two volumes of the catalog are concerned with the instrument collection. Vol. 1: Besaitete Tasteninstrumente. Orgel und orgelartige Instrumente. Vol. 2: Zupf- und Streichinstrumente. Vol. 3 (not published) was intended to cover the wind instruments. The Heyer instrument collection, one of the finest in the world, was transferred to Leipzig in 1926, where it was destroyed in World War II.

Kinsky's catalog is a mine of information for the student of early instruments; copiously illustrated, rich in detail.

See also no. 2479.

2533. Universität. Musikinstrumenten-Museum. Führer durch das Musikinstrumenten-Museum der Karl-Marx-Universität Leipzig. Von Paul Rubardt. Leipzig: Breitkopf & Härtel, 1955. 84 p. 16 plates.

2534. Universität. Musikinstrumenten-Museum. Führer durch das Musikwissenschaftliche Instrumente-Museum der Universität Leipzig. Hrsg. von Helmut Schultz. Leipzig: Breitkopf & Härtel, 1929. 85 p. 19 plates.
A classified catalog organized according to the ground plan of the display.

2535. Universität. Musikinstrumenten-Museum. Kataloge des Musikinstrumenten-Museums der Karl-Marx-Universität zu Leipzig. Leipzig: Deutscher Verlag für Musik, 1978– . 6 v. to date.
Contents:
Vol. 1. *Flöten* [von] Herbert Heyde.
Vol. 2. *Kielinstrumente* [von] Hubert Henkel.
Vol. 3. *Trompeten, Posaunen, Tuben* [von] Herbert Heyde.
Vol. 4. *Clavichorde* [von] Hubert Henkel.
Vol. 5. *Hörner und Zinken* [von] Herbert Heyde.
Vol. 6. *Orgelinstrumente, Harmoniums* [von] Klaus Gernhardt, Hubert Henkel [und] Winfried Schrammek.
Scientific studies of instruments in the Karl Marx University in Leipzig. Precise measurements provided.

LINZ, AUSTRIA

2536. Landesmuseum. Die Musikinstrumentensammlung des Oberösterreichischen Landesmuseums. Bearbeitet von Othmar Wessely. Linz: Demokratische Druck- und Verlags-Gesellschaft, [n.d.]. 47 p. (Kataloge des Oberösterreichischen Landesmuseums, 9)
A collection of 188 items, classified and described briefly.

LONDON, ENGLAND

2537. British Museum. Department of Western Asiatic Antiquities. Ancient musical instruments of Western Asia in the Department of Western Asiatic Antiquities, the British Museum. By Joan Rimmer. London: British Museum, 1969. 51 p. 26 plates.
Actual instruments as well as depictions are described. Treats the use of string, wind, and percussion instruments in Sumerian, Babylonian, Anatolian, Assyrian, and Hellenistic Asiatic societies. Corrects several inaccurate reassemblies. Appendix gives a classified list of instruments and a table of musical references in the Old Testament.

2538. Fenton House. Benton Fletcher Collection. Catalogue of the Benton Fletcher collection of early keyboard instruments at Fenton House, Hampstead. London: Country Life, Ltd., for the National Trust, 1957. 26 p.
A descriptive brochure by Raymond Russell for a collection of early keyboard instruments maintained in playing condition in a late 17th-century house in Hampstead, London.

2539. Galpin Society. British musical instruments. 7–30 August 1951. [London: Galpin Society, 1951.] 35 p.
A classified exhibition catalog of instruments, chiefly of British make or

use. Includes 151 woodwind, 61 brass, 27 keyboard, 62 of the violin family, 16 of the viol family, and 16 miscellaneous. Brief descriptions, with short introductions for each class of instruments.

See also the Galpin Society exhibition catalog, Edinburgh, 1968 (no. 2519).

2540. Horniman Museum. The Adam Carse collection of old musical wind instruments [now in the Horniman Museum, London]. London: Staple Press for the London County Council, 1951. 88 p.

A collection of 320 instruments, briefly described, with historical notes for each family. Illustrated by drawings.

2541. Horniman Museum and Library. Musical instruments: handbook to the museum's collection. By Jean L. Jenkins. 2nd ed. London: Inner London Education Authority, 1970. 104 p.

First edition published in 1958.

A catalog that is at the same time a handbook for the study of musical instruments, chiefly non-Western. 32 plates; bibliography, discography, and index.

2542. Royal College of Music. Catalogue of historical musical instruments, paintings, sculpture, and drawings. [London: Royal College, 1952.] 16 p.

Foreword by George Dyson.

Contains the Donaldson collection of musical instruments. Brief inventory with minimum description.

2543. Royal Military Exhibition, 1890. A descriptive catalogue of the musical instruments recently exhibited at the Royal Military Exhibition, London, 1890. Compiled by Charles Russell Day. London: Eyre & Spottiswoode, 1891. 253 p.

An exhibition confined to wind and percussion instruments. 457 wind instruments (percussion not inventoried). Plates.

2544. South Kensington Museum. A descriptive catalogue of the musical instruments of the South Kensington Museum. By Carl Engel.... London: Printed by G. E. Eyre and W. Spottiswoode for H. M. Stationery Office, 1874. 402 p.

Preceded by an essay on the history of musical instruments. This museum became the Victoria and Albert Museum.

2545. Victoria and Albert Museum. Catalogue of musical instruments. London: Her Majesty's Stationery Office, 1978–85. 2 v.

First published in 1968.

Vol. 1: Keyboard instruments, by Raymond Russell. 94 p. and 47 plates. Detailed descriptions of 52 keyboard instruments, including pianos and organs described by Austin Niland. Appendix B: The decoration of keyboard instruments by Peter Thornton; biographical notes on the makers, bibliography, and index.

Vol. 2: Non-keyboard instruments, by Anthony Baines. 121 p., 138 plates. The instruments are grouped as stringed instruments and wind instruments, with 16 subgroups of the former, 8 of the latter. Full technical descriptions, with clear plates of details; bibliography and index. Review of the 1968 ed. by Don L. Smithers in *Notes*, 26 (1969), p. 47–48.

2546. Victoria and Albert Museum. Musical instruments as works of art. London: Victoria and Albert Museum, 1968. 50 unnumbered leaves.

Illustrated with more than 100 plates showing details of early musical instruments characterized by fine workmanship. All from the instrument collection of the Victoria and Albert.

LOS ANGELES, CALIFORNIA

2547. Lachmann Collection. Erich Lachmann collection of historical stringed musical instruments, by Erich Lachmann. Los Angeles: Allan Hancock Foundation, University of Southern California, 1950. 53 p.

A handsome catalog of 42 items; noteworthy for its photographic illustrations by Irvin Kershner.

LUCERNE, SWITZERLAND

2548. Richard Wagner Museum. Katalog der städtischen Sammlung alter Musikinstrumente im Richard-Wagner-Museum, Tribschen, Luzern. Erstellt im Auftrag der Museum-Kommission von René Vannes.... Luzern: Otto Dreyer, 1956. 40 p.

A catalog of 95 stringed instruments, 46 wind, 11 idiophones, 37 exotic instruments. 16 plates.

LUTON, ENGLAND

2549. Museum and Art Gallery. The Ridley collection of musical wind instruments in the Luton Museum. [Luton: Corporation of Luton, Museum and Art Gallery, 1957.] 32 p.

65 wind instruments. Historical note, p. 1–21. Plates.

MILAN, ITALY

2550. Conservatorio di Musica "Giuseppe Verdi." Gli strumenti musicali nel Museo del Conservatorio di Milano. Ed. E. Guarinoni. Milano: Hoepli, 1908. 109 p.

A collection of 278 instruments, 177 European and 91 non-European. Index of donors and of instruments.

2551. Museo degli Strumenti Musicali. Catalogo, a cura di Natale Gallini e Franco Gallini. [Milano]: Castello Sforzesco, [1963]. 448 p.

An earlier catalog of the same collection issued in 1958 under the title: *Civico Museo di Antichi Strumenti Musicali.* The 1963 catalog, completely reorganized, lists 641 items, well described and illustrated in 141 plates.

2552. Museo degli Strumenti Musicali. Mostra di antichi strumenti musicali della Collezione N. Gallini (Maggio, 1953). Milano: Villa Comunale (Ex Reale), [1955]. 43 p.

An exhibition catalog of 200 items dating from the time when the Gallini collection was in private hands. It has since become the property of the city of Milan, and its complete catalog appears above. Preface signed by Natale Gallini; 32 plates.

MUNICH, GERMANY

2553. Bayerisches Nationalmuseum. Ausstellung alter Musik, Instrumente, Noten und Dokumente aus drei Jahrhunderten. Veranstaltet durch die Stadt München im Bayerischen Nationalmuseum, November–Dezember, 1951. Katalog. München: Musikverlag Max Hieber, 1951. 71 p. 23 plates.

An exhibition devoted to music in cultural history. 636 items, of which the majority are early instruments.

NEW HAVEN, CONNECTICUT

2554. Yale University. Checklist, Yale collection of musical instruments. New Haven: Yale University, 1968. 43 p.

Preface signed by Richard Rephann, Curator, 1968.

Checklist of 310 instruments comprising items from the Morris Steinert, the Belle Skinner, and the Emil Herrmann collections as well as gifts from private donors and Friends of Music at Yale. Brief descriptions, no bibliography, chiefly Western instruments.

2555. Yale University. Art Gallery. Musical instruments at Yale, a selection of Western instruments from the 15th to 20th centuries. Catalog by Sibyl Marcuse.... [New Haven]: Yale University Art Gallery, [1960]. 32 p.

An exhibition, 19 Feb.–27 March 1960, of 26 instruments as well as paintings, drawings, prints, and manuscripts. Illustrated.

2556. Yale University. Morris Steinert Collection. The Morris Steinert collection of keyed and stringed instruments. New York: Tretbar, [1893].

NEW YORK, NEW YORK

2557. Metropolitan Museum of Art. Catalog of keyboard instruments. New York: Metropolitan Museum of Art, 1903. 313 p.

2558. Metropolitan Museum of Art. Keyboard instruments in the Metropolitan Museum of Art, a picture book. By Emanuel Winternitz. New York: Metropolitan Museum of Art, 1961. 48 p.

Not a catalog, but a book of photo reproductions of keyboard instruments from the Metropolitan's collection, including details, with commentary by the former Curator.

2559. Metropolitan Museum of Art. Crosby Brown Collection. Catalog of the Crosby Brown collection of musical instruments of all nations.... New York: Metropolitan Museum of Art, 1903–1907. 3 v. in 4.

Vol. 1: Europe (1904). Vol. 2: Asia (1903). Vol. 3: Instruments of savage tribes and semicivilized peoples: Pt. 1, Africa (1907); Pt. 2, Oceania (1907); Pt. 3, Historical groups (1905).

See the article by Emanuel Winternitz, "The Crosby Brown collection of musical instruments: its origin and development," in *Metropolitan Museum Journal*, 3 (1970). Also printed separately. 20 p.

NUREMBERG, GERMANY

2560. Nuremberg. Germanisches Nationalmuseum. Musikinstrumente: von der Antike bis zur Gegenwart [von] John Henry van der Meer. München: Prestel-Verlag, 1983. 301 p. (Bibliothek des Germanischen Nationalmuseums Nürnberg zur deutschen Kunst- und Kulturgeschichte, 2)

A history of musical instruments based, in large measure, upon the collections of the Germanisches Nationalmuseum, Nuremburg.

2561. Nuremberg. Germanisches Nationalmuseum. Verzeichnis der europäischen Musikinstrumente im Germanischen Nationalmuseum Nürnberg; [Hrsg. von] John Henry van der Meer. Wilhelmshaven, Hamburg, Locarno, and Amsterdam: Heinrichshofen, 1979– . 1 v. (to date) (Instrumentenkataloge des Germanischen Nationalmuseums, Nürnberg, 1) (Quellenkataloge zur Musikgeschichte, 16)

Bd. 1: *Hörner und Trompeten, Membranophone, Idiophone.* 1979. 220 p. 195 plates.

A classified index. Bibliography and index to makers.

Review by Malou Haine in *Fontes Artis Musicae*, 28 (1981), p. 255–56.

2562. Nuremberg. Germanisches Nationalmuseum. Wegweiser durch die Sammlung historischer Musikinstrumente, Germanisches Nationalmuseum Nürnberg; 2. Aufl. [Hrsg. von] John Henry van der Meer. Nürnberg: Germanisches Nationalmuseum, 1976. 96 p.

First published 1971.

A guide to the collections.

OXFORD, ENGLAND

2563. Ashmolean Museum. Catalogue of the Hill collection of musical instruments in the Ashmolean Museum, Oxford. By David D. Boyden. London: Oxford University Press, 1969. 54 p. 57 plates.

Review by Joan Rimmer in *Notes*, 26 (1970), p. 741–44.

PARIS, FRANCE

2564. Conservatoire National. Le Musée du Conservatoire National de Musique. Catalogue descriptif et raisonné, par Gustave Chouquet. Nouvelle édition. Paris: Firmin-Didot, 1884. 276 p.

First published in 1875. Supplements by Léon Pillaut, in 1894, 1899, and 1903.

A catalog of 1,006 instruments, subdivided into European and non-European sections. Index of instruments and of names. Catalogers of musical instruments owe much to the classification established by Chouquet in this catalog.

ROME, ITALY

2565. Museo nazionale strumenti musicali. Antichi strumenti musicali in un moderno museo: Museo nazionale strumenti musicali, Roma [a cura di] Luisa Cervelli. 2a ed. Roma: Gela, 1986. 75 p.

A catalog of the older instruments in the museum. Includes index and bibliography.

SALZBURG, AUSTRIA

2566. Museum Carolino-Augusteum. Alte Musik-Instrumente im Museum Carolino-Augusteum Salzburg. Führer und beschreibendes Verzeichnis von Karl Geiringer. Leipzig: Breitkopf und Härtel, 1932. 46 p.

A catalog of 288 instruments, with an index of makers and 4 photographic plates showing 48 different instruments.

TOKYO, JAPAN

2567. Musashino Academia Musicae. Catalogue, museum of musical instruments. On the 40th anniversary of the Institute. Tokyo: 1969. 108 p. 4 p. of illustrations.

Text in Japanese and English.

The collection was established in 1953. The catalog is classified by national origins of the instruments, with a taxonomy according to method of sound production. Part 2 is a catalog of accessories; part 3, a catalog of mechanical devices.

2568. Ueno Gakuen College. Institute for the Study of Musical Instruments. Catalogue of the European musical instruments of the XVIIth, XVIIIth and XIXth centuries in the Ueno Gakuen collection. Tokyo: Ueno Gakuen Educational Foundation, 1980. 243 p.

Text in Japanese and English. 82 pages of photographs incorporating 3 to 6 views of each of 71 instruments. Text references to photographs by number.

TORONTO, CANADA

2569. Royal Ontario Museum. Musical instruments in the Royal Ontario Museum, by Ladislav Dselenyi. Toronto: Royal Ontario Museum, 1971. 96 p.

A well-illustrated catalog of more than 100 instruments. The instruments come from the bequest of R. S. Williams, beginning in 1913.

VERONA, ITALY

2570. Accademia Filarmonica di Verona. Catalogo degli strumenti musicali dell'Accademia filarmonica di Verona [per] John Henry van der Meer [e] Rainer Weber. Verona: Accademia filarmonica di Verona, 1982. 146 p.
Catalog of the instrument collections of one of the oldest continuously operating musical organizations in Italy.
Review by Malou Haine in *Fontes Artis Musicae*, 31 (1984), p. 135–37.

VIENNA, AUSTRIA

2571. Gesellschaft der Musikfreunde. "Musikinstrumente," in *Zusatz-Band zur Geschichte der K.K. Gesellschaft der Musikfreunde in Wien. Sammlung und Statuten*, p. 154–85. By Dr. Eusebius Mandyczewski. Wien: 1912.
Catalog of a collection of 355 instruments, of which 221 are of Western origin. The remaining are of ethnic interest: from Turkey, Africa, Arabia, Persia, Siam, India, China, Japan, etc.

2572. Kunsthistorisches Museum. Alte Musikinstrumente; die Sammlung des Kunsthistorischen Museums in der neuen Burg zu Wien. [By Victor Luithlen.] Wien: H. Bauer, 1954. 28 p.
A brief visitor's guide to the collection described in no. 2572.

2573. Kunsthistorisches Museum. Katalog der Sammlung alter Musikinstrumente. I. Teil. Saitenklaviere. Wien: Kunsthistorisches Museum, 1966. 95 p. 32 plates.
Classified catalog and description of 76 keyboard instruments. Full of detailed information respecting instrument makers, dimensions of the instruments, bibliographical references. The catalog is the work of the music instrument collection's director Victor Luithlen and his assistant Kurt Wegerer. This volume is the first of three that will eventually cover all of the museum's holdings.
Review by Friedrich Ernst in *Die Musikforschung*, 21 (1968), p. 506–507.

2574. Kunsthistorisches Museum. Die Sammlung alter Musikinstrumente. Beschreibendes Verzeichnis von Julius Schlosser. Wien: Anton Schroll, 1920. 138 p.
The catalog describes 361 instruments, most of which are illustrated in 57 plates. 31 Asian and folk instruments. Western instruments are entered in chronological order, grouped according to type, with full descriptions and an informative introduction to each major section: i.e., "Das Orchester des 16. und 17. Jahrhunderts"; "Die Entwicklung des Instrumentenbaus seit dem 18. Jahrhundert." Much useful historical information given, such as a supplement quoting the descriptions of 20 early instruments from Mattheson's *Neu-eröffnetes Orchester* (1713).

2575. Museum für Völkerkunde. Aussereuropäische Musikinstrumente. Wien: Museum für Völkerkunde, [1961]. 89 p.
Foreword by Alfred Janata.
Illustrated, classified catalog of 654 non-European instruments.

WASHINGTON, DISTRICT OF COLUMBIA

2576. Library of Congress. Music Division. Musical instruments in the Dayton C. Miller flute collection at the Library of Congress, a catalog. Washington, D.C.: Library of Congress, 1982– .
Vol. 1: *Recorders, Fifes, and Simple System Transverse Flutes of One Key.* Compiled by Michael Seyfrit.
This catalog, when complete, will cover the 6,000 instruments in the collection in 7 v. The catalog was preceded by a checklist: *Dayton C. Miller Flute Collection, a Checklist of the Instruments* by Laura E. Gilliam and William Lichtenwanger, 1961.
Vol. 1 treats 273 instruments. 56 photographs. Indexes of instrument makers, cities, symbols, and sources.
Review by Jane P. Ambrose in *Notes*, 39 (1983), p. 853.
See also Dayton C. Miller's catalog of literature on the flute (no. 947).

2577. Library of Congress. Music Division. Three masters: the stringed instrument collection in the Library of Congress. Text by Rembert Herbert; additional research by Paula Forrest; photographs by Paula Forrest, Michael Seyfrit and Dane Penland. Washington, D.C.: Library of Congress, 1983. 28 p.
A brief guide to the collection.

2578. Library of Congress. Music Division. Gertrude Clarke Whittall Foundation. The Stradivari memorial at Washington, the national capital, by William Dana Orcutt. Washington: Library of Congress, Gertrude Clarke Whittall Foundation, [1938]. 49 p.
Description of the matched set of Stradivarius instruments donated to the Library of Congress.

2579. Smithsonian Institution. Division of Musical Instruments. A checklist of keyboard instruments at the Smithsonian Institution. Washington: Smithsonian Institution, 1967. 79 p.
Full description lacking, but remarkably rich in information: maker, place of origin, date, type, compass, etc. 5 plates.

2580. Smithsonian Institution. Division of Musical Instruments. Handbook of the collection of musical instruments in the United States National Museum. By Frances Densmore. Washington: Government Printing Office, 1927. 164 p. 49 plates. (Smithsonian Institution U. S. National Museum. Bulletin 136)

2581. Smithsonian Institution. Division of Musical Instruments. Harpsichords and clavichords. By Cynthia A. Hoover. Washington: Smithsonian Institution Press, 1969. 43 p.
A guide to the instruments in the Smithsonian Institution.

Histories and Bibliographies of Music Printing and Publishing

Included here are bibliographies of the output of some of the major early music printers and publishers, such as Petrucci, Playford, Walsh, Ballard, etc.; studies of music publishing in particular regions or countries (England, Italy, Paris, Vienna, etc.); and a few works concerned with the technical processes of music printing or engraving and historical studies of copyright law (for contemporary law, see "Music Business and Law," nos. 3008–3021). An extensive, but now dated bibliography on the history of music printing has been compiled by Åke Davidsson (no. 2596). For the best one-volume, English-language summary, see *Music Printing and Publishing* (no. 2674).

2582. Bergmans, Paul. "La typographie musicale en Belgique au XVIe siècle." In *Histoire du Livre et de l'Imprimerie en Belgique des Origines à Nos Jours*, 5 (Bruxelles, 1929), p. 47–75.

An illustrated account of 16th-century Belgian music printers and printing.

2583. Bernstein, Jane A. "The burning salamander: assigning a printer to some sixteenth-century music prints." In *Notes*, 42 (1986), p. 483–501.

Concerning the attribution of a number of printed works to the Venetian music publisher Girolamo Scotto.

2584. Berz, Ernst-Ludwig. Die Notendrucker und ihre Verleger in Frankfurt am Main von den Anfängen bis etwa 1630. Eine bibliographische und drucktechnische Studie zur Musikpublikation. Kassel: International Association of Music Libraries and International Musicological Society, 1970. 336 p. (Catalogus musicus, 5)

A thoroughly documented study of music printing in Frankfurt to 1630, with a bibliography of 258 printed works by some 43 printers.

2585. Bobillier, Marie. "La librairie musicale en France de 1653 à 1790, d'après les Registres de privilèges." [Par Michel Brenet, pseud.] In *Sammelbände der Internationalen Musikgesellschaft*, 8 (1906–1907), p. 401–466.

An examination with extensive transcriptions from the archives in the Bibliothèque Nationale pertaining to licenses granted for the publication of music and books on music in Paris from 1652 to 1790. Thorough discussion of the inception of the royal *privilège*, with transcriptions of sample 17th-century *privilèges*. Supplemented by Cucuel (no. 2595).

The Breitkopf thematic catalogue.... See no. 1715.

2586. Calderisi, Maria. Music publishing in the Canadas, 1800–1867. L'Édition musicale au Canada, 1800–1867. Ottawa: National Library of Canada, 1981. 128 p.

A bibliographic study with a list of imprints beginning about 1800.

Reviewed by Donald W. Krummel in *Fontes Artis Musicae*, 29 (1982), p. 90.

2587. Castelain, Raoul. Histoire de l'édition musicale; ou, du droit d'éditeur au droit d'auteur, 1501–1793. Pref. de André Siegfried. Paris: H. Lemoine, 1957. 92 p.

Brief history of music publishing, with emphasis on legal aspects.

2588. Il Catalogo numerico Ricordi 1857 con date e indici; [per] Agostina Zecca-Laterza; prefazione di Philip Gossett. Roma: Nuovo istituto editoriale italiano, 1984– . Vol. 1– . (Bibliotheca musicae; 8)

Originally published in Florence by Presso Ricordi e Jouhaud, 1857.

A plate number catalog for the most important Italian publishing firm, covering the first 50 years of Ricordi's output, annotated with approximate dates of publication. Introduction in English.

2589. Chrysander, Friedrich. "A sketch of the history of music—printing, from the fifteenth to the nineteenth century." In *Musical Times*, 18 (1877), p. 265–68, 324–26, 375–78, 470–75, 524–27, 584–87.

Also published in German as "Abriss einer Geschichte des Musikdruckes vom fünfzehnten bis zum neunzehnten Jahrhundert" in *Allgemeine musikalishe Zeitung*, 14 (1879), cols. 161–67, 177–83, 193–200, 209–214, 225–32, 241–48.

2590. Cinq catalogues d'éditeurs de musique à Paris (1824–34): Dufaut et Dubois, Petit, Frère, Delahante-Erard, Pleyel. Avec une introduction de François Lesure. Genève: Minkoff Reprint, 1976. (Archives de l'édition musicale française, 2)

Reprints of the catalogs of the five publishers, each classified, some with tables of contents. The introduction provides information on each firm's history. The Pleyel catalogs provide plate numbers.

Review by Rita Benton in *Fontes Artis Musicae*, 25 (1978), p. 198–99.

2591. Cinque secoli di stampa musicale in Europa. Naples: Electa Napoli, 1985. 299 p.

Illustrated catalog for an exhibition at the Museo di Palazzo Venezia celebrating the 400th anniversary of the founding of the Accademia Nazionale di Santa Cecilia.

The exhibition was segmented into chronological periods. The catalog follows this design with introductory essays before entries for a particular period. Each entry provides a title-page transcription, collation, and indications of the library or archive holding the item. Then there is a short explanation of the significance of the item for the history of music printing. There were at least 620 scores exhibited, a large number of documents concerning music printing, many catalogs of music publishers from the

18th-century forward, and at least two dozen prints and paintings with musical themes. Each of these is described. The catalog concludes with a bibliography of works concerning the iconographic items in the exhibition and a general bibliography. The emphasis was upon Italian music printing, but all of the major European developments were represented.

2592. Cipolla, Wilma Reid. A catalog of the works of Arthur Foote, 1853–1937. Detroit, Michigan: Information Coordinators, 1980. 214 p. (Bibliographies in American music, 6)
A thorough bibliography of the published and unpublished compositions, documenting quite well some of the work of the publisher A. P. Schmidt.

2593. Cohen, Paul. Musikdruck und Drucker zu Nürnberg im 16. Jahrhundert erschienenen Noten- und Musikbücher.... Nürnberg: H. Zierfuss, 1927. 63 p.
Also issued as a dissertation (Erlangen) under the title, *Die Nürnberger Musikdrucker im sechzehnten Jahrhundert*, 1927. Historical study, with brief accounts of the individual printers, followed by a chronological listing of 443 works published in Nürnberg from 1501 to 1600.

2594. Cucuel, Georges. "Notes sur quelques musiciens, luthiers, éditeurs et graveurs de musique au XVIIIe siècle." In *Sammelbände der Internationalen Musikgesellschaft*, 14 (1912–13), p. 243–52.

2595. Cucuel, Georges. "Quelques documents sur la librairie musicale au XVIIIe siècle." In *Sammelbände der Internationalen Musikgesellschaft*, 13 (1911–12), p. 385–92.
A further study of the archives related to the licensing of music publications in France. Supplements the article by Bobillier (no. 2585).

2596. Davidsson, Åke. Bibliographie zur Geschichte des Musikdrucks. Uppsala: Almquist & Wiksell, 1965. 86 p. (Studia musicologica Upsaliensia, Nova Ser., 1)
A bibliography of 598 items related to the history of music printing and publishing, with a brief introductory survey of the literature. The expansion of a bibliography first issued as a part of the author's *Musikbibliographische Beiträge* (no. 2598).

2597. Davidsson, Åke. Danskt musiktryck intill 1700-talets mitt. Dänischer Musikdruck bis zur Mitte des 18. Jahrhunderts. Uppsala: [Almquist & Wiksell], 1962. 100 p. (Studia musicologica Upsaliensia, 7)
A historical study of early Danish music printing, with a chronological listing of Danish printed editions issued during the period under consideration. Bibliography and index of names.
Review by Martin Geck in *Die Musikforschung*, 18 (1965), p. 346–47.

2598. Davidsson, Åke. "Die Literatur zur Geschichte des Notendrucks." In his *Musikbibliographische Beiträge*, p. 91–115. Uppsala: A. B. Lundequistska Bokhandeln, 1954. (Uppsala Universitets Årsskrift, 1954:9)

A survey of writings on the history of music printing, with a bibliography of 268 items.

Superseded by the author's *Bibliographie zur Geschichte des Musikdrucks* (no. 2596).

Review by Edward N. Waters in *Notes*, 12 (1955), p. 604; by Vincent H. Duckles in *Library Quarterly*, 26 (1956), p. 73–74.

2599. Davidsson, Åke. Studier rörande svenskt musiktryck före ar 1750. Studien über schwedischen Musikdruck vor 1750. Uppsala: [Almquist & Wiksell], 1957. 167 p. (Studia musicologica Upsaliensia, 5)

Part I (Allmän del) is a general survey of early Swedish music printing. Part II (Speciell del) is a bibliography of 124 Swedish imprints issued between 1585 and 1750, in chronological order. Text in Swedish, summary in German. General bibliography and index of persons.

Review by Rudolph Gjelsness in *Notes*, 15 (1958), p. 569–70.

2600. Day, Cyrus L. and Eleanore Boswell Murrie. English song-books, 1651–1702; a bibliography with a first-line index of songs. London: Bibliographical Society, 1940. 439 p.

Lists and describes the contents of 252 secular songbooks published in England and Scotland. Arrangement is chronological; non-extant works included. First-line index of 4,150 songs by about 250 composers. Also indexed by composer, author of text, performer, tunes and airs, sources, titles of collections, printers, publishers, and booksellers. A model of descriptive bibliography, particularly valuable for its coverage of the publishing activity of John and Henry Playford and their contemporaries.

Day and Murrie also published "English song-books, 1651–1702, and their publishers," in *Library*, ser. 4, vol. 16, no 4 (March 1936).

2601. Deaville, James. "The C. F. Kahnt archive in Leipzig: a preliminary report." In *Notes*, 42 (1986), p. 502–517.

Concerning the survival and contents of the papers of one of the lesser Leipzig publishing houses.

2602. Deutsch, Otto E. Musikverlags-Nummern. Eine Auswahl von 40 datierten Listen. Zweite, verbesserte und erste deutsche Ausgabe. Berlin: Merseburger, 1961. 32 p.

Revision and expansion of a list originally published in the *Journal of Documentation*, 1 (1946), under the title "Music publishers' numbers, a selection of 40 dated lists, 1710–1900."

Treats 20 German, 14 Austrian, 3 Dutch, 1 English, 1 French, and 1 Swiss firm. Index of places and individual publishers. Supplemented by the author's "Musikverlags-Nummern, ein Nachtrag," in *Die Musikforschung*, 15 (1962), p. 155.

Review by Donald W. Krummel in *Notes*, 19 (1961), p. 76–77; by Richard Schaal in *Die Musikforschung*, 16 (1963), p. 389.

2603. Devriès, Anik. "Un éditeur de musique 'à la tête ardenté,' Maurice Schlesinger." In *Fontes Artis Musicae*, 27 (1980), p. 125–36.

A brief recounting of the publishing career of the person responsible for the *Revue et Gazette Musicale*.

2604. Devriès, Anik. Édition et commerce de la musique gravée à Paris dans la première moitié du XVIIIe siècle: les Boivin, les Leclerc. Genève: Minkoff, 1976. 274 p. (Archives de l'édition musical française, 1)

A study of Parisian music engraving in the early 18th century with particular regard for one of the principal engravers.

"Catalogue général de la production des Leclerc": p. [127]–272, an extensive catalog of the production of the Leclercs.

Review by Neal Zaslaw in *Notes*, 33 (1977), p. 825–26.

2605. Devriès, Anik. "Les Éditions musicales Sieber." In *Revue de Musicologie*, 55 (1969), p. 20–46.

Concerns the publishing history of the Parisian firm of Sieber between 1771 and 1847. Includes a table of the Sieber firm's addresses in Paris. Among others, Sieber published works by Stamitz, J. Haydn, W. A. Mozart, and J. Pleyel.

2606. Devriès, Anik and François Lesure. Dictionnaire des éditions de musique française des origines à environ 1820. Genève: Minkoff, 1979. 2 v. (Archives de l'édition musicale française, 4)

Volume 1 contains the dictionary of music publishers and dealers in France from the 16th century to 1820, including in each a biography, lists of successive addresses, lists of published catalogs, citations of privileges received, and a bibliography. The volume 2 presents facsimiles of more than 200 catalogs by 50 publishers and forms a supplement to Cari Johansson's *French Music Publishers Catalogs* (no. 2637). There is an index to insignia. Indexes to composers and titles in the reproduced catalogs. Source for each catalog and the rationale for attribution of date are given in a list preceding the reproductions.

Reviews by Eugene K. Wolf in *Journal of the American Musicological Society*, 33 (1980), p. 592–96, and by Lenore Coral in *Notes*, 37 (1980), p. 61–62.

2607. Donà, Mariangela. La stampa musicale a Milano fino all'anno 1700. Firenze: Olschki, 1961. 167 p. (Biblioteca di bibliografia italiana, 39)

Milanese music publishers given in alphabetical order, with chronological listings of their publications. Copies of rare works located in major European libraries. Index of composers and works, index of persons to whom works are dedicated.

Review by Richard Schaal in *Die Musikforschung*, 17 (1964), p. 183.

2608. Dunning, Albert. De muziekuitgever Gerhard Fredrik Witvogel en zijn fonds. Een bijdrage tot de geschiedenis van de Nederlandse muziekuitgeverij in de achttiende eeuw. Utrecht: A. Oosthoek's Uitgevermaatschappij N.V., 1966. 64 p. (Muziekhistorische Monografieen, 2)

"Uitgegeven door de Vereniging voor Nederlandse Muziekgeschiedenis."

Discussion of the life and works of Witvogel, with an annotated bibliography of 95 music publications by the firm. Locations of copies given, list of composers whose works were published, bibliography, and index of names.

2609. Eitner, Robert. Buch- und Musikalienhändler, Buch- und Musikaliendrucker nebst Notenstecher, nur die Musik betreffend nach den Originaldrucken verzeichnet.... Leipzig: Breitkopf & Härtel, 1904. 248 p. (Monatshefte für Musikgeschichte, Beilage)

Compiled as a by-product of the *Quellen-Lexikon*; limited to material before 1850. Alphabetical listing of publishers, printers, and dealers, their dates of location at various addresses, changes in name, branches (if any). International coverage.

2610. Elvers, Rudolf. "Musikdrucker, Musikalienhändler und Musikverleger in Berlin 1750–1850." In *Festschrift Walter Gerstenberg zum 60. Geburtstag*, p. 37–44. Wolfenbüttel: Möseler Verlag, 1964.

Lists 155 Berlin music printers, dealers, and publishers active during the century under consideration.

2611. Epstein, Dena J. Music publishing in Chicago before 1871; the firm of Root and Cady, 1858–1871. Detroit, Michigan: Information Coordinators, 1969. 243 p. (Detroit studies in music bibliography, 14)

This is an especially careful study illuminating the work of a firm of central importance in the history of American music publishing.

Review by Klaus Hortschansky in *Die Musikforschung*, 24 (1971), p. 464–65.

2612. Fisher, William A. 150 years of music publishing in the U.S.; a historical sketch with special reference to the pioneer publisher Oliver Ditson Co., 1783–1933. Boston, Massachusetts: Oliver Ditson, [1934]. 156 p.

A revision and extension of portions of the author's *Notes on Music in Old Boston*. Boston: 1918.

2613. Fog, Dan. Dänische Musikverlage und Notendruckereien. Beiträge zur Musikaliendatierung. Kopenhagen: 1972. 27 p.

Basic factual information concerning 60 Danish music printers and publishers. Important events in the history of these firms are given chronologically.

2614. Fog, Dan. Notendruck und Musikhandel im 19. Jahrhundert in Dänemark. Ein Beitrag zur Musikaliendatierung und zur Geschichte der Musikvermittlung. Copenhagen: Dan Fog Musikverlag, 1986. 336 p.

A revised and shortened edition of the first edition (1984) in Danish of the 2 volumes: *Musikhandel og Nodetryk I Danmark efter 1750: I: Musikhandel 1700–1754; II: Nodetryk efter 1750*.

A guide to music publishing and music trades in Denmark after 1750 until roughly 1899, incorporating a brief section on dating music of the period by plate numbers and other characteristics. Includes a dictionary of music dealers and publishers citing plate numbers. Bibliography and indexes.

2615. Fog, Dan. "Random thoughts on music dating and terminology." In *Fontes Artis Musicae*, 24 (1977), p. 141–44.

"My main purpose in voicing these observations is to suggest that the two principal preoccupations of our present work, dating and terminology, call for a new and different way of thinking. We must break free from the conventional, book-infected concepts that are often transferred to music bibliography."

2616. Fog, Dan and Kari Michelsen. Norwegian music publication since 1800. A preliminary guide to music publishers, printers, and dealers. Copenhagen: Dan Fog Musikforlag, 1976. 30 p.
Brief sketches of the activity of 38 Norwegian music publishers, printers, and dealers. Plate numbers given where known. Cites rental libraries. In English, with an informative introduction.

2617. Forney, Kristine Karen. Tielman Susato, sixteenth-century music printer: an archival and typographical investigation. Ph.D. dissertation, University of Kentucky, 1978. 356 p.
An investigation of the technical aspects of Susato's output and his contributions to single-impression music printing. Susato was active in Antwerp from 1543 to 1561. Includes a survey of music printing in the Low Countries prior to Susato. There is a chapter on "the making of a Renaissance music book" and another presenting an adaptation of the techniques of descriptive bibliography to identify and describe editions of chanson books issued by Susato.
Bibliographies of primary and secondary sources.

2618. Fraenkel, Gottfried S. Decorative music title pages; 201 examples from 1500 to 1800. Selected, introduced, and annotated by Gottfried S. Fraenkel. New York: Dover, 1968. 230 p.
Introduction, p. 1–15, an historical survey of the items in the collection. 201 plates with historical and descriptive annotations.

2619. Fuld, James J. and Frances Barulich. "Harmonizing the arts: original graphic designs for printed music by world-famous artists." In *Notes*, 43 (1987), p. 259–71.
A bibliography of the works of well-known artists created as illustrations to printed music. Arranged in alphabetical order by artist.

2620. Gamble, William. Music engraving and printing; historical and technical treatise.... London and New York: Pitman, 1923 [1922]. 266 p.
Reprinted by Arno Press, New York, 1979.
Discusses the technical processes of music printing and engraving, with emphasis on contemporary practices. Illustrated.

2621. Gericke, Hannelore. Der Wiener Musikalienhandel von 1700 bis 1778. Graz: H. Böhlaus Nachf., 1960. 150 p. (Wiener musikwissenschaftliche Beiträge, 5)
Contents: Wiener Buchhändler als Verkäufer von Musikalien; Privatverkäufer; Kopisten; Kupferstecher; Verzeichnis der Wiener Musikdrucke von 1700–1778; Liste der verbotenen Musikbücher; Zusammenfassung; Literaturverzeichnis.
Review by Donald W. Krummel in *Notes*, 18 (1961), p. 229–30.

2622. Göhler, Albert. Verzeichnis der in den Frankfurter und Leipziger Messkatalogen der Jahre 1564 bis 1759 angezeigten Musikalien. Leipzig: C. F. Kahns Nachf., 1902. 4 parts in 1 v.

Reprint by Frits Knuf, Hilversum, 1965.

A major source of information on the activities of early music dealers, printers, and publishers. It lists music entered in the Frankfurt and Leipzig trade catalogs from 1564 to 1759.

2623. Goovaerts, Alphonse J. M. A. Histoire et bibliographie de la typographie musicale dans les Pays-Bas. Anvers: P. Kockx, 1880. 608 p. (Extrait des Memoires de l'Academie Royale de Belgique, Collection in-8; tome XXIX)

Reprint issued by Frits Knuf, Hilversum, 1963.

Part I (historical): a chronological discussion of music publishing in The Netherlands from 1539. Part II (bibliographical): chronological list of 1,415 music publications from 1539 to 1841. Full descriptions. Index of personal names, titles, and places.

2624. Grand-Carteret, John. Les titres illustrés et l'image au service de la musique. Turin: Bocca, 1904. 269 p.

Première partie (p. 3–120): Le titre de musique sous la Révolution, le Consulat et le premier Empire (1500–1800). Deuxième partie: Le titre de musique et la lithographie; 1. 1817–30, 2. 1830–50.

Abundantly illustrated with facsimiles of title pages, printers' devices, and pages of music.

2625. Hase, Oskar von. Breitkopf & Härtel. Gedenkschrift und Arbeitsbericht. 5. Aufl. Wiesbaden: Breitkopf & Härtel, 1968. 2 v. in 3.

Bd. 1: 1542–1827. Bd. 2: 1828–1918. Bd. 3: 1918–68.

Thorough documentation of the activities of the great Leipzig publishing house of Breitkopf & Härtel. Reviews the history of the firm, its business relationships, its dealings with the great composers of the late 18th and 19th centuries; editorial work on the *Denkmäler* and *Gesamtausgaben*. Bd. 3, by Hellmuth von Hase, reviews the history of the firm through World War II to its establishment in Wiesbaden.

2626. Heartz, Daniel. "La chronologie des recueils imprimés par Pierre Attaingnant." In *Revue de Musicologie*, 44 (1959), p. 178–92.

Brief survey of Attaingnant's activity as a music printer, followed by a chronological tabulation of all collections published by him from 1528 to 1537. Superseded by Heartz's magisterial study (no. 2627).

2627. Heartz, Daniel. Pierre Attaingnant, royal printer of music: a historical study and bibliographical catalogue. Berkeley and Los Angeles: University of California Press, 1969. 451 p.

P. 1–204: Historical study treating the founding of the Attaingnant press, new techniques of music printing, commercial and artistic relationships, together with selected documents, dedications, and privileges.

P. 207–377: Bibliographical catalog of 174 works issued by the press, with precise bibliographical descriptions, listings of contents, and location of surviving copies. 16 black-and-white plates, with a frontispiece in color.

An outstanding work in book design and subject coverage. Chronological and alphabetical short-title lists. Index of Latin and French first lines, and of composers.

Review by Nicolas Barker in *Book Collector* (Summer 1971), p. 261–70; by Samuel Pogue in *Notes*, 27 (1970), p. 258–60; by G. Dottin in *Revue de Musicologie*, 57 (1971), p. 87–88; by Howard M. Brown in *Journal of the American Musicological Society*, 24 (1971), p. 125–26; by Frank Dobbins in *Music and Letters*, 51 (1970), p. 447–49.

2628. Henle, Günter. 25 Jahre G. Henle Musikverlag 1948–1973. München: G. Henle, 1973. 75 p.

A history of the firm, chiefly a reprint from part of the author's autobiography, *Weggenosse des Jahrhunderts*, published in 1968.

2629. Hill, Richard S. "The plate numbers of C. F. Peters' predecessors." In *Papers ... of the American Musicological Society ...* 29 and 30 Dec. 1938 [c. 1940], p. 113–34.

Surveys the publishing activities of F. A. Hofmeister and A. Kuhnel, 1784–1814, with a detailed analysis of their production in 1801–1802, plate numbers 1–102.

2630. Hoffmann-Erbrecht, Lothar. "Der Nürnberger Musikverleger Johann Ulrich Haffner." In *Acta Musicologica*, 26 (1954), p. 114–26, and *Acta Musicologica*, 27 (1955), p. 141–42.

A biography and chronologically ordered bibliography of works published by Haffner between 1742 and 1765. Index to composers.

2631. Hoogerwerf, Frank W. Confederate sheet-music imprints. Brooklyn: Institute for Studies in American Music, Conservatory of Music, College of the City University of New York, 1984. 158 p. (I.S.A.M. monographs, 21)

A study on music printing in the Confederate States of America during the American Civil War.

2632. Hopkinson, Cecil. A dictionary of Parisian music publishers, 1700–1950. London: Printed for the author, 1954. 131 p.

Reprinted in 1979 by Da Capo, New York.

Describes some 550 printers, tabulating their name forms and addresses where they were active during specific periods. A useful tool for determining date of undated French publications.

Review by Inger M. Christensen in *Notes*, 11 (1954), p. 550–51; by Vincent H. Duckles in *Journal of the American Musicological Society*, 8 (1955), p. 62–64.

See nos. 2637 and 2638 for another approach to the dating of 18th-century French music publications. The IAML *Guide for Dating Early Published Music* provides more references and techniques. (no. 2651)

2633. Hopkinson, Cecil. Notes on Russian music publishers. Printed for the author for private distribution to the Members of the I.A.M.L. at the Fifth International Congress, Cambridge, England, 29 June–4 July 1959. 10 p.

"This edition limited to 125 numbered copies."

2634. Humphries, Charles and William C. Smith. Music publishing in the British Isles, from the beginning until the middle of the nineteenth century; a dictionary of engravers, printers, publishers, and music sellers, with a historical introduction. 2nd ed. with suppl. New York: Barnes and Noble; Oxford: B. Blackwell, 1970. 392 p.

First published in 1954 by Cassell and Co., London. The 2nd edition differs only in the addition of a 36-page supplement.

This work supersedes the Kidson volume (no. 2641). It covers more than 2,000 persons and firms associated with British music printing and publishing. An introductory essay gives an excellent survey of the field. Indexes of firms outside London and of makers and repairers of musical instruments. 25 plates.

Review of the 1st edition by J. M. Coopersmith in *Notes*, 11 (1954), p. 549–50; of the 2nd edition by William Lichtenwanger in *Notes*, 27 (1971), p. 489–90.

2635. Hunter, David. "Music copyright in Britain to 1800." In *Music and Letters*, 67 (1986), p. 269–82.

A historical summary of the evolution of concepts of copyright and intellectual property rights in Britain, focusing principally on the 18th century, for which period documentation is more plentiful. Provides insights also on the sociological and commercial shifts affecting composers and publishers.

2636. Imbault, Jéan-Jerôme. Catalogue thématique des ouvrages de musique. Avec un index des compositeurs cités. [Réimpression de l'édition de Paris, c. 1792.] Genève: Minkoff Reprint, 1972. 284 p.

Classified thematic catalog of works published by Imbault. Each section has its own pagination.

2637. Johansson, Cari. French music publishers' catalogues of the second half of the eighteenth century. Uppsala: Almquist & Wiksell, 1955. 2 v.

Vol. 1 (octavo): Textband. 228 p. Vol. 2 (folio): Tafeln. 145 facsimiles from catalogs by French music publishing houses.

The first volume analyzes and describes the contents of the catalogs and their use for dating purposes. Compare Johansson's method with that of Hopkinson (no. 2632). Index of names, of titles, and of catalogs chronologically under name of firm.

Review by Donald W. Krummel in *Notes*, 17 (1960), p. 234–35; by A. Hyatt King in *Music and Letters*, 37 (1956), p. 376–77; by Wolfgang Schmieder in *Die Musikforschung*, 10 (1957), p. 180–82.

2638. Johansson, Cari. J. J. & B. Hummel. Music-publishing and thematic catalogues. Stockholm: Almquist & Wiksell, 1972. 3 v. (Publications of the Library of the Royal Swedish Academy of Music, 3)

Vol. 1: Text, containing essays on the life and work of the Parisian brothers J. J. and B. Hummel; "Aids to the dating of Hummel prints," transcription of the Hummel catalogs 1762–1814; list of plate numbers; index of names and titles; index of catalogs. Vol. 2: Music publishing catalogs in facsimile. Vol. 3: Thematic catalog 1768–74 in facsimile.

Review by Rita Benton, in the *Journal of the American Musicological Society*, 27 (1974), p. 530–32.

2639. Journal général d'annonces des œuvres de musique, gravures, lithographies, publié en France et à l'étranger. Avec un index des noms cités. Genève: Minkoff Reprint, 1976. 1 v. (Archives de l'édition musicale française, 3)

Reprint of weekly editions of a trade paper published in 1825. Most heavily weighted to French publications.

2640. Kast, Paul. "Die Musikdrucke des Kataloges Giunta von 1604." In *Analecta Musicologica,* 2 (1965), p. 41–47.

Transcribes the music portion of a general catalog issued by the Florentine music dealer and publisher Giunta in 1604. Contains masses, motets, and secular works of the late 16th century as well as a small selection of instrumental and theoretical works.

2641. Kidson, Frank. British music publishers, printers and engravers ... from Queen Elizabeth's reign to George IV, with select bibliographical lists of musical works printed and published within that period. London: W. E. Hill & Sons, 1900. 231 p.

Unaltered reprint by Benjamin Blom, Inc., New York, 1967.

The pioneer work on English music publishing. Not as comprehensive as Humphries and Smith (no. 2634), but many of Kidson's entries are fuller and are accompanied by lists of publications. Entries arranged alphabetically by place. No index.

2642. King, A. Hyatt. "English pictorial music title-pages, 1820–1885, their style, evolution and importance." In *Library,* ser. 5, vol. 4 (1949–50), p. 262–72.

2643. King, A. Hyatt. Four hundred years of music printing. 2nd ed. London: Trustees of the British Museum, 1979. 48 p.

1st edition, 1964. 48 p.

A short, well-written account of the history of music printing, with a selected bibliography of 29 items on the subject. Illustrated with facsimile pages of early music printing.

2nd edition, 1968, incorporating a few changes in the text and additions to the bibliography.

Review of the 1st edition by Harry Carter in *Library,* ser. 5, vol. 20 (June 1965), p. 154–57; by Donald W. Krummel in *Notes,* 22 (1965–66), p. 902–903.

2644. Kinkeldey, Otto. "Music and music printing in incunabula." In *Bibliographic Society of America, Papers,* 26 (1932), p. 89–118.

For other discussions of music incunabula, see nos. 2668 and 2743.

2645. Kinsky, Georg. "Beethoven-Erstdrucke bis zum Jahre 1800." In *Philobiblon,* 3 (1930), p. 329–36.

2646. Kinsky, Georg. "Erstlingsdrucke der deutschen Tonmeister der Klassik und Romantik." In *Philobiblon,* 7 (1934), p. 347–64.

Also printed separately by H. Reichner, Vienna, 1934.

2647. Kinsky, Georg. Die Originalausgaben der Werke Johann Sebastian Bachs; ein Beitrag zur Musikbibliographie. Wien: H. Reichner, [1937]. 134 p.

This and the two preceding items are contributions by one of the leading specialists in music printing of the 18th and 19th centuries.

2648. Krohn, Ernst Christopher. Music publishing in the Middle Western States before the Civil War. Detroit, Michigan: Information Coordinators, 1972. 44 p. (Detroit studies in music bibliography, 23)

2649. Krummel, Donald W. English music printing, 1553–1700. London: Bibliographical Society, 1975. 188 p.

This book is a history, a typographical study, and a bibliographical study. It is *not* a bibliography, although it is filled with useful bibliographic references. It is included here as a model of bibliographic investigation. Uses the concept of "bibliographical forms." Appends "A chronological synopsis of music type faces." A successor to Steele (no. 2704).

Review by Lenore Coral and Stanley Boorman in *Notes*, 34 (1977), p. 65–67.

2650. Krummel, Donald W. "Graphic analysis, its application to early American engraved music." In *Notes*, 16 (1959), p. 213–33.

Discussion of the history of early American music publishing in terms of the printing processes used, with special reference to the work of Blake and Willig. 7 plates.

2651. Krummel, Donald W. Guide for dating early published music: a manual of bibliographical practices. Hackensack, New Jersey: Joseph Boonin; Kassel: Bärenreiter, 1974. 267 p.

"Supplement to the *Guide for Dating Early Published Music*," in *Fontes Artis Musicae*, 24 (1977), p. 175–84, by Donald W. Krummel, adds and corrects information in the *Guide*.

Krummel was the chair of the IAML Commission for Bibliographical Research, which created this very important compilation of information on the dating of early editions of music bearing no date of publication. There is a synopsis, or systematic outline, of the methodology. Plate numbers, publishers' and dealers' addresses, publishing practices, and other kinds of evidence are discussed. There is a section organized by country discussing specifics of music publishing: studies; directories; important publishers, printers, and engravers; plate number files; catalogs. Also considered in each national report are copyright, announcements of music publications, design and printing practices, paper, units of currency and pricing practices, important collections, and other evidence. The first section is followed by footnotes and a bibliography, which the second section incorporates by references in each of the national reports. Index of composers.

The contents of the IAML *Guide* is made more accessible by Linda I. Solow's "An index to publishers, engravers, and lithographers and a bibliography of the literature cited in the IAML *Guide for Dating Early Published Music*" in *Fontes Artis Musicae*, 24 (1977), p. 81–95. Solow's work is, in effect, an appendix to the IAML *Guide*.

Review by Rita Benton in the *Journal of the American Musicological Society*, 29 (1976), p. 138–40.

2652. Krummel, Donald W. "Late 18th-century French music publishers' catalogs in the Library of Congress." In *Fontes Artis Musicae,* 7 (1960), p. 61–64.

Krummel, Donald W., ed. Music printing and publishing. See no. 2674.

2653. Krummel, Donald W. "Musical functions and bibliographical forms." In *Library,* (1976), p. 327–50.

A most important concept, that of grouping editions into "bibliographical forms," is presented.

2654. Layer, Adolf. Katalog des Augsburger Verlegers Lotter von 1753. Kassel: Bärenreiter, 1964. 44 p. (Catalogus musicus, 2)

Facsimile edition of the 1753 catalog of the music publications of the firm of Johann Jacob Lotter in Augsburg. Lists some 370 titles by 170 composers of the late 17th and early 18th centuries. Index and "Nachwort" provided by the editor.

2655. Lenneberg, Hans. "The haunted bibliographer." In *Notes,* 41 (1985), p. 239–48.

Concerning lack of understanding of the importance of stereotypography and lithography in music printing in the 19th century.

2656. Lenz, Hans U. Der Berliner Musikdruck von seinen Anfängen bis zur Mitte des 18. Jahrhunderts. Lippstadt, Westf: Buchdruckerei Thiele, 1932. 116 p.

Also issued as a dissertation, Rostock, 1932.

Discussion of the Berlin music printers, their output, their techniques. P. 27–35: chronological listing of 126 printed works.

2657. Lesure, François. Bibliographie des éditions musicales publiées par Estienne Roger et Michel-Charles Le Cène (Amsterdam, 1696–1743). Paris: Heugel, 1969. 173 p. (Publications de la Société Française de Musicologie. Sér. 2, Tome 12)

Documents the production of one of the most active music publishers of the early 18th century, some 700 volumes of vocal and instrumental music for French and Italian musicians.

Contains a transcription of the catalog by Roger published in 1716 and a facsimile of a Le Cène catalog printed in Amsterdam in 1737.

2658. Lesure, François. "Cotages d'éditeurs antérieurs à c. 1850: Liste préliminaire." In *Fontes Artis Musicae,* 14 (1967), p. 22–37.

A list by country of late 18th- and 19th-century music publishers who used plate numbers.

2659. Lesure, François and G. Thibault. Bibliographie des editions d'Adrian le Roy et Robert Ballard (1551–98). Paris: Société française de musicologie, Heugel et Cie, 1955. 304 p. (Publications de la Société française de musicologie. 2 sér., tome 9)

An exemplary bibliography of 319 musical editions issued by the Le Roy-Ballard press, cited chronologically with full bibliographical descriptions, lists of contents, and locations in public and private collections. Brief historical introduction, and an anthology of the most important prefaces, dedications, and other documents. First-line index of texts, index of titles and personal names. 9 facsimile plates.

Review by Kenneth Levy in *Journal of the American Musicological Society*, 8 (1955), p. 221–23; by Vincent H. Duckles in *Notes*, 15 (1957), p. 102–103.

2660. Lesure, François and G. Thibault. "Bibliographie des éditions musicales publiées par Nicolas Du Chemin (1549–1576)." In *Annales Musicologiques*, 1 (1953), p. 269–373.

Bibliography similar in scope and format to the preceding work. Covers 100 editions published by Du Chemin, with full descriptions, listings of contents, and locations of copies. Numerous facsimiles of title pages. First-line index of Latin and of French texts, and of titles and names.

2661. Littleton, Alfred H. A catalogue of one hundred works illustrating the history of music printing from the 15th to the end of the 17th century, in the library of Alfred H. Littleton.... London: Novello, 1911. 38 p. 12 facsimile plates.

Includes both musical and theoretical works grouped by nationality, with annotations directing attention to their interest as examples of music printing.

2662. Macmillan, Barclay. "Tune-book imprints in Canada to 1867: a descriptive bibliography." In the *Papers of the Bibliographical Society of Canada*, 16 (1977), p. 31–57.

Complements the Calderisi study (no. 2586) and covers imprints of Canada up to the Confederacy, thus omitting any publications from the Maritime Provinces.

2663. Mailliot, Sylvette. "Un couple de marchands de musique au XVIIIe siècle: Les Boivin." In *Revue de Musicologie*, 54 (1968), p. 106–113.

Concerns the life and career of the music publisher François Boivin and his wife, née Elizabeth Catherine Ballard, between 1721 and 1753. Ballard was the daughter and granddaughter of the famous printers of music for the king.

2664. Marco, Guy A. The earliest music printers of continental Europe, a checklist of facsimiles illustrating their work. [Charlottesville]: Bibliographical Society of the University of Virginia, 1962. 20 p.

An index of facsimile plates of the work of early music printers to be found in a variety of music histories, monographs, and other reference works. 101 printers from the late 15th century to 1599 are included.

2665. Matthäus, Wolfgang. Johann André Musikverlag zu Offenbach am Main; Verlagsgeschichte und Bibliographie, 1772–1800. [Nach dem Tode des Verfassers hrsg. von Hans Schneider]. Tutzing: H. Schneider, 1973. 401 p.

A history and description of the publishing house of Johann André, including a chronological survey of the publications listing plate numbers. There follows an extensive annotated bibliography of the publications in chronological order. Index to composers in the bibliography.

Reviewed by Thomas Heck in *Notes*, 31 (1971), p. 62–63, and by Rita Benton in the *Journal of the American Musicological Society*, 27 (1974), p. 530–32.

2666. Matthäus, Wolfgang. "Quellen und Fehlerquellen zur Datierung von Musikdrucken aus der Zeit nach 1750." In *Fontes Artis Musicae*, 15 (1967), p. 37–42.

A discussion of the three criteria that should be used to ascertain the date of a printed work.

2667. Meissner, Ute. Der Antwerpener Notendrucker Tylman Susato. Eine bibliographische Studie zur niederländischen Chansonpublikation in der ersten Hälfte des 16. Jahrhunderts. Berlin: Merseburger, 1967. 2 v. (Berliner Studien zur Musikwissenschaft, 11)

Vol. 1 contains biographical information and an analysis of Susato's activity as a music printer. Vol. 2 is a chronological bibliography of all of Susato's publications, with indexes of composers and a first-line index of compositions.

Review by Winfried Kirsch in *Die Musikforschung*, 22 (1969), p. 237–38; by Donald W. Krummel in *Notes*, 25 (1969), p. 500–501.

2668. Meyer-Baer, Kathi. Liturgical music incunabula, a descriptive catalog. London: Bibliographical Society, 1962. 63 p.

257 entries, arranged alphabetically by title, treating some 800 items. References made to the standard bibliographies of incunabula and to locations of copies in major libraries. 12 plates illustrating types of notation. Chronological index and index of printers and places.

See also the author's preliminary study, "Liturgical music incunabula in the British Museum," in *Library*, ser. 4, vol. 20 (1939), p. 272–94.

Review, anon., in *Times Literary Supplement*, 16 Nov. 1962, p. 880; and by Donald W. Krummel in *Notes*, 21 (1964), p. 366–68.

2669. Meyer, Kathi and Eva J. O'Meara. "The printing of music, 1473–1934." In *Dolphin*, 2 (1935), p. 171–207.

A well-illustrated sketch of the history of music printing. Includes a bibliography of works on the subject.

2670. Meyer, Kathi and Inger M. Christensen. "Artaria plate numbers." In *Notes*, ser. 1, no. 15 (1942), p. 1–22.

A painstakingly assembled list of Artaria (Jean as well as Mathias) plate numbers citing composers, brief title, and approximate date of printing. Supplementary list of Artaria plates without numbers in the copies they examined.

2671. Mischiati, Oscar. Indici, cataloghi e avvisi degli editori e librai musicali italiani dal 1591 al 1798. Firenze: Leo S. Olschki Editore, 1984. 553 p. (Studi e testi per la storia della musica, 2)

Transcriptions of lists of published Italian music from contemporaneous sources with descriptions of the sources, a composer-title index to the transcriptions, an index to names cited in the text, and a list of libraries cited in the text with page references.

Review by François Lesure in *Fontes Artis Musicae*, 32 (1985), p. 186.

2672. Molitor, Raphael. "Italienische Choralnotendrucke." In his *Die nach-tridentische Choral-Reform zu Rom*, v. 1, p. 94–119. Leipzig: 1901.

Reprinted by Olms, Hildesheim, 1982.

A general discussion of Italian printers of liturgical books of the later 15th and 16th centuries.

2673. Müller, Hans Christian. Bernhard Schott, Hofmusikstecher in Mainz: die Frühgeschichte seines Musikverlages bis 1797. Mit einem Verzeichnis der Verlagswerke 1779–1898. Mainz: Schott, 1977. 219 p. (Beiträge zur mittelrheinischen Musikgeschichte, 16)

A historical sketch of the publishing house of Schott until 1797, followed by a bibliographic study of musical works published up to that time.

Review by Rita Benton in *Fontes Artis Musicae*, 25 (1978), p. 194–95.

2674. Music printing and publishing. Edited by Donald W. Krummel and Stanley Sadie. New York: W. W. Norton; London: Macmillan, 1990. 615 p. (The Norton/Grove handbooks in music)

This volume incorporates material on the printing and publishing of music that appeared in *The New Grove Dictionary of Music and Musicians* and *The New Grove Dictionary of American Music* (1986), brought up-to-date and substantially supplemented.

Part 1 is based on the *New Grove* article "Printing and publishing," by H. Edmund Poole and Donald W. Krummel (no. 2683). Part 1, "Music printing," includes a new article, "Music printing by computer," by Richard Vendome. Part 2 is a dictionary of music publishers and printers. This is based on the roughly 500 entries on music publishers and printers in the 1980 and 1986 sets, supplemented by over 150 additional entries. Part 3 is a glossary of music printing and publishing, contributed by Stanley Boorman.

There is an entirely re-worked and expanded classified bibliography, p. 553–63, and a single index (a first in a *New Grove* volume) of corporate and personal names and cities.

Review by Corey Field in *Notes*, 47 (1991), p. 725–27, and by John May in *Brio*, 28 (1991), p. 37–38.

2675. Music publishing, copyright, and piracy in Victorian England: a twenty-five year chronicle, 1881–1906, from the pages of the *Musical Opinion & Music Trade Review* and other English music journals of the period. Gathered by James B. Coover. London and New York: Mansell, 1985. 169 p.

Includes bibliography and index.

Review by Miriam Miller in *Fontes Artis Musicae*, 33 (1986), p. 219–20.

2676. Neighbour, Oliver W. and Alan Tyson. English music publishers' plate numbers in the first half of the 19th century. London: Faber, 1965. 48 p.

Review by Klaus Hortschansky in *Die Musikforschung*, 21 (1968), p. 102.

2677. Novello. A century and a half in Soho; a short history of the firm of Novello, publishers and printers of music, 1811–1961. London: Novello, [1961]. 85 p.

A popular history of the music publishing house that has exercised a wide influence on public taste in England through the printing of inexpensive editions of the classics.

Review by Donald W. Krummel in *Notes*, 19 (1961), p. 60–61; by Richard Schaal in *Die Musikforschung*, 17 (1964), p. 183–84.

2678. Oldman, Cecil B. Collecting musical first editions. London: Constable, 1938. 29 p. (Aspects of book collecting)

Reprinted from *New Paths in Book Collecting*, edited by John Carter, London, 1934, p. 95–124.

An informal and inviting discussion of the pleasures of collecting early music. Bibliography, p. 120–24.

2679. Pattison, Bruce. "Notes on early music printing." In *Library*, ser. 4, vol. 19 (1939), p. 239–421.

A survey of the state of knowledge of the printing of music from 1481 to 1630, updating an earlier article by George Barclay Squire, "Notes on early music printing," in *Bibliographica*, 3 (1897), p. 99–122.

2680. Plesske, Hans-Martin. "Bibliographie des Schrifttums zur Geschichte deutscher und österreichischer Musikverlage." In *Beiträge zur Geschichte des Buchwesens*, Band III (1968), p. 135–222.

A bibliography of 755 items listed alphabetically under the names of the firms. The first section is devoted to information in general reference works, the second to histories of music publishing.

2681. Pogue, Samuel F. Jacques Moderne, Lyons music printer of the sixteenth century. Genève: Librairie Droz, 1969. 412 p. (Travaux d'humanisme et renaissance, 101)

> The book includes an extensive bibliography of all of Moderne's output, with full bibliographical descriptions of the non-musical books, and contents with concordances of the music books—a total of 149 entries, of which 59 are for books of music. [from the introductory remarks]

Includes music.

Review by Albert Dunning in *Notes*, 29 (1972), p. 46–47; by Frank Dobbins in *Journal of the American Musicological Society*, 24 (1971), p. 126–31; by Charles Cudworth in *Music and Letters*, 51 (1970), p. 85–86.

2682. Poole, H. Edmund. "New music types: invention in the eighteenth century." In *Journal of the Printing Historical Society*, 1 (1965), p. 21–38.

Reviews the history of music printing, with special emphasis on the contribution of Breitkopf.

2683. Poole, H. Edmund and Donald W. Krummel. "Printing and publishing of music." In *The New Grove Dictionary of Music and Musicians*, edited by Stanley Sadie, v. 15, p. 232–74. London: Macmillan, 1980.

A review of the history of printing from the early stages to modern practices and a survey of publishing practices from 1501 to the present. Followed by an excellent classified bibliography on the subject.

See no. 2674 for a revised and expanded version.

2684. Pougin, Arthur. "Notes sur la presse musicale en France." In *Encyclopédie de la musique et dictionnaire du Conservatoire*, pt. 2, v. 6 (1931), p. 3841–3859. Paris: Librarie Delagrave, 1931.

2685. Probleme des Musiknotendrucks. Papers from a session of the *Gutenberg-Symposion in der Johannes Gutenberg-Universität in Mainz vom 12.-14. Oktober 1981*. In the *Gutenberg-Jahrbuch*, 58 (1983), p. 105–141.

Anik Devriès, "La stéréomélotypie procédé d'impression musicale." Describes a method of printing music.

Rosemary Hilmar, "Nach den hinterlassenen endgültigen Korrekturen des Komponisten revidiert." A study of the printing of Berg's *Wozzeck*.

Helmut Rösing and Joachim Schlichte, "Die Serie A/I des RISM." Describes RISM A/I as documentation for the printing of music from the beginning to 1800.

2686. Przywecke-Samecka, Maria. Drukarstwo muzyczne w Polsce do kónca XVIII wieku. Kraków: Polskie Wydawnictwo Muzyczne, 1968. 263 p. 40 plates.

A study of music printing and publishing in Poland from the 16th through the 18th centuries.

Bibliography of early printers' works, arranged under location (p. 181–240). Bibliography of literature on music printing.

2687. Redway, Virginia L. Music directory of early New York City; a file of musicians, music publishers and musical instrument makers listed in N. Y. directories from 1786 through 1835, together with the most important New York music publishers from 1836 through 1875. New York: New York Public Library, 1941. 102 p.

Three main sections: (1) musicians and teachers; (2) publishers, printers, lithographers, and dealers, with names and addresses as they appeared in successive years; (3) instrument makers and dealers. Appendices include chronological list of firms and individuals, 1786–1811, and a list of musical societies, 1789–99.

2688. Reese, Gustave. "Printing and engraving of music." In *The International Cyclopedia of Music and Musicians*, 9th ed., p. 1441–43 (no. 63).

2689. Rheinfurth, Hans. Der Musikverlag Lotter in Augsburg (c. 1719–1845). Tutzing: Schneider, 1977. 344 p. (Musikbibliographische Arbeiten, 3)

2690. Ricordi. Casa Ricordi, 1808–1958; profile storico a cura di Claudio Sartori.... Milano: G. Ricordi, 1958. 116 p. 48 plates.

16 of the plates are facsimile pages of composers' autographs; the remainder are chiefly reproductions, in color, of cover designs for noteworthy Ricordi music publications.

Review by Donald W. Krummel in *Notes*, 17 (1960), p. 400–401.

2691. Robert, Henri. Traité de gravure de musique sur planches d'étain et des divers procédés de simili gravùre de musique ... precédé de l'historique du signe, de l'impression et de la gravùre de musique. 2e éd. Paris: Chez l'auteur, 1926. 151 p.

First published in 1902.

A rather sketchy historical survey of music writing, printing, and engraving, followed by a description of the technical processes involved in preparing engraved plates.

2692. Rochester Museum and Science Center. Music publishing in Rochester, 1859–1930: a checklist of the sheet music printed in Rochester in the collection of the Rochester Museum and Science Center. Compiled by Stuart A. Kohler. Rochester, New York: Rochester Museum and Science Center, 1975. 75 leaves in various foliations.

2693. Romero de Lecea, Carlos. Introducción a los viejos libros de musica. Madrid: Joyas Bibliográficas, 1976. 138 p. (Collección de estudios y ensayos, 4)

A history of music printing in Spain in the 15th and 16th centuries, with numerous facsimile plates. Provides a list of the earliest known examples of printed music, 1492–1511.

2694. Ross, Ted. The art of music engraving and processing; a complete manual, reference and text book on preparing music for reproduction and print. Miami: Hansen Books, 1970. 278 p.

Full of historical and technical information. Well-illustrated.

Sadie, Stanley, ed. Music printing and publishing. See no. 2674.

2695. Sartori, Claudio. Bibliografia delle opere musicali stampate da Ottaviano Petrucci. Firenze: Olschki, 1948. 217 p. (Biblioteca di bibliografia italiana, 18)

Chronological bibliography of Petrucci's work, with full descriptions, contents of each publication. Index of titles, lists of libraries, and their holdings of works printed by Petrucci. Bibliography.

2696. Sartori, Claudio. Dizionario degli editori musicali italiani (tipografi, incisori, librai-editori). Firenze: Olschki, 1958. 215 p. (Biblioteca di bibliografia italiana, 32)

Italian music printers, editors, and publishers from the 16th century to the present. Some bibliographical references given. The principal issues of the publishers are noted but no complete catalogs given. Index of names, but no chronology. 8 plates of early title pages.

Review by Dragan Plamenac in *Notes*, 16 (1959), p. 242–43; by Gerhard Croll in *Die Musikforschung*, 12 (1959), p. 255–56.

2697. Schaal, Richard. Die Kataloge des Augsburger Musikalien-Händlers Kaspar Flurschütz, 1613–1628. Mit einer Einleitung und Registern zum ersten Mal hrsg. von Richard Schaal. Mit einer Bibliographie zur Augsburger Musikgeschichte 1550–1650. Wilhelmshaven: Heinrichshofen's Verlag, 1974. 159 p. (Quellen-Kataloge zur Musikgeschichte, 7)

A catalog with introduction and index to the publisher/music seller Flurschütz. Includes a bibliography of the history of music in Augsburg from
1550–1650.

2698. Schaefer, Hartmut. Die Notendrucker und Musikverleger in Frankfurt
am Main von 1630 bis um 1720: eine bibliographisch-drucktechnische Un-
tersuchung. Kassel: Bärenreiter, 1975. 2 v. (711 p.) (Catalogus musicus, 7)
Bibliography: p. 663–87.

2699. Schmid, Anton. Ottaviano dei Petrucci da Fossombrone, erster Erfin-
der des Musiknotendruckes mit beweglichen Metalltypen, und seine Nach-
folger im sechzehnten Jahrhunderte. Wien: P. Rohrmann, 1845. 342 p.
Reprint by B. R. Gruner, Amsterdam, 1968. 356 p. with 4 folded leaves.
One of the first scholarly studies of early music printing. Contains important information about Petrucci's contemporaries in other European
centers of music printing.

2700. Schmidt-Phiseldeck, Josef. "Datierung der Musikalien." In *Beethoven-
Zentenarfeier. Wien, 1927*, p. 279–82. Wien: Universal Edition, 1927.
A short article on the importance of dating music publications.

2701. Smith, William C. A bibliography of the musical works published by
John Walsh during the years 1695–1720. London: Bibliographical Society,
1948. 215 p. 38 plates.
Reissued with corrections in 1968.
622 Walsh publications cited for the period under consideration, with
numerous descriptive annotations. Index of titles and works and general
index.
Review by J. Coopersmith in *Notes*, 7 (1949), p. 104–106; by A. Hyatt
King in *Music and Letters*, 30 (1949), p. 273–76.

2702. Smith, William C. and Charles Humphries. A bibliography of the musical
works published by the firm of John Walsh during the years 1721–1766.
London: Bibliographical Society, 1968. 351 p.
Review by J. Merrill Knapp in *Notes*, 26 (1969), p. 274–75; by Lenore
Coral in *Journal of the American Musicological Society*, 23 (1970), p. 141–
43; by Charles Cudworth in *Music and Letters*, 50 (1969), p. 416–17.

Squire, William Barclay. "Notes on early music printing." See no. 2679.

2703. Squire, William Barclay. "Publishers' numbers." In *Sammelbände der
Internationalen Musikgesellschaft*, 15 (1913–14), p. 420–27.
Refers to music publishers' plate numbers.

2704. Steele, Robert. The earliest English music printing; a description and
bibliography of English printed music to the close of the 16th century.
London: Printed for the Bibliographical Society, 1903. 102 p. (Illustrated
monographs, 11)
Brief introduction covers methods of printing, and the book includes a
chapter on early English printers of music. The bibliography of 197 items

is arranged chronologically from 1495 to 1600, giving full title and collation, library locations, and notes on typography. Bibliography of 34 items on music printing.

Reprinted in London, 1965, with a new appendix of addenda and corrigenda.

See also no. 2649.

2705. Steele, Robert. "Early music printing, 1601–1640." In *Transactions of the Bibliographical Society*, 11 (1909), p. 13–15.

Describes a project of extending his *Earliest English Music Printing* (no. 2704).

2706. Stellfeld, J. A. Bibliographie des éditions musicales plantiniennes. [Bruxelles: Palais des Academies, 1949.] 248 p. (Academie royale de Belgique. Classe des beaux-arts. Memoires, T. 5, fasc. 3)

Brief historical account of the Plantin Press, with detailed bibliographical description and discussion of the 21 music items printed by the press at Antwerp and at Leiden. 21 plates.

Toledo (Ohio). Museum of Art. The printed note.... See no. 2372.

2707. Tyson, Alan. The authentic English editions of Beethoven. London: Faber and Faber, 1963. 152 p.

An important work, one of the first to apply detailed bibliographical analysis to early 19th-century music printing. The author is able to make significant revisions in the chronology of Beethoven's works.

Review by Dagmar von Busch-Weise in *Die Musikforschung*, 17 (1964), p. 443–44; by Albi Rosenthal in *Music and Letters*, 45 (1964), p. 256–58; by Donald W. MacArdle in *Notes*, 22 (1965–66), p. 920.

2708. Valentin, Erich. 50 Jahre Gustav Bosse Verlag: Streiflichter aus der Verlagsarbeit, statt einer Festschrift. Regensburg: G. Bosse, 1963. 161 p.

"Verzeichnis der im Gustav Bosse Verlag erschienenen Werke": p. 149–61.

2709. Vernarecci, D. Augusto. Ottaviano dei Petrucci da Fossombrone, inventore dei tipi mobili metalli fusi della musica nel secolo XV. Seconda edizione. Bologna: Romagnoli, 1882. 288 p.

2710. Vol'man, B. Russkie pechatnye noty XVIII veka. Leningrad: Gosudarstvennoe muzykal'noe izdatel'stvo, 1957. 293 p.

Russian printed music of the 18th century.

2711. Weinhold, Liesbeth. "Musiktitel und Datierung." In *Fontes Artis Musicae*, 13 (1966), p. 136–40.

2712. Weinmann, Alexander. Beiträge zur Geschichte des Alt-Wiener Musikverlages. 1948– .

A series of studies related to Viennese music publishing of the late 18th and early 19th centuries. They appear under varied imprints and in two sub-series: Reihe 1, *Komponisten*; Reihe 2, *Verleger*. The volumes are listed below in series order.

2713. Weinmann, Alexander. Beiträge zur Geschichte des Alt-Wiener Musik-verlages. Reihe 1, Folge 1: Verzeichnis der im Druck erschienenen Werke von Joseph Lanner, sowie Listen der Plattennummern der Originalausgaben für alle Besetzungen.... Wien: Leuen, [1948]. 31 p.
Tables listing the work of Lanner (1801–43) in opus number order, with plate numbers of the first editions. Alphabetical index of works by title.

2714. Weinmann, Alexander. Beiträge zur Geschichte des Alt-Wiener Musik-verlages. Reihe 1, Folge 2. Verzeichnis sämtlicher Werke von Johann Strauss, Vater und Sohn. Wien: Musikverlag L. Krenn, 1956. 171 p.

2715. Weinmann, Alexander. Beiträge zur Geschichte des Alt-Wiener Musik-verlages. Reihe 1, Folge 3: Verzeichnis sämtlicher Werke von Josef und Eduard Strauss. Wien: Ludwig Krenn, 1967. 104 p.

2716. Weinmann, Alexander. Beiträge zur Geschichte des Alt-Wiener Musik-verlages. Reihe 2, Folge 1a. Verzeichnis der Verlagswerke des Musika-lischen Magazins in Wien, 1784–1802, Leopold (und Anton) Kozeluch. 2., erg. und vollständig umgearb. Aufl. Wien: L. Krenn, 1979. 53 p.
First published in 1950 by Österreichischer Bundesverlag, Vienna. 31 p.
Works without plate numbers, and with questionable plate numbers, in chronological order; works with plate number in numerical order, followed by an alphabetical list by composer of Kozeluch's catalog, published in 1800.

2717. Weinmann, Alexander. Beiträge zur Geschichte des Alt-Wiener Musik-verlages. Reihe 2, Folge 2. Vollständiges Verlagsverzeichnis Artaria & Comp. 2. erg. Aufl. Wien: L. Krenn, 1978. 201 p.
First edition published 1952.
A history of the Artaria firm, with a classified list, chronological within classifications, of its publications, giving in most cases exact dates of publication. Index by composers.
Review of the 1st ed. by Richard S. Hill in *Notes*, 10 (1953), p. 449–50.

2718. Weinmann, Alexander. Beiträge zur Geschichte des Alt-Wiener Musik-verlages. Reihe 2, Folge 3: "Vollständiges Verlagsverzeichnis der Musikalien des Kunst- und Industrie-Comptoirs in Wien, 1801–1819." In *Studien zur Musikwissenschaft; Beihefte der DTÖ*, 22 (1955), p. 217–52.
Contains a listing of 802 plate numbers in numerical order, with composer, title, and date of publication of the corresponding works. Composer index.
Review by William Klenz in *Notes*, 14 (1956), p. 117.

2719. Weinmann, Alexander. Beiträge zur Geschichte des Alt-Wiener Musik-verlages. Reihe 2, Folge 4: "Verzeichnis der Musikalien des Verlages Johann Traeg in Wien, 1794–1818." In *Studien zur Musikwissenschaft; Beihefte der DTÖ*, 23 (1956), p. 135–83.
Lists all works published by the firm, in chronological order.

2720. Weinmann, Alexander. Beiträge zur Geschichte des Alt-Wiener Musikverlages. Reihe 2, Folge 5: Wiener Musikverleger und Musikalienhändler von Mozarts Zeit bis gegen 1860; ein firmengeschichtlicher und topographischer Behelf. Wien: Rohrer, 1956. 72 p. (Österreichische Akademie der Wissenschaft ... Veröff. der Kommission für Musikforschung, 2)

Lists and discusses 38 music dealers and publishers and 19 related general book dealers and publishers. Tables showing early and existing addresses of the firms. Useful in dating Viennese musical imprints.

Review by Richard S. Hill in *Notes*, 15 (1958), p. 396–97.

2721. Weinmann, Alexander. Beiträge zur Geschichte des Alt-Wiener Musikverlages. Reihe 2, Folge 6: Verzeichnis der Musikalien aus dem K.K. Hoftheater-Musik-Verlag. Wien: Universal Edition, [1961]. 130 p. (Wiener Urtext Ausgabe)

Brief history of the firm and biographical notes on the men associated with it. List of publications from 1796 to c. 1820, with plate numbers and dates of issue if known.

Review by Donald W. Krummel in *Notes*, 19 (1961), p. 76.

2722. Weinmann, Alexander. Beiträge zur Geschichte des Alt-Wiener Musikverlages. Reihe 2, Folge 7: Kataloge Anton Huberty (Wien) und Christoph Torricella. Wien: Universal Edition, 1962. 135 p.

Brief histories of the firms, followed by detailed listings of their publications, giving composer, title, date of publication if known, location of copies in European libraries.

Review by Richard Schaal in *Die Musikforschung*, 18 (1965), p. 83.

2723. Weinmann, Alexander. Beiträge zur Geschichte des Alt-Wiener Musikverlages. Reihe 2, Folge 8: Die Wiener Verlagswerke von Franz Anton Hofmeister. Wien: Universal Edition, 1964. 252 p.

Contains a biography of Hofmeister; a dated list of plate numbers; entries, largely thematic, for all of the firm's publications; brief historical discussions of aspects of the firm's history.

2724. Weinmann, Alexander. Beiträge zur Geschichte des Alt-Wiener Musikverlages. Reihe 2, Folge 8a. Addenda und Corrigenda zum Verlagsverzeichnis Franz Anton Hoffmeister. Wien: L. Krenn, 1982. 46 p.

2725. Weinmann, Alexander. Beiträge zur Geschichte des Alt-Wiener Musikverlages. Reihe 2, Folge 9: Verlagsverzeichnis Tranquillo Mollo (mit und ohne Co.). Wien: Universal Edition, 1964. 111 p.

Biography of the Mollo family and history of the firm. Transcriptions of catalogs, with plate numbers. Alphabetical indexes by composers. The firm was a successor to Artaria.

2726. Weinmann, Alexander. Beiträge zur Geschichte des Alt-Wiener Musikverlages. Reihe 2, Folge 9a, p. 112–50. Ergänzungen zum Verlags-Verzeichnis Tranquillo Mollo. Wien: Universal Edition, 1972.

2727. Weinmann, Alexander. Beiträge zur Geschichte des Alt-Wiener Musik-verlages. Reihe 2, Folge 10: Verlagsverzeichnis Pietro Mechetti quondam Carlo (mit Portraits). Wien: Universal Edition, 1966. 205 p.

Review by Harald Heckmann in *Die Musikforschung*, 21 (1968), p. 507–508.

2728. Weinmann, Alexander. Beiträge zur Geschichte des Alt-Wiener Musik-verlages. Reihe 2, Folge 11: Verlagsverzeichnis Giovanni Cappi bis A. O. Witzendorf. Wien: Universal Edition, 1967. 210 p.

Review by Imogen Fellinger in *Die Musikforschung*, 25 (1972), p. 371.

2729. Weinmann, Alexander. Beiträge zur Geschichte des Alt-Wiener Musik-verlages. Reihe 2, Folge 12: Verzeichnis der Musikalien des Verlages Joseph Eder-Jeremias Bermann. Wien: Universal Edition, 1968. 78 p.

2730. Weinmann, Alexander. Beiträge zur Geschichte des Alt-Wiener Musik-verlages. Reihe 2, Folge 13: Wiener Musikverlag "Am Rande." Ein lücken-füllender Beitrag zur Geschichte des Alt-Wiener Musikverlages. Wien: Universal Edition, 1970. 155 p.

2731. Weinmann, Alexander. Beiträge zur Geschichte des Alt-Wiener Musik-verlages. Reihe 2, Folge 14: Verzeichnis der Musikalien des Verlages Maisch-Sprenger-Artaria. Mit 2 Supplementen: I. Die Firma Mattias Artar-ias Witwe u. Compagnie. II. Supplement zum Verlagsverzeichnis des Mu-sikalischen Magazins in Wien (Kozeluch). Wien: Universal Edition, 1970. 95 p.

2732. Weinmann, Alexander. Beiträge zur Geschichte des Alt-Wiener Musik-verlages. Reihe 2, Folge 15. Verlagsverzeichnis Ignaz Sauer (Kunstverlag zu den Sieben Schwestern), Sauer und Leidesdorf und Anton Berka & Comp. Wien: Universal Edition, 1972. 100 p.

2733. Weinmann, Alexander. Beiträge zur Geschichte des Alt-Wiener Musik-verlages. Reihe 2, Folge 16. Verlagsverzeichnis Johann Traeg (und Sohn). 2. verm. und verb. Aufl. Wien: Universal Edition, 1973. 89 p.

2734. Weinmann, Alexander. Beiträge zur Geschichte des Alt-Wiener Musik-verlages. Reihe 2, Folge 17. Johann Traeg; die Musikalienverzeichnisse von 1799 und 1804 (Handschriften und Sortiment). Wien: Universal Edition, 1973. 133 p.

Facsimiles of the two lists: *Verzeichniss alter und neuer sowohl ge-schriebener als gestochener Musikalien* and *Erster Nachtrag zu dem Ver-zeichniss alter und neuer sowohl geschriebener als gestochener Musika-lien.*

2735. Weinmann, Alexander. Beiträge zur Geschichte des Alt-Wiener Musik-verlages. Reihe 2, Folge 19. Vollständiges Verlagsverzeichnis Senefelder, Steiner, Haslinger. München and Salzburg: Musikverlag Katzbichler, 1979–83. vols. 1 and 3. (Musikwissenschaftliche Schriften, 14 and 16)

Contents: Bd. 1. A. Senefelder, Chemische Druckerey, S. A. Steiner, S. A. Steiner & Comp. (Wien, 1803–1826); Bd. 3. Tobias Haslingers Witwe und Sohn und Carl Haslinger qdm. Tobias (Wien, 1843–75).

2736. Weinmann, Alexander. Beiträge zur Geschichte des Alt-Wiener Musikverlages. Reihe 2, Folge 20. Verzeichnis der Musikalien des Verlages Anton Pennauer. Wien: Krenn, 1981. 58 p.

2737. Weinmann, Alexander. Beiträge zur Geschichte des Alt-Wiener Musikverlages. Reihe 2, Folge 21. Verzeichnis der Verlagswerke J.P. Gotthard. Wien: L. Krenn, 1981. 55 p.

2738. Weinmann, Alexander. Beiträge zur Geschichte des Alt-Wiener Musikverlages. Reihe 2, Folge 22. Verzeichnis der Musikalien des Verlages Thadé Weigl. Wien: L. Krenn, 1982. 178 p.

2739. Weinmann, Alexander. Beiträge zur Geschichte des Alt-Wiener Musikverlages. Reihe 2, Folge 23. Verlagsverzeichnis Peter Cappi und Cappi & Diabelli (1816 bis 1824). Wien: Krenn, 1983. 150 p.

2740. Weinmann, Alexander. Beiträge zur Geschichte des Alt-Wiener Musikverlages. Reihe 2, Folge 24. Verlagsverzeichnis Anton Diabelli & Co. (1824 bis 1840). Wien: L. Krenn, 1985. 494 p.

2741. Weinmann, Alexander. Der Alt-Wiener Musikverlag im Spiegel der *Wiener Zeitung.* Tutzing: Schneider, 1976. 71 p. (Institut für Österreichische Musikdokumentation. Publikation, 2)

2742. Weinmann, Alexander. Die Anzeigen des Kopiaturbetriebes Johann Traeg in der Wiener Zeitung zwischen 1782 und 1805: Bd. 2 zu seinen Musikalienverzeichnissen von 1799 und 1804 aus der Reihe *Beiträge zur Geschichte des Alt-Wiener Musikverlags.* Wien: L. Krenn, 1981. 109 p. (Wiener Archivstudien, 6)

2743. Wolf, Johannes. "Verzeichnis der musiktheoretischen Inkunabeln mit Fundorten." In Francesco Caza, *Tractato vulgare de canto figurato....,* p. 64–92. Berlin: M. Breslauer, 1922. (Veröffentlichungen der Musikbibliothek Paul Hirsch, 1)
　　Wolf lists 104 incunabula in the field of music theory, with the locations where copies are preserved, as a supplement to his edition of Caza's treatise.

2744. Young, James Bradford. "An account of printed musick, ca. 1724." In *Fontes Artis Musicae,* 29 (1982), p. 129–36.
　　A description of one of the earliest catalogs of printed music published in England. No publisher is named on the catalog, but evidence suggests that it was produced with connection to the revival of the Estienne Roger music publishing enterprise by Michel Le Cène. Considers "the essential place of commercial factors in the development of music publishing."

2745. Zur Westen, Walter von. Musiktitel aus vier Jahrhunderten; Festschrift anlässlich des 57 jährigen Bestehens der Firma C. G. Röder. Leipzig: [1921]. 116 p.

A study of musical title pages from the Renaissance to the end of the 19th century, with 96 facsimile illustrations.

Discographies

Within the last few decades the field of recorded sound has given rise to an abundance of documentation of interest to librarians, teachers, research scholars, and private collectors. One effort to bring these diverse interests together has resulted in an Association for Recorded Sound Collections, which issued in 1967 *A Preliminary Directory of Sound Recording Collections in the U.S. and Canada* (no. 2917). More recently, the International Association of Sound Archives has issued a directory of member archives covering the holdings, services, and staffs of institutions globally (no. 2942).

Recorded music has a particular attraction for the collector, whether his interests lie in early vocal discs or cylinders or in jazz recordings. There has been a proliferation of record reviews, listeners' guides, manufacturers' catalogs and numerical lists, and journals devoted almost exclusively to discography. Some indication of the scope and variety of the bibliographical coverage is suggested by the *Bibliography of Discographies* edited by Michael Gray and Gerald D. Gibson (no. 2747) in 3 volumes. No effort has been made here to list more than a few recent representative examples of the major types of reference tools available to the specialist in recorded sound. Some outmoded works are included to suggest the distance traveled by specialists in the course of this century.

Gordon Stevenson, in his article "Discography: scientific, analytical, historical and systematic," in *Trends in Archival and Reference Collections of Recorded Sound* (*Library Trends*, 21, *1* [1972], p. 101–135), has provided some of the basic theoretical principles of discography. There have been a number of articles in the *Journal of Jazz Studies* that have discussed some of these same philosophical and methodological points in the course of careful examinations of discographic questions concerning jazz recordings. The *Journal* is well worth perusal even for those not engaged in jazz studies.

In the organization following, "Encyclopedias of Recorded Music" have been distinguished from "Collectors' Guides." The distinction is perhaps an arbitrary one, but it is intended to separate the few comprehensive discographies from those directed toward the interests of collectors of classical music, jazz, or early discs.

BIBLIOGRAPHIES OF DISCOGRAPHIES

2746. Association for recorded sound collections. Journal. Vol. 1– (1968–).

In addition to the regular appearance of discographies as articles in the

Journal, there are reviews of discographies and citations of discographies not reviewed in every issue. The journal of the professional discographer.

2747. Bibliography of discographies. New York: Bowker, 1977–83. 3 v. to date.

Vol. 1: *Classical Music, 1925–1975*, by Michael H. Gray and Gerald D. Gibson.

Vol. 2: *Jazz*, by Daniel Allen.

Vol. 3: *Popular Music*, by Michael H. Gray.

Not yet issued are vol. 4, which will treat discographies of ethnic and folk music, and vol. 5, which will cover general discographies of music, label lists, speech recordings, and natural sounds.

These bibliographies are the most complete and scholarly in the field of discography. They include entries for monographs as well as for discographies appearing as articles or appended to articles. Each volume is separately indexed.

Vol. 1 contains 3,307 entries arranged in subject order. Each citation includes complete bibliographic information and annotations.

Vol. 1 has been supplemented by *Classical Music Discographies, 1976–1988: A Bibliography*, by Michael Gray (Westport, Connecticut: Greenwood Press, 1989. 334 p.) (Discographies, 34). This recent work is an explicit supplement to vol. 1, adding:

> entries for record labels citing significant numbers of classical recordings, discographies included in dissertations, and discographies appearing in program notes on sound recordings. Although the period of coverage for the most part is from 1976 to 1988, a number of citations for discographies overlooked in the earlier volume are included here as well. [from the introductory remarks]

Vol. 2 cites discographies of jazz, blues, ragtime, gospel, and rhythm and blues music published between 1935 and 1980. It excludes record company catalogs, works primarily of a critical nature, and lists of records, whether to support an accompanying text or for popular consumption. Entries are ordered by subject. A list of subject headings other than personal names or names of groups is provided. There is a list of periodicals cited and an index.

Vol. 3 cites discographies of pop music, rock and country, hillbilly and blue grass, motion picture and stage show music. Excludes record company catalogs, but includes pricing guides to out-of-print records and lists of charted popular music. There is a list of periodical titles cited and an index.

Vol. 1 reviewed by Jean-Michel Nectoux in *Fontes Artis Musicae*, 25 (1978), p. 418–19.

Updated to an extent by the discographies published in no. 2746.

2748. Cooper, David Edwin. International bibliography of discographies: classical music and jazz & blues, 1962–1972; a reference book for record collectors, dealers and libraries. Preface by Guy A. Marco. Littleton, Colorado: Libraries Unlimited, 1975. 272 p.

Brief review by Stephen M. Fry in *Notes*, 32 (1976), p. 554–55.

2749. Dearling, Robert and Celia Dearling with Brian Rust. The Guinness book of recorded sound. London: Guinness, 1984. 225 p.

A vast assemblage of facts about the history of recorded sound.

2750. Foreman, Lewis. Systematic discography. London: Clive Bingley, 1974. 144 p.

This is a comprehensive guide to the compilation of discographies. Includes a short chapter on the importance of sound recordings in documenting 20th-century history. There is a now-dated list of dealers in out-of-print recordings, a list of pirate record labels, a bibliography of relevant journals, another bibliography of discographies arranged by subject (wildlife, jazz, ethnic, etc.), and a general bibliography on sound recording and discography.

2751. Ritchie, Verna Ford. "A burgeoning in the world of discography." In *Reference Quarterly*, 21 (1982), p. 254–67.

An annotated, classified bibliography of some 70 discographies, most published in the late 1970s. Includes art music, jazz, and popular music. Lists journals and other publications that carry reviews of recorded music.

2752. Robbins, Donald C. "Current resources for the bibliographic control of sound recordings." In *Trends in Archival and Reference Collections of Recorded Sound*, edited by Gordon Stevenson, *Library Trends*, 21, no. 1 (July 1972), p. 136–46.

Incorporates a review of then-current discographies. Also cited as part of 2754.

2753. Rust, Brian A. L. Brian Rust's guide to discography. Westport, Connecticut: Greenwood Press, 1980. 133 p. (Discographies, 4)

Contents: purposes and functions of discography; short history of the science of discography; creation of a discography; securing information about discographies; labels; bibliography of book-length discographies.

2754. Stevenson, Gordon. Trends in archival and reference collections of recorded sound. Edited by Gordon Stevenson. Vol. 21, no. 1 of *Library Trends*. Urbana: University of Illinois Press, 1972. 155 p.

Contents:

"Introduction" by Gordon Stevenson.

"Sound scholarship: scope, purpose, function and potential of phonorecord archives" by Edward E. Colby.

"The struggle of sound archives in the United States" by Carlos B. Hagen.

"Recorded sound in the Library of Congress" by Donald L. Leavitt.

"Oral history" by Norman Hoyle.

"Preservation and restoration of authenticity in sound recordings" by William L. Welch.

"Discography: scientific, analytical, historical and systematic" by Gordon Stevenson.

"Current resources for the bibliographic control of sound recordings" by Donald C. Robbins.

"Copyright and archival collections of sound recordings" by Abraham A. Goldman.

ENCYCLOPEDIAS OF RECORDED MUSIC

2755. Clough, Francis F. and G. J. Cuming. The world's encyclopedia of recorded music. London: Sidgwick & Jackson, 1952. 890 p.

First Supplement (April 1950 to May–June 1951) bound with the main volume.

Second Supplement (1951–52). London, 1952. 262 p.

Third Supplement (1953–55). London, 1957. 564 p. Reprint by Greenwood Press, Westport, Connecticut, 1970.

The World's Encyclopedia is a useful reference tool for record specialists. Arrangement is alphabetical by composer, with a subclassification of works under prolific composers. Full information given as to content and labels. Special section for anthologies. (Focused on "art" music.)

Review by Philip Miller in *Notes*, 10 (1952), p. 94–95; review of the *Third Supplement* by Richard S. Hill in *Notes*, 14 (1957), p. 357–59.

2756. Eastman School of Music, Rochester. Sibley Music Library. Catalog of sound recordings. Boston, Massachusetts: G. K. Hall, 1977. 14 v.

Photo reproduction of the dictionary catalog of an extensive LP collection. Until the time of publication, the Sibley Music Library had a collection development policy to collect all current LPs of art music issued in the U.S. This catalog provides excellent coverage with numerous cross-references and added entries, but with no subject entries. Pre-Baroque coverage limited.

2757. Gramophone Shop, Inc., New York. The Gramophone Shop encyclopedia of recorded music. New York: Gramophone Shop, Inc., 1936. 574 p.

Compiled by R. D. Darrell. 2nd ed., New York, Simon & Schuster, 1942; George C. Leslie, supervising editor. 558 p. 3rd ed., rev. and enl., New York, Crown, 1948; Robert H. Reid, supervising editor. 639 p.

Reprint of the 3rd ed. (1948) by Greenwood Press, Westport, Connecticut, 1970.

The prototype for all encyclopedias of recorded music in its organization and coverage. Works arranged alphabetically under composer and partially classified. Brief biographical accounts of composers. All three volumes must be consulted, since the later editions are not fully cumulative. Coverage restricted to 78 rpm discs.

2758. Johnson, William W. The gramophone book, a complete guide for all lovers of recorded music. London: Hinrichsen, [1954]. 169 p.

A compendium of miscellaneous information useful to record collectors. British emphasis. Lacks an index.

2759. New York Public Library. Rodgers and Hammerstein Archives of Recorded Sound. Dictionary catalog of the Rodgers and Hammerstein Archives of Recorded Sound. Boston, Massachusetts: G. K. Hall, 1981. 15 v.

Photoreproduction of the card catalog of the enormous collection at Lincoln Center. Entries under composer, important performers, titles, and subjects.

2760. The Penguin guide to compact discs, cassettes and LPs. [By] Edward Greenfield, Robert Layton, Ivan March; edited by Ivan March. Harmondsworth and New York: Penguin, 1986. 1,168 p.

First published in 1975 as *The Penguin Stereo Record Guide.* Subsequently published as *The New Penguin Stereo Record and Cassette Guide* (1982) and *The Complete Penguin Stereo Record and Cassette Guide* (1984).

A successor to the *Stereo Record Guide* (no. 2785).

The authors are reviewers for *Gramophone.* This is a catalog of about 4,000 recordings in order by composer (or medium, then title for collective recordings). Each entry supplies copious discographical and performance information and the authors' opinions of the recording. Focused principally on recordings marketed in Great Britain.

COLLECTORS' GUIDES TO CLASSICAL MUSIC

Works on recordings of classical music cited in this section are useful to scholars because they generally include brief reviews featuring comments on the performances and often on the technical quality of the recordings. Few books intended for the amateur collector are included; the following listing is confined to more comprehensive English-language works. Journals such as *Gramophone,* the *American Record Guide,* and *Fanfare* provide numerous reviews of current releases.

2761. Basart, Ann Phillips. The sound of the fortepiano: a discography of recordings on early pianos. Berkeley, California: Fallen Leaf Press, 1985. 472 p. (Fallen Leaf reference books in music, 2)

"All of the pianos cited in this discography are either predecessors of the modern piano or are authentic reproductions of such pianos. Included here are commercially produced recordings released up through 1984."

> The discography is arranged in four main parts: composer-title list, giving individual compositions (this list contains the most complete information in general); pianists; piano manufacturers; and recordings, by record manufacturer and label number (this list has the most complete information on titles of albums and reissues). In addition, there are indexes to the full Composer-Title list by: performance medium (e.g., concertos, music for piano four-hands); performers other than pianists; date of piano; and instrument collections (e.g., the Colt Clavier Collection) and individual owners (e.g., Paul Badura-Skoda). The index of titles of record albums is keyed to the List of Record Manufacturers and Numbers. The appendix lists some incomplete citations of fortepiano recordings. [from the introductory remarks]

Recordings of the so-called "Siena" piano have been excluded. Entries under composer include make and model of piano, performer, place recorded, label, date of recording, title of album, and notes on program notes.

2762. Blyth, Alan, ed. Opera on record. Opera on record 2. Opera on record 3. Discographies compiled by Malcolm Walker. London: Hutchinson, 1979–84. 3 v.

Simultaneous publication in the U.S.: *Opera on Record*. New York: Harper and Row, 1982; *Opera on Record 2*. New York: Beaufort Books, 1983; *Opera on Record 3*. Dover, New Hampshire: Longwood Press, 1984.

A series of extended critical essays on recorded performances of operas by composers from Monteverdi to Britten, each accompanied by chronologically ordered discographies. Each volume has an index of performing artists.

2763. Blyth, Alan, ed. Song on record. Cambridge: Cambridge University Press, 1987–88. 2 v.

Discursive commentary on the repertory of recorded solo vocal music beginning with the works of Haydn and Mozart. Not a discography *per se*, though the text is liberally laced with references to particularly favored recordings and there are occasional lists of recordings. Each section is an independent essay written by a group of distinguished music critics, among them David Hamilton, Will Crutchfield, Robin Holloway, and Michael Kennedy. Index of singers' names.

2764. Cohn, Arthur. Recorded classical music; a critical guide to compositions and performances. New York: Schirmer Books, 1981. 2,164 p.

Entries arranged by composer, then title.

Review by Cohn of recordings of thousands of compositions. Record-label index enables the reader to discover which works appear on the same disc.

2765. Coover, James B. and Richard Colvig. Medieval and Renaissance music on long-playing records. [Detroit, Michigan: Information Service, Inc.], 1964. 122 p. (Detroit studies in music bibliography, 6)

Supplement, 1962–71 (1973). 258 p. (Issued as Detroit studies in music bibliography, 26.)

A well-organized guide to the recorded resources in medieval and Renaissance music. Part I of the *Supplement* analyzes 901 anthologies, as compared with the 322 analyzed in the 1964 edition. Part II: index to anthologies and individual discographies by composer. Part III: performer index.

The journal *Early Music* (1973–) features listings and reviews of recordings of early music and is a complement to this work in the period 1973–79. See also no. 2766.

Reviews of the 1964 edition by George F. DeVine in *Journal of Research in Music Education*, 13 (1965), p. 260, and by Ludwig Finscher in *Die Musikforschung*, 20 (1967), p. 84–85.

2766. Croucher, Trevor. Early music discography: from plainsong to the sons of Bach. Phoenix, Arizona: Oryx Press, 1982. 2 v.

First published by the Library Association, London.

Lists 3,164 recordings in a classified arrangement by period. Liturgical chant is in a separate section. In each section, entries are alphabetical by composer. There are analytics for titles of works and entries indicate performing ensemble, conductor, and basic discographic data. Indexes to names, plainsong melodies, and titles (of anonymous works).

Coover and Colvig (no. 2765) treated 901 anthologies, but there seems to be little overlap between the two discographies, perhaps because

Coover and Colvig were examining a different era of record production (LP recordings up to 1972) than Croucher (c. 1977 to 1980).

2767. Deays, Carl. La discothèque idéale. Rev. éd. Paris: Éditions Universitaires, 1973. 443 p.
First published in 1970.
Categorized entries of recommended recordings with evaluative comments. Of interest because of the inclusion of recordings marketed principally in Europe. Indexes to names of performers and composers.

2768. Discography series. Utica, New York: J. F. Weber, 1970– . Nos. 1– . Editors: nos. 1–4, 8–10, 12– , J. F. Weber; nos. 5–7, 11, Peter Morse. Contents:

   1. *Schubert Lieder.* 49 p.
   2. *Hugo Wolf Complete Works.* 2nd ed. 85 p.
   3. *Schumann Lieder.* 20 p.
   4. *Brahms Lieder.* 20 p.
   5. *Schubert, Schumann, Brahms, Choral Music.* 26 p.
   6. *Mendelssohn Vocal Music.* 2nd ed. 30 p.
   7. *Strauss Lieder.* 2nd ed. 46 p.
   8. *Loewe and Franz.* 20 p.
   9. *Mahler.* 2nd ed. 48 p.
  10. *Bruckner.* 34 p.
  11. *Debussy and Ravel Vocal Music.* 38 p.
  12. *Edgard Varèse.* 13 p.
  13. *Leonard Bernstein.* 16 p.
  14. *Alban Berg.* 16 p.
  15. *Pfitzner and Marx.* 18 p.
  16. *Benjamin Britten.* 58 p.
  17. *Richard Strauss Opera.* 51 p. By Alan Jefferson.
  18. *Leoš Janáček.* 65 p. By William D. Curtis.
  19. *Carter and Schuman.* 20 p.
  20. *A Gregorian Chant Discography.* 2 v. (fully described as no. 2901)

Each number is preceded by an informative introduction, including reference to bibliographical sources. These are lists of all recordings known to have been made of the genre(s) of works specified in the title. The arrangement varies; occasionally it is chronological in order of composition, and in other lists it is alphabetical by title. The chronological lists have title indexes. Often the lists are keyed to a standard catalog or lists of the composer's works. The manufacturer's name and catalog numbers are provided as well as the date of release, when known. Musicians and ensembles are identified where known, but there are no indexes to them. These are carefully and thoroughly researched discographies reflecting the state of knowledge at the time of compilation.

2769. Gilbert, Richard. The clarinetists' solo repertoire: a discography. New York: Grenadilla Society, 1972. 100 p.
A supplement, *The Clarinetists' Discography II*, was published in 1975. 150 p.
These are more than discographies. They include reviews and critiques, portraits of leading clarinetists, bibliographies, and lists of record publishers and their addresses.

2770. The guide to long playing records. New York: Knopf, 1955. 3 v.

Reprinted by Greenwood Press, Westport, Connecticut, 1978.

Vol. 1: Irving Kolodin, *Orchestral Music.* 268 p. Vol. 2: Philip L. Miller, *Vocal Music.* 381 p. Vol. 3: Harold C. Schonberg, *Chamber and Solo Instrument Music.* 280 p.

2771. Hall, David. The record book, a music lover's guide to the world of the phonograph. New York: Smith & Durrell, 1940. 771 p.

Supplement. 1941. (Continuing pagination, 772–886.)

Second Supplement. 1943. (Continuing pagination, 887–1013.)

Complete Edition. New York: Citadel Press, 1946. 1,063 p. Incorporates the two preceding supplements.

2772. Hall, David. The record book. International edition. A guide to the world of the phonograph. New York: Durrell, 1948. 1,394 p.

First edition published in 1940. There was a revised edition in 1946.

Part 1 is an encapsulated history of European classical music to the mid-20th century. Part 2 is a collection of reviews of recordings arranged alphabetically by composer. There are lists of recordings for each piece discussed. Each composer is given a short biography. There is a general index to the reviews and a composer index.

2773. Hall, David. Records: 1950 edition. New York: Knopf, 1950. 524 p.

Hall's books are addressed to the private collector with an interest in serious music. In the earlier editions the material is classified by medium. Beginning with the *International Edition* (no. 2772) the arrangement is alphabetical by composer. Much general information for the record collector is included. The 1950 edition is the first to direct attention to long-playing discs.

2774. Halsey, Richard Sweeney. Classical music recordings for home and library. Chicago, Illinois: American Library Association, 1976. 340 p.

Intended to provide guidance to librarians and amateur collectors in building a basic collection of classical music. Arranged by genre and within genre by composer. Indexes to title and manufacturers' names and numbers. Readers should ignore the ratings provided by the compiler.

2775. Hermil, Hélène. Musique: 10,000 compositeurs du XIIe au XXe siècle, répertoire chrono-ethnique. Saint-Mandè, France: Production et distribution Groupe de Recherche et d'Études Musicales, 1983. 842 p.

An alphabetical list of composers with dates and places of birth and death, followed by a chronological list of composers by country, showing ethnic origin. Lists of women composers. Lists of composers related by familial, marital, or other significant ties. Entries give record label and numbers. A product of the Bibliothèque Internationale de Musique Contemporaine.

2776. Lory, Jacques. Guide des disques; l'aventure de la musique occidentale, du chant grégorien à la musique électronique. 3ème éd. Paris: Buchet-Chastel, 1971. 416 p.

First published in 1967.

Arranges entries in historical order with comments on each historical period as well as upon the recordings. Recordings by European and American manufacturers.

2777. Opern auf Schallplatten, 1900–1962: ein historischer Katalog vollständiger oder nahezu vollständiger Aufnahmen als Beitrag zur Geschichte der Aufführungspraxis. Red. Irmgard Bontinck-Küffel, Mitarb., Kurt Blaukopf, Manfred Wagner. Wien: Universal Edition, 1974. 184 p.
One of the first attempts to apply discography to historical research. The editors identify the first recording of each opera with information as to cast, orchestra, and label. Discography arranged by composer and title. Alternative titles given as well as complete discographical information. Bibliography. No index!

2778. Pirie, Peter J. 20th century British music: a collector's guide. Beverly Hills, California: Theodore Front Musical Literature, 1980. 20 p. (Front musical publications, 2)
A discography covering "The English musical renaissance" of the 20th century.

2779. Purcell, Ronald C. Classic guitar, lute and vihuela discography. Melville, New York: Belwin-Mills, 1976. 116 p.

2780. "Recordings." In *Early Music*, vol. 1–6 (1973–79).
A quarterly checklist of commercial recordings of early music. Organized by composer's name if a single-composer collection; otherwise, listed under name of performer or ensemble. After 1979, only the section of record reviews continues.

2781. Rowell, Lois. American organ music on records. Braintree, Massachusetts: Organ Literature Foundation, 1976. 105 p.
415 entries of recorded organ music by American composers, arranged by performer, giving: title, performer, location and maker of organ recorded, and discographic citation. Indexes to performers, organ makers and locations, album titles, record labels and numbers, authors of program notes, and series.
Brief review by Stephen M. Fry in *Notes*, 33 (1976), p. 306.

2782. Russcol, Herbert. Guide to low-priced classical records. New York: Hart, (1969). 831 p.
"Over 300 composers covered; over 1,500 works appraised; over 3,000 records evaluated; a wealth of solid information" [from the book jacket]. A classic case of a publisher's underestimation of his readers' perspicacity.

2783. Sackville-West, Edward and D. Shawe-Taylor. The record year, a guide to the year's gramophone records, including a complete guide to long playing records. Assisted by Andrew Porter. London: Collins, [1952]. 383 p.
Succeeded by *The Record Guide* in 1956 (957 p.) and compiled with the assistance of Andrew Porter and William Mann. The revision of 1956 was itself brought up to date in 1956 with a *Supplement* of 191 p.

The Sackville-West guides are designed for British record collectors. The commentary is literate and well informed. Arrangement is by composer, with special sections devoted to collections and a performer index.

2784. Stahl, Dorothy. A selected discography of solo song: cumulation through 1971. Detroit, Michigan: Information Coordinators, 1972. 137 p. (Detroit studies in music bibliography, 24)
    Supplement, 1971–1974. Detroit, 1976. 99 p. (Detroit studies in music bibliography, 34)
    Supplement, 1975–1982. Detroit, 1984. 236 p. (Detroit studies in music bibliography, 52)
    First published in 1968 and supplemented in 1970.
    Review by Jean-Michel Nectoux in *Notes*, 42 (1985), p. 228.

2785. The stereo record guide. By Edward Greenfield, Ivan March, and Denis Stevens. London: Long Playing Record Library, Ltd., 1960–72. 8 v.
    An ancestor of no. 2760.
    The main arrangement for each volume is by composer, followed by special sections devoted to concerts, recitals, light music, etc. Vol. 1 contains a selection of 50 outstanding records for 1958–59; vol. 2, a selection of 100 outstanding records for 1960–61. The third volume supplements the two preceding, but it relists the important recordings from the earlier books, with page references to earlier commentary. The guide is distinguished by its intelligent, highly readable annotations.

2786. Turner, Patricia. Afro-American singers: an index and preliminary discography of long-playing recordings of opera, choral music, and song. Minneapolis, Minnesota: Challenge, 1977. 255 p.
    A 44-p. supplement was issued by the author in 1980.

COLLECTORS' GUIDES TO EARLY RECORDINGS

The field of discs and cylinder recordings of the period from 1898 to 1925 has long been the province of private collectors. Emphasis is usually placed on the performer, particularly the vocalist, rather than on the composer. The importance of collecting in this area has been recognized on a large scale by libraries and research institutions throughout the world, as, for example, at the New York Public Library, the Library of Congress, the British Institute of Recorded Sound, the Stanford University Archive of Recorded Sound, the Yale University Collection of Historical Sound Recordings, and Syracuse University. Lately there have been increasing numbers of musicological studies based on early recordings. To pursue this research most effectively, discographers are discovering the value of research in the catalogs issued by recording manufacturers and in their archives of contracts and logs of studio work.

2787. Bauer, Robert. The new catalogue of historical records, 1898–1908/09. 2nd ed. London: Sidgwick and Jackson, [1947]. 494 p.
    Reprinted, 1970. 1st edition, 1937.

Recordings listed under performer, grouped under label and year of pressing. Serial numbers given. Brief entries for composer and title of work.

2788. Bescoby-Chambers, John. The archives of sound, including a selective catalogue of historical violin, piano, spoken, documentary, orchestral, and composer's own recordings. Lingfield, Surrey: Oakwood Press, 1964. 153 p.

> Vocal recordings are fairly well documented today.... Violin, piano, and orchestral recordings are rarely written about, and there is a vast, almost uncharted sea of piano roll recordings that are almost forgotten today. [from the introductory remarks]

A valuable contribution to the discography and player piano resources for instrumental music. Brief biographies of performers, and listings of their recordings. Some chapter headings: "The violin on record," "Historical piano recordings," "Orchestral recordings," and "The composer's own interpretation."

2789. Deakins, Duane D. Cylinder records; a description of the numbering systems, physical appearance, and other aspects of cylinder records made by the major American companies, with brief remarks about the earliest American companies and the foreign record manufacturers. [2nd ed.] Stockton, California: Duane D. Deakins, [1958]. 35 p.

2790. Deakins, Duane D., Elizabeth Deakins and Thomas Grattelo. Comprehensive cylinder record index. Stockton, California: Duane D. Deakins, 1966.

> 1st edition produced in 1956. 2nd edition appeared in 1958.
> Pt. 1. Edison amberol records.
> Pt. 2. Edison standard records.
> Pt. 3. Edison blue amberol records.
> Pt. 4. Indestructible records.
> Pt. 5. U.S. everlasting records.

A discography of the earliest commercially distributed recordings, drawing together information from surviving catalogs, company documents, and the cylinders themselves. The concern in these works is for the objects, the companies, and the manufacturing process, not for the music recorded.

2791. Girard, Victor and Harold M. Barnes. Vertical-cut cylinders and discs; a catalogue of all "hill-and-dale" recordings of serious worth made and issued between c. 1897–1932. London: British Institute of Recorded Sound, 1971. 196 p.

> Facsimile reprint (corrected) of the original 1964 edition.

A major contribution to the discography of early recordings. Arranged in three major categories: (1) vocal recordings; (2) speech recordings; (3) instrumental and orchestral recordings. Appendixes devoted to complete operas and to anonymous Pathé discs. The approach is mainly by performer.

2792. Hurst, P. G. The golden age recorded. New and revised edition. Lingfield, Surrey: Oakwood Press, 1963. 187 p.

> First published by Sidgwick and Jackson, London, 1946.

A manual for private collectors. General discussions of record collecting followed by biographical notices of the major artists classified by voice. Appendix, p. 147–87: a selected list, by performer, of important early recordings.

2793. Karlin, Fred J. Edison Diamond Discs 50001–52651. Santa Monica, California: Bona Fide Publishing Co., [n.d.]. 160 p.

A numerical listing of every Edison Diamond Disc issued in the 50,000 series from 1912 to 1929. Cites 5,200 titles as well as the performing artists, composers, and lyricists.

2794. Koenigsberg, Allen. Edison cylinder records, 1889–1912, with an illustrated history of the phonograph. New York: Stellar Productions, 1969. 159 p.

Review by Edward Colby in *Notes*, 27 (1971), p. 499–500.

2795. Methuen-Campbell, James. Catalogue of recordings by classical pianists. Chipping Norton, Oxfordshire: Disco Epsom, 1984. 66 p.

A second volume is projected.

This catalogue aims to list all released recordings by classical pianists who were born up to, and including, 1872.... The lay-out of the catalogue is simple: matrix numbers where known, are given in the left-hand column — catalogue numbers in the right-hand column. The centre column is reserved for the composer and the title of the work recorded. A brief biography prefaces the recording of each artist. [from the introductory remarks]

In order by pianist. Includes private or never-released recordings and some reissues on LP recordings, especially those of the International Piano Archive. Occasional notes on individual recordings. Reported but not examined recordings are mentioned. In the catalog, among others, are: Richard Strauss, Florent Schmitt, Camille Saint Saëns, Hans Pfitzner, Ignace Paderewski, Vincent D'Indy, Edvard Grieg, Alexander Gretchaninov, Enrique Granados, Claude Debussy, Johannes Brahms, and Eugen d'Albert. No index.

2796. Moogk, Edward B. Roll back the years: history of Canadian recorded sound and its legacy: genesis to 1930. Ottawa: National Library of Canada, 1975. 443 p. and 7-inch disc.

Issued also in French as *En Remontant les Années*, 1975.

A history, but includes discographies of Canadian performers, composers, and early recordings.

2797. Moses, Julian M. Collector's guide to American recordings, 1895–1925. Foreword by Giuseppe di Luca. New York: American Record Collectors' Exchange, [1949]. 199 p.

Reprinted by Dover, New York, 1977. 1st edition, Concert Bureau, 1936. 44 p.

Discs arranged under performers by serial or matrix number. P. 172–95: numerical guide, Columbia and other labels. Index of operas and instrumental index.

2798. Moses, Julian M. Price guide to collectors' records, with new value chart. New York: American Record Collectors' Exchange, 1976. 31 p.

First published in 1952.

Discs identified by matrix number under performer, with estimates of value on the contemporaneous market. Designed to accompany the author's *Collector's Guide* (no. 2794).

2799. RAI-Radiotelevisione Italiana. Direzione Programmi Radio. Discoteca centrale. Catalogo della discoteca storica. Rome: RAI, Servizio archivi, 1969. 3 v.

A catalog of the 78 rpm recordings in the collection arranged by genre. Includes popular and folk music recordings. The collection is particularly strong, of course, in Italian recordings.

2800. Rigler and Deutsch Record Index. Washington, D.C.: Association for Recorded Sound Collections, 1981–83. 977 microfiche.

Originally issued on 36 reels of microfilm.

This is an index to the 78 rpm recordings held by five of the largest recorded-sound collections in the United States: New York Public Library, Rodgers and Hammerstein Archives of Recorded Sound; Yale University, Collection of Historical Sound Recordings; Syracuse University, Belfer Audio Laboratory and Archives; Stanford University, Archive of Recorded Sound; Library of Congress, Motion Picture, Broadcasting, and Recorded Sound Division. A total of 615,000 recordings held among these institutions are reflected in the *Rigler and Deutsch Record Index.*

The index is in several parts: an author-composer section, a title section, a performer section, a label name and issue number section, a label name and matrix number section, and a section in which label name and issue numbers are arranged by institution. There is an introduction to the *Index* on the first microfiche explaining the innovative methodology used to gather the data from the discs. No attempt has been made to bring the names and titles into consistency or under authority control. Many scholars who have used the *Index* have been rewarded for the extra effort needed to ensure that all possible forms of names and titles have been seached. Inevitably, numerous previously unknown or unlisted recordings have come to light, thanks to the *Rigler and Deutsch Record Index.*

The Association of Recorded Sound Collections and the Associated Audio Archives, the name of the group of five contributing collections, have converted the *Index* to machine-readable form, thereby vastly improving the ease of use, even if no attempt is made to bring the forms of names and titles into consistency. The *Index* is available on RILN (no. 1207).

There is an excellent, if brief, article on the *Index* by David Hamilton, entitled "A new way to find old records," in *Opus* (December 1985), p. 12–13. Review by Richard Koprowski in *Notes*, 42 (1986) p. 536–37.

2801. Rust, Brian A. L. Discography of historical records on cylinders and 78s. Westport, Connecticut: Greenwood Press, 1979. 327 p.

In fact, a history of the earliest period of sound storage. Includes index.

2802. Voices of the Past. [Lingfield, Surrey: Oakwood Press, 1955– .] Vol. 1– .

Vol. 1: A catalogue of vocal recordings from the English catalogues of the Gramophone Company, 1898–1899; the Gramophone Company Limited, 1899–1900; the Gramophone & Typewriter Company Limited, 1901–1907; and the Gramophone Company Limited, 1907–1925; by John R. Bennet. [1955]. Reprinted 1978 by Greenwood Press, Westport, Connecticut.

Vol. 2: A catalogue of the vocal recordings from the Italian catalogues of the Gramophone Company Limited, 1899–1900; the Gramophone Company (Italy) Limited, 1899–1909; the Gramophone Company Limited, 1909; Compagnia del Grammofono, 1912–1925; by John R. Bennett. [1957].

Vol. 3: Dischi Fonotipia, including supplement (1958) and addenda (1964), by John R. Bennett. [1964?].

Vol. 4: The international red label catalogue of "DB" & "DA" His Master's Voice recordings, 1924–1956; book 1: "DB" (12-inch), by John R. Bennett and Eric Hughes. [1961].

Vol. 5: The catalogue of "D" & "E" His Master's Voice recordings, by Michael Smith. [1961].

Vol. 6: The international red label catalogue of "DB" & "DA" His Master's Voice recordings, 1924–1956; book 2: "DA," by John R. Bennett and Eric Hughes. [1967?].

Vol. 7: A catalogue of vocal recordings from the 1898–1925 German catalogues of the Gramophone Company Limited, Deutsche Grammophon A.-G., by John R. Bennett and Wilhelm Wimmer. [1967]. Reprinted 1978 by Greenwood Press, Westport, Connecticut.

Vol. 8: Columbia Gramophone Company, Ltd.; English celebrity issues: D and LB series, L and LX series. (By Michael Smith.) [1968?].

Vol. 9: A catalogue of vocal recordings from the 1898–1925 French catalogues of the Gramophone Company Limited, Compagnie française du gramophone, by John R. Bennett. [1971?].

Vol 10: Plum label "C" series (12-inch), by Michael Smith and Frank Andrews.

Vol. 11: A catalogue of vocal recordings from the Russian Catalogues of the Gramophone Company Limited: Obshchestvo Grammofon c Ogr. Otv. 1899–1915, by John R. Bennett. [1977].

Vol. LP1: Columbia (blue and green labels), Oct. 1952–Dec. 1962, compiled by Alan J. Poulton. [1975].

Vol. LP2: H.M.V. (red label), Oct. 1952–Dec. 1962. [1975].

Vol. LP3: H.M.V. (plum label), Oct. 1952–Dec. 1962. [1975].

Reissue of supplement: HMV/Columbia Great Recordings of the Century (Oct. 1957–Dec. 1966); HMV Golden Treasury of Immortal Performances (Sept. 1956–June 1957). [1975].

These catalogs list the early recordings, chiefly vocal, in numerical order under their respective labels. Most of the volumes also provide an artist index. These are invaluable tools for organizing and identifying early vocal discs.

COLLECTORS' GUIDES TO JAZZ RECORDINGS

The jazz record collector lives in a world of his own and is well equipped with reference tools designed to meet his needs. The impetus toward documentation has come from European rather than American enthusiasts: see Delaunay (no. 2809) and Panassie (no. 2815). Daniel Allen's *Jazz* volume in the Gibson and Gray *Bibliography of Discographies* (no. 2747) provides entries for almost 4,000 discographies. Only some of the most important ones are cited in this section.

2803. Allen, Walter C. Studies in jazz discography I– . Introduction by William M. Weinberg. New Brunswick, New Jersey: Institute of Jazz Studies, Rutgers University, 1971– .

A periodical consistently presenting serious and important jazz discographic work. Lists of recordings and actual discographic investigations are featured as well as reviews of similar works published elsewhere.

Review by James Patrick in *Notes*, 29 (1972), p. 236–39.

2804. Bruynincx, Walter. Jazz: modern jazz, be-bop, hard bop, West Coast. Mechelen, Belgium: 60 Years of Recorded Jazz Team, 1985– . Vol. 1– .

5 volumes issued to date.

2805. Bruynincx, Walter. Modern jazz: modern big band. Mechelen, Belgium: 60 Years of Recorded Jazz Team, 1986?– . Vol. 1– .

Apparently to be issued in several volumes.

2806. Bruynincx, Walter. Progressive jazz: free third-stream fusion. Mechelen, Belgium: 60 Years of Recorded Jazz Team, 1984– . Vol. 1– .

Three volumes issued to date covering A–S.

2807. Bruynincx, Walter. 60 years of recorded jazz, 1917–1977. Mechelen, Belgium: Printed for the author, 1980. 16 v. (various pagings, issued unbound)

Originally issued between 1967 and 1975 as *50 Years of Recorded Jazz*.
Supplement volume issued 1980.
Update M–P issued 1986.

Focused primarily on LPs, entries, arranged by name of performer or group, includes brief biographical or historical information. Discographies cite all recordings with personnel and individual titles, including dates and places of recording sessions. Gives unissued and alternate takes when known. A few major artists (e.g., Louis Armstrong and Duke Ellington) have comprehensive discographies that include 78 rpm discs as well as LPs. There is a separate artist index, not subjected to authority control, which treats every musician listed anywhere in the set. Although intended for the avid amateur, Bruynincx's work is a substantial asset to the jazz scholar.

2808. Carey, David A. and Albert M. McCarthy. The directory of recorded jazz and swing music. London: Cassel, 1950–57. 6 v.

Cover title: *Jazz Directory.* Vols. 2–4 have appeared in 2nd editions, 1955–57.

An alphabetical listing of performers and ensembles, with detailed information as to their recorded output. Informative annotations.

The work has progressed through six volumes (as of 1957), paged continuously through p. 1112, as far as the entry "Longshaw."

Vols. 1–4 published by the Delphic Press, Fordingbridge, Hants. The 2nd editions of vols. 2–4 and vols. 5 and 6 are published by Cassell, London.

Continued in Jepsen (no. 2812) and McCarthy (no. 2814).

2809. Delaunay, Charles. New hot discography, the standard dictionary of recorded jazz. Edited by Walter E. Schaap and George Avakian. New York: Criterion, 1948. 608 p.

First published in France in 1936. Reprinted 1982.

Separates the "pioneers of jazz" from "post-1930 jazz." Subdivided by region. An elaborate classification system groups recordings by major jazz personalities. Complete index of names.

2810. Harris, Rex and Brian Rust. Recorded jazz. [Harmondsworth, Middlesex]: Penguin Books, 1958. 256 p.

> It must not be regarded as a comprehensive discography, but nevertheless the authors have presented a reasonable cross-section of real jazz, together with biographical notes of performers and a critical assessment of the records listed. [*Preface*]

2811. Jazz on record: a critical guide to the first 50 years: 1917–1967. By Albert McCarthy, Alun Morgun, Paul Oliver, and Max Harrison. London: Hanover Books; New York: Oak Publications, 1968. 416 p.

> *Jazz on Record* is not a gramophone catalogue but a reference book to the best, the most significant, or occasionally simply the most typical recorded works of the leading jazz and blues artists to come to prominence during the last half century. [Authors' *Introduction*]

Much biographical and critical commentary. Arranged mainly by jazz artists, with additional sections devoted to styles and traditions.

Supersedes a work published under the same title by C. Fox, P. Gammond, and A. Morgan, London: Hutchinson, 1960.

Review by Frank Tirro in *Notes*, 26 (1970), p. 756–58.

2812. Jepsen, J. G. Jazz records: A–Z, 1942–1969; a discography. Holte, Denmark: Knudsen, 1963–70. 11 v. in 8.

A major reference work covering recorded jazz from 1942 to 1969. Vols. 5 and 6 published by Nordisk Tidskrift Forlag, Copenhagen.

2813. Lange, Horst H. Die deutsche Jazz-Discographie. Eine Geschichte des Jazz auf Schallplatten von 1902 bis 1955. Berlin: Bote & Bock, 1955. 652 p.

One of several recent European compilations of jazz records. Includes a number of English and Continental performers.

2814. McCarthy, Albert J. Jazz discography 1: an international discography of recorded jazz, including blues, gospel, and rhythm-and-blues for the year January–December 1958. London: Cassell, 1960. 271 p.

The first volume of a projected yearbook to cover all jazz recordings issued throughout the world. New releases are listed alphabetically by country. Full contents of each disc listed, with personnel, place, and date of recording if known.

This volume was an attempt to carry on the work stated by Carey and McCarthy in their *Directory of Recorded Jazz* (no. 2808). Only one volume was published, but supplements appeared in McCarthy's periodical *Jazz Monthly*.

2815. Panassié, Hughes. Discographie critique des meilleurs disques de jazz. Paris: Robert Laffont, [1958]. 621 p.
An earlier edition, Paris, Corréa, 1951. 371 p.
The author is a prolific writer on jazz and one of the first important discographers in the field. Arrangement is by performer, with an analytical index by medium and an index of names.

2816. Rust, Brian. Jazz records, 1897–1942. 5th ed., rev. and enl. Chigwell, England: Storyville Publications, 1982. 2 v.
Vol. 1: A–Kar. Vol. 2: Kar–Z.
This work supersedes an earlier edition issued under the title *Jazz Records A–Z (1961–65)*.

> This set of two books covers in the fullest possible detail all known records made in the years between 1897 and 1942 in the ragtime, jazz and swing idioms.... Only records made by American and British musicians are listed. [Compiler's *Introduction*]

Performers and groups are listed alphabetically with their records identified by matrix numbers and titles. Introduction and index of abbreviations for musical terms and record labels. Artists' index compiled by Mary Rust. A rich source of information on jazz history and recording activity for the period specified.

2817. Smith, Charles E. The jazz record book ... with Frederic Ramsey, Jr., Charles Payne Rogers and William Russell. New York: Smith and Durrell, 1942. 515 p.
P. 1–125: a survey of the history of jazz in its various regional styles. P. 130–508: record listings by major performers and ensembles, with critical and descriptive commentary. Selected bibliography of jazz; index of bands.

2818. Tudor, Dean and Nancy Tudor. Jazz. Littleton, Colorado: Libraries Unlimited, 1979. 302 p. (American popular music on Elpee)
A discography of American jazz on long-playing records for the amateur aficionado. For an update, see no. 2837.

2819. Tulane University. William Ransom Hogan Jazz Archive. Catalog of the William Ransom Hogan Jazz Archive: the collection of seventy-eight rpm phonograph recordings, Howard-Tilton Memorial Library, Tulane University. Boston, Massachusetts: G. K. Hall, 1984. 2 v.
Photoreproduction of the card catalog for older recordings of one of the most significant jazz archives in the U.S.

COLLECTORS' GUIDES TO POPULAR RECORDINGS

2820. Aeppli, Felix. Heart of stone, the definitive Rolling Stones discography. Ann Arbor, Michigan: Pierian Press, 1985. 535 p. (Rock and roll reference series, 7)
Provides a chronological list of all Rolling Stones recordings from July 1962 through 1983, whether recorded by the group or by its individual

musicians. Separate catalogs of group recordings and solo recordings are followed by a catalog of unverified studio recordings and bootleg recordings. Includes indexes by names of musicians and by titles of both individual songs and albums.

2821.   Albris, Jon and Anders Laurson. "Zydeco & cajun." In *Fontes Artis Musicae*, 31 (1984), p. 108–112.
A brief discography with references to two periodical articles on the subjects.

2822.   Bennetzen, Jørgen. "Reggae." In *Fontes Artis Musicae*, 29 (1982), p. 182–86.
A brief discography with bibliographies of literature and music.

2823.   Cooper, B. Lee. A resource guide to themes in contemporary American song lyrics 1950–1980. Westport, Connecticut: Greenwood Press, 1986. 458 p.

> This resource guide contains more than 3,000 popular recordings organized to support fifteen pre-determined social, political and personal themes. Each of these major themes, which form the chapters in this reference work, is subdivided into a number of related sub-themes. A discographic section listing individual songs, performers, record company names and disc numbers, and years of release accompanies each major theme. Preceding these song lists is a brief essay describing each theme.... The function of this resource guide is to stimulate further thought and to provide factual material for future examination of lyrics as pieces of oral history. [from the introductory remarks]

The 15 themes are: characters and personality (e.g., heroes, rebels, and outcasts); communications media; death; education; marriage, family life, and divorce; military conflicts; occupations, materialism, and workplaces; personal relationships, love, and sexuality; political protest and social criticism; poverty and unemployment; race relations; religion; transportation systems; urban life; and youth culture.
There is an audio profile of the rock era, 1950–85, which is a discography. The "selected" bibliography is a classified 18-page list of books, dissertations, song lyric collections, discographies, encyclopedias, articles, reviews and record reviews, and conference proceedings. There is a song title index and a recording artist index.
Review by Ann P. Basart in *Cum Notis Variorum*, no. 115 (August–September 1987), p. 13–14.

2824.   George, Nelson. Top of the charts, the most complete listing ever. Piscataway, New Jersey: New Century, 1983. 470 p.
Lists of the top 10 best-selling records in various genres. Arranged chronologically for the 1970s and early 1980s, as listed in *Record World* weekly.

2825.   Godrich, J. and R. M. M. Dixon. Blues and gospel records, 1902–1942. 2nd ed., revised. London: Storyville Publications, 1969. 912 p.
First published by Brian Rust.

> In this volume we have attempted to list every distinctive Negroid folk music record made up to the end of 1942. These records were mostly made by large

536

national record companies, and issued for an almost exclusively Negro audience. In later years some of the records have been reissued, this time for a predominantly white public. Full issue and reissue details of all 78 rpm records are included in the main listing, as are the few microgroove issues involving the first appearance of previously unissued material.... We have also included details of the blues and gospel recordings made for the Library of Congress by John Lomax and others.... Sessions involving artists [in the Library of Congress recordings] whose names begin with M–Z were able to be included in the main listing; those with names beginning with letters A–L will be found in an Appendix. [*Introduction*]

Each artist is listed alphabetically by surname, unless the artist is known only by a pseudonym. Information about accompanying musicians is included. Dates of recording sessions are provided when known. Matrix numbers are supplied. Take numbers are supplied when known. Issue numbers are supplied as well. There are explanatory entries on the recording companies, an index to accompanists, and a small section of late additions. Many entries include a brief disquisition on the artists and their relationships to the recording companies. There are explanations of the pseudonyms as well.

Review by Frank J. Gillis in *Ethnomusicology*, 14 (1970), p. 499–500.

2826. Guralnick, Peter. Sweet soul music; rhythm and blues and the Southern dream of freedom. New York: Harper and Row, 1986. 438 p.

A history of blues and its roots. Of particular use is the selected, annotated, and chronologically classified discography of blues recordings (p. 415–30). Bibliography of sources.

2827. Helander, Brock. Rock 'n' roll to rock: a discography. Sacramento, California: Brock Helander, 1978. 328 p.

An alphabetical list of "significant and noteworthy" rock and roll records in order by performer. Entries provide album titles, record manufacturers' names and numbers, release dates, and number of discs, but do not analyze contents. Releases from the 1950s to 1978 are indexed.

2828. Hounsome, Terry and Tim Chambre. Rock record. New York: Facts On File, 1981. 526 p.

First published in a limited edition (*Rockmaster*, 1978) and revised, expanded edition (Rock Record, 1979), produced and published in the United Kingdom by Terry Hounsome. This edition published in the United Kingdom in 1981 by Blandford Books Ltd., as *New Rock Record*.

Listings of rock records with names of groups and individual musicians.

2829. Hummel, David. The collector's guide to the American musical theatre. [New rev., enl. ed.] Metuchen, New Jersey: Scarecrow Press, 1984. 2 v.

First published by the author in Grawn, Michigan, 1978 and 1979.

An extensive discography of recordings arranged by the title of the show. Each entry gives performance dates and titles of the principal members. Extensive notes. Preceded by four essays:

Rexton S. Bunnet, "The British musical."

Peter Pinne, "Australian theatre on disc."

Glenn Atchison, "The musical theatre in Canada—on-stage and on record."

Larry Warner, "Researching the pre-LP original cast recording."
Appendix of sources of excerpts. Vol. 2 is an index of all personal names cited.
Review by Ed Glazier in *Notes*, 43 (1986), p. 301–303.

2830. Jay, Dave, pseud. The Irving Berlin songography; 1907–1966. New Rochelle, New York: Arlington House, [1969]. 172 p.
A chronological list of Berlin's songs with annotations and lists of recordings, not including songs recorded in anthologies, which are separately analyzed. No indexes. Based on the compiler's *Jolsonography*.

2831. Leadbitter, Mike and Neil Slaven. Blues records, January 1943 to December 1966. London: Hanover Books, Ltd., 1968. 381 p.
A listing by artist and ensembles with discographies as complete as the compilers could make them. Gives instrumentation for the groups and dates of recordings where known.
Review by Frank Tirro in *Notes*, 26 (1970), p. 756–58.

2832. Marsh, Dave and John Swenson. The new Rolling Stone record guide. Rev., updated ed. New York: Random House/Rolling Stone Press, 1983. 648 p.
Revised edition of *The Rolling Stone Record Guide*, 1979. 631 p.
"Reviews and rates over 12,000 rock, pop, soul, country, blues, folk, and gospel albums" [*Preface*]. Citations, with critical ratings. It is, in effect, a survey of a large swath of recorded popular music.
Review of the original edition by William H. Tallmadge in *American Music*, 1 (1983), p. 92–94.

2833. Raymond, Jack. Show music on record from the 1890s to the 1980s; a comprehensive list of original cast and studio cast performances issued on commercial phonograph records, covering music of the American stage, screen and television, with composer performances and other collateral recordings. New York: Frederick Munger, 1982. 253 p.
Shows arranged chronologically. Lists 784 source recordings. "Artist albums" and anthologies separately listed. Artist index.

2834. Rohde, H. Kandy, ed. The gold of rock & roll, 1955–1967. New York: Arbor House, 1970. 352 p.
A discography listing the 10 most popular rock and roll recordings for each week during the years covered. "The top 50" for each individual year are extracted. Brief commentary for each year's activity. Indexed by song titles and artists.

2835. Rust, Brian. The American dance band discography 1917–1942. New Rochelle, New York: Arlington House, 1975. 2 v.
Contents: vol. 1. Irving Aaronson to Arthur Lange; vol. 2. Arthur Lange to Bob Zurke.
Covering 2,300 dance orchestras and listing their 78 rpm recordings with matrix and label numbers, dates of recording, personnel, arrangers, vocal-

ists, etc. 50,000 records cited, artist index of about 8,000 names. Black ensembles, Glenn Miller, and Benny Goodman are omitted. No title index. Brief review by Stephen M. Fry in *Notes*, 32 (1976), p. 782.

2836. Smolian, Steven. A handbook of film, theater, and television music on record, 1948–1969. New York: Record Undertaker, 1970. 64-p. alphabetical listing and 64-p. index.
A handbook for collectors of show and soundtrack recordings.

> This book should assist the reader in two basic ways—to outline what has been issued: what can be bought through regular record shops, and when he will either have to do some "bin hunting" or call on the services of a specialist dealer in cut-outs, and also to identify the records in his collection and tell him something about them. [Compiler's *Introduction*]

2837. Tudor, Dean. Popular music; an annotated guide to recordings. Littleton, Colorado: Libraries Unlimited, 1983. 647 p.

> ... a thorough updating and revision of the four separate volumes published by Libraries Unlimited in 1979 as *Jazz, Black Music, Grass Roots Music, and Contemporary Popular Music*. [*Preface*]

Arranged by categories as indicated by the predecessor volumes, but also includes popular religious music. Index of artists.
Earlier separate volumes also cited as nos. 2818, 2867, and 2868.

2838. Whitburn, Joel. Top pop albums, 1955–1985. Compiled from *Billboard's* pop album charts, 1955–85. Menomonee Falls, Wisconsin: Record Research, 1985. 508 p.

2839. Whitburn, Joel. Top pop records, 1940–1955. Menomonee Falls, Wisconsin: Record Research, 1973. 88 p.

> Facts about 1700 recordings listed in *Billboard's* "Best selling singles" pop charts, grouped under the names of the 400 recording artists. [from the introductory remarks]

2840. Whitburn, Joel. Top pop records, 1955–1982. Compiled from *Billboard's* pop singles charts, 1955–82. Menomonee Falls, Wisconsin: Record Research, 1983. 692 p.
Previously published by Gale Research in Detroit, Michigan, as *Top Pop Records, 1955–1970* in 1972.

> This publication is a complete factual record of the most successful popular music in the United States for the past 16 years. [Editor's *Note*]

2841. Whitburn, Joel. Top rhythm & blues (soul) records, 1949–1971. Menomonee Falls, Wisconsin: Record Research, 1973. 184 p.

> Facts about 4,000 recordings listed in *Billboard's* "Best selling rhythm and blues (soul) singles" charts, grouped under the names of the 1,200 recording artists. [from the introductory remarks]

A series of supplements issued since 1974 keep the discography up to date.

2842. Whitburn, Joel. Top rhythm & blues (soul) records, 1972–1973. Menomonee Falls, Wisconsin: Record Research, 1974. 48 p.

Supplement to no. 2841. Includes index.

ETHNIC AND FOLK MUSIC ON RECORDS

The use of recorded materials is basic to the techniques of modern ethnomusicology. Here the scholar is concerned less with commercially recorded discs and tapes than he is with recordings made in the field by research institutions and by individual collectors. The problem of bringing these diverse materials under "bibliographical control" is a difficult one. A good start has been made with the cooperation of UNESCO in two series published under the general title *Archives of Recorded Music.* Series B is concerned with Oriental music; Series C, with ethnographical and folk music. (Series A, not under consideration here, is devoted to Occidental music and has produced a general discography of the works of Frederic Chopin.)

2843. Archives of Recorded Music. (Archives de la Musique Enregistrée). Series B: Oriental Music. A catalogue of recorded classical and traditional Indian music. General discography and introduction by Alain Danielou. Paris: UNESCO, [1952]. 236 p.

The main organization is by region, subdivided by instrumental and vocal music, and listed under the performing artists. Chapter V is devoted to the songs of Rabindranath Tagore. Index of names. Bilingual (English-French).

2844. Archives of Recorded Music.... Series C: Ethnographical and Folk Music. 1. Collection Phonothèque Nationale (Paris). Catalogue prepared by the International Commission on Folk Arts and Folklore. Paris: UNESCO, [1952]. 254 p.

Lists 4,564 discs in groups as acquired by the Phonothèque. Recordings for any particular national group are scattered throughout the volume. There is an index of countries, however. Bilingual (French-English).

2845. Archives of Recorded Music.... Series C: Ethnographical and Folk Music. 2. Collection Musée de l'Homme (Paris). Catalogue prepared by the International Commission on Folk Arts and Folklore. Paris: UNESCO, [1952]. 74 p.

Catalog of a collection of 1,007 recordings, chiefly made in the field in various parts of Asia and Africa. Grouped under the name of the collector or expedition.

2846. Archives of Recorded Music.... Series C: Ethnographical and Folk Music. 3. Katalog der europäischen Volksmusik im Schallarchiv des Instituts für Musikforschung Regensburg. Bearbeitet von Felix Hoerburger. Regensburg: Gustav Bosse, [1952]. 189 p.

Material grouped by country and province.

2847. Archives of Recorded Music.... Series C: Ethnographical and Folk Music. 4. International catalogue of recorded folk music.... Edited by Norman Fraser, with a preface by R. Vaughan Williams and introduction by Maud Karpeles. London: Prepared and published for UNESCO by the International Folk Music Council in association with Oxford University Press, 1954. 201 p.

Part I: "Commercial records," a listing of the commercially recorded discs of ethnic and folk music, arranged by continent and by country. Part II: "Recordings held by institutions," a survey of the major collections of ethnic and folk music in libraries and research institutions throughout the world. Statistical summary of their holdings; addresses, names of chief administrators.

2848. Barnett, Elise B. A discography of the art music of India. Ann Arbor, Michigan: Society for Ethnomusicology, 1975. 54 p.

315 numbered items arranged alphabetically by record label. Indexed by sacred chants, art music (sacred and secular), Hindustāni rāg, Tāl, performers, performing forces, dance music, folk music, and composers.

2849. Briegleb, Ann, ed. Directory of ethnomusicological sound recording collections in the U.S. and Canada. Ann Arbor, Michigan: Society for Ethnomusicology, 1971. 46 p. (Special series, 2)

Not a discography, but a survey of the resources of 124 collections, public and private. Arranged alphabetically by state. Includes a list of institutions with "no holdings in ethnomusicology."

2850. Cohen, Norm and Paul F. Wells. "Recorded ethnic music: a guide to resources." In *Ethnic Recordings in America: A Neglected Heritage*, p. 175–250. Washington, D.C.: American Folklife Center at the Library of Congress, 1982.

A survey of printed, recorded, and archival resources for the use and study of music of ethnic Americans (Native Americans, Europeans and Eurasians, Asians, and Jews). There are sections on each major ethnic group within the broad categories just listed. As linguistic and regional ethnic groups are mixed, Afro-American materials are found in the European and Eurasian section. Each section begins with an introduction and then discographies, bibliographies, and citations of archival holdings are presented. There is a directory of record companies appended and a directory of archives holding materials of interest in the United States, Canada, and Finland (!).

2851. Etnomusica. Catalogo della musica di tradizione orale nel reistrazioni dell'Archivio Etnico Linguistico-Musicale della Discoteca di Stato. A cura di Sandro Biagiola. Roma: Discoteca di Stato, 1986. 886 p.

Succeeds the first catalog, published in 1970.

Covers over 11,000 recordings, of which perhaps 9,000 are of Italian music "of the oral tradition" and liturgical music of Judaism and Christianity in Italy. Indexes genres, occasions, regions, and localities.

Review by Giovanni Giuriati in *Musica/Realtà*, 23 (Agosto 1987), p. 155–56.

2852. Gillis, Frank. "The incunabula of instantaneous ethnomusicological sound recordings, 1890–1910: a preliminary list." In *Problems and Solutions; Occasional Essays in Musicology Presented to Alice D. Moyle*, p. 322–355. Edited by Jamie C. Kassler and Jill Stubington. Sydney: Hale and Iremonger, 1984.

Includes a list organized by Murdoch's *Outline of World Cultures* of the earliest known ethnomusicological recordings and their present locations.

2853. Hickmann, Hans and Charles Grégoire, Duc de Mecklenbourg. Catalogue d'enregistrements de musique folklorique égyptienne. Strasbourg: Heitz, 1958. 78 p. (Collection d'études musicologiques, 37)

Description and analysis of the contents of a recorded collection of Egyptian folk music assembled in 1955. 211 items. Preceded by a discussion of the music and instruments employed.

2854. Indiana. University. Archives of Traditional Music. A catalog of phono-recordings of music and oral data held by the Archives of Traditional Music. Boston, Massachusetts: G. K. Hall, 1975. 541 p.

Photoreproduction of the card catalog of this extensive collection. The reduction ratio is so great that reading is difficult. Indexes recording companies, collectors, depositors, performers, and "informers."

2855. Indiana. University. Archives of Traditional Music. Native North American music and oral data: a catalogue of sound recordings, 1893–1976. By Dorothy Sara Lee; foreword by Willard Rhodes. Bloomington: Indiana University Press, 1979. 463 p.

A guide to native North American music and oral data holdings at the Indiana University Archives of Traditional Music. Includes indexes.

2856. International Institute for Comparative Music Studies and Documentation, Berlin, compiler. Oriental music: a selected discography. New York: Foreign Material Center, University of the State of New York, State Education Department and National Council of Associations for International Studies, 1971. 100 p. (Foreign Area Material Center: Occasional Publication, 16)

2857. Library of Congress. Music Division. Archive of American Folk Song. Checklist of recorded songs in the English language in the Archive ... to July 1940. Washington, D.C.: Library of Congress, Division of Music, 1942. 3 v. in 1.

A guide to the holdings of one of the world's great folk song collections. Songs listed by title, with name of singer, collector, and date of recording. The third volume is a geographical index of titles arranged by state and country.

2858 Library of Congress. Music Division. Recording Laboratory. Folk music: a catalog of folk songs, ballads, dances, instrumental pieces, and folk tales of the United States and Latin-America on phonograph records. Washington, D.C.: Library of Congress, [1964]. 107 p.

Earlier listings of the same nature appeared in 1943, 1948, 1953, and 1959.

A catalog of recordings available for purchase from the Archive of American Folk Song at the Library of Congress. Presents a sampling of American folk music and tales recorded for the most part in their native environment.

2859. Lumpkin, Ben G. and N. L. McNeil. Folksongs on records.... Issue three, cumulative, including essential material in issues one and two. Boulder, Colorado: Folksongs on Records, 1950. 98 p.

Lists 700 commercially recorded discs and albums of folk songs and folk music, chiefly American. Contents of discs given, with informal annotations. Useful indexes to English and Scottish ballads, spirituals, work songs, Irish songs, Mexican and Latin American songs; numerical list of albums.

2860. Merriam, Alan P. African music on L.P. An annotated discography. Evanston, Illinois: Northwestern University Press, 1970. 200 p.

Describes and inventories the contents of some 389 recordings of African music, excluding the Hugh Tracy "Sound of Africa" series since it has been documented elsewhere (no. 2867). Entries are grouped by record labels. 18 indexes permit a wide variety of approaches to the information.

2861. Museums für Völkerkunde. Katalog der Tonbandaufnahmen M1-M2000 der Musikethnologischen Abteilung des Museums für Völkerkunde Berlin. Hrsg. von Dieter Christensen unter Mitarbeit von Hans-Jürgen Jordan. Berlin: Museum für Völkerkunde, 1970. 355 p.

2862. Musics of the world: a selective discography. Edited by Nancy Dols; compiled under the auspices of the Ethnomusicology Archive, University of California, Los Angeles. Los Angeles: UCLA Music Library, 1977– . 4 v. to date. (UCLA Music Library Discography Series, 1–)

Volumes 2–4 are entitled *Musics of the World.*

Vol. 1 covers sub-Saharan Africa, Bulgaria, Ethiopia, Guatemala, Japan, Romania, Tibet, U.S.S.R., United States, Yugoslavia.

Vol. 2, edited by Don Niles, covers Indonesia, Korea, Oceania, Taiwan, and Thailand.

Vol. 3, edited by Nora Yeh, covers the United States: Afro-American, European-American, Hispanic-American, and Native American musics.

Vol. 4, edited by Kenneth Culley, includes an index.

2863. La musique traditionnelle. Établié par Chantal Nourrit et William Pruitt. Paris: Radio-France Internationale, 1979–83. 20 v. in 2 series.

Each volume provides introductory essays on aspects of music in the area in question, followed by annotated discographies of 78 rpm and 33 1/3 rpm discs arranged by record manufacturer. There are indexes to ethnic groups, instruments, performers and authors, locations; to historic and legendary people; to subjects; and to record titles. Each volume includes a bibliography. The volumes range from 60 p. to 260 p. There are two series:

La musique traditionnelle de l'Ocean Indien: vol. 1—Ile Maurice; vol. 2—Seychelles; vol. 3—Madagascar.

La musique traditionnelle de Afrique Noire: vol. 1—Mali; vol. 2—Haute-Volta; vol. 3—Mauritanie; vol. 4—Senegal/Gambia; vol. 5—Niger; vol. 6—Côte D'Ivoire; vol. 7—Benin; vol. 8—Togo; vol. 9—Cameroun; vol. 10—Tchad; vol. 11—Centrafrique; vol. 12—Gabon; vol. 13—Congo; vol. 14—Zaire; vol. 15—Burundi; vol. 16—Rwanda; v. 17—Djibouti.

2864. Quinn, Jennifer Post. An index to the field recordings in the Flanders Ballad Collection at Middlebury College, Middlebury, Vermont. Middlebury: Middlebury College, 1983. 242 p.

An index to a collection focused on New England folk song, which was gathered by Helen Hartness Flanders and others during the period 1930–58. There is a history of the collection and a bibliography of sources. Entries include title as given by the performer, uniform title (or the commonly known title), name and location of the performer, and location of the recording in the collection. Indexes to titles, uniform titles, performers, and locations.

See the article "The Helen Hartness Flanders Ballad Collection, Middlebury College" by Dale Cockrell in *Notes*, 39 (1983), p. 31–42, for description of the collection.

2865. Spottswood, Richard K. Ethnic music on records: a discography of ethnic recordings produced in the U.S., 1893–1942. Urbana: University of Illinois Press, 1990. 7 v.

The aim of this work is to document all production of foreign language records made in the United States and its possessions in its entirety from 1893 to 1942, with the following exceptions: 1. operatic and other classical recordings; 2. language instruction records; 3. humorous material; 4. Hawaiian music; 5. reissues of non-U.S. matrices on U.S. labels; 6. instrumental recordings; 7. American Indian recordings of private or institutional origin.   All known issues from each matrix are given in whatever configuration they may be in (disc, cylinder, tape, or compact disc).... Whenever possible, matrix numbers are grouped together, documenting a single recording session, with each session followed by a collation giving date, place and whatever is known about instrumentation and individual performer names. [from the introductory remarks]

Vol. 1 on music of Western Europe, vol. 2 on Slavic music, vol. 3 on music of Eastern Europe, vol. 4 on music of Spanish, Portuguese, Philippine, and Basque origin, vol. 5. on Middle-Eastern, Far Eastern, Scandinavian, Irish, Scottish, Welsh, West Indian, American Indian, and "International" origin. Vol. 6 contains indexes to authors and titles. Vol. 7 contains indexes to record numbers and matrix numbers.

Entries are arranged by performer.

2866. Stone, Ruth and Frank J. Gillis. African music and oral data: a catalog of field recordings, 1902–1975. Bloomington: Indiana University Press, 1976. 412 p.

Includes a catalog of collectors. Indexes to countries, cult repositories, and subjects.

Review by Gilbert Rouget in *Fontes Artis Musicae*, 28 (1981), p. 254–55.

2867. Tracey, Hugh. Catalogue of the Sound of Africa series; 210 long playing records of music and songs from Central, Eastern, and Southern Africa.

Roodepoort, South Africa: International Library of African Music, 1973. 2 v.

Volume 1 is an extensive introduction to the recordings in the *Sound of Africa* series and thus to the musical cultures; it includes data on instruments, language zones, and scales. Volume 2 is the catalog. Recordings were made in the field, 1929–c. 1963.

2868. Tudor, Dean and Nancy Tudor. Black music. Littleton, Colorado.: Libraries Unlimited, 1979. 262 p. (American popular music on Elpee)
A discography of Afro-American music.
Later edition, no. 2837.

2869. Tudor, Dean and Nancy Tudor. Grass roots music. Littleton, Colorado: Libraries Unlimited, 1979. 367 p. (American popular music on Elpee)
A discography of American folk music and folk songs, including country music and bluegrass music.
Later edition, no. 2837.

2870. Waterhouse, David. "Hogaku preserved: a select list of long-playing records issued by Japanese record companies of the national music of Japan." In *Recorded Sound*, 33 (Jan. 1969), p. 383–402.

CURRENT OR ANNUAL DISCOGRAPHIES

Current listings and record reviews are in abundant supply. There are periodicals, such as the *American Record Guide*, *Fanfare*, and the *Gramophone*, devoted exclusively to the interests of record collectors.

2871. Bielefelder Katalog; Katalog der Schallplatten klassischer Musik. Bielefelder Katalog Jazz; Verzeichnis der Jazz-Schallplatten. Bielefeld: Bielefelder Verlagsanstalt, 1953– .
The German equivalent to *The Schwann* series, with superior analytics and indexing. Issued semiannually.

2872. Deutsche Bibliographie: Musiktonträger-Verzeichnis. Frankfurt am Main: Buchhändler-Vereinigung, 1978– .
Successor to the Deutsche Bibliographie *Schallplatten-Verzeichnis*, the *Musiktonträger-Verzeichnis* is a monthly publication with an annual composer/title index.
The premiere national discography, recording sound recordings not only published in the Bundes-Republik Deutschland but also distributed there. The depth and accuracy of indexing is impressive.

2873. Diapason: catalogue général. Paris: Diapason-microsillon, 1956– .
Title varies: *Catalogue Disques et Cassettes Diapason; Catalogue Général de Musique Classique et de Diction.*
The French equivalent to *The Schwann* series issued as an annual.
All issues include a classical music catalog with composer and anthology sections, occasionally with a section devoted to chant. Some issues

also include spoken word recordings. Entries provide full analysis of contents of albums. Composers and titles recorded in anthologies are entered with cross-references in the composer section. Entries show performer, album title, manufacturer's name and number, as well as contents. Beginning in 1977 there is an index to performers in the catalog. A list of French record manufacturers is provided.

2874. Gramophone classical catalogue. Harrow, Middlesex: General Gramophone Publications, 1953– .

In 1990, merged with *Gramophone compact disc audio guide and catalogue* to form *Classical catalogue.*

Title varies: *Gramophone long playing classical record catalogue.*

The British version of *The Schwann*, with substantially better analysis of anthologies and more extensive indexing. Now published in cumulating issues twice each year interspersed with issues updating the semi-annual cumulations. The up-dating issues are themselves cumulating.

2875. Gramophone Shop, Inc., record supplement. Vol. 1, no. 1 (Jan. 1938) to vol. 17, no. 2 (Feb. 1954).

Title varies: 1939, *Record Reviews.* (Cover title: *Record Supplement.*)

Extensively annotated listing of the major releases in the field of serious music. Confined chiefly to 78 rpm discs. A monthly publication.

2876. High Fidelity record annual. Edited by Roland Gelatt. Philadelphia, Pennsylvania: J. B. Lippincott, 1955–81. Vols. 1–26.

Title varies: from 1957, *Records in Review.* Great Barrington, Massachusetts, Wyeth Press. Editor, 1957: Joan Griffiths. Editor, 1958–60: Frances Newbury. The set through volume 12 (1972) has been reprinted by the AMS Press, Inc., 1972– .

Reviews from *High Fidelity*, compiled annually from monthly issues of the previous year, generally authoritative and signed by the reviewer. The main listing is by composer, followed by nine categories of collections: vocal, piano, organ and harpsichord, strings, woodwinds and brass, guitar, orchestra, medieval and Renaissance, miscellaneous. Index of performers.

2877. "Index of record reviews, with symbols indicating opinions of reviewers." In *Notes*, 5 (March 1948)– .

Since its inception, this index has been a regular feature. Compiled chiefly by Kurtz Myers until recently with the assistance of various specialists from time to time. A valuable guide to record selection for libraries and for private collectors. The quarterly appearances of this column have been cumulated; see no. 2878.

The next compiler for the column in *Notes* was Richard Le Sueur. He was succeeded by Paul Cauthen and Mark Palkovic. Beginning with Le Sueur, compact discs were included and now the *Index* indexes only compact discs.

2878. Myers, Kurtz. Index to record reviews; based on material originally published in *Notes, the Journal of the Music Library Association* between 1949 and 1977. Boston, Massachusetts: G. K. Hall, 1978. 5 v.

Supersedes the edition of Crown Publishers by Myers and Richard S. Hill issued in 1956. Continued by *Index to Record Reviews, 1978–1983,* compiled and edited by Kurtz Myers and issued by G. K. Hall, 1985. (873 p.) and by the monthly column in *Notes*.

Index to Record Reviews is a guidebook to a huge body of critical writing about recordings. Reviews from about 50 periodicals and other sources, specialized in music and general, have been indexed.

> The index has two sections. The first and longer is primarily a listing by composer. The second section, "composite releases," is necessary for handling records containing works by more than one composer. The entries here are arranged alphabetically under the name of the manufacturer, and then serially by the manufacturer's number. The names of composers appearing in this second list are indexed in volume five which also affords access to the first four volumes by manufacturer's label and number, and by performer. [*Introduction*]

The compiler has taken great pains to clarify and verify information about discs and their contents. This is a major reference work in the field of discography.

Review by David Hall in *Notes*, 37 (1981), p. 845–47.

2879. Phonolog reporter. Los Angeles, California: Trade Service Publications, Phonolog Publishing Division, 1948– .

A loose-leaf service with weekly distribution of new pages to enable audio stores to stay current with new releases. Valuable for discerning currently available audio releases in the North American market. In two large divisions, one for classical music and another for popular music. Each page is numbered and dated, but the actual pagination is difficult to discern as page numbers are alpha-numeric.

The classical division consists of three sections: one for entries by composer and then title, each entry providing title of album, names of principal performers, and manufacturer's name and number of disc or tape; a second for anthologies arranged by album title, providing brief titles of works featured in each anthology; and a third devoted to performing artists by name, but referring entries under conductors to the citations for the ensembles each has conducted. In the past, there were cross-references to individual titles from one section to another.

The popular division features many sections, the largest of which is entitled "popular titles" and arranged by album title. The other sections cover: Christmas music; Hawaiian albums; Latin albums; international albums; children's music; movie sound tracks and show tunes; sacred music; specialties; and miscellaneous.

A CD-ROM version has been released as *Billboard/Phonolog Music Reference Library* by BPI Communications of New York. It adds vastly improved searching possibilities to the contents of *Phonolog*.

2880. Polart index to record reviews. Detroit: Polart, 1960–67. 8 v.

An annual publication indexing all record and tape reviews published in the major journals. No evaluations, but the length of the review is indicated. Main entries under composer, with separate sections for collections and for "pop and jazz" recordings.

2881. Schwann opus. Santa Fe, New Mexico: Stereophile, 1991– . Vol. 2, no. 4– .

Also known as *Opus*. Succeeds *The Schwann Record and Tape Guide* and its several variant titles (*New Schwann Record and Tape Guide*,

Schwann-1 Record and Tape Guide, and *Schwann-2 Record and Tape Guide*), issued in Boston beginning in 1949 as monthly publications.

A quarterly publication listing over 40,000 currently available classical recordings on compact discs and cassette tapes. Listed alphabetically by composer, then by title, then by principal artist. Anthologies are listed in a separate section and are arranged by instrument or "music type" (i.e., ballet music, choral music, vocal music, guitar, organ, etc.). New releases are listed separately. Each issue includes articles, often with discographies of currently available discs. There is a list of manufacturers providing addresses and prices.

There is an *Annual Artist Issue.* It lists available discs arranged by performers and is organized in sections: orchestras and ensembles; conductors; instrumental soloists; choral groups; vocalists.

2882. Schwann spectrum. Santa Fe, New Mexico: Stereophile, 1991– . Vol. 2, no. 4– .

Also known as *Spectrum.*

A quarterly listing of over 60,000 recordings on compact discs, long-playing records, and cassette tapes of popular music, arranged alphabetically by performing group. Includes sections on: rock and pop individual releases and collections; jazz and jazz anthologies; musicals, movies, and TV; gospel and religious music; New Age music; spoken-word and miscellaneous recordings; children's music; international pop music, arranged by country and then by performer or group; sampler discs; Christmas music; and laser discs. New releases are so labeled in the margins.

Each issue includes articles, often with discographies of current releases.

SPECIALIZED DISCOGRAPHIES

2883. American music on records. A catalogue of recorded American music currently available. Prepared in cooperation with the Committee on Recordings of American Music of the National Music Council. New York: American Music Center, 1956. 39 p.

A composer listing in alphabetical order, with references to published scores and parts, if available.

2884. American Society of Composers, Authors and Publishers. 30 years of motion picture music, the big Hollywood hits from 1928–1958. New York: ASCAP, 1959. 122 p.

2885. American Society of Composers, Authors and Publishers. 40 years of show tunes, the big Broadway hits from 1917–57. New York: ASCAP, 1958. 149 p.

Chronological list of recorded show tunes arranged alphabetically under year of production. Composer, publisher, performing artist, and record number given. Title index.

2886. Band Record Guide. Alphabetical listing of band records by title of composition, composer, performing group, and record title. 1969 edition. Evanston, Illinois: Instrumentalist Co., 1969. 102 p.

Indexes 1,480 works by title, 574 composers, 170 bands. There is also a listing of record manufacturers and distributors.

2887. Celletti, Rodolfo. Il teatro d'opera in disco. Milano: Rizzoli, 1976. 614 p.

"The first catalog of all complete opera recordings with commentary on execution and interpretation" [*Foreword*].

Each citation provides original and reissue numbers. Anthologies of recorded excerpts are included.

2888. Cohn, Arthur. The collector's twentieth-century music in the Western Hemisphere. Philadelphia, Pennsylvania: Lippincott, [1961]. 256 p.

One of the best discographies of contemporary music. Well annotated; full coverage for American composers.

2889. Cohn, Arthur. Twentieth-century music in Western Europe, the compositions and the recordings. Philadelphia, Pennsylvania, and New York: J. B. Lippincott, [1956]. 510 p.

Part I, p. 3–345: discussion of the compositions of 30 contemporary European composers. Part II, p. 349–510: entries for the recordings of the works discussed in the preceding section. The records are graded from "poor" to "exceptional" in performance quality. The annotations in this section are devoted almost entirely to observations on performance.

2890. Creighton, James. Discopaedia of the violin, 1889–1971. Toronto: University of Toronto Press, 1974. 987 p.

A discography of the recordings of nearly 1,800 violinists. Main entries by artist, with recorded works listed alphabetically by composer. Indexed by composer and by popular names of the compositions.

2891. Davies, Hugh. "A discography of electronic music and musique concrète." In *Recorded Sound, Journal of the British Institute of Recorded Sound*, 14 (April 1964), p. 205–224.

Fully annotated listings of records and tapes; addresses of distributors and index of compositions.

2892. Davis, Elizabeth A. Index to the *New World Recorded Anthology of American Music*; a user's guide to the initial one hundred records. New York: Norton, 1981. 235 p.

A guide to the contents of a series of recordings of concert music by American composers supported by the Rockefeller Foundation as part of the American Bicentennial celebration. There is a master index providing a description of each record in numerical order and four indexes: names and titles of all recorded works; subjects and authors in the liner notes; genres and performing forces; dates of composition.

Frasier, Jane. Women composers; a discography. See no. 2981.

2893. International Roman Catholic Association for Radiodiffusion and Television. Catalogue du disque de musique religieuse. Préf. de J. Schneuwly; introd. de Jean-Michel Hayoz. Edité par UNDA, Association catholique internationale pour la radiodiffusion et la télévision. Fribourg: [1956]. 300 p.

2894. Kondracki, Miroslaw, Marta Stankiewicz and Frits C. Weiland. International Diskographie elektronischer Musik. International electronic music discography. Discographie internationale de la musique électronique. Mainz, etc.: Schott, 1979. 174 p.

A computer-generated discography arranged by composer, entries providing title, date of issue, name of studio, university, broadcasting station or institution where composition was produced, and the title of the complete recording or album. List of abbreviations of record companies. List of electronic studios. Index of composers.

2895. Kratzenstein, Marilou and Jerald Hamilton. Four centuries of organ music; an annotated discography. Detroit, Michigan: Information Coordinators, 1984. 308 p. (Detroit studies in music bibliography, 51)

Analyzing recordings of organ music from the Robertsbridge Codex through J. S. Bach. Indexes of organs, performers, and composers.

Review by Jean-Michel Nectouz in *Fontes Artis Musicae*, 32 (1985), p. 222.

2896. Kroó, György. "New Hungarian music." In *Notes*, 39 (1983), p. 43–71.

An annotated discography of the works of contemporary Hungarian composers in the period 1969–82. 100 works are described in detail, together with a discussion of the place of Hungarian music in the Western tradition.

2897. Laster, James H. A discography of treble voice recordings. Metuchen, New Jersey: Scarecrow Press, 1985. 147 p.

2898. Maleady, Antoinette, O. Record and tape reviews index 1971–74. Metuchen, New Jersey: Scarecrow Press, 1972–75. 4 v.

16 periodicals indexed. Section I: a listing of reviews by composer. Section II: reviews of music in collections, listed under record labels. Section III: spoken recordings.

Succeeded by her *Index to Record and Tape Reviews, a Classical Music Buying Guide*, published by Chulain Press in San Anselmo, California, 1976–82.

2899. Schweizer Musik auf Schallplatten. Musique suisse sur disques. Swiss music on records. Zürich: Schweizerisches Musik-Archiv, 1979. 79 p.

2900. Smart, James R. The Sousa band: a discography. Washington, D.C.: Library of Congress, 1970. 123 p.

2901. Weber, Jerome F. A Gregorian chant discography. Utica, New York: J. F. Weber, 1990. 2 v. (Discography series, 20)

This book is a practical guide to Gregorian chant on records. The contents are represented as nothing more than a list of pieces that have been offered on records as Gregorian chants. [*Introduction*]

Organized into two lists, each in one volume. Volume 1 lists recordings with each entry showing recording format, country recorded, label name and number, title, performing ensemble, date of recording, type of chant, title of chant, mode, chant book source, page number of chant in printed source, and duration of chant. The second volume provides entries in order by chant book source, then by order of the chants in each book; entries show type of chant, mode, and the recordings made of the chant. There is a table of chant recordings in chronological order, an appendix on non-Gregorian Latin chants, and records not available for analysis (a very small section). There is a performer list, a directory of performers, a conductor index, and an index to titles of all recorded chants in alphabetical order. This work brings order and clarity to what has been heretofore unholy chaos.

COMPOSER DISCOGRAPHIES

DEBUSSY, CLAUDE

2902. Cobb, Margaret G. Discographie de l'œuvre de Claude Debussy (1902–1950). Geneva: Editions Minkoff, 1975. 120 p. (Publications du Centre de Documentation Claude Debussy, 1)
Brief review by Stephen M. Fry in *Notes*, 32 (1975), p. 301. Review by James R. Briscoe in *Notes*, 34 (1978), p. 862–65.

FAURÉ, GABRIEL

2903. Nectoux, Jean Michel. Gabriel Fauré: 1900–1977. Paris: Bibliothèque nationale, Département de la phonothèque nationale et de l'audiovisuel, 1979. 262 p. (Phonographies, 1)
Review by Michael H. Gray in *Fontes Artis Musicae*, 32 (1985), p. 150–51; by David Hall in *Notes*, 37 (1980), p. 324–26.

IVES, CHARLES

2904. Warren, Richard. Charles E. Ives: discography. New Haven, Connecticut: Yale University Library, 1972. 124 p. (Historical Sound Recordings Publication Series, 1)
A discography of every recording in the Charles E. Ives Collection of the Jackson Music Library of Yale University, including all known commercial recordings. Arranged in alphabetical order by title of work, entries include Kirkpatrick's numbers for the works of Ives, names of performers, and recording information. There is a supplement listing radio and TV broadcasts about Ives and another listing recorded interviews and comments on Ives and/or his music. Index of performers.

POULENC, FRANCIS

2905. Bloch, Francine. Francis Poulenc, 1928–1982. Paris: Bibliothèque nationale, Département de la phonothèque nationale et de l'audiovisuel, 1984. 255 p. (Phonographies, 2)

An extensive discography arranged by opus. Index to names of performers. Includes a discography of Poulenc as performer.

SCHOENBERG, ARNOLD

2906. Shoaf, R. Wayne. The Schoenberg discography. Berkeley, California: Fallen Leaf Press, 1986. 200 p. (Fallen Leaf reference books in music)

STRAVINSKY, IGOR

2907. Igor Strawinsky (1882–1971) Phonographie. Seine Eigeninterpretation auf Schallplatten und in den europäischen Rundfunkanstalten, zusammen mit einem Verzeichnis der in den deutschen Rundfunkanstalten und im Deutschen Rundfunkarchiv vorhandenen Rundfunkproduktionen und historischen Schallplattenaufnahmen von Strawinsky-Werken. Frankfurt am Main: Deutsches Rundfunkarchiv, 1972. 216 p.

A discography of recordings of Stravinsky conducting his own works and the works of others. Includes citations of other conductors' interpretations of Stravinsky. In six sections, the most prominent of which lists Stravinsky's works chronologically and cites names of performers and conductors, describes the works, lists recordings, and gives timings. A subsequent section lists Stravinsky as conductor or performer of the works of other composers, in order by composer. There is a small list of recorded interviews with Stravinsky. Indexes to: sound recording archives cited; authors of texts; dedicatees; performers. Chronological lists of recordings by date of session and of first performances.

Yearbooks and Directories

Publications appearing under the title "Yearbook" can take a variety of forms. They may be annual volumes issued by learned societies, as, for example, the Spanish *Anuario Musical*, the British *Proceedings of the Royal Musical Association*, the Swiss *Schweizerisches Jahrbuch für Musikwissenschaft*, or the *Jahrbuch für Liturgik und Hymnologie*. They may be annual volumes issued by music publishing houses such as C. F. Peters, Simrock, or Breitkopf & Härtel; or they may be publications of societies devoted to the work of a particular composer, as, for example, *Bach Jahrbuch, Händel Jahrbuch, Mozart Jahrbuch*, or *Haydn Jahrbuch*. Finally, they may be directories or compilations of factual information covering a specific year. Works of this latter kind have been emphasized in the following, highly selective list. Yearbooks in this sense are often useful for reference purposes, since they provide data on current musical activities and personalities difficult to find otherwise. It should be remembered that the titles listed in this chapter are exemplars of their types; conscientious bibliographic sleuthing should reveal the presence of works of this genre on many subjects, societies, regions, and persons not found here.

Directories are useful in discovering current practical information about people, organizations, societies, institutions, and locations of musical interest. In particular, the annual directories of members of the American Musicological Society, the Music Library Association, and the International Association of Music Libraries are useful. Out-of-date directories help to place people geographically and chronologically for a variety of purposes in the writing of history. Adelmann (no. 2908) and Brody and Brook (nos. 2921–2924) are assets for the traveler seeking musical solace while away from the usual homes and haunts. The minimal directory is a dated list of names and address organized around a theme or some kind of association. Many are more elaborate and convey a variety of useful information.

2908. Adelmann, Marianne. Musical Europe; an illustrated guide to musical life in 18 European countries. New York: Paddington Press, 1974. 447 p.

Listings by country of the institutions of musical life giving names, addresses, telephone numbers, ticket office addresses, days and hours of opening, and principal festivals and seasons at or concerning: concert halls, opera houses, theaters; music festivals; residences, monuments, and portraits of composers and musicians; notable collections of musical instruments; organs; music archives and libraries; conservatories, master courses, and institutes; research and electronic music centers; instrument makers; music publishers; and gramophone companies.

2909. The American musical directory, 1861. With a new introduction by Barbara Owen. New York: Da Capo Press, 1980. 260 p.

Reprint of the original published in New York by Hutchinson, 1861.

Arranged by state and then by city, this directory lists persons involved in performance, teaching, commerce, and instrument making or repair. The largest sections are devoted to New York and New England, but coverage is truly continental, including Canada as well as most of the U.S. Two useful appendixes: one on music in the church, in order by denomination, describing the church organs and listing the church musicians and singers; the other on music societies, each entry describing the societies' purposes and activities.

2910. American Musicological Society. Directory of members and subscribers. Philadelphia, Pennsylvania: American Musicological Society, 1983– . Pagination varies.

Annual publication listing members and subscribers separately.

2911. L'année musicale. Publiée par Mm. Michel Brenet [pseud. used by Marie Bobillier], J. Chantavoine, L. Laloy, L. de La Laurencie ... 1.–3. année; 1911–13. Genève: Minkoff Reprints, 1972. 3 v.

Reprinting of Paris editions, 1912–14. No more published.

Includes section "Bibliographie" and "Bibliographie des bibliographies musicales": vol. 3, p. [1]–152.

2912. Annuaire du spectacle, cinéma, théâtre, télévision & radio, musique, variétés. [1.]–27. année; 1942/43–1973. Paris: Éditions Roault, 1942–73. 27 v.

With numerous pages of photos and indexes.

A yearbook of the French world of entertainment, emphasizing the commercial aspects. All areas are treated, including theater, cinema, music, radio, and television.

2913. Annuaire national de la musique, 1967–68. Paris: Annuaire National de la Musique, [1970]. 677 p.

Classified listings of names, with addresses, of people associated with musical activities, including performers of all kinds, editors, printers, societies, and associations.

2914. Annuaire OGM, 1970. Industries et commerces de radio, télévision, electronique, electroacoustique, musique. Paris: Horizons de France. 61e année, 1970. 532, 880 p.

An annual directory of the French audio-television industries. Includes listings of dealers and manufacturers of musical instruments.

2915. Annuario generale della musica italiana. Rassegna delle attività lirico-concertistiche in Italia. Prima edizione 1968–69. (Tito Chelazzi, direttore. Alberto Calcagno, condirettore. Roma, 1970. 174 p.

2916. Annuario musicale italiano, 1981– . Rome: Centro Italiano di Iniziativa Musicale (CIDIM), 1981– .

1981—353 p. 1982/83—590 p.

Divided into 9 sections, the annual cites events of importance in the Italian musical scene. There are short essays on matters of current interest (e.g., "Rock e jazz in Italia," "Ethnomusicologia in Italia").

The 9 sections are: *Produzione e distribuzione* (citing programs at opera theaters, concert halls, and the like); *stato e regioni* (covering laws and governmental matters); *sindacati e associazioni; didattica e aggiornamento* (including a directory of music libraries and archives); *autori e interpreti* (directories arranged by specialty); *editoria e stampa* (directories including musicologists, periodicals, and publishers); *negozie e fabbriche* (directories); *Europa musica* (including a very useful list of national and international musical associations of all sorts); *Italia: altre espressioni musicali* (a section of essays).

The second year (1982/83) featured more sections, including a list of books on music published since 1981 and a list of periodicals on music with extensive descriptions.

2917. Association for Recorded Sound Collections. A preliminary directory of sound recordings collections in the United States and Canada. Prepared by a committee of the Association for Recorded Sound Collections. New York: New York Public Library, 1967. 157 p.

Preface written "for the Committee" by Jean Bowen.

Collections listed alphabetically by state. Addresses given; brief information as to content of collections. Many private collectors listed.

2918. Australian Directory of Music Research. Edited by Philip J. Drummond. With a foreword by Barry S. Brook. Sydney: Australia Music Centre, 1978. 399 p.

A publication celebrating the birth of interest in music research in Australia. The *Directory* consists of three parts: a section of biographies of Australian scholars; abstracts of current literature; and a subject/author index.

2919. Bowles, Garrett H. Directory of music library automation projects. 2nd ed. Philadelphia, Pennsylvania: Music Library Association, 1979. 23 p. (MLA technical reports, 2)

A listing of automated information storage and retrieval systems projects under way in North American music libraries.

2920. British music yearbook. London [etc.]: Bowker, 1975– .

Beginning in 1984, published simultaneously in London by Classical Music and in New York by Schirmer Books.

Continues *The Music Yearbook* (begun in 1972–73) and its numbering scheme.

Arthur Jacobs, editor. "A survey and directory with statistics and reference articles." Covers most aspects of musical life in London and the rest of Great Britain, including radio and television performances. Directories of performers, associations, concert and rehearsal halls, music publishers, critics, festivals, and competitions. Includes directories of British libraries and musical museums, by categories (national libraries, church and cathedral libraries, etc.) and then by place, giving addresses and telephone numbers. *The Musical Yearbook* included occasional topical essays (e.g., "The musician and income tax").

Marianne Barton succeeded Jacobs as editor in 1981.

2921. Brody, Elaine and Claire Brook. The music guide to Austria and Germany. New York: Dodd Mead, 1975. 271 p.

This guide and the three following titles describe concert halls, conservatories, libraries, museums, musical organizations, and musical businesses of the major cities of each country. Included also is information about festivals, competitions, societies, journals, and available services. Addresses, telephone numbers, schedules, hours of opening are provided. For the musical tourist, scholar, and reference librarian.

Review by Stephen M. Fry in *Notes*, 34 (1978), p. 619.

2922. Brody, Elaine and Claire Brook. The music guide to Belgium, Luxembourg, Holland and Switzerland. New York: Dodd Mead, 1977. 156 p.

See annotation to no. 2921.

2923. Brody, Elaine and Claire Brook. The music guide to Great Britain: England, Scotland, Wales, Ireland. New York: Dodd Mead, 1975. 240 p.

See annotation to no. 2921.

2924. Brody, Elaine and Claire Brook. The music guide to Italy. New York: Dodd Mead, 1978. 233 p.

See annotation to no. 2921.

2925. Contemporary music almanac 1980/81. Edited by Ronald Zalkind. New York: Schirmer Books, 1980. 947 p.

"The *Contemporary Music Almanac* is about rock music and the people who make it."

Rock events of 1979, monthly lists of rock albums, directories of record companies, producers, studios, managers, agents, awards. Bibliography of books on the subject by R. Serge Denisoff. Projected on an annual basis; only this volume issued. Contains a variety of facts, biographical notices, and the like about rock, popular, and other commercial music.

Review by Victor Cardell in *Notes*, 37 (1980), p. 329–30.

2926. Directory of American and foreign contemporary operas and American opera premieres, 1967–1975. New York: Central Opera Service, 1975. 66 p.

An issue of the *Central Opera Service Bulletin*, vol. 17, no. 2 (Winter 1975).

A listing of operas by American composers premiered and operas by foreign contemporary composers presented in the period 1967–75.

Brief review by Stephen M. Fry in *Notes*, 32 (1976), p. 555.

2927. Directory of music faculties in colleges and universities, U.S. and Canada. 1967/68– ; 1st ed.– . Boulder, Colorado: College Music Society, 1968– .

A biennial. Originally compiled and edited as *Directory of Music Faculties in American Colleges and Universities* by Harry B. Lincoln. Craig R. Short subsequently edited the *Directory*.

A directory of 11,800 teachers of music in 1,100 institutions. Part I: departmental listing by state and school. Part II: listings by areas of specialization. Part III: national alphabetical listings.

Review of the 1967–68 edition by Rey M. Longyear in *Journal of Research in Music Education*, 16 (1968), p. 220–21.

2928. **Directory of music librarians in the United States and Canada;** a preliminary edition compiled by the Membership Committee of the Music Library Association. Edited by Don Phillips. Ann Arbor, Michigan: Music Library Association, 1976. 46 p.

An alphabetical list identifying each librarian's area(s) of special responsibility.

2929. **"Directory of national music centers."** Compiled by Keith MacMillan, with a foreword by Andre Jurres. In *Notes*, 27 (1971), p. 680–693.

Describes the history, organization, and services of 19 music information centers: Australia, Austria, Belgium, Canada, Czechoslovakia, Denmark, Finland, France, Federal Republic of Germany, Iceland, Israel, The Netherlands, Norway, Poland, Portugal, Sweden, Switzerland, United Kingdom, and United States.

2930. **Douglas, John R.** "Musician and composer societies: a world directory." In *Notes*, 34 (1978), p. 39–51.

An updated version of the 1974 directory. Arranged alphabetically by names of composers and musicians.

Supplemented by Douglas in "Societies devoted to individual musicians and composers: a world directory" in *Cum Notis Variorum*, 83 (June 1984), p. 5–12.

2931. **Farrell, Susan Caust.** Directory of contemporary musical intrument makers. Columbia: University of Missouri Press, 1981. 216 p.

Alphabetical directory, list of makers by instrument and state. Appendixes list schools and societies. Bibliography.

2932. **Felton, Gary S.** Record collector's international directory. New York: Crown, 1980. 365 p.

An international directory of record dealers, but with a focus on those in English-speaking countries. Lists journals and newsletters. List of directories and guides. Index of dealers by specialties.

2933. **Finnell, Judith Greenberg.** The contemporary music performance directory; a listing of American performing ensembles, sponsoring organizations, performing facilities, concert series and festivals of 20th-century music. New York: American Music Center, 1975. 238 p.

A useful contact guide produced under the auspices of the American Music Center.

Brief reviews by Stephen M. Fry in *Notes*, 32 (1976), p. 780–81; by Ann P. Basart in *Cum Notis Variorum*, 1 (1976), p. 2.

2934. **Flemming, Bill.** Directory of Australian music organisations. 3rd ed. Sydney: Australia Music Centre, 1985. 67 p.

Previously published in 1978 and 1980.

Indexed.

2935. **Gardeton, César.** Annales de la musique: ou, Almanach musical pour l'an 1819 et 1820. Genève: Minkoff Reprint, 1978. 322, 318 columns. (Archives de l'Édition musicale française, 5)

Reprint of the edition of Paris, 1819–20.

An almanac of musical events, including the publishing of music in Paris.

Review by Rita Benton, in *Fontes Artis Musicae*, 26 (1979), p. 313.

2936. Gids van muziekbibliotheken en fonotheken in Nederland. Samengesteld onder auspiciën van de sektie muziekbibliotheken en fonotheken. 2e herz. druk. 's-Gravenhage: Nederlands Bibliotheek en Lektuurcentrum, 1976. 1 v. (unpaged)

First edition issued in 1975. Also known as *Muziekbibliotheken en Fonotheken.*

A directory of Dutch music libraries and phonorecord collections. Describes collections in basic terms; relates services, hours of opening, addresses, and telephone numbers.

2937. Goertz, Harald. Musikhandbuch für Österreich; Struktur und Organisation in 2,500 Stichworten, Namen, Addressen, Information. Eine Publikation des Österreichischen Musikraten. Wien; München: Doblinger, 1983. 157 p.

Previously published in 1971 by Jugend und Volk Verlag, Munich. 349 p.

A classified directory. Entries provide brief descriptions of organizational function. Index to designated historical sites by composers' names. Index to names of organizations.

2938. Guía de la música argentina. 1971/72– . Buenos Aires: Instituto Luccheli Bonadeo, n.d.

An annual that serves as a directory of music and musicians in the Argentine republic.

2939. Gusikoff, Lynne. Guide to musical America. New York: Facts On File, 1984. 347 p.

> ... Historic highlights of different styles of music as they developed in particular regions of the United States at various times; and to certain geographical locations where one may hear different styles of music today.... [*Introduction*]

Entries displayed by geographic area, each section beginning with an explanatory essay. Directories of performing arts centers, festivals, and other public musical locations.

Review by Paula Morgan in *Notes*, 41 (1985), p. 516–17.

2940. Hewlett, Walter B. and Eleanor Selfridge-Field. Directory of computer assisted research in musicology. Menlo Park, California: Center for Computer Assisted Research in the Humanities, 1986– . 86 p.

Originally issued in 1985 in 56 p. Subsequently issued with the following titles: *Bibliographical Databases for Music Research* (1988); *Computing in Musicology: A Directory of Research* (1989).

Includes a review article, "Printing music by computer," and numerous illustrations of the state of the art. There is a section devoted to brief notices on activities and studies pertaining to computer-assisted musicology. Current applications are categorized and described in some detail.

There is a short bibliography of recent literature and a list of names and addresses cited in the directory.

Review by Richard Koprowski in *Notes*, 42 (1986), p. 364–65.

2941. Hinrichsen's musical year book, 1944–61. London: Hinrichsen Edition, Ltd., 1944–61. 11 v.

A series of volumes edited by Max Hinrichsen, issued at irregular intervals, remarkably varied in content. The articles range from trivia to substantial contributions by recognized authorities. Most of the volumes contain bibliographies of current music publications as well as numerous lists, illustrations, chronologies. More recent volumes have been organized about some central theme, i.e., vol. 7, "The fore-runners of the *Grove-Blum*" (1955); vol. 8, "The organ of Bach and matters related to this subject" (1956); vol. 9, "John Gay and the Ballad Opera" (1956); vol. 10, "Organ and choral aspects and prospects" (1958). Vol. 11 (1961) contains the papers read at the Joint Congress of the International Association of Music Libraries and the Galpin Society, Cambridge, 1959.

2942. International Association of Sound Archives. Directory of member archives. Compiled by Grace Koch. London: International Association of Sound Archives, 1982. 174 p. (Special publication, 3)

First edition edited by Ann Briegleb and Don Niles and published 1978. 94 p.

Extensive entries modeled on the *RISM* Series C directories to music collections.

2943. International Council of Museums. International directory of musical instrument collections. Edited by Jean Jenkins [for the International Council of Museums]. Buren: F. Knuf for [the] International Council of Museums, 1977. 166 p.

A predecessor was *Ethnic Musical Instruments: Identification-Conservation....* Edited by Jean Jenkins. (London: H. Evelyn for the International Council of Museums, 1970. 59 p.)

2944. International directory of music education institutions. Paris: UNESCO, 1968. 115 p.

A source book of information compiled by the International Society for Music Education for UNESCO. Covers 10 categories:

1. Conservatories and academies of music.
2. Music and music education schools or faculties in universities.
3. Other music institutions.
4. International music and music education workshops, summer courses, teacher-training courses.
5. International competitions.
6. International music festivals.
7. Music libraries, archives, and documentation centers of international standing.
8. Collections of musical instruments.
9. Organizations, societies, and institutions of music and music education.
10. National and international music periodicals.

2945. International Folk Music Council. The international folk directory of ethnic music and related traditions: a world listing of regional archives, institutes, and organizations, together with individual collectors, concerned wholly, or in part, with recording, documenting, and disseminating information about authentic local folk music and related traditional arts, crafts, and customs, etc. Totnes, England: Published for the International Folk Music Council, with the assistance of the Calouste Gulbenkian Foundation by the Dartington Institute of Traditional Arts, 1973. c. 200 p.

First published in 1964 under title *Directory of Institutions and Organisations Concerned Wholly or in Part with Folk Music.*

2946. International music guide, 1977–85. Edited by Derek Elley. London: Tantivy Press; South Brunswick, New Jersey, and New York: A. S. Barnes, 1976–86. 9 v.

Publisher varies. Continued by *International Music and Opera Guide.*

Intended to be "a readable annual surveying internationally all points of interest to the modern concert goer and general music-lover." Edited successively by Elley (through 1981), Jane Dudman (1981–85), and Hugh Canning (1986–).

Several sections: musicians of the year; world survey (arranged by country); music festivals and competitions; musical necrology; nonclassified reports (by genre); recorded music scene; audio reports; music shops; music schools; book reviews; music in print; music magazines.

No section attempts comprehensive or systematic coverage. Sections have been added and deleted through the course of this annual publication. Usually includes a guide to music festivals.

2947. Jackson, Paul T. Collectors' contact guide, 1975. Peoria, Illinois: Recorded Sound Research, 1975. 58 p. (Record collectors' source book, 3)

Bibliography: p. 46–58.

Brief review by Stephen M. Fry in *Notes*, 32 (1975), p. 302.

2948. Jackson, Paul T. Sound search: recording occasional papers. Peoria, Illinois: Recorded Sound Research, 1976. 35 p. (Record collectors source book, 5)

How to find out if something has been recorded, and if so, who has done it. For radio broadcasts, Watergate recordings, the women's movement, organ music, etc. [*Preface*]

2949. Jahrbuch der Musikwelt. The yearbook of the music world. Annuaire du monde musical. 1. Jahrgang, 1949–50. Bayreuth: Verlag Julius Steeger, 1949. 696 p.

Only one volume published. Contains a vast amount of information regarding musicians and musical institutions throughout the world. Contents include a classified listing of German music dissertations, 1885–1948; a chronology of music dictionaries and encyclopedias; a list of European music periodicals, 1945–48; a bibliography of German music and writings on music, etc.

2950. Kajanef, Marc. L'année de la musique. Paris: Éditions Stock, 1979. 560 p.

An almanac beginning with a very large directory of persons and events important in the French, and particularly Parisian, musical scene. Other sections cover special topics (e.g., Musique à lire, Profil de France musique). Index to names.

2951. Kemp's international music & recording industry year book; a comprehensive reference and marketing guide to the music and recording industry in Great Britain and overseas. vols. 1– ; 1965– . London: Kemps Group, 1965– .

Title varies: 1965–197?, *Kemp's Music & Recording Industry Yearbook.* Known also as the *International Music & Recording Industry Year Book* and the *Music & Recording Industry Year Book.*

Brief review by Stephen M. Fry in *Notes*, 32 (1975), p. 302–303.

2952. Mapp, Edward. Directory of blacks in the performing arts. Metuchen, New Jersey: Scarecrow Press, 1978. 428 p.

A classified directory with entries including brief biographical and career information for about 800 performers. Most of these persons are American and contemporary, but persons from other countries and historical figures are listed. Much of the information about living persons was gathered by questionnaire.

2953. Music industry directory. 7th ed., 1983. Chicago, Illinois: Marquis, 1983. 678 p.

Formerly the *Musician's Guide*, issued 1954–80.

... provides comprehensive coverage of the music industry. It contains descriptive listings for service and professional organizations, schools and colleges, competitions, periodicals, festivals, libraries, and foundations, as well as addresses and 'phone numbers for hundreds of music businesses. [*Preface*]

A classified directory of names connected with all phases of commercial music activity. Contains more than 50 rosters of persons, organizations, activities, and businesses concerned with the musical profession.

Review of the 1957 edition by Richard S. Hill in *Notes*, 14 (1957), p. 111–13; of the 1968 edition by Thor Wood and Neil Ratliff in *Notes*, 25 (1969), p. 736–37; also reviewed in *Booklist and Subscription Books Bulletin*, 1 Dec. 1972, p. 307–308.

Index to music publishers and general index.

2954. Music Library Association. New England Chapter. Directory of music libraries and collections in New England. Compiled and edited by the Publications Committee of the Music Library Association, New England Chapter. 7th ed. New London: Greer Music Library, Connecticut College, 1985. 100 p.

A guide to the holdings, services, and facilities of music libraries in New England.

2955. Music Library Association. Southeast Chapter. Directory of music collections in the Southeast. 2nd ed. compiled by Shirley Marie Watts and Mark D. Squire. Nashville, Tennessee: Music Library Association, Southeast Chapter, 1984. 27 p.

First edition compiled by Jeanette M. Drone, 1978.

A guide to the holdings, services, and facilities of music libraries in the southeastern states of the United States of America.

2956. Music Library Association. Southern California Chapter. A directory of special music collections in Southern California libraries and in the libraries of the University of California and the California State Universities and Colleges. Compiled by the Music Library Survey Committee. Edited by Don L. Hixon. Rev. ed. Music Library Association, Southern California Chapter, 1976. 36 p.

2957. The Music Magazine/Musical Courier. The annual directory of the concert world. Evanston, Illinois: Summy-Birchard Co., 1957–63.

Editions for 1957–61 published as the mid-January issue of *Musical Courier*, with title *Directory Issue of the Musical Arts and Artists*.

The 1963 issue, edited by Max D. Jones, contains pertinent information on American and foreign music organizations, artist and concert managers, artist availability, current series and associations, orchestras, opera booking organizations, festivals, foundations, schools of music, publishers, periodicals, recording firms, and music dealers.

2958. Musical American International directory of the performing arts. New York: K-III Publishing Co., 1993– .

Continues *Musical America Directory of Performing Arts* and was first issued as a special issue of *Musical America*, which ceased in January 1992.

International in scope, but focused most heavily on North America. Intended for use by agents, impresarios, and concert hall managers, the directory lists orchestras, dance and opera companies, choral groups, festivals, music schools, contests, foundations and awards, publishers, professional organizations, managers, and magazines and trade papers amid a welter of advertisements. Index of advertisers.

2959. Musiol, Karol. "Bibliothèques des conservatoires, académies, et écoles de musique." In *Fontes Artis Musicae*, 22 (1975), p. 97–154.

A compendium of information on such libraries. International in scope.

2960. The national directory for the performing arts and civic centers. Beatrice Handel, editor; Janet W. Spencer, associate editor, [*et al.*]. 3rd ed. New York: J. Wiley, 1978. 1,049 p.

First edition published in Dallas by Handel, 1973. 604 p.

Covers the United States. Organized by state and then by locality. Data on facilities, organizations devoted to instrumental music, vocal music, theater, dance, etc. Key management personnel listed.

2961. Neue Musik in der Bundesrepublik Deutschland. Dokumentation. 1953– . Köln: Gesellschaft für Neue Musik, Sektion Bundesrepublik Deutschland der Internationalen Gesellschaft für Neue Musik, 1953– .

A biennial sourcebook of information about the performance of new music in Germany. Preliminary group of essays; the accomplishments and the programs of regional radio centers are described. New music festivals and activities supporting or featuring new music are listed by cities.

2962. Norris, Gerald. A musical gazetteer of Great Britain and Ireland. Newton Abbot, England, and North Pomfret, Vermont: David and Charles, 1981. 352 p.

Like a literary gazeteer, but dealing entirely with the homes and haunts of composers and other musicians. Arranged concentrically by region, county, and place.

2963. Opera Annual. Edited by Harold Rosenthal. London: John Calder, 1953/54– . No. 1– .

Articles on aspects of the opera world during the current year. Attention focused on developments in Great Britain.

2964. Pavlakis, Christopher. The American music handbook, a guide to organized musical activity in the United States. An inventory of musical resources: the people, places, and organizations. New York: Free Press, 1974. 836 p.

A directory focused on professional musicianship in the United States: organizations, vocal and instrumental ensembles, performers, composers, festivals and awards, education, radio and television, music industries, periodicals, and management. A foreign supplement treats international festivals and contests, music publishers. Helpful index.

Review by Susan T. Sommer in *Notes*, 31 (1975), p. 770–71.

2965. Penney, Barbara. Music in British libraries: a directory of resources. 3rd ed. London: Library Association, 1981. 452 p.

Maureen W. Long edited the 1st and 2nd editions (1971 and 1974).

The results of a broad survey of music holdings in Great Britain. Includes information about services, personnel, and hours of opening. Collections are described in some detail. Index to locations and names of libraries. Index to composers, names of collections, and nature of collections.

2966. Pierre Key's music year book, the standard music annual, 1924–38. New York: Pierre Key, Inc., 1925–38. 6 v.

A directory of musical organizations and musicians, chiefly performers; issued irregularly over a period of 13 years. The earlier volumes are international in scope; the later are restricted to U.S. coverage.

2967. The purchaser's guide to the music industries. Annual edition, 1897– . New York: Music Trades, 1897– .

Title varies: after 1958, *Directory Issue....*

Annual classified directory of instrument manufacturers, music publishers, engravers, and printers, retail music stores, dealers in music merchandise, etc. Excludes performers and performing groups.

2968. Rabin, Carol Price. A guide to music festivals in America. Rev. and enl. ed. Stockbridge, Massachusetts: Berkshire Traveller, 1983. 286 p.

Covers over 150 classical and popular music festivals, providing some history on each, names of current directors, and the focus of each. Addresses provided for tickets and for accommodations near each festival. Rock music events are not included. Index to names of festivals.

2969. Rabin, Carol Price. Music festivals in Europe and Britain. Stockbridge, Massachusetts: Berkshire Traveller, 1984. 191 p.
Similar to the preceding title.

2970. "Register of early music." In *Early Music*, vols. 1–4 (1973–76).
An annual "list of names, addresses, phone numbers and instruments ..." of persons engaged in playing early music, as amateurs or professional musicians. Intended to stimulate performance of early music.

2971. Ross, Anne. The opera directory. London: John Calder; New York: Sterling Publishing Co., [1961]. 566 p.
A source book of contemporaneous opera facts and figures. Introductions and headings in six languages (English, French, German, Italian, Spanish, Russian). Material organized under 13 headings, the most important of which are opera singers, conductors, producers and designers, technical staff, theaters and producing organizations, festivals, living composers, works by living composers, librettists, colleges and schools of music, casting index, glossary.
Identical volumes were issued with various foreign title pages under the imprints of publishers in Paris, Geneva, Berlin, London, New York, etc.

2972. Samuel, Harold E. "Societies, musical." In *The New Harvard Dictionary of Music*, p. 773–78. Edited by Don M. Randel. Cambridge, Harvard University Press, 1986.
A list of current professional societies citing titles and dates of principal publications.

2973. Steinbeck, Hans. "Directory of music information centres." In *Fontes Artis Musicae*, 26 (1979), p. 147–59.
Provides information on each organization including support, publications, agencies, services, and projects.

2974. Steinbeck, Hans. Schweizer Musik-Handbuch: Informationen über Struktur und Organisation des Schweizer Musiklebens. Guide musical suisse: informations sur la structure et l'organisation de la vie musicale suisse. Guide musicale svizzera: informazioni sulla struttura e l'organizzazione della vita svizzera. Zürich: Schweizerisches Musik-Archiv, 1985. 222 p.
Previously published in 1979 and 1983.

A survey of musical instrument collections in the United States and Canada. See no. 2496.

2975. The year in American music, 1946/47–1947/48. New York: Allen, Towne & Heath, [1947–48]. 2 v.

1946/47 edited by Julius Bloom; 1947/48 by David Ewen.

The first part of each volume is a chronological survey of the important musical events of the year; this is followed by a miscellany of factual information, biographical and bibliographical.

2976. The year's work in music, 1947/48–1950/51. Edited by Alan Frank. London and New York: Published for the British Council by Longmans, Green & Co., 1948–51. 3 v.

Each volume contains a series of essays by various specialists on aspects of British musical life during the year: musical research, the making and playing of instruments, the British Broadcasting Corporation and contemporary music, etc. Contains an annual bibliography of published music and musical literature compiled by A. Hyatt King.

Women in Music

James B. Coover's work on music dictionaries has shown that the first of this genre devoted entirely to women was the Michaelis *Frauen als schaffende Tonkünstler: ein biographisches Lexikon* (Stettin: Leipzig, 1888). In the recent few years, there has been substantial new work on the subject, and while many of the works cited in this chapter are relevant to other sections of this book, they are brought together here to demonstrate the extent and rapid growth of scholarship on women in music.

2977. Block, Adrienne Fried and Carol Neuls-Bates. Women in American music; a bibliography of music and literature. Westport, Connecticut: Greenwood, 1979. 302 p.

A classified bibliography of 5,024 entries organized on the *RILM* model with abstracts. Author-subject index to the literature. Composer-author index to music. Index to recordings. Thorough indexing and annotating.

2978. Bowers, Jane. "The emergence of women composers in Italy, 1566–1700." In *Women Making Music; the Western Art Tradition, 1150–1950*, p. 116–67. Edited by Jane Bowers and Judith Tick. Urbana: University of Illinois Press, 1986.

Includes a bibliography of compositions by Italian women published 1566–1700, p. 162–167.

2979. Claghorn, Charles Eugene. Women composers and hymnists. Metuchen, New Jersey: Scarecrow, 1984. 272 p.

A "comprehensive biographical dictionary of [755] women hymnists and composers of church and sacred music covering all leading Protestant denominations, many Roman Catholics and a few Jewish hymnists." Bibliography.

Reviews by Gillian Anderson in *Fontes Artis Musicae*, 32 (1985), p. 221–22, and by Paula Morgan in *Notes*, 42 (1986), p. 552–53.

2980. Cohen, Aaron I. International encyclopedia of women composers. 2nd ed. New York and London: R. R. Bowker, 1987. 2 v.

Provides brief biographical coverage with lists of compositions for 6,196 women composers. Appendix of composers listed by country and century. Extensive bibliography of works about women composers.

2981. Frasier, Jane. Women composers; a discography. Detroit, Michigan: Information Coordinators, 1983. 308 p. (Detroit studies in music bibliography, 50)

Covering 337 composers or art music. Indexes to recording company, genres, titles. Bibliography.

Review by Gillian Anderson in *Fontes Artis Musicae*, 32 (1985), p. 89–90.

2982. Handy, D. Antoinette. Black women in American bands & orchestras. Metuchen, New Jersey: Scarecrow Press, 1981. 319 p.

Includes an extensive bibliography, p. 254–73.

Review by Deane L. Root in *Notes*, 38 (1982), p. 832–35.

2983. Hixon, Donald L. and Don Hennessee. Women in music: a bio-bibliography. Metuchen, New Jersey: Scarecrow Press, 1975.

Indexes articles in 48 standard reference works about women involved in classical music. Classified list of women musicians provided.

2984. Laurence, Anya. Women of note, 1,000 women composers born before 1900. New York: Richards Rosen Press, 1978. 101 p.

An extensive "biographical bibliography" of women composers active before 1900. Arranged by country of origin and then alphabetically. Short bibliography of sources. Discography.

2985. Le Page, Jane Wiener. Women composers, conductors, and musicians of the twentieth century; selected biographies. Metuchen, New Jersey: Scarecrow Press, 1980. 2 v.

Extensive articles on significant women engaged in various aspects of making music. Discographies, lists of compositions, and many quotations about each person are included. Each volume is provided with an index to corporate and personal names.

2986. Meggett, Joan M. Keyboard music by women composers: a catalog and bibliography; foreword by Nancy Fierro. Westport, Connecticut: Greenwood Press, 1981. 210 p.

A catalog of the work of 290 composers, including brief biographies and lists of sources. Discography. Extensive annotated bibliography of sources referring to more than one woman composer.

2987. Rogal, Samuel J. Sisters of sacred song: a selected listing of women hymnodists in Great Britain and America. New York and London: Garland, 1981. 162 p.

Lists women hymnodists and their hymns, classifying them by nationality and denominations. Cites collections of hymns. Title index to hymns cited.

2988. Schmidt, Siegrun. Komponisten; Verzeichnis lieferbarer Noten. 2. Aufl. Aarau, Schweiz: Musikhaus Pastorini, 1983– . 1. teil (100 p.)

This is a classified list of music by women composers citing titles, publishers, and places of publication. Women composers of all periods are included. There is a name index.

2989. Skowronski, JoAnn. Women in American music: a bibliography. Metuchen, New Jersey: Scarecrow Press, 1978. 183 p.

Arranged in four sections covering periods of American history, and contains two genre bibliographies: general history and reference works. Some entries are annotated. Name index.

Review by Carol Neuls-Bates in *Notes*, 35 (1979), p. 635–36.

2990. Smith, Julia, ed. Directory of American women composers, with selected music for senior and junior clubs. 1st ed. Chicago, Illinois: National Federation of Music Clubs, 1970. 51 p.

> Here is a first *Directory of American Women Composers....* The *Directory* contains the names of over 600 composers who have written, or are now writing music that ranges from very easy to the most difficult and experimental, including electronic music. [Editor's *Foreword*]

No work lists, but type of music composed is indicated for each composer as well as for the publishers who have issued their works. Key to music publishers and distributors (p. 48–51).

2991. Stern, Susan. Women composers: a handbook. Metuchen, New Jersey: Scarecrow Press, 1978. 191 p.

Entries provide very brief biographical data and references to sources of further information. The sources are separately listed. Cross-references are provided for women who had or used more than one name. There is a supplementary list of women composers for whom no information could be found. There is a supplementary bibliography of works that provide information about women composers in general. Covers more women than those cited in Hixon and Hennessee (no. 2983) and more sources of information as well.

Reviews by Judith Tick in *Notes*, 36 (1979), p. 99–100, and by A. F. Leighton Thomas in *Music Review*, 42 (1981), p. 61–67.

2992. Stewart-Green, Miriam. Women composers: a checklist of works for the solo voice. Boston, Massachusetts: G. K. Hall, 1980. 296 p.

In the general section, lists 3,746 women who have composed "classical" music. Cites song titles and publishers or locations when known. Separate lists for: operas, cantatas, oratorios, masses, cycles and collections, works for voice with instruments, dramatic scenes. Bibliography and index of names.

2993. Women in music: an anthology of source readings from the Middle Ages to the present. Edited by Carol Neuls-Bates. New York: Harper & Row, 1982. 351 p.

Concerning the work of women in Western art music, from Hildegard of Bingen to Elizabeth Lutyens. There are introductory and explanatory remarks establishing contexts. Sources are cited and there is a useful bibliography complementing the sources of the readings.

2994. Zaimont, Judith Lang and Karen McNerney Famera. Contemporary concert music by women; a directory of the composers and their works. A project of the International League of Women Composers. Westport, Connecticut: Greenwood, 1981. 355 p.

Half-page biographies, including photographic portraits and manuscript samples, of over 60 composers and 6 other musicians. Classified lists of music. Addresses of composers and publishers. Discography and index.

Miscellaneous and Bibliographical Tools

The "Miscellaneous" chapter has been shortened by the displacement of entries for music bibliographies in series to a separate index and reorganized to bring titles on the same general topic together. The resulting sections of this chapter are: Studies in Music Bibliography; Music Business and Law; Music Librarianship; Music Cataloging and Classification; and Miscellaneous.

STUDIES IN MUSIC BIBLIOGRAPHY

2995. Coover, James B. "The current status of music bibliography." In *Notes*, 13 (1956), p. 581–93.

A survey of the accomplishments, progress, and lacunae in the field of music bibliography as of 1956. The paper takes its point of departure from A. Hyatt King's statement in *Library* (1945) (no. 3001).

2996. Deutsch, Otto Erich. "Music bibliography and catalogues." In *Library*, 23 (1943), p. 151–70.

Concerning the importance to music bibliographers and scholars for library and other catalogers to include more information rather than less in entries. Discusses the confusion arising from varying numbering schemes for important composers' works. Mentions the utility of publishers' plate numbers and cites the variety of printing techniques used to reproduce music. Concludes with a short bibliography. Overall, a description of the state of music bibliography and music cataloging of the time.

2997. Duckles, Vincent H. "Music literature, music, and sound recordings." In *Bibliography, Current State and Future Trends*, p. 158–83. Edited by Robert B. Downs and Frances B. Jenkins. Urbana: University of Illinois Press, 1967.

First published in *Library Trends*, January 1967.

2998. Fischer, Wilhelm. "Verzeichnis von bibliographischen Hilfswerken für musikhistorische Arbeiten." In Guido Adler, *Methode der Musikgeschichte*, p. 200–222. Leipzig: Breitkopf & Härtel, 1919.

Classified list, including general bibliographical works, general musical works, and bibliographies of single aspects of music history. Some inaccurate dates and incomplete titles for French and English works, which are less well covered.

2999. Hoboken, Anthony van. "Probleme der musikbibliographischen Terminologie." In *Fontes Artis Musicae*, 1958:1. p. 6–15.

A discussion centered on the dificulties of establishing music bibliography as an "exact science" in view of the variety and complexity of the materials with which it is concerned.

3000. Hopkinson, Cecil. "The fundamentals of music bibliography." In *Fontes Artis Musicae*, 1955:2. p. 122–31.

An attempt to stimulate discussion of some basic points as to the nature, content, and procedures of music bibliography as it serves the needs of collectors, musicians, and historians.

3001. King, A. Hyatt. "Recent work in music bibliography." In *Library*, vol. 26, no. 2 (Sept.–Dec. 1945), p. 99–148.

Surveys the accomplishments in music bibliography during the period just prior to and during World War II.

3002. Krohn, Ernest C. "The bibliography of music." In *Musical Quarterly*, 5 (1919), p. 231–54.

One of the first surveys of the state of music bibliography by an American scholar. Useful as a statement of the accomplishments in the field at the time of writing. Incomplete citations. Narrative style.

3003. Krummel, Donald W. "Bibliography of music." In *The New Grove Dictionary of Music and Musicians*, edited by Stanley Sadie, v. 2, p. 682–92. London: Macmillan, 1980.

Divided into three sections: analytical and descriptive bibliography; reference bibliography; history of music bibliography. This article provides an overview of the subject and mentions some of the principal sources. It is particularly helpful in placing music bibliography in the context of general bibliography and in a historical perspective. Excellent classified bibliography and numerous references to related articles.

3004. Luther, Wilhelm-Martin. "Bibliographie." In *MGG*, edited by Friedrich Blume, v. 1, cols. 1831–39. Kassel: Bärenreiter, 1949–51.

Recounts the history and surveys the concepts of music bibliography, with an extensive listing of titles pertaining to the field.

3005. Mathiesen, Thomas J. "Towards a corpus of ancient Greek music theory: a new catalogue raisonné planned for RISM." In *Fontes Artis Musicae*, 25 (1978) p. 119–34.

Prospectus for a new *RISM* catalog (B, XI). Includes bibliographical references.

3006. Music and bibliography: essays in honour of Alec Hyatt King. Edited by Oliver W. Neighbour. New York: K. G. Saur, C. Bingley, 1980. 256 p.

Contents:

"Venetian Baroque music in a London bookshop: the Robert Martin catalogues, 1633–50" by Donald W. Krummel.

"The Chapel Royal part-books" by Margaret Laurie.

"The harpsichord music of John Blow: a first catalogue" by Watkins Shaw.

"A Dresden opera-goer in 1756: Johann Christian Trömer, called 'Der Deutsch-Franzos'" by David Paisey.

"Henric Fougt, typographer extraordinary" by John A. Parkinson.

"Music engraving practice in eighteenth-century London: a study of some Forster editions of Haydn and their manuscript sources" by H. Edmund Poole.

"The origins of Mozart's 'Hunt' quartet, K. 458" by Alan Tyson.

"Some aspects of music publishing in nineteenth-century Berlin" by Rudolf Elvers.

"The early Novello octavo editions" by Miriam Miller.

"Meyerbeer's Italian operas" by Winton Dean.

"Chélard's 'Palladium des artistes': a project for a music periodical" by Richard Macnutt.

"Musical periodicals in 'Bourgeois Russia'" by Gerald Abraham.

"Alfred Cortot as collector of music" by Albi Rosenthal.

"The past, present, and future of the music library thematic catalogue" by Barry S. Brook.

"Problems in teaching the bibliography of music" by Brian Redfern.

3007. Musica e filologia: contributi in occasione del festival "Musica e filologia" Verona, 30 settembre–18 ottobre 1982, a cura di Marco Di Pasquale con la collaborazione di Richard Pierce. Verona: Edizioni della Società Letteraria, 1983. 212 p. (Quaderni della società letteraria, 1)

Contents:

"La filologia musicale e la tradizione musicologica italiana" by Giorgio Pestelli.

"Gli attuali indirizzi della storiografia e degli studi musicali in Italia" by Enrico Fubini.

"Il luogo della musica" by Giovanni Calendoli.

"The editing and publication of Baroque music in Hungary: principles and practice" by István Máriássy.

"Concordanze letterarie e divergenze musicali intorno ai Madrigali a cinque voci [...] Libro primo di Claudio Monteverdi" by Paolo Fabbri.

"Altro non è 'l mio cor: canzonetta del Seicento" by Ivano Cavallini.

"Due quadri musicali di scuola caravaggesca" by Franca Trinchieri Camiz.

"La Cappella musicale del Duomo di Verona, 1620–1685: qualche integrazione" by Marco Materassi.

"The application and usefulness of 'rastrology' with particular reference to early eighteenth-century Italian manuscripts" by Paul Everett.

"Le 'Liste de' musici e sonatori': fonti d'archivio sulla prassi esecutiva della musica strumentale romana del primo Settecento" by Franco Piperno.

"Antonio Vivaldi e la cantata profana" by Piero Mioli.

"Il copista raggiratore: un apocrifo durantiano conservato presso la British Library" by Carlo Vitali e Pinuccia Carrer.

"Estetica e prassi della musica sacra nei documenti di Benedetto XIV" by Osvaldo Gambassi.

"'Prend ton Metastase et travaille!': per una indagine melodrammaturgica di Julie ou la Nouvelle Héloïse" by Giovanni Morelli.

MUSIC BUSINESS AND LAW

3008. Basart, Ann P. "Copyright." In *Cum Notis Variorum*, 56 (October 1981), p. 25–26.
A brief but valuable bibliography on the subject of copyright in the United States.

3009. Baskerville, David. Music business handbook and career guide. Los Angeles, California, and Denver, Colorado: Sherwood, 1975. 669 p.
An extensive, but now dated, introduction to the customs and procedures of various aspects of the music business, including advice on various relationships. Includes sections on: songwriting; publishing and copyright; business affairs; the record industry; music in broadcasting and film; career planning and development. There is an appendix of useful forms, a copy of the 1976 U.S. copyright act, a directory of professional organizations and trade associations, and a brief bibliography of sources.

3010. Erickson, J. Gunnar, Edward R. Hearn and Mark E. Halloran. Musician's guide to copyright. San Francisco, California: Bay Area Lawyers for the Arts, 1979. 86 p.
A brief review intended for the layman of the laws and regulations governing copyright of printed and recorded music.

3011. Karlin, Fred and Rayburn Wright. On the track: a guide to contemporary film scoring. Includes a complete CLICK BOOK by Alexander R. Brinkman. New York: Schirmer; London: Collier Macmillan, 1990. 856 p.
This book is not only a handbook to assist composers, conductors, directors, and editors in composing music for contemporary films, but it is also a comprehensive and practical manual including valuable information on the business of film music. Includes a filmography of the 150 films discussed in the course of the book and a classified bibliography with sections on commercials, conducting, film and television production, recording, and songwriting. Index.

3012. Orobko, William. The musician's handbook: a practical guide to the law and business of music. Vancouver: International Self-Counsel Press Ltd.; Seattle, Washington: Self-Counsel Press, 1985. 189 p.
A popular introduction to practice in the music business and to Canadian and American laws relating to that business.

3013. Pohlmann, Hansjörg. Die Frühgeschichte des musikalischen Urheberrechts (c. 1400–1800). Neue Materialien zur Entwicklung des Urheberrechtsbewusstseins des Komponisten. Kassel: Bärenreiter, 1962. 315 p. (Musikwissenschaftliche Arbeiten, 20.)
One of the few studies in the history of music copyright practice treating the sociological and psychological aspects of composers' rights, plagiarism, the history of honoraria for composers. An appendix gives 31 original documents in transcription.
Review by Werner Braun in *Die Musikforschung*, 17 (1964), p. 298–99.

3014. Rachlin, Harvey. The encyclopedia of the music business. New York: Harper & Row, 1981. 524 p.

Entries on terms and topics pertinent to the making and marketing of music for commercial reasons. Extensive appendixes, including winners of some of the more famous awards.

3015. Rapaport, Diane Sward. How to make and sell your own record: the complete guide to independent recording. Rev. 3rd ed. Jerome, Arizona: Jerome Headlands Press; New York: Perigee Books and Music Sales, 1988. 183 p.

First edition of 167 pages appeared in 1979, published by Harmony Books in New York. A revised edition of 183 pages was published by the Headlands Press in Tiburon, California, in 1984.

Comprehensive guide to promotion, sales, printing, graphics, manufacturing, recording procedures, recording options, recording time and money, song rights, business and planning. Brief bibliography and index.

3016. Rothenburg, Stanley. Copyright and public performance of music. The Hague: Martinus Nijhoff, 1954. 188 p.

A survey of the current status of music copyright and performers' rights in the United States and Europe.

3017. Schulze, Erich. Urheberrecht in der Musik. Dritte, neubearbeitete Auflage. Berlin: Walter de Gruyter, 1965. 474 p.

First published in 1951; 4th revised edition, 1972.

A sourcebook of information on music copyright practice. European orientation. 37 appendixes of codes and other documents related to copyright. The bibliography, p. xii–xxiv, provides an international listing of performers' rights organizations.

3018. Shemel, Sidney and M. William Krasilovsky. More about this business of music. Rev. and enl. 4th ed. New York: Billboard Publications, 1989. 240 p.

Previously published in 1967, 1974, and 1982.

Focuses on the business of serious music, religious music, and jazz.

> This book consists of additional topics and materials not contained in *This Business of Music.* The fourth edition helps participants in the music and recording industries comprehend the intricacies of the business and their rights and obligations. Economic facts deemed significant for daily operations as well as common legal concepts which guide business decisions are presented. The book is not designed to be a substitute for expert legal and accounting advice. [*Preface*]

Includes a large variety of useful forms and lists in the appendixes. Index.

3019. Shemel, Sidney and M. William Krasilovsky. This business of music. Rev. and enl. 6th ed. New York: Billboard Publications, 1990. 688 p.

Previously published in 1964, 1971, 1977, 1979, and 1985.

The companion to the previous work, focusing on the popular and commercial music trades. The standard source of information on recording contracts, copyright, clubs, licensing, performing rights, mechanized rights, music publishing, trademarks, and taxation. Includes an appendix of forms for copyright deposit, contracts, and licenses as well as some lists of reference sources.

3020. Taubman, Joseph. In tune with the music business. New York: Law-Arts Publishers, 1980. 279 p.

Based on Taubman's lectures on the music business at the New School for Social Research. Emphasizes the legal and regulatory aspects of the music trades.

3021. Wadhams, Wayne. Dictionary of music production. New York: Schirmer Books, 1988. 257 p.

Definitions of terms used by professionals making music for commercial purposes accompanied by codes indicating industry sources or categories for each term. Includes names and acronyms of trade organizations with statements of goals or intents of each organization. There is a separate set of definitions of standard units and measures used in the business. Select bibliography of sources. The introduction is invaluable.

MUSIC LIBRARIANSHIP

3022. Bayne, Pauline Shaw. A basic music library: essential scores and books. 2nd ed. Compiled by the Music Library Association, sub-committee on the basic music collection, under the direction of Pauline Shaw Bayne. Edited by Robert Michael Fling. Chicago, Illinois: American Library Association, 1983. 357 p.

First published in 1978. 173 p.

Review by Margaret F. Lospinuso in *Notes*, 36 (1979), p. 94–95.

3023. Bradley, Carol June. Music collections in American libraries: a chronology. Detroit, Michigan: Detroit Information Coordinators, 1981. 249 p. (Detroit studies in music bibliography, 46)

A chronological approach to the history of music librarianship in the United States.

Reviews by Paula Morgan in *Notes*, 39 (1983), p. 357–58, and by Vincent H. Duckles in *Fontes Artis Musicae*, 29 (1982), p. 147–48.

3024. Bryant, Eric Thomas and Guy A. Marco. Music librarianship: a practical guide. 2nd ed. Metuchen, New Jersey, and London: Scarecrow, 1985. 449 p.

First edition published in London: James Clarke; New York: Hafner Publishing, 1959. Reprinted by Stechert-Hafner, 1963.

Includes chapters on administration, reference books and periodicals, cataloging, classification, and sound recordings. The book is intended primarily for British practitioners.

The chapter on reference work includes *inter alia* an annotated bibliography of works that might constitute a reference collection in small to medium-size music libraries. The chapter on cataloging presents an overview of the principal codes for cataloging material for music libraries, and similarly the chapter on classification covers the main classification schemes. The sound recording chapter is an extended guide to the contents of recordings collections and is particularly relevant to British situations.

There is a bibliography and a brief index.

First edition reviewed by Alfons Ott in *Fontes Artis Musicae*, 7 (1960), p. 72–73, and by Rita Benton in *Notes*, 17 (1960), p. 397–98.

Second edition reviewed by Susan T. Sommer in *Notes*, 43 (1986), p. 44–45, and by David Hunter in *Libraries and Culture*, 24 (1989), p. 506–507.

3025. Currall, Henry F. J. Gramophone record libraries, their organization and practice.... With a preface by A. Hyatt King. 2nd ed. Published for the International Association of Music Libraries, United Kingdom Branch. London: Crosby Lockwood and Son, 1970. 303 p.

The work was first published in 1963.

A manual for the administration of a record library, with contributions by British librarians and sound recording experts. P. 131–46: "A basic stock list"; p. 171–76: "Gramophone librarianship: a bibliography." Illustrated.

Directory of music library automation projects. See no. 2919.

3026. Duckles, Vincent H. Music libraries and librarianship. *Library Trends*, 8 (April 1960), p. 495–617. [Published by the University of Illinois, School of Librarianship.]

15 specialists discuss various aspects of music librarianship, covering the areas of training for the profession, bibliography and selection, cataloging, services, and administration.

Review by Vladimir Fedorov in *Fontes Artis Musicae*, 8 (1961), p. 30–31.

3027. Folter, Siegrun H. "Library restrictions on the use of microfilm copies." In *Fontes Artis Musicae*, 24 (1977), p. 207–243.

A codification of information on restrictions placed on the use of microfilm copies of sources by the libraries holding the originals. A very useful and compact delineation of various practices. The International Association of Music Libraries Research Libraries Commission issued a "Report on the supply and use of microfilms" in *Fontes Artis Musicae*, 27 (1980), p. 207–209.

3028. McColvin, Lionel R. and Harold Reeves. Music libraries, including a comprehensive bibliography of music literature and a select bibliography of music scores published since 1957.... Completely rewritten, revised, and extended by Jack Dove. London: Andre Deutsch, 1965. 2 v.

First published in 1937–38.

Vol. 1 is made up of a series of chapters on various aspects of music library administration and practice: staff, binding, classification, cataloging, etc. There are chapters devoted to British public libraries, British university and special libraries, overseas libraries, etc.

Vol. 2 consists of bibliographies and indexes of music literature and scores that are cited elsewhere.

Reviews by Harold Spivacke and by K. H. Anderson in *Notes*, 22 (1965–66), p. 872–77.

3029. Music librarianship and documentation. Report of the Adelaide Seminar, May 1970. Adelaide: Department of Adult Education, University of Adelaide, 1970. 145 p.

A stimulating series of papers reporting on various aspects and problems of music librarianship and documentation in a part of the world where these disciplines had been established only in the mid-twentieth century.

3030. Music Library Association. Committee on Information and Organization. Manual of music librarianship. Edited by Carol June Bradley. Ann Arbor, Michigan: Music Library Association Executive Office, 1966. 150 p.

3031. Ott, Alfons. "Die Musikbibliotheken." In Fritz Milkau's *Handbuch der Bibliothekswissenschaft*, 2nd ed., vol. 2, p. 222–42.

Also printed separately by Harrassowitz, Wiesbaden, 1959.

Review by Cecil B. Oldman in *Fontes Artis Musicae*, 7 (1960), p. 71–72.

3032. Reader in music librarianship. Edited by Carol June Bradley. Washington, D.C.: Microcard Editions Books, 1973. 340 p.

Reprints of 53 seminal articles on the practice of music librarianship encompassing general philosophies and operational concerns, collection development and acquisitions, cataloging and classification, bibliography and exhibitions, binding, sound recordings and equipment, facilities, and education for music librarianship. Most chapters begin with a selected bibliography on the subject immediately following. A useful sourcebook, now somewhat dated. "The index comprehends concepts, subjects, library names, personal names, and titles of reprinted articles as well as the bibliographic citations throughout the book."

Reviews by Donald W. Krummel and by John W. Tanno in *Notes*, 31 (1974), p. 286–88.

3033. Wassner, Hermann. "Untersuchungen zur musikbibliothekavischen Arbeit: Ein Überblick über neure Veröffentlichungen gegenwärtige Aktivitäten und vorzuchlagende Arbeitsziele. (Beiträge aus der Bundesrepublik und aus West-Berlin)." In *Fontes Artis Musicae*, 30 (1983), p. 82–98.

A survey of publications from West Germany, including West Berlin, on the profession of music librarianship since 1975. Includes a classified bibliography of 167 works on the subject.

3034. Watanabe, Ruth. "American music libraries and music librarianship: an overview in the eighties." In *Notes*, 38 (1981), p. 239–56.

An overview of the American experience following World War II with particular attention to the challenges of the 1980s in automation, sound recordings, collection development, and conservation.

MUSIC CATALOGING AND CLASSIFICATION

3035. Bradley, Carol June. The Dickinson classification; a cataloguing and classification manual for music. Including a reprint of the George Sherman

Dickinson *Classification of Musical Compositions.* Carlisle, Pennsylvania: Carlisle Books, 1968. 176 p.

A classification system developed by George Sherman Dickinson, music librarian at Vassar College, 1927–53. This volume contains a reprint of the Dickinson classification, originally published in 1938, together with a manual of cataloging procedures based on it.

For a description of the classification and a demonstration of its applications, see Carol Bradley's article "The Dickinson classification for music" in *Fontes Artis Musicae*, 19 (1972), p. 13–22.

3036. The British catalogue of music classification. Compiled for the Council of the British National Bibliography, Ltd., by E. J. Coates. London: Council of the British National Bibliography, Ltd., British Museum, 1960. 56 p.

The classification scheme developed for use in the *British Catalogue of Music* (no. 1210).

3037. Code international de catalogage de la musique. I. Der Autorenkatalog der Musikdrucke. The author catalog of published music. By Franz Grasberger; translated by Virginia Cunningham. Frankfurt and London: C. F. Peters, 1961. 53 p.

This and the following four volumes are the result of the work of the Commission on Music Cataloguing of the International Association of Music Libraries. Later volumes projected include a code for the cataloging of music manuscripts and sound recordings.

Review by Richard S. Angell in *Notes*, 15 (1957), p. 110–11.

3038. Code international de catalogage de la musique. II. Code restreint. Rédigé par Yvette Fédoroff ... Kurzgefasste Anleitung—Limited Code. Übersetzung von Simone Wallon. Translated by Virginia Cunningham. Frankfurt and London: C. F. Peters, 1961. 53 p.

Review by Minnie Elmer in *Notes*, 19 (1961), p. 247–49; by Richard Schaal in *Die Musikforschung*, 17 (1964), p. 295–96.

3039. Code international de catalogage de la musique. III. Rules for full cataloging — Rules de catalogage detaillé — Regeln für die vollständige Titelaufnahme, compiled by Virginia Cunningham. Frankfurt: C. F. Peters, 1971. 116 p.

3040. Code international de catalogage de la musique. IV. Rules for cataloging music manuscripts. Compiled by Marie Louise Göllner. Translation [French] by Yvette Fédoroff, [German] by Horst Leuchtmann. Frankfurt and London: C. F. Peters, 1975. 56 p.

A result of the work of a committee of the International Association of Music Libraries.

3041. Code international de catalogage de la musique. V. Le catalogage des enregistrements sonores. The cataloging of sound recordings. Rédigé par Simone Wallon, Kurt Dorfmüller, avec la collaboration [de] Yvette Fédoroff, et Virginia Cunningham. Frankfurt and New York: C. F. Peters, 1983. 105 p.

Parallel text in English, French, and German.

3042. Gaeddert, Barbara Knisley. The classification and cataloging of sound recordings, 1933–1980; an annotated bibliography. 2nd ed. Philadelphia, Pennsylvania: Music Library Association, 1981. (Music Library Association Technical Reports, 4)

First published in 1977.

1st edition reviewed by Kären Nagy in *Notes*, 34 (1977), p. 88.

3043. International Association of Music Libraries. Deutsche Gruppe. Systematik der Musikliteratur und der Musikalien für öffentliche Musikbüchereien. Erarbeitet von der Kommission für Musiksystematik bei der Arbeitsgemeinschaft für Musikbüchereien in der Deutschen Gruppe der Association Internationale des Bibliotheques Musicales (AIBM). [Reutlingen]: Bücherei und Bildung, 1963. 39 p.

A system of music classification devised for German public library practice.

3044. Laforte, Conrad. Le catalogue de la chanson folklorique française. Québec: Les Presses Universitaires Laval, 1958. 397 p. (Publications des archives de folklore, Université Laval)

Demonstrates a method for establishing an alphabetical catalog, by title, of French folk songs, with appropriate cross-references to permit the grouping of variants under a common title. Based on material in Canadian archives and collections.

3045. Music Library Association. Code for cataloging music and phonorecords. Prepared by a Joint Committee of the Music Library Association and the American Library Association, Division of Cataloging and Classification. Chicago, Illinois: American Library Association, 1958. 88 p.

The five major divisions of the now considerably dated code are entry, description, phonorecords, simplified rules, and filing rules for conventional titles. Glossary and index.

3046. New York Public Library. Reference Department. Music subject headings, authorized for use in the catalogs of the Music Division. Boston, Massachusetts: G. K. Hall, 1959. 512 p.

Reproduced from cards in the subject heading file of the New York Public Library. An important tool for music catalogers, since it represents the practice of one of the great American music libraries.

3047. Pethes, Iván. A flexible classification system of music and literature on music. Translated by Mihaly Sandory. Budapest: Centre of Library Science and Methodology, 1968. 49 p.

In Hungarian and English.

3048. Regeln zur Katalogisierung der in der deutschen Bücherei eingehenden Musikalien. Entwurf. Leipzig: Deutsche Bücherei, 1959. 35 p.

Cataloging rules developed for German libraries.

Review by Virginia Cunningham in *Notes*, 16 (1959), p. 567.

3049. Schmidt-Phiseldeck, Kay. Miuskalienkatalogisierung; ein Beitrag zur Lösung ihrer Probleme. Leipzig: Breitkopf & Härtel, 1926. 44 p.

A plea for standards and rules for the cataloging of music.

3050. Smiraglia, Richard P. Cataloging music: a manual for use with AACR 2. [Edited by Edward Swanson.] 2nd ed. Lake Crystal, Minnesota: Soldier Creek Press, 1986. 181 p.

An excellent guide to the cataloging of music under the new terms of *Anglo-American Cataloging Rules*, 2nd ed., and MARC. Bibliography, p. 153–60.

3051. Smiraglia, Richard P. Shelflisting music: guidelines for use with the Library of Congress classification M. Philadelphia, Pennsylvania: Music Library Association, 1981. 21 p. (MLA technical reports, 9)

A brief but excellent guide to some of the mysteries of classification.

3052. U.S. Library of Congress. Subject Cataloging Division. Classification. Class M: music and books on music. 3rd ed. Washington, D.C.: 1978. 228 p.

First issued in 1904, revised 1917. 2nd edition, with supplementary pages, issued in 1963.

Largely the work of Oscar Sonneck, this classification schedule has been accepted, with various modifications, in many American music libraries, chiefly in colleges and universities.

3053. U.S. Library of Congress. Subject Cataloging Division. Music subject headings used on printed catalog cards of the Library of Congress. Washington, D.C.: Government Printing Office, 1952. 133 p.

MISCELLANEOUS

3054. Berner, A., J. H. van der Meer and G. Thibault. Preservation and restoration of musical instruments. Provisional recommendations. The International Council of Museums, 1967. 76 p.

Not a full-scale treatise on its subject, but suggests the problems to be encountered in the restoration and preservation of instruments. Illustrated with plates from early treatises on musical instruments. P. 23–29: bibliography.

3055. Bloesch, Ethel. "Music autographs and first editions on postage stamps." In *Fontes Artis Musicae*, 25 (1978), p. 250–63.

A checklist of 50 stamps from 24 countries.

3056. Crawford, Richard. The American Musicological Society 1934–84; an anniversary essay with lists of officers, winners of awards, editors of the *Journal*, and honorary and corresponding members. Philadelphia, Pennsylvania: American Musicological Society, 1984. 46 p.

A publication marking the 50th anniversary of the founding of the AMS.

3057. Crofton, Ian and Donald Fraser. A dictionary of musical quotations. London and Sydney: Croom Helm, 1985. 191 p.

More than 3,000 "notable, often celebrated, utterances by and about musicians," some of them quite extensive. Multilingual, but principally in English, with all foreign quotations translated to English. Arranged in a single alphabetical sequence of topics and composers. Some cross-references. In each topic or under each composer, the quotations are listed chronologically. Sources of quotations and dates of sources provided.

There is an index of authors and speakers of quoted material. A "subject index, consisting of significant keywords, linked to a short identifying phrase, from the quotations" is provided.

3058. Dadelsen, Georg von. Editionsrichtlinien musikalischer Denkmäler und Gesamtausgaben. Im Auftrag der Gesellschaft für Musikforschung.... Kassel and Basel: Bärenreiter, 1967. 143 p. (Musikwissenschaftliche Arbeiten, 22)

Presents standards and techniques for editorial practice as employed in the German critical editions.

Review by Robert L. Marshall in *Notes*, 25 (1969), p. 733–35.

3059. Dearling, Robert and Celia Dearling. The Guinness book of music facts and feats. 3rd ed. Compiled with the assistance of Brian Rust. Enfield, Middlesex: Guinness Superlatives, 1986. 288 p.

1st edition, 1976. Published in a Dutch translation by Charles Fabius in Haarlem by De Haan, 1978. 2nd edition, 1981.

A list of curious and wondrous musical facts and feats in music. Well arranged for reference use. Includes a bibliography of 50 titles and a good index.

3060. Encyclopedia of quotations about music. Compiled and edited by Nat Shapiro. Garden City, New York: Doubleday, 1978. 418 p.

Over 2,000 quotations, all originally in or translated to English, arranged in subject categories. Indexes to persons and sources, and to keywords.

3061. Fuchs, Albert. Taxe der Streichinstrumente; Anleitung zur Einschätzung von Geigen, Violen, Violoncelli, Kontrabässen usw. nach Herkunft und Wert. 12. Auflage. Neubearbeitet von Rudolf E. Pliverics. Hofheim am Taurus: Friedrich Hofmeister, 1985. 206 p.

First published in 1906.

A handbook for appraising the origins and values of string instruments. Brief entries on luthiers. Index to places.

3062. Grimsey, A. H. R. Checklist of postage stamps about music. London: National Philatelic Society, 1977.

A checklist of over 4,000 stamps portraying music instruments, composers, and other musical subjects.

3063. Harrison, David B. Computer applications to music and musicology: a bibliography. Waterloo, Ontario: University of Waterloo, 1977. 116 p.

3064. International Music Centre. Music in film and television: an international selective catalogue, 1964–1974: opera, concert, documentation. Compiled and edited by the International Music Centre, Vienna. Paris: UNESCO Press, 1975. 197 p.

Provides information on 223 films that employ music. Indexed by titles, composers, librettists, authors, translators, producers and directors, conductors, performing artists, orchestras and ensembles, organizations and companies.

3065. Karkoschka, Erhard. Notation in new music; a critical guide to interpretation and realization. Translated from the German by Ruth Koenig. New York: Praeger, 1972.

First published as *Das Schriftbild der Neuen Musik* by Moeck in 1966. Also published in London by Universal Edition in 1972.

A summary of notational problems and solutions with a method for looking up specific notational symbols. Extensive section of examples of new notations with annotations. Indexes to subjects and to names and works.

3066. Kupferberg, Herbert. The book of classical music lists. New York: Facts On File, 1985. 240 p.

A collection of statistics and other information, serious and trivial, unlikely to be found easily elsewhere.

3067. Miller, Philip L., comp. and tr. The ring of words; an anthology of song texts. The original texts selected and translated, with an introduction by Philip L. Miller. New York: W. W. Norton, 1973. 518 p.

Reprint of the 1963 and 1966 editions of Doubleday.

German, French, Italian, Spanish, Russian, Norwegian, and Swedish, with English translations of song texts most likely to be heard in recitals.

3068. Modern musical scholarship. Edited by Edward Olleson. Stocksfield, England: Oriel Press, 1980. 246 p.

Proceedings of the Oxford International Symposia, held at Christ Church, Oxford, 1977, published under the title *Modern Musicology and the Historical Tradition of Musical Scholarship.*

3069. Philips, Lois. Lieder, line by line and word for word. New York: C. Scribner's Sons, 1980. 365 p.

Presents the original German lyrics with a literal English translation below each word, and, alongside, an English prose version for Lieder by Beethoven, Schubert, Schumann, Wagner, Brahms, Wolf, Mahler, and Strauss. Index to German titles and first lines.

3070. Schaal, Richard. Musiker-Monogramme: ein Verzeichnis mit einem Quellen-Anhang, Kataloge und Literatur. Wilhelmshaven: Heinrichshofen, 1976. 122 p. (Taschenbücher zur Musikwissenschaft, 27)

In two parts: an index of monograms with their explanations; an index of persons with the monograms associated with them. Appendix lists library catalogs, national and international; dictionaries of anonymous and pseudonymous works; and representative source studies.

3071. Sharp, Harold S. and Marjorie Z. Sharp, comp. Index to characters in the performing arts. Metuchen, New Jersey: Scarecrow Press, 1966–1973. 4 v. in 6.

Contents: pt. 2. Operas and musical productions; pt. 3. Ballets A–Z and symbols.

3072. Siddons, James. "A librarian's guide to musical Japan." In *Fontes Artis Musicae*, 24 (1977), p. 59–68.

A brief introduction with sections on Japanese musical life and its relation to the West, a historical survey of music collections in Japan, and useful information about Japanese books and related matters.

3073. Slonimsky, Nicolas. Lexicon of musical invective: critical assaults on composers since Beethoven's time. 2nd ed. Seattle: University of Washington Press, 1969. 325 p.

First edition of 296 pages published in New York by Coleman-Ross, 1953. Coleman-Ross also brought out the second edition in 1965.

> This is an anthology of critical assaults upon composers since the time of Beethoven. The *Lexicon* cites biased, unfair, ill-tempered, and singularly unprophetic judgments. Its animating purpose is to demonstrate that music is an art in progress, and that objections leveled at every musical innovator are all derived from the same psychological inhibition, which may be described as Non-Acceptance of the Unfamiliar.
>
> To preserve the documentary value of the quotations, the reviews from French and German sources are given in the original languages as well as in translation. The separate entries under each composer's name are arranged chronologically to establish historic perspective. [introductory pages]

Arranged in order by name of composer. Includes an "Invecticon," an index of vituperative, pejorative, and deprecatory words and phrases. Index of names and titles.

3074. Voorhees, Anna Tipton. Index to symphonic program notes in books. Kent, Ohio: Kent State University Press, 1970. 136 p. (Keys to music bibliography)

See also Diamond (no. 693) and Wenk (no. 736).

Index of Authors, Editors, and Reviewers

Only names of persons are indexed here; institutional names will be found in the Index of Titles. Citation numbers in italics refer to reviewers.

Index of Authors, Editors, and Reviewers

Ecorcheville, Jules, 2282
Edmunds, John, 861
Edson, Jean Slater, 1342
Edwards, George Thornton, 203
Edwards, J. Michele, 1397
Edwards, Warwick, 1737
Eggebrecht, Hans Heinrich, 14, *53*, 54, 363, 636
Ehinger, Hans, *43*
Eigeldinger, Jean-Jacques, *1589*
Eimert, Herbert, 364
Einstein, Alfred, 53, 102, 521, 536, 566, 575, 1633, 1807
Eisen, Margret, 1608
Eisen, Walter, 1608
Eisler, Paul E., 609
Eitner, Robert, 79, 695, 1688, 1738, 1739, 1904, 1905, 2000, 2110, 2609
Eive, Gloria, 1896
Elley, Derek, 2946
Ellinwood, Leonard W., *359*, 780, 1828, 1829, 2449
Elliott, Robert, 2374
Ellis, Charles, *857*
Elmer, Minnie, 1891, 1896, *2385*, *3038*
Elschek, Oskár, 918
Elsner, Jürgen, 587, 1596
Elste, Martin, 696
Elvers, Rudolf, 754, 1907, 1910, 1911, 2610, 3006
Emerson, John A., 1712, *1724*
Emery, Frederic B., 1332,
Emery Walter, *1888*
Emmanuel, Maurice, 22
Emrich, Duncan, *901*
Emsheimer, Ernst, 293, 897
Engel, Carl, 2544
Engel, Hans, 548, *596*
Enrico, Eugene, 1927
Epstein, Dena J., *850*, *1412*, 2611
Erb, James, *1833*
Erdely, Stephen, 637
Erichsen, Joergen Poul, 771
Erickson, J. Gunnar, 3010
Erlebach, Rupert, 802, 2152
Ernst, Friedrich, *2528*, *2573*
Eskew, Harry, *1802*, 1837, *2160*
Eslinger, Gary R., 1204
Espina, Noni, 1398, 1399
Esses, Maurice, 1853
Estrada, Julio, 1089
Etzkorn, K. Peter, 702
Eubanks, Charles G., *777*
Evans, Charles, 1299
Evans, Joan, 2308
Evans, Mary Anne, 937
Evans, Peter, *566*
Evans, Tom, 937
Everett, Thomas G., 1483
Ewald, Konrad, 1424

Ewen, David, 81, 82, 83, 204, 239, 460, 461 1514, 2975
Ewing, Douglas C., 2247
Expert, Henry, 22, 2279

Fabbri, Paolo, 3007
Fabius, Charles, 3059
Fabricius, Georg, 1850
Fabris, Dinko, 1784
Fairfield, John H., 288
Fairley, Lee, 822, *219*
Falk, Marguerite, 1539
Fallou, Robert, 938
Fallows, David, *663*, 1019, 1020, 1712, *2387*
Famera, Karen McNerney, 2236, 2994
Fanna, Antonio, 1670
Fanti, Napoleone, 1924
Färber, Sigfrid, 2311
Farish, Margaret K., 1204, 1412
Farkas, András, 2105
Farkas, Andrew, 1127
Farkas, Ferenc, 2105
Farmer, Henry George, 78, 587, 1145
Farrell, Susan Caust, 2931
Farwell, Brice, 1597
Fassett, Charles K., 1378
Faurot, Albert, 1355
Faustini, R., 2070
Favati, Guido, 141
Fayolle, F. J. M., 76
Feather, Leonard G., 240, 241, 242
Feder, Georg, 525, 1681
Federhofer, Hellmut, *43*
Féderoff, Yvette, 3038, 3040, 3041
Fedorov, Vladimir, 21, *3026*
Fehr, A., 2472
Feininger, Laurence, 2475
Feinland, Alexander, 1416, 1417
Feist, Milton, *1275*
Felch, Patricia, *787*, *1519*
Fellerer, Karl Gustav, 144, 638, 2222, 2328
Fellinger, Imogen, 783, 810, 823, 824, 825, 826, *1395*, *1853*, *2007*, *2728*
Fellowes, E. H., 2364, 2365, 2366
Felton, Gary S., 2932
Fenlon, Iain, 1957
Fenlon, Ian, 1916
Ferguson, Donald N., 537
Fernández De La Cuesta, Ismael, 1740
Ferrari, Alberto, 3
Ferretti, Paolo M., 2198
Ferris, Sharon Paugh, 717
Fétis, François J., 84
Fey, Hermann, 145
Fichter, Heinz-Lothar, 746
Fidler, Linda, *796*
Fiedler, Arthur, 1512
Field, Corey, *2674*
Fierro, Nancy, 2986

Filippis, Felice de, 1540
Fine, Sheldon, 1489
Fink, Robert, 366
Finnell, Judith Greenberg, 2236, 2933
Finney, Ross Lee, *570*
Finney, Theodore M., 538, 2299, 2300
Finscher, Ludwig, 43, 525, 563, *801*, 1681, 2325, *2765*
Finson, Jon W., *46*
Finzi, Vittorio, 2197
Fischer, Albert. F., 406
Fischer, Kurt von, *43, 520*, 1712, 1741, 1783, 1988
Fischer, Peter, 1150
Fischer, Wilhelm, 521, 623, 2998
Fisher, William A., 2612
Fitzgerald, Gerald, 1553
Flanders, Peter, 1638
Fleischer, Oskar, 2503
Fleischhauer, Günter, 587
Flemming, Bill, 2934
Flesch, Siegfried, 1608
Flindell, E. Fred, 2493
Fling, Robert Michael, 3022
Forimo, Francesco, 1541
Flotzinger, Rudolf, 1009
Flower, Desmond, 255
Floyd, Samuel A., 1107, *1117*
Fog, Dan, 1542, 1623, 2613, 2614, 2615, 2616
Folter, Siegrun H., 2467, 3027
Foote, Henry W, 407, 442
Forbes, Elizabeth, 462
Ford, Robert, 2233
Ford, Terence, 1742
Ford, Wyn K., 1070
Foreman, Lewis, 2750
Forkel, Johann Nikolaus, 380, 539, 697
Fornatale, Peter, 976
Forney, Kristine Karen, 2617
Forrest, Paula, 2577
Forsyth, Ella Marie, 1317
Forte, Allen, *46*
Fortune, Nigel, 564, 1020, 1743
Fosner, Helmut, 1215
Foster, Myles B., 1830
Fox, C., 2811
Fox, Charles Warren, *6, 35, 43, 63, 564*
Fraenkel, Gottfried S., 2618
Framery, Nicholas Étienne, 23
Frank, Alan, 2976
Frank, Paul, 94, 97
Frankel, Walter A., 1204
Fraser, Donald, 3057
Fraser, Norman, 2847
Frasier, Jane, 2981
Frati, Lodovico, 1923
Frecot, Dieter J., 746
Fredricks, Jessica M., 827
Freed, Dorothy, 1852, 1853
Freedman, Frederick, 103

Freeman, Larry, 449, 1510
Freitag, Wolfgang M., 1105
French, Richard, *1158*
Frenzel, Herbert A., 472
Frequin, B., 2527
Frere, W. H., 427, 1709
Freunsch, Gail L., 2444
Freystätter, Wilhelm, 810, 828
Friedlaender, Max, 1744
Friedrich, Gary, 229
Frost, Maurice, 427, 1831
Fruchtman, Caroline S., 1627
Fry, Stephen M., *53, 62, 208, 370, 404, 418, 510, 656, 745, 803, 1110, 1191, 1297, 1308, 1355, 1398, 1402, 1480, 1519, 1622, 2054, 2088, 2159, 2748, 2781, 2835, 2902, 2921, 2926, 2933, 2947, 2951*
Fubini, Enrico, 3007
Fuchs, Albert, 3061
Fuchs, Aloys, 1614, 2476, 2477
Führer, Rudolf H., 1456
Fukuda, Naomi, 1079
Fuld, James J., 1128, 1516, 1517, *1667, 1678*, 1745, 2619
Fuller-Maitland, A. J., 568, 1955
Furnivall, Frederick J., 1403
Fuszek, Rita M., 1356

Gable, Frederick K., 2061
Gaeddert, Barbara Knisley, 3042
Gaeddert, William K., 1389
Gagnepain, Bernard, 608
Gai, Vincio, 2522
Gal, Hans, 2009
Gallego Gallego, Antonio, 602
Gallini, Franco, 2551
Gallini, Natale, 2551, 2552
Gallo, F. Alberto, 983, 1026
Gallo, Franca, 2076
Gallusser, Werner, 1852
Galvani, Livio Niso, (pseud.), 1551
Gambassi, Osvaldo, 3007
Gamber, Klaus, 2031
Gamble, William, 2620
Gammond, Peter, 243. 2811
Gandolfi, Riccardo, 2018, 2023, 2067
Gangi, Mario, 284
Gangwere, Blanche, 610
Gansemans, Jos, 587
Gänzl, Kurt, 463
Garbelatto, Antoni, 2172, 2268
García Fraile, Dámaso, 2332
Garcia Marcellan, Jose, 2180
García Muñoz, Carmen, 2361
Gardavský, Čeněk, 136
Gardeton, César, 698, 2935
Garfield, Ann M., 717
Gargan, William, 1518
Garlington, Aubry S., *46*, 2362

Index of Selected Music Bibliographic Series

In this index citation numbers follow the colons.

Bibliographies in American music, 6 (A
catalog of the works of Arthur Foote,
1853–1937. By Wilma Reid Cipolla,
1980): 2592
Bibliographies in American music, 7
(Louis Moreau Gottschalk, 1829–1869;
a bibliographical study and catalog of
works. By John G. Doyle, 1982): 1604
Bibliographies in American music, 8
(American music studies; a classified
bibliography of master's theses. By
James R. Heintze, 1984): 1109
Bibliographies in American music, 9
(American piano concertos; a
bibliography. By William Phemister,
1985): 1367
Bibliographies in American music, 10
(Music in higher education; an
annotated bibliography. By Edward
Brookhart, 1988): 996
Bibliographies and Indexes in Latin
American and Caribbean Studies, 2:
1083
Bibliographische Mitteilungen, Nr. 12,
1954–55; Nr. 16, 1956–57; Nr. 19, 1958–
60: 752
Bibliographische Veröffentlichungen der
Musikbibliothek der Stadt Leipzig:
2113
Biblioteca degli studi mediolatine e
volgari, 3: 141
Biblioteca dell'archivio delle tradizioni
popolari baresi. Civiltà musicale
pugliese: 1078, 1129
Biblioteca di bibliografia italiana, 18:
2695
Biblioteca di bibliografia italiana, 23:
1794
Biblioteca di bibliografia italiana, 32:
2696
Biblioteca di bibliografia italiana, 39:
2607
Biblioteca di bibliografia italiano, 47:
2223
Biblioteca di bibliografia italiana, 68:
2191
Biblioteca di bibliografia italiana, 83:
2168
Biblioteca "Historiae musicae cultores,"
45: 2399
Biblioteca Nazionale Universitaria di
Torino, I: 2381
Bibliotheca bibliographica Aureliana, 6:
686
Bibliotheca bibliographica aureliana, 9:
1143
Bibliotheca musica Bononiensia, I, 3: 345
Bibliotheca musica Bononiensis, I, 6:
380
Bibliotheca musica bononiensis, I, 11:
2015

Bibliotheca musica Bononiensis, III, 9:
1541
Bibliotheca musica Bononiensis, III, 64:
454
Bibliotheca musica Bononiensis, VI, 2:
2201
Bibliotheca musica bononiensis, VI, 3:
1926
Bibliotheca musicae, 1: 1865
Bibliotheca musicae, 2: 2320
Bibliotheca musicae, 3: 2164
Bibliotheca musicae, 4: 2035
Bibliotheca musicae, 7: 2254
Bibliotheca musicae, 8: 2588
Bibliotheca organologica, 51: 939
Bibliothek des Germanischen
Nationalmuseums Nürnberg zur
deutschen Kunst- und
Kulturgeschichte, 2: 2560
Bio-bibliographies in music, 1: 1635
Bio-bibliographies in music, 2: 1168
Bio-bibliographies in music, 3: 1568
Bio-bibliographies in music, 4: 1665
Bonner Beitrage zur Anglistik, 4: 382
Brass research series, 3: 1479
Brass research series, 6: 1483
Bulletin of the University of Utah, 45:10:
2333

Cambridge readings in the literature of
music: 557, 558
Canadian Association of Music Libraries,
Publications, 1: 1060
Carmina medii aevi posterioris latina, 1:
1808
Catalog of the American Music Center
Library, 3: 1434
Cataloghi di fondi musicali italiani, 4:
2406
Cataloghi di fondi musicali italiani, 5:
1928, 1938
Cataloghi di fondi musicali italiani, a
cura della Società Italiana di
Musicologia in collaborazione con il
Répertoire International des Sources
Musicales, 7: 2381
Catalogi van de muziekbibliotheek en de
collectie muziekinstrumenten: 2048
Catalogo dei fonti storici della biblioteca
del Conservatorio di musica
Benedetto Marcello, Venezia, I: 2399
Catálogos de la música antiqua
conservada en España, 1–3: 2176
Catalogue of printed books in the British
Museum. Accessions, 3rd ser., Pt.
291B: 2141
Catalogue of printed music in the British
Museum. Accessions, Pt. 53: 2142
Catalogues of Australian compositions:
1228–1235

Index of Subjects

Libraries and collections can be located by searching under the names of their cities or towns. Institutions, including libraries, are also entered directly under their names.

18th-century music—History and criticism, 804
18th-century music—Italy—Bibliography, 2385
18th-century music—Jonköpking, Sweden, 2086, 2202, 2287, 2300
18th-century music—Thematic catalogs, 1197
18th-century music—U.S.—Index, 1304
18th-century musical aesthetics, 557
18th-century opera—France—Bibliography, 1538
18th-century symphony—France—Thematic catalogs, 1719
Einstein, Alfred, *The Italian Madrigal*—Indexes, 1772
Einzeldrucke vor 1800—Indexes, 1753
Eisenach, Bachmuseum—Musical instruments—Catalogs, 2520
Eisenach, Richard Wagner Museum—Bibliography, 1189
Eisenach, Richard Wagner Museum—Catalog, 2010
Eisenmann, Will—Bio-bibliography, 1293
Eisler, Hanns—Catalogs, 1596
Electrical music—Bibliography, 943
Electronic data processing—Folklore—Bibliography, 925
Electronic data processing—Music—Bibliography, 925
Electronic data processing in music—Directories, 2940
Electronic music—Bibliography, 855, 859, 1485
Electronic music—Dictionaries—Terms, 364
Electronic music—Discographies, 2891, 2894
Electronic music, Australian, 1232
Electronic music with voices, 1397
Emory University Library, John Hill Hewitt Collection, Atlanta, 1619
Encyclopedia Britannica (11th ed.)—Music articles, 399
Encyclopedias—Bibliography, 688
England—Bath, 1884
England—Directories, 2923
England—History—Pre-1800—Bibliography, 1070
English church music—Bibliography, 1726
English Folk Dance and Song Society, Library, London—Catalog, 2147
English horn—Bibliography, 276
English horn music—Bibliography, 1453
English Madrigalists—Indexes, 1690
English music—18th-century, 2339
English music, 17th-century—Catalogs, 2300
English music, 18th-century—Catalogs, 2300
English music—Bibliography, 1197

English music—Exhibition catalogs, 2259
English music—To 1800—Bibliography, 2371
English music manuscripts—Catalog, 2233
English newspapers—Indexes, 804
English poetry—Musical settings, 1400, 1401, 1402
English School of Lutenist Song Writers—Indexes, 1690
English songs—Bibliography—Catalogs, 2490
English songs—Medieval—Catalog, 1774
English songs—17th-century—Bibliography, 1735
English vocal music—Bibliography, 1792
Episcopal Church music—Bibliography, 1839
Erzabtei St. Peter, Salzburg—Catalogs, 2336
Escorial, Archivo de Música, 2011
Eskimo music—Bibliography, 891
Essen Stadtbibliothek—Catalogs, 2012
Estense Collection, Österreichische Nationalbibliothek—Thematic catalogs, 2417
Esterházy Opernsammlung—Catalog, 1950
Ethnic American music, 2850
Ethnology—Africa—Bibliography, 928
Ethnomusicological collections—Directories, 2849
Ethnomusicology, 563, 631, 637, 644, 645, 651, 664
Ethnomusicology—Bibliography, 651, 753, 889, 892, 894, 895, 897, 899, 905, 906, 918, 919, 920, 921, 925, 926
Ethnomusicology—Discography, 2851, 2852
Ethnomusicology—Great Britain, 1020
Ethnomusicology—Iconography—Bibliography, 603
Ethnomusicology—Latin America—Bibliography, 1086
Ethnomusicology—Sources, 583
Euing Collection, Glasgow—Catalog, 2038
European festivals—Directories, 2969
European folk music—Bibliography, 918
European libraries—Anthologies—Thematic catalogs, 1209
European music—Directories, 2908
European music—Discographies, 2889
European regional music history—Bibliography, 1065
Evangelical and Reformed Church—Hymns—History and criticism, 431
Evangelisches Kirchengesangbuch—Index, 1347
Evans, Charles—*American bibliography*—Excerpts, 1108

Index of Subjects

Italian libraries—Catalogs, 2062
Italian libraries—Descriptions, 2081, 2082
Italian libraries—Early music— Bibliography, 1795
Italian manuscripts—Netherland compositions, 2083
Italian monody—Bibliography, 1743
Italian music—Bari—Bibliography, 1078
Italian music—Bibliography, 1078, 1552, 1800
Italian music—Discography, 2851
Italian music—18th-century— Bibliography, 2385
Italian music—15th-century— Bibliography, 1741
Italian music—14th-century— Bibliography, 1741
Italian music—Yearbooks, 2915, 2916
Italian music literature—Bibliography, 765
Italian opera—Bibliography, 1134
Italian recorded music—Discographies, 2799
Italian vocal music—Bibliography, 1807
Italy—Brescia—Bibliography, 1767
Italy—Directories , 2924
Italy—Naples, 1541
Italy—Opera—Bibliography, 1534
Ives, Charles E.—Discography, 2904
Ives, Charles Edward—Catalogs, 1621, 2234
Ivory Coast—Discography, 2863

Jackson Music Library, Filmer Collection, Yale University, 2233
Jacob Coopersmith Collection of Handeliana, 1975
Jacobi, Erwin R.—Collection, 1139, 2481
Jagielloński, Bibljoteka, Krakow— Catalogs, 2093
James Weldon Johnson Memorial Collection of Negro Arts and Letters, 2232
Japan, 3072
Japanese music—Bibliography, 1210, 1276
Japanese music—Discographies, 2870
Japanese music—History and criticism—Bibliography, 927
Japanese music libraries—Collected works—Union lists, 1697
Japanese music libraries—Periodicals— Union lists, 834, 835, 836
Japanese music literature, 2438
Japanese music literature—Bibliography, 723
Japanese musical studies—Bibliography, 1028

Japanese periodicals—Bibliography, 830
Jazz, Australian, 1233
Jazz dictionaries—Terms, 369, 370
Jazz literature, 968
Jazz literature—Bibliography, 961, 965, 969
Jazz musicians, 1510
Jazz musicians—Bio-bibliography, 250
Jazz—Bibliography, 250, 785
Jazz—Bibliography, 960, 963, 964, 966
Jazz—Bibliography, 1510, 1532
Jazz—Bio-bibliography, 242
Jazz—Biographies, 230, 231, 240, 241, 255, 259
Jazz—Dictionaries, 230, 231, 240, 241, 253, 255, 266, 370
Jazz—Discographies, 242, 1510, 2803, 2807, 2808, 2809, 2810, 2811, 2812, 2813, 2814, 2815, 2816, 2817, 2818, 2819, 2832, 2879, 2882
Jazz—Discography—Bibliography, 2748
Jazz—Films, 242
Jazz—Moving pictures, 967
Jazz—New Orleans, 259
Jazz—Periodicals—Indexes, 785
Jazz—Terminology, 370
Jazz, West Coast—Discography, 2804
Jena, Universitätsbibliothek—Catalogs, 2084
Jenny, Albert—Bio-bibliography, 1293
Jerusalem, Idelsohn Archives—Catalog, 2085
Jewish music—Bibliography, 418, 914, 1076, 1272, 1273, 1274, 1275
Jewish music studies—Bibliography, 2085
Jewish musicians, 163, 164, 165, 166, 167, 418, 540
Jews and music—Bibliography, 1077
Jirák, Karel Boleslav—Catalog, 1622
Joachimsthalsches Gymnasium, Bibliothek, Berlin—Catalog, 1904, 1905
João IV, King of Portugal, Collection— Catalogs, 2125
Johann André (firm), 2665
Johannesburg, Kirby Collection— Musical instruments—Catalogs, 2530
Jonköpking, Per Brahegymnasiet— Catalogs, 2086
José Antonio Echeverría Library, Havana, 1277
José Martí Library, Havana, 1277
Joseph Haydn, Thematisch-bibliographisches Werkverzeichnis, Bd 1 & 3—Indexes, 1613
Josquin des Pres, 1173
Journal of Aesthetics and Art Criticism—Indexes, 786
Journalism—Bibliography, 839
Judaism—Music—Bibliography, 418

Musical revue, comedy, etc.—England—
London, 463
Musical revue, comedy, etc.—Excerpts—
Bibliography, 1521
Musical revue, comedy, etc.—Great
Britain—Dictionaries, 451
Musical revue, comedy, etc.—New York
(City)—Chronology, 449
Musical revue, comedy, etc.—U.S., 233,
464, 447, 460, 468, 492, 2829
Musical societies, 2972
Musical theater, Australian—
Discography, 2829
Musical theater, British—Discography,
2829
Musical theater, Canadian—Discography,
2829
Musical theater, Italian, 1123
Musical theater—Bibliography, 1138,
1524
Musical theater—Discography, 2829,
2833, 2879, 2882, 2885
Musician societies—Directory, 2930
Musicians, American, 202, 263
Musicians, Australia and New Zealand,
121
Musicians, French—18th-century, 2594
Musicians, Italian, 110, 1541
Musicians, Jewish—Bibliography, 1275
Musicians, Paris—Directories, 698
Musicians, Slavic, 109
Musicians, Tuscan, 171
Musicians—Austria, 147
Musicians—Bavaria, 149
Musicians—Bio-bibliography, 35, 55, 63,
64, 65, 71–82, 84, 86, 88, 91, 92, 93, 103,
106–108, 110, 111, 112, 114, 117, 143,
178, 254, 311, 321, 384, 504, 1739, 1766,
1777
Musicians—Biographies—
Bibliographies, 1160
Musicians—Biography, 220, 481
Musicians—Cremona, Italy—Bio-
bibliography, 1985
Musicians—Cuba, 133
Musicians—Czechoslovakia—
Bibliography, 1098
Musicians—Directories, 1059, 2958
Musicians—East Germany, 151
Musicians—France, 138, 2271
Musicians—France—Bio-bibliography,
143
Musicians—France—Correspondence—
Catalogs, 2281
Musicians—Germany, 147
Musicians—Germany—Berlin, 148
Musicians—Paraguay, 180
Musicians—Paris, 138
Musicians—Periodicals, 810, 820
Musicians—Portraits, 2227, 2412
Musicians—Rhineland, 144

Musicians—Schleswig-Holstein, 145
Musicians—Silesia, 146
Musicians—Slovakia—Bibliography,
1097
Musicians—South Africa—Biography,
194
Musicians—Switzerland, 147
Musicological Archives for Renaissance
Studies, Urbana—Catalogs, 2387
Musicology, 525, 550, 551, 563, 623, 624,
626–631, 633–635, 638, 639, 643, 646–
650, 652–655, 658–670, 2653, 3007,
3068
Musicology—Addresses, essays, lectures,
636, 657
Musicology—Australia, 1008
Musicology—Australia—Directory, 2918
Musicology—Austria, 1009, 1010
Musicology—Belgium, 1011
Musicology—Bibliography, 635, 864, 866,
870–872, 875, 877, 884, 885
Musicology—Brazil, 1057
Musicology—Canada, 1012
Musicology—Czech Republic, 1013
Musicology—Data processing, 2940
Musicology—Denmark, 1014, 1039
Musicology—Directories, 2910, 2940
Musicology—Finland, 1015
Musicology—France, 1016
Musicology—Germany, 1017
Musicology—Germany (GDR)—
Bibliography, 677
Musicology—Germany—Bibliography,
1068
Musicology—Great Britain, 1018, 1019,
1020
Musicology—Greece, 1074
Musicology—Guides, handbooks, 636,
666
Musicology—Hungary, 1075
Musicology—India—Sources, 565
Musicology—Iran, 1021
Musicology—Iraq, 1022
Musicology—Israel, 1023, 1024
Musicology—Italy, 1025, 1026, 3007
Musicology—Japan, 1027, 1028
Musicology—Korea, 1029
Musicology—Latin America, 1030
Musicology—Norway, 1033, 1034, 1039
Musicology—Philippines, 1035
Musicology—Poland, 1090, 1091
Musicology—Poland—Bibliography, 722
Musicology—Portugal, 1036, 1037
Musicology—Romania, 1090
Musicology—Russia, 1038
Musicology—Scandinavia, 1039
Musicology—Serbia, 1306
Musicology—South Africa, 1040
Musicology—South America, 1041
Musicology—Soviet Union, 1038
Musicology—Spain, 1042

Quellen-Lexikon—Supplement, 1766, 1777
Quotations—Dictionaries, 3057, 3060

R. Istituto Musicale, Florence—Catalogs, 2067
Rachmaninoff, Sergei—Bibliography, 1177
Radio station commissions—West Germany, 856
Ragas, 1271
Ragas—Thematic catalogs, 1269
Ragtime—Bibliography, 1526
Ragtime—Bio-bibliography, 1526
Ragtime—Discography, 1526
Rainbeau, Doctor, 2487
Rameau, Jean-Philippe—Exhibition catalogs, 2277
Ransom Humanities Research Center, Austin, Texas, 1870
La Rassegna Musicale—Indexes, 798
Rastrology, 3007
Rattsschulbibliothek, Zwickau—Catalogs, 2466
Ravel, Maurice—Manuscripts, 1870
Ravel, Maurice, Vocal music—Discography, 2768
Razumovskii Collection—Catalogs, 2203
Real Colegio de Corpus Christi Patriarca, Valencia—Catalog, 2388
Record libraries, 3025
Recorded music—Catalogs, 2875
Recorded music—Discographies, 2755, 2757, 2758, 2759, 2767, 2771, 2772, 2773, 2774, 2776, 2782, 2783, 2785
Recorded music—Reviews, 2876
Recorded music—Reviews—Indexes, 2877, 2880, 2898
Recorded sound—Directories, 2932
Recorder—Bibliography, 1470
Recorder—Catalogs and collections, 2535
Recorder music—Bibliography, 1470, 1471, 1472
Recording music, 3015
Redlich, Hans Ferdinand, Collection, 2095
Regensburg, Fürst Thurn und Taxis Hofbibliothek—Catalogs, 2310, 2311
Regensburg, Instituts für Musikforschung, Schallarchiv, 2846
Reger, Max—Bibliography, 1178
Reggae—Bibliography, 2822
Reggae—Discography, 2822
Reggio-Emilia, Libraries—Catalogs, 2064
Regional music history—Europe—Bibliography, 1065
Regnart, Jacob—Catalogs, 1643
Reichel, Bernard—Bibliography, 2102
Reichel, Bernard—Bio-bibliography, 1293

Religious music, popular—Discographies, 2837
Renaissance music, 525, 564, 566, 568, 570, 631
Renaissance music—Bibliography, 764, 984, 988, 989, 1720, 1750, 1803, 2265, 2387
Renaissance music—Chronology, 610
Renaissance music—Dictionaries, 54
Renaissance music—Discography, 2766
Renaissance music—Italian manuscripts, 2083
Renaissance music—Sources—Catalogs, 1783, 2387
Renaissance music—Terms, 398
Renaissance music, Czech—Bibliography, 1988
Renaissance studies—Bibliography, 1978
Répertoire international de la presse musicale du XIXe siècle, 769
Research Libraries Group, 1207
Research Libraries Information Network, 1207
Revista de estudios musicales—Index, 1055
La Revista de musica—Index, 1055
Reznicek, Emil Nikolaus von, 2429
Rhode Island musicians, 209
Rhyming dictionaries, 517
Rhythm, 515
Rhythm—Bibliography, 712, 740
Rhythm and blues—Discography, 2814, 2841, 2842
Richard Aldrich Collection, Cambridge—Catalog, 1961
Richard Wagner Museum, Eisenach—Catalog, 1189
Richard Wagner Museum, Lucerne—Musical instruments—Catalogs, 2548
Ricordi (firm), 2690
Ricordi (firm)—Catalogs, 1199, 2588
Ridley Collection—Wind instruments—Catalogs, 2549
Rimbault, Edward Francis, 2487
Rio de Janeiro, Biblioteca Nacional—Catalogs, 2312, 2313, 2314
RISM, 2685
RISM A/I—Indexes, 1753
RISM A/II, 2097
RISM B/XI—Prospectus, 3005
Ritter-Akademie, Legnica—Catalogs, 2110, 2111
River Forest, Concordia Teachers College, Klinck Memorial Library—Catalogs, 2315
Rivington's New York Gazette—Indexes, 773
Rivista Musicale Italiana—Indexes, 801
RLG Conspectus in Music, 2436
RLIN, 1207, 1892

Index of Titles

Including names of institutions.

The A.S.T.A. dictionary of bowing terms for string instruments, 367
A. Z. Idelsohn archives at the Jewish National and University Library, Catalogue, 2085
Aarhus, Denmark. Statsbiblioteket, 771
Aaron Copland: a bio-bibliography, 1168
Abkürzungen in der Musik-Terminologie, 389
"Abriss einer Geschichte des Musikdruckes vom fünfzehnten bis zum neunzehnten Jahrhundert," 2589
Accademia di Santa Cecilia, Rome. Biblioteca, 2317
Accademia Filarmonica, Bologna, 1921, 1922
Accademia Filarmonica, Verona, 2403, 2570
"An account of printed musick, ca. 1724," 2744
Acta musicologica, 741
Addenda und Corrigenda zum Verlagsverzeichnis Franz Anton Hoffmeister, 2724
Additions to Steven D. Westcott, A comprehensive bibliography of music for film and television, 737
"Adriano Banchieri (1568–1634): Profilo biografico e bibliografia," 1567
Die älteren Musikalien der Stadt Freiberg in Sachsen, 2032
African music, 742
African music, a briefly annotated bibliography, 926
African music and oral data: a catalog of field recordings, 1902–1975, 2866
African music on L.P., 2860
African native music: an annotated bibliography, 928
Afro-American religious music: a bibliography and catalogue of gospel music, 1155
Afro-American singers: an index and preliminary discography, 2786
The age of Bach and Handel, 568

The age of Beethoven (1790–1830), 564
The age of enlightenment (1745–1790), 564
The age of humanism, 1540–1630, 564
"Aggiunte e correzioni ai dizionari biografici dei musicisti," 1777
Ägypten, 587
The Alexander Broude comprehensive guide to orchestral literature, 1334
"The Alfred Cortot collection at the University of Kentucky Libraries," 2118
L'allemand musicologique, 401
"Alfred Cortot as collector of music," 3006
Algemeene muziekgeschiedenis, 580
Algemene Muziekencyclopedie, 2
Allgemeine Geschichte der Musik, 539
Allgemeine Litteratur der Musik, 380, 697
Allgemeine Musikgesellschaft, Zürich, 2464, 2581
Allgemeines biographisches Lexikon alter und neuer geistlicher Liederdichter, 421
Allgemeines historisches Künstlerlexikon für Böhmen, 135
Allmänt musiklexikon, 47
Almanach musical pour l'an 1819 et 1820, 2935
An alphabetical index to Claudio Monteverdi: *Tutte le opere*, 1629
An alphabetical index to Hector Berlioz: *Werke*, 1572
An alphabetical index to Tomas Luis de Victoria: *Opera omnia*, 1668
Alt-Amerika; Musik der Indianer in präkolumbischer Zeit, 587
Der Alt-Wiener Musikverlag im Spiegel der *Wiener Zeitung*, 2741
Alte Drucke der Werke von tschechischen Komponisten des 18. Jahrhunderts in der Universitätsbibliothek in Brno, 1940
Alte Musik für Hausmusikanten, 1316

A bibliographical thematic catalogue of the works of John Field, 1782–1837, 1598

"Bibliographie," 860, 3004

Bibliographie der ältesten französischen und lateinischen Motetten, 1748

Bibliographie des altfranzösischen Liedes, 1779

"Bibliographie der Aufsätze zur Musik in aussermusikalischen Italienischen Zeitschriften," 779

Bibliographie zur Augsburger Musikgeschichte 1550–1650, 2697

Bibliographie de Belgique, 1945

"Bibliographie des bibliographies musicales," 682

Bibliographie des chansonniers français des XIIIe et XIVe siècles, 1779

Bibliographie der deutschen Arbeiterliedblätter 1844–1945, 1251

Bibliographie des editions d'Adrian le Roy et Robert Ballard (1551–98), 2659

Bibliographie des éditions musicales plantiniennes, 2706

Bibliographie des éditions musicales publiées par Estienne Roger et Michel-Charles Le Cène (Amsterdam, 1696–1743), 2657

"Bibliographie des éditions musicales publiées par Nicolas Du Chemin (1549–1576)," 2660

Bibliographie zur ethnomusikologischen Literatur der Schweiz, 889

"Bibliographie générale," 991

Bibliographie zur Geschichte des deutschen Kirchenliedes im XVI. Jahrhundert, 1849

Bibliographie zur Geschichte des Musikdrucks, 2596

Bibliographie einiger Grenzgebiete der Musikwissenschaft, 686

Bibliographie internationale de la littérature sur Wagner 1945–1955, 1184–1187

Bibliographie Musicale Française, 1248

Bibliographie musicale de la France et de l'étranger, 698

Bibliographie musikalischer thematischer Werkverzeichnisse, 738

Bibliographie der Musik-Druckwerke bis 1700 welche in der Stadtbibliothek, der Bibliothek des Acad. Inst. für Kirchenmusik, und der K. und Universitäts-Bibliothek zu Breslau, 2457

Bibliographie der Musik-Sammelwerke des XVI. und XVII. Jahrhunderts, 1738

Bibliographie des Musikschrifttums, 746

Bibliographie der musiktheoretischen Drucke des 16. Jahrhunderts, 1143

Bibliographie der Musikwerke in der Ratsschulbibliothek zu Zwickau, 2466

Bibliographie der Orgel; Literatur zur Geschichte der Orgel bis 1968, 951

Bibliographie des poésies de P. de Ronsard mises en musique au XVIe siècle, 1806

Bibliographie rétrospective des périodiques françaises de littérature musicale 1870–1954, 846

"Bibliographie der Schriften über Musik aus der Deutschen Demokratischen Republik, 1945–59," 679

"Bibliographie des Schrifttums zur Geschichte deutscher und österreichischer Musikverlage," 2680

Bibliographie der Troubadours, 1775

Bibliographie unselbständiger Jazz-literatur, 785

Bibliographien, musikwissenschaftliche Literatur sozialistischer Länder, 677

"Bibliographies, lexicons, guides, histories, and other works dealing with opera," 1130

"Bibliographies of wind music: a check-list," 1488

Bibliographische Mitteilungen, 752

Bibliographischer und thematischer Musikkatalog des Päpstlichen Kapellarchives im Vatikan zu Rom, 2394

Bibliographisch-thematisches Verzeichnis der Kompositionen von Karl Friedrich Abel (1723–1787), 1562

Bibliography Committee, New York Chapter, MLA, 1572, 1629, 1668

A bibliography for medieval and renaissance musical manuscript research, 1978

A bibliography for the study of American folk songs, 902

Bibliography of American hymnals, 1828

"Bibliography of Asiatic musics," 930

A bibliography of bagpipe music, 1310

Bibliography of black music, 1104

The bibliography of books and articles on Jewish music, 1077

Bibliography of cello ensemble music, 1427

A bibliography of Chicano and Mexican dance, drama and music, 1285

Bibliography on Chinese music, 1241

A bibliography of computer applications in music, 711

A bibliography of computer music, 862, 1487

Bibliography of concertos for organ and orchestra, 1337

A bibliography of contemporary music in the Music Library of North Texas State, 1997

Index of Titles

A descriptive catalogue of rare manuscripts and printed books, chiefly liturgical, 2149
Detroit Public Library. Hackley Collection, 1999
Detroit studies in music bibliography, 2765
Deutsche Bibliographie, 2872
Deutsche Demokratische Republik 1945–1970, 677
Die deutsche Jazz-Discographie, 2813
Das Deutsche Kirchenlied, 1841
Das deutsche Kirchenlied von der ältesten Zeit bis zu Anfang des 17. Jahrhunderts, 1850
Das deutsche Lied, geistlich und weltlich bis zum 18. Jahrhundert, 1716
Das deutsche Lied im 18. Jahrhundert, Quellen und Studien, 1744
Deutsche Musikbibliographie, 751
Deutsche Oratorien, 1800 bis 1840, 1746
Deutsche Staatsbibliothek, Berlin, 752, 1898–1902
Deutschen Musikarchiv der Deutschen Bibliothek, 1193
Deutschen Musiker-Lexikons, 147
Deutschen Musikverleger-Verband, 1193
Deutscher Bibliotheksverband. Sektion Musikbibliotheken, 2037
Deutscher Büchereiverband. Arbeitsstelle für das Büchereiwesen, 782
Deutsches Historische Institut in Rom, 2328
Deutsches Musiker-Lexikon, 147
Deutsches Musikgeschichtliches Archiv, 2088
Deutsches Rundfunkarchiv, 2026
Die deutschsprachigen Musikperiodica, 1945–57, 841
"The development of modern musicology," 662
The Diagram Group, 287
Diamonds & rust: a bibliography and discography on Joan Baez, 1531
Diapason: Catalogue général, 2873
Diccionario biográfico, bibliográfico, histórico, critico de guitarras, 326
Diccionario biográfico de la música, 106
Diccionario biographico de musicos portuguezes, 187
Diccionario Enciclopédico de la Música, 16
Diccionario folclórico de Colombia; musicos, instrumentosy danzas, 235
Diccionario Harvard de música, 384
Diccionario de la música cubana, 132
Diccionario de la música, histórico y técnico, 356
Diccionario de la música ilustrado, 16
Diccionario de la música Labor, 49

Dicionário bio-bibliográfico musical (brasileiro e internacional), 173
Dicionário biográfico de musicos do norte de Portugal, 184
Dicionário biográfico de musicos portugueses, 185
Dicionário de música ilustrado, 10
Dicionário músical, 392
Dicionnaire critique de la musique ancienne et moderne, 12
The Dickinson classification, 3035
"The Dickinson classification for music," 3035
"Dictionaries and encyclopedias of music," 688
Dictionarium musica, 374
Dictionary of American hymnology, 1828, 1829
Dictionary of American pop/rock, 262
A dictionary of church music, 422
The dictionary of composers and their music, 87
Dictionary of contemporary music, 116
A dictionary of early music: from the troubadors to Monteverdi, 54
Dictionary of famous music and musicians, 108
A dictionary of foreign musical terms, 402
Dictionary of guitarists, 326
A dictionary of hymnology, 411
A dictionary of Middle English musical terms, 359
A Dictionary of Modern Music and Musicians, 77
Dictionary of music, 53
Dictionary of music production, 3021
Dictionary of musical biography, 220
A dictionary of musical information, 99
A dictionary of musical morphology, 379
A dictionary of musical quotations, 3057
Dictionary of musical terms, 354, 394, 398
A dictionary of musical terms in four languages, 393
A dictionary of musical themes, 499
A Dictionary of Musicians, from the earliest ages to the present time, 78
A dictionary of old English music and musical instruments, 383
The dictionary of opera, 481
A dictionary of opera and song themes, 500
Dictionary of organs and organists, 343
A dictionary of Parisian music publishers, 1700–1950, 2632
A dictionary of pianists, 311
Dictionary of pipe organ stops, 299
Dictionary of popular music, 243
A dictionary of Protestant church music, 404

Fürst Thurn und Taxis Hofbibliothek, 2310, 2311
Fürstlich Hohenlohe-Langenburg'sche Schlossbibliothek, 2097
"Fürstlich Hohenlohe-Langenburg'sche Schlossbibliothek. Katalog der Musikhandschriften," 2097

Gabriel Fauré, 2275
Gabriel Fauré: 1900–1977, 2903
Gads musikleksikon, 27
Galerie des Beaux-Arts, Bordeaux, 1933
Galleria degli Uffizi, Florence, 2020–2022
Galpin Society, 2539
Galston-Busoni Archive, University of Tennessee, Knoxville, 2092
The Garland library of the history of western music, 639
Die gedruckten englischen Liederbücher in der Zeit Shakespeares, 1711
Die gedruckten mehrstimmigen Chansons von 1500–1600, 1729
"Das gegenwärtige Geschichtsbild der mittelalterlichen Musik," 990
"Der gegenwärtige Stand der jugoslawischen Musikwissenschaft," 1053
Gegenwartsfragen der Musik in Afrika und Asien, 908
Die Geigen- und Lautenmacher vom Mittelalter bis zur Gegenwart, 309
Geigenbauer der deutschen Schule des 17. bis 19. Jahrhunderts, 291
Geïllustreerd muzieklexicon, 34
Geist und Form im musikalischen Kunstwerk, 525
Die geistlichen Musikhandschriften der Universitätsbibliothek Jena, 2084
Gemeentemuseum, The Hague, 2048, 2049, 2524–2527
General bibliography for music research, 656
General catalog of music publishing in France, 1250
General catalog of published and unpublished works by instrumental category, 1448
A general history of music, 526
A general history of the science and practice of music, 546
A general index to modern musical literature, 680
General repertory of pieces and educational literature for the saxophone, 1473
"Die Genere des Webern-Archivs," 1878
George Frideric Handel. The Newman Flower collection in the Henry Watson Music Library, 2183
George Gershwin; a selective bibliography and discography, 1602

The George Pullen Jackson collection of southern hymnody, 2160
German and Austrian violin makers, 303
German violin makers, 290
"Gesamtausgaben," 1702
Gesamtausgaben: a checklist, 1685
"Gesamtausgaben und Publikationsreihen in Übersichten," 1700
Geschichte des Dirigierens, 551
Geschichte der europäisch-abendländischen oder unserer heutigen Musik, 549
Geschichte der evangelischen Kirchenmusik, 525
Geschichte der Gesellschaft der Musikfreunde in Wien, 1912–1927, 2408
Geschichte des Instrumentalkonzerts, 551
Geschichte der K.K. Gesellschaft der Musikfreunde in Wien, 1146
Geschichte der Kantate und des geistlichen Konzerts, 551
Geschichte des Kirchenliedes, 433
Geschichte des Klaviers, 320
Geschichte des Kontrabasses, 1431
Geschichte der Messe, 551
Geschichte der Motette, 551
Geschichte der Musik, 522, 574, 586
Geschichte der Musik in Bildern, 595
Die Geschichte der Musik des 17. 18. und 19. Jahrhunderts in chronologischem Anschlusse, 555
Geschichte der Musiktheorie im IX.-XIX. Jahrhunderts, 728
Geschichte des neuen deutschen Liedes, 551
Geschichte der Oper, 551
Geschichte des Oratoriums, 551
Geschichte der Ouvertüre und der freien Orchesterformen, 551
Geschichte der Sinfonie und Suite, 551
Geschichte als Weg zum Musikverständnis, 550
Geschichte der weltlichen Solokantate, 551
Geschichte der Zither, 320
Gesellschaft der Freunde des vaterländischen Schul- und Erziehungswesens, Hamburg. Ausschuss für Musik, 2052
Gesellschaft der Musikfreunde, 2408–2411, 2571
Giacomo Carissimi, catalogo delle opere attribuite, 1587
Gids van muziekbibliotheken en fonoteken in Nederland, 2936
Giovanni Battista Pergolesi, 1710–1736; a thematic catalogue, 1639
Die Gitarre und ihr Bau, 301

Index of Titles

Gitarre-Musik; ein internationaler Katalog, 1501

Gitarren-Lexikon, 325

Glasbeni Rokaposo in Tiski na Slovenskem do Leta 1800, 2349

Glossary of Hausa music and its social contexts, 270

The gold of rock & roll, 1955–1967, 2834

The golden age recorded, 2792

Gospel music encyclopedia, 224

The Gottfried Galston Music Collection, 2092

Göttweig. Graphisches Kabinett, 2041

Der Göttweiger thematische Katalog von 1830, 2042

Gramophone classical catalogue, 2874

Gramophone compact disc audio guide and catalogue, 2874

Gramophone record libraries, their organization and practice, 3025

Gramophone Shop, Inc., New York, 2757

Gramophone Shop, Inc., Record Supplement, 2875

Le grand livre de la guitare, de la Renaissance au rock, 937

Les grandes dates de l'histoire de la musique, 608

Le Grandi Voci, 88

Les grands violinists du passé, 274

"Graphic analysis, its application to early American engraved music," 2650

Grass Roots Music, 2837, 2869

Les gravures musicales dans l'Illustration, 1843–1899, 589

Great guitarists; the most influential players in jazz, country, blues and rock, 249

Great masters of the violin, 337

The great song thesaurus, 1520

The great songwriters of Hollywood, 233

Great violinists in performance, 331

Greene's Biographical Encyclopedia of composers, 89

A Gregorian chant discography, 2901

Griechenland, 587

Grosse Geiger unserer Zeit, 294

Grosser Chor-Katalog, 1374

Grosser Duetten-Katalog, 1390

Grosser Lieder-Katalog, 1391

Grossherzogliche Regierungsbibliothek, Schwerin, 2344, 2345

"A group of English manuscript volumes at the University of Pittsburgh," 2300

"Grove V and MGG," 43

"The growth and influence of musicology in the United States," 1047

Grundlage einer Ehren-Pforte, 96

Grundlagen der Musikgeschichte, 633

Grundriss der Musikwissenschaft, 659

Gruuthusemuseum, Bruges, 2510

Guía bibliográfica, 1089

Guía de la música argentina, 2938

Guide des disques, 2776

Guide du violoniste, 1415

"A guide to available jazz films," 242

Guide to the best in contemporary piano music, 1354

A guide to Byzantine hymnography, 1157

A guide to Canada's composers, 1059

Guide for dating early published music: a manual of bibliographical practices, 2651

A guide to English folk song collections, 1817

Guide to the hymns and tunes of American Methodism, 439

A guide to international congress reports in musicology, 1900–1975, 733

A guide to the Jacob Coopersmith Collection of Handeliana, 1975

Guide to Japanese reference works, 1080

Guide to jazz, 255

Guide to Latin American music, 1278

Guide to the Lester S. Levy collection of sheet music, 1873

The Guide to Long Playing Records, 2770

Guide to low-priced classical records, 2782

A guide to music festivals in America, 2968

A Guide to the music of Arthur Farwell, 1597

A guide to the music of Latin America, 1278

Guide to musical America, 2939

Guide musical suisse, 2974

Guide musicale svizzera, 2974

A guide to organ music, 1345

A guide to research in music education, 1005

The guide to the performing arts, 778

Guide to the pianist's repertoire, 1359

Guide to the Pilgrim hymnal, 443

"Guides to piano music: a check-list," 1353

Guildhall Library. Gresham Music Library, 2148

The Guinness book of music facts and feats, 3059

Guitar bibliography, 955

The guitar and mandolin, 278

Guitar music index, 1499

The guitarist's resource guide, 1504

"Guitarretabulaturen," 1811

Guitars: music, history, construction, and players from the Renaissance to rock, 937

Gustav Mahler Dokumentation, Sammlung Eleonore Vondenhoff, 2430

Gutenberg-Museum, 2181

Gymnasium, Heilbronn. Bibliothek, 2055

Michigan Music Theory Society, 704

Military and brass band music, 1234

Milton S. Eisenhower Library, 1873

Miscellanea Musicae Bio-Bibliographica, 1766

Mr. and Mrs. C. W. Best collection of autographs, 2252

Mittelasien, 587

The modern age (1890–1960), 564

Modern jazz: modern big band, 2805

Modern Music published by the League of Composers, 1924–1945; an analytic index, 803

Modern musical scholarship, 3068

Modern musicology and the historical tradition of musical scholarship, 3068

Die moderne Musik seit der Romantik, 525

Monarchs of minstrelsy, 257

Monasterio de Guadalupe, Badajoz, Spain, 1872

Monasterio de San Lorenzo El Real, Escorial, 2011

"The monastic manuscript microfilm library," 1977

Monumenta Monodica Medii Aevi, 1769

Moravsk Muzeum, Brno, 1939

More about this business of music, 3018

Mosaik-Opernführer, Konzertführer mit Operetten und Musicals, 111

Mostra autografi musicali della scuola napoletana, 2227

Mostra bibliografica di musica italiana dalle origini alla fine del secolo XVIII, 2014

Mostra bibliografica dei musicisti cremonesi, 1985

Mostra internazionale di musica in Bologna 1888, 1922

Mostra di strumenti musicali in disegni degli "Uffizi," 2021

"The motet in New France: some 17th- and 18th-century manuscripts in Quebec," 2309

"Die Motette von Franko von Köln bis Philipp von Vitry," 1708

Motion picture moods for pianists and organists, 1528

"Mozart alla Biblioteca del Conservatorio di Napoli," 2228

Mozart-Bibliographie 1971–1975 mit Nachträgen zur Mozart-Bibliographue bis 1970, 1176

Mozart-Bibliographien (bis 1970), 1176

Mozart in the British Museum, 2132

Mozart en France, 2278

Musashino Academia Musicae, Tokyo. Biblioteca, 2367, 2368

Il Museo Donizettiano, 1890

Il Museo storico musicale di S. Pietro a Majella, 2229

Museo Teatrale alla Scala, 2194

Museum of Art, Toledo, Ohio, 2372

Museums für Völkerkunde, 2861

"Music," 729

Music, a catalog of selected doctoral dissertation research, 876

Music: a dissertation bibliography, 877

Music, printed and manuscript, in the James Weldon Johnson Memorial Collection of Negro Arts and Letters: an annotated catalog, 2232

Music, [Section R] in volume 3 of *Arts in America, a bibliography*, 1106

"Music, the unknown," 641

Music A to Z, 388

Music and aesthetics in the eighteenth and early nineteenth centuries, 557

Music in American education, 1004

Music analyses; an annotated guide to the literature, 693

The music of ancient Greece: an encyclopaedia, 1073

"Music in the archives of the Basilica of Santa Maria in Trastevere," 2318

Music Article Guide, 789

"Music autographs and first editions on postage stamps," 3055

Music in the Baroque, 993

Music in the Baroque era, 1140

Music in the Baroque era, from Monteverdi to Bach, 566

Music in Belgium: contemporary Belgian composers, 125

Music bibliographies for all instruments, 1308

"Music . . . Bibliography," 1083

Music and bibliography: essays in honour of Alec Hyatt King, 3006

"Music bibliography and catalogues," 2996

Music, books on music, and sound recordings, 1219

Music in British libraries, 2965

Music business handbook and career guide, 3009

Music for children's choirs, 1203

Music in the classic period, 570

Music collection of the British Library, London, 2133

The music collection of Christ Church, Oxford, 2266

The music collection of the Royal College of Music, London, 2154

Music collections in American libraries: a chronology, 3023

Music collections and archives in the CSSR, 1990

"The music collections of the British Library Reference Division," 2145

Music Computation Conference II, 1486